5/6

C.G. JUNG LETTERS

selected and edited by · GERHARD ADLER

in collaboration with · ANIELA JAFFÉ

translations from the German by · R. F. C. HULL

in two volumes · 2: 1951–1961

BOLLINGEN SERIES XCV : 2 · PRINCETON UNIVERSITY PRESS

THIS TWO-VOLUME WORK IS THE
NINETY-FIFTH IN A SERIES OF BOOKS
SPONSORED BY BOLLINGEN FOUNDATION

The letters in these two volumes were published, with some variations, in *C. G. Jung: Briefe*, edited by Aniela Jaffé, in collaboration with Gerhard Adler, three volumes, © Walter-Verlag AG, Olten (Switzerland), 1972 and 1973. The following letters have been previously published either in Jung's original English or in R.F.C. Hull's translation. (Copyright in the letters prefixed by an asterisk has been assigned to Princeton University Press.) — To Louis S. London, 24 Sept. 26, in London, *Mental Therapy: Studies in Fifty Cases*, copyright, 1937, by Louis S. London; * to Mary Foote, 19 Mar. 27, 28 Mar. 33, 18 Dec. 29, 12 July 37, in *Spring*, 1974, copyright © 1974, The Analytical Psychology Club of New York Inc.; to James Joyce, 27 Sept. 32, in Richard Ellmann, *James Joyce*, © by Richard Ellmann, 1959; * to Sally M. Pinckney, 30 Sept. 48, in the *Bulletin of the Analytical Psychology Club of New York*, X (Sept. 1948), copyright 1948 by the Analytical Psychology Club of New York Inc.; to Emanuel Maier, 24 Mar. 50, in *The Psychoanalytic Review*, vol. 50 (1963), copyright ©, 1963, by the National Psychological Association for Psychoanalysis, Inc.; to Ernest Jones, 22 Feb. 52, 19 Dec. 53, and to K. R. Eissler, 20 July 58, in *The Freud/Jung Letters*, copyright © 1974 by Princeton University Press (for Sigmund Freud Copyrights Ltd. and Erbengemeinschaft Prof. Dr. C. G. Jung); * to Upton Sinclair, 3 Nov. 52, 7 Jan. 55, in *New Republic*, copyright 1953 and 1955 in the USA by New Republic, Inc.; to James Kirsch, 18 Nov. 52, in *Psychological Perspectives*, the letter being copyright © 1972 by Princeton University Press; to Carl Seelig, 25 Feb. 53; A. M. Hubbard, 15 Feb. 55; Theodor Bovet, 9 Nov. 55; Anon., 19 Nov. 55; the Earl of Sandwich, 10 Aug. 60, in *Spring*, 1971, the letters being copyright © 1971 by Princeton University Press; to Patricia Graecen, 29 June 55, in Patricia Hutchins, *James Joyce's World*, Methuen, 1957, and in *James Joyce*, © by Richard Ellmann, 1959; to Simon Doniger, Nov. 55, in *Pastoral Psychology*, VI:60 (Jan. 1956), copyright 1955 by Pastoral Psychology Press; to H. L. Philp, 11 June 57, in Philp, *Jung and the Problem of Evil*, © H. L. Philp, 1958; to John Trinick, 15 Oct. 57, in Trinick, *The Fire-Tried Stone*, © John Trinick, 1967; to Gustav Steiner, 30 Dec. 57, (the present tr. by R.F.C. Hull with minor variations), in the editor's introduction to *Memories, Dreams, Reflections* by C. G. Jung, recorded and edited by Aniela Jaffé, copyright © 1961, 1962, 1963 by Random House, Inc., and published by Pantheon Books, a division of Random House, Inc.; * to Joseph R. Rychlak, 27 Apr. 59, in Rychlak, *A Philosophy of Science for Personality Theory*, copyright © 1968 by Joseph R. Rychlak; * to Valentine Brooke, 16 Nov. 59, (partially) in Aniela Jaffé, *The Myth of Meaning*, © 1971 by the C. G. Jung Foundation; * to A. D. Cornell, 9 Feb. 60, (in tr. by Hildegard Nagel), in *Spring*, 1961, copyright 1961 by the Analytical Psychology Club of New York Inc.; to Melvin J. Lasky, 31 Mar. 60, 14 Sept. 60, in *C. G. Jung and Hermann Hesse*, © Miguel Serrano 1966; to Melvin J. Lasky, 19 Oct. 60, in *Encounter*, Feb. 1961, © 1961 by Encounter Ltd.; to Edward Thornton, 1 Dec. 60, *The Diary of a Mystic*, © George Allen & Unwin Ltd., 1967; * to William G. Wilson, 30 Jan. 61, in two issues of AA *Grapevine*, © 1963 and 1968 by AA Grapevine.

*Library of Congress Catalogue Card
Number: 74-166378*
ISBN 0-691-09724-0

TABLE OF CONTENTS

LIST OF ILLUSTRATIONS

Frontispiece

C. G. Jung: Bollingen, 1959. *Hugo Charteris*

Plates

Illustrations in the Text

INTRODUCTION

In May 1956—Jung was then nearly 82—I broached to him the question of the publication of his letters. Jung's ready response made it clear that this project had been on his mind for some time. Thus my inquiry came at a favourable moment, and Jung asked his secretary, Mrs. Aniela Jaffé, to select two file folders of letters, all of them to clergymen, labelled "Pfarrerbriefe" in Jung's own handwriting, for my opinion concerning the advisability of their publication.

Over many years Jung had frequently used the medium of letters to communicate his ideas to the outside world and to rectify misinterpretations about which he felt sufficiently strongly, quite apart from answering people who approached him with genuine problems of their own and corresponding with friends and professional colleagues. In this way many of his letters contained new creative ideas and a running commentary on his work.

In his later years it became his practice to send copies of letters which he regarded as important to people whose judgment he trusted. This he did partly to communicate ideas to them which, on account of his age, he no longer felt willing or able to put into book form, and partly because the question of the publication of his letters had been on his mind for some time.

Originally the idea of such publication had come not from himself but from friends who were aware of the unique literary and psychological value of Jung's correspondence. At first Jung had reacted against the whole notion, since he felt that the spontaneity and immediacy of his letters were not for the general public; but in his later years he changed his attitude, and he even mentioned occasionally in a particular letter that it was not only directed to the addressee but was also meant for later publication.

Thus it was just the right moment when I put my own thoughts to Jung, and he responded by asking me if I were willing to undertake the editorial task. The final result of my talk and of the ensuing correspondence with him was formulated in Jung's decision, stated in a letter to me of 15 November 1957, to appoint an Editorial Committee consisting of his daughter Mrs. Marianne Niehus-Jung as representative of the family, Mrs. Aniela Jaffé, who had been Jung's secretary since the autumn of 1955 and was familiar with the archives kept at his house in Küsnacht, and finally myself as chairman of the Committee and chief editor who was to direct the whole project. The matter was formalized in a letter of 29 January 1959 from Jung to Mr. John D. Barrett, president of the Bollingen Foundation, which sponsored the publication of Jung's Collected Works. The original plan had been to bring out the letters as part of the Collected Works, a plan which was later modified so as to publish the letters independently.

There the matter rested until after Jung's death in 1961. Active work on the project started in January 1962, and early in 1963 appeals for Jung's letters were published in various newspapers and journals in the United States, Great Britain and Switzerland. This appeal was all the more important since the archives in Küsnacht were, to put it conservatively, incomplete. For years, Jung had no regular secretary, except for occasional help from his unmarried sister Gertrud. He wrote most letters in longhand and apparently kept no file copies. It was not until April 1931, when his daughter Marianne (later Mrs. Walther Niehus-Jung) began helping her father with secretarial work, that carbon copies of typewritten letters sent out were kept and filed together with letters received. But it was only in 1932, with the advent of Marie-Jeanne Schmid (later Mrs. Marie-Jeanne Boller-Schmid, daughter of Jung's friend Dr. Hans Schmid-Guisan), that files were established in a systematic way. Marie-Jeanne Schmid remained Jung's secretary until her marriage in 1952.* Without her accuracy and devoted care, the publication of these letters would have been virtually impossible, and to her is due the gratitude of all interested in Jung's work.

Marie-Jeanne once told me that one of the reasons why Jung did not bother to keep his addressees' letters or copies of his own was that he realized only later in life that he was a "famous man" in whose correspondence people might some day be interested. He was particularly neglectful of letters of a more personal and intimate nature—in short, of letters not immediately connected with his scientific work. The situation was complicated by Jung's habit of writing many letters by hand, particularly from his country retreat,

---

* Between her departure in 1952 and Aniela Jaffé's arrival in 1955 Jung had three other secretaries who, however, stayed only for short periods.

his Tower at Bollingen, without having them copied, although later on Mrs. Jaffé succeeded in saving many such letters from oblivion by typing copies before they were sent off.

This explains the relative dearth of letters before 1931–32. For earlier letters we were almost completely dependent on the result of published appeals. Thanks to the generosity of individuals and several libraries or archives, about sixty letters of the early period, up to the end of 1930, were received, not counting the letters to Freud (about which more later on). So small a number must be very disappointing, considering that it covers a period of several decades, and it is to be hoped that the publication of these volumes will lead to the discovery of more letters of the early period. This period could have been much more adequately covered with regard to both quantity and valuable material had the Jung heirs, to my deepest regret, not proscribed the publication of any of Jung's letters to his family (the earliest, to his mother, dating from 1896), the great majority of them to his wife. I can only hope that this embargo will be lifted at a later time, since these letters, on account of their personal character, warm feeling, and gay tone, are a very necessary complement to the letters published here with their predominantly scientific content. (It seemed superfluous to republish the seven letters to his wife printed in Jung's *Memories, Dreams, Reflections*.) The only letters to his closer family are two to his daughter Marianne, which were given to me by her personally. There exist also many intimate and very personal letters to other recipients, mostly analysands or pupils, who, however, felt it too early to allow their publication. Jung's letters to his close friend and collaborator Miss Toni Wolff were returned to him after her death in 1953 and were destroyed by Jung, together with her letters to him.

The correspondence between Freud and Jung is of particular importance. It consists of 167 letters from Freud to Jung and of 196 letters from Jung to Freud. It starts with Freud's letter of 11 April 1906, thanking Jung for the present of a volume of his *Diagnostische Assoziationsstudien*, and ending with Jung's letter of 27 October 1913, announcing his resignation as editor of the *Jahrbuch für psychoanalytische und psychopathologische Forschungen*. When Jung agreed to the plan for the publication of his letters he explicitly excluded these to Freud, which he did not want to be published until at least thirty years after his death (a period which he later reduced to twenty years). In a letter to me of 24 May 1956 he wrote: "Separate treatment of this correspondence is justified, because it touches in parts upon very personal problems, whereas the planned publication refers to scientific subjects. I consider it inopportune to expose the personal material as long as the waves of animosity are still running so high (*so lange die Wogen der Gehässigkeit noch so hoch schlagen*). At the date suggested by me Freud and I will be 'historical personalities,' and the necessary detachment from events will prevail by then." For these reasons I felt justified in publishing only a very few and quite uncontroversial letters of Jung's to Freud, eight in all.* However, Jung's heirs, in conjunction with the heirs of Freud, decided for an earlier publication of the Freud/Jung correspondence. In consequence the two sons met in London in 1970, and Ernst Freud and Franz Jung exchanged the letters of their respective fathers. As a result of these changed conditions the complete Freud/Jung correspondence has now been published in translation in the United States by Princeton University Press, and in the United Kingdom in a joint edition by Hogarth Press and Routledge & Kegan Paul; and in the German original by S. Fischer Verlag, Frankfurt.

After eliminating all purely "business" letters, such as routine correspondence with publishers, notes of appointments with patients, etc., I had in the end to choose from about 1600 letters. Since these letters were frequently written in Jung's capacity as a psychiatrist in answer to people's personal questions, the first principle of selection had to be that of medical discretion, and many such letters had perforce to be omitted. Furthermore, there are numerous references to people who themselves, or whose relatives, are still alive, which necessitated either omissions or the substitution of initials for names. Besides this principle of discretion the chief criterion of selection was that of intrinsic interest, whether scientific, personal, or historical. Some letters which were too long or too technical have been omitted but will be published in volume 18 of the Collected Works. The long correspondence between Jung and H. L. Philp and David Cox, published in Philp's book, *Jung and the Problem of Evil* (1958), has also been omitted, with the exception of three short letters; most of the letters on Jung's side are in volume 18. The correspondence between Jung and Dr. Löy has been published in volume 4 of the Collected Works.

The reader may notice a certain repetitiveness. Although I have

* Seven letters of Freud's to Jung were included in a selection edited by E. L. Freud (1960). See Freud, 5 Oct. 06, n. □.

tried to eliminate this to some extent, I felt that such repetitions—apart from Jung's frequent complaint about too much work or correspondence—tended to emphasize his great concern with certain problems. They also show his feeling of being constantly misunderstood (as on the distinction between God and God-image, or on his empirical approach to psychological problems) and his equally constant attempt—sometimes expressed with great patience and tolerance, sometimes with some affect—to clear up such misunderstandings.

As far as humanly possible, I, with the help of Mrs. Jaffé, tried to obtain permission for publication from every single addressee after the year 1930. The same applies to dream material or other data mentioned in the notes. Since the earlier letters date back many decades, some degree of liberty had to be taken with letters to people who we knew had died. In some cases, arrangements were made through friendly relations with families or estates of addressees (such as Countess Keyserling and the Hermann Hesse and Richard Wilhelm archives); in others, where the contents seemed to justify and allow it, we had to take personal responsibility for publication. As far as living addressees are concerned, we tried to consult every one who could be identified. In this task we were only partially successful, since many of the inquiring letters we sent out were returned marked "addressee unknown" or "addressee moved." This is not surprising. But it was gratifying to receive almost exclusively positive answers from those who responded, very often with kind personal remarks and helpful information, and I want to express my thanks to all these people for their cooperation. Only a handful of outright refusals were received. Some of the addressees requested anonymity, or the omission of certain passages, or the anonymity of some person mentioned in a letter; some letters were sent in with deletions made by the addressees. Others asked specifically for inclusion of their name or of certain passages which it had been my intention to treat differently. A few omissions have been made where the meaning was too obscure. This was the case with untraceable allusions, as when a letter referred to previous correspondence which could not be recovered, or to a conversation with the addressee.

The annotations are intended to provide the reader with facts it might prove difficult for him to find out for himself. I had started off with considerably more detailed and extensive notes than those I decided to include in the end. Such elaborate annotation would have burdened the volumes with facts that were not absolutely necessary or about which the reader could be expected to inform himself without too much trouble. Some notes which may appear unduly elaborate or unnecessary are included for personal or historical interest: the more time passes, the more difficult it will become to elicit the information given in them. On the other hand, many a time I had to admit defeat: there will be quite a few places in Jung's letters where the reader might look in vain for a numeral signalling a note. In such places, lengthy editorial research has failed to elucidate the reference. This regrettable fact is often due to Jung's habit of not keeping the addressees' letters; and he usually returned the numerous manuscripts and related material to the sender, so that very often identification was impossible. A special problem is that of giving details concerning addressees. This has been done wherever possible in a preliminary note designated with a □ ; in some cases, discretion precluded such annotation, and in many more cases the addressee could not be located. It should be borne in mind that many of the letters Jung received were from people completely unknown to him.

As a matter of principle and in order to prevent the notes from becoming too bulky, publications by addressees are included chiefly in the □ notes referring to analytical psychologists (and even here occasionally only in selection; generally only published books are cited). However, a few exceptions are made where it seems desirable for the understanding of the correspondence. Where the requisite information is available, biographical notes on addressees are regularly attached to the first letter, but the index contains every reference to them in other letters. The aim has been, when nothing else is known of an addressee, to give in the □ note at least the city or town to which the letter was addressed or, when the addressee is anonymous, the country. Such a place may not, obviously, have been a permanent residence. In so far as possible, the professional status of recipients is indicated, as well as the birth and death dates of those who are deceased; correspondents whose photographs appear as illustrations are limited to close friends who are no longer living. Names, book-titles, events, and subjects of importance are, with a few exceptions, annotated at their first occurrence; here again the index can be consulted for information on subsequent occurrences. While the notes are as concise as possible, abbreviations are at a minimum, the chief being CW for the Collected Works (20 vols., including a vol. of miscellany, *The Symbolic Life*, and the bibliography and index vols.) and *Memories* for the autobiographical *Memories*,

Dreams, Reflections, by Jung in collaboration with Aniela Jaffé. As the London and New York editions of the latter differ in pagination, double page references are given.

In spite of the great care taken and much time-consuming research, a fair number of gaps remain. I would be most grateful for any important information or corrections to letters and notes which readers might be able to provide.

The sources of the letters are varied. The largest group, from the files at Küsnacht, consists of carbon copies of dictated and typed letters and secretarial typed copies of handwritten letters. A second category includes letters sent to us by the recipients or their heirs, some in the original, some in xerox copies, some in the recipient's own typed copy. Handwritten letters are so indicated in the □ notes, and likewise previously published letters, but it has not been possible to give full details of the various documentary states of typed letters —originals with signature, xerox copies of the same, file carbon copies, typed copies of holograph letters, etc.

Although the greatest care has been taken to establish the authentic text, this was not always possible owing to Jung's habit of writing in corrections and adding handwritten postscripts. These changes were as a rule transferred by the secretaries to the carbon now in the files. However, some omissions of this procedure cannot be ruled out, e.g., where Jung's letters were posted at the village of Bollingen. Another problem was Jung's habit of filling in by hand Greek words or phrases for which a blank space had been left by the secretary. In most cases inquiries have enabled us to fill in these gaps; sometimes, however, clarification has not been possible. All such omissions, as well as doubtful restitutions, are mentioned in the notes. There are also instances of letters published by an addressee, who changed Jung's English, sometimes rightly and sometimes wrongly.

Occasionally we received copies of letters through third hands without knowing the name of the addressee. In such cases we had no means of checking the text. I have nevertheless assumed the accuracy of the copies.

Omissions are of two kinds: of repetitive or quite unimportant passages, and of passages of a too intimate or confidential nature. All omissions are indicated by ". . .". Changes in the letters written in English are limited mainly to punctuation (Jung's followed the German style and would be confusing to the English reader), obvious spelling mistakes, and corrections of secretarial errors (for instance, the incorrect "septem reges lapis" in the letter to Miss Nanavutty of 11 Nov. 1948, or a hearing mistake in a letter to Schoening of 24 Mar. 1955: the incorrect "what are they giving an aim to" for "what are they giving a name to"). We may suppose that such secretarial errors were corrected by Jung on the top copies. More important changes concern Jung's English style, which because of Germanisms and other idiosyncrasies makes Jung's difficult to understand for the English reader, particularly if he is unfamiliar with German. Un-English locutions like "in a hundred miles distance," "I wish you would elucidate me," "according to my humble idea," "on the one side/on the other side" have been changed to "a hundred miles away," "I wish you would enlighten me," "in my humble opinion," "on the one hand/on the other hand." Typically German is Jung's use of prepositions: "I object against," "independent from," "with other words," and similar phrases have been regularly altered to the customary English usage. Germanisms like "I succeeded to find" and "incapable to do" have also been changed. Jung's use of tenses is often highly erratic, and he frequently uses the classical subjunctive after "if"; these have been normalized. Jung's use of capitals in English (Anima, Unconscious, Psychology, Man, etc.) was so irregular that I felt justified in standardizing it and bringing it into line with the Collected Works. The same applies to the uniform use of forms like "psychic" instead of Jung's "psychical." In revising, I have followed the advice of Mr. R.F.C. Hull, the translator of the Collected Works. I am sure that Jung would not only not have objected but would have approved such changes, seeing that he submitted all of his English lectures and writings to the criticism of English-speaking people for revision. On the other hand, where Jung's English is highly personal and idiosyncratic but clearly understandable, no changes have been made, so that the English reader may come across passages that sound slightly strange to his ears.

In both the original English and the translated letters, certain conventions have been adopted. Titles of books have uniformly been put in italics, those of articles and essays have been put in quotation marks. For quotations in Latin, French, etc., italics are regularly used. As a rule, titles of Jung's works (and non-English works in general) are given in their translated forms. Paragraphs—often very long, as is usual in German—have occasionally been subdivided in order to make the text easier to read. Jung's address is not given except in the case of letters not written from his home at Seestrasse

228, Küsnacht. In a few cases, the address is uncertain, e.g., where Jung wrote letters from Bollingen, Locarno, etc., without the place being mentioned in the letter. Dates are conventionalized to the form "1 January 1909" (in notes, abbreviated "1 Jan. 09"). Jung's letters were dated almost without exception. To save space, the complimentary closings have usually been run in with the body of the letter and the signature.

A special problem is raised by the German salutations and complimentary closings. It is quite impossible to find precise equivalents in English. "Sehr geehrter Herr Doktor" and "Lieber Herr Doktor" are both bound to become "Dear Dr. —," "Verehrter Herr Graf" (Honoured Count) must be reduced to "Dear Count," and "Liebe gnädige Frau" (Dear gracious lady) to the prosaic "Dear Frau —." Recipients without honorifics are addressed "Dear Herr/Frau/Fräulein" or "Dear Mr./Mrs./Miss" according to language. Letters to Swiss, German, or French Protestant clergymen begin "Dear Pastor —," as the formal English "Dear Mr. —" would be inappropriate. The names of anonymous recipients are replaced by "N."; in the few cases where he or she received several letters, another capital has been substituted. As for the comparatively elaborate nuances of the German and French endings, often untranslatable, we have had in the main to use the conventional English forms that come closest while having a natural, idiomatic ring. No English translation can, most unfortunately, do complete justice to the nuances of the Continental formalities and distinctions.*

In some cases the reader may find it regrettable that the letter of the addressee is not published as well. However, I have tried to give in the notes the gist of the essential points—sometimes at considerable length—and to fill in the background wherever it seemed necessary for an understanding of Jung's answer. Here again, unfortunately, explanations are lacking only too frequently, because it was impossible to recover the addressee's letter.

*

As mentioned at the outset, the original Editorial Committee consisted of three members: Mrs. Marianne Niehus-Jung, Mrs. Aniela Jaffé, and myself. It was a very sad loss when Marianne Niehus died

---

* The availability of the Swiss edition of these Letters facilitates the comparison of the texts for those interested in the precise nuances. Cf. p. xviii.

in March 1965 after a prolonged illness. By that time the task of collecting the letters had virtually come to an end, but the work of selection and annotation was just beginning, and her co-operation was sorely missed. I would like to express my profound appreciation of her warmth and generosity, her tact and understanding, and her constant willingness to further my work. I am deeply grateful to her for all she had done right up to the end of her life.

After her death I had to carry the full responsibility with the support of Aniela Jaffé. Here again I would like to express my deep gratitude for the help she has given me all through the many years of the work. Her intimate knowledge of Jung's later years, her close contact with him both as his secretary and as his collaborator, her complete grasp of his ideas, were of the greatest assistance to me. I regularly sent her my notes for possible additions or corrections; and equally the selection and omission of letters were the subject of continuous correspondence. Thus a most friendly co-operation developed over more than ten years of work on these letters. It was the natural consequence of this co-operation that Aniela Jaffé from 1968 onwards assumed responsibility for the Swiss edition of the *Briefe*, published by the Walter-Verlag, Olten and Freiburg (which, in 1971, took over the interests of Rascher Verlag, Zurich, in the publication of Jung's works). With a very few exceptions, owing to the relative interest of some letters to the British/American or the German/Swiss reader, the selection of letters in the two editions is identical, though the Swiss edition (1972–73) has been divided into three volumes.

I am also much indebted to all those scholars in various fields who helped me in the formulation of notes. Jung's immense range of interests as shown in his letters makes it practically impossible for *one* person to provide the necessary annotations, and here I have been greatly helped in my researches by many experts, too numerous to be mentioned individually. However, I want to single out the Rev. W. Baddeley, of Cambridge, England, who gave me invaluable help with the Greek and Latin quotations. Particular thanks are due to Mr. R.F.C. Hull, the translator of the Collected Works. His remarkable knowledge of Jung's texts, terminology, and style and his wide interest in other fields were a constant stimulus to me and occasioned many improvements. Mrs. Jane A. Pratt very kindly contributed the English translation of the letters written in French. Equally helpful was Mr. William McGuire, of Bollingen Series and Princeton University Press, whose editorial and research experience was of the greatest value and who succeeded in locating a consider-able number of letters, in particular of correspondents in the U.S.A. Mr. Kurt Niehus, Jung's son-in-law, accepted responsibility on be-half of the family for reading and approving the final selection of letters. I wish also to thank my faithful secretary Mrs. Hertha Manheimer, who over many years of complicated work never lost patience in spite of the continuous changes, deletions, and additions and my all but illegible handwriting.

Last but certainly not least, my particular thanks are due to the Bollingen Foundation, without whose moral and financial support these letters could not have been collected, edited, and published in their present form.

London, 1971   GERHARD ADLER

Several letters of the 1906–1950 period which came to light after the publication of volume 1 are included as addenda in the present vol-ume. I am deeply indebted to Miss Hildegard Nagel for translating several of these, owing to the illness of Mr. R.F.C. Hull.

London, 1974   G. A.

CHRONOLOGY

1875   26 July: born to Johann Paul Achilles Jung (1842–1896), then parson at Kesswil (Canton Thurgau), and Emilie, née Preiswerk (1848–1923).

1879   The family moves to Klein-Hüningen, near Basel.

1884   Birth of sister Gertrud (d. 1935).

1895–1900   Medical training (and qualification) at Basel U.

1900   Assistant Staff Physician to Eugen Bleuler at the Burghölzli, the insane asylum of Canton Zurich and psychiatric clinic of Zurich U.

1902   Senior Assistant Staff Physician at the Burghölzli. — M.D. dissertation (Zurich U.): *Zur Psychologie und Pathologie sogenannter occulter Phänomene* (= "On the Psychology and Pathology of So-called Occult Phenomena," CW 1).

1902–1903   Winter semester with Pierre Janet at the Salpêtrière in Paris for the study of theoretical psychopathology.

1903   Marriage to Emma Rauschenbach, of Schaffhausen (1882–1955); one son and four daughters.

1903–1905   Experimental researches on word associations, published in *Diagnostische Assoziationsstudien* (1906, 1909) (= *Studies in Word-Association*, 1918; CW 2).

1905–1909   Senior Staff Physician at the Burghölzli; after that in private practice at his home, 1003 (later 228) Seestrasse, Küsnacht (Zurich).

1905–1913   Lecturer (Privatdozent) on the Medical Faculty of Zurich U.; lectures on psychoneuroses and psychology.

1907   *Über die Psychologie der Dementia Praecox* (= *The Psychology of Dementia Praecox*, 1909; CW 3). — First meeting with Freud in Vienna.

1908   First International Psychoanalytic Congress, Salzburg.

1909   First visit to U.S.A. with Freud and Ferenczi on the occasion of the 20th anniversary of Clark University, Worcester, Mass., where Jung lectures on the association experiment and receives hon. degree of LL.D.

1909–1913   Editor of *Jahrbuch für psychoanalytische und psychopatho-logische Forschungen.*

1910   Second International Psychoanalytic Congress, Nurem-berg.

1910–1914   First President of the International Psychoanalytic Asso-ciation.

1911   Third International Psychoanalytic Congress, Weimar.

1912   Another visit to U.S.A. for series of lectures at Fordham U., New York, on "The Theory of Psychoanalysis" (CW 4). — "Neue Bahnen der Psychologie" (= "New Paths in Psychology," later revised and expanded as "On the Psychology of the Unconscious"; both CW 7). — *Wandlungen und Symbole der Libido* (= *Psychology of the Unconscious,* 1916; for revision, see 1952) leading to

1913   break with Freud. — Fourth International Psychoanalytic Congress, Munich. — Jung designates his psychology as "Analytical Psychology" (later also "Complex Psychology"). — Resigns his lecturership at Zurich U.

1913–1919   Period of intense introversion: confrontation with the un-conscious.

1916   "VII Sermones ad Mortuos"; first mandala painting. — *Collected Papers on Analytical Psychology.* — First descrip-tion of process of "active imagination" in "Die transzen-dente Funktion" (not publ. until 1957; in CW 8). — First use of terms "personal unconscious," "collective/su-prapersonal unconscious," "individuation," "animus/an-ima," "persona" in "La Structure de l'inconscient" (CW 7, App.). — Beginning of study of Gnostic writings.

1918   "Über das Unbewusste" (= "The Role of the Uncon-scious," CW 10).

1918–1919   Commandant of camp for interned British soldiers at Château d'Oex (Canton Vaud). — First use of term "archetype" in "Instinct and the Unconscious" (CW 8).

1920   Journey to Algeria and Tunisia.

1921   *Psychologische Typen*; first use of term "self" (= *Psy-chological Types,* 1923; CW 6).

1922   Purchase of property in village of Bollingen.

1923   First Tower in Bollingen. — Death of mother. — Richard Wilhelm's lecture on the *I Ching* at the Psychological Club, Zurich.

1924–1925 Visit with Pueblo Indians in New Mexico.

1925 First English seminar at the Psychological Club, Zurich.

1925–1926 Expedition to Kenya, Uganda, and the Nile; visit with the Elgonyi on Mt. Elgon.

1928 Beginning of encounter with alchemy. — *Two Essays on Analytical Psychology* (= CW 7). — *Über die Energetik der Seele* (various essays, now in CW 8).

1928–1930 English seminars on "Dream Analysis" at the Psychological Club, Zurich.

1929 Publication, with Richard Wilhelm, of *Das Geheimnis der goldenen Blüte* (= *The Secret of the Golden Flower;* Jung's contribution in CW 13). — *Contributions to Analytical Psychology.*

1930 Vice-President of General Medical Society for Psychotherapy, with Ernst Kretschmer as president.

1930–1934 English seminars on "Interpretation of Visions" at the Psychological Club, Zurich.

1931 *Seelenprobleme der Gegenwart* (essays in CW 4, 6, 8, 10, 15, 16, 17).

1932 Awarded Literature Prize of the City of Zurich.

1933 First lectures at the Eidgenössische Technische Hochschule (E.T.H.), Zurich (Swiss Federal Polytechnic), on "Modern Psychology." — *Modern Man in Search of a Soul.* — Eranos lecture on "A Study in the Process of Individuation" (CW 9, i). — Visit to Egypt and Palestine.

1934 Founds International General Medical Society for Psychotherapy and becomes its first president. — Eranos lecture on "Archetypes of the Collective Unconscious" (CW 9, i). — *Wirklichkeit der Seele* (essays in CW 8, 10, 15, 16, 17).

1934–1939 English seminars on "Psychological Aspects of Nietzsche's *Zarathustra*" at the Psychological Club, Zurich.

1934–1939 Editor of *Zentralblatt für Psychotherapie und ihre Grenzgebiete* (Leipzig).

1935 Appointed Professor at the E.T.H., Zurich. — Founds Schweizerische Gesellschaft für Praktische Psychologie. — Eranos lecture on "Dream Symbols of the Individuation Process" (expanded to Part II of *Psychology and Alchemy,* CW 12). — Tavistock Lectures at the Institute of Medical Psychology, London (not published until 1968: *Analytical Psychology; Its Theory and Practice;* CW 18).

1936   Receives hon. doctoral degree from Harvard U. — Eranos lecture on "Ideas of Redemption in Alchemy" (expanded as part III of *Psychology and Alchemy*); "Wotan" (CW 10).

1937   Terry Lectures on "Psychology and Religion" (CW 11) at Yale U., New Haven, Conn. — Eranos lecture on "The Visions of Zosimos" (CW 13).

1938   Invitation to India by the British Government on the 25th anniversary of the Indian Science Congress; hon. doctorates from the universities of Calcutta, Benares, and Allahabad. — International Congress for Psychotherapy at Oxford with Jung as President; he receives hon. doctorate of Oxford U. — Appointed Hon. Fellow of the Royal Society of Medicine, London. — Eranos lecture on "Psychological Aspects of the Mother Archetype" (CW 9, i).

1939   Eranos lecture on "Concerning Rebirth" (CW 9, i).

1940   Eranos lecture on "A Psychological Approach to the Dogma of the Trinity" (CW 11).

1941   Publication, together with Karl Kerényi, of *Einführung in das Wesen der Mythologie* (= *Essays on a Science of Mythology*; Jung's contribution in CW 9, i). — Eranos lecture on "Transformation Symbolism in the Mass" (CW 11).

1942   Resigns appointment as Professor at E.T.H. — *Paracelsica* (essays in CW 13, 15). — Eranos lecture on "The Spirit Mercurius" (CW 13).

1943   Hon. Member of the Swiss Academy of Sciences.

1944   Appointed to the chair of Medical Psychology at Basel U.; resigns the same year on account of critical illness. —*Psychologie und Alchemie* (CW 12).

1945   Hon. doctorate of Geneva U. on the occasion of his 70th birthday. — Eranos lecture on "The Psychology of the Spirit," expanded as "The Phenomenology of the Spirit in Fairy Tales" (CW 9, i).

1946   Eranos lecture on "The Spirit of Psychology" (expanded as "On the Nature of the Psyche," CW 8). — *Die Psychologie der Übertragung* (= "The Psychology of the Transference," CW 16); *Aufsätze zur Zeitgeschichte* (= *Essays on Contemporary Events*; in CW 10); *Psychologie und Erziehung* (CW 17).

1948	*Symbolik des Geistes* (essays in CW 9, i, 11, 13). — Eranos lecture "On the Self" (expanded to ch. IV of *Aion*, CW 9, ii). — Inauguration of the C. G. Jung Institute, Zurich.
1950	*Gestaltungen des Unbewussten* (essays in CW 9, i and 15).
1951	*Aion* (CW 9, ii). — Eranos lecture "On Synchronicity" (CW 8, App.).
1952	Publication, with W. Pauli, of *Naturerklärung und Psyche* (= *The Interpretation of Nature and Psyche*; Jung's contribution "Synchronicity: An Acausal Connecting Principle," CW 8). — *Symbole der Wandlung* (= *Symbols of Transformation*, CW 5: 4th, greatly revised edition of *Psychology of the Unconscious*). — *Antwort auf Hiob* (= "Answer to Job," CW 11).
1953	Publication of the 1st vol. of the American/British edition of the *Collected Works* (tr. by R.F.C. Hull): *Psychology and Alchemy* (CW 12).
1954	*Von den Wurzeln des Bewusstseins* (essays in CW 8, 9, i, 11, 13).
1955	Hon. doctorate of the E.T.H., Zurich, on the occasion of his 80th birthday. — Death of his wife (27 November).
1955–1956	*Mysterium Coniunctionis* (CW 14); the final work on the psychological significance of alchemy.
1957	*Gegenwart und Zukunft* (= "The Undiscovered Self (Present and Future)," CW 10). — Starts work on *Memories, Dreams, Reflections* with the help of Aniela Jaffé (pub. 1962). — BBC television interview with John Freeman.
1958	*Ein moderner Mythus* (= "Flying Saucers: A Modern Myth," CW 10). — Publication of initial vol. in Swiss edition of Gesammelte Werke: *Praxis der Psychotherapie* (Bd. 16).
1960	Hon. Citizen of Küsnacht on the occasion of his 85th birthday.
1961	Finishes his last work 10 days before his death: "Approaching the Unconscious," in *Man and His Symbols* (1964). — Dies after short illness on 6 June in his house at Küsnacht.

ADDENDA 1906–1950

To Poul Bjerre

17 July 1914

The present situation is worse, or better, than before. Freud's last regrettable enunciation in the *Jahrbuch*,[1] which clearly bases ΨA on the principle of authority, has not passed unnoticed here. Our president Dr. Maeder has taken the initiative and proposed to the Zurich group that they resign *in toto* from the International Association. This has been done. In explaining the resignation a protest is being made against the principle of authority promulgated by Freud. Consequently we shall not attend the Dresden Congress.[2] Our moves are merely reactions to the papal policies of the Viennese. Naturally one should do what one can to open people's eyes. But they want to be blind, as was indubitably clear in Munich.[3] Vienna is working against me with methods which are so unfair that I cannot defend myself. Personal insinuations are being bandied about—for instance, I had tried at Deuticke's to take over the *Jahrbuch*, and other such shameless lies. In a breach of medical discretion, Freud has even made hostile use of a patient's letter—a letter which the person concerned,

□ (Handwritten.) See Bjerre, 22 Jan. 34 (in vol. 1). For B.'s participation in the early psychoanalytic movement, see *The Freud/Jung Letters*, ed. William McGuire (1974), index, under his name.

[1] This refers to a passage in "On the History of the Psycho-Analytic Movement" (Standard Edn. 14, p. 43; originally written Jan.–Feb. 1914) where Freud, discussing the problem of his successor, says: ". . . in favour of Jung were his exceptional talents, the contributions he had already made to psycho-analysis, his independent position and the impression of assured energy which his personality conveyed. In addition to this, he seemed ready to enter into a friendly relationship with me and for my sake to give up certain racial prejudices which he had previously permitted himself. I had no inkling at that time that in spite of all these advantages the choice was a most unfortunate one, that I had lighted upon a person who was incapable of tolerating the authority of another, but who was still less capable of wielding it himself, and whose energies were relentlessly devoted to the furtherance of his own interests."

[2] On account of the outbreak of the First World War the Congress, planned for Sept. 1914, did not take place until Sept. 1918, when it was held in Budapest.

[3] In a letter to Bjerre of 30 Sept. 13, Jung had written: "In the psychoanalytic world there has been a great uproar since Munich. From Vienna the watchword goes forth: We in Zurich have never had any notion of true and correct analysis, we are theological occultists, we introduce ethical demands into the patient which are not his own (!), etc. Not a trace of any desire to understand our viewpoint. Further I have heard that the Viennese did not let things come to an open break in Munich only because they did not want to endanger the existence of the newly founded [1912] *Internationale Zeitschrift für ärztliche Psychoanalyse*."

whom I know very well, wrote in a moment of resistance against me.[4] Supposing I were to publish what people have already told me about Freud!!! These practices are characteristic of Viennese policies. Such an enemy is not worth the name.

I am most grateful to you for the promise of your valuable assistance in connection with our publication.[5] We shall not have very much to publish, since we are a relatively small group in which not all members are active as writers. This is something to be glad about, really, because nowadays too much is written and too little read.

Perhaps it would be worthwhile for the others if you went to the Dresden Congress and spoke your mind bluntly. It may be that a few people's eyes would then be opened after all.

Yours very sincerely, JUNG

[4] The letter is published in "On the History of the Psycho-Analytic Movement," pp. 63f.
[5] Cf. Maeder, 29 Oct. 13 (where, however, the first volume of the *Psychologische Abhandlungen*, published by Deuticke in 1914, is erroneously attributed to Rascher Verlag, which published the volumes that followed). This first volume of "publications of the Zurich school" contained papers by various writers, but later volumes were devoted almost entirely to Jung's papers.

To Oskar A. H. Schmitz

Dear Herr Schmitz,   7 January 1927

. . .

I, too, have been struck by the fact that people are not responding to the last part of your book.[1] There is something there. In some way it does not take hold. It is hard to say why. But I believe it is because you have not found the right "potential." There is too little difference between levels, at least so one feels. Either you have brought the incomprehensible too close to the comprehensible, or you have lifted yourself by means of an inflated balloon to the height of visions. Somehow you are too much on a level with them, so that no tension results. But just here there should be tension, for two worlds, two forms of experience that are in some way incommensurable, are colliding here. These visions formerly constituted the uttermost secret of the mystery! Since you have presented the subject in a very deco-

□ (Handwritten. Translated by Hildegard Nagel.) See Schmitz, 26 May 23 (in vol. 1).
[1] Unascertainable.

rous and dignified manner I cannot say that you have banalized the unexpressible. You have spoken only of the expressible, but in such a way that no one can guess that behind or beneath it the unexpressible secret lies buried, or that you yourself have any such notion. Your method of presentation is apparently complete and satisfying, but it lacks a sense of what lies beyond; one might say also that it is "unimpassioned" and probably hit the mark. *The experience lacks corporeality*, that is why it does not grip us. Somebody has even contested the authenticity of your experience and taken it for a made-up fantasy. This reaction seems to me important. It always seems to me that one says such things more effectively by leaving them unsaid. There is an art, not of speaking of such things, but of keeping silent. But I myself have no assured judgment about this, merely a marked reluctance to present anything in this direction to the public.

I have already pretty well worked out my Darmstadt lecture[2] and found that I am scarcely able to include everything that would be desirable.

With the best wishes for the New Year,

Yours sincerely, C. G. JUNG

[2] Cf. Keyserling, 21 May 27, n. ☐.

To Mary Foote

[ORIGINAL IN ENGLISH]

Dear Miss Foote,   19 March 1927

I rather prefer to have you come to Zurich about the middle of October for the winter term. Age is of no importance. As long as you live, you have all the problems of the living, only different ones than with 20.

Sincerely yours, C. G. JUNG

☐ (1887–1968), American portrait painter, living in Peking in 1927. In Zurich 1928–1958. Beginning in 1929, she edited and supervised the private publication of most of the transcripts ("Notes") of Jung's English seminars. — This letter and those of 28 Mar. 33, 18 Dec. 29, and 12 July 37 are published by courtesy of the Beinecke Library, Yale U. They were previously published in an article by Edward Foote, "Who Was Mary Foote," *Spring*, 1974.

To Oskar A. H. Schmitz

Dear Herr Schmitz,   21 July 1927

. . .

There is something still a little unclear about the relation to woman, in spite of the great "hit" you made with Fräulein Wolff.[1] In this direction something needs to be added. This belongs to that idea that constantly obtrudes itself in you, about the man who "is master of all his functions." Goethe, too, was a great bluffer. Not only during his lifetime but in particular posthumously he has had an increasingly bedazzling effect. I doubt the genuineness of the "complete man." It is too much of a concoction. What was his marriage really like?

Because of your negative mother complex, all sorts of unrealized safeguards against feminine influence were still to be expected. The penitent's shirt beneath and the red habit outside[2] are surely necessary forms of transition, but at the same time symbols of the bodily and spiritual celibate. Woman is world and fate, that is why she is so important to the man. Your present image in this respect is still eighteenth century. It is remarkable how Keyserling, too, connects with Cagliostro[3]—to say nothing of Faust.

I still have to gather breath to get started. I ought to write, but the sunshine is still too good to be sitting at a desk. With best wishes,

Yours truly, C. G. JUNG

☐ (Handwritten. Translated by Hildegard Nagel.)
[1] Cf. Kirsch, 28 May 53, n. 1.
[2] This seems to refer to a dream which cannot be ascertained.
[3] Count Allesandro Cagliostro (1743–95), Italian adventurer who posed as a physician, alchemist, magician, etc.

To James Kirsch

Dear Colleague,   temporarily at Bollingen, 19 August 1929

The picture is really unsatisfactory and seriously dissociated. In such cases it is always advisable not to analyse too actively, and that means letting the transference run its course quietly and listening sympathetically. The patient obviously needs you as a father and you have to take up the attitude of a father towards her. Really as a

☐ (Handwritten.) Cf. Kirsch, 26 May 34 (in vol. 1). — Published (in K.'s tr.) in *Psychological Perspectives*, III:1 (spring 1972).

father, with exhortation, reproof, loving care, paternal interest, etc. No technical-analytic attitude, please, but an essentially human one. The patient needs you in order to unite her dissociated personality in your unity, calm, and security. For the present you must only stand by without too many therapeutic intentions. The patient will get out of you what she needs. Without rectification of her relationship to the father she cannot put her love problem in order either. She must first become at peace with the father in a human relationship built on confidence.

Yours ever, C. G. JUNG

To Mary Foote

[ORIGINAL IN ENGLISH]

My dear Miss Foote,   Bollingen, Ct. St. Gallen, 18 December 1929

Here is one Seminar.[1] Now please do tell me whether you gave me more than one, f.i. the Astrology Seminar. I can't find it here. I thought I had taken all with me that you gave me—but it *might* be that I have left something more at home. If that is the case, please tell Mrs. Jung, who is actually at home, that the missing parts are either in my studio or on the big desk in my library. She should send them right away. I hope I forgot nothing.

Cordially yours, C. G. JUNG

□ (Handwritten.) Cf. Foote, 19 Mar. 27, n. □.

[1] Evidently the Notes on either the Autumn 1928 or Winter and Spring 1929 part of Jung's seminar on *Dream Analysis*, prepared by F. and other members of the seminar. Content indicates that the "Astrology Seminar" mentioned in the next sentence is the Autumn 1929 part. The *Dream Analysis* seminar continued into Spring 1930.

To Mary Foote

[ORIGINAL IN ENGLISH]

[Rhodes,] 28 March 1933

Dear Mary, here are some greetings from the enchanted island of roses; more than that—here I found a piece of my spiritual ancestry.

Affectionately yours, C. G.

□ (Handwritten.) Postcard, showing a photograph of the city of Rhodes; postmarked Cyprus, 29 March. Jung was on a trip to Egypt and Palestine.

To Mary Foote

Dear Mary, [ORIGINAL IN ENGLISH] Bollingen, 12 July 1937

The hut is erected and looks good as a studio. There are no trees and bushes close to the window.

I shall be in all Thursday and any time will suit me for you to come and deposit your tools. Then on the 17th I am ready for you to start work.[1]

Very sincerely yours, C. G.

[1] Mary Foote painted a portrait of Jung, now hanging in the Beinecke Library, Yale U.

To Henry A. Murray

My dear Murray, [ORIGINAL IN ENGLISH] 6 October 1938

You have misunderstood my letter completely. I didn't suspect you for one moment of having talked such nonsense about me. I only wanted to get a written statement from you which I could use to prove that you never said such a thing and that the "man from Princeton" was a positive liar. Maybe my letter was too short and I took it too much for granted that you would understand it. I can only assure you that the thought never entered my head that you could have been the fountainhead of childish rumours.

I don't think that I have paranoic delusions about persecution. The difficulty is very real. Whatever I touch and wherever I go I meet with this prejudice that I'm a Nazi and that I'm in close affiliation with the German government. I had very real proof of this and corresponding difficulties this summer in England. Even in India[1] I discovered that a faked photograph with my name had been sent to scientific societies years ago from Vienna. On this photo, which I possess, I'm represented as a Jew of the particularly vicious kind. Such experiences are no delusions.

Hoping that my more longwinded explanations this time have allayed your suspicions, I remain,

Yours cordially, C. G. JUNG

☐ See Murray, 2 May 25 (in vol. 1).

[1] During his visit to India earlier in 1938 for the Silver Jubilee Session of the Indian Science Congress. Cf. *Memories*, pp. 274ff./256ff.

xxxiv

To Henry A. Murray

[ORIGINAL IN ENGLISH]

My dear Murray,   19 December 1938

The origin of the story about myself being seldom at home and a frequent guest at Berchtesgaden has been traced back to Dr. Hadley Cantril.[1] He is the head of the Institute of Propaganda Analysis at Princeton University and he told Dr. Beatrice Hinkle[2] at a luncheon that the tale was "so sincerely believed because Dr. Murray told him Freud himself told it to Dr. Murray."

I should like very much to know what on earth has prompted this man to tell such a cock and bull story, mixing up your name with it. Could you write and ask Dr. Cantril what his idea was? It isn't ordinary fussiness that I insist upon knowing of such tales that are spread over the world. There must be something behind it.

With best wishes for the new year, I remain,

Yours cordially, C. G. JUNG

[1] Hadley Cantril (1906–1969), professor of psychology, Princeton U., president of the Institute for Propaganda Analysis and later director of the Princeton Public Opinion Research Council; author of *The Invasion from Mars: A Study in the Psychology of Panic* (Princeton, 1940); cf. CW 9, i, par. 227, n. 22.
[2] See Hinkle, 6 Feb. 51.

To Henry A. Murray

[ORIGINAL IN ENGLISH]

My dear Murray,   6 March 1939

Thank you very much for the thorough exploration of the Hitler case. Quite a number of Germans who have heard the story said that they wished it were true. I recently had news from Germany which confirm that all is not well in Berchtesgaden.

Cordially yours, C. G. JUNG

To H. K. Fierz

Dear Colleague,   Bollingen, 16 September 1943

I have read your paper[1] with interest and pleasure. You will find a few notes in the margin. I have been busying myself with the 3 of the princess:[2] the 3, being uneven, is masculine; also the 5. Here the 3 cannot refer to the functions but has the significance of a set of three. From the archaic point of view that is a unity, namely "the *one* set of three," therefore a *triad* and, better still, a *Trinity* (*triunus!*). The princess is the Lady Soul, in the *Orient* (for example, the ὄρνις περσικός,[3] the rooster, comes from Persia). The three as the masculine companion of the anima is, on the chthonic level, the phallus + 2 testes = 3, and on the psychic level a divine triad that has creative cosmogonic significance. Hence the three is nothing less than the divinity, the *demiurge*. The *fight* is that of *Jacob with the angel* (i.e., with the might of Yahweh) at the ford of the Jabbok. He himself had previously behaved demiurgically, i.e., deceptively (Esau!), and had to wrestle with an angry God. He was able to hold his own against the angel. Then, in Gen. 32:28 comes the new name (Israel = warrior of God); then comes in 30f.: "And Jacob called the name of the place Peniel (i.e., the face of God) for *I have seen God face to face*, and *my life is preserved.*" 31: "And as he passed over Peniel *the sun rose upon him; and he halted upon his thigh* (motif of dislocating the arm! Cf. *Wandlungen und Symbole der Libido*).[4] The 3 consists of three equal units; there you see the natural foundation of the ὁμοούσία (τῷ πατρι),[5] Christi, Patris & Spir. Sancti, and at the same time you see why Arius[6] was an arch heretic, for the doctrine of ὁμοούσία (ομοουσιος τῷ πατρι) is just false. And the liberal parsons who deny the divinity of Christ are even more damnable heretics. *Anathema sit!*

I will recommend your MS to Morgenthaler.[7] But I am afraid it is

☐ (Handwritten. Translated by Hildegard Nagel.) Heinrich Karl Fierz, M.D., Swiss psychiatrist and analytical psychologist, medical director of the Klinik am Zürichberg; cf. his *Klinik und analytische Psychologie* (1963).

[1] "Zur Entstehung und Bedeutung von Zwangsgedanken," paper read to the Swiss Society for Practical Psychology.

[2] The initial dream of the male patient, discussed in the lecture, was about the dismemberment of a young girl. The final dream of the treatment to which Jung refers was of the patient's wedding to a Persian princess in a great castle. He had to defend her, successfully, against her three brothers. — In Dr. F.'s discussion of the dream with the patient he pointed out that a legitimate relationship to the anima had been achieved which, however, had still to be protected, with regard to both the sexual and the spiritual aspects.

[3] = Persian bird.

[4] Cf. *Symbols of Transformation*, CW 5, pars. 356, n. 50, and 524.

[5] Cf. Niederer, 23 June 47, n. 6.

[6] Arius of Alexandria (c. 260–336), founder of Arianism, the doctrine of homoiousia, was condemned as heretic at the Councils of Nicaea (325) and Constantinople (381).

too long. You will have to arrange that somehow with him. Send it to him direct. I am no longer on the editorial staff, but merely "collaborator"—*Dei gratia*. With best wishes,

Yours sincerely, C. G. JUNG

7 W. Morgenthaler, Swiss psychiatrist, editor of the *Schweizer Zeitschrift für Psychologie*, which he had founded together with Jung and the Geneva psychologist Jean Piaget. — The paper was eventually published in the *Schweizer Medizinische Wochenschrift*, 1944, and again in Fierz's book (n. □).

To Philip Wylie

[ORIGINAL IN ENGLISH]

Dear Mr. Wylie: 19 February 1947

I have owed you a letter for a long time. Unfortunately your *Generation of Vipers*[1] has been hidden from my sight for quite a time, and when I began to read it last fall I fell seriously ill—your book was not the cause of it!—and now I'm just slowly recovering. No sooner could I open my eyes again that I continued reading your book and have read it from cover to cover with the most intense interest. You can shock people sky-high, and apparently they need it.

I have enjoyed your book thoroughly, although I must confess I felt critical at certain passages. For instance: The affair of the ecclesiastical Jesus is not so damn simple as your critique seems to suggest. Half of the picture you paint is absolutely true and I can subscribe to every word of it. All that dogmatic stuff heaped around the figure of the Redeemer can be brushed aside easily if you swing your rationalistic broom, but you overlook entirely the fact that out of that philosophic and speculative scholasticism something has grown which you cannot wipe off the slate, and that is science and the scientific attitude, which is characterized by sincerity, devotion, and honesty. As William James rightly said: "Our scientific temper is devout."[2]

Although your book is modest enough not to claim to be more than a *Kulturkritik* of America, it is valid also for our European civiliza-

□ (1902–1971), American author. Jung had met him in the U.S.A. in 1936 and had visited him at the time of his Terry Lectures on "Psychology and Religion" at Yale U. in 1937. — This letter and Wylie 27 June 47 are published by courtesy of Princeton University Library and Mrs. Philip Wylie.
1 Pub. 1942. Cf. White, 19 Dec. 47, for further comment.
2 *Pragmatism* (1907), p. 15.

tion, if one is still allowed to speak of such a thing. With some slight variations your book is applicable to almost any cultured nation. I'm now busy spreading its fame over here in Switzerland, and I try to get it known as much as possible.

At the moment when I had finished reading the *Generation of Vipers* your book *On Morals*[3] arrived, which I'm going to read at once.

In a further edition of your *Generation of Vipers* you should add an illustration of Grant Wood's wonderful painting: Daughters of Revolution.[4]

I hear complaints from all sides that my books are not getatable in the U. S. I can tell you now that an English firm is going to publish all my books in a decent form as a complete edition.[5] But that will take its time, particularly under the present economic conditions prevailing in England.

There is a real need of books like yours, because somebody ought to wake up, since mankind has now reached the straight road to hell.

Thank you for your honesty and courage!

Yours sincerely, C. G. JUNG

[3] *An Essay on Morals* (1947); see Wylie, 27 June 47, par. 2.
[4] Wood (1891–1942) was known for his paintings of the American scene. *Daughters of Revolution* satirizes bigoted mother-types.
[5] Routledge & Kegan Paul Ltd., London, and the Bollingen Foundation, through Pantheon Books Inc., New York, collaborated in publishing the Collected Works.

To Philip Wylie

[ORIGINAL IN ENGLISH]

Dear Mr. Wylie: 27 June 1947

Through Mrs. Baumann[1] I became acquainted with your letter to her. It was most enlightening! You must take into account that we have been cut off from the rest of the world for about five years, and I had no possibility to get informed about the remarkable intelligence of your countrymen. I'm just beginning to open my eyes. I understand your point of view thoroughly now. You are quite right and I beg to inform you of the fact that I agree completely with your attitude. Your way is obviously the right one, which I didn't know before, being, as I said, uninformed about American public opinion.

In the meantime I have read your book *An Essay on Morals*.[2] I

[1] Carol F. Baumann, an American pupil of Jung's, living in Zurich.
[2] See Wylie, 19 Feb. 47, n. 3.

think it's a perfectly heroic attempt to teach a nation a simple truth. I must say your book is difficult. I have read it carefully from cover to cover and time and again I was struck by the fact that I couldn't imagine how you can hope to overcome the prejudice and short-sightedness of your public by a rather abstract demonstration of the moral issues of my ideas. I think the most comprehensible point is the fact you hammer in, namely that man is an animal. And even this most obvious of all facts collides in the most violent way with the most sacred prejudices. It is such a simple truth that it is exceedingly difficult to grasp it, because people are twisted and not simple. I definitely cannot see how you lead them on from the state of such an insight to a state of humanity. In other words: how can man become human? This is the problem that has confronted me every day in my practical work. When I was in Africa in the Kavirondo country,[3] the older people said of the younger ones, who, under the influence of the missions, didn't submit any longer to the traditional initiations (circumcision etc.), that they remained mere animals. Now where are our initiations, or the equivalent of them? I find that without a very thorough analysis people cannot even see that they have a shadow—and from the shadow down to the animal there is a very long way indeed. People don't know that the only true servants of God are the animals. Now what are you going to do to bring up your Methodists and Baptists and so on to the understanding that any lousy dog is much more pious than they are? But please don't get discouraged! I'm profoundly grateful to you for your valiant attempt and I fervently hope that you will succeed for the good of our foolish and hopelessly blindfolded humanity.

I'm sorry I never acknowledged personally the receipt of your former books (*When Worlds Collide, After Worlds Collide, Gladiator,* and *Finnley Wren*).[4] They were sent to me by Farrar & Rinehart and I was under the impression that it was their initiative and not yours. I have read them and I can tell you that after the many years that have gone by since, the picture of the colliding worlds is still vividly impressed upon my mind. It has hit the head of an unconscious nail in me, which I hadn't succeeded in eradicating completely.

Sincerely yours, C. G. JUNG

[3] For Jung's visit to East Africa in winter 1925–26, see Kuhn, 1 Jan. 26, and *Memories*, ch. IX, iii.
[4] Published respectively 1933, 1934, 1930, and 1934. The first two are "science fiction" fantasies. Cf. Jung, "Flying Saucers: A Modern Myth of Things Seen in the Skies" (1958; CW 10).

To Medard Boss

Dear Colleague, 27 June 1947

Please forgive me for not thanking you sooner for the inaugural dissertation[1] you so kindly sent me. And also many thanks for the inaugural lecture[2] which has arrived in the meantime. I have now studied
them both and am allowing myself a few comments.

As regards your book on sexual perversions, I find your observations
very good and to the point. I am less able to say the same of your
theoretical disquisitions, since their philosophical language shows a
striking disproportion to the exactness of your observations.

The same thing struck me in your lecture. For example, the case of
anxiety neurosis you describe (p. 14)[3] is in my opinion quite insufficiently explained by your general philosophical views. There you dealt
in detail with Freud's way of looking at things, but not with how I
would see such a case. Of course I would not expect anything of that
sort, except that you had already referred to me critically.[4]

It is going rather too far that you feel you have to reproach me for a
certain narrow-minded prejudice. Obviously you are not aware that as
long as 30 years ago I expressed, against Freud, doubts about a purely
causalistic interpretation, in consequence of which the Freudians pil-
loried me as totally unscientific. It seems equally unknown to you that
I have suggested a conditional approach. Archetypes have never been
for me pure *causae*, but conditions [*Bedingungen*]. From your conclusions I find that you have completely misunderstood my concept of
archetypes. You are utterly mistaken in saying that I have described
the archetypes as given with the brain structure. Is the fact that the
body also expresses character totally unknown to you, or do you be-

---

☐ (Translated by Hildegard Nagel.) Medard Boss, M.D. (1903–   ), Swiss existential psychoanalyst; professor of psychotherapy at the U. of Zurich. Cf. his *Psychoanalysis and Daseinsanalysis* (New York, 1963).

[1] *Sinn und Gehalt der sexuellen Perversionen* (Bern, 1947). — The English tr.,
Meaning and Content of Sexual Perversions (New York, 1949), is a second edition and contains many changes.

[2] "Psychotherapie in daseinsanalytischer Sicht," unpublished.

[3] In ibid.

[4] This seems to refer to a passage in the unpublished lecture. The preface to the
2nd, English edition, after some appreciative remarks on Jung's concepts of the
self and individuation, has a sentence (on p. xi) which may contain the gist of
B.'s criticism: "Jung's descriptions, however, were still loaded with the remnants
of the old mechanistic exact-scientific way of thinking and with many outdated
biological theories."

lieve that the pattern of behaviour familiar to biologists is not some-how expressed in the biological structure? You yourself say that the human body is not only a thing of nature, but "one of the possible manifestations of human nature itself." The body as a whole, so it seems to me, is a pattern of behaviour, and man as a whole is an archetype. You believe you have discovered a contradiction when you find that I think of the archetype at one time as structure and at other times as psychic organ, or vessel, or quality [*Eigenschaft*], or as instinct, etc., and do not perceive that I am giving just as many descriptions of the archetype as can be illustrated by facts, as you might have learned, for instance, from our curatorium meetings.[5] I have no theory about the archetype and have never maintained that it is pure causality. It is a condition [*Bedingung*] and as such it has a certain *efficacitas causalis*, for only that which has effects has reality.[6] If it had none it would be mere show. But this does not mean that it is limited to a causal effect. On the contrary it has many modalities, expressed in a variety of symbols. Here I am supported by verifiable phenomena and not merely by such things as fantasies. I have no philosophy regarding the archetype, only the experience of it.

You believe that you have discovered something entirely new and unknown to psychology in your "pre-given world pattern"[7] and are not aware that by this somewhat fulsome phrase you are describing exactly what I mean by the archetype. It has also escaped you that in the description of the self presented more than once at curatorium meetings—quite apart from my published work—I made a connection between the subject and the world and said that here lies the special significance of the self as opposed to the purely subjectivistic ego. It happened with you as with our colleague Trüb,[8] who also did not notice that I differentiate between ego and self, though I have said it plainly in I don't know how many pages in I don't know how many books.

You will understand, dear colleague, that such elementary misun-

---

[5] Jung and others founded (May 1938) a "Teaching Institute for Psychotherapy" at Zurich U., directed by a curatorium of 9 doctors including Boss. Its aim was to foster cooperation among various analytical schools; however, it did not succeed and was dissolved in 1948. Cf. van der Hoop, 14 Jan. 46, n. 1.

[6] The German play on words "nur was wirkt ist wirklich" is untranslatable.

[7] B. took over the term "pre-given world pattern" (*vorgegebener Weltentwurf*) from Martin Heidegger's *Sein und Zeit* (1947; tr., *Being and Time*, 1962).— The German philosopher Heidegger, greatly influenced by the writings of Kierkegaard, has exerted an important influence on modern existentialism.

[8] Cf. Bovet, 9 Nov. 55, n. 3.

derstandings are not very encouraging to me. I have taken all possible trouble, as witnesses assure me, to say these things as clearly as possible, not only in the curatorium, but also in my books and indeed so often that in the end I felt that I was repeating myself to an odious degree. But it still seems to have been insufficient. This is one of the reasons why I feel that the discussions in the curatorium are unsatisfactory. You, for example, though you have a different viewpoint, have never tried to interpret for us one of the fantasy-series in terms of existential philosophy and prove that this approach hits the core of the matter better than my modest comparative-psychological efforts. Similarly, Herr Trüb has never been moved to announce that he sees no difference between the ego and the self. I should not want to be maneuvered into a situation where it would look as if I wanted *à tout prix* to preach my doctrine (which isn't one) to unwilling listeners who later, in my absence, hold a discussion, and eventually present their lack of understanding in writings and lectures to the public. I had pictured these discussions as something quite different. As I always said, it was never my intention to promulgate my ideas, it was rather to collaborate. But when the other side does not participate and essential things are left outside, no fruitful discussion can develop. I have therefore written Dr. Bally[9] that my collaboration is illusory if no contrasting opinions or better concepts on the part of others are brought into the discussion.

Please allow me a few more details: on p. 9[10] I would simplify "body and vital sphere inaccessible to all conscious decision and responsibility. . . ." One could as well say "unconscious." Instead of "existential centre" one could say "centre of the personality." You mean by this something similar to what I expressed as the self.

Freud's dilemma, conscious–unconscious,[11] is no *abbreviation* but a powerful fact, into which in my opinion he has not "squeezed" anything whatever, but which he met with and which could not be stated better nor more clearly.

In closing I may perhaps allow myself the observation that in spite of all existential philosophy the opposition between ego and world, subject and object, is not annulled. That would be too simple. Then

[9] Cf. van der Hoop, 14 Jan. 46, n. 1.
[10] of the unpublished lecture.
[11] Ibid. — This, according to a communication from Prof. Boss, refers to "Freud's belief that objects could only become conscious when connected with a word. At the same time he admitted that children frequently had not yet words for objects but that nevertheless one could not call them unconscious."

we would need no further psychotherapeutic efforts; instead, intoxicated with the prodigiously stilted jargon of this philosophy we could reach the point of national community.[12]

With best thanks I am enclosing the MS you were kind enough to send me. With collegial greetings,

Sincerely, C. G. JUNG

[12] This is an allusion to the Nazi concept of the "people's community" (the German term used by Jung is "Volksgemeinschaft"). — Regarding Jung's negative attitude to Heidegger (who had been sympathetic to National Socialism) cf. Meinertz, 3 July 39, and Künzli, 16 Mar. 43.

To Medard Boss

Dear Colleague,   5 August 1947

Many thanks for your informative letter,[1] which I have read very attentively. It shows me that assuredly you had no intention of expressing yourself polemically. Had that been so, I should not have objected. All I permitted myself to remark was that for me it was a great disappointment to learn of such opinions only indirectly and not in the curatorium,[2] where, as it seemed to me, I had offered every opportunity for discussion and gladly welcomed every stimulating response from you.

Your "interpretations" in the light of existential philosophy are so entirely different from Freud's or my approach, which seeks only to "interpret" facts, that I do not even understand what you mean by them. In my view you could easily have brought up your divergent opinions for discussion in the curatorium. I should not like to be maneuvered into a false position in which I would appear as the one with whom it is impossible to discuss any divergent opinion whatever. Under these conditions it seemed the only course for me to withdraw from the meetings. Discussion has no meaning unless all participants contribute the best knowledge they have to offer. That is all I do myself. I admit without further ado that I do not comprehend your

☐ (Translated by Hildegard Nagel.)
[1] B., in a long letter of 17 July 47, expressed his feeling that Jung had misunderstood his true intention, which had been only to clarify certain formulations of Jung's, and that in fact he had "the greatest possible admiration for your scientific achievement."
[2] Cf. Boss, 27 June 47, n. 5.

existential philosophy but will gladly let myself be taught better if this can be done in a logical way and sustained by facts.

I believe I may conclude from your letter that you wish to continue the curatorium sessions. If that is the case I will ask Dr. Katzenstein[3] to lend us again the picture series which I used to develop my concepts. Then I would have to ask you to elucidate the methods and interpretations of existential philosophy by discussion of this case. For no participant is to get the feeling that I have rejected his possibly divergent ideas in a bossy fashion. Dr. Trüb[4] has already accused me of a flagrant disregard of his opinions. Have you ever seen Dr. Trüb let himself be drawn into presenting his opinions? You will understand that such an attitude makes any discussion impossible.

I have tried seriously to form some picture of your philosophical concepts from your letter but found myself step by step entangled in contradictions. I am just no philosopher. For example, I do not know the difference between "explaining" and "interpreting," nor can I recognize anything tangible in the "world-image" of a patient. And in your inaugural address I never found out what you mean by an "existential-analytic" way of looking at things. That implies, if I understand you rightly, somehow concepts of a new and different sort that do not agree with previous ones which you therefore oppose. Surely one is glad to hear something new and more comprehensive about these things that have brought on so many headaches. For a long time I have marvelled how philosophers can make so many apparently enlightening statements about facts they have no knowledge of, and how stupid we are never to notice it. How, for instance, does Heidegger know so much about the world plan and *the* world image? I have not achieved those heights by a long shot. But these are just the things we philosophers should know something about. It would certainly be worth while if you no longer withheld this knowledge from us. You can see what trouble I take to learn more than has been possible with the methods so far available. You must not let yourself become discouraged, but have patience with our lack of understanding and show us how and where our horizon will be expanded by the existential-philosophical approach. That can probably be best achieved by the absolutely objective Katzenstein material. For I did not pick it out in order to illustrate my own concepts.

You can grasp the extent of my non-comprehension by the fact that

[3] Erich Katzenstein, M.D., Zurich neurologist.
[4] Cf. Bovet, 9 Nov. 55, n. 3.

I do not in the least understand why you ascribe to me exist.-phil. assumptions. Man as archetype is after all a purely empirical matter, without a tinge of philosophy. You are acquainted with the ubiquitous image of the Ἄνθρωπος. It is also an empirical fact that the archetype has a causal or conditional effect. If this were not so, it could never have been observed at all. So it is not a theory but pure observation of facts. Is there any exist.-phil. reason why this should not be so? Or why do you think it is a theory? It is only a formulation of observable connections that naturally, like macrophysics, cannot get along without the concept of causality. Causality is inapplicable only in the realms of microphysics and unconscious processes. Neither is *any longer directly observable.*

I refer to this only to show how far our concepts differ and how advisable it would be for you to acquaint us with the exist.-phil. approach. With collegial regards,

Yours sincerely, C. G. JUNG

To Christian Stamm

Dear Herr Stamm,   23 April 1949

Best thanks for your kind letter. I would answer your questions[1] as follows:

It is better not to try to loosen up the unconscious, though "an honest drink would none forbid" has been held sacrosanct from time

□ Gächlingen, Switzerland.
[1] The addressee had sent Jung a list of questions, as follows. (Those which are not of general interest have been omitted together with Jung's answers.)

"Do you consider the loosening up of the unconscious through the moderate enjoyment of alcohol or other narcotics as relatively useful or as a mistake?

How does a person born blind dream of mandalas?

Might not mandalas be derived from actual factors: roundness of the pupil of the eye, and projection of a general striving for harmony into space (geometry) and time (rhythm), both united in mechanical representations?

How far do individuation dreams depend on race, tradition, character, experience? Are there, besides psychological types, also dream-types?

Do you know Bunyan's *Pilgrim's Progress*, a dream elaborated in literary form? (The city shone so dazzlingly that people could look at it only through (!) mirrors that lay around for this purpose.)

My six-year-old boy dreamt of a painting-book with a beautiful picture in it: a ring and a blue flower. Isn't that too early to dream of a mandala?

When I 'should' dream of a horse, it is generally a motorcycle!"

immemorial. Wine = son of the earth (Christ the vine, Dionysus the wine, soma in India).

I do not know how a blind person dreams of mandalas. Mandalas are also formed with the hands, danced, and represented in music (for instance Bach's *Art of Fugue*, on which as we know he was working when he died).

When a mandala is being formed, everything round and square known to man works on it too. But the impetus for its formation comes from the unconscious archetype *per se*.

Everything living dreams of individuation, for everything strives towards its own wholeness. This has nothing whatever to do with race and other things. There are typical dreams but no dream-types, since the collective unconscious is not a type but contains types, namely the archetypes.

Bunyan's *Pilgrim's Progress*[2] is a literary book of devotion making use chiefly of Christian symbolism. The symbol of the mirror refers to Paul's "For now we see through a glass, darkly; but then face to face."[3] The symbol of the mountain is found among the Victorines.[4]

It is quite in order that your boy should have a mandala dream. Such dreams occur normally and not too infrequently between the ages of 4 and 6. The mandala is an archetype that is always present, and children, who are not yet spoiled, have a clearer vision for divine things than adults, whose understanding is already ruined. The mandala should really have 4 colours to be complete. The reason for the absence of the fourth colour may be either that he is already going to school, or that he is the son of a teacher who has an instinctive interest in the differentiation of the functions.

Nowadays animals, dragons, and other living creatures are readily replaced in dreams by railways, locomotives, motorcycles, aeroplanes, and suchlike artificial products (just as the starry sky in the southern hemisphere, discovered relatively late by European navigators, contains many nautical images).[5] This expresses the remoteness of the modern mind from nature; animals have lost their numinosity; they

[2] John Bunyan (1628–88), *The Pilgrim's Progress from This World to That Which is to Come* (1678). Cf. M. Esther Harding, *Journey into Self* (New York, 1956).

[3] I Cor. 13:12.

[4] Cf. van Dijk, 25 Feb. 46, n. 2.

[5] Among the southern constellations are: Octans (Octant), Sextans (Sextant), Telescopium, Microscopium, Triangulum, Circinus (Compass for describing a circle).

have become apparently harmless; instead we people the world with hooting, booming, clattering monsters that cause infinitely more damage to life and limb than bears and wolves ever did in the past. And where the natural dangers are lacking, man does not rest until he has immediately invented others for himself.

Yours sincerely, C. G. JUNG

Letters 1951-1961

_____

To Beatrice M. Hinkle

[ORIGINAL IN ENGLISH]

Dear Dr. Hinkle,   6 February 1951

I owe you many thanks for kindly sending me Donald Keyhoe's book about the Flying Saucers.[1] I have read several books about this subject now, and I think the best of them is Gerald Heard's *The Riddle of the Flying Saucers*,[2] which I can recommend to you.

I think it is most astonishing that such a phenomenon that has apparently been witnessed by at least hundreds of people has not produced more photos and hasn't been dealt with in a more adequate way yet—particularly so in view of its possible immense importance. Of course we know that ever so often it has happened that things of greatest importance have been inadequately dealt with at the time. But it is most curious nevertheless that—as far as my knowledge goes —no really satisfactory evidence has been produced yet.

I'm puzzled to death about these phenomena, because I haven't been able yet to make out with sufficient certainty whether the whole thing is a rumour with concomitant singular and mass hallucination, or a downright fact. Either case would be highly interesting. If it's a rumour, then the apparition of discs must be a symbol produced by the unconscious. We know what such a thing would mean seen from the psychological standpoint. If on the other hand it is a hard and concrete fact, we are surely confronted with something thoroughly out of the way. At a time when the world is divided by an iron curtain— a fact unheard-of in human history—we might expect all sorts of funny things, since when such a thing happens in an individual it means a complete dissociation, which is instantly compensated by symbols of wholeness and unity. The phenomenon of the saucers might even be both, rumour as well as fact. In this case it would be what I call a synchronicity. It's just too bad that we don't know enough about it.

Thank you also for the kind offer to send me the Betty Books.[3] I

□ M.D., (1874–1953), New York; analytical psychologist and psychiatrist, translator of *Wandlungen und Symbole der Libido* = *Psychology of the Unconscious* (1916); revised and tr. R.F.C. Hull as *Symbols of Transformation*, CW 5. (See pl. VII.)

[1] Donald Edward Keyhoe, *Flying Saucers Are Real* (1950).

[2] Gerald Heard, *Is Another World Watching? The Riddle of the Flying Saucers* (1950).

[3] Cf. Künkel, 10 July 46, n. 1.

think I have them all. It's really remarkable how that woman has smelt the kind of psychology that is compensatory to our modern state of consciousness. That girl was a real prophetess. I have written a short preface to the German edition of *The Unobstructed Universe* which appeared in Switzerland.

The revised edition of the *Psychology of the Unconscious* is being printed now at last, i.e., the German edition of course. It is going to appear under the new title *Symbols of Transformation (Symbole der Wandlung).*

Except for the *Essays on a Science of Mythology* (the joint book with Kerényi) nothing is out in English yet, but please let me know if and what I can send you of my German books.

I'm still working a bit, as you see, but also trying to get as much rest as possible. I hope you are doing the same. With many thanks and best wishes,

Yours cordially, C. G. JUNG

To Heinrich Boltze

Dear Herr Boltze,   13 February 1951

For your orientation: I am a psychiatrist and not a philosopher, merely an empiricist who ponders on certain experiences. *Psyche* for me is an inclusive term for the totality of all so-called psychic processes. *Spirit* is a qualitative designation for certain psychic contents (rather like "material" or "physical"). *Atlantis*: a mythical phantasm. *L. Frobenius*: an imaginative and somewhat credulous original. Great collector of material. Less good as a thinker.

God: an inner experience, not discussable as such but impressive. Psychic experience has two sources: the outer world and the unconscious. *All immediate experience is psychic.* There is physically transmitted (outer world) experience and inner (spiritual) experience. The one is as valid as the other. God is not a *statistical* truth, hence it is just as stupid to try to prove the existence of God as to deny him. If a person feels happy, he needs neither proof nor counterproof. Also, there is no reason to suppose that "happiness" or "sadness" cannot be experienced. God is a universal experience which is obfuscated only by silly rationalism and an equally silly theology. (Cf. my little book *Psychologie und Religion*, Rascher-Verlag, Zurich 1940, where you will find something on this theme.)

What mankind has called "God" from time immemorial you ex-

4

perience every day. You only give him another, so-called "rational" name—for instance, you call him "affect." Time out of mind he has been the psychically stronger, capable of throwing your conscious purposes off the rails, fatally thwarting them and occasionally making mincemeat of them. Hence there are not a few who are afraid "of themselves." God is then called "I myself," and so on. *Outer world and God are the two primordial experiences* and the one is as great as the other, and both have a thousand names, which one and all do not alter the facts. The roots of both are unknown. The psyche mirrors both. It is perhaps the point where they touch. Why do we ask about God at all? God effervesces in you and sets you to the most wondrous speculations.

People speak of *belief* when they have lost *knowledge*. Belief and disbelief in God are mere surrogates. The naïve primitive *doesn't believe, he knows*, because the inner experience rightly means as much to him as the outer. He still has no theology and hasn't yet let himself be befuddled by boobytrap concepts. He adjusts his life—of necessity—to outer and inner *facts*, which he does not—as we do—feel to be discontinuous. He lives in *one* world, whereas we live only in one half and merely believe in the other or not at all. We have blotted it out with so-called "spiritual development," which means that we live by self-fabricated electric light and—to heighten the comedy—believe or don't believe in the sun.

Stalin in Paris[1] would have become *une espèce d'existentialiste* like Sartre, a ruthless doctrinaire. What generates a cloud of twaddle in Paris causes the ground to tremble in Asia. There a potentate can still set himself up as the incarnation of reason instead of the sun.

Yours very truly, c. g. jung

☐ Western Germany.
[1] B. expressed his regret that Stalin had not been born in Paris.

To Fowler McCormick

[ORIGINAL IN ENGLISH]

Dear Fowler,   22 February 1951

It is very kind of you to send me news about the flying saucers again.

☐ (Handwritten.) Harold Fowler McCormick (1898–1973), Chicago industrialist, was an old friend of Jung's. He accompanied Jung on his journeys to the

I have read Gerald Heard's book in the meantime which is a very emphatic apology for the saucers' existence. Unfortunately he is preaching his cause a bit too much for my taste.

The new statements about the saucers being nothing but weather balloons unfortunately does not chime in with the alleged observations, but maybe the latter are also just fake and hallucination. It is very funny indeed that it seems to be so difficult to establish the truth about the reality of this phenomenon. I think it is chiefly an obstinate rumour, but the question whether there is something real behind it is not answered.

Apart from some rheumatism I feel pretty well and I'm doing my work as usual. I suppose you are very busy! I appreciate it all the more that I get some token of your existence from time to time. Many thanks!

Yours ever cordially, c. g.

Pueblos of New Mexico (1924–25) and to India (1938) and was a frequent companion in later years in Zurich. He often took Jung and Ruth Bailey (who acted as Jung's housekeeper after Mrs. Jung died, 1955) on auto excursions (cf. McCormick, Christmas 1960). "The Undiscovered Self," CW 10, bears the dedication "To my friend Fowler McCormick." (See pl. v.)

To Dr. H.

Dear Dr. H., 17 March 1951

To answer your long and meaty letter one must have time. My answer therefore comes a bit late.

Psychology as a natural science must reserve the right to treat all assertions that cannot be verified empirically as projections. This epistemological restriction says nothing either for or against the possibility of a transcendent Being. Projection is an unavoidable instrument of cognition. That the Christological projection remained attached to the "historical" man Jesus is of the greatest symbological significance, it seems to me. Attachment to the concrete man was necessary because otherwise the incarnation of God—most important! —could never have come about. The conception, already growing up on the Osiris tradition, of an Osiris belonging to the individual[1] is

☐ (Handwritten.) Western Germany.
[1] Cf. Michaelis, 20 Jan. 39, n. 1.

6

continued in the Judaeo-Christian idea of the *imago Dei* and in the Christian idea of the υἱότης.[2] Docetism was a relapse into the pagan view of the world. Bultmann's attempt at demythologization[3] is a consequence of Protestant rationalism and leads to the progressive impoverishment of symbolism. What is left over does not suffice to express the prodigal (and dangerous) world of the unconscious, to join it to consciousness or, as the case may be, to hold it in check. As a result, Protestantism will become even more boring and penurious than it already is. It will also continue, as before, to split up endlessly, which is actually the unconscious purpose of the whole exercise. With the Reformation it has lost one leg already, the essential ritual. Since then it has stood on the hypertrophied other leg, faith, which is beset with difficulties and gradually becoming inaccessible. Thanks to this defoliation of the symbolic tree religion will increasingly become a purely private affair, but the greater the spiritual poverty of the Protestant the more chance he has of discovering the treasure in his own psyche. At any rate he has better prospects in this regard than the Catholic, who still finds himself in full possession of a truly collective religion. His religion is developing by leaps and bounds. The Assumption of the B.V.M. is an eloquent example of this. It is the first step in Christianity towards wholeness, i.e., the quaternity.[4] We now have the old formula $3 + 1$,[5] the 1 representing 98% a goddess and a mediatrix coordinated with the Trinity. Dreams referring to the Assumption are extremely interesting: they show that behind the *luna plena* or the sun woman[6] the dark new moon is rising up with its mystery of the *hierosgamos* and the chthonic world of darkness. That is why, as early as the 16th century, Gerardus Dorneus attacked the quaternity so fiercely,[7] because the acceptance of the *binarius*[8] ($=$ devil) in the form of the feminine principle, represented by the

---

[2] $=$ sonship.

[3] Rudolf Karl Bultmann (1884–), German Protestant theologian, then professor at the U. of Marburg. He rejected the authenticity of large portions of the NT (e.g., the events on Good Friday and at Easter) as purely mythical and demanded the "demythologization of the Christian message."

[4] In Jung's view the Trinity is an incomplete quaternity, lacking the feminine element, earth, or body. Cf. *Psychology and Alchemy*, CW 12, pars. 26, 31, 319ff.; "Psychology and Religion," CW 11, par. 107.

[5] The quaternity is expressed by the formula $3 + 1$, where 3 represents the Trinity and 1 the fourth person—be it the inferior function, the anima, the feminine element in the deity, or, in another context, the devil.

[6] Rev. 12:1. Cf. "Answer to Job," CW 11, pars. 710ff., 737f.

[7] "Psychology and Religion," pars. 103f. & n. 47, par. 120 & n. 11.

even numbers 2 or 4, would break up the Trinity. The Pope probably did well to discourage the psychologizing tendency (chiefly among the French Jesuits). The Trojan horse should be kept hidden as long as possible. All in all, I consider the declaration of the Assumption the most important symbological event since the Reformation, and I find the arguments advanced by Protestant critics lamentable because they all overlook the prodigious significance of the new dogma. The symbol in the Catholic Church is alive and is nourished by the popular psyche and actually urged on by it. But in Protestantism it is dead. All that remains is to abolish the Trinity and the *homoousia*.[9]

Since the time of Clemens Romanus,[10] Jakob Boehme was the first to come to grips adequately with evil. I do not fight for a recognition of the "Fourth." Nowadays it doesn't need any recognizing—it's too obvious. I merely point to the existence of a problem which is of great importance in the history of symbols. I only fight *for* the reactivation of symbolic thinking, because of its therapeutic value, and *against* the presumptuous undervaluation of myth, which only a very few people have the least understanding of anyway.

I don't quite understand why you call a venture "faith."[11] A venture is a misnomer when you are convinced that it is going to turn out all right in the end anyhow. A venture is when you neither know nor believe. When her travelling carriage overturned, St. Teresa of Avila, lifting her arms to heaven, cried: "Now I know why you have so few friends."[12] It can also turn out like that.

I "believe" only when I have sufficient grounds for an assumption. The word "belief" means no more to me than that. Leaps into the dark I know very well. For me they have everything to do with courage and nothing with belief, but not a little with hope (i.e., that all will go well).

---

[8] Ibid.; cf. also "Dogma of the Trinity," CW 11, pars. 256, 262; *Mysterium Coniunctionis,* CW 14, par. 238.

[9] Cf. Niederer, 23 June 47, n. 6.

[10] Pope Clement I, *fl.* 96, apostolic Father, who is erroneously credited with the conception of Christ as the right hand and the devil as the left hand of God (cf. "Foreword to Werblowsky's *Lucifer and Prometheus,*" CW 11, par. 470). Actually it goes back to Pseudo-Clement, author of the Clementine Homilies, a collection of Gnostic-Christian writings dating from the middle of the 2nd cent. (cf. *Aion,* CW 9, ii, par. 99).

[11] In his letter to Jung of 29 Jan., Dr. H. wrote that in the most extreme situations of distress in life he would describe "the last leap into the depths, the venture of decision," as "faith."

[12] Cf. "Good and Evil in Analytical Psychology," CW 10, par. 883.

This summer a new work of mine will appear, which is concerned with Christian symbology (especially the figure of Christ), under the title *Aion*. Then I'll be ripe for an auto-da-fé. I can say with Tertullian: "*Novum testimonium advoco immo omni litteratura notius, omni doctrina agitatius . . . toto homine maius . . . Consiste in medio anima!*"[13] But the soul is anathema to holy theology. "Demythologization"! What hybris! Reminiscent of the disinfection of heaven with sublimate of mercury by a crazy doctor who then declared God could [not] be found.[14] Yet God is the mythologem *kat 'exochen.* Christ was no doubt a moral philosopher—what else remains of him if he is not a mythologem? With best regards,

Yours sincerely, C. G. JUNG

[13] "I summon a new witness, or rather a witness more known than any written monument, more debated than any doctrine . . . greater than the whole of man. . . . Approach then O my soul . . . !" Tertullian, *De Testimonie animae*, I. Full text in *Psychological Types*, CW 6, par. 18.
[14] The "not" is missing in the file copy, but has been inserted because Jung frequently told this anecdote in that sense. Cf. *Two Essays*, CW 7, par. 110.

To Adolf Keller

Dear friend,   20 March 1951

   . . .

What you feel as my anti-Protestant complex is an admittedly violent criticism of Protestantism, for it is not where I would want it to be. Now that the Catholic Church has taken the momentous step of the Assumption, Protestantism is really and truly nailed fast to the Patriarchal line of the Old Testament and way behindhand in the matter of dogmatic development. The Catholic at least believes in continuing revelation, but the Protestant sees himself committed to an—oh so contradictory!—document like the Bible, and consequently cannot construct but merely demolish—*vide* the famous "demythologization" of Christianity. As though statements about sacred history were not—mythologems! *God always speaks mythologically.* If he didn't, he would reveal reason and science.

I fight against the *backwardness* of Protestantism. I don't want it to lose the lead. I don't want to turn back to the unconsciousness,

☐ Th.D., (1872–1963), lectured at the U. of Zurich, later in Los Angeles. He was one of Jung's oldest friends. Cf. *The Freud/Jung Letters*, 133 J, n. 4.

the nebulosity, of Catholic concretism, so I also fight against the Protestant concretism of historicity and the vacuity of the Protestant message, which can only be understood today as an historical vestige. If Christ means anything to me, it is only as a *symbol*. As an historical figure he could just as well have been called Pythagoras, Lao-tse, Zarathustra, etc. I do not find the historical Jesus edifying at all, merely interesting because controversial.

I say this so that you may know where I stand. I'd be glad if you would nevertheless have a talk with me. So if ever you can find the time I shall be ready.

Again with best thanks for your attentive and good-natured letter,

CARL

To Adolf L. Vischer

Dear Colleague,   21 March 1951

I am sorry I am thanking you only now for your very kind letter of 26.XII.50. Your sympathy over the death of my last close friend, Albert Oeri,[1] was veritable balm. One can indeed feel the pain of such a loss without making oneself guilty of undue sentimentality. One notices on all such occasions how age gradually pushes one out of time and the world into wider and uninhabited spaces where one feels at first rather lonely and strange. You have written so sympathetically and perceptively in your book[2] of the peculiarities of old age that you will have an understanding heart for this mood. The imminence of death and the vision of the world *in conspectu mortis* is in truth a curious experience: the sense of the present stretches out beyond today, looking back into centuries gone by, and forward into futures yet unborn. With heartfelt thanks,

Affectionately yours, C. G. JUNG

☐ See Vischer, 10 Oct. 44 (in vol. 1).
[1] Cf. Oeri, 12 Feb. 20, n. ☐.
[2] *Das Alter als Schicksal und Erfüllung* (1942).

To Pastor Fritz Pfäfflin

Dear Pastor Pfäfflin,   22 March 1951

I was very glad to hear from you again. Unfortunately I cannot fulfill your wish.[1] I have so many other things to do and I can't do nearly as much as I did before. Nor am I allowed to overwork.

I don't know what kind of dream material you could mean, and how it is supposed to link up with the unarmed neutrality of Germany. The disarmament of Germany is itself a dream which could only occur in a sleeping nation—the very nation which has overrun its neighbours twice in a quarter of a century. It is the dream of a profoundly warlike nation that consciously considers itself harmless and peace-loving. It must indeed be dreaming if one thinks one can live unarmed in an anarchic world where only guile and force count. Every German who is not asleep and dreaming knows that it is time, highest time to rearm, and the more consciously he does so the better it will be for peace. The really dangerous ones are the harmless dreamers who don't know that they want to perish gloriously yet again through their accursed playing the saviour. One time they strike their fellow men dead in order to convert them to the new religion of Naziism; the next time they preach disarmament in order to hand over their own country to Russian tyranny. How would it have gone with us in Switzerland if we had had no army! People like Herr Noack[2] would have got a pension for doing useful preparatory work, and the rest of us would simply have been stood up against the wall by the culture-bringers. And that's how it would be for you too with the Russians, for they also are universal saviours who want to cure the whole world with their own disease, just as the Nazis did. Do you seriously believe that any robber would be scared off by German disarmament? You know very well: "I feel provoked," said the wolf to the lamb.

One can also be neutral when armed, without falling a victim to militarism. But unarmed neutrality seems to me, and probably to all non-Germans as well, the acme of failed instinct, to which I would add, from my intimate acquaintance with the German national character, German crankiness, which is something out of this world. The

☐ See Pfäfflin, 5 Jul. 35 (in vol. 1).

[1] For a contribution to the journal *Versöhnung* (Reconciliation) on the subject of German unarmed neutrality, possibly "on the basis of some dream material."

[2] Ulrich Noack, professor of history at the U. of Würzburg, had written an article in *Versöhnung* advocating unarmed neutrality.

11

dangerous thing about Noack's proposal is that it represents yet another attempt at national suicide. Whence comes the recklessness or "intemperance" of the Germans, whence their love of national downfall? When Jacob Burckhardt heard of the declaration of Empire at Versailles,[3] he exclaimed: "That means the downfall of Germany." Since then there has been no let-up in these downfalling attempts. One might, it seems to me, try to be reasonable for a change.

I hope, my dear Pastor, you will pardon these humble opinions. They may make it clear to you why it seems to me quite out of the question—even if it were possible on other grounds—to give serious consideration to your proposal. Please regard this letter as a private expression of my views. I have no wish to insult the German nation in the shape of its individual representatives.

To have arms is an evil; to have no arms is a still greater evil. The reasonable man is modestly content with the lesser evil; he prefers to look at heroic Götterdämmerungen and suchlike Herostratic gestures[4] in the theatre, to lock up madmen betimes and not worship them as leaders and saviours. My words and warnings in this connection are as futile and useless as Jacob Burckhardt's. "Si non crediderunt tibi neque audierunt sermonem signi prioris,"[5] then only God speaks the word. But let man, mindful of his hybris, be content with the lesser evil and beware of the Satanic temptation of the grand gesture, which is only intended for show and self-intoxication. Best regards,

Yours sincerely, C. G. JUNG

[3] Wilhelm, King of Prussia, was crowned Emperor of Germany 18 Jan. 1871 at Versailles.
[4] Herostratus, in order to make his name immortal, burnt down the temple of Artemis in Ephesus, 356 B.C.
[5] Exodus 4:48: ". . . and if they will not believe thee, neither hearken to the voice of the first sign."

To Adolf Keller

Dear friend,   Easter Monday [26 March] 1951

At the end of this week I am spending April in Bollingen, where I have all sorts of work to attend to. So this week is still open should

☐ (Handwritten.)

12

you be here again. Best thanks for your two letters! They swarm with questions and possible misunderstandings which we can only settle by talking. Otherwise I would have to write whole treatises. I would only remark now that I haven't become "more Christian," it's just that I now feel better prepared to contribute something to the psychology of Christianity. *Dreams* can be many things, but we have only *one* theoretical premise for their explanation. The scientific axiom *principia explicandi non sunt multiplicanda praeter necessitatem* should be taken very seriously. We must therefore try to get as far as we can with the compensation theory.[1]

The *quaternity* is an empirical fact, not a *doctrine*. Until now Christianity, like so many other systems, had 4 metaphysical figures: Trinity $+$ πύρινος θεὸς ἀριθμῷ τέταρτος.[2] The unconscious expresses itself chiefly in quaternities, irrespective of Christian tradition. The quaternity is of Old Testament as well as Egyptian origin. Vishnu has four faces, etc. *Theologia naturalis*[3] must take account of this fact, or it will make no contact with psychology. The quaternity is not a doctrine that can be discussed but a fact which, *ut supra demonstravimus*, also underlies dogmatics.

Since the *incarnatio Dei* conveys nothing intelligible to modern man, σάρξ ἐγένετο[4] has to be translated for better of worse, e.g., "has assumed definite empirical form." This formula would serve as a bridge to psychology. Meanwhile best greetings,

CARL

[1] One of the most important discoveries of Jung's is that of the psyche as a self-regulating system in which one-sided attitudes of the conscious mind are compensated by emphasis on the opposite (compensatory) tendency, mainly through the medium of dreams.

[2] The "fiery god, the fourth by number," was the demiurge of the Naassenes. Cf. *Aion*, CW 9, ii, par. 128.

[3] Natural theology attempts to gain knowledge of God by means of natural reason (i.e., not enlightened by faith) through the contemplation of his creation. Akin to Paracelsus's *lumen naturae*, light of nature.

[4] = become flesh.

To Pastor Werner Niederer

Dear Pastor Niederer,   Easter Monday [26 March] 1951

While tidying up my MSS I came across your kind gift[1] of Feb. 1949. I doubt whether I ever thanked you for it. Though I have a

13

secretary upon whom it is incumbent to protect me from the consequences of my absent-mindedness and forgetfulness, she too occasionally drowns in the floods of paper which pour down upon me
without cease. At any rate I will now make good my thanks and
beg you for indulgence and forgiveness of sins.

At the end of your lucid exposé you inquire about the "merit" of
Christ, which you no longer understand as a magical occurrence,
replacing it, so to speak, by the integration of projections. This is
rationally correct but, it seems to me, scarcely an adequate answer.
The psychological "merit" (or rather, significance) of Christ consists in the fact that, as the "firstling," he is the prototype of the
τέλειος, the integral man.[2] This image, as history testifies, is *numinous*
and can therefore be answered only by another numinosity. It touches
the *imago Dei*, the archetype of the self in us, and thereby awakens
it. The self is then "constellated" and by virtue of its numinosity
compels man towards wholeness, i.e., towards the integration of the
unconscious or the subordination of the ego to a holistic "will,"
which is rightly conceived to be "God's will." Τελείωσις in the psychological sense means the "completeness," not the "perfection" of man.
Wholeness cannot be conscious, since it also embraces the unconscious. Hence at least half of it is a *transcendental* state, mystical
and numinous. Individuation is a transcendental goal, an incarnation
of the ἄνθρωπος. The only part of this we can understand *rationally*
is the holistic religious striving of consciousness, i.e., the *religiose
observare* of the holistic impulses in the unconscious, but not the
existential reality of wholeness or of the self, which is prefigured by
εἶναι ἐν χριστῷ.[3]

. . .

Very sincerely, C. G. JUNG

☐ (Handwritten.) See Niederer, 23 June 47 (in vol. 1).
[1] One of his sermons.
[2] The "perfect" man (Phil. 3:12 & 15). Cf. *Aion*, CW 9, ii, par. 333 & n. 110.
[3] = being in Christ.

To Bernard Aschner

Dear Colleague,   28 March 1951

I still have vivid memories of our meeting in Vienna, since it was
from you that I took over, in my own way, your interest in Paracelsus.

During the war, especially, I was much concerned with him, in particular with his *religio medica* as expounded in his treatise *De Vita Longa*.

As for your question[1] I can only tell you that I fully stand by my earlier remarks. Sooner or later it will grow into a question of first-class importance for humanity, since we are rapidly approaching the time when the feeding of the world's population will come up against a barrier that cannot be crossed. Even now India is so near the brink that a single bad season is enough to precipitate a famine, and today, thanks to modern hygiene, the whole world is multiplying unchecked. This surely cannot go on much longer, for the problem will then arise that already confronts all primitive societies: limitation of progeny through food shortages. This danger of overpopulation, already staring us in the face, still hasn't reached the consciousness of the public at large, least of all our legislators, who are smitten by a special blindness. Your initiative has my undivided applause. With collegial regards,

Yours sincerely, C. G. JUNG

☐ M.D., (1883–1960), Austrian gynaecologist, after 1938 in U.S.A. Edited and translated into modern German the works of Paracelsus (*Sämtliche Werke*, 4 vols., 1926–32).
[1] At a meeting in Vienna 1931 Jung remarked privately that "there are few things which have caused as much anxiety, unhappiness, and evil as the compulsion to give birth." A. asked permission to quote these words in the 7th edn. of his *Lehrbuch der Konstitutionstherapie*.

To R. J. Zwi Werblowsky

Dear Herr Werblowsky,   28 March 1951

I hope that in the meantime you have received my short foreword.[1] I am sorry that I am only now getting down to saying a few words about some points in your book.

P. 80. I should propose a somewhat different wording: instead of saying "pushing the process of individuation"—exactly the thing you cannot do because it instantly leads into an inflation or into an identification with archetypes—I should recommend something like

☐ Then lecturer at Leeds U. and at the Institute of Jewish Studies, Manchester; now professor of comparative religion at the Hebrew U. of Jerusalem.
[1] "Foreword to Werblowsky's *Lucifer and Prometheus*," CW 11.

15

"becoming too recklessly selfish." The term individuation ought to be reserved for the legitimate evolution of the individual entelechy.[2]

Your singling out of hybris[3] as the specific vice of the Greeks is very illuminating. It corresponds to Augustine's conception of *superbia*. As you know, he said there are two cardinal sins: *superbia and concupiscentia*.[4] It is therefore to be supposed that if the specific Greek vice is *superbia*, *concupiscentia* falls to the lot of the Jews. We see this very clearly in Freud, namely in his "pleasure principle," in its turn corresponding to the castration complex which, incidentally, plays a much smaller role with non-Jews. In my practice I very seldom have occasion even to speak of it. Hybris actually looms much larger with the Gentiles.

P. 84. Here I would recommend a revision of the text. Hybris can hardly be described as a "hypertrophy of masculinity," since this would not apply in the case of a woman. Hybris is an inflation of the human being in general. It is also extremely doubtful whether Greek homosexuality can be derived from it. Homosexuality is more a social phenomenon which develops wherever a primitive society of males has to be cemented together as a stepping-stone to the State. This is particularly evident in Greece.

Nor can one impute without qualification a contempt of women to homosexuals. Very often they are good friends to them. For instance, a young homosexual bachelor is a welcome guest among women of uncertain age, and he feels happy in their company because it surrounds him with mothers. Most homosexuals are suspended or potential males still clinging to their mother's apron strings.

The castration complex, which you mention in this connection, really has nothing to do with homosexuality but very much to do with the meaning of Jewish circumcision which, as a most incisive operation on a sensitive organ, is a reminder of *concupiscentia*. And because it is an act prescribed by divine law, it bridles concupiscence for the purpose of consolidating man's affinity with the Law or with God as a permanent state. It is a kind of κατοχύ,[5] an expression of Yahweh's marriage with Israel. When the idea of God's marriage becomes obsolete, the alleged castration, which circumcision is under-

---

[2] This paragraph is written in English.

[3] Presumptuous encroachment on the rights of others, particularly of the gods, leading to the tragic downfall of the transgressor.

[4] Pride and concupiscence are the "twin moral concepts of Saint Augustine" (Jung, "The Undiscovered Self," CW 10, par. 555).

[5] = imprisonment.

16

stood to be, regresses to dependence on the mother (Attis myth![6]). But in so far as the mother signifies the unconscious pure and simple, the unconscious takes Yahweh's place. It is, however, correct to say that homosexuality comes in here indirectly as the result of an almighty mother complex. The mother-fixated son, because of his "aloofness from women," is constantly in danger of autoerotism and exaggerated self-esteem. The characteristic arrogance of adolescent youths towards the female sex is simply a defence mechanism against domination by the mother and can hardly be interpreted as hybris.

"Greek" homosexuality occurs, as said, in all primitive societies of males though it never led them to the soaring flights of Greek culture. The real foundation of the Greek spirit is not to be found in these primitive phenomena but in the specific endowments of the people. One must, I think, be very chary of the assumption that the genius of a culture has anything to do with "masculinity."

P. 85, note 21. You say an antisexual tendency is inherent in the Virgin Mother archetype. This can hardly be maintained since the cult of the Oriental love-goddess is notoriously anything but antisexual.

I have read your book with great pleasure and found the difference between Jewish and Greek psychology particularly instructive. I must confess that I have never read the whole of *Paradise Lost* any more than I have read the *Messias* of Klopstock.[7] I have learnt a lot from your work and have tried in my foreword to see the emergence of the figure of Satan in the 17th century in historical perspective.

Many thanks for the notes about Blake you enclosed in your letter. I am no particular friend of Blake,[8] whom I am always inclined to criticize. With kind regards,

Yours sincerely, C. G. JUNG

[6] Cf. *Symbols of Transformation*, CW 5, pars. 659ff.
[7] Friedrich Gottlieb Klopstock (1724–1803), German poet.
[8] Cf. Nanavutty, 11 Nov. 48.

To Aniela Jaffé

Dear Aniela,   Bollingen, 29 May 1951

So it goes all the time: memories rise up and disappear again, as it suits them. In this way I have landed the great whale; I mean "An-

□ (Handwritten.) See Jaffé, 22 Dec. 42 (in vol. 1).

swer to Job." I can't say I have fully digested this *tour de force* of the unconscious. It still goes on rumbling a bit, rather like an earthquake. I notice it when I am chiselling away at my inscription (which has made good progress). Then thoughts come to me, as for instance that consciousness is only an organ for perceiving the fourth dimension, i.e., the all-pervasive meaning, and itself produces no real ideas. I am getting much better. Only my sleep is still rather delicate. I oughtn't to talk much, or intensely. Luckily occasions for this are rare.

How are you? I hope you are not overstraining yourself at the Institute. I won't make any false promises about a visit from you, but I am thinking of it. Meanwhile with cordial greetings,

C. G.

To S. Wieser

Dear Colleague,   6 July 1951

Thank you for telling me about your interesting experience. It is a case of what we would call clairvoyance. But since this is just a word that signifies nothing further, it explains nothing. You can get a bit nearer to understanding such happenings only if you observe them in a wider context of the same or similar events. Surveying the sum of experiences of this kind you come to the conclusion that there is something like an "absolute knowledge"[1] which is not accessible to consciousness but probably is to the unconscious, though only under certain conditions. In my experience these conditions are always provided by emotion. Any emotion that goes at all deep has a lowering effect on consciousness, which Pierre Janet called "abaissement du niveau mental." The lowering of consciousness means on the other hand an approach to the unconscious, and because the unconscious seems to have access to this "absolute knowledge," information can be mediated which can no longer be explained rationally and causally. This occasional failure of the seemingly absolute law of causality is due to the fact that even this law has only statistical validity, with the implication that exceptions must occur.

If you are interested in the theory of these acausal connections of

□ Switzerland.

[1] Knowledge not connected with the ego "but rather a self-subsistent 'unconscious' knowledge." Cf. "Synchronicity," CW 8, par. 931.

events I would mention that a little book of mine will shortly be published by Rascher under the title *Die Synchronizität als ein Prinzip akausaler Zusammenhänge.* With collegial regards and best thanks,

Yours sincerely, c. g. j u n g

To Karl Kerényi

Dear Professor Kerényi, 12 July 1951

The rapid appearance and handsome format of *Einführung in die Mythologie*[1] came as a surprise. It is pleasant to know that this book has now found its niche.

The experiences you are having[2] will inevitably befall anyone who knowingly dips into the primordial world of eternal images. He reaches beyond himself and bears out the truth of the old alchemist's saying: *maior autem animae pars extra corpus est.*[3]

You are right: seen in relation to their archetypal background, banal dream-images are usually more instructive and of greater cogency than "mythologizing" dreams, which one always suspects are prompted by reading. The case you report is very interesting: it is a consistent working out of the archetypal model. I would be extremely interested to hear more details of your experiences sometime. I can imagine that for a mythologist the collision with living archetypes is something quite special. It was the same with me; only for me it was the encounter with mythology. It means an intensification and enhancement of life—with a pensive side-glance at the genius *vultu mutabilis, albus et ater.*[4]

That the ripples of your life and work are spreading far and wide is in the highest degree gratifying and an occasion for hearty congratulation! With very best regards,

Yours sincerely, c. g. j u n g

☐ (Handwritten.) See Kerényi (1897–1973), 26 July 40 (in vol. 1). (See pl. v.)
[1] 2nd edn., 1951, with a foreword by K.
[2] K. described certain experiences with dreams of students at the C. G. Jung Institute who reacted to his lectures on Greek mythology with dreams of an archetypal nature.
[3] "The greater part of the soul is outside the body." Sendivogius, "De sulphure," *Musaeum Hermeticum* (1678). Cf. *Psychology and Alchemy,* CW 12, pars. 396, 399.
[4] "Of changeful countenance, both white and black." Horace, *Epistulae,* II, 2.

To Aniela Jaffé

Dear Aniela,   18 July 1951

. . .

I am especially pleased that you could get into such close relationship with the second part of my book.[1] So far most people have remained stuck in the first. I personally have the second more at heart
because it is bound up with the present and future. If there is anything like the spirit seizing one by the scruff of the neck, it was the
way this book came into being.

. . .

☐ (Handwritten.)
[1] "Answer to Job," CW 11. The second part probably begins at sec. 8, pars. 649ff.

To Dr. S.

Dear Colleague,   8 August 1951

Heartiest thanks for kindly remembering my birthday!

I see with regret from your letter that you are suffering very much
from your noises in the ear. The unconscious often uses symptoms of
this kind in order to make psychic contents audible, i.e., the symptoms are intensified by a psychogenic afflux and only then do they
acquire the proper tormenting character that forces your attention
inwards, where of course it gets caught in the disturbing noises. Obviously it should turn inwards but not get caught in the noises;
rather it should push on to the contents that are acting on it like a
magnet. The little word "should" always means that one doesn't
know the way to the desired goal. But often it is at least helpful to
know that on top of the organic symptom there is a psychic layer
that can be lifted off. I know from experience that the demand of
the unconscious for introversion—in your case the ability to listen
inwards—is unusually great. And equally great is the danger that instead of *being able* to listen inwards one is *compelled* to listen inwards. My own otosclerosis has presented me with all manner of
noises, so I am fairly well informed on this matter. You are quite
right to remember the storm that interrupted our conversation. In a

☐ See Dr. S., 16 Oct. 30 (in vol. 1).

20

quite irrational way we must be able to listen also to the voice of nature, thunder for instance, even if this means breaking the continuity of consciousness. With best wishes,

Yours sincerely, c. g. j u n g

To Dr. H.

Dear Dr. H.,   30 August 1951

You must pardon my long silence. In the spring I was plagued by my liver, had often to stay in bed and in the midst of this *misère* write a little essay[1] (ca. 100 typed pages) whose publication is causing me some trouble. I am afraid of stirring up a hornets' nest. It is about the question you raised in your letter of 1 May. I myself have the feeling that I have not yet found the right way to formulate my answer, i.e., the kind of presentation that would convey my views to the public without provoking too many misunderstandings.

My *modus procedendi* is naturally empirical: how to give a satisfactory description of the phenomenon "Christ" from the standpoint of psychological experience?

The existing statements about Christ are, in part, about an empirical man, but for the other and greater part about a mythological God-man. Out of these different statements you can reconstruct a personality who, as an empirical man, was identical with the traditional Son of Man type, as presented in the then widely read Book of Enoch.[2] Wherever such identities occur, characteristic archetypal effects appear, that is, *numinosity* and *synchronistic phenomena*, hence tales of miracles are inseparable from the Christ figure. The former explains the irresistible suggestive power of his personality, for only the one who is "gripped" has a "gripping" effect on others; the latter occur chiefly in the field of force of an archetype and, because of their aspatial and atemporal character, are acausal, i.e., "miracles." (I have just lectured at Eranos on synchronicity.[3] The

☐ Württemberg.
[1] "Answer to Job."
[2] The (Ethiopic) Book of Enoch, 2nd–1st cent. b.c., the most important of the apocryphal or pseudo-apocryphal Biblical writings. (There is also a Slavonic Book of Enoch and a Book of the Secrets of Enoch.) In Charles, *The Apocrypha and Pseudepigrapha of the Old Testament in English*, II (1913).
[3] "Über Synchronizität," *Eranos Jahrbuch* 1951; now "On Synchronicity," CW 8, Appendix, pars. 969ff.

21

paper will soon appear in the acts of the Institute.[4] This remarkable
effect points to the "psychoid"[5] and essentially transcendental nature
of the archetype as an "arranger" of psychic forms inside and outside
the psyche. (In theoretical physics the archetype corresponds to the
model of a radioactive atom, with the difference that the atom consists of quantitative, the archetype of qualitative, i.e., *meaningful*,
relationships, the *quantum*[6] appearing only in the *degree of numinosity*. In physics the *quale* appears in the irreducible quality of the
so-called discontinuities,[7] as for instance in the quantum or in the
half-life[8] of radioactive substances.)

In consequence of the predominance of the archetype the personality that is "gripped" is in direct contact with the *mundus archetypus*,[9] and his life or biography is only a brief episode in the eternal
course of things or in the eternal revolution of "divine" images. That
which is eternally present appears in the temporal order as a succes-
sion. "When the time was fulfilled" the solitary creator-god transformed himself into a father and begot himself as a son, although
from eternity, i.e., in the non-time of the Pleroma or in his transcendental form of being, he is father-son-spirit-mother, i.e., the suc-
cession of archetypal manifestations.

Although the psychoid archetype is a mere model or postulate,
archetypal effects have just as real an existence as radioactivity. Anyone who is gripped by the archetype of the Anthropos lives the God-
man—one can very well say that he *is* a God-man. Archetypes are
not mere concepts but are entities, exactly like whole numbers,

---

[4] *Studien aus dem C. G. Jung-Institut*, in which Jung's paper on synchronicity,
together with Pauli's paper, appeared as vol. IV (1952), *Naturerklärung und
Psyche*.

[5] A term coined by Jung to describe "quasi-psychic 'irrepresentable' basic forms,"
i.e., the archetypes *per se* in contradistinction to archetypal images (cf. Devatmananda, 9 Feb. 37, n. 1). They belong to the transconscious areas where psychic
processes and their physical substrate touch. Cf. "On the Nature of the Psyche,"
CW 8, pars. 368, 417.

[6] "A discrete unit quantity of energy proportional to the frequency of radiation"
(SOED).

[7] Discontinuity is a concept stemming from Max Planck's quantum theory, according to which the course of nature does not advance continuously but "by tiny
jumps and jerks" (Jeans, *The Mysterious Universe*, Pelican Books, pp. 31f.; cf.
also "Synchronicity," par. 966).

[8] The half-life of a given radioactive element is the time required for the disintegration of one half of the initial number of atoms.

[9] The archetypal, potential world as underlying pattern of the actual world. In the
psychological sense, the collective unconscious. Cf. *Mysterium*, CW 14, par. 761.

which are not merely aids to counting but possess irrational qualities that do not result from the concept of counting, as for instance the prime numbers and their behaviour. Hence the mathematician Kronecker[10] could say: Man created mathematics, but God created whole numbers: ὁ θεὸς ἀριθμητίζει.[11]

This description of Christ satisfies me because it permits a non-contradictory presentation of the paradoxical interplay of his human and divine existence, his empirical character and his mythological being.

The wordless or formless "gripping" is no argument against the presence of the archetype, since the very numinosity of the moment is itself one of its manifestations (and the most frequent), a primordial form of archetypal seizure, cf. *kairos*[12] and Tao or (in Zen) *satori*. On account of its transcendence, the archetype *per se* is as irrepresentable as the nature of light and hence must be strictly distinguished from the archetypal idea or mythologem (see "Der Geist der Psychologie"[13] in *Eranos-Jahrbuch* 1946). In this way the transcendence of the theological premise remains intact.

In the hope that I have answered your question at least to some extent, with best regards,

Yours sincerely, c. g. jung

[10] Leopold Kronecker (1823–91), German mathematician.
[11] "God arithmetizes," a saying attributed to the German mathematician Karl Friedrich Gauss (1777–1855). Cf. "Synchronicity," par. 943 & n. 72.
[12] The right or proper time, the favourable moment.
[13] Cf. "On the Nature of the Psyche," CW 8, par. 417.

To Aniela Jaffé

Dear Aniela,   Bollingen, 8 September 1951

Here comes a sign of life! After Eranos I was very tired. Have recovered a bit now, and again a thought has caught me, this time with reference to synchronicity. I must rework the chapter on astrology. An important change has to be made—Knoll[1] put me on to it. Astrology is not a mantic method but appears to be based on proton

□ (Handwritten.)
[1] Max Knoll (1897–1970), German physicist, 1948–55 professor of electrical engineering at Princeton U.; after 1956 director of the Institute for Technical Electronics, Munich.

radiation[2] (from the sun). I must do a statistical experiment in order to be on sure ground. This preys on my mind but not so much that I forget you. How are you? I hope better. Please let me have a word from you. After Eranos I missed the daily exchange of ideas and the warmth of life lapping me round.

I'm sorry I have to stop. My son has just arrived by sailing boat.

Meanwhile with cordial greetings,

C. G.

[2] According to Knoll, solar proton radiation is strongly influenced by planetary constellations. Cf. Knoll, "Transformation of Science in Our Age," *Man and Time*, Papers from the Eranos Yearbooks, 3 (1957); Jung, "On Synchronicity," CW 8, Appendix, par. 987, and "Synchronicity," par. 875.

To Father Victor White

[ORIGINAL IN ENGLISH]

Dear Victor,   Bollingen, 21 September 1951

I have seen Mrs. X. and I assure you she is quite an eyeful and beyond! We had an interesting conversation and I must admit she is quite remarkable. If ever there was an anima it is she, and there is no doubt about it.

In such cases one had better cross oneself, because the anima, particularly when she is quintessential as in this case, casts a metaphysical shadow which is long like a hotel-bill and contains no end of items that add up in a marvellous way. One cannot label her and put her into a drawer. She decidedly leaves you guessing. I hadn't expected anything like that. At least I understand now why she dreams of the Derby winners: it just belongs to her! She is a synchronistic phenomenon all over, and one can keep up with her as little as with one's own unconscious.

I think you ought to be very grateful to St. Dominicus that he has founded an order of which you are a member. In such cases one appreciates the existence of monasteries. It is just as well that she got all her psychology from books, as she would have busted every decent and competent analyst. I sincerely hope that she is going on dreaming of winners, because such people need money to keep them afloat.

If you see Mrs. X., please tell her how much I've enjoyed her

□ See White, 26 Sept. 45 and pl. VI (in vol. 1).

visit—but keep quiet about my other expectorations! She must not be frightened too soon.

Don't work too much!

Yours cordially, c. g. jung

P.S. Please don't forget to tell your Swiss friend and co-frater at the Vatican Library to inquire about unpublished MSS of St. Thomas!!![1]

c. g.

[1] Cf. von Franz, *Aurora Consurgens: A Document Attributed to Thomas Aquinas* (tr., 1966), p. 431, n. 130. (The postscript was handwritten.)

Anonymous

[original in english]

Dear Mrs. N.,   13 October 1951

It isn't easy or simple to answer your question,[1] because much depends upon your faculty of understanding. Your understanding on the other hand depends upon the development and maturity of your personal character.

It isn't possible to kill part of your "self" unless you kill yourself first. If you ruin your conscious personality, the so-called ego-personality, you deprive the self of its real goal, namely to become real itself. The goal of life is the realization of the self. If you kill yourself you abolish that will of the self that guides you through life to that eventual goal. An attempt at suicide doesn't affect the intention of the self to become real, but it may arrest your personal development inasmuch as it is not explained. You ought to realize that suicide is murder, since after suicide there remains a corpse exactly as with any ordinary murder. Only it is yourself that has been killed. That is the reason why the Common Law punishes a man that tries to commit suicide, and it is psychologically true too. Therefore suicide certainly is not the proper answer.

As long as you don't realize the nature of this very dangerous impulse you block the way to further development, just as a man who intends to commit a theft, without knowing what he is intending and without realizing the ethical implication of such a deed, cannot develop any further unless he takes into account that he has

☐ U.S.A.

[1] N., a woman of 47, in a state of nervous collapse and depression, asked whether an attempted suicide at the age of 21 could have killed part of her "self."

a criminal tendency. Such tendencies are very frequent, only they don't always succeed and there is hardly anybody who must not realize in this or any other way that he has a dark shadow following him. That is the human lot. If it were not so, we might get perfect one day which might be pretty awful too. We shouldn't be naïve about ourselves and in order not to be we have to climb down to a more modest level of self-appreciation.

Hoping I have answered your question, I remain,

Yours sincerely, C. G. JUNG

Thank you for the fee.
Nothing more is needed.

Anonymous

[ORIGINAL IN ENGLISH]

Dear Mr. N.,   Bollingen, 1 November 1951

I'm sorry to be so late with my answer. Your letter arrived while I was away from home for my vacations. I couldn't have seen you anyhow during that time.

If you hadn't this relapse of tuberculosis I should have said that you'd better come once again to Zurich so that one could find out about that snag you seem to run into with your women analysts. Perhaps it is just that they are women!

While you are in your plaster cast you have time to think and to read and I should advise you to make ample use of it. Try to find out about yourself as much as possible with the aid of literature. It could give you some masculine courage which you seem to be in need of. In the long run the psychological influence of women isn't necessarily helpful. The more helpless a man is, the more the maternal instinct is called upon, and there is no woman who could resist such a call. But a man's psychology gets badly undermined by too much motherliness. Anything you acquire by your own effort is worth a hundred years with a woman analyst.

Unfortunately I'm unable to interpret your dream.[1] I wouldn't dare to let my intuitions handle your material. But, since I appear in your dream, I cannot refrain from making the remark that I like

☐ (Handwritten.) England.
[1] The dream has not been preserved.

26

thick walls and I like trees and green things, and I like many books. Perhaps you are in need of these three good things.

My best wishes!

Yours sincerely, C. G. JUNG

Anonymous

Dear Herr N.,   1 November 1951

I am sorry to be late with my answer. I was away on holiday and your letter was lying around for some time.

You have experienced in your marriage what is an almost universal fact—that individuals are different from one another. Basically, each remains for the other an unfathomable enigma. There is never complete concord. If you have committed a mistake at all, it consisted in your having striven too hard to understand your wife completely and not reckoning with the fact that in the end people don't want to know what secrets are slumbering in their souls. If you struggle too much to penetrate into another person, you find that you have thrust him into a defensive position, and resistances develop because, through your efforts to penetrate and understand, he feels forced to examine those things in himself which he doesn't want to examine. Everybody has his dark side which—so long as all goes well—he had better not know about. That is no fault of yours. It is a universal human truth which is nevertheless true, even though there are plenty of people who will assure you that they'd be only too glad to know everything about themselves. It is as good as certain that your wife had many thoughts and feelings which made her uneasy and which she wanted to hide even from herself. That is simply human. It is also the reason why so many elderly people withdraw into their own solitude where they won't be disturbed. And it is always about things they would rather not be too clearly conscious of. Certainly *you* are not responsible for the existence of these psychic contents. If nevertheless you are still tormented by guilt feelings, then consider for once what sins you have not committed which you would have liked to commit. This might perhaps cure you of your guilt feelings towards your wife. With kind regards,

Yours sincerely, C. G. JUNG

☐ Germany.

27

To Hans Schär

Dear Dr. Schär, 16 November 1951

Best thanks for your friendly letter. I am glad you have not damned me. What offends you bothered me too. I would have liked to avoid sarcasm and mockery but couldn't, for that is the way I felt and if I had not said so it would have been all the worse, but hidden. I realized only afterwards that they have their place as expressing resistance to God's nature, which sets us at odds with ourselves. I had to wrench myself free of God, so to speak, in order to find that unity in myself which God seeks through man. It is rather like that vision of Symeon the Theologian,[1] who sought God in vain everywhere in the world, until God rose like a little sun in his own heart. Where else, after all, could God's antinomy attain to unity save in the vessel God has prepared for himself for this purpose? It seems to me that only the man who seeks to realize his own humanity does God's will, but not those who take to flight before the bad fact "man," and precipitately turn back to the Father or have never left the Father's house. To become man is evidently God's desire in us.

Sarcasm is certainly not a pretty quality, but I am forced to use even means I find reprehensible in order to deliver myself from the Father. God himself uses very different means to jolt these human beings of his into consciousness. It has not yet been forgotten, I hope, what happened in Germany and what is happening day after day in Russia. Job's suffering never ceases and multiplies a millionfold. I cannot avert my eyes from that. By remaining with the Father, I deny him the human being in whom he could unify himself and become One, and how can I help him better than by becoming One myself? (*Nunquam unum facies, nisi prius ex te ipso fiat unum.*)[2] God has quite obviously not chosen for sons those who hang on to him as the Father, but those who found the courage to stand on their own feet.

□ (1910–68), Swiss Protestant theologian, late professor of theology at the U. of Bern. (Cf. Neumann, 5 Aug. 46, n. 2.) He officiated at the funerals of Mrs. Jung and Prof. Jung, and also at that of Toni Wolff. (Part of this letter is published in Ges. Werke, XI, pp. 685f.)

[1] Symeon Metaphrastes, 10th cent., Byzantine hagiographer.

[2] "Thou wilt never make (from others) the One (that thou seekest), except there first be made one thing of thyself." A much-quoted saying from Gerhard Dorn, "Philosophia meditativa," *Theatrum chemicum*, I (1602). Cf. *Psychology and Alchemy*, CW 12, par. 358.

Sarcasm is the means by which we hide our hurt feelings from ourselves, and from this you can see how very much the knowledge of
God has wounded me, and how very much I would have preferred to
remain a child in the Father's protection and shun the problem of
opposites. It is probably even more difficult to deliver oneself from
good than from evil. But without sin there is no breaking away from
the good Father; sarcasm plays the corresponding role in this case.
As I hinted in the motto, *Doleo super te*,[3] I am sincerely sorry to
wound praiseworthy feelings. In this regard I had to overcome misgivings aplenty. I shall have to suffer anyway for being one against an
overwhelming majority. Every development, every change for the
better, is full of suffering. It is just the Reformers who should know
this best. But what if they themselves are in need of reform? One
way or another certain questions have to be openly asked and
answered. I felt it my duty to stimulate this. Again with best thanks,

Yours sincerely, C. G. JUNG

[3] II Samuel 1:26: "I am distressed for thee, my brother," forms the motto to
"Answer to Job."

To M. Esther Harding

[ORIGINAL IN ENGLISH]

My dear Dr. Harding,   5 December 1951

I am most awfully sorry to be so late with my answer to your letter
of September 6th. The reason is that I just cannot keep up with my
correspondence. There is simply too much of it. Moreover I need my
time for my own work with the last chapter of the big book on the
Mysterium Coniunctionis. It keeps me so busy that I have to disregard the world as much as I can.

You ask me in your letter about the spook phenomena. Well, this
is a point where I have to give up. I cannot explain the locally bound
spook phenomena. There is a factor in it that is just not psychological. We have to look elsewhere for a proper explanation. I'm
inclined to believe that something of the human soul remains after
death, since already in this conscious life we have evidence that the
psyche exists in a relative space and in a relative time, that is in a
relatively non-extended and eternal state. Possibly the spook phenomena are indications of such existences.

· · ·

☐ See Harding, 28 Sept. 39 (in vol. 1). (See pl. VI in the present vol.)

Concerning synchronicity I can tell you that my paper about it will be printed in the course of this winter and is going to appear together with a paper by Professor W. Pauli about the archetypal foundations of Kepler's astronomy. The title of the book will be *Naturanschauung und Psyche*.[1] We hope that it will also appear in an English translation soon.

With kind regards and best wishes also to Dr. Bertine,[2]

Yours cordially, c . g . j u n g

[1] *Naturerklärung und Psyche*, tr. as *The Interpretation of Nature and the Psyche* (1955). Jung's contribution was "Synchronicity: An Acausal Connecting Principle," Pauli's "The Influence of Archetypal Ideas on the Scientific Theories of Kepler."
[2] See pl. vii.

To Dr. S.

Dear Colleague,   5 December 1951

Frankly I am surprised at your letting yourself be impressed by T. S. Eliot.[1] Becoming conscious does not in itself lead to hell by any means. It leads to this unpleasant place only if you are conscious of certain things and not of others. You must always ask yourself *what* ought to become conscious. In the case of both these two, Eliot and above all Sartre, the talk is always of consciousness, never of the objective psyche, the unconscious. It is quite natural that if in your consciousness you are always running round in a circle you will finally end up in hell. And that is just what Sartre is after and what Eliot would like to prevent with obviously ineffective measures.

I have no desire to argue with these two. I made my position clear long before they did in their writings, so that anybody who wishes to know it can. With collegial regards,

Yours sincerely, c . g . j u n g

[1] *The Cocktail Party* (1950).

To Maria Folino Weld

[O R I G I N A L   I N   E N G L I S H]

Dear Miss Weld,   5 December 1951

I must apologize for not having answered your letter for such a long time. I was ill in the early part of the summer and then my

30

correspondence has accumulated to such an extent that I couldn't see my way through it any more.

Your letter is interesting. If done in the right way such a Journal[1] may be quite interesting, provided you get the right kind of collaborators who try to be objective and refrain from merely airing their neurosis.

Glover's book[2]—apart from its more venomous qualities—is quite amusing: it is exactly like those pamphlets people used to write against Freud in the early days. It was quite obvious then that they were merely expressing their resentments on account of the fact that Freud had trodden on their toes. The same is true of Glover. A critique like his is always suspect as a compensation for an unconscious inclination in the other direction. He is certainly not stupid enough not to see the point I make, but I touched upon a weak spot in him, namely where he represses his better insight and his latent criticism of his Freudian superstition. He is just a bit too fanatical. Fanaticism always means overcompensated doubt. He merely shouts down his inner criticism and that's why his book is amusing.

Wishing you every success, I remain,

Yours sincerely, C. G. JUNG

☐ Watertown, Massachusetts.
[1] W. asked Jung's "blessing" for her project to publish a journal "for non-professional students of Jungian psychology."
[2] Edward Glover, *Freud or Jung* (1950); an extremely biased critique of Jung's concepts.

To Alice Lewisohn Crowley

[ORIGINAL IN ENGLISH]

Dear N.,   Bollingen, 30 December 1951

Thank you ever so much for your juicy collection of culinary delights! I arrived here only yesterday and I still feel a bit tired after the labours of Xmas celebrations. I am practising the gentle art of sleeping. After a while I will try my hand on the third stage of *coniunctio*,[1] but for the time being I am undergoing the curse of letter-writing. Only through submission to detestable duties does one gain a

☐ See Crowley, 20 Dec. 41 (in vol. 1).
[1] Cf. *Mysterium*, pars. 759ff. For Dorn the third and highest stage of the *coniunctio* was "the union of the whole man with the *unus mundus*," par. 760 (or *mundus archetypus*, cf. Dr. H., 30 Aug. 51, n. 9. For *unus mundus* cf. Schmid, 11 June 58, n. 4).

certain feeling of liberation which induces a creative mood. In the long run one cannot steal creation.

.   .   .

I am glad you enjoyed our club-meeting.[2] It was correctly on the shortest day. Now the light increases again. I have greeted it with the ancient salute:

Chaire nymphie neon phos!

(Welcome bridegroom new light)[3]

There is great excitement in the Catholic church and much discussion about the new dogma. I am just reading about it. The pope has caught them neatly at their own game of fostering creeds that have no foundation in the scriptures.

Best wishes for the New Year,

Yours affectionately, c. g.

[2] At the Psychological Club, Zurich.

[3] According to Firmicus Maternus (4th cent.) this was the way Dionysos was greeted at the celebration of his mysteries. Cf. *Symbols of Transformation*, CW 5, par. 274, n. 20.

To Erich Neumann

My dear Neumann,   Bollingen, 5 January 1952

Very many thanks for your kind letter and the way you have understood me. This compensates for 1,000 misunderstandings! You have put your finger on the right spot, a painful one for me: I could no longer consider the average reader. Rather, he has to consider *me*. I had to pay this tribute to the pitiless fact of my old age. With the undimmed prospect of all-round incomprehension I could exercise no suasions and no *captatio benevolentiae*; there was no hope of funnelling knowledge into fools. Not in my livery, but "naked and bare I must go down to the grave," fully aware of the outrage my nakedness will provoke. But what is that compared with the arrogance I had to summon up in order to be able to insult God? This gave me a bigger bellyache than if I had had the whole world against me. That is nothing new to me any more. I have expressed my sorrow and condolence in my motto, *Doleo super te, fratri mi.*

☐ (Handwritten.) See Neumann (1905–1960), 29 Jan. 34 (in vol. 1). (See pl. IV in the present vol.)

Your questions: The book is about the Canonical God-image.[1] This is our prime concern, and not a general philosophical concept of God. God is always specific and always locally valid, otherwise he would be ineffectual. The Western God-image is the valid one for me, whether I assent to it intellectually or not. I do not go in for religious philosophy, but am held in thrall, almost crushed, and defend myself as best I can. There is no place for Gnosis or the Midrashim[2] in this image, for there is nothing of them in it. Only my intellect has anything to do with *purusha-atman* or Tao, but not my living thraldom. This is local, barbaric, infantile, and absymally unscientific.

The "vacillation between theological and psychological formulation" is indeed "involuntary." I have much more sympathy with Sophia[3] than with the demiurge,[4] but faced with the reality of both my sympathy counts for nothing.

God is a contradiction in terms, therefore he needs man in order to be made One. Sophia is always ahead, the demiurge always behind. God is an ailment man has to cure. For this purpose God penetrates into man. Why should he do that when he has everything

---

[1] N. had read the MS of *Answer to Job* and besides asking a few questions wrote in a letter of 5 Dec. 51: "It is a book that grips me profoundly, I find it the most beautiful and deepest of your books, a statement which has to be qualified by saying that in reality it is no longer a 'book.' In a certain sense it is a dispute with God, similar to Abraham's when he pleaded with God on account of the destruction of Sodom. In particular it is—for me personally—also a book against God, who let 6 million of 'his' people be killed, for Job is really Israel too. I do not mean this in any 'petty' sense; I know we are only the paradigm for the whole of humanity in whose name you speak, protest, and console. And it is precisely the conscious one-sidedness, indeed often the wrongness of what you say, that is for me an inner proof of the necessity and justice of your attack—which is naturally not an attack at all, as I well know."

[2] Part of the "oral" teachings of Judaism as distinct from the "written" teachings of the Bible.

[3] Sophia, or Sapientia Dei, the Wisdom of God, figures in Proverbs, Ecclesiasticus, and the Wisdom of Solomon, quoted in "Answer to Job," pars. 609ff.; in par. 609 she is defined as "a coeternal and more or less hypostatized pneuma of feminine nature that existed before the Creation," and as God's "friend and playmate from the beginning of the world" (par. 617).

[4] *Demiourgos* (lit., artisan), in Platonic philosophy (*Timaeus*, 40) the creator of the world. The Gnostics took over the word, but the status of the demiurge varies greatly in the various Gnostic systems. Sometimes he corresponds to the God of the OT, sometimes he is the creator only of the material world and subordinate to the highest God, sometimes he is the creator of evil.

already? In order to reach man, God has to show himself in his true form, or man would be everlastingly praising his goodness and justice and so deny him admission. This can be effected only by Satan, a fact which should not be taken as a justification for Satanic actions, otherwise God would not be recognized for what he really is.

The "advocate"[5] seems to me to be Sophia or omniscience. Ouranos and Tethys[6] no longer sleep together. Kether and Malkhuth[7] are separated, the Shekhinah is in exile; that is the reason for God's suffering. The *mysterium coniunctionis* is the business of man. He is the *nymphagogos*[8] of the heavenly marriage. How can a man hold aloof from this drama? He would then be a philosopher, talking *about* God but not *with* him. The first would be easy and would give man a false sense of security, the second is difficult and therefore extremely unpopular. Just that was my lamented lot, wherefore I needed an energetic illness to break down my resistance.[9] I have to be everywhere *beneath* and not *above*. How would Job have looked had he been able to keep his distance?

Although I am talking of the Western, specifically Protestant God-image, there are no texts one can turn to for a more or less reliable interpretation. They have to be taken in the lump. One doesn't shoot at sparrows with cannons, i.e., the God-image is a *représentation collective*[10] which everyone knows something about.

As for the *nigredo*,[11] it is certain that no one is redeemed from a

[5] Translation of the German word *Anwalt*, used by Jung with reference to Job 19:25. The word occurs in the *Zürcher Bibel*; the Luther Bible has *Erlöser* corresponding to AV "redeemer." In RSV the alternative reading for "redeemer" is "vindicator," very close to "advocate."

[6] The reference is to Okeanos (not Ouranos) and Tethys, who according to legend no longer cohabited on account of a quarrel. Cf. Iliad, XIV, 300ff.; *Mysterium*, CW 14, par. 18, n. 121.

[7] Kether (= crown) and Malkhuth (= kingdom) are the highest and lowest *Sefiroth* of the Kabbalah. What Jung had in mind is the *unio mystica* of Malkhuth (also called Shekhinah) and Tifereth (= beauty), the sixth *Sefira* (cf. Fischer, 21 Dec. 44, n. 5) and the abandonment of Malkhuth by Tifereth (*Mysterium*, par. 18).

[8] The "bridal guide" or "best man," who gives away the bride to the bridegroom. Thus man, through greater consciousness, unites the masculine and feminine aspects of the Deity, or the opposite aspects of the self.

[9] Cf. Corbin, 4 May 53.

[10] A term coined by Lévy-Bruhl for the symbolical figures and ideas of primitives.

[11] Blackness, the first stage of the alchemical opus (cf. White, 24 Sept. 48, n. 8); in a psychological sense, the encounter with the dark side of the personality, or shadow.

sin he has not committed, and that a man who stands on a peak cannot climb it. The humiliation allotted to each of us is implicit in his character. If he seeks his wholeness seriously, he will step unawares into the hole destined for him, and out of this darkness the light will rise. But the light cannot be enlightened. If anyone feels he is in the light, I would never talk him into the darkness, for with his light he would seek and find something black which is not him at all. The light cannot see its own peculiar blackness. But if it dims, and he follows his twilight as he followed his light, then he will get into the night that is *his*. If the light does not dim he would be a fool not to abide in it.

Your *Psyche*[12] has arrived—many thanks—and I have begun reading it. I will write about it later. So far I am very impressed and am enjoying it.

Job and *Synchronicity* are now in the press. At present, with my unfortunately very limited working capacity, I am still struggling with the last chapter of *Mysterium Coniunctionis*. The book will run to 2 volumes, followed by a third, containing *Aurora Consurgens* (attributed to Thomas Aquinas) as an example of the interpenetration of Christianity and alchemy.

Again many thanks!

Yours sincerely, C. G. JUNG

[12] *Amor and Psyche* (1956; orig. 1952). Cf. Neumann, 28 Feb. 52.

To Donal A. Rajapakse

[ORIGINAL IN ENGLISH]

Dear Mr. Rajapakse,   22 January 1952

As you see I am hastening to your rescue,[1] hoping that you did not get yourself into too much of a jam by your making yourself particularly obnoxious to your Vice-Chancellor. You know that one of the unfortunate qualities of introverts is that they so often cannot help putting the wrong foot forward. At all events I must say that it is a pretty daring attitude to risk a dispute with the Vice-Chancellor of your University. Obviously this gentleman is not quite informed

□ Mount Lavinia, Ceylon.
[1] R. asked for advice concerning his controversy with the Vice-Chancellor of the U. of Ceylon on how to conduct interviews. He maintained that introverts and extraverts should be treated differently.

about the situation. Presumably he has never read my book *Psychological Types*, otherwise he couldn't have made that mistake to assume that it is based upon "a premise" at all. I'm an alienist and I have an experience of over 50 years with a great number of patients and people in general, and—together with a number of other pioneers in the field of psychology—I couldn't help noticing that there is a very characteristic difference in the attitude and outlook of people. As a matter of fact the forum of science has accepted not only the facts I described, but also my terminology practically all over the world. It therefore seems rather preposterous to me that the Vice-Chancellor of your University shouldn't be acquainted with these facts. Of course the practical application you make is a method that would appeal only to a psychologist, i.e., a man who knows and appreciates the practical value of psychological classification. That is a thing one cannot expect of everybody. If your man should belong to a different discipline, then you have to tread softly, because people as a rule are very sensitive when it comes to the recognition of psychological truth. People don't like psychology and they don't want to be saddled with psychological qualities. So you can only try to call his attention to certain difficulties people have with their attitudes, i.e., you ought to present it to him as if it were one of your own shortcomings, not his. Tell him you are an introvert and explain to him what an introvert is and ask for his sympathetic understanding and his patience. But be careful not to suggest that he ought to know how to handle extraverts and introverts. No person in authority can be expected to know about psychology or to apply a psychological truth—particularly not when he is a European. They underrate the human soul in an appalling way.

That's about all I can tell you concerning your question. I wish you good luck!

Sincerely, C. G. JUNG

To A. Galliker

Dear Herr Galliker,   29 January 1952

I don't think you are seeing too black. You are quite right when you say that the modern world prefers living *en masse* and thus forgets the bond with the past which is characteristic of every culture.

The young people are not to blame, for it is quite understandable that they should keep an eye open for what is new and impressive about our so-called cultural achievements. But one must also realize that the real cultural good, the legacy of the past, is very often presented in such a boring and uninteresting way that it is almost a miracle if anyone can muster any enthusiasm for it. Those for whom tradition means mere knowledge and book-learning will not be able to interpret the past as the living present. I myself have experienced as a doctor how one had to brush aside the whole previous presentation of religion, mythology, and history as so much junk in favour of new living things, and how later one can find access again to what was lost if one reflects on its living meaning. In order to understand what is going on now I had to return to the distant past and dig up the very things I thought were finally buried in the rubbish heap. It seems to me perfectly possible to teach history in the widest sense not as dry-as-dust, lifeless book-knowledge but to understand it in terms of the fully alive present. All these things should be presented as coming out of our contemporary experience and not as dead relics of times outlived. This certainly faces the teacher with a hard and responsible task, but that's what a teacher is for.

A more than specialist education is always useful. I have never regretted knowing things outside my specialty, on the contrary: renewals never come from over-sophisticated specialized knowledge but from a knowledge of subsidiary subjects which give us new points of view. A wider horizon benefits all of us and is also more natural to the human spirit than specialist knowledge that leads to a spiritual bottleneck.

Yours very truly, C. G. J U N G

☐ Editor of the Swiss journal *Der Jungkaufmann* ("The Young Business-Man"); he had written to several leading authors (including also Einstein, Hesse, and Kerényi) asking the question "Do books still live?" which, he stated, the poet Friedrich Hölderlin had put to his contemporaries. The replies were published in *Der Jungkaufmann*, XXVII:3 (March 1952). — The words attributed to Hölderlin (1770–1843) are a misquotation of "Leben die Bücher bald?" in his ode "An die Deutschen"; the sense is, in the future will books now begin to live? Cf. tr. by Michael Hamburger, *Hölderlin: Poems and Fragments* (1967), p. 58.

To J. M. Thorburn

[ORIGINAL IN ENGLISH]

My dear Thorburn,   6 February 1952

Thank you very much for your two letters. Unfortunately I cannot remember whether I answered the first one by hand while my secretary was away. I know I wanted to but it may be that I was prevented from actually writing. I simply cannot cope with my correspondence any longer. But I want to answer your second letter at once and let you know what I feel about that biography.[1]

First of all I dislike biography because it is seldom true and then it is only interesting when something has happened in the human life that people understand. As long as people don't understand what I have done with psychology there is little use for a biography. My psychology and my life are interwoven to such an extent that one cannot make my biography readable without telling people at the same time about the things I have found out about the unconscious.

What you tell me about your interest in astrology has interested me greatly. My thoughts have been hovering over similar problems lately for several years and I assume that they still are in a way, i.e., my unconscious thinking is definitely rotating round the problem of time. I cannot say what I am thinking exactly, however, because I only get glimpses from time to time of what it thinks. In a way it is connected with the subject of a recent discussion in the Society for Psychical Research, where a Dr. J. R. Smythies[2] has proposed a new theory of absolute space or absolute space-time. It is a pretty complex conception of not less than 7 dimensions, i.e., 3 dimensions of physical space, 3 dimensions of psychic space, the latter at right angles to physical space, and one time-dimension common to both. How he is going to explain the astrological or the ψ-phenomena is dark to me, also I'm unable to find out what the questions fertilizing future experimental work and issuing from this conceptual basis might be.

Well, if I were you I shouldn't bother about my biography. I don't want to write one, because quite apart from the lack of motive I wouldn't know how to set about it. Much less can I see how anybody else could disentangle this monstrous Gordian knot of fatality, dense-

---

□ (d. 1970), formerly lecturer in philosophy, Cardiff U.; cf. Oswald, 8 Dec. 28, n. 2.

[1] T. suggested that Jung commission someone to write his biography.

[2] Cf. Smythies, 29 Feb. 52, n. □.

ness, and aspirations and what-not! Anybody who would try such an adventure ought to analyse me far beyond my own head if he wants to make a real job of it.

Good luck for your trip to America! I wish I could still travel, but that is pretty much out of the question. I have to be content with mental flights—indeed more adventurous than what you could do on this globe that harbours no place any longer which would be sheltered from the devastating foolishness of man. Even Tibet is going to the dogs![3]

Cordially yours, C. G. JUNG

[3] The Chinese had occupied Tibet in 1950 and begun to destroy its theocracy.

To Pastor Walter Uhsadel

Dear Pastor Uhsadel,   6 February 1952

It is extraordinarily kind of you to wish to dedicate your book[1] to me, and I would gladly accept this dedication if I were certain that you would be equally pleased in the future.[2] My wife has pointed out that this might possibly not be the case and I have to agree with her. A controversial book of mine is to appear shortly, entitled Answer to Job. Unfortunately I cannot tell you in detail what I have written in it, but can only hint that this book is a very critical discussion of the Old Testament Yahweh and of the Christian appropriation of this God-concept. I have shown the MS to three theologians and they were shocked. On the other hand many younger people had a very positive reaction. But I can imagine that in circles where thinking and feeling are orthodox my book could have a devastating effect —both for me and for all those with whom I have close relationships. I wouldn't like to expose you to this danger without cause. Therefore I would ask you to think twice about it.

The motive for my book was an increasingly urgent feeling of responsibility which in the end I could no longer withstand. Nor could

☐ See Uhsadel, 4 Aug. 36 (in vol. 1).
[1] Der Mensch und die Mächte des Unbewussten. Studien zur Begegnung von Psychotherapie und Seelsorge (1952). The book carried the dedication: "To Dr. Carl Gustav Jung, dedicated in gratitude."
[2] Jung sent Uhsadel Answer to Job with a handwritten dedication: "To Pastor W. Uhsadel with friendly feelings, but just for that reason with hesitation from the author, March 1953."

I, like Albert Schweitzer, seek suitable refuge far away from Europe and open a practice there. On the time-honoured principle *Hic Rhodus, hic salta*, I had to resign myself to looking the problem of the modern Christian in the eye. So perhaps you had better wait until the book is out.

Meanwhile with kind regards and best thanks,

Yours sincerely, C. G. JUNG

To J. Wesley Neal

[ORIGINAL IN ENGLISH]

Dear Sir,   9 February 1952

It is not so easy to answer your question about the "Island of Peace."[1] I seem to have quite a number of them, a sort of peaceful archipelago. Some of the main islands are: my garden, the view of distant mountains, my country place where I withdraw from the noise of city life, my library. Also small things like books, pictures, and stones.

When I was in Africa the headman of my safari, a Mohammedan Somali, told me what his Sheik had taught him about Chadir.[2] He said: "He can appear to thee like light without flame and smoke, or like a man in the street, or like a blade of grass."

I hope this will answer your question.

Yours sincerely, C. G. JUNG

☐ Long Beach, California.
[1] N. asked if Jung had an "island of peace" which offered him a "refuge in the stream of daily living."
[2] Cf. Irminger, 22 Sept. 44, n. 3. For the quotation cf. "Concerning Rebirth," CW 9, i, par. 250.

To Ernest Jones

[ORIGINAL IN ENGLISH]

Dear Jones,   22 February 1952

Freud's letters in my possession are not particularly important. They chiefly contain remarks about publishers or the organization of

☐ M.D., (1879–1958), British psychoanalyst, founder of the British Psycho-Analytical Society (1913); Freud's biographer: *Sigmund Freud: Life and Work*, 3 vols. (1953–57). (See pl. II in vol. 1.)

the Psychoanalytical Society.[1] And some others are too personal. As a matter of fact I don't care for their publication. On the whole they wouldn't be an important contribution to Freud's biography.

My personal recollections on the other hand are a chapter for itself. They have very much to do with Freud's psychology, but since there is no witness except myself I prefer to refrain from unsubstantiated tales about the dead.

Hoping you will understand my motives, I remain,

Very truly yours, C. G. JUNG

[1] I.e., the International Psychoanalytic Association, of which Jung was first president. — *The Freud/Jung Letters* have subsequently been published (1974); see introduction by the editor, W. McGuire, pp. xxiff. (where this letter is published), introduction to the present vol., pp. xif., and infra, Jones, 19 Dec. 53.

To Erich Neumann

Dear Neumann,   28 February 1952

I should have written to you long since but in the meantime I have been banished to bed again with flu. At 77 this is no light matter, for though *facilis descensus Averno, revocare gradum*[1] is all the more difficult, i.e., the motives for returning to the upper air gradually lose their plausibility. Today I am up for the first time and am writing to you as one does in the three-dimensional world. I must tell you straight out how very much I have enjoyed your *Amor and Psyche*. It is brilliant and written with the most impassioned inner participation. I think I now understand why, with Apuleius, you have let Psyche's fate and her femininity[2] unfold on the distant shores of the pristine world of heroes. With the utmost scrupulosity and lapidary precision you have shown how this drama, rooted in an anonymous

[1]   ". . . facilis descensus Averno;
noctes atque dies patet atri ianua Ditis;
sed revocare gradum superasque evadere ad auras,
hoc opus, hic labor est . . ."
(. . . easy is the descent to Avernus: night and day the door of gloomy Dis stands open; but to recall thy steps and pass out to the upper air, this is the task, this the toil!). — Virgil, *Aeneid*, VI, 126–29 (tr. H. R. Fairclough, Loeb edn.). Motto to *Psychology and Alchemy*, CW 12, Part II.
[2] The book is a psychological commentary, subtitled "The Psychic Development of the Feminine," on the Amor and Psyche episode in *The Golden Ass* of Apuleius.

world of aforetime and far removed from all personal caprice, unrolls before our eyes in exemplary fashion when Apuleius, imitating Psyche, descends to the nether gods and experiences his perfection as Sol,[3] thus attaining the "supreme masculine authority." This "noonday sun"[4] is a triumph, and with it the hero's career begins: his voluntary abdication before "the human and feminine, which by its superiority in love has proved itself equal to the divine."[5]

Your depression seems to me to go together with the mystery of the noonday. In the case of bad books, it is enough that they get written. But good books want to achieve a reality beyond that and start posing questions one would rather leave others to answer. It seems to me the dialogue has already begun. "Ten pairs of tortoises cannot oppose it."[6] Even unfortunate events turn out for the best if one is kind from inner necessity. One should indeed be presented before God, then the thing for which one strives will assuredly be recognized as the truth. I have seldom seen a more fitting oracle. You have only to listen quietly, then you will hear what is expected of you if you "keep the heart constantly steady."

Paramahansa Yogananda: *Autobiography of a Yogi.*[7] 100% pure coconut oil, starting at 105 F. in the shade and 100% humidity, it gets more and more believable as the best psychological tourist-guide to regions south of the 16th parallel; presupposes a bit too much amoebic dysentery and malarial anaemia so as to make changes of moral scenery and the high frequency of miraculous intermezzi more endurable; huge success along with Amy McPherson[8] and her ilk as a metaphysical Luna Park on the Pacific coast south of San Francisco; is no

---

[3] The highest stage of initiation into the mysteries of Isis as described by Apuleius, the so-called "solificatio." Cf. *Psychology and Alchemy,* pars. 66f., and *Symbols of Transformation,* CW 5, par. 130, n. 14.

[4] *Amor and Psyche,* pp. 43f., 98ff.

[5] Ibid., p. 125.

[6] Cf. the *I Ching,* Hexagram 42, "Increase":
   "Six in the second place means:
   Someone does indeed increase him;
   Ten pairs of tortoises cannot oppose it.
   Constant perseverance brings good fortune.
   The King presents him before God.
   Good fortune."
The rest of this passage contains allusions to other places in the hexagram and the comments on them.

[7] London, n.d. (the author's "Note to the London Edition" is dated 25 Oct. 1949).

[8] Aimee Semple McPherson (1890–1944), Canadian-born American evangelist and founder of the International Church of the Foursquare Gospel. A woman of

ordinary substitute but authentically Indian for all five senses; guaranteed offer of 100-year treks into the great hinterland with increasing obfuscation of the hitherland; makes all illusionistic arts superfluous and offers all that could be desired for a negative existence; unsurpassed as an antidote to the disastrous population explosion and traffic jams and the threat of spiritual starvation, so rich in vitamins that albumen, carbohydrates, and suchlike banalities become supererogatory. At that rate Martin Buber[9] could make his beard grow 2 metres longer. Yes, what other fancies might come crowding into one's head? Happy India! Halcyon coconut palm-fringed elephantiasis isles, chupatties reeking of hot oil—oh my liver can't bear them any more! Yogananda fills the yawning gap. But I won't write him a foreword. Well, that's me.

Best greetings and no offence meant!

C. G. JUNG

---

great magnetism, charm, and energy, she was given to high drama which she used successfully for self-promotion and for her evangelistic activities. Died of an overdose of sleeping pills.

[9] Martin Buber had published an article "Religion und modernes Denken," *Merkur* (Stuttgart), VI:2 (Feb. 1952), in which he attacked Jung's religious position and labelled it "Gnosticism." Jung—who felt completely misunderstood and misinterpreted—replied in an article "Religion und Psychologie," *Merkur*, VI:5 (May 1952). Buber's rejoinder was published in the same issue; both it and the original article were later incorporated in his *Gottesfinsternis: Betrachtungen zur Beziehung zwischen Religion und Philosophie* (Zurich, 1953); tr. in *Eclipse of God* (1952). Jung's reply is in CW 18 (and in Ges. Werke, XI, Anhang, pp. 657ff.).

To John Raymond Smythies

[ORIGINAL IN ENGLISH]

Dear Dr. Smythies,   29 February 1952

I hardly dare to write a letter to the Editor of the *S.P.R. Journal*, as you suggest.[1] I am afraid my English is too poor, too ungrammatical, and too colloquial. Amongst very learned and illustrious philosophers my simple argumentation would have no show. Moreover I know from experience that philosophers don't understand my un-

☐ English psychiatrist, later consultant and senior lecturer at the Department of Psychological Medicine, U. of Edinburgh. Author of many papers on the theoretical bases of extra-sensory perception.

[1] S. suggested a contribution to a symposium "On the Nature of Mind," to be published in the *Journal of the Society for Psychical Research*, 1952.

couth language. I prefer therefore, if you allow, to write a letter to yourself, and leave it to you to make that use of it you see fit.

Concerning your own proposition I have already told you how much I welcome your idea of a perceptual, i.e., "subtle" body. Your view is rather confirmed, as it seems to me, by the peculiar fact that on the one hand consciousness has so exceedingly little direct information of the body from within, and that on the other hand the unconscious (i.e., dreams and other products of the "unconscious") refers very rarely to the body and, if it does, it is always in the most roundabout way, i.e., through highly "symbolized" images. For a long time I have considered this fact as negative evidence for the existence of a subtle body or at least for a curious gap between mind and body. Of a psyche dwelling in its own body one should expect at least that it would be immediately and thoroughly informed of any change of conditions therein. Its not being the case demands some explanation.

Now concerning your critique of the space concept:[2] I have given a good deal of thought to it. You know perhaps that the helium atom is characterized by 2 x 3 space factors and 1 time factor.[3] I don't know whether there is something in this parallel or not. At all events the assumption of a perceptual body postulates a corresponding perceptual space that separates the mind from physical space in the same way as the subtle body causes the gap between the mind and the physical body. Thus you arrive logically at two different spaces, which however cannot be entirely incommensurable, since there exists—in spite of the difference—communication between them. You assume that time is the factor they have in common. Thus time is assumed to be the same physically as well as perceptually. Whereas Ψ-phenomena bear out clearly that physical and psychic space differ from each other. I submit that the factor of time proves to be equally "elastic" as space under ESP conditions. If this is the case, we are confronted with two four-dimensional systems in a contingent contiguity. Please excuse the awfully tortuous ways of putting it. It shows nothing more than my perplexity.

The obviously arbitrary behaviour of time and space under ESP conditions seemingly necessitates such a postulate. On the other hand one might ask the question whether we can as hitherto go on thinking in terms of space and time, while modern physics begins to relinquish these terms in favour of a time-space continuum, in which

[2] Cf. Smythies, *Analysis of Perception* (1956).
[3] The helium atom has two electrons, each of which has three space coordinates, and the whole system has one time coordinate.

44

space is no more space and time no more time. The question is, in short: shouldn't we give up the time-space categories altogether when we are dealing with psychic existence? It might be that psyche should be understood as *unextended intensity* and not as a body moving with time. One might assume the psyche gradually rising from minute extensity to infinite intensity, transcending for instance the velocity of light and thus irrealizing the body. That would account for the "elasticity" of space under ESP conditions. If there is no body moving in space, there can be no time either and that would account for the "elasticity" of time.

You will certainly object to the paradox of "unextended intensity" as being a *contradictio in adiecto*. I quite agree. Energy is mass and mass is extended. At all events, a body with a speed higher than that of light vanishes from sight and one may have all sorts of doubts about what would happen to such a body otherwise. Surely there would be no means to make sure of its whereabouts or of its existence at all. Its time would be unobservable likewise.

All this is certainly highly speculative, in fact unwarrantably adventurous. But ψ-phenomena are equally disconcerting and lay claim to an unusually high jump. Yet any hypothesis is warrantable inasmuch as it explains observable facts and is consistent in itself. In the light of this view the brain might be a transformer station, in which the relatively infinite tension or intensity of the psyche proper is transformed into perceptible frequencies or "extensions." Conversely, the fading of introspective perception of the body explains itself as due to a gradual "psychification," i.e., intensification at the expense of extension. Psyche = highest intensity in the smallest space.

In my essay on synchronicity I don't venture into such speculation. I propose a new (really a very old) principle of explanation, viz. synchronicity, which is a new term for the time-hallowed συμπάθεια[4] or *correspondentia*. I go back in a way to Leibniz, the last mediaeval thinker with holistic judgment: he explained the phenomenon by four principles: space, time, causality, and correspondence (*harmonia praestabilita*).[5] We have dropped the latter long ago (though Schopenhauer took it up again, disguised as causality). I hold that *there is no causal explanation for ψ-phenomena*. Terms like thought-transmission, telepathy, clairvoyance, mean nothing. How can one imagine a causal explanation for a case of precognition?

[4] = sympathy. Cf. Kling, 14 Jan. 58, n. 2.
[5] "Pre-established harmony"; according to Leibniz, the divinely arranged harmonious relationship between body and soul, and the "absolute synchronism of psychic and physical events." Cf. "Synchronicity," CW 8, pars. 937ff., also 828f.

Ψ-phenomena, I hold, are contingencies beyond mere probability, "meaningful coincidences" (*sinngemässe Koinzidenzen*) due to a specific psychic condition, namely, a certain emotional mood called interest, expectation, hope, belief, etc., or an emotional objective situation like death, illness, or other "numinous" conditions. Emotions follow an instinctual pattern, i.e., an archetype. In the ESP experiments f.i. it is the situation of the *miracle*. It looks as if the collective character of the archetypes would manifest itself also in meaningful coincidences, i.e., as if the archetype (or the collective unconscious) were not only inside the individual, but also outside, viz. in one's environment, as if sender and percipient were in the same psychic space, or in the same time (in precognition cases). As in the psychic world there are no bodies moving through space, there is also no time. The archetypal world is "eternal," i.e., outside time, and it is everywhere, as there is no space under psychic, that is archetypal conditions. Where an archetype prevails, we can expect synchronistic phenomena, i.e., *acausal correspondences*, which consist in a parallel arrangement of facts in time. The arrangement is not the effect of a cause. It just happens, being a consequence of the fact that causality is a merely statistical truth. I propose, therefore, 4 principles for the explanation of Nature:[6]

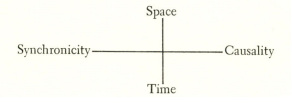

Or taking into account modern physics:[7]

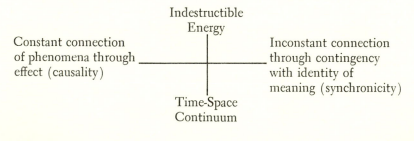

[6] Ibid., pars. 961f.
[7] Ibid., pars. 963f.

Contingency is usually without meaning, but Ψ-phenomena prove that occasionally it has meaning.

One can introduce synchronicity as the necessary supplement to a merely statistical causality, which is a negative way of doing it. A positive demonstration however demands facts, which I cannot provide in a letter. They are in my book. Nevertheless I hope that I have succeeded in giving you some idea at least of what I mean by synchronicity. If you think of it as being something not unlike Leibniz' *harmonia praestabilita* you are not far off the truth. But whereas it is a constant factor with Leibniz, it is a thoroughly inconstant one with me and mostly dependent upon an archetypal psychic condition.

Sorry to be a bit late with my answer. I had a grippe in the meantime and I still feel somewhat under the weather.

Yours sincerely, C. G. JUNG

To C. H. Josten

[ORIGINAL IN ENGLISH]

Dear Sir, 6 April 1952

Thank you ever so much for letting me see Ashmole's dreams![1] Such a series is indeed unique. One has to go right back to the 3rd cent. A.D. to find something that would bear comparison, namely the dream-visions of Zosimos of Panopolis. These are indubitably alchemistic, while Ashmole's dreams have nothing—on the surface at least—reminiscent of alchemy. They are, though, of considerable interest inasmuch as they contain a problem which played a great role in the generation immediately before Ashmole's time: It is the so-called "Mysterium Coniunctionis" represented in a literary document, viz. Christian Rosencreutz: *Chymische Hochzeit*, 1616. It is also the foundation of Goethe's *Faust* and one of the most important items in Gerardus Dorneus' "Speculativa Philosophia" (end of XVIth cent. Printed in *Theatr. Chemi.*,[2] Vol. I, 1602).

☐ Then curator of the Museum of the History of Science, Oxford.
[1] J. was preparing a critical edition of the autobiographical notes of the English archaeologist and alchemist Elias Ashmole (1617–92), founder of the Ashmolean Museum, Oxford (1683). These notes contained a number of dreams which J. had sent Jung. Cf. *Elias Ashmole 1617–1692: His autobiographical and historical notes, his correspondence, and other contemporary sources relating to his life and work*, ed. with biographical introduction by C. H. Josten, 5 vols. (1966).
[2] *Theatrum chemicum*, one of the classics of alchemy, a compilation of alchemical treatises in 6 vols. The first three vols. were published in Ursel 1602, the following

47

The "Mysterium" reaches its culmination in the dream of Dec. 29th 1646. The *peripeteia*[3] follows in the dream of March 1st 1647 and the catastrophe in the dream of May 16th 1647.[4] The subsequent dreams show the turning over from the feminine to the masculine side, i.e., from the attempt at *coniunctio s. compositio* to the suppression of the feminine factor in favour of a onesided masculinity. This amounts to a complete disregard of the "left" side,[5] i.e., the unconscious, and the equally complete restoration of the former state of consciousness. We describe this process as an *intrusion of unconscious contents* into the conscious world of an individual. It is setting in with Sept. 11th 1645: ♀ in the IX house = a personification of the alchemistic "Sapientia" (parallel to the Gnostic "Sophia"!). All the subsequent erotic and semi-erotic dreams aim at a *coniunctio* with the feminine, i.e., unconscious side (called "anima"). The "bridegroom" is always, curiously enough, also the cipher chosen for Ashmole himself, quite correctly, because it is his "mystery." March 1, 1647, a "young man" poisons him, i.e., he himself as a younger person than he is, less experienced, his inferior, insinuates a younger, more masculine idea over against an older, wiser attitude, inclined to integrate his more "feminine" trends which aim at the completion of the Self ("process of individuation"). The latter is expressed in dream June 21st 1646[6] by paradise on the Northpole, the 4 springs (quaternity!) and the "chapel of Our Lady," also by dream of Dec. 29th 1646: "all my affections terminate in thee," i.e., the Anima-Sapientia. In the

---

three in Strasbourg 1613, 1622, 1661 (they are in Jung's library). Vol. I contains nine treatises by Dorn, of which "Speculativa philosophia" is the first.

[3] = change, dénouement.

[4] The dream of 29 Dec. 1646 is not Ashmole's; he reports the dream of a Mrs. March (with whom he was in love at the time): "At night she dreamed / that I had written something round, and she was to fill it up in the middle / Thereupon I wrote this in a ring of paper / 'All my affections terminate in thee' / and she wrote a verse in the middle." — In the dream of 1 March 1647 he had poisoned himself "with eating poyson in with butter (that a young man had given me)"; finally, on 16 May 1647, he dreamt of the sudden death of a Jonas Moore (? a friend of his) which he "much lamented."

[5] For instance, on 10 Dec. 1647 Ashmole reports a dream in which his "left hand was suddenly rotted off."

[6] "Morning that I was near paradise which seemed to be toward the North Pole / and 4 springs issued out of a hill upon which was a chapel erected to our lady Mary / but I could not be come nearer but 4 or 5 miles because of the cold and frost." (The "4 springs" refer to Gen. 2:10–14, the 4 rivers of paradise: Pison, Gihon, Hiddekel, Euphrates.)

Northpole dwells the *cor Mercurii*.[7] A. describes here a mandala, a well-known symbol of the Self. (You will find all the necessary amplifications and evidence in my book *Psychologie u. Alchemie*, 1944 and in *Symbolik des Geistes*, 1948, here especially about ☿.[8] Concerning the "North"[9] *vide* my book *Aion*, 1951.)

On account of a complete lack of personal material I am unable to say anything about the personalistic aspect of the dreams. It would be however nothing more than a bit of personal or "all-too-human (!) *chronique scandaleuse*,"[10] not altogether interesting. I have confined myself therefore to the archetypal and impersonal aspect exclusively. Here we have ample material for comparison at our disposal and a fairly conclusive one at that.

The whole dream-episode pictures in a remarkably neat way the experience of an "unconscious" invasion compensating a somewhat impulsive and rather onesided masculine attitude, characteristic of the XVI and XVII cent. in the northern countries. A parallel document in Italy is the famous *Ipnerotomachia* of Poliphilo (XVth cent.) with very much the same psychology. (Cf. the book by L. Fierz-David: *Der Liebestraum des Poliphilo*[11] [1947] Zurich.)

I have given you a very rough draft indeed of what one could say about A.'s dreams. There is quite a lot more of detail I have not dealt with here. To do so would require half a small book. I only want to draw your attention to the *Faust* parallel: in the beginning of the series a number of women symbolize the approach of the unconscious; he is unable to establish a relationship with the female partner (his unconscious side, viz. his "anima"), he then gets poisoned through his shadow (alchem.: "familiaris," as a rule ☿, in *Faust* Mephisto) and through death and murder and fraud he regains his former masculine attitude with its ambitions: honour and wealth. Another solution even in those unpsychological times would have been possible if A. had carefully observed the ethical rules as well as the "Philosophia Meditativa"[12] of alchemy. It does not seem as if the publication of the

---

[7] Cf. *Psychology and Alchemy*, CW 12, par. 265: "In the Pole is the heart of Mercurius."

[8] The astrological sign for the planet Mercury.

[9] *Aion*, CW 9, ii, pars. 156ff., 188ff.

[10] J. confirmed Jung's reaction in a letter of 29 Apr.: "Your interpretation of Ashmole's dreams corresponds in a remarkable way with the events in Ashmole's life during the same period. . . . The dreams are surrounded by much information which, as you rightly presume, is mostly 'chronique scandaleuse.'"

[11] Cf. *The Dream of Poliphilo* (tr., 1950).

[12] Treatise by Dorn, *Theatrum chemicum*, I.

Theatrum Chemicum Britannicum[13] had been the right answer. However the dream series was an episode which might have had another effect if repeated later in his life.

I have dealt with this classical alchemistic problem in a special treatise *Mysterium Coniunctionis,* that is not yet published. But my *Psych. and Alch.* gives you a general orientation at least.

Could you enlighten me about Mr. Lilly?[14] Was he a sort of sorcerer? and about the *"Negative Oath"*?[15] I know nothing about it.

Thank you again for your kindness!

Yours sincerely, C. G. JUNG

P.S. Are you going to publish the dreams? It would be interesting material for a psychologist of my brand.

[13] Edited by Elias Ashmole (London, 1652).
[14] William Lilly (1602–81), English astrologer and magician, was a close friend of Ashmole's. — In a dream of "♃," 2 Jan. 1647, "Mr. Lilly has assured me he would procure me [i.e., Mrs. March] by his art." (♃ is the astrological sign for Jupiter which Ashmole used for Mrs. March.)
[15] The negative oath was the oath to be taken by Royalists who wanted to secure their property from sequestration under Cromwell.

To Father Victor White

[ORIGINAL IN ENGLISH]
pro tempore Locarno, Ticino, Park Hotel

Dear Victor,   [? Spring, 1952][1]

Thank you very much for your offprints! You have been obviously busy. I have read them all and I think the one about the "Dying God"[2] is particularly good. The one about Freud[3] is clever and remarkably open-minded. Your meditation about the way of the Cross[4] contains nothing I could not subscribe to. It is psychologically "correct." This amounts to a sincere compliment. Does the book you are planning[5] contain these articles?

□ (Handwritten.)
[1] This letter has no date but must, from internal evidence, have been written before 9 Apr. ["? Spring, 1952"] is added in W.'s handwriting.
[2] An article which was incorporated as ch. XIII: "The Dying God," in W.'s *God and the Unconscious.*
[3] Incorporated as ch. III: "Freud, Jung and God" in ibid.
[4] Most likely W.'s contribution to *What the Cross Means to Me: A Theological Symposium* (1943).
[5] *God and the Unconscious.*

I hope you have received my *Antwort auf Hiob*.[6] I had a pretty miserable time throughout March on account of a grippe, from which I am recovering very slowly. I came down here to pick up again. Although we are in the sun, the air is still pretty cold and windy. I have finished the dreaded last chapter of my *Mysterium Coniunctionis*. It has knocked me flat, and my head is tired. Well, I am approaching my 78th year, and complaints are pointless. My next goal seems to be a thorough contemplation of the spiritual life of lizards and similar cold-blooded animals. But the world does not let me go so easily. After this letter I have to write another one about understanding and believing to a Protestant *theologus*.[7] I am afraid I cannot conceive of any religious belief which is less than a violation of my ego-consciousness. Otherwise I would be hardly aware of believing anything at all. If belief does not come to me as a shock, it would not convince me. I don't know whether they are going to like my opinion or not.

The Curator of the Museum of the History of Science in Oxford has sent me a rather long series of dreams which he has unearthed from the Elias Ashmole MSS, the editor of the *Theatrum Chemicum Britannicum* 1646 (?).[8] They extend over about 5 years and contain the remarkable story of an invasion of unconscious contents aiming at a *coniunctio* with the unconscious. The attempt fails, i.e., is superseded by a return of the former one-sided masculine consciousness. It is an unconscious parallel to *Faust*. The attempt culminates in a symbol of the self: Paradise on the North Pole, 4 springs, and on a hill the chapel of Our Lady. The series begins with Venus in the IX house = *Sapientia*. It ends with death, fraud, and murder. A fine example of an individuation that did not come off.

Hoping to see you in summer again!

Yours cordially, c . g .

[6] W. confirmed the receipt of the book in a letter of 5 April, where he speaks of it as "the most exciting and moving book I have read in years: and somehow it arouses tremendous bonds of sympathy between us, and lights up all sorts of dark places both in the Scriptures and in my own psyche." This reaction is the more surprising in view of his later severe criticism of the book (cf. White, 2 Apr. 55, n. 1).

[7] No such letter has been preserved. Cf. White, 30 Apr. 52, n. 6.

[8] Actually 1652. See preceding letter, n. 13.

To Father Victor White

[ORIGINAL IN ENGLISH]

Dear Victor,   Park Hotel, Locarno, 9 April 1952 until 14th

Thank you for your human letter.[1] It gives me some idea of what is happening inside of you.

The *privatio boni* does not seem to me such a particular puzzle, but I understand that it is of the greatest importance. It is perhaps best if I set forth my point of view, so that you can see how I look at it. At the same time I shall try to consider your standpoint too.

I think you agree with me that within our empirical world good and evil represent the indispensable parts of a logical judgment, like white and black, right-left, above-below, etc. These are equivalent opposites and it is understood that they are always relative to the situation of the one that makes the statement, a person or a law. Empirically we are unable to confirm the existence of anything absolute, i.e., there are no logical means to establish an absolute truth, except a tautology.

Yet we are moved (by archetypal motifs) *to make such statements,* viz. religious or metaphysical assertions such as the Trinity, the Virgin Birth and other exceedingly improbable and physically impossible things. One of these assertions is the *Summum Bonum*[2] and its consequence, the *privatio boni.* The latter is logically as impossible as the Trinity. It is therefore a truly religious statement: *prorsus credibile quia ineptum.*[3] Divine favour and daemonic evil or danger are archetypal. Even if you know that your judgment is entirely subjective and relative you are nevertheless forced to make such statements more than a dozen times every day. And when you are religious you talk in terms of impossibilities. I have no arguments against these facts. I only deny that the *privatio boni* is a logical statement, but I admit the obvious truth that it is a "metaphysical" truth based upon an archetypal "motif."

The way in which opposites are reconciled or united in God we just don't know. Nor do we understand how they are united in the self.

□ (Handwritten.)

[1] Cf. preceding letter, n. 6. In the same letter of April 5 W. expressed his desire to find some common ground on the problem of the *privatio boni,* "which must affect one's value-*judgments* on almost everything (alchemy, gnosticism, Christ and anti-Christ, the Second Coming, the whole orientation of psychotherapy), without there being any dispute about the *facts.*"

[2] God as the Summum Bonum, the Ultimate Good, is "the effective source of the concept of the *privatio boni*" (*Aion,* CW 9, ii, par. 80).

[3] = "immediately credible because absurd." Cf. Wegmann, 20 Nov. 45, n. 2.

The self is transcendental and is only partially conscious. Empirically it is good and evil. The same as the "acts of God" have decidedly contradictory aspects. This fact however does not justify the theological judgment that God is either good or evil. He is transcendental, just as much as the self and therefore not subject to human logic.

The supreme powers are assumed to be either indifferent or more often good than evil. There is an archetypal accent upon the good aspect, but only slightly so. This is understandable, because there must be some sort of equilibrium, otherwise the world could not exist.

The great difficulty seems to consist in the fact that on the one hand we must defend the sanity and logic of the human mind, and on the other hand we have to accept and to welcome the existence of illogical and irrational factors transcending our comprehension. We must deal with them as rationally as we can, even if there is no hope of ever getting on top of them. As we can't deal with them rationally we have to formulate them symbolically. A symbol when taken literally is nearly always impossible. Thus I should say that the *privatio boni* is a *symbolic truth*, based on archetypal motivation, not to be defended rationally any more than the Virgin Birth.

Excuse my bad writing. I am in the garden and there is no table but my knee. Answer not expected. I will try to help you as much as possible.

Yours, c. g.

To H. Haberlandt

Dear Colleague,   23 April 1952

Very many thanks for kindly sending me your review of *Aion*.[1] It stands out from all the others because it is obvious that its author has really read the book, which is something I am grateful for. I therefore venture to ask you to let me know in what sense you use the term "Gnosis." You can hardly mean γνῶσις = knowledge in general, but more specifically the Christian γνῶσις θεοῦ or even that of Gnosticism. In both the latter cases it has to do with *metaphysical* assertions or postulates, i.e., it is assumed that γνῶσις actually consists in the knowledge of a metaphysical object. Now I state expressly and repeatedly in my writings that psychology can do no more than concern itself with

□ A professor in Vienna.
[1] Published in *Wissenschaft und Weltbild* (Vienna), IV (1952).

assertions and anthropomorphic images. The possible metaphysical significance of these assertions is completely outside the bounds of empirical psychology as a science. When I say "God" I mean an anthropomorphic (archetypal) God-image and do not imagine I have said anything about God. I have neither denied nor affirmed him, unlike the Christian or Gnostic γνῶσις which thinks it has said or has to say something about a metaphysical God.

The difficulty which gives rise to misunderstandings is that archetypes are "real." That is to say, effects can be empirically established whose cause is described hypothetically as *archetype*, just as in physics effects can be established whose cause is assumed to be the *atom* (which is merely a model). Nobody has ever seen an archetype, and nobody has ever seen an atom either. But the former is known to produce numinous effects and the latter explosions. When I say "atom" I am talking of the model made of it; when I say "archetype" I am talking of ideas corresponding to it, but never of the thing-in-itself, which in both cases is a transcendental mystery.[2] It would never occur to a physicist that he has bagged the bird with his atomic model (for instance Niels Bohr's planetary system).[3] He is fully aware that he is handling a variable schema or model which merely points to unknowable facts.

This is scientific gnosis, such as I also pursue. Only it is news to me that such knowledge is accounted "metaphysical." You see, for me the psyche is something real *because it works*,[4] as can be established empirically. One must therefore assume that the effective archetypal ideas, including our model of the archetype, rest on something actual even though unknowable, just as the model of the atom rests on certain unknowable qualities of matter. But science cannot possibly establish that, or to what extent, this unknowable substrate is in both cases God. This can be decided only by dogmatics or faith, as for instance in Islamic philosophy (Al-Ghazzali), which explained gravitation as the will of Allah. This is Gnosticism with its characteristic overstepping of epistemological barriers. The Church's proofs of God likewise come under this heading, all of which beg the question if looked at logically.

---

[2] Cf. Devatmananda, 9 Feb. 37, n. 1.

[3] (1885–1962), Danish physicist, head of the Copenhagen Institute for Theoretical Physics; received the Nobel Prize for Physics in 1922. He elaborated the model of the atom as a miniature solar system first put forward by the English physicist Ernest Rutherford (1871–1937) on the basis of the spectrum of hydrogen.

[4] The German play on words, "wirklich" (real) and "wirkt" (works), cannot be rendered satisfactorily in English. "Actual because it acts" is a lame duck. [Tr.]

By contrast I pursue a scientific psychology which could be called a comparative anatomy of the psyche. I postulate the psyche as something real. But this hypothesis can hardly be called "gnostic" any more than the atomic theory can.

So my question is: Wherein consists my "gnosis" in your view, or what do *you* understand by "gnosis"?

Excuse me for bothering you with such a long letter. But I wonder how it comes that so many people think I am a gnostic while equally many others accuse me of being an agnostic. I would like to know whether I am making a fundamental mistake somewhere that occasions such misunderstandings. I would be sincerely grateful to you if you could lighten my darkness. With collegial regards,

Yours very sincerely, C. G. JUNG

To N. Kostyleff

Dear Dr. Kostyleff,   25 April 1952

Naturally some knowledge of modern psychopathology and psychotherapy as they have developed over the last 50 years is presupposed in order to understand my writings. The dream series you refer to in *Psychology and Alchemy* is given there only to illustrate the origin and development of the mandala motif. That has nothing to do with a clinical history or with therapy. It is therefore completely irrelevant what sort of anamnesis the patient had or what was the result of the treatment. But I can tell you that he is a cultured and extremely intelligent man in his middle years who gradually got himself into anxiety states, psychogenic alcoholism, and general moral dissipation. The effect of the treatment was that he didn't have anxiety states any more, didn't drink, and could adapt to life again.[1] Part of the wearisome process of development depicted itself in his dreams, as you might have gathered from my book. — The patient with the dream of the crab[2] suffered from hysterical depressions. At the end of the cure the depressions ceased.

I would like to remark that it is not an arbitrary assumption on my part to regard the ego as a precarious unity. We see all the time

☐ France.
[1] For details of this case see *Analytical Psychology: Its Theory and Practice* (1968), pp. 195–97 = "The Tavistock Lectures," CW 18, pars. 402ff.
[2] Cf. *Two Essays on Analytical Psychology*, CW 7, pars. 123ff.

how easily ego-consciousness gets dissociated, in neurosis as well as in schizophrenia, and also in primitive psychology.

What the unconscious is in itself cannot possibly be established precisely because it is unconscious. Only when it becomes conscious can we establish that a lot of different contents are present, among them a type of unity which is represented by the mandala motif.

Descriptions based entirely on case material are practically impossible. I once analysed the prodromal stage of schizophrenia and the result was a book of 820 pages.[3] Moreover each case is so individual and the individual aspects are so important for the person concerned that less penetrating analyses are much too general and superficial. I have therefore given up expositions of case material.

I must confess I have never heard of your "reflexology,"[4] but shall find out about it.

Yours sincerely, C. G. JUNG

[3] *Symbols of Transformation*, CW 5. The German text runs to 820 pp.
[4] A school of psychology, founded by I. P. Pavlov and W. Bechterev, which interprets all human and animal behaviour in terms of simple or complex reflexes. K.'s contribution remains untraced.

To Vera von Lier-Schmidt Ernsthausen

Dear Frau Ernsthausen,   25 April 1952

I have read your detailed letter with attention. I am not a philosopher but a doctor and empiricist. I practise psychology in the first place as a science, in the second place as an instrument of psychotherapy. Since neurosis is an attitudinal problem, and the attitude depends on, or is grounded in, certain "dominants,"[1] i.e., the ultimate and highest ideas and principles, the problem of attitude can fairly be characterized as a religious one. This is supported by the fact that religious motifs appear in dreams and fantasies for the obvious purpose of regulating the attitude and restoring the disturbed equilibrium. These experiences compelled me to come to grips with religious questions, or rather to examine the psychology of religious statements more closely. My aim is to unearth the psychic facts to which religious statements refer. I have found that, as a rule, when "archetypal" con-

☐ Netherlands.
[1] A term occasionally used for archetypes, e.g., "On the Nature of the Psyche," CW 8, par. 403 & n. 117.

56

tents spontaneously appear in dreams, etc., numinous and healing effects emanate from them. They are *primordial psychic experiences* which very often give patients access again to blocked religious truths. I have also had this experience myself.

I am far from thinking of "self-redemption" since I am wholly dependent on whether such an experience will come my way or not. I am in the position of Saul, who does not know what will happen to him on the road to Damascus. If nothing happens, a Paul will never be made of him. He must then go on persecuting the Christians until the revelation finally smites him. Thus it happens with my patients and thus it happened with me. Just as I can hold back or actually stop the *influxus divinus* (wherever it may come from) with preconceived opinions, so also by suitable behaviour I can draw closer to it and, when it happens, accept it. I can win nothing by force, but can only try to do everything for and nothing against it. The psyche for me is something objective that sends up effects into my consciousness. The unconscious (the *objective psyche*) doesn't belong to me; rightly or wrongly I belong to it. By making it conscious I separate myself from it, and by so objectivating it I can integrate it consciously. Thus my personality is made complete and is prepared for the decisive experience, but no more than that. What can, but need not, happen then is the spontaneous action from the unconscious, an action which is symbolized by the alchemists, Paracelsus, Boehme and the modern unconscious as *lightning*. (Cf. *Gestaltungen des Unbewussten*,[2] pp. 102ff.)

I hope the foregoing has answered your question. I must apologize for the tardiness of my answer. First I had to recover from flu.

Yours sincerely, C. G. JUNG

[2] Cf. "A Study in the Process of Individuation," CW 9, i, pars. 531ff.

To Linda Veladini

Dear Fräulein Veladini,   25 April 1952

I would gladly corroborate your interesting observations[1] if I were in a position to do so. But I lack the necessary experience in this spe-

□ Child psychotherapist, of Locarno.
[1] V. submitted her observations of several cases of poliomyelitis in which distortion of the child's ego-development played a decisive role at the onset of illness.

cialized field. In my practice I have had only one case of infantile paralysis. It was that of a young man, who fell ill with severe polio-myelitis at the age of 4. He still remembered an impressive dream he had shortly before the onset of the illness. He dreamt he was sitting at his mother's feet, playing with some toy or other. Suddenly a wasp flew out of the mother, which stung him, and immediately he felt his whole body poisoned and awoke in terror. I knew the patient's mother and she was a very domineering personality and a burden to her children. An elder brother of the patient had a formidable mother-complex which overshadowed his later life.

The situation was entirely in keeping with your view that the suppression of the child's individuality under the parental influence can at least be a psychic precondition for a paralytic illness. However, we do not have sufficient documentary evidence at present to conclude that infantile paralysis is psychogenic. We only know that certain psychic disturbances cause a lowering of the body's resistance and hence a proneness to infections. We know this quite definitely in the case of tonsilitis, and in the case of tuberculosis there is at least a well-founded suspicion. I have treated several cases of chronic pulmonary tuberculosis for psychic disturbances and observed, coincidentally so to speak, a complete cure of the tuberculosis without specialist treatment. For this reason I have long advocated that sanatoria for consumptives be staffed with psychologically trained doctors because these places positively swarm with neuroses. At all events, psychic treatment would give substantial support to the specific treatment of tuberculosis.

Hoping that these remarks may be of some service to you, I remain,

Yours sincerely, C. G. JUNG

To Father Victor White

[ORIGINAL IN ENGLISH]

Dear Victor,   30 April 1952

The *privatio boni* seems to be a puzzle.[1] A few days ago I had an interesting interview with a Jesuit father from Munich (Lotz is his name). He is professor of dogmatics (?) or Christian philosophy. He

---

[1] Cf. White, 9 Apr. 52, to which he sent a short reply on 20 Apr., complaining of "the deadlock of assertion and counter-assertion" in spite of good will. "We move in different circles, and our minds have been formed in different philosophical climates."

58

was just in the middle of *Antwort auf Hiob* and under the immediate impact of my argument against the *privatio*. He admitted that it is a puzzle, but that the modern interpretation would explain "Evil" as a "disintegration" or a "decomposition" of "Good." If you hypostatize —as the Church does—the concept or idea of Good and give to it metaphysical substance (i.e., *bonum = esse* or having *esse*), then "decomposition" would be indeed a very suitable formula, also satisfactory from the psychological standpoint, as Good is always an effort and a composite achievement while Evil is easily sliding down or falling asunder. But if you take your simile of the good egg,[2] it would become a bad egg by decomposition. A bad egg is not characterized by a mere decrease of goodness however, since it produces qualities of its own that did not belong to the good egg. It develops among other things H_2S, which is a particularly unpleasant substance in its own right. It derives very definitely from the highly complex albumen of the good egg and thus forms a most obvious evidence for the thesis: Evil derives from Good.

Thus the formula of "decomposition" is rather satisfactory in so far as it acknowledges that Evil is as substantial as Good, because H_2S is as tangibly real as the albumen. In this interpretation Evil is far from being a μὴ ὄν. Pater Lotz therefore had my applause. But what about the *privatio boni?* Good, by definition, must be good throughout, even in its smallest particles. You cannot say that a small good is bad. If then a good thing disintegrates into minute fragments, each of them remains good and therefore eatable like a loaf of bread divided into small particles. But when the bread rots, it oxidizes and changes its original substance. There are no more nourishing carbohydrates, but acids, i.e., from a good substance has come a bad thing. The "decomposition" theory would lead to the ultimate conclusion that the Summum Bonum can disintegrate and produce H_2S, the characteristic smell of Hell. Good then would be corruptible, i.e., it would possess an inherent possibility of decay. This possibility of corruption means nothing less than a tendency inherent in the Good to decay and to change into Evil. That obviously confirms my heretical views. But I don't even go as far as Pater Lotz: I am quite satisfied with non-hypostatizing Good and Evil. I consider them not as substances but as

---

[2] In his letter of 20 Apr. W. wrote: "The validity of any particular judgment of value is surely quite another question from the meaning of the terms [good and evil] employed. There is surely nothing religious or archetypal in my motivation, nor anything illogical or transcendental, when I call an egg 'bad' because it *lacks* what I think an egg ought to have."

59

a merely psychological judgment since I have no means of establishing them as metaphysical substances. I don't deny the possibility of a belief that they are substances and that Good prevails against Evil. I even take into consideration that there is a large consensus in that respect, for which there must be important reasons (as I have pointed out in *Aion*).[3] But if you try to make something logical or rationalistic out of that belief, you get into a remarkable mess, as the argument with Pater Lotz clearly shows.

You know, I am not only empirical but also practical. In practice you say nothing when you hold that in an evil deed is a small Good: there is big Evil and a little bit of Good. In practice you just can't deny the ὀυσία of Evil. On the metaphysical plane you are free to declare that what we call "substantially evil" is in metaphysical reality a small Good. But such a statement does not make much sense to me. You call God the Lord over Evil, but if the latter is μὴ ὄν, He is Lord over nothing, not even over the Good, because He is it Himself as the Summum Bonum that has created only good things which have however a marked tendency to go wrong. Nor does evil or corruption derive from man, since the serpent is prior to him, so πόθεν τὸ κακόν???[4]

The necessary answer is: Metaphysically there is no Evil at all; it is only in man's world and it stems from man. This statement however contradicts the fact that paradise was not made by man. He came last into it, nor did he make the serpent. If even God's most beautiful angel, Lucifer, has such a desire to get corrupt, his nature must show a considerable defect of moral qualities—like Yahweh, who insists jealously on morality and is himself unjust. No wonder that His creation has a yellow streak.

Does the doctrine of the Church admit Yahweh's moral defects? If so, Lucifer merely portrays his creator; if not, what about the 89th Psalm,[5] etc.? *Yahweh's immoral behaviour rests on biblical facts. A morally dubious creator cannot be expected to produce a perfectly good world,* not even perfectly good angels.

I know theologians always say: one should not overlook the Lord's greatness, majesty, and kindness and one shouldn't ask questions any-

[3] Cf. pars. 81ff., 100f.

[4] = whence evil?

[5] In *Aion*, par. 169, Jung mentions a story told by Abraham ben Meier ibn Ezra (Jewish scholar and poet, 1092–1167) of "a great sage who was reputed to be unable to read the 89th Psalm because it saddened him too much." The story occurs in Ibn Ezra's Commentary on the Psalms. — Psalm 89 deals with Yahweh's lack of loyalty toward King David; to Jung this was a parallel to the tragedy of Job.

how. I don't overlook God's fearful greatness, but I should consider myself a coward and immoral if I allowed myself to be deterred from asking questions.

On the practical level the *privatio boni* doctrine is morally dangerous, because it belittles and irrealizes Evil and thereby weakens the Good, because it deprives it of its necessary opposite: there is no white without black, no right without left, no above without below, no warm without cold, no truth without error, no light without darkness, etc. If Evil is an illusion, Good is necessarily illusory too. That is the reason why I hold that the *privatio boni* is illogical, irrational and even a nonsense. The moral opposites are an epistemological necessity and, when hypostatized, they produce an amoral Yahweh and a Lucifer and a Serpent and sinful Man and a suffering Creation.

I hope we can continue worrying this bone in the summer!

Cordially yours, C. G.

P.S. Unfortunately I have no copy of the letter to the Prot. theologian.[6] But I will send you an offprint of my answer to Buber,[7] who has called me a Gnostic. He does not understand psychic reality.

[6] Cf. White, Spring 52, n. 7.
[7] Cf. Neumann, 28 Feb. 52, n. 9.

To Paul Billeter

Dear Herr Billeter,   3 May 1952

I am returning Buri's article[1] to you with best thanks. It has already been sent me by various people. I shall refrain from taking up a position in public. I have said all that is necessary in my little book[2] and in my experience it is quite hopeless to argue with people who can't or won't see certain simple truths. Buri imputes false opinions to me and does not understand my epistemological standpoint, although the situation is as simple as could be wished. When someone talks so long and so emphatically about his 100 thalers this is no proof whatever that he has them in his pocket. I even do theology the honour of taking its statements perfectly seriously, but I cannot in all conscience

☐ Zurich.
[1] Fritz Buri, "C. G. Jungs 'Antwort auf Hiob,' " *Basler National-Zeitung*, 27 Apr. 1952. Cf. Buri, 5 May 52.
[2] *Antwort auf Hiob* (1952) = "Answer to Job," CW 11.

know whether they correspond exactly to the metaphysical facts, and anyway it is utterly impossible for us to know these facts. I do not by any means dispute their existence, but I maintain for good reasons that they are first of all statements. Even the Bible was written by human beings. I cannot possibly suppose that God himself was its author. Since we cannot know the metaphysical truth, we must be content with statements and at least take them seriously, and this means criticizing them if they contain gross contradictions. So if I compare the behaviour of the Old Testament God with a Christian conception of God, I must point out that these statements do not agree in many respects and that this can upset a devout heart, which certainly not all theologians possess. It is a fact that the Jews acknowledged the amorality of Yahweh, as you can see from the Midrashim. I have cited the relevant passages in *Aion*[3] (1951, pp. 93ff.). These things are generally unknown to theologians, however. I once met a professor of theology who hadn't even read the Book of Enoch.

Yours sincerely, C. G. JUNG

[3] CW 9, ii, pars. 106ff.

To C. H. Josten

[ORIGINAL IN ENGLISH]

Dear Mr. Josten,   3 May 1952

Your elucidating remarks about the Ashmolean Dreams have been most welcome. I was quite particularly interested, of course, to hear that the dream of December 29th is not from Ashmole himself.[1] (I hadn't understood the note in your report.) That makes the case particularly interesting. The dream itself is of an unusual clarity compared with Ashmole's own dreams. His whole psychological situation then almost demanded the presence of the female, because usually these individuation processes are accompanied by the relationship with a *soror mystica*. That is the reason why a number of alchemists are reported to have been related to what I call an anima figure; like Nicolas Flamel and Péronelle,[2] Zosimos and Theosebeia,[3] Mrs. At-

[1] Cf. Josten, 6 Apr. 52, n. 4.
[2] Nicolas Flamel, b. *ca.* 1330, French alchemist; married Péronelle Lethas, who became his faithful helpmeet and *soror mystica*.
[3] Zosimos of Panopolis, 3rd cent. A.D., the earliest alchemist to write books in his own name, addressed his most extensive work to a lady named Theosebeia.

wood and her father,[4] John Pordage and Jane Lead,[5] etc. The royal nuptial in alchemy represents such a relationship. As it is a common experience that couples have often remarkable coincidences of thought, so they have the same parallelism in dreams. They can even exchange dreams. One finds the same between parents and their children. I have observed the case of a man who had no dreams, but his nine-year-old son had all his father's dreams which I could analyse for the benefit of the father.[6] In the course of this work the father began to dream and the son ceased to have such adult dreams. This peculiar phenomenon is at the base of Rhine's famous ESP experiments, as you know. Such facts point to the relativity of space in the unconscious.

I'm glad to know that my supposition of Lilly being a magician is borne out by the facts.

The obvious identification of Ashmole with Mercury,[7] Mercury being the arch-personification of alchemy, makes it most probable that Mercury was a symbol of the self, with which Ashmole tried to identify. Such an attempt, as far as it succeeds, invariably causes an inflation of the ego. I should assume therefore that Ashmole must have shown signs of a hypertrophied ego. — The allegorical use of Mercury is indeed a symptom of Ashmole's inflation.

Thank you for your explanation about the Negative Oath.

Unfortunately I don't possess a copy of Ashmole's *Fasciculus Chemicus*.[8] I only have the *Theatrum Chemicum Britannicum*.

Your proposition that I should write a paper about Ashmole's dreams is tempting. I really shouldn't accept it, because I have to be very careful not to overwork and I have to take care of a great amount of mental work already. But I will consider it, without giving you a formal promise, however, if you don't mind.

Travelling is a somewhat complicated matter for me, unfortunately, and it is not likely that I shall ever go to England again. But if you

---

[4] Mary Anne Atwood, A *Suggestive Inquiry into the Hermetic Mystery* (1850). Cf. "The Psychology of the Transference," CW 16, par. 505.

[5] Cf. Pelet, Jan. 44, n. 1.

[6] "Child Development and Education," CW 17, par. 106.

[7] Cf. Josten, Apr. 52, nn. 7 & 8. In reply to that letter he stated: "Ever since Ashmole started studying astrology (1644) he was obsessed by his own 'Mercurial complexion.' Mercury and the sun in Gemini occupied the first house of his nativity and this may have been the origin of the idea [of his identification]."

[8] London, 1650.

should come to Switzerland I would be most interested to see your material.

Thank you again for all the useful information!

Yours sincerely, c. g. jung

To Fritz Buri

Dear Professor Buri,   5 May 1952

Since you were kind enough to send me your review,[1] I am taking the liberty of going more closely into a few points in it.

As you know, I apply my method not only to my patients but also to all historical and contemporary products of the mind. With regard to Yahweh's "cure" it should be noted that anything that happens in our consciousness has a retroactive effect on the unconscious archetype. Submission to the archetype that appears as an unjust God must bring about a change in this "God." And this, as subsequent history proves, is what actually happened. Yahweh's injustice and amorality were known to the Jews and were a source of disquiet and distress. (Cf. the drastic passages cited in *Aion*, pp. 93ff.)[2] The transformation of the God of the Old Testament into the God of the New is not my invention but was known long ago in the Middle Ages.[3]

I am in truth concerned with the "depths of the human psyche," as I expressly point out. But I cannot make statements about a metaphysical God, nor do I imagine that with the term "God" I have "posited" anything metaphysical. I speak always and exclusively only of the anthropomorphic God-image. The verbal inspiration of the Bible seems to me an implausible and unprovable hypothesis. I do not by any means dispute the existence of a metaphysical God, but I allow myself to put human statements under the microscope. Had I criticized the *chronique scandaleuse* of Olympus this would have caused an uproar 2500 years ago. Today nobody would bat an eyelid.

I do not pretend to know anything tenable or provable about a metaphysical God. I therefore don't quite understand how you can smell "gnostic" arrogance in this attitude. In strictest contrast to Gnosticism *and* theology, I confine myself to the psychology of an-

☐ Basel. Cf. Buri, 10 Dec. 45 (in vol. 1).
[1] Cf. Billeter, 3 May 52, n. 1.
[2] Pars. 106ff.
[3] Cf. *Psychology and Alchemy*, CW 12, pars. 522f.

thropomorphic ideas and have never maintained that I possess the slightest trace of metaphysical knowledge. Just as the physicist regards the atom as a model, I regard archetypal ideas as sketches for the purpose of visualizing the unknown background. One would hardly call a physicist a Gnostic because of his atomic models. Nor should one want to know better than God, who himself *regrets* his actions and thereby plainly says what *he himself* thinks of them.

Anyway I am very grateful to you for having expounded my shocking thought-processes so objectively—a rare experience for me!

Yours sincerely, c. g. j u n g

To Dorothee Hoch

Dear Dr. Hoch,   28 May 1952

The conjecture that I have succumbed to a personal complex does indeed spring to mind when one knows that I am a clergyman's son.[1] However, I had a good personal relationship with my father, so no "father complex" of the ordinary sort. True, I didn't like theology because it set my father problems which *he* couldn't solve and which *I* felt unjustified. On the other hand, I grant you my personal mother complex.

It is always a risky business to attribute unproven personal motives to an opponent before one has sufficiently weighed or understood the nature of his argument.

It does not seem to be quite clear to you that I am dealing with ideas and images. God-images, for instance, can be discussed. I consider it unfortunate that most theologians believe they have named God when they say "God." The rabbi, for instance, hardly means the Christian God, the Protestant definitely the God who was incarnate, the Catholic the God who has revealed the Assumptio B.V.M. to the Church. Under these rather distressing circumstances the empiricist, regardless of his religious convictions, has no choice but to deal with the ideas of God, without deciding the metaphysical issue. He makes

□ Protestant minister, Basel.
[1] H. sent Jung her review of "Answer to Job" in *Kirchenblatt für die reformierte Schweiz* (Basel), 22 May 1952. In an accompanying letter she expressed the opinion that the book might be explained partly "from personal motives of the author," suggesting that Jung, as the son of a clergyman, might "carry with him vengeful sentiments against a 'fatherly God.' "

no decisions based on faith. Ideas of God are first of all *myths*, statements about things that are philosophically and scientifically indeterminable; that is, they are psychological objects which are amenable to discussion. Anyone who holds that God is named and expressed when he says "God" is hypostatizing Yahweh, Allah, Quetzalcoatl, Jupiter, etc. That puts an end to all discussion. All religious objects become taboo. Not only can Christians not agree among themselves but the denominationally uncommitted layman dare not open his mouth because of the danger of blasphemy.

As a psychologist I have to speak of ideas professionally and if necessary criticize them when they behave too objectionably. I don't imagine that by so doing I have affected God; I merely try to put my own ideas in order. I can think about my ideas but not about a metaphysical God who is beyond the range of human understanding. I move exclusively in the domain of psychological empiricism, not in that of denominational metaphysics.

I don't turn Christ into "the animus" (cf. *Aion*, ch. V), but Christ can be brought into relation with the concept of the "self," as the symbolism proves.

The "black son" is definitely not "harmless," as you would infer from my Job book.[2]

Everyone is *reckless* who unleashes a world catastrophe,[3] whatever he may imagine by this.

I know no "most perfect" man but only a relatively complete one.

I have never asserted that God is only an intrapsychic potency. If I say I am a captain in the Swiss Army Medical Corps, as I have a perfect right to do, you will hardly conclude that this is my only qualification.

I share your opinion entirely that man lives wholly when, and only when, he is related to God, to that which steps up to him and determines his destiny.

My documentation is concerned with the historical development of ideas in Western culture. It cannot be disputed that the Book of Enoch and other apocrypha were read in the Near East and were not without influence. The same is true of ancient Egyptian influences as well as of Catholic dogmas. You ought to have noticed that I don't go in for dogmatics but submit the psychology of Western ideas of

[2] She opined that Jung regarded the "black son," Satan, as harmless.
[3] She cited "Answer to Job," par. 734: "The decision of an ill-considered moment . . . can suffice to unleash the world cataclysm."

God to critical discussion. Presumably you won't think I am criticizing the metaphysical God? After all, we are not living in the Middle Ages when people still believed they could do God an injury. The Protestants will, I hope, not fall into the error of thinking they are the only Christians in the world? Every real Christian must recognize that he lives in a schism. One is not just a Protestant or a Catholic but a human being with paganism still ingrained in his very bones. Hence I write of universally Christian ideas and do not touch the—for me—inaccessible question of metaphysical truth. I don't know, either, why you want to prove that an "irruption into myth"[4] has occurred. It doesn't look to me that way at all. The myth goes on, now as before, as the Assumptio proves, which obviously belongs to the Christian world of ideas and not to that of Islam or Buddhism.

If you will conscientiously reread what I have said about individuation you cannot possibly conclude that I mean Nirvana or that I overlook the Resurrection. It would be too cheap to credit me with such stupidity. I understand why you are annoyed. It really is very distressing that the majority of educated people today eschew talk of religious matters. I hold theologians responsible for this up to a point, because they obstinately refuse to admit that they, as much as the rest of us, are talking of anthropomorphic ideas about which we do not know how exactly or inexactly they depict a possible metaphysical fact. In this way they slaughter every discussion from the start, so that one is obliged to avoid, politely, any conversation with theologians, *very much to the detriment of the religious life*! What good is it to anyone when a theologian "confesses" that he has "met the living Lord"? The wretched layman can only turn green with envy that such an experience never happened to him. In my practice I often had to give elementary school lessons in the history of religion in order to eliminate, for a start, the disgust and nausea people felt for religious matters who had dealt all their lives only with confession-mongers and preachers. The man of today wants to *understand and not be preached at*. The need for understanding and discussion is as great as it is unconscious (at least in most cases). That is why my little Job book has the (unexpected) effect of getting people who know the Bible only from hearsay to turn to it with curiosity. It is of burning interest for them to hear something understandable about religion, so much so that often I am hard put to it to draw a distinction between myself and a director of conscience.

---

[4] She spoke of the life of Christ as an "irruption into myth."

For me personally religion is a matter of first-rate importance; that is why I accept all the odium that is heaped upon the critic of tabooed area. And that is also why I disturb the sleep of the just, who won't take the trouble to rouse themselves out of their subjectivism, their preacher role, and their irresponsibility in the face of the demands of the time. It would perhaps be worth the effort to make Christianity comprehensible to educated people today instead of leaving this urgent task to the psychiatrist. To this end I have set forth in my little book what a thoughtful contemporary can read out of the Christian tradition. Let him forget the arrogance of clerics who deem themselves in possession of the sole truth and who contrive to spread the schism of Christendom still further, and reflect on the only question of importance: *What is religion all about?* Only a fraction of white humanity is Christian, and yet Christianity indulges in the luxury of not having any truck with human intelligence.

I don't want to annoy people needlessly, but in this case my conscience compelled me to say out loud what so many think in silence. I hope I have started the ball rolling. "Il faut casser les œufs pour faire une omelette!"

I enclose my reply to M. Buber,[5] who also thinks he can talk of God without saying which, and without proving that this is the only right one. These absurdities have to be cleared up for once.

This all-too-long letter may clarify for you the standpoint of an empiricist who is doing his best to understand the language of theologians.

Yours sincerely, c . g . j u n g

[5] Cf. Neumann, 28 Feb. 52, n. 9.

To Gerd Rosen

Dear Herr Rosen,   16 June 1952

Taken in the spirit of the age, the *Malleus Maleficarum*[1] is not so gruesome. It was an instrument whereby it was supposed that one of

☐ Berlin.
[1] R. asked for information concerning psychoanalytic literature on belief in and persecution of witches. *Malleus Maleficarum* (Hammer of the Witches), written by two Catholic inquisitors, Heinrich Kramer and Jakob Sprenger, and published in 1489 (tr. Montague Summers, 1928), is the classic textbook on the evil deeds of witches and how to combat them.

those great psychic epidemics could be stamped out. For that age it represented a work of enlightenment which was, admittedly, prosecuted with very drastic measures. The psychology of the witch-hunting epidemic has never been worked out properly. There are only rather inept opinions about it. It can only be understood in the total context of the religious problem of the time and in particular in the context of the German psyche under mediaeval conditions. The solution of this problem makes unusual demands on our knowledge of the spiritual undercurrents which preceded the Reformation. Although I have some knowledge of them I would scarcely venture to tackle the problem. For a German it must be quite particularly difficult because it is connected with specifically German psychological assumptions. You can get some idea of them by comparing the women in German literature with those in French and English literature during the past 200 years. The Rhine forms not only a political frontier but also a psychological one.

Yours very truly, C. G. JUNG

To R. J. Zwi Werblowsky

Dear Dr. Werblowsky,   17 June 1952

Many thanks for kindly sending me your critical reflections.[1] For me they are valuable and interesting as the reactions of an (almost) non-participant. From touching lightly on psychology you have already acquired a "golden finger"[2] and must now give forthright answers before the world. This happens even with people who have said "good day" to me only once.

I don't know whether I ought to be glad that my desperate attempts to do justice to the reality of the psyche are accounted "ingenious ambiguity."[3] At least it acknowledges my efforts to reflect, as best I can, the "ingenious ambiguity" of the psyche.

For me the psyche is an almost infinite phenomenon. I absolutely don't know what it is in itself and know only very vaguely what it is *not*. Also, I know only to a limited degree what is individual about

[1] On the controversy between Buber and Jung.
[2] A fairytale motif: a child looks into a forbidden room and is given away by a finger turning golden. Cf. "Our Lady's Child" and "Iron Hans," *Grimm's Fairy Tales* (Pantheon edn., 1944), pp. 23ff. and 612–15.
[3] A remark of Buber's in his reply to Jung. Cf. Neumann, 28 Feb. 52, n. 9.

the psyche and what is universal. It seems to me a sort of all-encompassing system of relationships, in which "material" and "spiritual" are primarily designations for potentialities that transcend consciousness. I can say of nothing that it is "only psychic," for everything in my immediate experience is psychic in the first place. I live in a "perceptual world" but not in a self-subsistent one. The latter is real enough but we have only indirect information about it. This is as true of outer objects as of "inner" ones, of material existents and the archetypal factors we could also call εἴδη.[4] No matter what I speak about, the two worlds interpenetrate in it more or less. This is unavoidable, for our language is a faithful reflection of the psychic phenomenon with its dual aspect "perceptual" and "imaginary." When I say "God" the dual aspect of the *ens absolutum* and the hydrogen atom (or particle + wave) is already implicit in it. I try to speak "neutrally." (Prof. Pauli would say: the "neutral language"[5] between "physical" and "archetypal.")

The language I speak must be ambiguous, must have two meanings, in order to do justice to the dual aspect of our psychic nature. I strive quite consciously and deliberately for ambiguity of expression, because it is superior to unequivocalness and reflects the nature of life. My whole temperament inclines me to be very unequivocal indeed. That is not difficult, but it would be at the cost of truth. I purposely allow all the overtones and undertones to be heard, partly because they are there anyway, and partly because they give a fuller picture of reality. Unequivocalness makes sense only in establishing facts but not in interpreting them; for "meaning" is not a tautology but always includes more in itself than the concrete object of which it is predicated.

I define myself as an empiricist, for after all I have to be something respectable. You yourself admit that I am a poor philosopher, and naturally I don't like being something inferior. As an empiricist I have at least accomplished something. If a man is a good shoemaker and knows he is one, people will not inscribe on his tombstone that he was a bad hatmaker because he once made an unsatisfactory hat.

I am, more specifically, simply a psychiatrist, for my essential problem, to which all my efforts are directed, is psychic disturbance: its phenomenology, aetiology, and teleology. Everything else is secondary for me. I do not feel called upon to found a religion, nor to proclaim my belief in one. I am not engaged in philosophy, but merely in think-

---

[4] = forms, species. Cf. "Synchronicity," CW 8, par. 942.
[5] Ibid., par. 960.

ing within the framework of the special task that is laid upon me: to be a proper psychiatrist, a healer of the soul. This is what I have discovered myself to be, and this is how I function as a member of society. Nothing would seem more nonsensical and fruitless for me than to speculate about things I cannot prove, let alone know. I am quite prepared to grant that others may know more about them than I. I do not know, for example, how God could ever be experienced apart from human experience. If I do not experience him, how can I say that he exists? But my experience is extremely small and narrow, and so, in spite of oppressive intimations of the infinite, what I experience is also small and in the likeness of man—a fact which emerges clearly when one tries to express it. In our experience everything gets tainted with the ambiguity of the psyche. The greatest experience is also the smallest and narrowest, and for that reason one hesitates to boast about it, let alone philosophize about it. One is after all too small and too incompetent to be able to afford any such arrogance. That is why I prefer ambiguous language, since it does equal justice to the subjectivity of the archetypal idea and to the autonomy of the archetype. "God," for example, is on the one hand an inexpressible *ens potentissimum,* and on the other hand an exceedingly inadequate token and expression of human impotence and perplexity—an experience, therefore, of the most paradoxical nature. The realm of the psyche is immeasurably great and filled with living reality. At its brink lies the secret of matter and of spirit. I do not know whether this schema means anything to you or not. For me it is the frame within which I can express my experience. With best regards,

Yours sincerely, C. G. JUNG

To Father Victor White

[ORIGINAL IN ENGLISH]

Dear Victor,   30 June 1952

First of all I should like to know whether the doctrine of *privatio boni* ranks as a dogma or as a *sententia communis.*[1] In the latter case it could be a disputable subject so far as I understand the ways of ecclesiastical thinking. At all events I have started the discussion on this

☐ (Typewritten and signed.)

[1] A theological statement which is generally accepted without being a dogma. Father White, in a letter of 9 July 52, replied that the *privatio boni* was a *sententia communis,* not a formal dogma.

assumption. If on the other hand it should be a defined and declared truth, I will not discuss it any more, but I shall try to understand the deeper reasons for its existence, as I have already tried at least tentatively.

The crux seems to lie in the contamination of the two incongruous notions of Good and of Being. If you assume, as I do, that Good is a moral judgment and not substantial in itself, then Evil is its opposite and just as non-substantial as the first. If however you assume that Good is Being, then Evil can be nothing else than Non-Being.[2] In my empirical thinking the *tertium quid* is always the observer, i.e., the one who makes the statement. Your example of light and darkness[3] is a subjective and relative statement, inasmuch as light is equal to motion and darkness equal to rest, that is, more or less frequency or more or less standstill. Darkness is certainly a decrease of light, as light is a decrease of darkness. Thus it amounts to a play of words to say that only Good *is*, i.e., has substance and Evil not. Standstill is just as real for an observer as movement. You could not even have a notion of movement if there were not standstill to compare it with.

Things are quite simple if you could only admit that Good and Evil are judgments, having nothing to do with the incommensurable concept of Being. It is true that motion is everything, since all things move, but it is equally true that certain things are less moving for a certain observer than other things. From this fact you form the notion of standstill, which in itself, as far as we know, does not occur in our empirical world. Thus you can hold that everything is good, but certain things are less good for a certain observer. But this argument also depends upon an observer and his statement, which is always subjective. What you call *fixed stars*, for instance, may move much faster in reality than our sun, and what you call good may be in other respects a great evil, that is, for another observer. The whole question may be a case like that of the earth, around which the sun revolved for the better part of 1900 years.[4] In recent times only it became an admissible truth that the earth is moving round the sun.

[2] Equivalent to μὴ ὄν.

[3] In his letter of 20 Apr. (cf. White, 30 Apr. 52, nn. 1 & 2) W. had written: "I [cannot] think of a single empirical specimen of real or alleged 'evil' in which the *privatio* definition is not verified—any more than I can think of an empirical darkness that is not a *privatio* of light." That Jung now, after over two months, takes up this question once more shows his besetting preoccupation with the problem of the *privatio boni* about which they had been arguing for 2½ years (White, 31 Dec. 49).

[4] That is, presumably, from the time of Aristarchus of Samos (b. *ca.* 320 B.C.), who first put forward the view that the planets and the earth revolved round the

If the *privatio boni* is merely a doctrine and not a dogma,[5] it can be discussed or is that not so? St. Thomas is not infallible. His views about the Assumptio for instance don't seem to agree with the new dogma.

Whereas Being is obviously a concept of +, Non-Being is one of —. But Evil is as substantial as Good, as the devil and his hell are substantial. If Evil should be a very small Good, it would nevertheless be good, however little, and not at all bad. If I am condemned to hell I am still nothing but good, in spite of the fact that I have lost 99% of goodness because Evil is *not*.

Is it quite impossible for a theologian to admit the obvious fact of Good and Evil being moral judgments and as such relative to an observer? There is not the faintest evidence for the identity of Good and Being. God is certainly Being itself and you call Him the Summum Bonum. Thus all Being is good, and even Evil is a minute Good, even Satan's disobedience is still good to a small degree and nothing else. For that small Good he is in hell. Why should Good be thrown into hell? And at which percentage of goodness are you liable to get condemned? Moreover there is no darkness in God and God is All— where in hell is the absence of light then, where the host of fallen angels, where the "evil-doers" (i.e., those having done a little good) and Satan himself? Why should a little good be against God? It is still with God, even Satan is. Whatever he is doing, it is always a little good and nothing else.

That is how the Christian doctrine gets out of its inherent dualism, i.e., Manicheism, by denying the existence of Evil. You do deny it by calling Evil a decreasing Good. Absolute Evil is for you a merely neutral condition, in which there is nothing at all, a μὴ ὄν, but inasmuch as Satan exists, he is nothing but good, because Being = Good.

It reminds me of St. Maël's baptism of the penguins and St. Catherine's advice: Donnez-leur une âme, mais une petite![6]

---

sun, but which was rejected by his successors and then sank into oblivion, until the rediscovery of the heliocentric system by Copernicus in *De revolutionibus orbium coelestium*, published Nuremberg 1543, the year of his death. The book passed almost unnoticed, and was not even put on the Index until 1616.

[5] Dogmas are statements of the Christian truth finally declared by the authorities of the Church; doctrines are explanations and elaborations of the faith not yet crystallized into dogmas.

[6] In Anatole France's *Penguin Island* (orig. 1908) the heavenly council cannot decide whether the penguins had acquired an immortal soul after being baptized by St. Maël, until St. Catherine of Alexandria (cf. Jacobi, 23 Dec. 32, n. 7) suggests the compromise cited in the letter. (Cf. *Penguin Island*, tr. Evans, 1948, p. 30.)

I'm looking forward to seeing you on the 16th or the 17th VII.[7] I shall be in Bollingen then.

Cordially yours, C. G.

[7] W. spent 17–27 July with Jung at Bollingen. His stay had been preceded by a long answer (July 9) to the present letter, in which he was highly critical of Jung's attitude. Evidently the discussions on the *privatio boni* during the ten days at Bollingen did not lead to any agreement, and the subsequent correspondence shows distinct and growing signs of estrangement. Apart from a few long letters of Jung's in Nov. 1953, Apr. 1954, and 1955, the correspondence almost ceased, and it came to a formal end with White, 6 May 55: "I am the cause of much discomfort to you." Only W.'s illness in early 1960, leading to his death, prompted the two last letters of 25 Mar. and 30 Apr. 60.

To Dorothee Hoch

Dear Dr. Hoch,   3 July 1952

I am very grateful that this time you have met my endeavour with more friendliness and understanding. I certainly admit that personal motives creep in everywhere in an exasperating way, but I still think it is a bit too glib to suspect an objective argument of personal resentment without closer and surer knowledge of the circumstances. Only at the end of a discussion, when all objective elements have run out, may one hazard the question whether personal motives have also had a hand in it. But I won't make any annotations to Knigge's *Umgang mit Menschen*.[1]

You are surprised at my reaction to your avowed faith in a personal meeting with Christ. I thought I ought not to conceal from you that such an avowal has a thoroughly intimidating effect on many people, because they feel (with good reason, I think) that this only happens to one of the elect, who has been singled out from the human community of the unblest, the wayward, the unbelievers, the doubters and the God-forsaken, and, especially if they are religious people, it makes them feel inferior. Many theologians make themselves unpopular on that account and so make the doctor, who is expected to have a better understanding of the ordinary, uninitiated person, appear as a more desirable proposition.

I do, to be sure, maintain that the Bible was written by man and is

[1] By Adolf Freiherr von Knigge (1752–96), an immensely popular book (1788) on etiquette and good manners.

74

therefore "mythological," i.e., anthropomorphic. God is certainly made *vivid* enough in it, but not *visible*. That would be a bit too much for our human inadequacy, even if we could see him in his incarnate form. This is the μορφὴ δούλου after the kenosis[2] had taken place, the well-attested pagan figure of the κάταχος[3] and the Old Testament "servant of God,"[4] or the unsuccessful, suffering hero like Oedipus or Prometheus.

The insistence on the uniqueness of Christianity, which removes it from the human sphere and doesn't even allow it a mythological status conditioned by history, has just as disastrous an effect on the layman as the afore-mentioned "avowal." The gospel becomes unreal; all possible points of contact with human understanding are abolished, and it is made thoroughly implausible and unworthy of belief. It is really and truly sterilized, for all the psychic propensities in us which would willingly accept it are brusquely thrust aside or suppressed and devalued. This short-sightedness is neither rational nor Christian and empties the Protestant churches in the most effective way; but it is very *convenient* because then the clergyman doesn't have to bother about whether the congregation understand the gospel or not but can comfortably go on preaching at them as before. Educated people, for instance, would be much more readily convinced of the meaning of the gospel if it were shown them that the myth was always there to a greater or lesser degree, and moreover is actually present in archetypal form in every individual. Then people would understand where, in spite of its having been artificially screened off by the theologians, the gospel really touches them and what it is talking about. Without this link the Jesus legend remains a mere wonder story, and is understood as little as a fairytale that merely serves to entertain. Uniqueness is synonymous with unintelligibility. How do you make head or tail of a ἅπαξ λεγόμενον?[5] If you are not fascinated at the first go, it tells you absolutely nothing. How can you "meet people in their lives" if you talk of things, and especially of unique events, that have *nothing* to do with the human psyche?

You refer me to your sermon. You talk there of rebirth, for instance, something the man of antiquity was thoroughly familiar with,

---

[2] = "emptying": cf. Phil. 2:7: ". . . Christ Jesus who . . . emptied himself, taking the form of a servant, being made in the likeness of men" (DV). Cf. also *Mysterium*, par. 29 & n. 195.
[3] = prisoner.
[4] Isaiah 42:1–7, 49:1–6, 50:4–9, 52:13, 53:12.
[5] An expression used only once.

but modern man? He has no inkling of the mysteries, which anyway are discredited by Protestant theology, because for it there is only *one* truth, and whatever else God may have done for man is mere bungling. Does modern man know what "water" and "spirit" signify? Water is *below*, heavy and material; wind above and the "spiritual" breath body. The man of antiquity understood this as a clash of opposites, a *complexio oppositorum*, and felt this conflict to be so impossible that he equated matter with evil outright. Christ forces man into the impossible conflict. He took himself with exemplary seriousness and lived his life to the bitter end, regardless of human convention and in opposition to his own lawful tradition, as the worst heretic in the eyes of the Jews and a madman in the eyes of his family. But we? We imitate Christ and hope he will deliver us from our own fate. Like little lambs we follow the shepherd, naturally to good pastures. No talk at all of uniting our Above and Below! On the contrary, Christ and *his* cross deliver us from our conflict, which we simply leave alone. We are Pharisees, faithful to law and tradition, we flee heresy and are mindful only of the *imitatio Christi* but not of our own reality which is laid upon us, the union of opposites in ourselves, preferring to believe that Christ has already achieved this for us. Instead of bearing ourselves, i.e., our own cross, ourselves, we load Christ with our unresolved conflicts. We "place ourselves under *his* cross,"[6] but by golly not under our own. Anyone who does this is a heretic, self-redeemer, "psychoanalyst" and God knows what. The cross of Christ was *borne by himself* and was *his*. To put oneself under somebody else's cross, which has already been carried by him, is certainly easier than to carry your own cross amid the mockery and contempt of the world. That way you remain nicely ensconced in tradition and are praised as devout. This is well-organized Pharisaism and highly un-Christian. Whoever imitates Christ and has the cheek to want to take Christ's cross on himself when he can't even carry his own has in my view not yet learnt the ABC of the Christian message.

Have your congregation understood that they must close their ears to the traditional teachings and go through the darknesses of their own souls and set aside everything in order to become that which every individual bears in himself as his individual task, and that no one can take this burden from him? We continually pray that "this cup may pass from us" and not harm us. Even Christ did so, but without success. Yet we use Christ to secure this success for ourselves. For all these reasons theology wants to know nothing of psychology, be-

[6] These words occur in a sermon of H.'s which she enclosed with her letter.

cause through it we could discover our own cross. But we only want to talk of Christ's cross, and how splendidly his crucifixion has smoothed the way for us and solved our conflicts. We might also discover, among other things, that in every feature Christ's life is a prototype of individuation and hence cannot be imitated: *one can only live one's own life totally in the same way with all the consequences this entails.* This is hard and must therefore be prevented. How this is done is shown among other things by the following example. A devout professor of theology (i.e., a lamb of Christ) once publicly rebuked me for having said "in flagrant contradiction to the word of the Lord" that it is unethical to *"remain"* a child. The "Christian" ought to remain sitting on his father's knee and leave the odious task of individuation to dear little Jesus. Thus naïvely, but with unconscious design, the meaning of the gospel is subverted, and instead of catechizing ourselves on the meaning of Christ's life we prefer, in *ostensible* agreement with the word of the Lord, to remain infantile and not responsible for ourselves. Thus an exemplary διδάσκαλος τοῦ Ἰσραήλ[7] who can't even read the New Testament properly.[8] No one but me protested because it suits everybody's book. This is only one of many examples of the way we are cheated in all godliness. Without anybody noticing it, Protestantism has become a Judaism *redivivus*.

Denominationalism has likewise become a flight from the conflict: people don't want to be Christians any more because otherwise they would be sitting between two stools in the middle of the schism of the Church. Allegiance to a particular creed is—heaven be praised!—unambiguous, and so they can skulk round the schism with a good conscience and fight "manfully" for a one-sided belief, the other fellow— alas—being always in the wrong. The fact that I as a Christian struggle to unite Catholicism and Protestantism within myself is chalked up against me in true Pharisaic fashion as blatant proof of lack of character. That psychology is needed for such an undertaking seems to be a nuisance of the first order. The resistance to and devaluation of the soul as "only psychic" has become a yardstick for Pharisaic hypocrisy. Yet people should be glad that dogmatic ideas have psychological foundations. If they hadn't, they would remain eternally alien to us and finally wither away, which they are already doing very speedily in Protestantism. But that is what people unconsciously want, because then they wouldn't be reminded of their own cross

---

[7] = teacher of Israel.
[8] Matthew 18:3: "Except ye . . . *become* as little children, ye shall not enter into the kingdom of heaven."

and could talk all the more uninhibitedly about Christ's cross, which takes them away from their own reality, willed by God himself. Therefore, by entrenching themselves behind a creed, they calmly perpetuate the hellish scandal that the so-called Christians cannot reach agreement even among themselves.

Even if you thought there is anything to my reflections you could hardly preach a sermon about them to your congregation. This "cross" would presumably be a bit too heavy. But Christ accepted a cross that cost him his life. It is fairly easy to live a praiseworthy truth, but difficult to hold one's own as an individual against a collective and be found unpraiseworthy. Is it clear to your congregation that Christ may possibly mean just this?

These reflections came to me as I read the sermon you have kindly placed at my disposal. I was particularly affected by your thesis of "total surrender." Is it clear to you what that means: *absolute exposure?* A fate without if's and but's, with no assurance that it will turn out harmlessly, for then one would have ventured nothing and risked nothing for God's sake. It was these rather sombre undertones, so true to reality, that I missed in your sermon. With best greetings,

Yours sincerely, C. G. JUNG

To Valerie Reh

Dear Frau Reh,   28 July 1952

Many thanks for your friendly letter and the character diagnosis.[1] It fits very well, even the details. The sensitiveness to noise persists. I always seek silence. I am a bundle of opposites and can only endure myself when I observe myself as an objective phenomenon. My capacity for work has fallen off very much—possibly a sign of fatigue, for in these last years I have worked very hard. I fear new ideas as they demand too much work from me. I now need a lot of rest. With best thanks and kind regards,

Yours sincerely, C. G. JUNG

□ Tel Aviv, Israel.

[1] R. sent Jung her diagnosis of his character, using the method of numerology, based on the principle that each letter of the alphabet has a certain numerical value. Numbers in themselves possess psychological values and meanings, and from their combination, particularly of name and date of birth, the characterological pattern is interpreted.

Anonymous

[ORIGINAL IN ENGLISH]

Dear N.,   28 July 1952

. . .

I still feel too tired to make up my mind for further adventures. For the time being I have to steel my mind against the battering I receive from my *Hiob*, which causes the weirdest misunderstandings. My birthday, though celebrated modestly in the family circle, was rather exhausting on account of too many letters and telegrams. On the whole I am picking up slowly, but my head is still unwilling to do serious work which ought to be done.

Hoping you are not eaten alive by your visitors, I remain,

Your grateful CG

To Father Victor White

[ORIGINAL IN ENGLISH]

Dear Victor!   Bollingen, 7 August 1952

I forgot to tell you that *I Ching* 16 place 1[1] refers to "putting in music" the problem of *priv. boni,* i.e., understanding it as a *feeling* problem. You would get a more complete picture if you contemplate such ideas not only from an intellectual but also from a feeling standpoint. In this case you could feel the "contrapunctum" very clearly. You were followed by a letter which I have re-addressed to Blackfriars.

Greetings!

Yours cordially, C. G.

☐ (Handwritten postcard.)

[1] Evidently W. had consulted the *I Ching* while in Bollingen on the *privatio boni* impasse. The title of Hexagram 16 is "Enthusiasm," and the comment on "The Image" (not place 1) speaks of the "power of music to ease tension" and "to purify the feelings of men." The comment on place 1 says: "Enthusiasm . . . is justified only when it is a general feeling that unites one with others."

To Joseph L. Henderson

[ORIGINAL IN ENGLISH]

Dear Henderson,   9 August 1952

Thank you for your kind letter! I am glad to have had the chance of talking to X.[1] She is better "knitted together" than I expected.

The balance is carefully yet a bit anxiously maintained. There is much insecurity and uncertainty about the volcanic chaos underneath. Consciousness ought to be strengthened, as it needs a strong ego to counterbalance the dormant affects. There is much uncertainty in her whether she will be able to disidentify from the collective unconscious. She is in need of *theoria*,[2] i.e., of symbolic concepts that would enable her to "comprehend" the contents of the unconscious. I would try to get her interested in a *general, theoretical* knowledge of the basic contents of the unconscious and of their significance for individuation. I have noticed some spark in her when the conversation touched upon related subjects. The more she knows and understands, the better are her chances. She should beware of too much activity of an extraverted kind. I have the impression that she is not yet congealed but still "fluid." My best wishes,

Yours cordially, C. G. JUNG

☐ Psychiatrist and analytical psychologist, in San Francisco. Cf. his *The Wisdom of the Serpent* (together with Maud Oakes; 1963); *Thresholds of Initiation* (1967).
[1] A patient in the early stages of a schizophrenic breakdown.
[2] The alchemical concept of *theoria* (counterpart of *practica*) is used here to express the patient's need for an understanding in the form of conceptual images. Cf. "The Psychology of the Transference," CW 16, pars. 471, 488.

To Hans Schär

Dear Dr. Schär,   15 August 1952

Hearty thanks for kindly sending me your review of *Job*.[1] I didn't envy you this difficult task. But you have done it in a very objective way and have also succeeded in introducing one or two things for the fine-eared.

Your idea of my spiritual affinity or at least sympathy with Jakob Burckhardt is amazingly true. Burckhardt's pessimistic forebodings were undoubtedly right. It doesn't pay not to see the dark side.

I am glad that such a carefully balanced review got into a theological journal. It may well be the first to have found its way there.

I hear you are coming to visit me sometime in September. All that month I shall be in Bollingen, where I can receive you at any time if

[1] "C. G. Jung und die Deutung der Geschichte," *Schweizerische Theologische Umschau* (Bern), VII (1952).

you let me know a few days beforehand. Meanwhile with kind regards,

Yours sincerely, C. G. JUNG

To Horst Scharschuch

Dear Herr Scharschuch,   1 September 1952

There can be no doubt that the unconscious comes to the surface in modern art[1] and with its dynamism destroys the orderliness that is characteristic of consciousness. This process is a phenomenon that can be observed in more or less developed form in all epochs, as for instance under primitive conditions where the habitual way of life, regulated by strict laws, is suddenly disrupted, either by outbreaks of panic coupled with wild lawlessness at solar and lunar eclipses, or in the form of religious license as in the Dionysian orgies, or during the Middle Ages in the monasteries with the reversal of the hierarchical order,[2] and today at carnival time. These episodic or regular disruptions of the accustomed order should be regarded as psycho-hygienic measures since they give vent from time to time to the suppressed forces of chaos.

At the present day such things are obviously taking place on the largest scale because the cultural order has suppressed the primitive disorderliness too long and too violently. If one views modern art prospectively, as I think one can, it plainly announces the uprush of the dissolvent forces of disorder. It clears the air by abolishing the constraints of order. I myself am inclined to view what rushes up as the opposite of art, since it very evidently lacks order and form. The uprushing chaos seeks new symbolic ideas which will embrace and express not only the previous order but also the essential contents of the disorder. Such ideas would have a magical effect by holding the destructive forces of disorder spellbound, as has been the case in Christianity and in all other religions. In ancient tradition this magic is called white magic; black magic, on the other hand, exalts the destructive forces into the only valid truth in contrast to the previous order, and moreover compels them to serve the individual in contrast

☐ Heidelberg, Germany.
[1] S. asked for a definition of the terms "magical" and "daemonic," with particular regard to artistic creation.
[2] Cf. "The Psychology of the Trickster Figure," CW 9, i, pars. 458ff.

to the collective. The means used for this purpose are primitive, fascinating, or awe-inspiring ideas and images, unintelligible incantations, outlandish words and shapes, savage rhythms, drumming and suchlike. In so far as modern art uses such means as ends in themselves and thereby increases the state of disorder it can be described outright as black magic.

The daemonic, on the contrary, rests entirely on the unconscious forces of negation and destruction and on the reality of evil. The existence of the daemonic is demonstrated by the fact that black magic is not only possible but uncannily successful, so much so that it is tempting to assume that black magicians are possessed by a daemon. Hitler's magic, for instance, consisted in his always saying what everybody was afraid to say out loud because it was considered too disreputable and inferior (resentment against the Jews). But his daemonism lay in the fact that his methods were uncannily effective and that he himself obviously became the victim of the daemon which had taken total possession of him.

The study of these questions must of course begin with a thorough knowledge of primitive magical practices. I would advise you to read the book by Mircea Eliade, *Le Chamanisme*,[3] also the *Philosophia Occulta* of Agrippa von Nettesheim[4] and some of the writings of Paracelsus, for instance *Liber Azoth*.[5] In Paracelsus especially you will find a lot about sympathetic magic. You will also find the same kind of suggestive neologisms that characterize the latest German philosophy—the incomprehensible words, signs, antics, etc. You may get something out of my little book *Paracelsica* (1942). I should also mention the theory of Albertus Magnus that when anyone gives free rein to violent emotion and in this state wishes evil, it will have a magical effect.[6] This is the quintessence of

---

[3] *Shamanism. Archaic Techniques of Ecstasy* (tr., 1964; orig. 1951).

[4] Heinrich Cornelius Agrippa von Nettesheim (1486–1535), German physician and mystic philosopher. *De occulta philosophia* was written about 1510, but on account of Agrippa's conflict with the Inquisition was published only in 1531 in Antwerp. It is a defence of magic. He is frequently cited in "Paracelsus as a Spiritual Phenomenon," CW 13, see index; see also "The Psychology of the Transference," CW 16, par. 414 & n. 7.

[5] Cited in "Paracelsus," pars. 161, 174, 180, 201, and in "Paracelsus the Physician," CW 15, par. 25.

[6] Albertus Magnus of Cologne (*ca.* 1193–1280), German Dominican theologian and scholastic philosopher; called "Doctor Universalis" on account of his eminence; teacher of Thomas Aquinas. Magical effect: cf. "Synchronicity," CW 8, pars. 859f.

82

primitive magic and of the corresponding mass phenomena like Naziism, Communism, etc. Ernst Robert Curtius[7] once described James Joyce's classic *Ulysses* as "infernal"[8]—quite rightly. I fear this description can also be applied to long stretches of modern art in all its forms.

Yours sincerely, C. G. JUNG

[7] Ernst Robert Curtius (1886–1956), German Romanist, professor in Marburg, Heidelberg, and Bonn.
[8] In his *James Joyce und sein Ulysses* (1929; tr. in *Critical Essays on European Literature*, Princeton, 1973) he called it "a work of Antichrist." Cf. *Mysterium*, par. 454.

To Don L. Stacy

[ORIGINAL IN ENGLISH]

Dear Mr. Stacy,   1 September 1952

If granite[1] were at hand I would use it, but in the place where I live we have a hard, bluish-green sandstone which for my purpose is just solid enough.

I'm no artist. I only try to get things into stone of which I think it is important that they appear in hard matter and stay on for a reasonably long time. Or I try to give form to something that seems to be in the stone and makes me restless. It is nothing for show, it's only to make these troublesome things steady and durable. There is not much of form in it, chiefly inscriptions and you would learn nothing from it.

Sincerely yours, C. G. JUNG

□ An artist, of New York City.
[1] S. asked for information about Jung's Bollingen sculptures. Cf. *Memories*, pp. 226ff./214ff., and Pl. VI/facing p. 305.

To Dorothee Hoch

Dear Dr. Hoch,   23 September 1952

You are quite right: in my last letter I said very much more than was warranted by your sermon. The theologians pick on me so much and misunderstand me so dismally that it would be unnatural if I didn't let off steam occasionally. But it was not meant personally.

If I stress the historical evolution of Christianity this does not mean that I overlook the news it brings. I only want to smooth the transition so that the meaning of the message can be understood. People are so different! Recently an elderly Swiss clergyman wrote me a touching letter emphasizing that through my writings I had *at last opened the way to the Bible for him*. I certainly never expected anything like that. But you can see from this that the figurative language of the Bible is not understood even by a clergyman. No doubt the archetypes are present everywhere, but there is also a *widespread resistance* to this "mythology." That is why even the gospel has to be "demythologized."

To be sure we are dealing with the meaning and content of mythologems. To be sure "Christ" gave the myth a new meaning for the *man of antiquity*. But when we still go on stressing the newness 2000 years later, we must point out what exactly is the *news for us*, which we *haven't yet heard and understood*. Then we could feel like primitive Christians again. But we hear only the same old words and, like Bultmann, get sick of mythology. *How far is the message new for us?* How far is Christ still unknown to us? We heard ages ago that he exists as a living person exempt from our arbitrariness, and all the rest of it. What we need is a new point of departure, and this cannot be found without the assignment of new meaning. The message is alive only if it creates new meaning. I don't believe at all that it has run dry, rather that theology has. Just how do you make it clear to your listeners that "the death and resurrection of Christ are *their* death and *their* resurrection"? Aren't you equating Christ with the self of man, and isn't this a view which is contested when *I* say it? If the death and resurrection of Christ are my death and resurrection, i.e., if a = b, then b = a. That Christ is the self of man is implicit in the gospel, but the conclusion Christ = self has never been explicitly drawn. This is an assignment of new meaning, a further stage in the incarnation or actualization of Christ. You are drawing near to this insight with rapid steps; indeed, you have already voiced it. And with it Christ becomes a formulable psychological experience: the self is a living person and has always been there. It is an insight upon which Hindu philosophy (the equivalent of Western theology), Buddhism, Taoism, mystical Islamic sects, and Christianity are all agreed. My psychology is a modest contribution to this illustrious assemblage, and from the Christian standpoint you have formulated the essential psychological principle in the words quoted above. Thanks to this insight and inner experience the figure of Christ has come alive for you, and means for you an ultimate and unshakable truth, because it issues from a universally disseminated, collective archetype, which is ἀχειροποίητος.[1] Every Christian should rejoice, but I fear the theologians will make a sour face. I, however, rejoice that the unconscious has put into your mouth the true meaning: θαρρεῖτε μύσται τοῦ θεοῦ σεσοσμένου.[2] As you may know, I have written in detail about this in *Aion* and *Answer to Job* and other works.

It goes without saying that I am not of the opinion that insights which only the individual can have should be *preached*. I realize that the sermon is a pressing affair for the clergyman, something he has to cope with somehow. But his psyche is perhaps an even more pressing task, and it is of this I speak. In this respect there is a general *flight outwards*, a wrinkling of the nose at "psychology," a terrifying ignorance of it, and the *cura animarum* has reached its nadir. Instead, one goes in for missions to the heathen. The first emissaries went into the great centres of civilization, but not to the sources of the Nile. That came in only with monasticism, which sprang from a disgust with the civilized world from which one had dropped out. A good example is Albert Schweitzer,[3] who is urgently needed in Europe but prefers to be a touching saviour of savages and to hang his theology on the wall. We have a justification for missionizing only when we have straightened ourselves out here, otherwise we are merely spreading our own disease. How is it with God's Kingdom in Europe? Not even savages are stupid enough not to see our lies. Shamelessly and childishly we parade our irreconcilable schisms before the wondering eyes of our black "brethren" and preach peaceableness, brotherliness, neighbourly love, etc. etc. through the mouths of Evangelists, Lutherans, High Church, Nonconformists, Baptists, Methodists, Catholics, all of whom are resolved to the death *not* to communicate with their brother. Is this fulfilling God's will?

These thoughts come to me unbidden when you speak of total commitment, for instance to missionary work. Of course people can be committed to everything and anything—even to Naziism, as we have seen. But whether the goal presupposed by us to be "right" also corresponds to God's will is another matter. About this only a very

---

[1] = made without hands (Mark 14:58).

[2] "Be of good cheer, mystes of the saved god." Julius Firmicus Maternus, *De errore profanorum religionum* (c. A.D. 346), 23.

[3] (1875–1965), French Protestant clergyman, music scholar, missionary physician. He directed a medical mission in Lambaréné, Gabon, west Africa.

85

small, still voice within us gives us any information. And not infrequently it contradicts our collective ideals (*vide* the way it called certain of the prophets!).[4]

One of the greatest obstacles to our psychic development, it seems to me, is the drowning out of the inner voice in the interests of some collective, conventional ideal which makes us insensitive to the damage done to our own house and gives us the right to impart good advice to our neighbours. If we go along with a so-called good cause, we can easily give ourselves the treat of not having to do something to improve our—oh so small and insignificant!—psyches. But that the right means in the hands of the wrong man then work mischief is something nobody thinks about. Don't you think we would have more cause to worry about the state of Christianity in Europe than about the hygienic precautions in and around Lambaréné? The first is naturally highly unpopular, but the second is exemplary idealism which guarantees a first-class good conscience and nowhere tarnishes the lordly feelings of the white man.

Please don't take my remarks personally but for what they are— footnotes to the religious question of the present.

Yours sincerely, C. G. JUNG

P.S.[5] I really owe you an explanation why it is that I bombard you with such long and repellent letters. I have, you see, to listen to so much idiotic and negative stuff about Christianity on the one hand, and am so grotesquely misunderstood by the theologians on the other, that I do my utmost to bring my criticism to bear only when I can count on goodwill, i.e., on a truly Christian attitude which may have not a little to do with neighbourly love. Besides that, your last letter has also moved me to show you how closely your religious views touch my own.

[4] For instance, the Lord commanded Hosea to marry a whore. Cf. Hosea, ch. 1.
[5] Handwritten.

To L. Stehli

Dear Frau Stehli,   31 October 1952

Were I not old and ill I would take the trouble to explain to you personally why human ideas of God are not necessarily right. God is

☐ Zurich.

something unknowable. An old German mystic has said: "God is a sigh in our souls." Paul, as you know, said something similar.[1] My personal religious convictions are not shaken in the slightest by the fearful contradictions in the Biblical texts. I just wanted to tell you this to set your mind at rest.

With kind regards, C. G. JUNG

---

[1] Conceivably Romans 8:26: ". . . the spirit himself intercedes for us with sighs too deep for words" (RSV).

To Upton Sinclair

[ORIGINAL IN ENGLISH]

Dear Mr. Sinclair,   3 November 1952

I have read your book A *Personal Jesus*[1] carefully and with great interest. It is certainly of great merit and will help your public to appreciate a religious figure from a new angle. I was curious to see in which way you would tackle such a difficult task as the reconstruction of a Jesus biography. Being the son of a parson, and having grown up in an atmosphere steeped in theology, I learnt about a number of attempts such as those of Strauss,[2] Renan,[3] Moore,[4] etc., and in later years I was an ardent reader of A. Schweitzer's work.[5] I have repeatedly, i.e., at different phases of my life, tried to realize what kind of personality—explaining the *whole effect* of its existence—could be reconstructed from the scanty historical evidence offered by the New Testament. Having had a good deal of psychological ex-

---

☐ (1878–1968), American writer. — This letter, with minor changes (some incorporated here), was published in *The New Republic* (Washington), vol. 128, no. 17, issue 2004, 27 Apr. 1953.

[1] New York, 1952.

[2] David Friedrich Strauss (1808–74), German theologian and philosopher. His *Das Leben Jesu, kritisch bearbeitet*, 1835–36 (tr. George Eliot, *The Life of Jesus*, 1846), produced a sensation by interpreting most of the history of Jesus as mythological and attempting to establish a life of Jesus free from all supernatural elements.

[3] Ernest Renan (1823–92), French philosopher. In his *Vie de Jésus* (1863), the first volume of his *Histoire des origines du Christianisme* (1863–81), he tried to combine positivistic science and Christianity and to explain the life of Jesus in purely human terms. (Tr. *Life of Jesus*, Everyman's Library, no. 805, 1927.)

[4] Presumably George Foot Moore (1851–1931), American Biblical scholar, author of a *History of Religions* (1913–19).

[5] *The Quest of the Historical Jesus* (1906; tr. 1910), in which he expounds the eschatological, messianic view of the life of Jesus.

perience, I should have been sufficiently equipped for such a task, but in the end I came to the conclusion that, owing on the one hand to the paucity of historical data, and on the other to the abundance of mythological admixtures, I was unable to reconstruct a personal character free from rather fatal contradictions.

You have certainly succeeded in presenting an acceptable picture of a certain Jesus. I should venture to say that it is even a likely portrait of such a presumably unique character. It may even be convincing to a modern American mind, but seen from the standpoint of a European scientist, your *modus procedendi* seems to be a bit too selective; that is, you exclude too many authentic statements for no other reason than that they do not fit in with your premises, for instance, predestination and esoterism, which cannot be excluded for textual reasons. They cannot be dismissed as mere interpolations. There is also incontestable textual evidence for the fact that Jesus foresaw his tragic end. Moreover, you exclude practically the whole overwhelming amount of eschatology, the authenticity of which is undeniable whether it offends our reason or not.

Then you paint a portrait; though of the highest literary quality, it is subject to the same critique you apply to John the Evangelist (p. 155 seq.): "We are going to learn what this Hellenized intellectual thinks about Jesus." We learn from your book what a modern American writer "thinks about Jesus." This is not meant to be derogatory; on the contrary, it merely shows my perplexity. Surely we can draw a portrait of Jesus that does not offend our rationalism, but it is done at the expense of our *loyalty* to the textual authority. As a matter of fact, *we can omit nothing* from the authentic text. We cannot create a true picture of Hermetic philosophy in the IVth century if we dismiss half of the *libelli* contained in the *Corpus Hermeticum*. The New Testament as it stands is the "Corpus Christianum," which is to be accepted as a whole or not at all. We can dismiss nothing that stands up to a reasonable philological critique. We cannot suppress any single contradiction because we have no anterior or better or more reliable evidence. We have to take the whole and make the best of it.

The "Corpus Christianum" tells the story of a God-Man and of the various ways in which His life and teaching were understood. If Jesus was, as you portray Him, a rationally understandable teacher of fine morals and a devout believer in a good Father-God, why should the Gospels be stuffed with miracle stories and He Himself saddled with esoteric and eschatological statements, showing Him in the role of a Son-God and cosmological saviour?

If Jesus had indeed been nothing but a great teacher hopelessly mistaken in His messianic expectations,[6] we should be at a complete loss in understanding His historical effect, which is so clearly visible in the New Testament. If, on the other hand, we cannot understand by rational means what a God-Man is, then we don't know what the New Testament is all about. But it would be just our task to understand what they meant by a "God-Man."

You give an excellent picture of a possible religious teacher, but you give us no understanding of what the New Testament tries to tell, namely the life, fate, and effect of a God-Man, whom we are asked to believe to be a divine revelation.

These are the reasons why I should propose to deal with the Christian *Urphänomen* in a somewhat different way. I think we ought to admit that we don't understand the riddle of the New Testament. With our present means we cannot unravel a rational story from it unless we interfere with the texts. If we take this risk we can read various stories into the texts and we can even give them a certain amount of probability:

1. Jesus is an idealistic, religious teacher of great wisdom, who knows that His teaching would make the necessary impression only if He were willing to sacrifice His life for it. Thus He forces the issue in complete foreknowledge of the facts which He intends to happen.

2. Jesus is a highly strung, forceful personality, forever at variance with His surroundings, and possessed of a terrific will to power. Yet being of superior intelligence, He perceives that it would not do to assert it on the worldly plane of political sedition as so many similar zealots in His days had done. He rather prefers the role of the old prophet and reformer of His people, and He institutes a spiritual kingdom instead of an unsuccessful political rebellion. For this purpose He adopts not only the messianic Old Testament expectations, but also the then popular "Son of Man" figure in the Book of Enoch. But meddling with the political whirlpool in Jerusalem, He gets Himself caught in its intrigues and meets a tragic end with a full recognition of His failure.

3. Jesus is an incarnation of the Father-God. As a God-Man He walks the earth drawing to Himself the ἐκλεκτοί[7] of His Father, announcing the message of universal salvation and being mostly misunderstood. As the crowning of His short career, He performs the

---

[6] Cf. Matthew 16:27f.

[7] = chosen (Matthew 22:14).

supreme sacrifice in offering Himself up as the perfect host, and thus redeems mankind from eternal perdition.

You can make out a pretty good case from the texts for each of these three highly different variants, with the necessary omissions and violations of scriptural authority. The first and second variants are "rational," i.e., they happen to be within the frame of our contemporary understanding, while the third is definitely outside it; although up to about 200 years ago nobody thought so.

If we avoid violations of the authentic texts, we have to take into consideration the three possibilities, and perhaps some more, and then we must try to find out which theory would fit the complete picture. Since the Gospels do not give, and do not even intend to give, a biography of the Lord, the mere reconstruction of a life of Jesus could never explain the picture given by the texts. The little we know of His biography must needs be supplemented by a very careful study of the peculiar mental and spiritual atmosphere of the time and place of the gospel writers. People at that time were highly Hellenized. Jesus Himself was under the influence of eschatological literature, as υἱὸς ἀνθρώπου[8] bears out. (Cf. also the synagogue of the Dura Europos,[9] which throws a new light on Jewish syncretism.)

What we call "Jesus Christ" is—I am afraid—much less a biographical problem than a social, i.e., collective, phenomenon, created by the coincidence of an ill-defined yet remarkable personality with a highly peculiar *Zeitgeist* that has its own no less remarkable psychology.

I must, dear Sir, apologize for the length of my letter. Having myself given a great deal of thought to the problem of Jesus, and having also done some spadework in this field, I felt I had to give you an account of how and where I slipped up in trying to cope with the challenge of the Christian enigma.

Sure enough, we must believe in Reason. But it should not prevent us from recognizing a mystery when we meet one. It seems to

---

[8] = Son of Man.

[9] Dura Europos, ancient city on the Euphrates, founded under Seleukos I (312–280 B.C.), rediscovered 1921, excavated 1928–37. Among the extremely valuable objects discovered is a synagogue dating back to the 3rd cent. A.D. It contains frescoes with scenes from the OT, thus infringing the orthodox Jewish law against the making of images and showing the influence of the local Oriental civilization. For details cf. E. R. Goodenough, *Jewish Symbols in the Greco-Roman Period* (13 vols., 1953–68), vols. 9–11.

me that no rational biography could explain one of the most "irrational" effects ever observed in the history of man. I believe that this problem can only be approached through his history and comparative psychology of symbols. Attempts in this direction have already yielded some interesting results. (Unfortunately there are no English publications yet to which I could refer.)

I am deeply obliged to you for your kind attention and I remain,

Yours sincerely, C. G. JUNG

To Friedrich Bach

Dear Herr Bach,   5 November 1952

I am most impressed by your suggestion.[1] That would be the answer a doctor would have to give in order to validate what the doctor has known from time immemorial—or thought he knew. Though I haven't *said* it, I have at least *done* it so far as my powers allowed me. But it takes more than one lifetime to hold out against the scientific influence in medicine. Your vision is amazingly right, and I marvel.

Yours sincerely, C. G. JUNG

☐ Schorndorf, Württemberg.
[1] That Jung should write on the spiritual aspect of illness and on the encounter it brings with the Transcendental.

To James Kirsch

[ORIGINAL IN ENGLISH]

Dear Kirsch,   18 November 1952

I am sending you an English letter this time as I am still unable to write longhand letters myself. I had another attack of arrhythmia and tachycardia due to overwork. I am now slowly recovering and my pulse is normal again for almost a week, but I am still tired and have to go slowly.

Your question[1] is a very important one and I think I can under-

☐ See Kirsch, 26 May 34 (in vol. 1). — Published in *Psychological Perspectives* (Los Angeles), III:1 (spring 1972).
[1] Regarding the role which Christ and the Christian mystery play in the Jewish psyche.

stand its full import. I would not be able to give you a satisfactory answer, yet having studied the question as far as is possible, I can call your attention to the extraordinary development in the Kabbalah. I am rather certain that the *sefiroth* tree[2] contains the whole symbolism of Jewish development parallel to the Christian idea. The characteristic difference is that God's incarnation is understood to be a historical fact in the Christian belief, while in the Jewish Gnosis it is an entirely pleromatic process symbolized by the concentration of the supreme triad of Kether, Hokhmah, and Binah in the figure of Tifereth.[3] Being the equivalent of the Son and the Holy Ghost, he is the *sponsus* bringing about the great solution through his union with Malkhuth. This union is equivalent to the *assumptio beatae virginis*, but definitely more comprehensive than the latter as it seems to include even the extraneous world of the Kelipoth.[4] X. is certainly all wet when he thinks that the Jewish Gnosis contains nothing of the Christian mystery. It contains practically the whole of it, but in its unrevealed pleromatic state.

There is a very interesting little Latin mediaeval book written either by Knorr von Rosenroth or at least under his direct influence. It is called *Adumbratio Kabbalae Christianae, Id est Syncatabasis Hebraizans, Sive Brevis Applicatio Doctrinae Hebraeorum Cabbalisticae Ad Dogmata Novi Foederis*. Francofurti, 1684. This little book is highly worth while; it contains a very useful parallel to the Christian and the Kabbalistic mystery and might give you much help as it has helped me in understanding this all-important problem of the Jewish religious development. It would be highly commendable to translate the book. I am pretty certain that the extraordinary and venomous response of the orthodox rabbis against the Kabbalah is based upon the undeniable fact of this most remarkable Judeo-Christian parallelism. This is hot stuff, and since the 17th century, as far as my knowledge goes, nobody has dared

---

[2] Cf. Fischer, 21 Dec. 44, n. 5. The ten *sefiroth* are usually arranged in the shape of a tree.

[3] Cf. ibid., also Neumann, 5 Jan. 52, n. 7. Hokhmah ("wisdom" of God) is the second *sefirah*; Binah ("intelligence" of God) the third. Malkhuth ("kingdom" of God) is the tenth, the mystical archetype of Israel's community, the Shekhinah. Cf. G. Scholem, *Major Trends in Jewish Mysticism* (1941), p. 209.

[4] The *kelipoth*, "shards" or "shells," are the daemonic forces of evil. According to the Kabbalist Isaac Luria (1534–72), they originated in the "breaking of the vessels" of the *sefiroth* which could not contain the power of God. The world of the *kelipoth* is the counterpole to the world of the *sefiroth*. Cf. "Answer to Job," CW 11, par. 595, n. 8, and Jaffé, *The Myth of Meaning*, pp. 122ff.

to touch it, but we are interested in the soul of man and therefore we are not blindfolded by foolish confessional prejudices.

. . .

Sincerely yours, C. G. JUNG

To Barbara Robb

[ORIGINAL IN ENGLISH]

Dear Mrs. Robb,   19 November 1952

Thank you very much for your kind letter which has given me some valuable information. My discussion of the *privatio boni* with Victor[1] was a very unsatisfactory experience. I am glad, therefore, to have some further news about this problem, this time apparently more positive, if I may assume that the flaw demonstrated in the doctrine of the *privatio boni* has become visible to Victor too. Your dream about the word "Evil"[2] is extraordinarily illuminating and, in a way, most unusual. It contains in a nutshell practically everything you can say about the problem of evil. It is certainly worth remembering. The second dream[3] contains an equally excellent demonstration of the dynamic structure of the moral opposites in general.

Unfortunately, my illness has nothing to do with the weather, or only indirectly, inasmuch as the brilliant summer seduced me into an activity surpassing my actual strength. I am just about to recover, but slowly, from my prostration.

Thank you again for your kind information, I remain,

Yours cordially, C. G. JUNG

☐ English psychotherapist; cf. her *Sans Everything: A Case to Answer* (1957).

[1] Cf. White, 30 June 52, n. 7.

[2] In the dream R. is playing anagrams with Jung who passes her the word "evil." She changes it into "live" which seems to please Jung. On waking, two alternatives occur to her: "veil" and "vile," the former showing blindness to the horrors of evil, the latter symbolizing the inability to appreciate "the good of evil."

[3] "A vision of a small lump of hair-like substance representing the psychic energy that I use for doing good or evil. When it spun round and round in a clockwise direction, it meant that I was doing good; when it spun in an anti-clockwise direction, I was doing evil. In changing from good to evil, and vice versa, there was an instant when it was absolutely still, and this neutral condition might be called the *privatio boni*, or, equally well, the *privatio mali*."

To Upton Sinclair

[ORIGINAL IN ENGLISH]

Dear Mr. Sinclair,   24 November 1952

Thank you ever so much for the kind reception you gave to my letter and to my apparent criticism.[1] I do not feel quite happy about my way of using the English language, since I seem to cause many misunderstandings. I want, therefore, to make it quite clear that I fully appreciate not only your masterful portrait of a personal Jesus, but also the laudable tendency of your work to show an apathetic world the possibility of a personal approach to a highly debatable religious figure. My letter has obviously given you cause to analyse the mental condition of its perpetrator.[2] Since it is a rule of thumb never to analyse any given subject without the pertinent association material (if there is any!), I want to support your analytic attempt by giving you some more necessary information: *I have a certain picture of a personal Jesus.* It has been dimly suggested to me through certain New Testament data. Yet the strongest impression came to me from the Linceul de Turin, the Saint Suaire.[3] Its stern and august countenance has confirmed my formerly vague expectations. I am, as a matter of fact, so profoundly impressed by the superiority of this extraordinary personality that I would not dare to reconstruct its psychology. I am not at all sure that my mental capacity would be up to such a task. That is why I must personally refrain from a biographical attempt.

You are quite right in contending that the world is entitled to demand something more positive from me than mere criticism. As

---

[1] In his appreciative answer to Jung's letter of 3 Nov., S. questioned the statement "your *modus procedendi* seems to me to be a bit too selective" (par. 2) and said: "It is my thesis that we have no other possible method of procedure because the texts are so undependable. . . . This makes it necessary for every person to do his own selecting. . . . The very title of the book indicates that A *Personal Jesus* means *my* Jesus. I offer you mine, and I invite you in return to give me yours."

[2] S. had written: "I am going to be very presumptuous and psychoanalyze one of the world's greatest psychoanalysts. I suspect that your willingness to write such a long letter is a confession of guilt because you yourself have not written the book on this subject. As a cure I prescribe that you should write it. . . ."

[3] In Catholic tradition, the image of Christ's face and body was sweated out and imprinted on the shroud (Linceul) in which the body was wrapped by Joseph of Arimathea. The Linceul ("Sudario" or "Suaire") is preserved in the cathedral of St. John the Baptist in Turin. Jung kept a copy of the face in his study, behind a curtain. (See illustration.)

The face of Christ on the Holy Shroud, or Linceul, in Turin: see Sinclair,
24 Nov. 52

a matter of fact (since 1948) I have published everything sustainable which I have thought about the *documentary phenomenon of Christ* and its psychological reconstruction. There are three essays:[4]

1. *Symbolik des Geistes*, 1948, p. 323–446: "Versuch einer psychologischen Deutung des Trinitätsdogmas."

2. *Aion*, 1951, p. 15–379: "Beiträge zur Symbolik der Selbst."

3. *Antwort auf Hiob*, 1952.

People mostly don't understand my empirical standpoint: I am dealing with psychic phenomena and I am not at all concerned with the naïve and, as a rule, unanswerable question whether a thing is historically, i.e., concretely, true or not. It is enough that it has been said and believed. Probably most history is made from opinions, the motives of which are factually quite questionable; that is, the psyche is a factor in history as powerful as it is unknown. In dealing with Christ, my *point de départ* is the Corpus Christianum in the first place. It consists of the canonical writings *exclusively*. From this source we learn not only of a personal and rational Jesus, but also and even foremost of an eschatological Christ. I use (as others) the term "eschatology" in the wider sense (i.e., not only with reference to the *parousia*),[5] viz. oneness with God, sonship, messianic mission, identity with the Anthropos ("Son of Man"), the glorified resurrected Christ, the κύριος τῶν ἀγγέλων καὶ τῶν δαιμόνιων[6] and the *iudex vivorum et mortuorum*,[7] not forgetting the pre-existent λόγος.

This irrational aspect is inseparable from the evangelical picture of Christ.

In the second place, in dealing with Christ's historical effects, I have to take into account not only the dogmata of the Church but the Gnostics, and the later heretics also, right down to late mediaeval alchemy.

No wonder people don't understand what it's all about. The trouble is they are still stuck with the silly question as to whether a metaphysical assertion is true or not, or whether a mythologem refers to a historical fact or not. They don't see, and they don't want to see, what the psyche can do. But there—alas—is the key.

---

[4] Respectively, "A Psychological Approach to the Dogma of the Trinity," CW 11; *Aion*, CW 9, ii; "Answer to Job," CW 11.

[5] = The Second Coming of Christ (cf. I Cor. 15:23).

[6] = Lord of angels and daemons.

[7] = Judge of the quick and the dead.

Thank you for letting me see Professor Einstein's highly complimentary letter.[8] I am duly impressed and feel quite low.

Yours very truly, c. g. jung

P.S. I would have gladly sent you a copy of my books but they are not translated.

[8] The letter expressed Einstein's appreciation of Sinclair's book.

To Nöel Pierre

Dear M. Pierre,   3 December 1952

Thank you for your book. I have succeeded in reading it from the first page to the last; a thing which does not happen often with me—or rather almost never—where modern poetry is concerned, or modern art in general. I am sick of those things, but I was able to read your poems, and even to read them more than once. Your verses have something alive and real in them, an adventure lived, a spark of celestial and infernal fire. This is not a pile of infantile débris produced by a life without vision or quest. For the first time I have been able to rejoice over a modern poem. I congratulate you on this totally unexpected success so far as I am concerned. Happily your poetry has something to say, and—praise God—it says it. It speaks the eternal language, the language of symbols which never cease to be true, and which are understood *semper, ubique, ab omnibus*. With thanks,

Yours very sincerely, c. g. jung

☐ (Translated from French.) Nöel Pierre, pseudonym of Comte Pierre Crapon de Caprona, had sent Jung a copy of his book of poems *Soleil noir* (1952). (Cf. Schmied, 5 Nov. 42, n. 1.) According to a communication by P., "of the 50 odd people on the press list," Jung was "the only one to acknowledge" the gift. Jung quotes some of P.'s verses in "The Philosophical Tree," CW 13, par. 348.

To O. Schrenk

Dear Professor Schrenk,   8 December 1952

I greatly enjoyed your interesting letter.[1] Naturally your "reaction" made a special impression on me. It was quite in keeping with the deeper meaning of the dream that you should write to me about it.

The "teacher" shows you the secret of his "daughter." Perhaps I may draw your attention to a small but, in its consequences, serious technical mistake in your interpretation of the dream. (It plays a greater role in the dream that follows.) The dream's extremely negative criticism of your "product"[2] may be connected with this.

The conscious starting-point of the dream is the reading of my book, or rather its affective impact which evokes the image of your one-time teacher. The dream leads away from me to Prof. Gaub, who is entirely *your* memory. Gaub didn't write *Job*, also he has no daughter, but he is an *ideal* teacher. Contrary to all expectations, the dream has concealed me and replaced me by Gaub.

Why does the dream make such an arrangement? Why does it say "eagle"[3] instead of Schrenk or Jung? The dream quite obviously means Gaub and eagle. It is only *we* who think it must actually mean Schrenk or Jung. In this respect your colleague has already corrected you, only to make the same mistake himself of wanting to know better than the dream. It is as if a doctor found sugar in a patient's urine and told him, "The sugar really means albumen," and then treated the patient for nephritis on the basis of a mere opinion. Freud himself made this fundamental mistake. It is the simplest way of killing the dream's meaning.

Of course we look round for figures in our world of experience to explain dreams. But the first thing to be established is that a dream is a natural phenomenon which we cannot interpret with a flick of the wrist, otherwise we are doing alchemy instead of chemistry. Since the second dream obviously means eagle, and neither you nor I are eagles circling round concentration camps, this interpretation is purely arbitrary. But what, then, is the eagle?

☐ Paris.

[1] S. wrote to Jung—whom he had never met—after reading "Answer to Job." He reported two dreams of his own and one of a colleague of his, all of them occasioned by reading the book. In the first two pars. of his letter Jung refers to S.'s second dream, in which a revered teacher says: "Today I shall show you my daughter sunbathing"; the dreamer has an intuition of a screen hiding the naked body of a woman.

[2] In the dream he urinates. The urine is highly unaesthetic.

[3] The eagle appears in the colleague's dream, which is quoted and interpreted in "The Philosophical Tree," CW 13, pars. 466ff. The dreamer—a young French Jew who had been in a concentration camp—is back in the camp and sees a mighty eagle circling overhead. When he told S. the dream, S. wondered if he himself might be meant by the eagle, but the colleague associated the eagle with Jung.

The eagle is here meant as a *threatening* factor which has to be "shot down." It is *all-seeing*, spying out its prey from above with a telescopic eye which nothing escapes. Understandably enough, this invigilation is particularly disagreeable to the rationalistic and atheistic Jew[4] as it reminds him of the *eyes of Yahweh*, which "run to and fro through the whole earth" (mentioned in my *Job!*)[5] and from which nothing remains hidden. The eagle "seizes" and "snatches up" (Ganymede[6] and the eagle of Zeus). Your colleague is reminded that he is still stuck in an *intellectualistic* concentration camp and feels the *liberator* as an enemy. Here we are dealing with an archetype and not with the writer Jung. The same is true of the teacher and even more so of the daughter. Here the figure of *Sophia* insinuates herself, divided into the "Wise Old Man" and his daughter, who stands for the virgin *soul*. The two dreams do not point back to the daytime impressions, but forwards into the world of living archetypal figures, which apparently or in fact we have long forgotten but which are always there if only we would think scientifically and not be satisfied with mere opinions.

Please don't take these remarks as schoolmasterish criticism; I only thought they might help you to understand my apparently very difficult and so often misunderstood psychology. With best thanks for your stimulating letter,

Yours sincerely, C. G. JUNG

[4] S. described his colleague as a follower of Sartre and an atheist.
[5] Cf. "Answer to Job," CW 11, par. 575, quoting those words from Zechariah 4:10.
[6] On account of his beauty, Ganymede was snatched up by Zeus in the shape of an eagle and made his cupbearer.

To Paul Campbell

[ORIGINAL IN ENGLISH]

Dear Mr. Campbell,   19 December 1952

Thank you very much for your kind letter and the programme of your Conference.[1] I fully realize that Catholic analysts are faced with very particular problems which, on the one hand, are an aggravation of the work which is difficult in itself already, yet on the other hand,

☐ Catholic analytical psychologist, of Glasgow.
[1] C. sent the programme of a Catholic Jungian Conference to be held in London, Jan. 1953.

an asset, since you start within a world of thought and feeling based upon archetypal realities.

I have had a number of TB patients[2] in my time and some really excellent results with psychotherapy, but it is true that the average somatic case generally has a resistance to a psychological approach, particularly the TB patients, since TB is, in a way a "pneumatic" disease,[3] that is, affecting the life-giving breath. It is in such cases often as if the patient had a pride and obstinacy in defending the achievement of a somatic answer to an insoluble psychological problem.

With every good wish for Christmas and the New Year, I remain,

Yours cordially, C. G. JUNG

[2] A tuberculosis specialist had referred several cases to C., believing in the value of analysis in effecting a cure.
[3] Cf. Swoboda, 23 Jan. 60.

To Stanislaw Komorowski

Dear Colleague,   19 December 1952

Many thanks for your friendly letter.

I know Suzuki personally. I have studied Zen not in the practical sense but only from the psychological angle.[1] I have had much more to do with the European developments that tend in the same direction. Many paths lead to the central experience. But the nearer one gets to the centre the easier it is to understand the other paths that lead there. I have no doubt that this study is the most important in our time.

With best wishes for the *natalis Solis invicti*,

Yours sincerely, C. G. JUNG

☐ Cracow, Poland.
[1] Cf. "Foreword to Suzuki's *Introduction to Zen Buddhism*," CW 11.

To Mitchel Bedford

[ORIGINAL IN ENGLISH]

Dear Dr. Bedford,   31 December 1952

Concerning Mr. Buber, I can tell you that to my knowledge there has never been the slightest personal friction between us and I do not

101

think that Buber has ever been impolite to me. The only trouble with him is that he does not understand what I am talking about. Concerning Kierkegaard, I am convinced that for many people it is an excellent thing to read him, because he gives voice to many deliberations which prove to be of great value inasmuch as they help people to think about such questions. I myself, quite personally, do not find a sufficient amount of meat in him. One hears too damn much of himself, but very little of that voice which I would prefer to hear.[1]

I have no personal opinion of Buber since I have met him only a few times and I dislike forming opinions on insufficient grounds.

Sincerely yours, C. G. JUNG

☐ Los Angeles, California.

[1] Cf. Künzli, 28 Feb. and 16 Mar. 43; Bremi, 26 Dec. 53.

To Elisabeth Metzger

Dear Frau Metzger,   7 January 1953

Man is notoriously not God, to whom alone is given the power to preserve and destroy life. Man has only very limited possibilities amongst which—so far as his consciousness extends—he can choose with practical freedom. If causality is axiomatic, i.e., absolute, there can be no freedom. But if it is only a statistical truth, as is in fact the case, then the possibility of freedom exists.

The paradoxical God-image is not an innovation in the sense that it is a *novum* in the world's history. The God of the Old Testament as well as all non-Christian deities are inwardly contradictory, and the non-Christians must also live and have always lived with the paradox. It is certainly true that a paradoxical God-image forces man to come to grips with his own paradoxicality. This is in fact our task which we have hitherto avoided.

Yours sincerely, C. G. JUNG

☐ See Metzger, 7 Feb. 42 (in vol. 1), 1953, at a home for the aged in Leonberg, Germany.

To Ignaz Tauber

Dear Colleague,   23 January 1953

Thanks for your friendly visit! I passed a good night. One Quidinal was enough to stop the tachycardia. Everything fine today, I am up again.

Yesterday I quite forgot to ask you what you think about smoking. Until now I have smoked 1 pipe with water condensation[1] on beginning work in the morning, a miniature cigar after lunch, equal to 1–2 cigarettes, another pipe at 4 o'clock, after supper another little cigar, and generally another pipe about 9:30. A little tobacco helps me to concentrate and conduces to my peace of mind.

Please do send me your bill. You were kind enough to bring the Corhomon along. I've already had an injection today. With many thanks for your advice,

Yours sincerely, C. G. JUNG

☐ (Handwritten.) T., of Winterthur, a general medical practitioner who also made use of analytical psychology, was treating Jung at the time.
[1] This type of pipe was Jung's favourite, and there were always several on his writing desk ready for smoking.

To William Hamilton Smith

[ORIGINAL IN ENGLISH]

Dear Mr. Smith,   26 January 1953

Everybody is free to believe anything which seems to fit about things of which we know nothing. Nobody knows whether there is reincarnation, and equally one does not know that there is none. Buddha himself was convinced of reincarnation, but he himself on being asked twice by his disciples about it, left it quite open whether there is a continuity of your personality or not.[1] Certainly we do not know where we come from, nor where we are going, or why we are here at the present time. I think it is right to believe that having done

☐ S., of Springfield, Massachusetts, who described himself as "just a little fellow 58 years old and employed as a packer in a government arsenal," and having "an intense desire to know where I came from, where I am going and why I am here at the present time," asked if it was "wrong for me to believe in the doctrine of reincarnation."
[1] Cf. *Samyutta-Nikaya*, Part II: "The Nidana Book," pp. 150f. (Tr. Rhys Davids and Woodward, 1922.)

the best we could do here, we are also best prepared for things to come.

Yours sincerely, c. g. jung

To James Kirsch

My dear Kirsch,   29 January 1953

I would like to thank you personally for the great honour[1] you have destined for me and the great pleasure this has given me. I hope and wish all the best for the future of your Society. If I had a *Doctor honoris causa* to bestow I would place the well-earned academic hat on your head in recognition of your truly remarkable and meritorious activity on behalf of "my" psychology, with regard to which, however, I presume to no proprietary rights. It represents a movement of the spirit which took possession of me and which I have had the privilege of serving all my life. It illuminates the evening of my days and fills me with joyful serenity that I was granted the favour of putting my best abilities at the service of a great cause.

What you write about the effect of *Job* on analysts accords with my own experience: the number of individuals capable of reacting is relatively very small and analysts are no exception. A second edition is already on the way, in which I have made the corrections you suggested.[2] I will send you a copy.

I am recuperating slowly, but now things are getting positively better. Today I finished a long essay on the "Philosophical Tree," which kept me company during my illness. I have discovered some interesting things. Writing it was an enjoyable substitute for the fact that so few of my contemporaries can understand what is meant by the psychology of the unconscious. You should have seen the press reviews of *Job*! The naïve stupidity of it all is beyond imagination.

Again with cordial thanks and kindest regards,

Yours sincerely, c. g. jung

☐ (Handwritten.) Published (in K.'s tr.) in *Psychological Perspectives*, III:2 (fall 1972).

[1] Jung had been made an honorary member of the Analytical Psychology Club of Los Angeles.

[2] K. had made his own translation of "Answer to Job" for members of his 1952–53 Seminar in Los Angeles. A number of his suggestions were incorporated in the 1954 London edition (cf. Priestley, 8 Nov. 54, n. 2) and K.'s help is acknowledged in Hull's "Translator's Note."

To Ignaz Tauber

Dear Colleague, 4 February 1953

For a time I faithfully observed the rigorous rules of abstinence until my impatience drove me again to a few pipes. Of the 2 evils the pipe seems to me the lesser. Everything went very well from the moment I gave up the digitalis. . . .

Yours sincerely, C. G. JUNG

To G. van Schravendijk-Berlage

Dear Frau Schravendijk-Berlage, 11 February 1953

I can only confirm the impression you have formed of the world-wide readiness to help. Here in Switzerland we are all deeply affected by the terrible catastrophe[1] that has befallen your country. On a superficial view, one must regard this response as a positive sign of the feeling of human solidarity. But as you have quite rightly seen there is something more behind it: the pressure weighing on all Europe and the more or less open fear of a still greater catastrophe. The present political situation is historically unique in that an Iron Curtain has split the world into two halves which virtually balance each other. Nobody knows the answer to this problem. But whenever man is confronted with an unanswerable question or situation, corresponding archetypes are constellated in his unconscious. The first thing this produces is a general unrest in the unconscious which manifests itself as fear and makes people seek closer union in order to ward off the danger. But when a catastrophe like the Dutch one occurs, they are reminded of the far greater danger under the threat of which they live. The breaking loose of the elements, tempest and flood, is a symbol of the possible end of our world.

Yours sincerely, C. G. JUNG

☐ Baarn, Netherlands.
[1] S.-B. asked about the psychological background of the extraordinary worldwide response to the catastrophic flood in the Netherlands during the first days of Feb.

To Henri Flournoy

Dear Colleague,   12 February 1953

I have always mistrusted autobiography, for one never can tell the truth. In so far as one is truthful, or believes one is truthful, that is an illusion—or bad taste. Recently, in line with a suggestion from America, I was asked to give my help to an attempt at biography in interview form. There was a person supposed to start work on this after the New Year, but so far nothing has happened. Personally, I have no wish to write any fiction or poetry about the bizarre experience called life. It is enough to have lived it! My health is not good and I am almost 78, which Cicero would have called *tempus maturum mortis*.[1] Regretting that I cannot give you more satisfactory information, I am,

Yours very sincerely, C. G. JUNG

☐ (Translated from French.) See Flournoy, 29 Mar. 49 (in vol. 1).
[1] = time ripe for death.

To J. B. Rhine

[ORIGINAL IN ENGLISH]

Dear Professor Rhine: 18 February 1953

Thank you for your kind letter![1] My state of health is unfortunately not so good as to allow me much work. The work I am planning on ESP does not concern the fact itself (which you have demonstrated up to the hilt), but rather the peculiar *emotional factor* that seems to be a very important condition deciding the success or failure of the ESP experiment. As a rule (though not always) spontaneous cases of ESP happen under emotional circumstances (accidents, death, illness, danger, etc.) which usually arouse the deeper archetypal and instinctual layers of the unconscious. I should like to examine the state of the unconscious in cases of minor or major events occurring not so rarely with our patients. I have observed a great many ESP cases with my patients in the course of time. The only trouble is to

☐ See Rhine, 27 Nov. 34 (in vol. 1).
[1] Acknowledging the gift of *Naturerklärung und Psyche* (1952). The essay on synchronicity contains a very appreciative review of R.'s work on ESP and PK. In his letter he suggested subjecting Jung's theory "to an adequately crucial experimental test" and offered his help in such a project.

find suitable methods by which the state of the unconscious can be established objectively. We have begun to try out such methods.[2] They are difficult and unorthodox, and need a very special training. I am most obliged to you for offering your help, but in the actual state of our research I would not know where the statistical method would come in, although I hope once to get to a point where statistics can be applied.

It is annoying that my recent works are not yet published in English. But what can you do when there are at least two committees occupied with the publication of my collected works? I have tried to kick them into life, but they have taken more than five years over one single book, and it is not yet out![3] I have written to Mr. Barrett of the Bollingen Press[4] concerning my essay on synchronicity. It could easily be translated and published.

Thanking you for your kind interest, I remain,

Yours sincerely, c. g. j u n g

[2] A group of researchers at the C. G. Jung Institute had for some time been investigating intuitive methods such as the *I Ching*, geomancy, Tarot cards, numerology, astrology. Cf. "Synchronicity," CW 8, pars. 863ff., and ch. 2: "An Astrological Experiment."

[3] *Psychology and Alchemy*, the first volume to appear in the Collected Works, was published in June 1953. Despite the exasperated tone of this paragraph, no doubt due to an insufficient appreciation of the immense problems involved in planning an edition of twenty volumes and setting up the administrative machinery for its production, Jung later paid generous tribute to the Bollingen Foundation for the speed with which the books were being published. Cf. Barrett, 11 Feb. 54.

[4] That is, Bollingen Series, published by Pantheon Books, New York, for the Bollingen Foundation. The essay on synchronicity was published in *The Interpretation of Nature and the Psyche* (Bollingen Series, 1955; also in London).

To John Weir Perry

[O R I G I N A L   I N   E N G L I S H]

Dear Dr. Perry,   24 February 1953

I have studied your manuscript[1] with great and continued interest. You present your stuff indeed very well, so I have no criticisms to make. Just because it is not an extraordinary case it makes a very good

☐ M.D., analytical psychologist in San Francisco. Cf. his *The Self in Psychotic Process* (1953); *Lord of the Four Quarters* (1966); *The Far Side of Madness* (1974).
[1] Of *The Self in Psychotic Process*. Jung's foreword is in CW 18, pars. 832ff.

introduction for the average alienist to the psychological understanding of schizophrenia. Case studies of this kind are really indispensable, and I earnestly hope that yours will be just the beginning of a number of such researches. Clinical psychiatry is very much in need of such case material, and at the same time it is also of the highest value to the psychologist, since we all know of a number of isolated cases but we have no comprehensive knowledge of the average psychological phenomenology in schizophrenia. I think it would be a good idea to start case research in many places with a number of co-workers, a thing which I always missed in Europe. You could really start a journal devoted exclusively to the psychology of schizophrenia, filled with case researches. It would be a most meritorious work and could form the basis of a real psychopathology—a science that has not been created yet. In America you are in a very much better position than I was over here, since you find there very much more assistance and willingness when you once have overcome the barriers of prejudice.

I hope my preface suits you. It is the best I could do under the prevailing circumstances. I am slowly recovering from my tachycardiaparoxysmalis,[2] which has bothered me now for about five months. My scientific work was only progressing slowly on account of this disturbance, but I hope to issue a new volume in the spring under the title of *Von den Wurzeln des Bewusstseins*.[3]

There is a rumour that *Psychology and Alchemy* will appear on April 15th, but I am not yet sure whether Mr. Barrett's prophetic word is authentic or not.

Hoping you keep in good health, I remain,

Yours cordially, C. G. JUNG

[2] Abnormal, convulsive rapidity of the action of the heart.
[3] Zurich, 1954. The essays are contained in CW 8, 9, i, 11, 13.

To Carl Seelig

Dear Dr. Seelig,   25 February 1953

I got to know Albert Einstein[1] through one of his pupils, a Dr. Hopf[2] if I remember correctly. Professor Einstein was my guest on

☐ (1894–1962), Swiss author, journalist, and theatre critic. Cf. his *Albert Einstein. Eine dokumentarische Biographie* (1952); *Albert Einstein, Leben und Werk eines Genies unserer Zeit* (1954). He asked Jung for his impressions of Einstein. — The letter was published in *Spring*, 1971.

several occasions at dinner, when, as you have heard, Adolf Keller[3] was present on one of them and on others Professor Eugen Bleuler, a psychiatrist and my former chief. These were very early days when Einstein was developing his first theory of relativity.[4] He tried to instil into us the elements of it, more or less successfully. As non-mathematicians we psychiatrists had difficulty in following his argument. Even so, I understood enough to form a powerful impression of him. It was above all the simplicity and directness of his genius as a thinker that impressed me mightily and exerted a lasting influence on my own intellectual work. It was Einstein who first started me off thinking about a possible relativity of time as well as space, and their psychic conditionality. More than thirty years later this stimulus led to my relation with the physicist Professor W. Pauli and to my thesis of psychic synchronicity. With Einstein's departure from Zurich my relation with him ceased, and I hardly think he has any recollection of me. One can scarcely imagine a greater contrast than that between the mathematical and the psychological mentality. The one is extremely quantitative and the other just as extremely qualitative.

　　With kind regards,

Yours sincerely, C. G. JUNG

[1] Einstein (1879–1955) had been living in Bern until 1909 as an examiner of patents at the Patent Office, during which period he took his Ph.D. at the U. of Zurich. After publishing several papers on physical subjects, he was appointed extraordinary professor of theoretical physics at the U. in 1909, and in 1912 professor at the Federal Polytechnic (E.T.H.). Cf. *The Freud/Jung Letters*, 230J, par. 1.

[2] Ludwig Hopf, theoretical physicist.

[3] Cf. Keller, 26 Mar. 51.

[4] In 1905 Einstein published his famous *On the Electrodynamics of Moving Bodies*, in which the principle of relativity is mentioned for the first time.

To Ignaz Tauber

Dear Colleague, 　　　　　　　　　　　　　　　13 March 1953

　　Excuse my tardiness! I should have reported to you some time ago. The Convenal worked well. As the result of a dream I completely laid off smoking five days ago. The last drop in the barometer yesterday did *not* affect me. I'm now waiting for the next. The fall of snow

☐ (Handwritten.)

would have been ideal otherwise. Best greetings to your wife. And thanks for your letter. At present I'm still in a foul mood. What would the gods do without smoke offerings?

Best regards, c. g. jung

To Josef Rudin

Dear Dr. Rudin,   14 March 1953

I owe you many thanks for kindly sending me your essay[1] about *Job*. Psychologically, the divine polarity is a question of *oppositio* and not *contradictio*,[2] hence Nicolaus Cusanus speaks of *opposita*. The non-reciprocity of the God-man relationship[3] is a hard doctrine. Creatures would then be things but not free individuals, and what in the world would be the motive for the Incarnation if man's fate didn't affect God? Also, no one has ever heard of a bridge that leads only to the *other* bank of the river. Isn't the original idea that man can exercise no *compulsion* on God? But that man's prayers can reach God? And that the Incarnation makes God still more reachable?

Please excuse these naïve questions. They don't need answering.

Yours sincerely, c. g. jung

☐ S.J., psychotherapist, since 1967 professor at the U. of Innsbruck. Cf. his *Psychotherapie und Religion* (1964); *Fanatismus* (1965).
[1] "Antwort auf Hiob. Zum gleichnamigen Buch von C. G. Jung," *Orientierung* (Zurich), 28 Feb. 1953.
[2] R. suggested that the problem of the dual aspect of God might be solved by introducing the scholastic distinction between "opposition" and "contradiction," in the sense that an inner opposition of divers attributes could be ascribed to God but no contradiction.
[3] The Catholic teaching admitting the relation of man to God as necessary but not of God to man.

To E. Roenne-Peterson

[ORIGINAL IN ENGLISH]

Dear Sir,   16 March 1953

Inseminatio artificialis[1] could indeed become a public and legal problem in a society where a merely rationalistic and materialistic

☐ Stockholm.

point of view has become predominant, and where the cultural values as to the freedom of human thoughts and of human relations have been suppressed. This danger is not so remote that one could disregard it. It is therefore a legitimate question when one asks what the possible consequences of the practice of the said procedure might be.

From the standpoint of psychopathology, the immediate effect would be an "illegitimate," i.e., fatherless pregnancy, in spite of the fact that the fertilization took place in wedlock and under legalized circumstances. It would be a case of *unknown paternity*. Since human beings are individual and not exchangeable, the father could not be artificially substituted. The child would suffer inevitably from the handicaps of illegitimacy, or of being an orphan, or of adoption. These conditions leave their traces in the psyche of the infant.

The fact that artificial insemination is a well-known cattle-breeding device lowers the moral status of a human mother to the level of a cow, no matter what she thinks about it, or what she is talked into. As any bull having the desired racial characteristics can be a donor, so any man appreciated from the breeder standpoint is good enough for anonymous procreation. Such a procedure amounts to a catastrophic devaluation of the human individual, and its destructive effect upon human dignity is obvious. Having no practical experience in this matter, I do not know what the psychological effect is of a conception brought about in such a cold-blooded "scientific" way, and what a mother who had to carry the child of a total stranger would feel. I can imagine that the effect would be like that of rape. It seems to me to be in itself an ominous symptom of the mental and moral condition of our world that such problems have to be discussed at all.

Sincerely yours, C. G. JUNG

¹ R.-P. was "psychological adviser" to a committee of scientists organized to protest against the introduction of artificial insemination in Scandinavia, and asked for Jung's views on the subject.

To Jakob Amstutz

Dear Pastor Amstutz,   28 March 1953

Excuse the delay in answering your kind letter of 9 March. It is indeed a pleasant exception. For there are exceptions. Otherwise dis-

□ (Handwritten.) See Amstutz, 8 Jan. 48 (in vol. 1).

mal darkness reigns. My criticism of the Yahwistic God-image is for you what the experience of the book was for me: a drama that was not mine to control. I felt myself utterly the *causa ministerialis* of my book. It came upon me suddenly and unexpectedly during a feverish illness.[1] I feel its content as an unfolding of the divine consciousness in which I participate, like it or not. It was necessary for my inner balance that I made myself conscious of this development.

Man is the mirror which God holds up to himself, or the sense organ with which he apprehends his being.

So-called progress makes possible a tremendous multiplication of man and leads simultaneously to a spiritual inflation and to an unconsciousness of God (*genetivus accusativus!*). Man confuses himself with God, is identical with the demiurge and begins to usurp cosmic powers of destruction, i.e., to arrange a second Deluge. He should become conscious of the tremendous danger of God becoming man, which threatens him with becoming God, and learn to understand the *mysteria Dei* better.

In the Catholic Church, faith is not so dangerous in practice. The Church stands on two feet, Protestantism only on *sola fide*, therefore faith is so important to it but not to the Catholic. Sometimes *semel credidisse*[2] is sufficient for him since he has the ritual graces. With best greetings,

Yours sincerely, C. G. JUNG

[1] For the genesis of "Answer to Job," cf. Corbin, 4 May 53.
[2] = once having believed. Cf. *Psychology and Alchemy*, CW 12, par. 12.

To R. A. McConnell

[ORIGINAL IN ENGLISH]

Dear Sir,   14 April 1953

I have read your interesting article: "ESP—Fact or Fancy?" in *The Scientific Monthly*,[1] to which Professor Pauli in Zurich has called my attention. I was very much impressed by the fact that the whole problem of ESP is taken up by physicists, as this science is most concerned with phenomena challenging the classical concepts of time

☐ Then assistant professor of physics at the U. of Pittsburgh (Pennsylvania); later research professor of biophysics.
[1] *The Scientific Monthly* (Lancaster, Pa.), LXIX:2 (1949).

and space. I have come across many cases of spontaneous ESP with my patients, and their theoretical implications have occupied my thoughts for the better part of thirty years, but only last year could I make up my mind to write about this bewildering problem.[2] An English translation has not yet appeared but the Bollingen Press seems eventually to have decided to publish the book.

I would be much obliged to you if you would kindly keep me *au courant* with your results; I expect no detailed report, but if you could give me the main lines that would be sufficient. With my best wishes, I am,

Sincerely yours, C. G. JUNG

[2] "Synchronicity."

To Dorothee Hoch

Dear Dr. Hoch,   30 April 1953

It was very kind of you to write to me again in spite of the fact that I never answered your letter of 5.XII.52. Since I have not been in the best of health for some time, and you are evidently not in a position to follow my line of thought,[1] I quailed at the prospect of answering you yet again. It is simply a question of something that the primitive Christians understood and that was understood again and again even in the Middle Ages and that the whole of India has understood from time immemorial. How very much you misunderstand me is evident from your remark that "psychanalysis (!)[2] tries to lead man to the discovery of his self as the ultimate goal." Maybe "psychanalysis" aims at something of the sort, but I intend no such futility, for the self is by definition a transcendental entity with which the ego is confronted. It is a total misunderstanding (and the opposite of what I have always emphasized) to say that the self is a "concentration on the Me." That is just what it is not. Whatever the ultimate fate of the self may be (and the Christian mystics have something to say

[1] H. misunderstood the concept of the self when she wrote in her letter of 5 Dec. 52: "It seems to me . . . a fallacy to believe that man's self can coincide with the divine self which alone carries life within itself."

[2] Despite the exclamation mark, this spelling was used by Jung in his early days. Cf. "Freud's Theory of Hysteria: A Reply to Aschaffenburg," CW 4, par. 2 & n. 3, and *The Freud/Jung Letters*, 7J, n. 2.

113

here), it means at any rate first the end of the ego. Indeed, you yourself say (as Orelli[3] said and I have always said[4]) that Christ is "the self of all selves." This is the correct definition of the self and means that just as Christ is related to all individuals, so all individuals are related to Christ. Every self has the quality of belonging to the "self of all selves," and the self of all selves consists of individual selves. The psychological concept fully agrees with this.

I have nothing against your theological formulations, and if I wanted to criticize them I would first have to acquire a lot more theological knowledge. You treat psychology cavalierly and do not notice how very much you misunderstand it. My aim was therefore to give you a fairer conception of my psychology. This is evidently not possible, as I must admit to my regret. It is really not easy to talk with theologians: they don't listen to the other person (who is wrong from the start) but only to themselves (and call this the Word of God). Perhaps this comes from their having to preach down from the pulpit, with nobody allowed to answer back. This attitude, which I met practically everywhere, has shooed me out of the Church like so many others. I like discussions with theologians, Protestant and Catholic, who understand and want to understand what I am talking about. But the discussion comes to an end when you bang your head against the walls of Church and credo, for there contumaciousness begins and the power-drive that countenances nothing except itself. That is why the devil laughs in the face of the 400 feuding Protestant sects and the great reformatory schism. If even the Christian Churches can't agree! What an infernal scandal! You have not exactly encouraged my attempt to build bridges. But I won't molest you any further with my paradoxes, rather I must ask your forgiveness for what must inevitably appear to you as unjustified aggressiveness. I have no wish whatever to offend or annoy you pointlessly, and therefore I repeat that I have nothing against your theological formulations but, on the contrary, find them justified in their fashion. My hope was only that I might inculcate into you a somewhat more reasonable and less distorted view of my psychology. I am evidently a bad advocate in my own cause and would therefore like to take leave of you with many apologies.

Yours sincerely, C. G. JUNG

[3] Cf. Orelli, 7 Feb. 50, n. ☐.
[4] *Aion*, par. 70: "Christ exemplifies the archetype of the self." Cf. also the section "Christ as Archetype" in "A Psychological Approach to the Dogma of the Trinity," CW 11, pars. 226ff.

To Henry Corbin

Dear M. Corbin, 4 May 1953

A few days ago I received an offprint of your essay "La Sophie Éternelle."[1] Unfortunately it is impossible for me to express all the thoughts and feelings I had upon reading your admirable presentation of your subject. My French is so rusty that I cannot use it to formulate exactly what I want to say to you. Yet I must tell you how delighted I was by your work. It was an extraordinary joy to me, and not only the rarest of experiences but even a unique experience, to be fully understood. I am accustomed to living in a more or less complete intellectual vacuum, and my *Answer to Job* has done nothing to diminish it. On the contrary, it has released an avalanche of prejudice, misunderstanding, and, above all, atrocious stupidity. I have received hundreds of critical reviews, but not a single one that comes anywhere near yours in its lucid and penetrating understanding. Your intuition is astounding: Schleiermacher[2] really is one of my spiritual ancestors. He even baptized my grandfather—born a Catholic—who by then was a doctor.[3] This grandfather became a great friend of the theologian de Wette,[4] who had connections of his own with Schleiermacher. The vast, esoteric, and individual spirit of Schleiermacher was a part of the intellectual atmosphere of my father's family. I never studied him, but unconsciously he was for me a *spiritus rector.*

☐ (Translated from French.) Henry Corbin, professor of Islamic religion at the École des Hautes Études, Sorbonne; directeur de département d'Iranologie de l'Institut Franco-Iranien, Teheran. Frequent lecturer at the Eranos meetings.

[1] *La Revue de culture européenne* (Paris), III:5 (1953).

[2] Friedrich Schleiermacher (1768–1834), German Protestant theologian and philosopher. His writings excel by their combination of deep religiosity, clear intellect, and vivid sense of reality. Cf. Jung, 30 Dec. 59.

[3] Cf. ibid. Jung's grandfather Carl Gustav Jung (1794–1864), a convert to Protestantism, had to leave Germany for Switzerland in 1820 on account of his liberal political activities, after spending over a year in prison. In 1822 he became professor of medicine at the U. of Basel. Cf. Jung and Jaffé, *Erinnerungen, Träume, Gedanken,* pp. 400ff. (This section on the Jung family by Jaffé is omitted in the American/English edns. of *Memories.*) For his portrait, see *Memories,* facing p. 110/64.

[4] Wilhelm de Wette (1780–1849), German theologian. He was dismissed as professor of theology at Berlin U. on account of his progressive political sympathies in 1819, but three years later was appointed professor of theology at the U. of Basel. He has been described (by Julius Wellhausen, the German biblical scholar and Orientalist, 1844–1918, famous for his critical investigations into OT history) as "the epoch-making opener of the historical criticism of the Pentateuch."

You say you read my book as an "oratorio." The book "came to me" during the fever of an illness. It was as if accompanied by the great music of a Bach or a Handel. I don't belong to the auditory type. So I did not hear anything, I just had the feeling of listening to a great composition, or rather of being at a concert.

I should mention that de Wette had a tendency, as he said, to "mythize" the "marvellous" Bible stories (that is, the shocking ones). Thus he preserved their symbolic value. This is exactly what I have been forced to do not only for the Bible but also for the misdeeds in our dreams.

I don't know how to express my gratitude but, once again, I must tell you how much I appreciate your goodwill and your unique understanding.

My compliments to Madame Corbin. The caviar is not forgotten. With grateful regards,

Sincerely yours, C. G. JUNG

To R. J. Zwi Werblowsky

Dear Dr. Werblowsky,   21 May 1953

Best thanks for kindly sending me your two lectures.[1] I have read them with great interest; the second even twice, as Father White came to Zurich the day before yesterday. Your critique is most interesting but not exactly easy reading. When I saw Father White he hadn't yet read it. But I hope I shall have an opportunity to discuss certain points with him. You are absolutely right about the hornet's nest.[2]

The two dark figures in Kafka[3] are a duplication of the shadow or of the self (the two white balls[4]). This duality attaches, for instance,

[1] "Psychology and Religion," *The Listener* (London), vol. 49, no. 1260 (23 Apr. 1953); "God and the Unconscious," ibid., no. 1262 (2 May 1953), a critical review of Victor White's book of the same name.

[2] In his second lecture W. said that in certain cases the psychologist "makes affirmations not merely of what 'appears' but of what 'really' is in spite of appearances," and that this "raises a hornet's nest of questions."

[3] A frequent theme in Kafka's work is the appearance of two dark and grotesque figures, e.g., in *The Trial* and *The Castle*.

[4] The two white balls occur in Kafka's *Description of a Struggle* (1931; tr., 1958), "Blumfeld, an Elderly Bachelor."

116

to the messengers from the underworld (Apocalypse of Peter[5]) or the "helpful animals."[6] As a rule the shadow appears only in the singular. If it occasionally appears as a duality this is, so to speak, a "seeing double": a conscious and an unconscious half, one figure above the horizon, the other below. So far as I know anything definite about it, the duplication seems to occur when the split-off figure is real in a special sense—real as a ghost. Duplications also occur in dreams, but less frequently than in fairytales and legends. The duplication is the origin of the motif of the hostile brothers.[7]

I read the Ibn Ezra passage[8] in a book I can't remember the name of for the moment. I hope to locate the quotation sometime. With best regards,

Yours sincerely, C. G. JUNG

[5] The Apocalypse of Peter was written A.D. 100–140. It is influenced by Oriental and Hellenistic conceptions of heaven and hell. Contained in James, *The Apocryphal New Testament*, pp. 505ff.
[6] A frequent motif in fairytales and legends. Cf. *Symbols of Transformation*, par. 264; "The Phenomenology of the Spirit in Fairytales," CW 9, i, par. 431.
[7] Cain and Abel, Jacob and Esau are examples of this archetypal motif. (Cf. Evans, 17 Feb. 54, n. 3.) For the duplication motif cf. "The Spirit in Fairytales," par. 608, and *Aion*, pars. 181ff.
[8] Cf. White, 30 Apr. 52, n. 5.

To James Kirsch

Dear Colleague,   Bollingen, 28 May 1953

At last I can find time to thank you personally for the kind letter you wrote me on the occasion of the death of Toni Wolff.[1] On the day of her death, even before I had received the news, I suffered a relapse and had a bad attack of my tachycardia. This has now subsided but it has left an arrhythmia which hampers my physical capacities very much. I have ventured out to Bollingen over Whitsun and hope to recuperate a bit more here.

☐ (Handwritten.) Published (in K.'s tr.) in *Psychological Perspectives*, III:2 (fall 1972).
[1] Toni Wolff (1888–1953), Swiss analytical psychologist, for over 40 years a close collaborator and friend of Jung's; 1928–44 and 1949–50, president of the Psychological Club, Zurich. Cf. her *Studien zu C. G. Jungs Psychologie* (1959);

117

Toni Wolff's death was so sudden, so totally unexpected, that one could hardly realize her passing. I had seen her only two days before. Both of us completely unsuspecting. The Hades dreams I had in the middle of February I related entirely to myself because nothing pointed to Toni Wolff. Nobody who was close to her had any warning dreams, and in England, Germany, and Zurich only people who knew her superficially.

At the beginning of my illness in Oct. 52 I dreamt of a huge black elephant that uprooted a tree. (Meanwhile I have written a long essay on "The Philosophical Tree.") The uprooting of a tree can signify death. Since then I have dreamt several times of elephants which I always had to treat warily. Apparently they were engaged in road-building.

Your news interested me very much. The Professor for the Old Testament at the University[2] here is giving a seminar on my *Job*. One can of course consider the Book of Job from various angles. What mattered to me this time was man's relationship to God, i.e., to the God-image. If God's consciousness is clearer than man's, then the Creation has no meaning and man no *raison d'être*. In that case God does not in fact play dice,[3] as Einstein says, but has invented a machine, which is far worse. Actually the story of the Creation is more like an experiment with dice than anything purposive. These insights may well involve a tremendous change in the God-image.

"Synchronicity" is soon to appear in English and *Psychology and Alchemy* is out at last.

The clinical practice of psychotherapy is a mere makeshift that does its utmost to prevent numinous experiences. To a certain extent you can also get along in this way. There will however always be cases which go beyond that, even among doctors.

The "white stone" (*calculus albus*)[4] occurs in the Apocalypse as a symbol of election.

The model of the self in *Aion* is based on the Ezekiel vision![5]

With best regards,

Yours sincerely, C. G. J U N G

Jung's introduction is in CW 10, pars. 887ff. (Cf. Brody, 18 Mar. 58.) (See pl. IV.)

[2] Prof. Dr. Victor Maag.

[3] K. quoted a saying of Einstein's: "I cannot believe that God plays dice with the world." From Lincoln Barnett, *The Universe and Dr. Einstein* (1948), p. 26.

[4] Rev. 2:17. This refers to a dream of K.'s in which he was given a white stone.

[5] Ezekiel 1:4ff. For the model, cf. *Aion*, CW 9, ii, pars. 410f.

To Aniela Jaffé

Dear Aniela,   29 May 1953

. . .

The spectacle of eternal Nature gives me a painful sense of my weakness and perishability, and I find no joy in imagining an equanimity *in conspectu mortis*. As I once dreamt, my will to live is a glowing daimon, who makes the consciousness of my mortality hellish difficult for me at times. One can, at most, save face like the unjust steward, and then not always, so that my Lord wouldn't find even that much to commend. But the daimon recks nothing of that, for life, at the core, is steel on stone.

Cordially, C. G.

□ (Handwritten.)

To R.F.C. Hull

[ORIGINAL IN ENGLISH]

Dear Mr. Hull,   [postmark: 3 August 1953]

No objection to using my ant and telephone analogy.[1] The whole experiment has indeed been bedevilled, even more so than I have said.[2] The old trickster[3] had a grand time. Two years ago when I worked out the statistics he stared at me out of a stone in the wall of my tower in Bollingen. By carving him out I discovered his identity. I have thought I have laid him, but I was obviously wrong again. Latest news is that "Synchronicity" will appear with Pauli!

Sincerely yours, C. G. JUNG

□ (Handwritten postcard.) Richard Francis Carrington Hull (1913–74), translator of Jung's collected works, these *Letters* (from German), and Jung's part of *The Freud/Jung Letters*. (See pl. v.)

[1] In a letter to H. of 16 July 53 Jung used the telephone analogy now to be found in "Synchronicity," CW 8, par. 901.

[2] A number of miscalculations had occurred in evaluating statistically the results of "An Astrological Experiment" (ch. 2 of "Synchronicity"), which Jung and Markus Fierz (cf. Fierz, 22 June 49, n. □) corrected for the English tr. (cf. pars. 901, n. 10 and 991, n. 8). The tr. also includes extensive additions made by Jung himself (pars. 904, 906–8).

[3] Jung "saw" the face of a trickster on the rough surface of the wall and subsequently sculptured it in bas-relief. Cf. the chapter on the Tower in *Memories* and Tauber, 13 Dec. 60.

Anonymous

Dear N.,   Bollingen, 3 August 1953

Hearty thanks for your kind birthday wishes! Unfortunately I can't remember here in Bollingen what you sent me. There was such a flood of letters, flowers, and things pouring in on me that I can remember absolutely nothing except your letter with its main point, the question of *prayer*. This was and still is a problem for me. Some years ago I felt that all demands which go beyond what *is* are unjustified and infantile, so that we shouldn't ask for anything that is not granted. We can't remind God of anything or prescribe anything for him, except when he tries to force something on us that our human limitation cannot endure. The question is, of course, whether such things happen. I think the answer is yes, for if God needs us as regulators of his incarnation and his coming to consciousness, it is because in his boundlessness he exceeds all the bounds that are necessary for becoming conscious. Becoming conscious means continual renunciation because it is an ever-deepening concentration.

If this is right, then it may be that God has to be "reminded." The innermost self of every man and animal, of plants and crystals, is God, but infinitely diminished and approximated to his ultimate individual form. In approximating to man he is also "personal," like an antique god, and hence "in the likeness of a man" (as Yahweh appeared to Ezekiel).

An old alchemist formulated the relation to God thus: "Help me, that I may help you!"[1]

                                With cordial greetings, C. G. JUNG

□ (A woman in Switzerland.) (Handwritten.)
[1] Cf. *Psychology and Alchemy*, CW 12, par. 155, where Jung quotes a passage from the *Rosarium philosophorum* (Frankfurt a. M., 1150) in which the *lapis* says, "Protege me, protegam te" (Protect me, I will protect you).

To Gerhard Zacharias

Dear Dr. Zacharias,   24 August 1953

The perusal of your MS[1] was very interesting and instructive. I think you have succeeded in assimilating from the theological standpoint the findings of the modern psychology of the unconscious with fair completeness, which amounts to an incarnation or realization of the Logos. Just as Origen understood the Holy Scriptures as the body of the Logos, so we can interpret the psychology of the unconscious as a medium for its assimilation. The Christ-image as we know it certainly did not appear as the result of human intervention, it was the transcendental ("total") Christ who created for himself a new and more specific body. The Kingdom of Christ or the realm of the Logos is "not of this world," it is an assignment of meaning above and beyond this world; therefore it is so lamentably wrong that theology, whenever it makes its inevitable assertions *contra naturam*, anxiously looks round for a rational excuse, as when the fire on Sinai is excused as being the remnants of volcanic activity in the Red Sea! This shows how far the transcendence of the Christian viewpoint has slipped down.

Please don't take it amiss if I say that your occasional approximations to the Heideggerean or neo-High German schizophrenic style (Auf-forstung, be-treten, An-rempelung, Unter-teilung) are hardly convincing (or con-vincing) to the reader. Also, you cite my name too often. Pardon!

Yours sin-cerely, C. G. J U N G

☐ (Handwritten.) Gerhard P. Zacharias, then German Greek-Orthodox clergyman, now analytical psychologist in Germany. Cf. his *Psyche und Mysterium* (1954); *Ballet—Gestalt und Wesen* (1962); *Satanskult und Schwarze Messe* (1964).
[1] Of *Psyche und Mysterium.*

To Countess Elisabeth Klinckowstroem

Dear Countess,   2 September 1953

I was very glad to hear from you again after all these many years. I am delighted, also, that my books have given you pleasure. The loss of Fräulein Wolff has hit me very hard indeed.[1] She has left behind in our circle a gap that can never be filled. My health rests on a shaky foundation. But when one is in one's 79th year, one need no longer be surprised at anything.

Eastern philosophy fills a psychic lacuna in us but without answering the problem posed by Christianity. Since I am neither an Indian

☐ Nassau, Germany. She had first met Jung in 1927 in Count Keyserling's circle.
[1] Cf. Kirsch, 28 May 53.

121

nor a Chinese, I shall probably have to rest content with my European presuppositions, otherwise I would be in danger of losing my roots for a second time.[2] This is something I would rather not risk, for I know the price one has to pay to restore a continuity that has got lost. But all culture is continuity.

I am glad you have met Jacobsohn.[3] Do you know his excellent essay on "The Dialogue of a World-Weary Man with His Ba"?

My wife sends you her kindest regards.

Yours sincerely, C. G. JUNG

[2] This could refer to the time of the break with Freud, of which Jung wrote in *Memories*, p. 170/165: ". . . I felt totally suspended in mid-air, for I had not yet found my own footing . . ."

[3] Dr. Helmuth Jacobsohn, Egyptologist at the U. of Marburg. His essay is published in James Hillman, ed., *Timeless Documents of the Soul* (Evanston, Illinois, 1968).

To R. J. Zwi Werblowsky

Dear Dr. Werblowsky,   2 September 1953

Best thanks for kindly sending me R. Gikatilla's text on dreams.[1] The identification of Chalom and Cholem with Kether[2] is very interesting for all its scurrility. When I read that, I had to think of the question recently raised by a mathematician, as to whether it was possible to produce *absolute chance groupings*. The same statements have to be made about each unit *qua* unit. To that extent all units are identical. The unit is necessarily the ἀρχή[3] and the origin of multi-

□ (Handwritten.)

[1] Josef ben Abraham Gikatilla (1248–1305), one of the greatest Kabbalistic scholars. He understood the original text of the OT as the unfolding or paraphrase of the various names of God. Central to his teaching is the mystical meaning of these names and of the alphabet. — Dr. W. had sent Jung an article of his, "Kabbalistische Buchstabenmystik und der Traum (Josef ben Abraham Gikatillas Exkurs über Herkunft und Bedeutung der Träume)," *Zeitschrift für Religions- und Geistesgeschichte* (Cologne), VIII: 2 (1956). In this article W. talks of the "scurrilous idea" (*skurriler Einfall*) of Gikatilla's in connecting the grammatical term *cholem*—the vowel ō, written as a dot—with the root *ch-l-m* (to dream). The vowel *cholem* is co-ordinated with the highest sefirah Kether and denotes also "the unity of all possibilities of language."

[2] Chalom = dream, Cholem = dreamer. Kether: cf. Neumann, 5 Jan. 52, n. 7.

[3] = beginning.

plicity. Because it is *undifferentiated* the unconscious is a unit and hence the ἀρχή μεγάλη[4] and indistinguishable from God.

I can understand that South Africa has no attractions for you. A colony nowadays is about the most disagreeable thing one can imagine. With best regards,

Yours sincerely, c. g. j u n g

[4] = great beginning.

To Maria Folino Weld

[ORIGINAL IN ENGLISH]

Dear Madam,   6 September 1953

A lexicon of dream symbols[1] is a nightmare to me, as I see this task from the standpoint of responsible science and I know its enormous difficulties. We have a large collection of material in our Institute in Zurich, but it is far from being a lexicon of symbols. It would be a well-nigh gigantic undertaking to work out the comparative significance of dream motifs. It should be done in the way of monographs. But this would cover only the archetypal background of dreams and would tell nothing of the actual meaning of dreams. Such a collection would indeed be helpful to professional psychologists trained in comparative psychology, but to the layman it would be a limitless jungle in which he would lose all orientation in no time. Last winter I worked out a sketchy and incomplete monograph about the Tree[2]—well, nobody will do more than a few of the kind.

A superficial collection of interpretations would be the worst as well as completely worthless. But the monographic study of the structure and objective meaning of motifs (mythologemata or archetypes) would be of highest importance, although it is a highly difficult and ambitious task. If you should intend to do some work over here, I am sure our Institute would gladly give you help and expert advice.

Sincerely yours, c. g. j u n g

[1] W. asked Jung to comment on her plan to publish a dictionary of symbols on which she had started work.
[2] "The Philosophical Tree," CW 13.

To Carleton Smith

[ORIGINAL IN ENGLISH]

Dear Sir,   9 September 1953

It is very kind of you to invite me to become an adviser to the National Arts Foundation.

Your plan to establish prizes in the fields of human activity not yet covered by the Nobel Prize is indeed a very fine idea. Whereas the Nobel Prize only considers discoveries or merits concerning natural sciences and medicine[1] (with the exception of the political "peace prize"), the psychic and spiritual welfare of man has been completely disregarded. Man's peace of mind, his mental balance and even his health largely depend upon mental and spiritual factors that cannot be substituted by physical conditions. If man's psychic health and happiness depended upon the proper food and other physical conditions of living, then all wealthy people should be healthy and happy, and all poor people mentally unbalanced, physically ill, and unhappy. But the contrary is true.

The great dangers threatening the life of millions are not physical factors, but mental folly and diabolical schemes causing mental epidemics in the mentally defenceless masses. There is no comparison between even the worst disease or the greatest natural catastrophe (such as earthquakes, floods, and epidemics) and that which man can do to man today.

A prize should be given to people who successfully suppress the outburst of political madness, or of panic (Churchill!), or who produce great ideas enlarging the mental and spiritual horizon of man. Great discoveries concerning the origin of man (palaeontology and archaeology), or about the structure of the universe (astronomy and astrophysics), or the nature of the psyche (for instance J. B. Rhine for his extra-sensory perception experiments), should be rewarded.

What you need above all are *good advisers*, namely representatives of the said spheres of knowledge and research, who are not mere specialists, but who have a wide horizon.

The great trouble is that new ideas are rarely recognized by con-

□ American author, founder and president of the National Arts Foundation (New York), which awarded fellowships in music, architecture, and painting, organized art exhibitions, etc. Jung's suggestion of a prize for the advance of the "psychical and spiritual welfare of man" was not taken up. — Conversations between Jung and Dr. Smith in 1956 led to Jung's writing "The Undiscovered Self (Present and Future)," CW 10.

[1] Jung seems to have overlooked the Nobel Prize for Literature.

temporaries. Most of them fight blindly all creative attempts in their special field. They thrive on things already known and therefore "safe." Universities are the worst in this respect. Yet one can find independent and intelligent personalities even among professors.

The best thing you could do would be to travel about and talk to the main representatives of the departments of history, archaeology, philology (theology?), psychology, biology, comparative religion, ethnology (anthropology), politics, and sociology. I don't mention philosophy as its modern variety does not include a corresponding way of life any more, and therefore consists of mere words.

Albert Schweitzer, by the way, would have deserved a reward for his most important and courageous book on the Jesus biography research,[2] but not for his African romance, which any little doctor could take care of just as well without being made into a saint. It is a mere escape from the problem called Europe.

This is an unofficial letter, giving you my subjective and private thoughts and opinions about your great enterprise.

My best wishes!

Sincerely yours, C. G. JUNG

[2] *The Quest of the Historical Jesus* (1906; tr. 1910). Schweitzer received the Nobel Prize for Peace in 1952.

To Aniela Jaffé

Dear Aniela,   Bollingen, 16 September 1953

Forgive me for answering your last letter only now. I was swamped with proof-reading and correspondence. On top of that the English proofs of "Synchronicity" with a lot of questions about terminology. I have at least 3 hours of writing to do 4 days a week. That is the maximum I can accomplish without having to pay for the excess with disturbed sleep and heart symptoms.

. . .

I have about 5 MSS to read here and besides that a lot of little jobs to do in and about the house. Everything goes slow, and I have to spare myself as my heartbeat is still arrhythmical. In general I'm getting better, as I can sleep properly again. Luckily the weather in the last weeks has been wonderfully kind to me.

☐ (Handwritten.)

125

Nothing doing with the mountains. It's all too complicated. I can walk only for ¼ hour at most and you get nowhere with that.

I see to my horror that I talk only of myself. Please excuse this senile egoism. The 79th year is 80 – 1, and that is a *terminus a quo* which you can't help taking seriously. The provisionalness of life is indescribable. Everything you do, whether watching a cloud or cooking soup, is done on the edge of eternity and is followed by the suffix of infinity. It is meaningful and futile at once. And so is oneself, a wondrously living centre and at the same time an instant already sped. One is and is not. This frame of mind encompasses me and hems me in. Only with an effort can I look beyond into a semi-self-subsistent world I can barely reach, or which leaves me behind. Everything is right, for I lack the power to alter it. This is the débâcle of old age: "Je sais bien qu'à la fin vous me mettrez à bas."

Cordially, c. g.

To J. B. Rhine

[ORIGINAL IN ENGLISH]

Dear Dr. Rhine,   25 September 1953

I am indeed very sorry to be so late in answering your letter.[1] I am no longer efficient. Everything takes its time, usually a long one.

I am not sure whether I can get together all my reminiscences concerning parapsychical events. There were plenty. The accumulation of such tales does not seem to be profitable. The collection by Gurney, Myers and Podmore[2] has produced very little effect. People who know that there are such things need no further confirmation, and people not wanting to know are free, as hitherto, to say that one tells them fairy tales. I have encountered so much discouraging resistance that I am amply convinced of the stupidity of the learned guild. A propos—you have probably heard that in Brussels a young mathema-

---

[1] In a letter of 24 July 53, R. suggested that Jung should make a record of all his experiences and observations of parapsychological phenomena. He also mentioned "a group in California who are working on the problem of control of ESP through deep hypnosis," and, with reference to the experiments of Aldous Huxley, another group, including "an English and Canadian psychiatrist . . . using the alkaloid-mescalin method to give them better access to the unconscious operations they seek to discover and control."

[2] *Phantasms of the Living* (1886). This pioneer work is a collection of cases of ESP, spook phenomena, apparitions, etc. which were corroborated to a considerable extent. Cf. "Synchronicity," CW 8, par. 830.

tician, a Mr. Brown (?) ventilated his view that since your ESP is a fact, the foundations of your probability-calculation must be wrong, inasmuch as there are no real chance groupings or series.[3] Everything seems to be arranged to a certain (small) extent. Well, I would not know it, but it would suit my synchronicity concept not at all badly.

The mescalin-man in Canada is Dr. Smythies[4] from Queen's Hospital in London. He is the originator of this enormous hypothesis of a 7-dimensional universe, the subject of a symposium in the Proc. of the SPR.[5] I could not ascertain what the good of such a hypothesis with reference to ESP might be.

I think the attempt to link up ESP with any personalistic psychology is absolutely hopeless.[6] I don't even think that the emotional factor has any causal, i.e., aetiological importance. As you say, personal factors can only hinder or help, but not cause. *The all-important aspect of ESP is that it relativizes the space as well as the time factor.* This is far beyond psychology. If space and time are psychically relative, then *matter* is too (telekinesis!) and then *causality is only statistically true,* which means that there are plenty of *acausal exceptions,* q.e.d.

As nobody knows what telepathy or precognition or clairvoyance are (except names for ill-defined groups of events), we could just as well designate them as x, y, z, i.e., 3 unknowns of which you could not give a definition, which means that you could not differentiate x from y and z, etc. Their only obvious characteristic would be that they are arbitrary designations *of an unknown factor.* It may even be x = y = z and probably is: *principia explicandi praeter necessitatem non sunt multiplicanda!!* But nobody seems to be aware of this snag. Hoping you are always in good health,

Yours cordially, c. g. jung

---

[3] G. Spencer Brown, "De la recherche psychique considerée comme un test de la théorie des probabilités," *Revue métapsychique* (Paris), 29/30 (May/Aug. 1954); *Probability and Scientific Inference* (1957). Brown claimed (first in two letters of July and Sept. 1953 to *Nature,* London) that ESP experiments showed that something was wrong with the probability calculus. His theory was repudiated by mathematicians. Cf. S. G. Soal and F. Bateman, *Modern Experiments in Telepathy* (1954).

[4] Smythies (cf. Smythies, 29 Feb. 52, n. □) was at that time psychiatrist at the Saskatchewan Hospital, Weyburn, Canada.

[5] Cf. ibid., n. 1.

[6] In his letter R. remarked that "psi functions . . . are not likely to be associated with personality characteristics or traits except as they are inhibited by the other operations of the personality."

127

To Pastor L. Memper

Dear Pastor Memper, 29 September 1953

Please excuse the lateness of my answer. Your letter was a great joy and brought back memories of old, long vanished times. It is now 59 years since I left the vicarage in Klein-Hüningen.[1] I thank you kindly for your invitation.[2] Formerly I would have accepted it without a qualm, because I feel a bond with all the stations of my way, but now I am too old and for reasons of health can no longer take on the responsibility of giving a difficult public address. It is a difficult art to speak to a simple public about a complicated matter. Anyway I would not have mounted the pulpit. This happened to me only once, at a teachers' congress in Bern, which without my previous knowledge was held in a church. To my terror I was forced into a pulpit, which gave me such a shock that I have never spoken in a church again. I hadn't realized how much a sacred and hallowed precinct meant to me. The profane use Protestants make of their churches I regard as a grave error. God may be everywhere, but this in no way absolves believers from the duty of offering him a place that is declared holy, otherwise one could just as well get together for religious purposes in the 3rd class waiting-room of a railway station. The Protestant is not even granted a quiet, pious place where he can withdraw from the turmoil of the world. And nowhere does there exist for God a sanctified *temenos*[3] which serves only one and a sacred purpose. No wonder so few people attend church.

Formerly, in spite of my willingness to oblige, I would also have had to stipulate that the meeting should not in God's name be held in a church, as I am a practising anti-profanist. I hope you will forgive me for taking your kind invitation as a pretext for voicing my subjective protest. But I know from my many years of psychological practice how painful the rationalistic profanation of our churches is for very many educated people.

[1] In 1879 Jung's father moved to Klein-Hüningen, near Basel, now M.'s parish. Cf. *Memories*, pp. 15ff./28ff.
[2] To address his congregation from the very pulpit from which Jung's father had preached.
[3] In Homer's usage, a king or a god's domain; in later times the sanctuary or precinct surrounding the altar. Jung makes frequent use of this term to describe a numinous area (cf. *Psychology and Alchemy*, CW 12, index). Mandalas often appear in this form.

128

I have heard that my father's tombstone was set up near the church. Unfortunately I did not know at the time when the stone was made that my father was described as Dr. theol. instead of Dr. phil. He graduated as an Orientalist, in Arabic.

I was very glad to hear once again of my old home where I spent at least 16 years of my youth. I hope you won't mind my scruples. I found a magnificent temple in India,[4] now standing derelict in the desert. It was desecrated by the Moslems 400 years ago, which resulted in permanent desacralization. It gave me some idea of the strength of this feeling for a sacred precinct, and for the emptiness which arises when the profane breaks in. With kindest regards,

Yours sincerely, C. G. JUNG

[4] Apparently the ruined temple at Konarak. Cf. Mees, 15 Sept. 47, n. 10.

To Pastor W. Niederer

Dear Pastor Niederer,   1 October 1953

I will answer your points[1] as best I can in writing.

1. My interest in the first place was to understand the meaning of the Christian message myself, in the second place to convey this understanding to those of my patients who felt a religious need, and in the third place to salvage the meaning of Christian symbols in general.

2. I don't do anything to God at all, how could I? I criticize merely our *conceptions of God*. I have no idea what God is in himself. In my experience there are only psychic phenomena which are ultimately of unknown origin, since the psyche in itself is hopelessly unconscious. My critics all ignore the epistemological barrier which is expressly respected by me. Just as everything we perceive is a psychic phenomenon and therefore secondary, so is all inner experience. We should be truly modest and not imagine we can say anything about God himself. Truly we are confronted with frightful enigmas.

We must in fact be conscious that an unconscious exists. I don't

[1] The points concerned 1. Jung's intention to make the Biblical message intelligible to modern people; 2. his critics' conviction that he "depersonalized" God, and similar misunderstandings; 3. the problem of the archetype in relation to God's power; 4. the condemnation of Jung as an "a-Christian psychologist of religion" by certain narrow-minded theologians.

129

dare to formulate what the theologian does, but what I do is try to make people conscious enough to know where they can exercise their will and where they are confronted with the power of a non-ego. So far as I can observe the workings of this non-ego it is possible for me to make statements about it. I have no real cognitive means (only arbitrary decisions) which would enable me to distinguish the unknowable non-ego from what men since the remotest times have called God (or gods, etc.). For instance the—so far as I can judge—supreme archetype of the self has a symbolism identical with the traditional Christ..an God-image. How all this can be understood without a knowledge of the psychology of the unconscious, or without self-knowledge, is utterly beyond me. In psychology one understands only what one has experienced.

The archetype is the ultimate I can know of the inner world. This knowledge denies nothing *else* that might be there.

3. If one assumes that God affects the psychic background and activates it or actually is it, then the archetypes are, so to speak, organs (tools) of God. The self "functions" like the Christ-image. This is the theological *Christus in nobis*. It is not only I who think this way, but all the ancients right back to Paul. I take my stand clearly on the empirical plane and speak a psychological language where the theologian speaks an analogous theological or mythological language.

Of course theological statements about the Christian aeon do not agree at all points with psychological empiricism, for instance in regard to God as the Summum Bonum or Christ as a one-sided pneumatic light-figure. But everything that is alive changes; it even develops, so that Christianity is no longer what it was 1000 let alone 1900 years ago. It can differentiate itself still further, i.e., go on *living*, but to do that it *must* be interpreted anew in every aeon. If that does not happen (it happens even in the Catholic Church) it suffocates in traditionalism. But the foundations, the fundamental psychic facts, remain eternally the same.

4. Here I can only say: *O sancta simplicitas!* I realize I am fit for the stake *ad maiorem Dei gloriam*. I consider myself a Christian, but that didn't do Savonarola[2] or Servetus[3] much good, and not even

---

[2] Girolamo Savonarola (1452–98), Italian Dominican monk and reformer. After the expulsion of the Medici, he tried to establish a theocratic and democratic republic in Florence. After initial successes he was defeated by the combined efforts of the Florentine nobility and Pope Alexander VI, whom he had severely criticized for abuses of his office. He was hanged in the marketplace of Florence in 1498.

Christ himself escaped this fate. "Woe to that man by whom the offence cometh!"[4] How about these parsons and the true *imitatio Christi?* Where are they crucified? They are redeemed scot-free of all pain, and Christ can take care of everything else.

With respects to your wife and kind regards,

Yours sincerely, C. G. JUNG

[3] Michael Servetus (Miguel Serveto; 1511–53), Spanish theologian and physician; burnt at the stake in Champel on the instigation of Calvin, French-Swiss theologian and reformer, for his unorthodox beliefs.
[4] Matthew 18:7.

To John Symonds

[ORIGINAL IN ENGLISH]

Dear Sir,   13 October 1953

The quotation[1] you have kindly sent me is indeed very interesting. Thank you very much for it. I know a case in my own experience where children who have been brought up in a too rationalistic way, that is have been deprived of a proper knowledge of the fairy world, have invented fairy tales all by themselves, obviously to fill the gap left by the stupid prejudices of the adults.

I know the book about *The Great Beast.*[2] It is indeed beastly beyon l words, and very good reading for people who have too optimistic a view of man. Thanking you,

Yours sincerely, C. G. JUNG

☐ London.
[1] Charles Lamb, "Witches and Other Night Fears," *The Essays of Elia* (1821): "Gorgons, and Hydras, and Chimaeras, dire stories of Celaeno and the Harpies, may reproduce themselves in the brain of superstition, but they were there before. They are transcripts, types—the archetypes are in us, and eternal. How else should the recital of that, which we know in the waking state to be false, come to affect us all?" S. submitted the quotation because of the surprising occurrence of the word "archetypes," employed in a way very similar to Jung's.
[2] Symonds, *The Great Beast: The Life of Aleister Crowley* (1951).

To O. Schrenk

Dear Professor Schrenk,   18 November 1953

Thank you very much for your friendly letter which I received in the spring of this year. I was ill then and unable to attend to my correspondence, so unfortunately your letter has remained unanswered. But I would like to take it up again now because it contains many things of importance. The "professor and his daughter"[1] is a well-known modern image for the archetype of the Old Man and his daughter in Gnosis: Bythos and Sophia.[2] You will surely remember the interesting love-story of Sophia in the *Adversus Haereses* of Irenaeus.[3] Of course it is unavoidable, if you read archetypal material, that the primordial images in your unconscious will be affected. When you read books that address you personally there is always the danger of mimicry, and there are far too many people who think that's all there is to it. But if you have an honest and critical attitude towards yourself, you will soon see how bogus this is. Everything wants to be lived, positively or negatively.

As for your colleague's dream,[4] I have since discovered that in the Midrashim the symbol of the eagle is ascribed to the prophet Elijah, who soars like an eagle over the earth and spies out the secrets of the human heart. I know from experience that for most Jews these old traditions have passed into oblivion, but come alive again at the slightest provocation and sometimes release the most intense feelings of anxiety.

. . .

Your remark about the Swabian vicarage[5] is on the right track in so far as my maternal grandmother was a Faber (Germanization of Favre du Faure) and, I think, came from Tuttlingen. She married my grandfather, Samuel Preiswerk, head of the reformed clergy in Basel.[6] I have always suspected that my blessed grandfather laid a very strange egg into my mixture.

Yours sincerely, C. G. JUNG

[1] Cf. Schrenk, 8 Dec. 52, par. 1.

[2] In the Gnostic system of Valentinus the perfect primal being, Bythos (= abyss), created the 30 Aeons of whom Sophia is the last. She longs to return to her father and becomes pregnant by him, giving birth to Christos, the saviour.

[3] Irenaeus (*ca.* 130–202), bishop of Lyons, the first great Catholic theologian and fierce opponent of Gnosticism. His *Adversus omnes Haereses* (or *Refutation and Overthrow of Gnosis, Falsely So Called*, orig. in Greek) is a key source for our knowledge of Gnosticism, especially the Gnosis of Valentinus.

[4] Cf. Schrenk, 8 Dec. 52, n. 3.

[5] Unidentifiable because S.'s letter has not been preserved.

[6] Cf. Jung and Jaffé, *Erinnerungen, Träume, Gedanken*, pp. 405f., and Jaffé, *From the Life and Work of C. G. Jung* (tr., 1971), p. 2.

To E. A. Bennet

[ORIGINAL IN ENGLISH]

My dear Bennet,   21 November 1953

Thank you very much for kindly sending me Jones's book about Freud. The incident on page 348 is correct, only the setting in which it occurred is entirely distorted.[1] It was a discussion about Amenophis IV and the fact that he scratched out his father's name on the monuments to put his own in its place, and in the famous manner this was explained as a negative father-complex owing to which everything Amenophis created—his art, his religion and his poetry—was nothing but resistance against the father. No notice was taken of the fact that other Pharaohs have done the same. Now, this derogatory way of judging Amenophis IV got my goat and I expressed myself pretty strongly. That was the immediate cause of Freud's accident. Nobody ever asks *me* how things really were; one only gives a one-sided and twisted representation of my relation to him.

.   .   .

I notice with great interest that the Royal Society of Medicine begins to get interested in my "contributions to the medical science."[2]

Hoping to see you again in the future, not too far away, I remain,

Yours cordially, C. G. JUNG

☐ M.D., English psychiatrist and analytical psychologist; close friend of Jung's. Cf. his *C. G. Jung* (1961); *What Jung Really Said* (1966).

[1] Freud's fainting spell on 24 Nov. 1912, in Munich (Jones, I, p. 348). Jones explains it as connected with the growing dissension between Freud and Jung. The incident is also described in *Memories*, p. 157/153 (cf. Jones, 19 Dec. 53). For further psychoanalytic comment see Nandor Fodor, "Jung, Freud, and a Newly-Discovered Letter of 1909 on the Poltergeist Theme," *The Psychoanalytic Review*, vol. 50, no. 2 (summer 1963), 119ff.

[2] The Royal Society of Medicine had asked B. to arrange a meeting in March 1954 on "Jung's Contribution to Psychiatric Theory and Practice."

To Father Victor White

[ORIGINAL IN ENGLISH]

Dear Victor,   24 November 1953

Forget for once dogmatics and listen to what psychology has to say concerning your problem: *Christ as a symbol is far from being invalid*,[1] although he is one side of the self and the devil the other. This pair of opposites is contained in the creator as his right and left hand,

133

as Clemens Romanus says.[2] From the psychological standpoint the experience of God the creator is the perception of an overpowering impulse issuing from the sphere of the unconscious.[3] We don't know whether this influence or compulsion deserves to be called good or evil, although we cannot prevent ourselves from welcoming or cursing it, giving it a bad or a good name, according to our subjective condition. Thus Yahweh has either aspect because he is essentially the creator (*primus motor*) and because he is yet unreflected in his whole nature.

With the *incarnation* the picture changes completely, as it means that God becomes manifest in the form of Man who is conscious and therefore cannot avoid judgment. He simply has to call the one good and the other evil. It is a historical fact that the real devil only came into existence together with Christ.[4] Though Christ was God, as Man he was detached from God and he watched the devil falling out of heaven,[5] removed from God as he (Christ) was separated from God inasmuch as he was human. In his utter helplessness on the cross, he even confessed that God had forsaken him. The Deus Pater would leave him to his fate as he always "strafes" those whom he has filled before with this abundance by breaking his promise.[6] This is exactly what S. Joannes a cruce describes as the "dark night of the soul." It is the reign of darkness, which is also God, but an ordeal for Man. The Godhead has a double aspect, and as Master Eckhart says: God is not blissful in his mere Godhead, and that is the reason for his incarnation.[7]

But becoming Man, he becomes at the same time a definite being, which is this and not that. Thus the very first thing Christ must do is

---

[1] In a letter of 8 Nov., W. said that Jung seemed to create a dilemma by maintaining that "Christ is no longer an adequate and valid symbol of the self"—a misunderstanding which Jung tries to correct here. (Most of this letter is published in German in Ges. Werke, XI, Anhang, pp. 681ff.)

[2] Cf. Dr. H., 17 Mar. 51, n. 10.

[3] "Psychology and Religion," CW 11, par. 137: ". . . it is always the overwhelming psychic factor that is called 'God.' "

[4] Jung was, of course, perfectly aware of the fact that the figure of Satan occurs in the OT. What he means is that, Christ being the incarnation of God's goodness, the devil becomes a psychological inevitability as the incarnation of evil—in other words the devil is the personification of Christ's split-off dark side. Cf. *Aion*, CW 9, ii, par. 113.

[5] Luke 10:18.

[6] Rev. 3:19.

[7] Cf. *Psychological Types*, CW 6, par. 418.

to sever himself from his shadow and call it the devil (sorry, but the Gnostics of Irenaeus[8] already knew it!).

When a patient in our days is about to emerge from an unconscious condition, he is instantly confronted with his *shadow* and he has to decide for the good, otherwise he goes down the drain. *Nolens volens* he "imitates" Christ and follows his example. The first step on the way to individuation consists in the discrimination between himself and the shadow.

In this stage the Good is the goal of individuation, and consequently Christ represents the self.

The next step is the *problem of the shadow*: in dealing with darkness, you have got to cling to the Good, otherwise the devil devours you. You need every bit of your goodness in dealing with Evil and just there. To keep the light alive in the darkness, that's the point, and only there your candle makes sense.

Now tell me how many people you know who can say with any verisimilitude that they have finished their dealings with the devil and consequently can chuck the Christian symbol overboard?

As a matter of fact, our society has not even begun to face its shadow or to develop those Christian virtues so badly needed in dealing with the powers of darkness. Our society cannot afford the luxury of cutting itself loose from the *imitatio Christi*, even if it should know that the *conflict with the shadow*, i.e., Christ versus Satan, is only the first step on the way to the far-away goal of the unity of the self in God.

It is true however that the *imitatio Christi* leads you into your own very real and *Christlike conflict* with darkness, and the more you are engaged in this war and in these attempts at peacemaking helped by the anima, the more you begin to look forward beyond the Christian aeon to the *Oneness of the Holy Spirit. He is the pneumatic state the creator attains to through the phase of incarnation.* He is the experience of every individual that has undergone the complete abolition of his ego through the absolute opposition expressed by the symbol Christ versus Satan.

The state of the Holy Spirit means a restitution of the original oneness of the unconscious on the level of consciousness. That is alluded to, as I see it, by Christ's logion: "Ye are gods."[9] This state is not quite understandable yet. It is a mere anticipation.

---

[8] *Aion*, par. 75, n. 23.
[9] John 10:34, referring to Psalm 82:6.

The later development from the Christian aeon to the one of the S. spiritus has been called the *evangelium aeternum* by Gioacchino da Fiori[10] in a time when the great tearing apart had just begun. Such vision seems to be granted by divine grace as a sort of *consolamentum*,[11] so that man is not left in a completely hopeless state during the time of darkness. We are actually in the state of darkness viewed from the standpoint of history. We are still within the Christian aeon and just beginning to realize the age of darkness where we shall need Christian virtues *to the utmost*.

In such a state we could not possibly dismiss Christ as an invalid symbol although we clearly foresee the approach of his opposite. Yet we don't see and feel the latter as the preliminary step toward the future union of the divine opposites, but rather as a menace against everything that is good, beautiful, and holy to us. The *adventus diaboli* does not invalidate the Christian symbol of the self, on the contrary: it complements it. It is a mysterious transmutation of both.

Since we are living in a society that is unconscious of this development and far from understanding the importance of the Christian symbol, we are called upon to hinder its invalidation, although some of us are granted the vision of a future development. But none of us could safely say that he has accomplished the assimilation and integration of the shadow.

Since the Christian church is the community of all those having surrendered to the principle of the *imitatio Christi*, this institution (i.e., such a mental attitude) is to be maintained until it is clearly understood what the assimilation of the shadow means. Those that foresee, must—as it were—stay behind their vision in order to help and to teach, particularly so if they belong to the church as her appointed servants.

You should not mind if some of your analysands are helped out of the church. It is their destiny and adventure. Others will stay in it anyhow. It does not matter whether the ecclesiastical powers-that-be

---

[10] Joachim of Flora (*ca.* 1145–1202), Italian mystic and theologian. He taught that there are three periods of world history: the Age of the Law, or of the Father; the Age of the Gospel, or of the Son; and the Age of the Holy Spirit, or of Contemplation. His teachings were condemned by the Fourth Lateran Council, 1215. Cf. *Aion*, pars. 137ff.

[11] The rite of "consoling" or "comforting," the central rite of the Cathars (cf. ibid., pars. 225ff.). It was baptism with the Spirit, considered to be the Paraclete sent by Christ (the "comforter which is the Holy Ghost," John 14:26). The *consolamentum* freed man from original sin.

approve of your vision or not. When the time is fulfilled a new orientation will irresistibly break through, as one has seen in the case of the Conceptio Immaculata[12] and the Assumptio which both deviate from the time-hallowed principle of apostolic authority,[13] a thing unheard-of before. It would be a lack of responsibility and a rather autoerotic attitude if we were to deprive our fellow beings of a vitally necessary symbol before they had a reasonable chance to understand it thoroughly, and all this because it is not complete if envisaged from an anticipated stage we ourselves in our individual lives have not yet made real.

Anybody going ahead is alone or thinks he is lonely at times, no matter whether he is in the church or in the world. Your practical work as *directeur de conscience* brings to you individuals having something in their character that corresponds with certain aspects of your personality (like the many men fitting themselves as stones into the edifice of the tower in the *Shepherd of Hermas*).[14]

Whatever your ultimate decision will be, you ought to realize beforehand that staying in the church makes sense as it is important to make people understand what the symbol of Christ means, and such understanding is indispensable to any further development. There is no way round it, as little as we can eliminate from our life old age, illness, and death, or Buddha's Nidana-chain of evils.[15] The vast majority of people are still in such an unconscious state that one should almost protect them from the full shock of the real *imitatio Christi*. Moreover we are still in the Christian aeon, threatened with a complete annihilation of our world.

As there are not only the many but also the few, somebody is entrusted with the task of looking ahead and talking of the things to be. That is partially my job, but I have to be very careful not to destroy the things that are. Nobody will be so foolish as to destroy the foun-

---

[12] The dogma of the Immaculate Conception pronounced as "of faith" by Pius IX in the bull *Ineffabilis Deus* (1854).

[13] The principle by which all that the Apostles were supposed to have taught was regarded as infallible, and by which nothing in religious teaching or practice was considered Christian unless it was of Apostolic origin.

[14] An early Christian text ascribed to Hermas, brother of Pope Pius I (*ca.* 140–55), containing lessons to be disseminated for the instruction of the Church. Cf. *Psychological Types*, pars. 381ff., esp. par. 390 for the building of the tower.

[15] The twelve *nidanas* of Buddhism, starting with "ignorance" and ending with "despair," form the *nidana*-chain, the conditions which keep man a prisoner in *samsara*, the endless chain of rebirth.

dations when he is adding an upper storey to his house, and how can he build it really if the foundations are not yet properly laid? Thus, making the statement that Christ is not a complete symbol of the self, I cannot make it complete by abolishing it. I must keep it therefore in order to build up the symbol of the perfect contradiction in God by adding this darkness to the *lumen de lumine*.[16]

Thus I am approaching the end of the Christian aeon and I am to take up Gioacchino's anticipation and Christ's prediction of the coming of the Paraclete. This archetypal drama is at the same time exquisitely psychological and historical. We are actually living in the time of the splitting of the world and of the invalidation of Christ.

But an anticipation of a faraway future is no way out of the actual situation. It is a mere *consolamentum* for those despairing at the atrocious possibilities of the present time. Christ is still the valid symbol. Only God himself can "invalidate" him through the Paraclete.

Now that is all I can say. It is a long letter and I am tired. If it is not helpful to you, it shows at least what I think.

I have seen X. She is as right as she can be and as she usually is, and just as wrong as her nature permits, altogether as hopeful as a hysterical temperament ever can be.

You have probably heard of the little celebration we had here round the Nag-Hamâdi Gnostic Codex[17] given to the Institute by a generous donor. There was even a note in the *Times*.[18] It was a disproportionate affair and neither my doing, nor liking. But I was manoeuvred into saying in the end a few words about the relation between Gnosticism and psychology.[19]

My best wishes![20]

Yours cordially, c. g.

---

[16] The Council of Nicaea (325) defined the everlasting Word, "the true light" (John 1:9), as *lumen de lumine*, light of the light.

[17] A Gnostic Papyrus in Coptic found in 1945 near the village of Nag-Hamâdi in Upper Egypt and acquired in 1952 for the C. G. Jung Institute. It is now known as the Codex Jung; its main part consists of the so-called "Gospel of Truth" attributed to Valentinus. This has been published under the editorship of M. Malinine, H. C. Puech, and G. Quispel as *Evangelium Veritatis* (Zurich, 1956). Two further parts: *De Resurrectione* (1963) and *Epistula Jacobi Apocrypha* (1968); the fourth part, *Tractatus Tripartitus*, is still unpublished.

[18] "New Light on a Coptic Codex," *The Times*, 16 Nov. 1953.

[19] Jung's address is in CW 18, pars. 1514ff.

[20] W. answered in a short note of 20 Nov., saying how "immensely grateful" he was for the letter, adding: ". . . the points that 'ring the bell' most immediately are those about the 'autoerotic attitude' and about 'an anticipation of a faraway future is no way out.' "

To the Rev. S.C.V. Bowman

[ORIGINAL IN ENGLISH]

Dear Sir,   10 December 1953

. . .

Your problem of the *liberum arbitrium*[1] has of course many aspects which I wouldn't know how to deal with in the frame of a letter. I only can say that as far as consciousness reaches, the will is understood to be free, i.e., that the feeling of freedom accompanies your decisions no matter if they are really free or not. The latter question cannot be decided empirically. Where you are not conscious, there can obviously be no freedom. Through the analysis of the unconscious, you increase the amount of freedom. A complete consciousness would mean an equally complete freedom and responsibility. If unconscious contents approaching the sphere of consciousness are not analysed and integrated, then the sphere of your freedom is even diminished through the fact that such contents are activated and gain more compelling influence upon consciousness than when they were completely unconscious. I don't think that there are any great difficulties in this line of approach. The actual difficulty, as I see it, begins with the problem of how to deal with the integrated formerly unconscious contents. This, however, cannot be dealt with by correspondence.

Hoping to see you in spring, I remain,

Yours sincerely, C. G. JUNG

☐ An American minister of the Episcopal Church, at that time studying in Canterbury, England.
[1] B. expressed the fear that Jung's psychology might destroy "man's divinely given free will."

To Pastor Willi Bremi

Dear Pastor Bremi,   11 December 1953

My very best thanks for the great and joyful surprise you have given me with your splendid book.[1] I am already reading it eagerly and have learnt much from it that I did not know very well before or even at all. You know how to present a synoptic view without glossing over

☐ Basel.
[1] *Der Weg des protestantischen Menschen von Luther bis Albert Schweitzer* (1953).

essentials. I am now about a third of the way through. It is interesting and positively thrilling to see how it comes to grips with the problems of our time. So far I can follow and agree with you everywhere, only Albert Schweitzer raises a few questions. I rate this man and his scientific achievements very highly and admire his gifts and versatility. But I can see no particular merit in his recognition that Christ and the apostles erred in their expectation of the parousia and that this disappointment had repercussions on the development of ecclesiastical dogma. We have known this for a long time. That he said it out loud was no more than scientific decency. This fact appears in such a glaring light only because it contrasts so strongly with the pusillanimity and dishonesty of others who knew it all along but did not want to admit it. So far as I know, Schweitzer has given no answer to the conclusion that Christ is thereby irremediably *relativized*. What has he to say to that?

What does he do with this shattering admission that Christ was wrong and therefore, perhaps, didn't see clearly in other matters too? For him Christ is the "supreme authority," *primus inter pares*, and one of the best founders of religion along with Pythagoras, Zarathustra, Buddha, Confucius, etc. But that was not how it was originally meant; at any rate no Christian creed and least of all Karl Barth would subscribe to such a judgment. Every well-meaning rationalist and even the Freemasons and anthroposophists with their mental sloppiness could endorse the formula "supreme authority" without hesitation.

Faced with the truly appalling *afflictio animae* of the European man, Schweitzer abdicated from the task incumbent on the theologian, the *cura animarum*, and studied medicine in order to treat the sick *bodies of natives*. For the native this is very gratifying, and I am the first to laud those doctors in the tropics who risked their lives, and frequently lost them, on lonely outposts and under more dangerous circumstances. Yet none of these dead who rest in African earth is surrounded by the halo of a Protestant saint. Nobody speaks of them. Schweitzer is doing no more than his professional duty, like any other medical missionary. Every doctor in the tropics would like nothing better than to build his own hospital on his lonely outpost, but unhappily he hasn't Schweitzer's talent for using money-making lectures and soul-stirring organ recitals for this purpose.

To put it the other way round: What would one think of a highly gifted surgeon and almost irreplaceable specialist who, coming upon a medical enigma, suddenly got himself trained as a Franciscan Father in order to read the Mass to peasants in the remotest corner of Löt- schental[2] and hear their confessions? The Catholic Church would perhaps beatify him and after a few hundred years canonize him *ad maiorem ecclesiae gloriam*. But what would Protestant reason, not to mention the Medical Association, have to say about it?

I'm afraid I can only feel it as painful that Schweitzer found the answer to catastrophic conclusion of his *Quest of the Historical Jesus* in abandoning the *cura animarum* in Europe and becoming a white saviour to the natives. A fatal analogy with Nietzsche springs to mind: "God is dead" and the Superman is born, fully in accordance with the old rule that people who repudiate the gods become gods themselves (example on a grand scale: Russia!). A relativized Christ is no longer the same as the Christ of the gospels. Anyone who relativizes him is in danger of becoming a saviour himself. And where can that best be done? Well, in Africa. I know Africa and I also know how the white doctor is worshipped there, how touchingly and how seductively!

Schweitzer has left it to the Christians in Europe to find out what can be done with a relativized Christ.

Allow me a few words on the ideal of *caritas christiana*. It is a gift or a charisma like faith. There are people who by nature are loving and kind, just as there are people who by nature believe and trust. For them love and faith are a natural expression of life which also benefits their fellow men. For the others, less gifted or not gifted at all, they are barely attainable ideals, a convulsive effort which is felt by their fellows too. Here we come up against the question that is always overlooked: *Who* does the loving and *who* does the believing? In other words, everything may very well depend on *who* performs a certain activity or *how* the agent of a function is constituted, for "the right means in the hands of the wrong man" works mischief, as Chi- nese wisdom rightly says. How induce the necessary *metanoia*[3] if a relativized Christ grips us as much as or as little as a Lao-tse or Mo- hammed? Does the religious relationship really mean nothing but sub- mission to an authority declared to be infallible? Should we all, fol- lowing Schweitzer's banner, emigrate to Africa and cure native diseases when our own *sickness of soul* cries to heaven?

When you write "from Luther to Schweitzer" this raises the ques-

[2] A valley in Canton Valais, on the river Lonza.
[3] = transformation of mind, rethinking; "repent" in Matthew 3:2.

tion: Do you put Luther and Schweitzer for comparison on the same plane? If yes, then the further question arises: What innovation or guidance has Schweitzer brought to the world? He is an eminent scholar and researcher, a brilliant organist, and a medical benefactor to the natives in Lambaréné. He has voiced the well-known fact that Christ was deceived about the parousia and has thus presented the world with a relativized and locally conditioned Christ. The same honour could also be accorded to Prof. Volz, who has given an impressive account of Yahweh's daemonism.[4] Is this Yahweh also the God of the New Testament?

It seems to me that the fate of Protestantism depends in large measure on the answer to these two questions.

In point of charity, Schweitzer's philanthropic activity hardly bears comparison with the achievements of Pastor von Bodelschwingh,[5] General Booth,[6] and countless other *Sancti minores* of Protestantism.

It seems to me, also, that the metaphysical foundations of belief as well as of ethical demands are not a matter of indifference. What one usually hears, "You should want to believe and love," stands in direct contrast to the charismatic character of these gifts. The doctor may occasionally tell a demoralized patient, "You can also want to get well," without seriously supposing that the illness is thereby cured and his *knowledge and skill* are superfluous. The *sermon* is utterly inept as a *cura animarum* since the sickness is an individual affair and cannot be cured in a lecture hall. The doctor has to take account of individual dispositions even when treating only the body. In even higher degree the *cura animarum* is an individual affair that cannot be dealt with from the pulpit.

The answer to the above questions seems to me urgent because no one interested in religion can help seeing in the long run that the Protestant conception of God is unclarified and the Reedemer a dubious authority. How can one pray to relativized gods when one is no longer a pre-Christian?

I beg you, my dear Pastor, not to take my layman's questions amiss. I am not out to criticize Schweitzer personally. I am personally not acquainted with him. But I *am* concerned about religious problems since they affect not only me myself but also my professional activity.

---

[4] Paul Volz, *Das Dämonische in Jahwe* (1924).
[5] Friedrich von Bodelschwingh (1831–1910), German Protestant theologian and social reformer; founded numerous welfare institutions.
[6] William Booth (1829–1912), English Methodist preacher, founder and "General" of the Salvation Army.

The book I have sent you[7] as a return gift may elucidate for you the points of contact between psychology and theological questions.

As a parallel to your mandala[8] I enclose a clipping from the BBC Journal.[9] Again with best thanks,

Very sincerely yours, C. G. JUNG

P.S. Perhaps you will allow me to draw your attention to p. 525. There you derive myth from rational reflections. This viewpoint is superseded. All mythological ascents and descents derive from primitive psychic phenomena, i.e., from the trance states of sorcerers as found in the universal dissemination of shamanism. The trance is regularly bound up with the recitation of journeys to heaven or hell. Other regular features are the climbing of the tree (world-tree, world-mountain, world-axis), reaching the heavenly abode (village, city), winning the heavenly bride (*nuptiae coelestes, hierosgamos*), or the descent to the underworld or world of the dead, or to the "Mother of Animals" at the bottom of the sea. All these are genuine psychic phenomena which can still be observed today in modified form. In the Christian tradition you find the same mythologem in St. Augustine (*Serm. Suppos.* 120, 8): "Procedit Christus quasi sponsus de thalamo suo, praesagio nuptiarum exiit ad campum saeculi . . . pervenit usque ad *crucis torum* et ibi firmavit *ascendendo* coniugium; ubi cum sentiret anhelantem in suspiriis creaturam commercio pietatis se pro coniuge dedit ad poenam . . . et copulavit sibi perpetuo iure matronam."[10] The *arbor crucis*[11] is here interpreted as "marriage bed" (*torus*). The

---

[7] *Aion*, CW 9, ii.

[8] Earlier in the year B. had sent Jung a photo of a mandala done in needlework by an educated schizophrenic woman of 45, a patient in an asylum where he had worked in 1924 as chaplain. The work on the mandala was done most intensively during periods when she felt particularly ill. It is reproduced in Bremi's above-mentioned book, p. 416.

[9] The clipping was from *The Listener*, 23 Apr. 1953, part of Werblowsky's BBC lecture "Psychology and Religion" (cf. Werblowsky, 21 May 53, n. 1), quoting the dream of a patient in analysis who dreamt of a mandala (a tabernacle) in which the centre was missing (the tabernacle was empty).

[10] Cf. *Symbols of Transformation*, CW 5, par. 411: "Like a bridegroom Christ went forth from his chamber, he went out with a presage of his nuptials into the field of the world . . . He came to the marriage bed of the cross, and there, in mounting it, he consummated his marriage. And when he perceived the sighs of the creature, he lovingly gave himself up to the torment in place of his bride . . . and he joined himself to the woman for ever."

[11] = tree of the cross. For the equation of crucifix and tree cf. "The Philosophical Tree," CW 13, chs. 17 and 18.

143

most recent and perhaps most complete collection of shamanistic phenomenology is M. Eliade's *Le Chamanisme*, 1951.[12] Here we have an archetypal psychic experience which can crop up *spontaneously* everywhere. The archetype is part of the psychic substructure and has nothing to do with astronomical or meteorological phenomena.

[12] Cf. Scharschuch, 1 Sept. 52, n. 3.

To Ernest Jones

[ORIGINAL IN ENGLISH]

Dear Jones,   19 December 1953

Of course you have my permission to read Freud's letters, copies of which are in the Freud Archives in New York.

Your biographical material is very interesting although it would have been advisable to consult me for certain facts. For instance you got the story of Freud's fainting attack quite wrong.[1] Also it was by no means the first one; he had such an attack before in 1909 previous to our departure for America in Bremen, and very much under the same psychological circumstances.

Hoping you are going on to continue enjoying old age, I remain,

Yours very truly, C. G. JUNG

☐ Published in *The Freud/Jung Letters* (1974), introduction, p. xxiii, with an account of the history of those letters. See also editor's introduction to the present work.
[1] Cf. Bennet, 21 Nov. 53, n. 1. Jones returned to these fainting fits in *Freud: Life and Work* (London), II, pp. 165f. This earlier attack is described in *Memories*, pp. 156f./152f.

To Pastor Willi Bremi

Dear Pastor Bremi,   26 December 1953

Well knowing how numerous and exacting the duties of a clergyman are during feast days, I had not expected such a prompt and comprehensive answer. There was no hurry at all.

It was very kind of you to explain what is the subjective significance of Schweitzer for you. The *volte face* he made is unquestionably impressive. But I must confess that nihilism[1] was never a problem for me. I had enough and more than enough reality on my own doorstep.

What interests me much more in the case of Schweitzer is the problem his critique has left behind for the religious-minded layman: the *relativized authority of the Christ figure. What does Protestant theology say about that?*

I know Bultmann's answer. It doesn't enlighten me. Karl Barth, like the Catholic Church, can overlook this problem (and for the same reasons).

Reading your detailed account of Kierkegaard, I was once again struck by the discrepancy between the perpetual talk about fulfilling God's will and reality: when God appeared to him in the shape of "Regina"[2] he took to his heels. It was too terrible for him to have to subordinate his autocratism to the love of another person. Nevertheless K. saw something very essential and at the same time very terrifying: that it is God's "passion to love and be loved." Naturally it was just this quality that struck K. most forcibly. One could ascribe plenty of other passions to God which are just as obvious and emphasize his old Jewish character even more strongly—which brings us back to Question 2: *Is Yahweh identical with the God of the New Testament?*

Please don't let yourself be rushed by my letters. I am quite content to hope for an occasional short answer. It is not intellectual curiosity that prompts such questions; I myself am asked so many things that I seize every favourable opportunity to be taught better. With best wishes for the New Year,

Very sincerely yours, C. G. JUNG

[1] B. had answered on 18 Dec., expressing his admiration for Schweitzer's having found his way through the modern crises of nihilism and the denial of religious and moral teachings.

[2] Kierkegaard's lifelong love was Regine Olsen; he was engaged to her but suddenly broke off the engagement. Jung's use of the Latinized form "Regina" is an allusion to the alchemical opus or, psychologically, the process of individuation, in which the partnership of Rex (king = animus) and Regina (queen = anima) is essential for its completion.

To E. L. Grant Watson

[ORIGINAL IN ENGLISH]

Dear Mr. Watson,   25 January 1954

Your dream[1] is remarkable. The dream of the horse represents the union with the animal soul, which you have missed for a long time.

□ (Handwritten.) British author (1885–1970).

145

The union produces a peculiar state of mind, namely an unconscious thinking that enables you to realize the natural progress of the mind in its own sphere. You can understand it as the natural thought-process in the unconscious or as an anticipation of postmortal mental life.[2] (This is a serious possibility inasmuch as the psyche is, at least partially, independent of space and time. Cf. Rhine's experiments with ESP.) The feet represent "standpoint"; Hindus = eastern standpoint. The dream shows your transmutation from the Western outlook to the Eastern realization of the atman = self and its identity with the universal atman. You proceed beyond the ego to ever-widening horizons, where the atman gradually reveals its universal aspect. You integrate your animal, your parents, all the people you love (they all live in you and you are no more separated from them). This is the secret of John XVII: 20 sqq. and at the same time the essential Hindu doctrine of the atman-purusha. Our unconscious definitely prefers the Hindu interpretation of immortality. There is no loneliness, but allness or infinitely increasing completeness.

Such dreams occur at the gateway of death. They interpret the mystery of death. They don't predict it but they show you the right way to approach the end.

Yours sincerely, C. G. JUNG

[1] G. W. reported two dreams. The first, of a magic horse that had been killed in battle, and whose entrails he carries around for many years. Then he goes down some stairs and meets the resuscitated horse coming up. The horse devours all its own entrails, and is ready for the dreamer to mount. — The second dream three or four months later consists of several scenes. The first is of a theatre; when the curtain goes up, all the people on the stage are lying down as though dead. They are, however, conversing with each other, though the dreamer cannot hear what they are saying. After a while he gets on to the stage and lies down too. In the next scene he is in a desert, led by two Hindu guides. He has difficulty in walking because his feet are those of an old man. They come to an open place where an initiation ceremony is going on; deep cuts are made on his feet and he has to stand in boiling water. Thereupon he sees his own idealized image emerge in a huge concave mirror and is told by the guides to continue the journey alone through the desert. He meets two new Hindu guides who lead him to a building where he finds many people, among them his father, stepfather, and his mother, who gives him a kiss of welcome. He has to go on a long climb ending at the edge of a deep precipice. A voice commands him to leap; after several desperate refusals he obeys and finds himself swimming "deliciously into the blue of eternity."

[2] Cf. *Memories*, ch. XI: "On Life After Death."

To Erich Neumann

Dear Neumann,   30 January 1954

Best thanks for your friendly letter. I was just writing to Hull, who is to insert a passage on your work in the English edition of *Symbole der Wandlung*.[1]

The transition to the New Year has not passed without difficulties: liver and intestine revolted against the too oily hotel cooking in Locarno, though this had its good side in that my holiday was 1½ weeks longer than expected.

I have already penetrated a good way into your "Kulturentwicklung"[2] and shall be able to read further as soon as the mountain of letters that have accumulated during my absence is cleared away.

I would abandon the term "Gnostic" without compunction were it not a swearword in the mouths of theologians. They accuse me of the very same fault they commit themselves: presumptuous disregard of epistemological barriers. When a theologian says "God," then God has to be, and be just as the magician wants, without the latter feeling in any way impelled to make clear to himself and his public exactly which concept he is using. He fraudulently offers his (limited) God-concept to the naïve listener as a special revelation. What sort of God is Buber talking about, for instance? Yahweh? With or without *privatio boni*? And if Yahweh, where does he say that this God is certainly not the God of the Christians? This underhand way of doing holy business I fling in the teeth of theologians of all colours. I do not maintain that my "gnostic" images are a faithful reflection of their transcendental background, binding on everyone, or that this is conjured up by my naming it. It is evident that Buber has a bad conscience, as he publishes only *his* letters[3] and does not represent me fairly, since I am a mere Gnostic, though he hasn't the faintest idea of what the Gnostic was moved by. Meanwhile with best regards and wishes,

Yours sincerely, c. g. j u n g

---

[1] Cf. *Symbols of Transformation*, CW 5, par. 3, where Jung refers to N.'s "massive contribution towards solving the countless difficult problems that crop up everywhere in this hitherto little explored territory [of historical and ethnological parallels]."

[2] *Kulturentwicklung und Religion* (1953), containing N.'s 1948–50 Eranos lectures.

[3] Cf. Neumann, 28 Feb. 52, n. 9.

To John Weir Perry

[ORIGINAL IN ENGLISH]

Dear Perry, 8 February 1954

I am sorry that you had to wait so long until you got my answer to your question.[1] All sorts of things have intervened in the meantime, and my health also has misbehaved. I will try to answer your question as simply as possible; it is a difficult problem as you probably realize.

First of all, the regression that occurs in the rebirth or integration process is in itself a normal phenomenon inasmuch as you observe it also with people that don't suffer from any kind of psychopathic ailment. When it is matter of a schizoid condition, you observe very much the same, but with the difference that there is a marked tendency of the patient to get stuck in the archetypal material. In this case, the rebirth process is repeated time and again. This is the reason why the classical schizophrenia develops stereotype conditions. Up to a certain point, you have the same experience with neurotic individuals. This is so because the archetypal material has a curious fascinating influence which tries to assimilate the individuals altogether. They are tempted to identify with any of the archetypal figures characteristic of the rebirth process. For this reason schizophrenic cases retain nearly always a certain markedly childish behaviour. You can observe approximately the same with neurotic patients; either they develop inflations on account of identification with the archetypal figures, or they develop a childish behaviour on account of the identity with the divine child. In all these cases the real difficulty is to free the patients from the fascination. Schizoid cases as well as neurotic ones very often repeat their personal infancy story. This is a favourable sign in so far as it is an attempt to grow up into the world again as they had done before, viz. in their infancy. They are children again after rebirth exactly as you say happened in the *Taurobolia*.[2]

As a rule, you haven't to take care of making patients revive their infantile reminiscences; generally they produce it all by themselves, because it is an unavoidable mechanism, and, as I said, a teleological attempt to grow up again. If you go quietly along with the material

---

[1] "Has it been your experience that in regression and rebirth, as the divine child emerges, the personal infantile complexes and needs tend to coincide and merge with it?"

[2] Ritual baths of initiation in the blood of a sacrificial bull. They were taken over from the cult of Kybele into that of the Indo-Iranian god Mithras. Cf. Perry, *The Self in Psychotic Process*, p. 118.

the patients produce, you will see that they can't help getting into their infantile reminiscences and habits and ways, and that they project particularly the parental images. Wherever there is a transference, you get unavoidably involved and integrated into the patient's family atmosphere. The insistence of the Freudians upon making people revive their past simply shows that in the Freudian analysis people don't naturally take to living their past again, simply because they have resistance against the analyst. If you let the unconscious have its natural way, then you may be sure everything the patient needs to know will be brought up, and you may be equally sure that everything you bring out from the patient by insistence on theoretical grounds will not be integrated into the patient's personality, at least not as a positive value, but maybe as a lasting resistance. Did it never occur to you that in my analysis we talked very little of "resistance," while in the Freudian analysis it is the term that most frequently occurs?

When it comes to schizoid patients, there of course the difficulty of liberating them from the grip of the unconscious is much greater than in ordinary neurotic cases. Often they can't find their way back from their archetypal world to the equivalent personal infantile world where there would be a chance for liberation. Not in vain Christ insists upon "becoming like unto children," which means a conscious resolution to accept the attitude of the child as long as such an attitude is demanded by the circumstances. Since it is always the problem of accepting the shadow, it needs the simplicity of a child to submit to such a seemingly impossible task. So when you find that the rebirth process shows a tendency to repeat itself, you must realize that the fascination of the archetypal material has still to be overcome, perhaps because your help has been insufficient or the patient's attitude was unfavourable to it. But this aetiological question matters little. You simply must try again to convert the archetypal fascination into a child-like simplicity. There are of course many cases where our help is insufficient or comes too late, but that is so in all branches of medicine. I always try to follow the path of nature and I avoid as much as possible the application of theoretical viewpoints, and I have never regretted this principle.

I include a *charming example*[3] of a particularly enlightened Amer-

---

[3] According to a communication from P., this is "a scurrilous and irresistibly witty diatribe called 'Jung Revisited' by Hiram Johnson, in a New Jersey psychiatric journal, of late '53 or early '54." It could not be traced.

ican doctor just for your amusement or as a sort of consolation in case you don't get the desired understanding from your contemporaries.

Hoping you are in good health, I remain,

Yours cordially, c. g. jung

P.S. I think we underrate in Europe the difficulties you have to put up with in America as soon as you try to communicate something to your audience that demands a certain humanistic education. I am afraid that your educational system produces the same technological and scientific one-sidedness and the same social welfare idealism as Russia. Most of your psychologists, as it looks to me, are still in the XVIIIth century inasmuch as they believe that the human psyche is *tabula rasa*[4] at birth, while all somewhat differentiated animals are born with specific instincts. Man's psyche seems to be less [differentiated] than a weaver bird's or a bee's.

---

[4] Jung repeatedly rejected the idea that the child is born with an "empty" psyche (*tabula rasa*, "erased tablet," is the wax writing tablet of the Romans on which the writing was erased after use). He held that "the child is born with a differentiated brain that is predetermined by heredity" ("Concerning the Archetypes, with Special Reference to the Anima Concept," CW 9, i, par. 136).

To John D. Barrett

[ORIGINAL IN ENGLISH]

Dear Barrett, 11 February 1954

Many thanks for kindly sending me my royalty statements. Recently I saw Kurt Wolff[1] and his wife; we talked about many things although not exactly about the things I want to mention in this letter.

From a number of mutually independent American reactions to the general purpose and activity of the Bollingen Foundation, I concluded that the said Foundation must be an unusual exception in the United States. I got the impression of a small island in an infinite sea of misunderstanding and flatness. I didn't realize what it means for the level of education when there is an almost complete absence of the humanities, and now can more appreciate the genius of Mrs.

□ President until 1969 of the Bollingen Foundation, New York, which sponsored the publication of the Collected Works and of the present selection; editor of Bollingen Series.
[1] Cf. Wolff, 1 Feb. 58, n. □.

Mellon[2] who planned the Bollingen Foundation with Paul Mellon's generous aid.

I just wanted to let you know that it is difficult for a European to size up such a mental condition which he does not know from his own country. When I hear of the difficulties of my pupils in the States whose main task is teaching, I am profoundly impressed by the effects of a one-sided education in natural sciences; all the more I know how to appreciate the cultural importance of your Foundation. It is a shining beacon in the darkness of the atomic age. I heard that my books are well on the way, and I am quite overwhelmed by the speed with which they are turned out from the press. Thank you personally for all the trouble you have had in getting the things on the way, and your patience with my impatience.

Hoping you have begun this new year with an optimistic outlook, I remain,

Yours cordially, C. G. JUNG

[2] Mary Conover Mellon, first wife of Paul Mellon; see Mellon, 19 June 40, n. □. Also cf. Thompson, 23 Sept. 49, n. 1.

To G. A. *van den Bergh von Eysinga*

[ORIGINAL IN ENGLISH]

Dear Sir,   13 February 1954

In the meantime, somebody helped me to a careful excerpt of your critique.[1] There seems to me some misunderstanding of my basic ideas.

First of all, I am not a philosopher and my concepts are not philosophical and abstract, but empirical, viz. *biological*. The concept generally misunderstood is that of the *archetype*, which covers certain biological facts and is not a hypostatized idea at all. The "archetype" is practically synonymous with the biological concept of the *behaviour pattern*. But as the latter designates external phenomena chiefly, I have chosen the term "archetype" for "psychic pattern." We don't know whether the weaver-bird beholds a mental image while it follows an immemorial and inherited model in building its nest, but there is

□ (1874–1957), Dutch professor of theology.
[1] Unidentifiable, but the context makes it clear that it was a critical review of *Answer to Job*.

151

no doubt that no weaver-bird in our experience has ever invented its nest. It is as if the image of nest-building were born with the bird.[2]

As no animal is born without its instinctual patterns, there is no reason whatever to believe that man should be born without his specific forms of physiological and psychological reactions. As animals of the same kind show the same instinctual phenomena all over the world, man also shows the same archetypal forms no matter where he lives. As animals have no need to be taught their instinctive activities, so man also possesses his primordial psychic patterns and repeats them spontaneously, independently of any kind of teaching. Inasmuch as man is conscious and capable of introspection, it is quite possible that he can perceive his instinctual patterns in the form of archetypal representations. As a matter of fact, these possess the expected degrees of universality (cf. the remarkable identity of shamanistic structures). It is also possible to observe their spontaneous reproduction in individuals entirely ignorant of traditions of this sort. Such facts prove the autonomy of the archetypes.

The pattern of behaviour is *autonomous* also inasmuch as it enforces its own application as soon as the general conditions allow. Nobody would assume that the biological pattern is a philosophical assumption like the Platonic idea or a Gnostic hypostasis. The same is true of the archetype. Its autonomy is an *observable fact* and not a philosophical hypostasis. I am a physician and I am practising as a psychiatrist, thus having plenty of opportunity to observe mental phenomena which are unknown to philosophy in spite of the fact that Pierre Janet's *Automatisme psychologique*[3] was published almost 70 years ago.

Your critique of my poetic licence: the *night* surrounding the *mulier amicta sole*,[4] is correct in so far as the text does not mention the night. But it isn't so far away when you can see the dragon removing one third of the stars from heaven.[5] My mythologem obviously points to Leto,[6] to the heroes' mothers in general, and to the matriarchal mother goddesses and their chthonic and nocturnal associations. But this is hardly of any importance.

To mention another point: if Yahweh was not influenced by Satan,

---

[2] Concerning the relation of archetype and pattern of behaviour, cf. "On the Nature of the Psyche," CW 8, pars. 398 & 435.

[3] *L'Automatisme psychologique* (1889).

[4] Rev. 12:1: "a woman clothed with the sun." Cf. "Answer to Job," par. 711.

[5] Rev. 12:4.

[6] "Answer to Job," pars. 711, 713.

as you apparently assume, then he tortured Job against his own better conviction, which makes his case only worse. Yahweh's amorality has nothing to do with a moral differentiation of the believers. It exists still today and is recognized even by theological textbooks although his uncontrolled affects and his injustice are swallowed without the consequences even drawn by the Midrashim[7] long ago. (F.i. the admonition to the Lord to remember his better qualities; the sounding of the shofar[8] to remind him of murderous attempt against Isaac, etc.)

It is regrettable that you did not read my introductory remarks. You might have discovered there my *empirical standpoint* without which—I grant you—my little book makes no sense at all. Envisaged from a philosophical point of view without consideration of its psychological premise, it is sheer idiocy, from a theological angle nothing but downright blasphemy and from the standpoint of rationalistic commonsense a heap of illogical and feeble-minded phantasmata. But psychology has its own proposition and its own working hypotheses based upon the observation of facts, i.e. (in our case) of the *spontaneous reproduction of archetypal structures* appearing in dreams as well as in psychoses. If one doesn't know of these facts, it will be difficult to understand what is meant by "psychic reality" and "psychic autonomy."

I agree with you that my statements (in *Antwort auf Hiob*) are shocking, but not more, rather less so, than the manifestations of Yahweh's demonic nature in the OT. The Midrashim are quite aware of it, and the Christian church had to invent that awful syllogism, the *privatio boni*, in order to annihilate the original ambivalence of the Jewish God. But while the Catholic Church has at least a sort of *sententia communis* explaining the transmutation of Yahweh, who *ad instar rhinocerotis*[9] had upset the world in the OT, into the God of love in the NT, Protestantism clings to an identity of the two gods and does not allow of a transformation of the One God. This is a

---

[7] Cf. *Aion*, pars. 106ff.

[8] The shofar is a kind of bugle made of a ram's horn. It has a loud tone useful for signalling (cf. Judges 3:27 and Job 39:24f.) and is blown on the Jewish New Year to announce its coming. The passage referred to is from J. Fromer and M. Schnitzer, *Legenden aus dem Talmud* (1922), pp. 34f., quoted in "Transformation Symbolism in the Mass," CW 11, par. 406, n. 25.

[9] Cf. ibid., par. 408 & n. 28: ". . . the learned Jesuit, Nicolas Caussin, declared that the unicorn was a fitting symbol for the God of the Old Testament, because in his wrath he reduced the world to confusion like an angry rhinoceros (unicorn), until, overcome by the love of a pure virgin, he was changed in her lap into a God of Love."

scandalum. But theologians suffer from the fact that when they say "God," then that God *is.* But when I say "God," I know I have expressed my image of such a being and I am honestly not quite sure whether he is just like my image or not, even if I believe in God's existence. When Martin Buber speaks of God, he does not tell us which God, but he assumes that his God is the only one. My God-image corresponds to an *autonomous* archetypal pattern. Therefore I can experience God as if he were an object, but I need not assume that it is the only image. I know I am dealing, as Kant says, with a "symbolical anthropomorphism" which concerns "language" (and mimic representation in general) but *not the object itself.*[10] To criticize intentional or unintentional anthropomorphism is neither blasphemy, nor superstition, but wholly within the province of psychological criticism. I remain, dear Sir,

Yours faithfully, C. G. JUNG

[10] Kant, *Prolegomena,* Part III, par. 57.

To James Kirsch

Dear Kirsch,   16 February 1954

. . .

I scarcely think that the Jews have to accept the Christ symbol. They need only understand its meaning. Christ wanted to change Yahweh into a moral God of goodness, but in so doing he tore apart the opposites (Satan falling from heaven, Luke 10:18) that were united in him (God) though in an inharmonious and unconscious way; hence the suspension between the opposites at the crucifixion. The purpose of the Christian reformation through Jesus was to eliminate the evil moral consequences that were caused by the amoral divine prototype. One cannot "strain at a gnat and swallow a camel" (Matt. 23:24) or "serve two masters" (Matt. 6:24) at the same time.

This moral differentiation is a necessary step on the way of individuation. Without thorough knowledge of "good and evil," ego and shadow, there is no recognition of the self, but at most an involuntary and therefore dangerous identification with it.

The Jew has roughly the same moral development behind him as the Christian European, consequently he has the same problem. A

□ (Handwritten.) Published (in K.'s tr.) in *Psychological Perspectives,* III:2 (fall 1972).

Jew can recognize the *self* in that hostile pair of brothers, Christ and Satan, as well as I can or perhaps even better, and with it the incarnation or Yahweh's assimilation to man. Naturally the status of man is profoundly altered because of this.

The Jew has the advantage of having long since anticipated the development of consciousness in his own spiritual history. By this I mean the Lurianic stage of the Kabbalah, the breaking of the vessels and man's help in restoring them.[1] Here the thought emerges for the first time that man must help God to repair the damage wrought by the Creation. For the first time man's cosmic responsibility is acknowledged. Naturally it is a question of the self and not the ego, although the latter will be deeply affected.

That is the answer I would give a Jew. With best regards,

Yours sincerely, c. g. j u n g

[1] Cf. Kirsch, 18 Nov. 52, n. 4.

To the Rev. Erastus Evans

[ORIGINAL IN ENGLISH]

Dear Mr. Evans,   17 February 1954

Allow me to tell you that I am profoundly grateful to you for your most remarkably objective review[1] of my uncouth attempt to disturb the obnoxious somnolence of the guardians. That is the way in which this damnable little book looks to me. *Habent sua fata libelli!* I would not have written this thing. I had kept away from it studiously. I had published before the volume *Aion* in polite language and as much man-made as possible. It was not sufficient apparently, because I got ill and when I was in the fever it caught me and brought me down to writing despite my fever, my age, and my heart that is none too good. I can assure you I am a moral coward as long as possible. As a good little bourgeois citizen, I am lying low and concealed as deeply as possible, still shocked by the amount of the indiscretions I have committed, swearing to myself that there would be no more of it because I want peace and friendly neighbourhood and a good conscience and the sleep of the just. Why should I be the unspeakable fool to jump into the cauldron?

☐ London.

[1] *An Assessment of Jung's "Answer to Job"* (Guild of Pastoral Psychology, Lecture No. 78; London, 1954).

Well, I don't want to be melodramatic. This is just for your personal information. I have no merit and no proper guilt since I got to it "like a dog to a kick," as we say. And the little moral coward I am goes on whining: why should I be always the one that collects all available kicks?

I tell you these things because you have been nice, just, and lenient with me. The attribute "coarse" is mild in comparison to what you feel when God dislocates your hip or when he slays the firstborn. I bet Jacob's punches he handed to the angel were not just caresses or polite gestures.[2] They were of the good hard kind; as you rightly say, "with the gloves off."

That is *one side* of my experiences with what is called "God." "Coarse" is too weak a word for it. "Crude," "violent," "cruel," "bloody," "hellish," "demonic" would be better. That I was not downright blasphemous I owe to my domestication and polite cowardice. And at each step I felt hindered by a beatific vision of which I'd better say nothing.

You have interpreted my thoughts most admirably. There is only one point where it seems to me you slipped up, viz. in attributing the traditional, dogmatic, and "colloquial" picture of Christ to me. This is not my personal idea of Christ at all, as I am quite in sympathy with a much darker and harsher image of the man Jesus. The dogmatic and traditional conception of Christ however must be and is made as bright as possible—*lumen de lumine*[3]—and the black substance all in the other corner.

You have probably been shocked by the idea of the "hostile brethren"[4] and the incomplete incarnation.[5] If it had been complete, the logical consequence, the *parousia*, would have taken place. But Christ was in error about it.

Practically, it makes no difference whether the Christ of the gospels

[2] Cf. *Memories*, p. 344/317, where the situation of the individual who is compelled by dire necessity to act with "savage fatefulness"—as Jung was when writing "Job"—is illustrated by the story of Jacob's fight with the angel (Gen. 32:24ff.).
[3] Cf. White, 24 Nov. 53, n. 16.
[4] In "Answer to Job," CW 11, pars. 628f., it is argued that Satan and Christ, following the pattern of Cain and Abel, correspond to the archetype of the hostile brothers. The parallel is quite explicit in "Dogma of the Trinity," CW 11, par. 254, n. 19.
[5] "Answer to Job," pars. 657f.: "God's Incarnation in Christ requires continuation and completion because Christ, owing to his virgin birth and his sinlessness, was not an empirical being at all. . . . Christ is the first-born who is succeeded by an ever-increasing number of younger brothers and sisters." Cf. Matt. 16:27f.

is undergoing an enantiodromia[6] into the relentless judge of the Revelations, or the God of love becoming the Destroyer.

Christ has an opposite—the Antichrist or (and) the Devil. If you see a bit too much darkness in his picture, you make him too much into the likeness of his father, and then it becomes difficult to understand why he taught a God so very different from the one of the OT. Or you disown the whole Christian tradition of the better part of 1900 years.

Christ is most decidedly not the whole Godhead as God is ἕν τὸ πᾶν.[7] Christ is the Anthropos that seems to be a prefiguration of what the Holy Ghost is going to bring forth in the human being. (I wish you would read my volume *Aion*, where you find most of the material behind *Answer to Job*.) In a tract of the *Lurianic Kabbalah*, the remarkable idea is developed that man is destined to become God's helper in the attempt to restore the vessels[8] which were broken when God thought to create a world. Only a few weeks ago, I came across this impressive doctrine which gives meaning to man's status exalted by the incarnation. I am glad that I can quote at least one voice in favour of my rather involuntary manifesto. Or don't you think that mankind should produce some adequate reflections before it blows itself up into eternity? I realized something when fire was raining upon German cities and Hiroshima was flashed out of existence. I thought it is a rather drastic world in which we live. There is a proverb that says: a coarse block wants a coarse wedge. No time for niceties! This is one of the troubles of our Christianity. I remain, dear Mr. Evans,

Yours gratefully, C. G. JUNG

[6] Literally, "running counter to," a philosophical term coined by Heraclitus, who conceived the universe as a conflict of opposites ruled by eternal justice. Jung used the term to describe "the emergence of the unconscious opposite in the course of time." Cf. *Psychological Types*, CW 6, Def. 18.
[7] = the One, the All.
[8] Cf. Kirsch, 18 Nov. 52, n. 4.

To E. Schwarz

Dear Dr. Schwarz, 2 March 1954

The concept of finality seems to me a logical complement of causality, and I therefore think that only the two aspects make up the sumtotal of causality.

Just as the connection between cause and effect is a necessity, so is the connection of the so-called final cause with the result. Without necessity there is neither causality nor finality, although there are not a few people nowadays who treat the concept of causality very incautiously.

Finality shows itself in the teleological character of biological phenomena; but I would not know where finality could be pointed out in the realm of the inorganic. The 4 aspects of causality[1] make possible a homogeneous causal viewpoint but not a total one. For this purpose, it seems to me, causality (in all its aspects) has to be complemented by acausality. Not simply because freedom also is guaranteed in a law-bound world, but because freedom, i.e., acausality, does in fact exist. In order to express such a proposition, however, one must have a "rigorous" concept of causality, using the term "causality" only when it is really a matter of necessary connections, and "acausality" only when a causal connection is not even thinkable, e.g., in *hysteron-proteron*,[2] where an event in the present appears to be caused by a future event.

As for your question about faith,[3] I must emphasize that there are apparently two realities: objective and subjective, by reason of the fact that objective reality can be established as being nonpsychic, whereas psychic reality cannot be established as being objective in the same sense. But this is due primarily to the unavoidable premise that perception and judgment are themselves psychic, and that consequently one cannot jump over one's own head. Nevertheless, the reality of the psyche can be established by means of verified statements or objectively verifiable symptoms. Hoping I have answered your questions, I remain,

Yours sincerely, C. G. JUNG

☐ Neustadt, Germany.

[1] Cf. Schopenhauer's "On the Fourfold Root of the Principle of Sufficient Reason," *Two Essays* (1889); also Aristotle's distinction between material, formal, efficient, and final causes necessary for a complete judgment.

[2] = the latter [put as] the former: a false argument in which what should come second is put first. Colloquially, "putting the cart before the horse."

[3] Concerning Jung's faith in God in relation to his statements in "Answer to Job."

To James Kirsch

Dear Kirsch, 5 March 1954

. . .

The integration of the collective unconscious amounts roughly to taking cognizance of the world and adapting to it. This does not mean that one would have to learn to know the whole world, or that one must have lived in all climates and continents of the world. The integration of the unconscious is always, of course, only a very relative affair, and refers only to the constellated material, not to its total theoretical scope. John of the Cross's "Dark Night of the Soul" has nothing to do with this.[1] Rather, integration is a conscious confrontation, a dialectical process such as I have described in my essay "The Relations between the Ego and the Unconscious." A great deal of fog seems to have spread itself over this point. With best regards,

Yours very sincerely, c. g. j u n g

☐ (Handwritten.) Published (in K.'s tr.) in *Psychological Perspectives*, III:2 (fall 1972).

[1] K. had asked whether individuation involved integrating the whole collective unconscious and whether "The Dark Night of the Soul" of St. John of the Cross (1542–91) described such an integration.

To D. Cappon

[ORIGINAL IN ENGLISH]

Dear Doctor Cappon, 15 March 1954

Concerning your question about the physical substratum of mental facts like archetypes, this is a problem I hardly dare to touch. It invites all sorts of funny speculations, and that is exactly what I try to avoid. If you say they repose on the genes, you can't go wrong. Everything depends upon them.

The same question would arise with instincts. Where are they localized? With the vertebrates, one would assume that they are based upon the brain and its annexes, but where are they localized in an insect that has no brain? Obviously, in the sympathetic nervous system. You can also hold that an instinctual pattern being identical

☐ Formerly professor of psychiatry, now professor of environmental studies, York University, Toronto. He wrote as "a lone exponent of 'dynamic' (analytical) psychology" who had "run across many problems and much resistance."

with an archetype is based upon our sympathicus. But all this is mythology, quite unwarrantable from an epistemological standpoint, and just as inadmissible as these ridiculous fantasies about intra-uterine psychological experiences.

I am personally convinced that our mind corresponds with the physiological life of the body, but the way in which it is connected with the body is for obvious reasons unintelligible. To speculate about such unknowable things is mere waste of time. If you want to be quite accurate, both statements, viz. that the psyche is founded upon an organic process of the body, or that the psyche is independent of the body, are unanswerable. The question of brain localization is an extremely delicate one, because when you destroy a certain part of the brain you destroy a certain function. Yet you do not know whether you have really destroyed the function because it is quite possible that you have only destroyed the transmitter of that function, as if you have taken away the telephone apparatus which does not mean that you have killed its owner. There is even no absolute certainty about the psyche being definitely dependent upon the brain since we know that there are facts proving that the mind can relativize space and time, as the Rhine experiments and general experience have proved sufficiently. As I have already pointed out, the archetypes are the psychological representations of instinctual patterns, and behave exactly like these. How did the instincts get into an individual? Instincts have been inherited since time immemorial, and presumably have developed with the different species. Thus, they are certainly in most cases millions of years old. Also with regard to instincts, it is questionable if they continue to exist when you have destroyed their transmitter, i.e., whether they have been killed themselves.

It is quite obvious that it is not at all necessary to uncover the archetypes in every treatment of neurosis. One can get along successfully with far less, but it is equally true that it is sometimes not at all in your hand to decide whether you will go into archetypes or not, since they turn up all by themselves, sometimes with a vehemence you wouldn't like. I never look for archetypes and don't try to find them; enough when they come all by themselves. This is almost regularly the case when an analysis lasts a bit long or when it is matter of a person with a somewhat vivacious mind.

1.[1] There is no point in trying to make a patient understand arche-

___

[1] C. made three points: 1. that although archetypal images emerged early in analysis they could be understood only much later; 2. that by then all symptoms

typal material as long as he has not yet gained some insight into his personal complexes, and particularly into the nature of his shadow.

2. The patient may be practically cured without ever having heard of an archetype.

3. One has cured neurosis by the most astonishing means long before our modern psychology. If there are no technical means, it is the sincerity of the doctor's attitude and his willingness to help that restore the impaired wholeness of the patient, but if you withhold a better technical knowledge, you wouldn't be able to get any proper result with less. The successful therapeutic attitude always expects of you that you really do your best, no matter how good or how bad it is, or what kind of technique you apply. Only you must be sure that you do the best you know.

I should not worry about all this localization talk. It's practically all foolishness, and a remnant of the old brain mythology like the explanation of sleep through the contraction of the ganglia, which is by no means more intelligent than the localization of the psyche in the pituitary gland.[2]

Hoping I have answered your question, I remain, dear Doctor Cappon,

Yours sincerely, c. g. jung

---

may have disappeared; 3. that psychoanalysis produced good results without using archetypal interpretations.

[2] The pituitary gland, located at the base of the brain, is intimately connected with the build, character, and behaviour of the individual. For Jung's views on "physiological or 'organic' hypotheses with respect to psychological processes" cf. *Psychological Types*, CW 6, par. 479.

To Philip Metman

Dear Mr. Metman,   27 March 1954

Many thanks for your kind letter, which interested me very much. I gather with great concern that you have had a hair-breadth escape from a car accident. The accident has affected only the outer shell, but evidently you and your wife were not affected physically by this broad hint. Naturally this may have an inner connection with what

□ (1893–1965), German-born analytical psychologist, practised in England from 1936. Cf. his *Mythos und Schicksal* (1936).

you are writing, for experience shows that accidents of this sort are very often connected with creative energy which turns against us because somehow it is not given due heed. This may easily happen, for we always judge by what we already know and very seldom listen to what we don't yet know. Therefore we can easily take a step in the wrong direction or continue too long on the right path until it becomes the wrong one. Then it may happen that in this rather ungentle way we are forced to change our attitude.

I shall soon turn to your manuscript,[1] for just now I am once again preoccupied willy-nilly with the question of synchronicity and astrology. I have had to suppress the chapter on astrology altogether in the English edition,[2] since apparently no one can understand it. I am now reducing it to a few pages without any tables. Maybe I shall succeed this time in making the risqué joke of an acausal arrangement accessible to my public. Meanwhile with best regards,

Yours sincerely, c. g. JUNG

P.S. I would be glad to welcome you here on October 10th, but you know how it is in old age: one promises something and knows that everything is only provisional.

[1] *Some Reflections on the Meaning of Illness* (Guild of Pastoral Psychology, Lecture No. 83; London, 1954).
[2] The chapter "An Astrological Experiment" was not suppressed but had to undergo certain changes (cf. Hull, 3 Aug. 53, n. 2; also Fordham, 24 Jan. 55, n. 1). A much abbreviated version, without tables, was subsequently published in *Zeitschrift für Parapsychologie und Grenzgebiete der Psychologie* (Bern), I:2/3 (May 1958). It is translated in CW 18, pars. 1174ff.

To Aniela Jaffé

Dear Aniela,   Bollingen, 6 April 1954

Best thanks for your excellent review[1]—I have nothing to correct in it! After all the rubbish that gets delivered to my house on my work, it is such a pleasure to find something understanding and friendly for once. I often ask myself why by far the most of my "critics" are so unfriendly and unobjective? Is my style so irritating, or what is it in

☐ (Handwritten.)
[1] MS of "C. G. Jung: 'Von den Wurzeln des Bewusstseins,'" *Tages-Anzeiger für Stadt und Kanton Zürich*, 29 Apr. 1954.

me that the world finds so offensive? This is understandable with *Job*, for that was its purpose. Now I have been irritated enough.

Your pious wishes for good weather were fulfilled only on Sunday, but then totally. Now the weather is beastlier than ever, so that one can only huddle behind the stove. I busy myself chiefly with cooking, eating and sleeping. In between I am writing a long letter to Pater White. He has—thanks be to God—chosen the better course of facing his difficulties with complete honesty. I now see clearly what a fatal challenge my psychology is for a theologian but, it seems, not only for him.

I observe myself in the stillness of Bollingen and with all my experience of nearly eight decades must admit that I have found no rounded answer to myself. I am just as much in doubt about myself as before, the more so the more I try to say something definite. It is as though familiarity with oneself alienated one from oneself still further. Cordially,

Yours ever, C. G.

To Father Victor White

[ORIGINAL IN ENGLISH]

Dear Victor,   Bollingen, 10 April 1954

Your letter[1] has been lying on my desk waiting for a suitable time to be answered. In the meantime I was still busy with a preface I had promised to P. Radin and K. Kerényi. They are going to bring out a book together about the figure of the *trickster*.[2] He is the collective shadow. I finished my preface yesterday. I suppose you know the Greek-Orthodox priest Dr. Zacharias?[3] He has finished his book representing a reception, or better—an attempt—to integrate Jungian psychology into Christianity as he sees it. Dr. Rudin S.J. from the Institute of Apologetics did not like it. Professor Gebhard Frei on the other hand was very positive about it.

[1] W. wrote a long letter on 3 Mar. 54 in answer to Jung's of 24 Nov. 53, expressing agreement with most of what he said. It deals largely with Jung's views on the problem of "Christ's shadow," which contradict the Catholic doctrine that Christ knew everything (and therefore could not have a shadow).
[2] Jung's commentary "On the Psychology of the Trickster Figure" (CW 9, i) for Paul Radin, *The Trickster* (1956; orig. *Der göttliche Schelm*, 1954). Kerényi wrote the other commentary.
[3] Cf. Zacharias, 24 Aug. 53.

163

I am puzzled about your conception of Christ and I try to understand it. It looks to me as if you were mixing up the idea of Christ being human and being divine. Inasmuch as he is divine he knows, of course, everything, because all things macrocosmic are supposed to be microcosmic as well and can therefore be said to be known by the self. (Things moreover behave as if they were known.) It is an astonishing fact, indeed, that the collective unconscious seems to be in contact with nearly everything. There is of course no empirical evidence for such a generalization, but plenty of it for its indefinite extension. The *sententia*, therefore: *animam Christi nihil ignoravisse*[4] etc. is not contradicted by psychological experience. *Rebus sic stantibus*, Christ as the self can be said *ab initio cognovisse omnia* etc. I should say that Christ knew his shadow—Satan—whom he cut off from himself right in the beginning of his career. The self is a unit, consisting however of two, i.e., of opposites, otherwise it would not be a totality. Christ has consciously divorced himself from his shadow. Inasmuch as he is divine, he is the self, yet only its white half. Inasmuch as he is human, he has never lost his shadow completely, but seems to have been conscious of it. How could he say otherwise: "Do not call me good . . ."?[5] It is also reasonable to believe that as a human he was not wholly conscious of it, and inasmuch as he was unconscious he projected it indubitably. The split through his self made him as a human being as good as possible, although he was unable to reach the degree of perfection his white self already possessed. The Catholic doctrine cannot but declare that *Christ even as a human being knew everything*. This is the logical consequence of the perfect union of the *duae naturae*. Christ as understood by the Church is to me a spiritual, i.e., mythological being; even his humanity is divine as it is generated by the celestial Father and exempt from original sin. When I speak of him as a human being, I mean its few traces we can gather from the gospels. It is not enough for the reconstruction of an empirical character. Moreover even if we could reconstruct an individual personality, it would not fulfil the role of redeemer and God-man who is identical with the "all-knowing" self. Since the individual human being is characterized by a selection of tendencies and qualities, it is a specification and not a wholeness, i.e., it cannot be indi-

---

[4] "Christ's soul was not ignorant of anything." This and the following *ab initio cognovisse omnia* ("from the beginning he knew everything") are two statements of the Holy Roman Office (one of the eleven departments of the Roman Curia) laid down in 1918 and quoted by W.

[5] Cf. Matthew 19:17, Mark 10:18, Luke 18:19.

vidual without incompleteness and restriction, whereas the Christ of the doctrine is perfect, complete, whole and therefore not individual at all, but a collective mythologem, viz. an archetype. He is far more divine than human and far more universal than individual.

Concerning the omniscience it is important to know that *Adam* already was equipped with supernatural knowledge according to Jewish and Christian tradition,[6] all the more so Christ.

I think that the great split[7] in those days was by no means a mistake but a very important collective fact of synchronistic correspondence with the then new aeon of Pisces. Archetypes, in spite of their conservative nature, are not static but *in a continuous dramatic flux.* Thus the self as a monad or continuous unit would be dead. But it lives inasmuch as it splits and unites again. There is no energy without opposites!

All conservatives and institutionalists are Pharisees, if you apply this name without prejudice. Thus it was to be expected that just the better part of Jewry would be hurt most by the revelation of an exclusively good God and loving Father. This novelty emphasized with disagreeable clearness that the Yahweh hitherto worshipped had some additional, less decorous propensities. For obvious reasons the orthodox Pharisees could not defend their creed by insisting on the bad qualities of their God. Christ with his teaching of an exclusively good God must have been most awkward for them. They probably believed him to be hypocritical, since this was his main objection against them. One gets that way when one has to hold on to something which once has been good and had meant considerable progress or improvement at the time. It was an enormous step forward when Yahweh revealed himself as a *jealous* God, letting his chosen people feel that he was after them with blessings and with punishments, and that God's goal was man. Not knowing better, they cheated him by obeying his Law literally. But as Job discovered Yahweh's primitive amorality, God found out about the trick of observing the Law and swallowing camels.[8]

The old popes and bishops succeeded in getting so much heathendom, barbarism and real evil out of the Church that it became much better than some centuries before: there were no Alexander VI,[9] no auto-da-fés, no thumbscrews and racks any more, so that the com-

---

[6] *Mysterium,* CW 14, pars. 570ff.

[7] The separation of Christ, the epitome of good, from his shadow, the devil.

[8] Matthew 23:24: "Ye blind guides, which strain at a gnat, and swallow a camel."

[9] Rodrigo Borgia (1431–1503), the most notorious of the corrupt and venal popes of the Renaissance.

pensatory drastic virtues (asceticism etc.) lost their meaning to a certain extent. The great split, having been a merely spiritual fact for a long time, has at last got into the world, as a rule in its coarsest and least recognizable form, viz. as the iron curtain, the completion of the second Fish.[10]

Now a new synthesis must begin. But how can absolute evil be connected and identified with absolute good? It seems to be impossible. When Christ withstood Satan's temptation, that was the fatal moment when the shadow was cut off. Yet it had to be cut off in order to enable man to become morally conscious. If the moral opposites could be united at all, they would be suspended altogether and there could be no morality at all. That is certainly not what synthesis aims at. In such a case of irreconcilability the opposites are united by a neutral or ambivalent bridge, a symbol expressing either side in such a way that they can function together.[11] This symbol is the *cross* as interpreted of old, viz. as the tree of life or simply as the tree to which Christ is inescapably affixed. This particular feature points to the compensatory significance of the tree: the tree symbolizes that entity from which Christ had been separated and with which he ought to be connected again to make his life or his being complete. In other words, the *Crucifixus* is the symbol uniting the absolute moral opposites. Christ represents the light; the tree, the darkness; he the son, it the mother. Both are *androgynous* (tree = phallus).[12] Christ is so much identical with the cross that both terms have become almost interchangeable in ecclesiastical language (f.i. "redeemed through Christ or through the cross" etc.). The tree brings back all that has been lost through Christ's extreme spiritualization, namely the elements of nature. Through its branches and leaves the tree gathers the powers of light and air, and through its roots those of the earth and the water. Christ was suffering on account of his split and he recovers his perfect

[10] The astrological sign of Pisces consists of two fishes which were frequently regarded as moving in opposite directions. Traditionally, the reign of Christ corresponds to the first fish and ended with the first millennium, whereas the second fish coincides with the reign of Antichrist, now nearing its end with the entry of the vernal equinox into the sign of Aquarius. Cf. *Aion*, CW 9, ii, pars. 148f., and "Answer to Job," CW 11, par. 725.

[11] The bridge is the "uniting symbol," which represents psychic totality, the self. Cf. *Psychological Types*, CW 6, par. 828.

[12] The tree often symbolizes the mother and appears as such in the numerous tree-birth myths (cf. *Symbols of Transformation*, CW 5, Part II, ch. V). But it is also a phallic symbol and thus has an androgynous character. (For Christ's androgyny cf. *Mysterium*, pars. 526, 565 & n. 63.)

166

life at Easter, when he is buried again in the womb of the virginal mother. (Represented also in the myth of Attis by the tree, to which an image of Attis was nailed, then cut down and carried into the cave of the mother Kybele.[13] The Nativity Church of Bethlehem is erected over an Attis sanctuary!)[14] This mythical complex seems to represent a further development of the old drama, existence becoming real through reflection in consciousness, Job's tragedy.[15] But now it is the problem of dealing with the results of conscious discrimination. The first attempt is moral appreciation and decision for the Good. Although this decision is indispensable, it is not too good in the long run. You must not get stuck with it, otherwise you grow out of life and die slowly. Then the one-sided emphasis on the Good becomes doubtful, but there is apparently no possibility of reconciling Good and Evil. That is where we are now.

The symbolic history of the Christ's life shows, as the essential teleological tendency, the crucifixion, viz. the union of Christ with the symbol of the tree. It is no longer a matter of an impossible reconciliation of Good and Evil, but of man with his vegetative (= unconscious) life. In the case of the Christian symbol the tree however is dead and man upon the Cross is going to die, i.e., the solution of the problem takes place after death. That is so as far as Christian truth goes. But it is possible that the Christian symbolism expresses man's mental condition in the aeon of Pisces, as the ram and the bull gods do for the ages of Aries and Taurus. In this case the post-mortal solution would be symbolic of an entirely new psychological status, viz. that of Aquarius, which is certainly a oneness, presumably that of the Anthropos, the realization of Christ's allusion: "*Dii estis.*"[16] This is a formidable secret and difficult to understand, because it means that man will be essentially God and God man. The signs pointing in this direction consist in the fact that the cosmic power of self-destruction is given into the hands of man and that man inherits the dual nature of the Father. He will [mis]understand it and he will be tempted to ruin the universal life of the earth by radioactivity. Materialism and

[13] Attis was one of the young dying gods, the lover of Kybele, the Great Mother goddess of Anatolia. In her rites, taking place in March, a pine tree, symbol of Attis, was carried into her sanctuary. Cf. White, 25 Nov. 50, n. 5.

[14] A sanctuary of Adonis, another young dying god closely related to Attis, existed since ancient times in a cave at Bethlehem. It is supposed to be identical with Christ's birthplace, over which Constantine the Great (*ca.* 288–337) had a basilica built.

[15] Cf. *Memories*, pp. 338f./312, and Neumann, 10 Mar. 59.

[16] "Ye are gods." John 10:34.

atheism, the negation of God, are indirect means to attain this goal. Through the negation of God one becomes deified, i.e., god-almighty-like, and then one knows what is good for mankind. That is how destruction begins. The intellectual schoolmasters in the Kremlin are a classic example. The danger of following the same path is very great indeed. It begins with the lie, i.e., the projection of the shadow.

There is need of people knowing about their shadow, because there must be somebody who does not project. They ought to be in a visible position where they would be expected to project and unexpectedly they do not project! They can thus set a visible example which would not be seen if they were invisible.

There is certainly Pharisaism, law consciousness, power drive, sex obsession, and the wrong kind of formalism in the Church. But these things are symptoms that the old showy and easily understandable ways and methods have lost their significance and should be slowly replaced by more meaningful principles. This indeed means trouble with the Christian vices. Since you cannot overthrow a whole world because it harbours also some evil, it will be a more individual or "local" fight with what you rightly call *avidya*. As "tout passe," even theological books are not true forever, and even if they expect to be believed one has to tell them in a loving and fatherly way that they make some mistakes. A true and honest introverted thinking is a grace and possesses for at least a time divine authority, particularly if it is modest, simple and straight. The people who write such books are not the voice of God. They are only human. It is true that the right kind of thinking isolates oneself. But did you become a monk for the sake of congenial society? Or do you assume that it isolates only a theologian? It has done the same to me and will do so to everybody that is blessed with it.

That is the reason why there are compensatory functions. The introverted thinker is very much in need of a developed feeling, i.e., of a less autoerotic, sentimental, melodramatic and emotional relatedness to people and things. The compensation will be a hell of a conflict to begin with, but later on, by understanding what *nirdvandva*[17] means, they[18] become the pillars at the gate of the transcendent function, i.e., the *transitus* to the self.

We should recognize that life is a *transitus*. There is an old cov-

[17] *Nirdvandva* (Skt.), "free from the opposites" (love and hate, joy and sorrow, etc.). Cf. *Psychological Types*, pars. 327ff.
[18] Here "they" refers to the compensatory (or inferior) functions. Cf. ibid., Def. 30.

ered bridge near Schmerikon[19] with an inscription: "Alles ist Uebergang."[20] Even the Church and her *sententiae* are only alive inasmuch as they change. All old truths want a new interpretation, so that they can live on in a new form. They can't be substituted or replaced by something else without losing their functional value altogether. The Church certainly expects of you that you assimilate its doctrine. But in assimilating it, you change it imperceptibly and sometimes even noticeably. Introverted thinking is aware of such subtle alterations, while other minds swallow them wholesale. If you try to be literal about the doctrine, you are putting yourself aside until there is nobody left that would represent it but corpses. If, on the other hand, you truly assimilate the doctrine, you will alter it creatively by your individual understanding and thus give life to it. The life of most ideas consists in their controversial nature, i.e., you can disagree with them even if you recognize their importance for a majority. If you fully agreed with them you could replace yourself just as well by a gramophone record. Moreover, if you don't disagree, you are no good as a *directeur de conscience*, since there are many other people suffering from the same difficulty and being badly in need of your understanding.

I appreciate the particular moral problem you are confronted with. But I should rather try to understand why you were put into your actual situation of profound conflict before you think it is a fundamental mistake. I remember vividly your *charta geomantica*[21] that depicts so drastically the way you became a monk. I admit there are people with the peculiar gift of getting inevitably and always into the wrong place. With such people nothing can be done except get them out of the wrong hole into another equally dubious one. But if I find

---

[19] A village in Canton St. Gallen, on the Upper Lake of Zurich, near the Tower at Bollingen.

[20] = "All is transition."

[21] In geomancy, an ancient method of divination still widely practised in the Orient, especially the Far East, earth or pebbles are thrown on the ground and the resultant pattern is interpreted. In Europe the pattern was known as the *charta geomantica*. A later development was to make dots at random on a piece of paper: the "Art of Punctation." (Cf. "Synchronicity," CW 8, par. 866.) Jung was fond of experimenting with all such mantic methods in order to test synchronistic events. He became acquainted with the *Ars Geomantica* through "De animae intellectualis scientia seu geomantica," *Fasciculus geomanticus* (Verona, 1687), by the English physician and mystical philosopher Robert Fludd (1574–1637), who is discussed in Pauli's "The Influence of Archetypal Ideas on the Scientific Theories of Kepler," *The Interpretation of Nature and the Psyche* (tr., 1955).

an intelligent man in an apparently wrong situation, I am inclined to think that it makes sense somehow. There may be some work for him to do. Much work is needed where much has gone wrong or where much should be improved. That is one of the reasons why the Church attracts quite a number of intelligent and responsible men in the secret (or unconscious?) hope that they will be strong enough to carry its meaning and not its words into the future. The old trick of law obedience is still going strong, but the original Christian teaching is a reminder. The man who allows the institution to swallow him is not a good servant.

It is quite understandable that the ecclesiastical authorities must protect the Church against subversive influences. But it would be sabotage if this principle were carried to the extreme, because it would kill the attempts at improvement also. The Church is a "Durchgang" [passage] and bridge between representatives of higher and lower consciousness and as such she quite definitely makes sense. Since the world is largely *sub principatu diaboli*, it is unavoidable that there is just as much evil in the Church as everywhere else, and as everywhere else you have got to be careful. What would you do if you were a bank-clerk or a medical assistant at a big clinic? You are always and everywhere in a moral conflict unless you are blissfully unconscious. I think it is not only honest but even highly moral and altruistic to be what one professes to be as completely as possible, with the full consciousness that you are making this effort for the weak and the unintelligent who cannot live without a reliable support. He is a good physician who does not bother the patient with his own doubts and feelings of inferiority. Even if he knows little or is quite inefficient the right *persona medici* might carry the day if seriously and truly performed for the patient. The grace of God may step in when you don't lose your head in a clearly desperate situation. If it has been done, even with a lie, in favour of the patient, it has been well done, and you are justified, although you never get out of the awkward feeling that you are a dubious number. I wonder whether there is any true servant of God who can rid himself of this profound insecurity balancing his obvious rightness. I cannot forget that crazy old Negro Mammy[22] who told me: "God is working in me like a clock—funny and serious." By "clock" seems to be meant something precise and regular, even monotonous; by "funny and

[22] Possibly a patient Jung interviewed during his work with mentally deranged Negroes at St. Elizabeth's Hospital in Washington, D.C., in 1912. Cf. *The Freud/Jung Letters*, 323J, n. 3. — And cf. Loeb, 26 Aug. 41, n. □.

serious" compensating irrational events and aspects—a humorous seriousness expressing the playful and formidable nature of fateful experiences.

If I find myself in a critical or doubtful situation, I always ask myself whether there is not something in it, explaining the need of my presence, before I make a plan of how to escape. If I should find nothing hopeful or meaningful in it, I think I would not hesitate to jump out of it as quick as possible. Well, I may be all wrong, but the fact that you find yourself in the Church does not impress me as being wholly nonsensical. Of course huge sacrifices are expected of you, but I wonder whether there is any vocation or any kind of meaningful life that does not demand sacrifices of a sort. There is no place where those striving after consciousness could find absolute safety. Doubt and insecurity are indispensable components of a complete life. Only those who can lose this life *really*, can gain it. A "complete" life does not consist in a theoretical completeness, but in the fact that one accepts, without reservation, the particular fatal tissue in which one finds oneself embedded, and that one tries to make sense of it or to create a cosmos from the chaotic mess into which one is born. If one lives properly and completely, time and again one will be confronted with a situation of which one will say: "This is too much. I cannot bear it any more." Then the question must be answered: "Can one really not bear it?"

Fidem non esse caecum sensum religionis e latebris subconscientiae erumpentem,[23] etc., indeed not! *Fides* in its ecclesiastical meaning is a construction expressed by the wholly artificial credo, but no spontaneous product of the unconscious. You can swear to it in all innocence, as well as I could, if asked. Also you can *teach*, if asked, the *solid* doctrine of St. Thomas Aquinas, as I could if I knew it. You can and will and must criticize it, yet with a certain discrimination, as there are people incapable of understanding your argument. *Quieta movere*[24] is not necessarily a good principle. Being an analyst, you know how little you can say, and sometimes it is quite enough when only the analyst knows. Certain things transmit themselves by air when they are really needed.

[23] On 1 Sept. 1910 Pius X edited a *motu proprio* (a document issued by the Pontiff on his own initiative) in which the sentence occurs: "Certissime teneo ac sincere profiteor fidem non esse caecum sensum religionis e latebris subconscientiae . . . erumpentem" (I maintain as quite certain and sincerely avow that faith is not a blind religious feeling which breaks out of the darkness of the subconscious).

[24] Lit. "to move what is at rest"; more colloquially, "rousing sleeping dogs."

I don't share at all X.'s idea that one should not be so finicky about conscience. It is definitely dishonest and—sorry—a bit too Catholic. One must be finicky when it comes to a moral question, and what a question! You are asked to decide whether you can deal with ambiguity, deception, "doublecrossing" and other damnable things for the love of your neighbour's soul. If it is a case of "the end justifying the means," you had better buy a through ticket to hell. It is a devilish hybris even to think that one could be in such an exalted position to decide about the means one is going to apply. There is no such thing, not even in psychotherapy. If you don't want to go to the dogs morally, there is only one question, namely "Which is the necessity you find yourself burdened with when you take to heart your brother's predicament?" The question is *how you are applied* in the process of the cure, and not at all what the means are you could offer to buy yourself off. It depends very much indeed upon the way you envisage your position with reference to the Church. I should advocate an analytical attitude, which is permissible as well as honest, viz. take the Church as your ailing employer and your colleagues as the unconscious inmates of a hospital.

Is the LSD-drug mescalin?[25] It has indeed very curious effects— *vide* Aldous Huxley![26]—of which I know far too little. I don't know either what its psychotherapeutic value with neurotic or psychotic patients is. I only know there is no point in wishing to *know* more of the collective unconscious than one gets through dreams and intuition. The more you know of it, the greater and heavier becomes your moral burden, because the unconscious contents transform themselves into your individual tasks and duties as soon as they begin to become conscious. Do you want to increase loneliness and misunderstanding? Do you want to find more and more complications and increasing responsibilities? You get enough of it. If I once could say that I had done everything I know I had to do, then perhaps I should realize a legitimate need to take mescalin. But if I should take it now, I would not be sure at all that I had not taken it out of idle curiosity. I should hate the thought that I had touched on the sphere where the paint is made that colours the world, where the light is created that makes shine the splendour of the dawn, the lines and shapes of all form, the

---

[25] W. mentioned that he had been invited to a lunatic asylum "to talk to the staff, and (as I found) try to lend a hand with religious-archetypal material which patients were producing under the L.S.D. drug." — Jung wrote "mescal."
[26] Aldous Huxley, *The Doors of Perception* (1954).

sound that fills the orbit, the thought that illuminates the darkness of the void. There are some poor impoverished creatures, perhaps, for whom mescalin would be a heavensent gift without a counterpoison, but I am profoundly mistrustful of the "pure gifts of the Gods." You pay very dearly for them. *Quidquid id est, timeo Danaos et dona ferentes.*[27]

This is not the point at all, to know of or about the unconscious, nor does the story end here; on the contrary it is how and where you begin the real quest. If you are too unconscious it is a great relief to know a bit of the collective unconscious. But it soon becomes dangerous to know more, because one does not learn at the same time how to balance it through a conscious equivalent. That is the mistake Aldous Huxley makes: he does not know that he is in the role of the "Zauberlehrling," who learned from his master how to call the ghosts but did not know how to get rid of them again:

> *Die ich rief, die Geister,*
> *Werd ich nun nicht los!*[28]

It is really the mistake of our age. We think it is enough to discover new things, but we don't realize that knowing more demands a corresponding development of morality. Radioactive clouds over Japan, Calcutta, and Saskatchewan point to progressive poisoning of the universal atmosphere.

I should indeed be obliged to you if you could let me see the material they get with LSD. It is quite awful that the alienists have caught hold of a new poison to play with, without the faintest knowledge or feeling of responsibility. It is just as if a surgeon had never learned further than to cut open his patient's belly and to leave things there. When one gets to know unconscious contents one should know how to deal with them. I can only hope that the doctors will feed themselves thoroughly with mescalin, the *alkaloid of divine grace*, so that they learn for themselves its marvellous effect. You have not finished with the conscious side yet. Why should you expect more from the unconscious? For 35 years I have known enough of the collective unconscious and my whole effort is concentrated upon preparing the ways and means to deal with it.

---

[27] "[Men of Troy, trust not the horse!] Be it what it may, I fear the Danaans, though their hands proffer gifts" (Virgil, *Aeneid*, I, 48).
[28] Goethe's poem "The Magician's Apprentice": "I cannot get rid / Of the spirits I bid."

Now to end this very long epistle I must say how much I have appreciated your confidence, frankness, courage and honesty. This is so rare and so precious an event that it is a pleasure to answer at length. I hope you will find a way out to Switzerland.

. . .

The winter, though very cold, has dealt leniently with me. Both my wife and myself are tired, though still active, but in a very restricted way.

I am spending the month of April in Bollingen *procul negotiis*[29] and the worst weather we have known for years.

Cordially yours, C. G.

[29] = away from work.

To Eugene M. E. Rolfe

[ORIGINAL IN ENGLISH]

Dear Mr. Rolfe,   1 May 1954

Thank you very much for your interesting article on "Rival Gods."[1] You ask a pertinent question[2] indeed. I am afraid there will be nobody to answer it, at least not in the way which we would expect following tradition. Can you imagine a real prophet or saviour in our days of television and press reportage? He would perish by his own popularity within a few weeks. And yet some answer will be expected. You rightly point out the emptiness of our souls and the perplexity of our mind when we should give an equally pat, simple-minded and understandable answer as f.i. Marxism. The trouble is that most of us believe in the same ideals or very similar ones. Mankind as a whole has not yet understood that the ultimate decision is really laid into its own hands. It is still possessed by wrathful gods and is doing their will. There are very few who realize the true position and its desperate urgency.

I am glad you asked the question!

Sincerely yours, C. G. JUNG

□ See Rolfe, 3 Mar. 49 (in vol. 1).

[1] In *The Hibbert Journal*, LII (Apr. 1954).

[2] R.'s article, dealing with the "rival gods" of the U.S.A. and the U.S.S.R., concluded with the question: "What right have we to preach to the devotees of a modern idolatry if . . . our souls are full of emptiness . . . . Where is the vision, the mystery, the living operative Truth for which we would joyfully live and die, with all the strength of heart and mind and spirit? What is His name, my friend?"

To André Barbault

Dear M. Barbault,   26 May 1954

First I must apologize for being so late in answering your letter of March 19th. I was away on holiday part of the time—or else ill. Besides, unfortunately, my advanced age no longer permits me to fulfil all my obligations as I would like to.

As for your questionnaire, here are my answers:

1. *The connections between astrology and psychology.* There are many instances of striking analogies between astrological constellations and psychological events or between the horoscope and the characterological disposition. It is even possible to predict to a certain extent the psychic effect of a transit. For example [. . .].[1] One may expect with a fair degree of probability that a given well-defined psychological situation will be accompanied by an analogous astrological configuration. Astrology, like the collective unconscious with which psychology is concerned, consists of symbolic configurations: the "planets" are the gods, symbols of the powers of the unconscious.

2. *The modus operandi of astrological constellations.* It seems to me that it is primarily a question of that parallelism or "sympathy"[2] which I call *synchronicity,* an acausal connection expressing relation-

☐ (Translated from French.) B.'s letterhead reads: "Centre International d'astrologie — Le Vice-président: André Barbault, Paris." He submitted the following questionnaire:

"1. What connections do you see between astrology and psychology?

2. In what way, physical, causal, or synchronous, do you think these connections can be established?

3. What is your attitude to the positions taken by astrologers who admit the existence of a psychological field from birth on, and by psychoanalysts who explain the aetiology of neuroses in terms of the earliest life experiences?

4. Astrology introduces the concept of qualitative time ('temps qualitatif') in the universe. Do you recognize its role in the individual psyche (problem of cycles and transits)?

5. In the course of analytical treatment, have you observed typical phases of either resistance or progress which would coincide with certain astrological constellations, e.g., transits?

6. What are your main criticisms of astrologers?

7. What orientation of astrological thought do you consider desirable?"

Jung's letter was published as an interview in *Astrologie Moderne,* ed. Barbault, which interview appeared in a somewhat erratic translation in the *Aquarian Agent,* I:13, Dec. 1970.

[1] Here the astrological symbols which Jung put in by hand are missing in the file copy and cannot be restored.

[2] Cf. Kling, 14 Jan. 58, n. 2.

ships that cannot be formulated in terms of causality, such as precognition, premonition, psychokinesis (PK), and also what we call telepathy. Since causality is a *statistical truth*, there are exceptions of an acausal nature bordering on the category of synchronistic (not synchronous) events. They have to do with "qualitative time."

3. *Attitude to positions taken by astrologers* [etc.]. The first experiences in life owe their specific (pathogenic) effect to environmental influences on the one hand, and on the other to the psychic predisposition, i.e., to heredity, which seems to be expressed in a recognizable way in the horoscope. The latter apparently corresponds to a definite moment in the colloquy of the gods, that is to say the psychic archetypes.

4. *Qualitative time*. This is a notion I used formerly[3] but I have replaced it with the idea of synchronicity, which is analogous to sympathy or *correspondentia* (the συμπάθεια of antiquity), or to Leibniz's *pre-established harmony*. Time in itself consists of nothing. It is only a *modus cogitandi* that is used to express and formulate the flux of things and events, just as space is nothing but a way of describing the existence of a body. When nothing occurs in time and when there is no body in space, there is neither time nor space. Time is always and exclusively "qualified" by events as space is by the extension of bodies. But "qualitative time" is a tautology and means nothing, whereas synchronicity (not synchronism) expresses the parallelism and analogy between events in so far as they are noncausal. In contrast, "qualitative time" is an hypothesis that attempts to explain the parallelism of events in terms of *causa et effectus*. But since qualitative time is nothing but the flux of things, and is moreover just as much "nothing" as space, this hypothesis does not establish anything except the tautology: the flux of things and events is the cause of the flux of things, etc.

Synchronicity does not admit causality in the analogy between terrestrial events and astrological constellations (except for the deflection of solar protons and their possible effect on terrestrial events),[4] and denies it particularly in all cases of nonsensory perception (ESP), especially precognition, since it is inconceivable that one could observe the effect of a nonexistent cause, or of a cause that does not yet exist.

What astrology can establish are the analogous events, but not that either series is the cause or the effect of the other. (For instance, the same constellation may at one time signify a catastrophe and at an-

---

[3] Cf. "Richard Wilhelm: In Memoriam," CW 15, par. 82: "Whatever is born or done at this particular moment of time has the quality of this moment of time." Also "Foreword to the *I Ching*," CW 11, pars. 970f.

[4] Cf. Jaffé, 8 Sept. 51, n. 2.

other time, in the same case, a cold in the head.) Nevertheless, astrology is not an entirely simple matter. There is that deflection of solar protons caused on the one hand by the conjunctions, oppositions, and quartile aspects, and on the other hand by the trine and sextile aspects, and their influence on the radio and on many other things.[5] I am not competent to judge how much importance should be attributed to this possible influence.

In any case, astrology occupies a unique and special position among the intuitive methods, and in explaining it there is reason to be dubious of both a causal theory and the exclusive validity of the synchronistic hypothesis.[6]

5. I have observed many cases where a well-defined psychological phase, or an analogous event, was accompanied by a transit (particularly when Saturn and Uranus were affected).

6. *My main criticisms of astrologers.* If I were to venture an opinion in a domain with which I am only very superficially acquainted, I would say that the astrologer does not always consider his statements to be mere possibilities. The interpretation is sometimes too literal and not symbolic enough, also too personal. What the zodiac and the planets represent are not personal traits; they are impersonal and objective facts. Moreover, several "layers of meaning" should be taken into account in interpreting the Houses.

7. Obviously astrology has much to offer psychology, but what the latter can offer its elder sister is less evident. So far as I can judge, it would seem to me advantageous for astrology to take the existence of psychology into account, above all the psychology of the personality and of the unconscious. I am almost sure that something could be learnt from its symbolic method of interpretation; for that has to do with the interpretation of the archetypes (the gods) and their mutual relations, the common concern of both arts. The psychology of the unconscious is particularly concerned with archetypal symbolism.

Hoping you will find this answer satisfactory, I remain,

Yours sincerely, C. G. JUNG

[5] "Synchronicity," CW 8, par. 875.
[6] Cf. Bender, 10 Apr. 48.

To Michael Fordham

[ORIGINAL IN ENGLISH]

Dear Fordham,   18 June 1954

Your letter brings bad news; I am really sorry that you didn't get the post at the Institute of Psychiatry,[1] although it may be a small consolation to you that they took at least your pupil, Dr. Hobson.[2] Well, after all, you are approaching the age when one has to become acquainted with the difficult experience of being superseded. Times go on and inexorably one is left behind, sometimes more, sometimes less, and one has to realize that there are things beyond our reach one shouldn't grieve for, as such grieving is still a remnant of too youthful an ambition. Our libido certainly would go on reaching for the stars if fate didn't make it clear beyond any reasonable doubt that we shouldn't seek completion without, but within—alas! One becomes aware that there is so much to improve in the field of the inner man that we must even be grateful to adversity that it helps us to have the necessary amount of free energy to deal with the defects of our development, i.e., with that which has been "spoiled by the father and by the mother."[3] In this respect, loss of such kind is pure gain.

Cordially yours, c. g. j u n g

☐ M.D., English analytical psychologist; co-editor of the Collected Works; editor (until 1971) of *The Journal of Analytical Psychology* (London). Cf. his *Life of Childhood* (1944); *New Developments in Analytical Psychology* (1957; Jung's foreword is in CW 18); *The Objective Psyche* (1958); *Children as Individuals* (1970).
[1] The Institute of Psychiatry, Maudsley Hospital, London, is the leading English psychiatric hospital.
[2] Robert F. Hobson, M.D., analytical psychologist.
[3] Cf. the *I Ching*, hexagram 18: "Work on What Has Been Spoiled."

To P. F. Jenny

Dear Herr Jenny,   1 July 1954

The appearance in public and the consequent overwhelming success of a child prodigy are decidedly dangerous, so a rare appearance not only does no harm but is to be recommended. The development of such a child is usually uneven; part of the personality often remains undeveloped for a long time, or even infantile, and this side has to be protected against too great an expenditure of psychic and physical energy, otherwise a premature drying up of the sources of the prodigy can set in. Gifted children are often pushed out into the world and its neurotic turmoil much too early for their situation, and then their gift is soon exhausted. So I think you would do well to keep a constant eye on this undeveloped side; genius can look after itself.

Yours sincerely, c. g. j u n g

☐ Zurich.

To Carol Jeffrey

[ORIGINAL IN ENGLISH]

Dear Mrs. Jeffrey,   3 July 1954

For the long delay of my answer I must ask for forgiveness. I have little time, and at times my energies are rather low. I have looked through your pictures with appreciation and admiration. I am rather astonished about your question: "For whom have I painted the pictures?" They belong to you, and you have painted them as a support for your own individuation process. As the *Jongleur de Notre-Dame*[1] plays his tricks in honour of the Madonna, so you paint for the self. In recognition of this fact, I am going to send the pictures back to you. They shouldn't be here, and nowhere else but with yourself, as they represent the approximation of the two worlds of spirit and body or of ego and self. The opposites seek each other so that the other side comes hither and the Here is swallowed up by the There. In the last picture, both aspects approximately assume identity in producing a single circle. One could say a lot of things about such a central process, but this is quite impossible in a letter.

I thank you at all events for having shown me your pictures. I suppose it would be useful if you could contemplate these pictures until you feel that they are understood, as they contain a development not only of subjective importance but also of a collective significance, viz. the development of the traditional and conventional Christian symbol in a symbol of totality. The latter is, as the church says, *implicite* in the Christian idea. From this point of view, you can see how much there is contained in your pictures. I have written quite a lot about it in my books, but they are not yet translated I am afraid.

Hoping things are all right with you, I remain,

Yours sincerely, C. G. JUNG

☐ English psychotherapist.
1 "The Jongleur de Notre-Dame" is a French story of the 13th cent. It tells of a juggler who, having entered a monastery in his old age and not knowing what to offer, juggled in front of a statue of the Virgin. She responded with a gracious smile.

To Fernando Cassani

Dear Herr Cassani,   13 July 1954

Best thanks for your friendly letter. I can only tell you that none of my books represents a "synthesis or foundation of my work," at least not in my view. I am not a philosopher who might be able to achieve something as ambitious as that, but an empiricist who describes the progress of his experiences; thus my work has no absolute beginning and no all-encompassing end. It is like the life of an individual, which suddenly becomes visible somewhere but rests on definite though invisible foundations, so has no proper beginning and no proper end, ceasing just as suddenly and leaving questions behind which should have been answered. You do not know my later (and perhaps more important) works yet. I therefore enclose a list of them.

As for the writings of Ouspensky[1] and Gurdjieff,[2] I know enough to satisfy me that I have no time for them. I seek real knowledge and therefore avoid all unverifiable speculation. I have seen enough of that as a psychiatrist. You might just as well recommend Mme. Blavatsky's *Isis Unveiled* or the compendious opus of Rudolf Steiner or Bô-Yin-Râ[3] (why not Schneiderfranken?). Anyway I thank you for your good intentions.

It is so difficult to establish facts that I detest anything that obscures them. You can attribute this to a *déformation professionelle*.

I naturally agree with what you say about freedom of thought. The Communist doesn't come into this category, since he doesn't think; but his actions are a danger to the public. If he thought, he would have found out his deceit long ago.

Hoping you will excuse my freedom of thought,

Yours sincerely, C. G. JUNG

☐ Caracas, Venezuela.

[1] Peter D. Ouspensky (1877–1947), Russian mathematician and author. Cf. his *In Search of the Miraculous* (1950); *A New Model of the Universe* (1953); *Tertium Organum* (1911). He was the most lucid expositor of Gurdjieff's teachings.
[2] George Ivanovitch Gurdjieff (1877–1949), Russian writer, traveller, student of esoteric doctrines in Central Asia, upon which he based his system of teaching and inner discipline; founder and director of the Institute for the Harmonious Development of Man, in Fontainebleau, near Paris, in 1922. Cf. his *All and Everything* (1950); *Meetings with Remarkable Men* (1963). From 1914 onwards he collaborated with Ouspensky.
[3] Pseudonym of the German writer and painter Joseph Anton Schneiderfranken (1876–1943), whose works have a spiritualistic character.

To J. B. Rhine

[ORIGINAL IN ENGLISH]

Dear Dr. Rhine,   9 August 1954

Thank you for your kind letter.

The English translation of "Synchronicity" will be published by the

Bollingen Press.[1] The translator is Mr. Hull, who is translating my Collected Works. He has a fair understanding of the synchronicity concept, which *au fond* is not complicated at all and has its long history reaching from high antiquity right down to Leibniz. He had still four principles for the explanation of Nature, viz. space, time, causality, and his *harmonia praestabilita*, an acausal principle.

My doctoral thesis[2] was published, if I am right, in my volume *Collected Papers on Analytical Psychology* (2nd edit., 1920). (I am actually not at home.)

The main difficulty with synchronicity (and also with ESP) is that one thinks of it as being produced by the subject, while I think it is rather in the nature of objective events. Although ESP is a gift of certain individuals and seems to depend upon an emotional perception, the picture it produces is that of an objective fact. This truth becomes highly problematical in the case of precognition, where a fact is perceived that apparently does not exist. As one cannot perceive a fact that does not exist, we must assume that it has some form of existence, so that it can be perceived nevertheless. To explain it we must assume that the (future) objective fact is paralleled by a similar or identical subjective, i.e., psychic, already existing arrangement which cannot be explained as an anticipatory causal effect. But it is quite possible and, as a matter of fact, you have shown it to be possible, that the subjective parallelism can be perceived as if it were the future fact itself. The *harmonia praestabilita* would be in this case the obvious explanation.

I think that all forms of ESP (telepathy, precognition, etc.) including PK have essentially the same underlying principle, viz. the identity of a subjective and an objective arrangement coinciding in time (hence the term "synchronicity").[3] With my best wishes,

Yours sincerely, C. G. J U N G

---

[1] I.e., in Bollingen Series, 1955; also by Routledge & Kegan Paul (London).

[2] "On the Psychology and Pathology of So-called Occult Phenomena," CW 1. First published (in tr.) in *Collected Papers* (1916).

[3] In a letter of 23 Nov. 71 R. wrote to Aniela Jaffé: "One of the reasons for my sincere admiration of Dr. Jung came from his forthright devotion to the findings of parapsychology with which he came into experience long ago before I began to give attention to them at Duke. When the experimental studies helped to bring the findings into a firm status he made no bones about taking the consequences seriously. Not many people in science are so straightforward in their intellectual life; they wait for someone else to stand in the front lines."

To Cécile Ines Loos

Dear Frau Loos,   7 September 1954

It was unexpectedly kind of you to remember my birthday. I am not surprised you forgot it at first, but I am astonished that you remembered.

With regard to the lack of appreciation of writers in Switzerland, one must never forget that Switzerland is a very small country and has never trusted its own taste in spite of cultural philistinism and the vogue for art, and anyway you can't expect publishers to be idealists. Rascher[1] for instance wastes his money on idiotic picture-books, but only because this is his hobby and not a well-founded artistic judgment.

As you wish, I am sending you a copy of my book *Von den Wurzeln des Bewusstseins.*

The petition for "daily bread" is appropriate under all circumstances, although in Matthew 6:11 it reads: *"Panem nostrum supersubstantialis da nobis hodie"* (Give us this day our supersubstantial bread[2]). At least that is how St. Jerome translated the Greek word, which occurs only in Matthew and has undergone various interpretations, banal or otherwise. But Jerome will have known what he was doing, especially when you see what is said in the ensuing verses, where Christ admonishes his disciples not to worry about their daily needs, which is naturally very much easier in a warm country than in our climate, of which Zola rightly said: "Mais notre misère a froid." With best wishes,

Yours sincerely, C. G. JUNG

☐ (1883–1959), Swiss author. Cf. her *Die leisen Leidenschaften* (1934); *Jehanne* (1946); *Leute am See* (1951).
[1] Jung's Swiss publisher at that time.
[2] So tr. in the Douay-Rheims (Catholic) version of the Vulgate.

To Josef Rudin

Dear Dr. Rudin,   1 October 1954

My very best thanks for kindly sending me your interesting essay on freedom.[1]

[1] "Die Tiefenpsychologie und die Freiheit des Menschen," *Orientierung* (Zurich), no. 16 (31 Aug. 1954).

The latest developments of scientific thinking, especially in physics, but recently also in psychology, make it clear that "freedom" is a necessary correlate to the purely statistical nature of the concept of causality. In particular it comes into the category of meaningful co-incidences, which I have discussed in my book on synchronicity. Freedom could be put in doubt only because of the one-sided and un-critical overvaluation of causality, which has been elevated into an axiom although—strictly speaking—it is nothing but a mode of thought.

Yours sincerely, C. G. JUNG

Anonymous

[ORIGINAL IN ENGLISH]

Dear Mr. N.,   2 October 1954

Not knowing the case of Mrs. N., I am quite unable to give you any advice how to treat her. At all events, at that age a psychosis is always a serious thing which transcends all human efforts. It all depends whether one can establish a mental and moral rapport with the patients. The shock treatment, as a rule, dulls their mental perception, so that there is usually little hope of gaining an influence on them. I certainly wouldn't know how you could set about giving her a religious outlook, since you yourself have a merely intellectual conception of the deity. I wouldn't go so far as to suggest that people with a religious outlook would be immune to psychosis. Such statement would only be true in borderline cases. The question of religion is not so simple as you see it: it is not at all a matter of intellectual conviction or philosophy or even belief, but rather a matter of inner experience. I admit that this is a conception which seems to be completely ignored by the theologians in spite of the fact that they talk a lot of it. St. Paul for instance was not converted to Christianity by intellectual or philosophical endeavour or by a belief, but by the force of his immediate inner experience. His belief was based upon it, but our modern theology turns the thing round and holds that we first ought to believe and then we would have an inner experience, but this reversal forces people directly into a wrong rationalism that excludes even the possibility of an inner experience. It is quite natural that they identify the deity with cosmic energy, which is evidently impersonal and almost physical, and to which nobody can pray, but the inner experi-

□ U.S.A.

ence is utterly different: it shows the existence of personal forces with which an intimate contact of a very personal nature is thoroughly possible. Nobody who is not really aware of an inner experience is able to transmit such a conviction to somebody else; mere talk—no matter how good its intention is—will never convey conviction. I have treated a great number of people without religious education and without a religious attitude, but in the course of the treatment, which as a rule is a long and a difficult undertaking, they inevitably had some inner experiences that gave them just the right attitude.

It is of course quite impossible to give you a short account of the way in which you attain that inner experience. It is particularly not true that anyone could say: it is so and so; it is not transmitted by words. I don't know whether you know something of my writings; there I say a lot about ways and means, but the danger is that when you read such things you get quite confused. You might have a talk with one of my pupils, e.g. Mrs. Frances G. Wickes,[1] 101 East 74th Street, New York. She could explain things to you better than I can do it in a letter.

Sincerely yours, C. G. JUNG

[1] Cf. Wickes, 9 Aug. 46.

To Calvin S. Hall

[ORIGINAL IN ENGLISH]

Dear Sir,   6 October 1954

Thank you for kindly giving me an opportunity to glimpse into the psychology of an American psychologist. Above all I am much encouraged by the fact that you were able to get something positive out of my incompetent work and I am deeply obliged to you 1) for your willingness to hear my impressions, 2) for the honesty and sincerity of your purpose, and 3) for your serious attempt to be impartial and to lay aside your prejudices.

You have left me however with a puzzle from which I can hardly extricate myself. In the first place I cannot understand the peculiar

☐ Then professor of psychology, Western Reserve U., Cleveland, Ohio; now at U. of California, Santa Cruz. Hall had sent Jung a draft of a chapter in his and Gardner Lindzey's *Theories of Personality* (1957; 2nd edn., 1970); Jung returned it "with 137 handwritten comments, on the basis of which the draft was drastically revised" (communication from Hall).

way in which you present my work. In order to make myself clear, I should like to use the following example:

Somebody sets out to present Mr. Evans' work in Crete to an ignorant audience. In order to do so he talks almost exclusively of Evans' conjectures with reference to Minoan history and culture. But why doesn't he mention what he has dug up in Knossos? His conjectures are irrelevant in comparison with the *facts* and results of his *excavations*, and moreover his audience not knowing about his main merit is in no way prepared to understand what his conjectures are all about.

Thus you chiefly deal with words and names instead of giving substance. I am thoroughly empirical and therefore I have no system at all. I try to describe facts of which you merely mention the names. I got the funny impression that, while you claim to present myself, you restrict yourself to my suit of clothes, which is altogether indifferent to me and is certainly not essential.

I have never claimed f.i. to know much about the nature of archetypes, how they originated or whether they originated at all, whether they are inherited or planted by the grace of God in every individual anew. You even adduce the old-fashioned sophism of the non-inheritance of acquired peculiarities. What about a *mutation* that maintains itself in the subsequent generations? What about the funny things you can see on the Galápagos?[1] If no change gets inherited, then nothing gets changed unless there is an infinite series of creative acts. But I don't insist, as you can easily see, upon such sophistications. Your harping on such utterly irrelevant conjectures probably hangs together with another puzzle which I should like to explain again by an example:

Somebody tries to present Mr. Plato's philosophical work. We in Europe should expect that anybody trying to carry out such a plan would read *all of Plato's writings* and not only barely half and chiefly the earlier part of them. Such a *procedere* would not qualify and could hardly be called responsible or reliable. One could not even advocate it with an author as insignificant as myself.

[1] The Galápagos Islands (belonging to Ecuador) in the Pacific show remarkable fauna with a large number of forms peculiar to the various islands. They attracted the attention of Charles Darwin and provided a base for his ideas of natural selection and evolution. Jung was particularly interested in the fact that a species of wingless insects had developed through mutation, and that this acquired characteristic had become hereditary (cf. Kristof, July 1956).

The last and greatest puzzle is the funny prejudice which reminds me vividly of that vulgar idea that an alienist must be necessarily crazy because he deals with lunatics. If you call me an occultist because I am seriously investigating *religious, mythological, folkloristic and philosophical fantasies* in modern individuals and ancient texts, then you are bound to diagnose *Freud as a sexual pervert* since he is doing likewise with sexual fantasies, and a psychologically inclined criminologist must needs be a gaol-bird. A typical example of my later work is *Psychology and Alchemy*. It is not my responsibility that alchemy is occult and mystical, and I am just as little guilty of the mystical delusions of the insane or the peculiar creeds of mankind. Perhaps you have noticed that I follow the well-known method of comparative anatomy or of comparative history of religions or that of deciphering difficult ancient texts, as you can easily see in *Psych. and Alch.* Dealing with such fantasies I have to adduce analogous material, which is to be found in mystical texts or in myths and religions. Or do you assume that psychopaths have no fantasies of this kind? Please cf. my book: *Symbols of Transformation*.

I cannot understand at all how dealing with sex fantasies should be more objective or more scientific than dealing with any other kind of fantasy, f.i. the religious one. But obviously the sex fantasy must be true and real, while the religious fantasy is not true, it is an error and should not be, and whoever deals with it is highly unscientific. Such logic transcends my horizon.

Being a physician and citizen I am not only justified but morally bound to warn or advise publicly when I see fit. I am not inclined to preach, but I feel socially responsible and I have made up my mind not to participate in the arch-sin of the intellectual, namely the *Trahison des clercs*[2] as a French author calls this particular form of infantile autoeroticism. This is the reason why I am interested in the social aspects of psychology.

It is most surprising to me that almost none of the critiques of my work ever mentions the facts I am producing. As a rule they ignore them completely. But I should like to know how they would explain the astounding parallelism of individual and historical symbolism not reducible to tradition. This is the real problem. To deny the facts is too simple and too cheap. It never pays to underrate new ideas or facts.

I hope you don't mind my giving you my impressions without po-

[2] *La Trahison des clercs* (1927) by the French philosopher Julien Benda (1867–1956).

lite detours. You can dismiss them as irrelevant, but it won't be to the advantage of the progress of science. I shall always remember the time when Freud disturbed the peaceful slumber of the medical and philosophical faculties by his shocking discoveries, which are now taken into serious consideration. A professor once repudiated my statements saying: "But your argument collides with the doctrine of the unity of consciousness. Therefore you are wrong." This is an answer worthy of the XIIIth century, but unfortunately it happened in the XXth century.

Your typescript with my notes follows.

Hoping that my criticism does not offend you, I remain,

Yours respectfully, C. G. JUNG

To a Young Greek Girl

[ORIGINAL IN ENGLISH]

Dear Miss N.,   14 October 1954

As to your question[1] whether it makes a difference to your dreams if one has read about similar subjects, I must say that dreams of the sort you give me an example of can occur whether you have read [my books] or not. It is, of course, quite natural that the dreams take suitable material from whatever source is available, either from books or from other experiences but this doesn't matter. There are people who can read my books and never have a dream of anything reminiscent of my writings, but it is true that if you understand what you have read, you get a frame of mind or a problematical outlook which you did not have before, and that, of course, influences your dreams.

I shouldn't assume that your dream[2] has been particularly influenced by what you have read. I dislike as a rule interpreting dreams of people whom I don't know personally; one can easily be led astray. I will make an exception in your case since I see that your dream has a meaning very important for you. The beginning of it shows a certain fear of an imminent catastrophic situation—the tempest and the darkness. The sudden discovery of the relief is something like a revelation, an unveiling of the compensatory background to your conscious

---

[1] N. asked whether the fact that she had read some of Jung's books might have influenced her dreams.

[2] The dream begins with sudden darkness and the starting up of a tempest; the dreamer seeks shelter in a building with a square room, where she finds a huge bas-relief representing "two feminine figures in their long Grecian robes, one of whom was the goddess Demeter."

psychology that has masculine (animus) inclinations.[3] It is the Eleusinian mystery of Demeter and her daughter Persephone.[4] The masculine element is paying homage to this maternal figure. It is quite obvious that the dream intends to call your attention to this great mythologem so important for a woman's psychology. It is particularly important to your case because you are very much on your mother's side and presumably partially identified with her, being her only daughter. Also you are remote from your father,[5] from whom you have not received what is due to a daughter. Therefore, you have developed a sort of substitute for the spiritual influence not coming forth from your father as it should. That is a great hindrance working either way to the masculine as well as to the feminine side of your personality. It would be wise, therefore, to follow the suggestion of the dream and to meditate on all the aspects of the myth of Demeter and Persephone. Also, Greece had its Eleusinian cult because it suffered from a very similar psychological condition: women too much under the influence of their mothers and spiritually starved by their fathers, men also too much influenced by the mother because of the uncontrolled emotionality of the fathers and victimized by the emotional appetites of their mothers, hence the widespread homosexuality particularly in the male population. At the time of Pericles there was even an epidemic of suicides among young girls feeling neglected by the men occupied with homosexual affairs. Try to find out what Demeter has to convey to you. You are obviously more attracted by the chthonic mystery represented by Demeter than by the spiritual and paternal trends of Christianity, from which you apparently have separated yourself. It is this critical attitude that has to be considered as the immediate cause of this dream with its definitely antique atmosphere.

This is about all I can safely say about your dream. If you give it your full attention, you will probably have other dreams elucidating the further steps of your way.

Sincerely yours, C. G. JUNG

[3] N. wrote of her "high appreciation of intellectual values" and "conscious cultivation of masculine traits."

[4] The Eleusinian mysteries were celebrated in honour of Demeter and her daughter Persephone, the "Kore" (girl), who in the myth is carried off to Hades by Pluto, god of the underworld. On the intervention of Zeus, she returns to earth for one half of the year, her return being celebrated in the mysteries. Cf. Kerényi, "Kore," in Jung and Kerényi, *Essays on a Science of Mythology* (tr. 1949; London edn.: *Introduction to a Science of Mythology*).

[5] An "extremely introverted and indifferent" man with whom she had conflicts.

188

To Aniela Jaffé

Dear Aniela,   22 October 1954

At last I have succeeded in assimilating coherently your 16 pages on *Der Tod des Vergil*.[1] It made a very powerful impression on me and I admired your careful hand, feeling its way along Broch's secret guidelines and from time to time bringing a treasure to light. You're quite right: *it's all there.*

I have wondered all the more about my reluctance which on all sorts of pretexts has hitherto held me back from letting this *Tod des Vergil* approach me too closely. This morning the insight came to me: I was *jealous* of Broch because he has succeeded in doing what I had to forbid myself on pain of death. Whirling in the same nether-world maelstrom and wafted to ecstasy by the vision of unfathomable images I heard a voice whispering to me that I could make it "aesthetic," all the while knowing that the artist in words within me was the merest embryo, incapable of real artistry.[2] I would have produced nothing but a heap of shards which could never have been turned into a pot. In spite of this ever-present realization the artist homunculus in me has nourished all sorts of resentments and has obviously taken it very badly that I didn't press the poet's wreath on his head.

I had to tell you quickly about this psychological intermezzo. Next week I shall try to go on holiday. You can imagine my letter chaos—with no secretary!

Cordial greetings,

Very sincerely, c. g. j u n g

P.S. Anyway why did it have to be *the death of the poet?*

☐ (Handwritten.)
[1] MS of an essay on Hermann Broch's novel *The Death of Vergil* (1945; tr. 1946). An expanded version of the essay was published in *Studien zur analytischen Psychologie C. G. Jungs,* II (1955).
[2] Cf. *Memories,* pp. 185ff./178f.

To Henry D. Isaac

Dear Herr Isaac,   25 October 1954

Your question is indeed most timely, for it is highly unlikely that any social measures and proposals will make the individual more conscious, more conscientious and more responsible but will have the opposite effect, because all agglomerations of individuals show a distinct tendency to lower the level of individual consciousness. Hence all advice that begins with "you ought" usually proves to be completely ineffective. This hangs together with the obvious fact that only the individual is the carrier of virtues but not the mass. Today this supremely important vehicle of the social function is imperilled by our whole culture, or rather unculture. If the individual could be improved, it seems to me that a foundation would be laid for an improvement of the whole. Even a million noughts do not add up to one. I therefore espouse the unpopular view that a better understanding in the world can come only from the individual and be promoted only by him. But considering the vast numbers involved, this truth looks like a counsel of despair and futility. Supposing, however, that anyone did want to make his infinitesimal contribution to the desired ideal, he would have to be in a position really to understand another person. The indispensable precondition for this is that he understands himself. If he doesn't, he will inevitably see the other person through the deceptive and distorting lens of his own prejudices and projections and will recommend and impute to him the very things he most needs himself. So we must understand ourselves to a certain extent if we want any real communication with others.

Today there are a whole lot of things which an adult ought to know in order to be equipped for life. He is supposed to have picked them up in his schooldays, but then he was much too young to understand them, and later there is nothing to prompt him to go back to school again. Usually he has no time for that. Nobody brings him any useful knowledge in this respect, and he remains in a state of childish ignorance. We should have schools for adults, where one could inculcate into them at least the elements of self-knowledge and knowledge of human nature. I have made this suggestion often enough, but it has remained a pious wish although everyone admits in theory that without self-knowledge there can be no general understanding. Ways and means would surely be found if it were some technological problem. But since it is merely the most important thing of all, the human psyche and human relationships, that is at issue, there are neither teachers nor pupils, neither schools nor refresher courses, and every-

☐ Stockbroker of New York City, originally from Germany and Palestine, who submitted the question "What is the best way for an individual to contribute to better understanding in the world?" to a number of prominent people and received many replies, which he did not publish.

190

thing is shrugged off with "you ought." That everyone ought to begin with himself is much too unpopular and so everything stays as it is. Only when people get so nervous that the doctor diagnoses a neurosis do they go to a specialist, whose medical horizon usually does not include social responsibility.

Unfortunately the so-called religions have never proved to be vehicles of general human understanding, since with few exceptions they suffer from totalitarian claims and in this respect at least hardly differ from any other -ism, and actually disrupt human relationships at the critical point.

If one is in the position of a doctor, as I am, to become intimately acquainted with very many educated people, one is continually amazed at the terrifying unconsciousness of modern civilized man. Contemporary science can give such people any amount of enlightening knowledge about things they should have known right at the beginning of their social life but had no chance to acquire. Instead of knowing, they had to be content with ridiculous prejudices and preconceived opinions. Our whole society is split up by specialism, and the self-serving professions are so differentiated that none of them knows what the other is doing. There's nothing to be hoped for from the universities, since they turn out only specialists. Even psychology gives no thought to the unity of man, but has split into countless subdivisions each with its own tests and specialist theories. Anyone who sought the wisdom that is needed would soon find himself in the situation of old Diogenes, who went looking for a man on the marketplace of Athens in broad daylight with a lantern in his hand.

I think this is all I have to say about the present state of human understanding.

Yours sincerely, C. G. JUNG

To Calvin S. Hall

[ORIGINAL IN ENGLISH]

Dear Prof. Hall,   8 November 1954

Thank you for your kind reply. I am much obliged that you took my criticism in a good spirit. The main point with me is that it is difficult having to deal with careless and superficial criticisms. None of my critics has ever tried to apply my method conscientiously. Anybody doing it cannot fail to discover what I call archetypal motifs. They appear in dreams just as much as in speech or in the writings of our poets. The only question is: are they wholly spontaneous or due to tradition? To answer this question one has to go into detail, and it's just that detail that is neglected by the critics. For many years I have carefully analysed about 2000 dreams p.a., thus I have acquired a certain experience in this matter.

As I already told you, I object to the term "system." If I had an invented system, I certainly should have constructed better and more philosophical concepts than those I am applying. Take for instance *animus* and *anima*. No philosopher in his senses would invent such irrational and clumsy ideas. When things fit together, it is not always matter of a philosophical system; sometimes it is the facts that fit together. Mythological motifs are facts; they never change; only theories change. There can never be a time which denies the existence of mythological motifs, it is not just a barbarous darkening of the mind. Yet the theory about them can change a great deal at any time.

By this same mail, I am sending you a list of all my writings so that you can compare it with your list of my books.

Apologizing for my impatience, I remain,

Yours very sincerely, c. g. jung

To J. B. Priestley

[ORIGINAL IN ENGLISH]

Dear Mr. Priestley,   8 November 1954

Friends have sent your two articles[1] to me. I am deeply touched by your kindness and understanding. You as a writer are in a position to appreciate what it means to an isolated individual like myself to hear one friendly human voice among the stupid and malevolent noises rising from the scribbler-infested jungle. I am indeed most grateful for your warm-hearted support and your generous appreciation. Your succour comes at a time when it is badly needed; soon a little book of mine will be published in England which my publishers in USA did not dare to print. Its title is: *Answer to Job*.[2] It deals with the

☐ See Priestley, 17 July 46 (in vol. 1).

[1] "Jung and the Writer," *The Times Literary Supplement*, 6 Aug. 1954 (a review of Ira Progoff, *Jung's Psychology and Its Social Meaning*, 1953), and "Books in General," *The New Statesman and Nation*, 30 Oct. 1954 (a review of CW 7, 12, 16, 17).

[2] First published late 1954 by Routledge & Kegan Paul, London, and in 1956 by the Pastoral Psychology Book Club, Great Neck, New York. It was incorporated in CW 11 in 1958. (Cf. Murray, Aug. 56.)

wholly unsatisfactory outcome of the Book of Job and what its further historical consequences for the development of certain religious questions including Christian views were. The book will be highly unwelcome in certain spheres and will be misunderstood and misinterpreted accordingly. The German edition over here has already upset the representatives of three religions, not because it is irreligious but because it takes their statements and premises seriously. Needless to say the best of the so-called free-thinkers are equally shocked. Sir Herbert Read, who is informed about its contents, wisely said: "You certainly understand how to put your foot in it." But I am really glad that they are willing to print it. I will tell my publishers to present a copy to you as soon as it comes out.

Hoping you are in good health and active as ever, I remain,

Yours gratefully and sincerely, C. G. JUNG

To H. Oswald

Dear Frau Oswald,   11 November 1954

I would gladly accept your invitation to devote myself to Hölderlin's work if I still felt up to this task. Unfortunately I am no longer energetic enough and am too old—in my 80th year—to do it justice. I know the lines you quote[1] from Hölderlin only too well. But I have worked so hard in these last decades that I must be wary of even relatively minor mental exertions. It is now up to the younger generation to open a few locked doors, perhaps with the help of the keys I have

☐ Munich.

[1] "Nah ist   (Near is God
Und schwer zu fassen der Gott.   And hard to apprehend.
Wo aber Gefahr ist, wächst   But where danger is, there
Das Rettende auch . . ."   Arises salvation also . . .)

The opening lines of Hölderlin's poem "Patmos." Jung was deeply interested in Hölderlin's work, and in *Symbols of Transformation*, CW 5, there is a lengthy interpretation of several poems (pars. 618–42), among them "Patmos" (pars. 630ff.). — In 1953 the Swiss writer Georg Gerster, who was preparing an anthology of the favourite poems of 30 famous contemporaries, had asked for Jung's three favourites. He replied: "A selection from the number of my superlatives appears almost impossible. . . . Any one of the countless Islands of the Blessed is enough for me. . . . Tentatively: Goethe's 'God and the Bayadere'; Nietzsche's 'From High Mountains,' and the first strophe of Hölderlin's 'Patmos.' . . . Most likely something else would occur to me tomorrow." Cf. Gerster (ed.), *Trunken von Gedichten. Eine Anthologie geliebter deutscher Verse* (1953), p. 63.

193

wrought. In any case I see no one at present who could tackle Hölderlin. Such a work is reserved for a distant future. A person carries the torch only a stretch of the way and must then lay it down, not because he has reached a goal but because his strength is at an end. It would be most unseemly to grab Hölderlin by the hair in senile impatience. I cannot deny that all sorts of thoughts run through my head, but that traitor the body leaves me in the lurch. Nevertheless I thank you for your pious wish, for which there is every justification.

Yours sincerely, c. g. jung

To Arvind U. Vasavada

[ORIGINAL IN ENGLISH]

Dear friend,   22 November 1954

Thank you for your kind letter and the beautiful "salutation to the perfect Master." In the guru, I perceive, you greet the infinitesimal God whose light becomes visible wherever a man's consciousness has made even the smallest step forward and beyond one's own horizon. The light of the Dawn praised by our medieval thinkers as the *Aurora consurgens*,[1] the rising morning light, is awe-inspiring, it fills your heart with joy and admiration or with irritation and fear and even with hatred, according to the nature of whatever it reveals to you.

The ego receives the light from the self. Though we know of the self, yet it is not known. You may see a big town and know its name and geographical position, yet you do not know a single one of its inhabitants. You may even know a man through daily intercourse, yet you can be entirely ignorant of his real character. The ego is contained in the self as it is contained in the universe of which we know only the tiniest section. A man of greater insight and intelligence than mine can know myself, but I could not know him as long as my consciousness is inferior to his. Although we receive the light of consciousness from the self and although we know it to be the source of our illumination, we do not know whether it possesses anything we would call consciousness.[2] However beautiful and profound the

☐ Indian analytical psychologist; studied at the Jung Institute, now in U.S.A. Cf. his *Tripura-Rahasya* (*Jnanakhanda*), English tr., comparative study of the process of individuation (Chowkhamba Sanskrit Studies, 50; Varanasi, 1965).
[1] Cf. M.-L. von Franz, ed., *Aurora Consurgens* (tr., 1966).
[2] Cf. Sickesz, 19 Nov. 59.

sayings of your Wisdom are, they are essentially outbursts of admiration and enthusiastic attempts at formulating the overwhelming impressions an ego-consciousness has received from the impact of a superior subject. Even if the ego should be (as I think) the supreme point of the self, a mountain infinitely higher than Mt. Everest, it would be nothing but a little grain of rock or ice, never the whole mountain. Even if the grain recognizes itself as being part of the mountain and understands the mountain as an immense agglomeration of particles like itself, it does not know their ultimate nature, because all the others are, like itself, *individuals*, incomparable and incomprehensible in the last resort. (The individual alone is ultimate reality and can know of existence at all.)

If the self could be wholly experienced, it would be a limited experience whereas in reality its experience is unlimited and endless. It is our ego-consciousness that is capable only of limited experience. We can only *say* that the self is limitless, but we cannot *experience* its infinity. I can *say* that my consciousness is the same as that of the self, but it is nothing but words, since there is not the slightest evidence that I participate more or further in the self than my ego-consciousness reaches. What does the grain know of the whole mountain, although it is visibly a part of it? If I were one with the self, I would have knowledge of everything, I would speak Sanskrit, read cuneiform script, know the events that took place in prehistory, be acquainted with the life of other planets, etc. There is unfortunately nothing of the kind.

You should not mix up your own enlightenment with the self-revelation of the self. When you recognize yourself, you have not necessarily recognized the self but perhaps only an infinitesimal part of it, though the self has given you the light.

Your standpoint seems to coincide with that of our medieval mystics, who tried to dissolve themselves in God. You all seem to be interested in how to get back to the self, instead of looking for what the self wants you to do in the world, where—for the time being at least—we are located, presumably for a certain purpose. The universe does not seem to exist for the sole purpose of man denying or escaping it. Nobody can be more convinced of the importance of the self than me. But as a young man does not stay in his father's house but goes out into the world, so I don't look back to the self but collect it out of manifold experiences and put it together again. What I have left behind, seemingly lost, I meet in everything that comes my way and I collect it, reassembling it as it were. In order to get rid

195

of opposites, I needs must accept them first, but this leads away from the self. I must also learn how opposites can be united, and not how they can be avoided. As long as I am on the first part of the road I have to forget the self in order to get properly into the mill of the opposites, otherwise I live only fragmentarily and conditionally. Although the self is my origin, it is also the goal of my quest. When it was my origin, I did not know myself, and when I did learn about myself, I did not know the self. I have to discover it in my actions, where first it reappears under strange masks. That is one of the reasons why I must study symbolism, otherwise I risk not recognizing my own father and mother when I meet them again after the many years of my absence.

Hoping I have answered your question, I remain,

Yours sincerely, c. g. jung

To V. Wittkowski

Dear Herr Wittkowski,   22 November 1954

Best thanks for your kind postcard. I am glad to know that you haven't let yourself be thrown into confusion by my *Answer to Job*. My defence of the Marian dogma[1] is certainly an unexpected joke in the world's history, but one with a significant background. Also, the Pope's latest Encyclical on the *Regina et Domina omnis creaturae*[2] is uncommonly important in view of coming developments. Moreover there is an intimation in it of that little door through which the co-Redemptrix can one day enter (*participationem filii sui efficacitas habens*).[3] I would give anything to know the innermost thoughts of the Holy Father . . .

Yours sincerely, c. g. jung

□ Location unknown.

[1] Cf. White, 25 Nov. 50, n. 2; Dr. H., 17 Mar. 51; and Sinclair, 7 Jan. 55.

[2] This refers to the Encyclical *Ad Caeli Reginam*, in which a quotation is given from St. John of Damascus (8th cent.) calling Mary "Regina, Hera, Domina et omnium creaturae Domina."

[3] This quotation seems to be a very free rendering of the words of the Encyclical: ". . . verum etiam aliquam illius *efficacitatis participationem qua eius Filius* . . ." (The sentence in the Encyclical is translated: "The Blessed Virgin has not only been given the highest degree of excellence and perfection after Christ, *but also shares in the power which her Son* and our Redeemer exercises over the minds and wills of men.")

196

To Fowler McCormick

[ORIGINAL IN ENGLISH]

Dear Fowler,   24 November 1954

Don't worry, I enjoyed myself the other evening and I had a very good sleep afterwards. An interesting conversation never disturbs my sleep. Only an arduous talk to no purpose disturbs it. What about Friday?[1] We might try Einsiedeln to get a bit of sunshine, say about 10 o'clock.

Cordially yours, C. G. JUNG

(sorry!) C.G.

[1] For a motor excursion.

To Bernhard Martin

Dear Dr. Martin,   7 December 1954

It is very kind of you to submit your manuscript to me for an opinion. I have taken the liberty of marking it with numbers in pencil where a change in the text seems necessary.

You "know" of that which is beyond the psyche only through belief, not through knowledge. I do not write for believers who already possess the whole truth, rather for unbelieving but intelligent people who want to *understand* something. Without the psyche you can neither know *nor believe*. Therefore everything about which we can speak at all lies in the psychic realm; even the atom is in this sense a psychic model. (. . .)[1]

I grant you that the believer will learn nothing from my *Answer to Job* since he already has everything. I write only for unbelievers. Thanks to your belief, you know much more than I do. Since my earliest youth I have been made to feel how rich and how knowing the believers are, and how disinclined even to listen to anything else. I do not hesitate to admit my extreme poverty in knowing through believing, and would therefore advise you to shut my book with a bang and inscribe on the inside of the jacket: "Nothing here for the believing Christian"—a sentiment with which I am in complete agreement. I am not concerned with what is "believable" but simply with what is knowable. It seems to me that we are not in a position

□ Kassel.

[1] Here follow three pages of comments, omitted because they are unintelligible without Martin's MS, which cannot be traced.

to "generate" or "uphold" belief, for belief is a charisma which God giveth or taketh away. It would be presumptuous to imagine that we can command it at will.

For the sake of brevity my comments are rather direct and outspoken. I hope you won't mind this, but will see how different are the two planes on which the discussion is moving. Without in any way impugning belief, I confine myself to its *assertions*. As you see, I even take the highly controversial new dogma at its face value. I do not consider myself competent to judge the metaphysical truth of these assertions; I only try to elucidate their content and their psychological associations. The assertions are, as you yourself admit, anthropomorphic and therefore can hardly be considered reliable with respect to their metaphysical truth. You as a believer take the stand that the proposition "God is" has as its inevitable corollary God's existence in reality, whereas Kant[2] irrefutably pointed out long ago (in his critique of Anselm's[3] proof of God) that the little word "is" can denote no more than a "copula in the judgment." Other religions make equally absolute assertions, but quite different ones. But as a psychologist on the one hand and a human being on the other I must acknowledge that my brother may be right too. I do not belong to the elect and the *beati possidentes* of the sole truth, but must give fair consideration to all human assertions, even the denial of God. So when you confront me as a Christian apologist you are standing on a different plane from me. You cling to "believing is knowing," and I must always be the loser because *de fide non est disputandum*[4] any more than one can argue about taste. One cannot argue with the possessor of the truth. Only the seeker after truth needs to reflect, to inquire, to deliberate, for he admits that he does not know. As a believer you can only dismiss me out of hand and declare that I am no Christian and what I say is useless, indeed harmful. Well, gunpowder was a dangerous invention, but it also has its useful applications. It is notorious that everything can be used for

[2] Kant's critique, essentially the same as that of Thomas Aquinas, is formulated in his *Critique of Pure Reason*, in the section "The Transcendental Dialectic," Book 2, ch. 3, sec. 4. It is quoted and discussed in *Psychological Types*, CW 6, pars. 63ff.

[3] Anselm of Canterbury (1033–1109), Scholastic thinker, canonized 1494. His ontological proof of God (in his *Proslogion*) states that God is the Being than whom nothing greater can be conceived and therefore necessarily has real existence. This "proof" was criticized by Aquinas on the ground that we cannot pass from an idea to its reality. It is discussed in *Psychological Types*, pars. 59ff.

[4] = one cannot argue about faith.

a good or a bad purpose. Hence there was no valid reason for me to keep silence, quite apart from the fact that the present state of "Christendom" arouses a host of doubts in people's minds. As a doctor I have to provide the answers which for many of my patients are not forthcoming from the theologian. I myself have politely requested the theologians to explain to me what the attitude of modern Protestantism is as regards the identity of the Old and the New Testament concept of God. Two didn't answer at all and the third said that nobody bothers any more about God-concepts nowadays. But for the religious-minded person this is a matter of burning interest, which was one of my motives for writing *Answer to Job*. I would like to recommend Prof. Volz's *Das Daemonische in Jahwe* to your attention, and as for the New Testament I pose the question: Is it necessary to placate a "loving Father" with the martyr's death of his son? What is the relation here between love and vindictiveness? And what would I feel about it if my own father exhibited that kind of phenomenology?

Such are the questions of the unbelieving religious man for whom I write. To him applies the amiable (predestinarian) principle of Matt. 13:12: "Whosoever hath, to him shall be given," etc. But "illis non est datum,"[5] these lost sheep of which another, equally authentic logion says that Christ was sent *only* to them.[6] Those who cannot believe would at least like to *understand*: "Putasne intelligis quae legis?"[7] (Acts 8:30). But understanding begins at the bottom of the mountain on top of which the believer sits. He already knows everything much better and can therefore say: "Lord, I thank thee that I am not so dumb and ignorant as those down below, who want to understand" (cf. Luke 18:11). I cannot anticipate a thing by believing it but must be content with my unbelief until my efforts meet with the grace of illumination, that is, with religious experience. I cannot *make-believe*.

To conclude with an indiscreet question: Don't you think that the angel of the Lord, wrestling with Jacob, also got a few hefty cuffs and kicks? (So much for my "scandalous" criticism of Yahweh!) I know my *Answer to Job* is a shocker for which I ought to offer a civil apology (hence my motto).

Yours sincerely, C. G. JUNG

[5] Matthew 13:11: ". . . but to them it is not given."
[6] Matthew 9:13: "I am not come to call the righteous, but sinners to repentance." Cf. also Mark 2:17, Luke 5:32.
[7] Acts 8:30: "Understandest thou what thou readest?"

To Aniela Jaffé

Dear Aniela,   26 December 1954

I don't know which I admire more: your patience, your feeling for essentials and your descriptive powers, or Broch's astonishingly profound insight into the mystery of transformation, his pertinacity and consistency, and finally his linguistic artistry. At any rate I must be thankful I lacked the latter, for had this capacity been mine in the years 1914 to 1918, my later development would have taken a quite different turn less congenial to my nature. Still, Broch and I do have something in common: overwhelmed by the numinosity of things seen, the one wrapped his vision in a well-nigh impenetrable mist of images, and the other covered it up with a mountain of practical experiences and historical parallels. Both wanted to tear away the veils and yet both, from an excess of motivations, shrouded the ineffable secret again and opened up new byways for error. It fared with us as with Faust: "For Nature keeps her veil inviolate / Mysterious still in open light of day."[1]

Nevertheless a few new lights have been lit, among them your essay on Broch, so that even in our time the seeker may find his way back to the essential.

I am greatly obliged to you for your Christmas present.[2] I have started reading it at once. The book is very well written and its content is having a beneficial influence. There are things in those photos of the night sky that are exceedingly strange and moving. I won't or can't say anything about it yet, as I still haven't found the right words. It affects me directly in some way or other, but I don't know how or where. With cordial thanks,

Yours ever, c. g.

□ (Handwritten.)
[1] *Faust, Part One* (tr. P. Wayne), p. 53.
[2] A book with photos of the night sky taken at Mount Palomar Observatory.

To Laurens van der Post

[ORIGINAL IN ENGLISH]

Dear van der Post,   26 December 1954

Thank you ever so much for kindly sending me your book *Flamingo Feather*.[1] It is the nicest thing the huge wave of Xmas mail has washed up on my shore. It brings back those already remote memories of 30 years ago ever so vividly, unforgettable colours, sounds, perfumes, of days and nights in the bush. I am grateful to the particular genius—*vultu mutabilis, albus et ater*[2]—that took it upon itself to weave the patterns of my fate, that he included the experience of Africa[3] and its glory.

I beg you to accept my booklet *Answer to Job* as a humble response to your generous gift.

My best wishes and regards to you and Mrs. van der Post,

Cordially yours, C. G. JUNG

☐ (Handwritten.) South African author and explorer, later living in England.
[1] London and New York, 1955.
[2] Cf. Kerényi, 12 July 51, n. 4.
[3] Cf. *Memories*, ch. 9, sec. 3.

To Upton Sinclair

[ORIGINAL IN ENGLISH]

Dear Mr. Sinclair,   7 January 1955

Having read your novel *Our Lady*[1] and having enjoyed every page of it, I cannot refrain from bothering you again with a letter. This is the trouble you risk when giving your books to a psychologist who has made it his profession to receive impressions and to have reactions.

☐ This letter was published, with minor changes and some omissions, in *New Republic*, vol. 132, no. 8, issue 2100 (21 Feb. 1955). — As some of Jung's comments will hardly be intelligible to readers unfamiliar with *Our Lady*, a brief summary is given: The heroine of the story is Marya, a widow and grandmother, a peasant woman of ancient Nazareth speaking only Aramaic. Her son Jeshu, who is depicted as a religious and social revolutionary, has gone away on a mission, and in an agony of fear as to his future she consults a sorceress. Under a spell, she awakens in a great city (Los Angeles), moving with the crowd into a stadium where she witnesses what she takes to be a battle: the football game between Notre Dame U., Indiana, and the U. of California. Sitting next to her is a professor of Semitic languages at Notre Dame; on addressing the utterly bewildered woman he learns to his astonishment that she speaks ancient Aramaic. He hears her story and takes her to the bishop, who exorcises the demons and sends her back to Nazareth with no enlightenment whatever. There she rebukes the sorceress, saying: "I asked to see the future of myself and my son: and nothing I saw has anything to do with us."
[1] Emmaus, Pennsylvania, 1938.

On the day after I had read the story, I happened to come across the beautiful text of the "Exultet" in the Easter night liturgy:

> O inaestimabilis dilectio caritatis
> Ut servum redimeres, Filium tradidisti!
> O certe necessarium Adae peccatum,
> Quod Christi morte deletum est!
> O felix culpa
> Quae talem ac tantum meruit habere Redemptorem![2]

Although I am peculiarly sensitive to the beauty of the liturgical language and of the feeling expressed therein, something was amiss, as if a corner had been knocked off or a precious stone fallen from its setting. When trying to understand, I instantly remembered the bewildered Marya confronted with the incongruities of the exorcism, her beautiful and simple humanity caught in the coils of a vast historical process which had supplanted her concrete and immediate life by the almost inhuman superstructure of a dogmatic and ritual nature, so strange that, in spite of the identity of names and biographical items, she was not even able to recognize the story of herself and of her beloved son. By the way, a masterful touch! I also remembered your previous novel[3] about the idealistic youth who had almost become a saviour through one of those angelic tricks well known since the time of Enoch (the earthly adventure of Samiasaz[4] and his angelic host). And moreover, I recalled your Jesus biography.[5] Then I knew what it was that caused my peculiarly divided feeling: it was your common sense and realism, reducing the Holy Legend to human proportions and to probable possibilities, that never fails in knocking off a piece of the spiritual architecture or in causing a slight tremor of the Church's mighty structure. The anxiety of the priests to suppress the supposedly satanic attempt at verisimilitude is therefore most con-

---

[2] The *Missale Romanum* (liturgy of the Roman Catholic Mass), has the following text for Holy Saturday: "Oh unspeakable tenderness of charity! In order to redeem the servant, Thou hast given the son. Oh truly necessary sin of Adam which has been redeemed through the death of Christ. Oh happy guilt which has found so great a Redeemer!" — The term "felix culpa" (happy fault) goes back to St. Augustine.

[3] *What Didymus Did* (London, 1954), the story of a young gardener in a suburb of Los Angeles who is visited by an angel and receives the power to perform miracles. (Didymus, "twin," is the name of the apostle Thomas. Cf. John 11:16.)

[4] In the Book of Enoch, Samiasaz is the leader of the angels who took human wives (Gen. 6:2). Cf. "Answer to Job," CW 11, par. 689.

[5] Cf. Sinclair, 3 Nov. 52: *A Personal Jesus*.

vincing, as the devil is particularly dangerous when he tells the truth, as he often does (*vide* the biography of St. Anthony of Egypt by St. Athanasius[6]).

It is obviously your *laudabilis intentio* to extract a quintessence of truth from the incomprehensible chaos of historical distortions and dogmatic constructions, a truth of human size and acceptable to common sense. Such an attempt is hopeful and promises success, as the "truth" represented by the Church is so remote from ordinary understanding as to be well-nigh inacceptable. At all events, it conveys nothing any more to the modern mind that wants to understand since it is incapable of blind belief. In this respect, you continue the Strauss-Renan tradition in liberal theology.

I admit it is exceedingly probable that there is a human story at the bottom of it all. But under these conditions I must ask: Why the devil had this simple and therefore satisfactory story to be embellished and distorted beyond recognition? Or why had Jesus taken on unmistakably mythological traits already with the Gospel writers? And why is this process continued even in our enlightened days when the original picture has been obscured beyond all reasonable expectation? Why the Assumptio of 1950 and the Encyclical Ad caeli Reginam[7] of Oct. 11, 1954?

The impossibility of a concrete saviour, as styled by the Gospel writers, is and has always been to me obvious and indubitable. Yet I know my contemporaries too well to forget that to them it is news hearing the simple fundamental story. Liberal theology and incidentally your *laudabilis intentio* have definitely their place where they make sense. To me the human story is the inevitable *point de départ*, the self-evident basis of historical Christianity. It is the "small beginnings" of an amazing development. But the human story—I beg your pardon—is just ordinary, well within the confines of everyday life, not exciting and unique and thus not particularly interesting. We have heard it a thousand times and we ourselves have lived it at least

---

[6] St. Athanasius (*ca.* 293–373), archbishop of Alexandria, wrote a biography of St. Anthony (*ca.* 250–350), the first Christian monk. St. Anthony is noted for his fights with the devil, who appeared to him under manifold disguises. In one story the devil admits defeat by the saint, hoping to seduce him into the sin of pride. A long excerpt from the biography, "Life of St. Anthony," in *The Paradise or Garden of the Holy Fathers* (1904), is in *Psychological Types*, CW 6, par. 82.
[7] After having promulgated the dogma of the bodily assumption of Mary into heaven in *Munificentissimus Deus*, Nov. 1950, Pius XII confirmed it in his Encyclical Ad Caeli Reginam, 11 Oct. 1954, which established a yearly feast in honour of Mary's "royal dignity" as Queen of Heaven and Earth.

in parts. It is the well-known psychological *ensemble* of Mother and beloved Son, and how the legend begins with mother's anxieties and hopes and son's heroic fantasies and helpful friends and foes joining in, magnifying and augmenting little deviations from the truth and thus slowly creating the web called the *reputation of a personality*.

Here you have me—the psychologist—with what the French call his *déformation professionnelle*. He is *blasé*, overfed with the "simple" human story, which does not touch his interest and particularly not his religious feeling. The human story is even the thing to get away from, as the small story is neither exciting nor edifying. On the contrary, one wants to hear the great story of gods and heroes and how the world was created and so on. The small stories can be heard where the women wash in the river, or in the kitchen or at the village well, and above all everybody lives them at home. That has been so since the dawn of consciousness. But there was a time in antiquity, about the fourth century B.C. (I am not quite certain about the date. Being actually away on vacation, I miss my library!), when a man Euhemeros[8] made himself a name through a then new theory: The divine and heroic myth is founded upon the small story of an ordinary human chief or petty king of local fame, magnified by a minstrel's fantasy. All-Father Zeus, the mighty "gatherer of clouds," was originally a little tyrant, ruling some villages from his *maison forte* upon a hill, and "nocturnis ululatibus horrenda Prosperpina"[9] was presumably his awe-inspiring mother-in-law. That was certainly a time sick of the old gods and their ridiculous fairy stories, curiously similar to the "enlightenment" of our epoch equally fed up with its "myth" and welcoming any kind of iconoclasm, from the *Encyclopédie*[10] of the XVIIIth century to the Freudian theory reducing the religious "illusion" to the basic "family romance" with its incestuous innuendos in the early XXth century. Unlike your predecessor, you do not insist upon the *chronique scandaleuse* of the Olympians and other ideals, but with a loving hand and with decency like a benevolent pedagogue, you take your reader by the hand: "I am going to tell you a

[8] Euhemeros, Greek philosopher (*fl.* 4th–3rd cent. B.C.). He taught that the Olympians were originally great kings and war heroes.
[9] "Proserpine striking terror with midnight ululations." — Apuleius, *The Golden Ass*, XI, 2.
[10] *Encyclopédie ou Dictionnaire raisonée des sciences, des arts et des métiers*, edited by Diderot (1713–84), became one of the most important influences in the French Enlightenment.

better story, something nice and reasonable, that anybody can accept. I don't repeat these ancient absurdities, these god-awful theologoumena[11] like the Virgin Birth, blood and flesh mysteries, and other wholly superfluous miracle gossip. I show you the touching and simple humanity behind these gruesome inventions of benighted ecclesiastical brains."

This is a kind-hearted iconoclasm far more deadly than the frankly murderous arrows from M. de Voltaire's quiver: all these mythological assertions are so obviously impossible that their refutation is not even needed. These relics of the dark ages vanish like morning mist before the rising sun, when the idealistic and charming gardener's boy experiments with miracles of the good old kind, or when your authentic Galilean grandmother "Marya" does not even recognize herself or her beloved son in the picture produced by the magic mirror of Christian tradition.

Yet, why should a more or less ordinary story of a good mother and her well-meaning idealistic boy give rise to one of the most amazing mental or spiritual developments of all times? Who or what is its *agens*? Why could the facts not remain as they were originally? The answer is obvious: The story is so ordinary that there would not have been any reason for its tradition, quite certainly not for its world-wide expansion. The fact that the original situation has developed into one of the most extraordinary myths about a divine *heros*, a God-man and his cosmic fate, is not due to its underlying human story, but to the powerful action of pre-existing mythological motifs attributed to the biographically almost unknown Jesus, a wandering miracle Rabbi in the style of the ancient Hebrew prophets, or of the contemporary teacher John the Baptizer, or of the much later Zaddiks of the Chassidim.[12] The immediate source and origin of the myth projected upon the teacher Jesus is to be found in the then popular Book of Enoch and its central figure of the "Son of Man" and his messianic mission. From the Gospel texts it is even manifest that Jesus identified himself with this "Son of Man." Thus it is the spirit of his time, the collective hope and expectation, which caused this astounding transformation and not at all the more or less insignificant story of the man Jesus.

[11] Teachings not part of Church dogma but supported by theologians; more generally, theological formulations of the nature of God.

[12] The Chassidim (or Hasidim) were a mystical sect of Judaism, founded shortly before the middle of the 18th cent. by the mystic Israel Baal Shem ("Master of the Holy Name"; 1700–1760). The leaders were called Zaddiks (righteous men).

The true *agens* is the archetypal image of the God-man, appearing in Ezekiel's vision[13] for the first time in Jewish history, but in itself a considerably older figure in Egyptian theology, viz., Osiris and Horus.

The transformation of Jesus, i.e., the integration of his human self into a super- or inhuman figure of a deity, accounts for the amazing "distortion" of his ordinary personal biography. In other words: the essence of Christian tradition is by no means the simple man Jesus whom we seek in vain in the Gospels, but the lore of the God-man and his cosmic drama. Even the Gospels themselves make it their special job to prove that their Jesus is the incarnated God equipped with all the magic powers of a κύριος τῶν πνευμάτων.[14] That is why they are so liberal with miracle gossip which they naïvely assume proves their point. It is only natural that the subsequent post-apostolic developments even went several points better in this respect, and in our days the process of mythological integration is still expanding and spreading itself even to Jesus' mother, formerly carefully kept down to the human rank and file for at least 500 years of early church history. Boldly breaking through the sacrosanct rule about the definability of a new dogmatic truth, viz., that the said truth is only *definibilis* inasmuch as it was believed and taught in apostolic times, *explicite* or *implicite*, the pope has declared the *Assumptio Mariae* a dogma of the Christian creed. The justification he relies on is the pious belief of the masses for more than 1000 years, which he considers sufficient proof of the work of the Holy Ghost. Obviously the "pious belief" of the masses continues the process of projection, i.e., of transformation of human situations into myth.

But why should there be myth at all? My letter is already too long so that I can't answer this last question any more, but I have written several books about it. I only wanted to explain to you my idea that in trying to extract the quintessence of Christian tradition, you have removed it like Prof. Bultmann in his attempt at "demythologizing" the Gospels. One cannot help admitting that the human story is so very much more probable, but it has little or nothing to do with the problem of the myth containing the essence of Christian religion. You catch your priests most cleverly in the disadvantageous position which they have created for themselves by their preaching a concrete historicity of clearly mythological facts. Nobody reading your admirable novel can deny being deeply impressed by the very dramatic confrontation of the original with the mythological picture, and very

[13] Ezekiel 1:26.
[14] = Lord of the spirits.

206

probably he will prefer the human story to its mythological "distortion."

But what about the εὐαγγέλιον, the "message" of the God-man and Redeemer and his divine fate, the very foundation of everything that is holy to the Church? There is the spiritual heritage and harvest of 1900 years still to account for, and I am very doubtful whether the reduction to common sense is the correct answer or not. As a matter of fact, I attribute an incomparably greater importance to the dogmatic truth than to the probable human story. The religious need gets nothing out of the latter, and at all events less than from a mere belief in Jesus Christ or any other dogma. Inasmuch as the belief is real and living, it works. But inasmuch as it is mere imagination and an effort of the will without understanding, I see little merit in it. Unfortunately, this unsatisfactory condition prevails in modern times, and in so far as there is nothing beyond belief without understanding but doubt and scepticism, the whole Christian tradition goes by the board as a mere fantasy. I consider this event a tremendous loss for which we are to pay a terrific price. The effect becomes visible in the dissolution of ethical values and a complete disorientation of our *Weltanschauung*. The "truths" of natural science or "existential philosophy" are poor surrogates. Natural "laws" are in the main mere abstractions (being statistical averages) instead of reality, and they abolish individual existence as being merely exceptional. But the individual as the only carrier of life and existence is of paramount importance. He cannot be substituted by a group or by a mass. Yet we are rapidly approaching a state in which nobody will accept individual responsibility any more. We prefer to leave it as an odious business to groups and organizations, blissfully unconscious of the fact that the group or mass psyche is that of an animal and wholly inhuman.

What we need is the development of the inner spiritual man, the unique individual whose treasure is hidden on the one hand in the symbols of our mythological tradition, and on the other hand in man's unconscious psyche. It is tragic that science and its philosophy discourage the individual and that theology resists every reasonable attempt to understand its symbols. Theologians call their creed a *symbolum*,[15] but they refuse to call their truth "symbolic." Yet, if

---

[15] A *symbolum*, in the theological sense, is the formulation of a basic tenet of Christian faith; the creeds were *symbola*. Cf. "Dogma of the Trinity," CW 11, pars. 210ff.

207

it is anything, it is anthropomorphic symbolism and therefore capable of re-interpretation.

Hoping you don't mind my frank discussion of your very inspiring writings,

I remain, with my best wishes for the New Year,

Yours sincerely, C. G. JUNG

P.S. Thank you very much for your kind letter that has reached me just now. I am amazed at the fact that you should have difficulties in finding a publisher.[16] What is America coming to, when her most capable authors cannot reach their public any more? What a time!

[16] In his letter S. spoke of his difficulties in finding a publisher for *What Didymus Did*. It was never published in America but only in England. — This postscript was added in handwriting.

To Pastor William Lachat

Dear Pastor Lachat,   18 January 1955

The book on *Le Bâpteme dans l'Église réformée*[1] which you were good enough to send me deals with an eminently theological theme. I feel that I am too much of a layman to be competent to touch upon it. The only problem that concerns me is that of the *rite* in Protestantism. As I see it, this is a problem of the highest importance. The *sola fide* standpoint seems to me insufficient for a complete religion. Every religion makes use of two feet: faith on one side and ritual on the other.

In the two Christian churches, the importance and the psychological significance of rites are not generally appreciated; to some people they are acts of faith or of habit; to others, acts of magic. But in reality there is a third aspect: the aspect of the rite as a symbolic act, giving expression to the *archetypal expectation* of the unconscious. What I mean by this is that every epoch of our biological life has a numinous character: birth, puberty, marriage, illness, death,

□ (Translated from French.) Neuchâtel.
[1] *Le Bâpteme dans l'Église réformée*, ed. Paul Attinger (1954). L. suggested that the Swiss Reformed Church should adopt a more liberal attitude to the administration of baptism. — Another letter to L., dated 27 Mar. 54, too long and technical to be included in this Selection, is in CW 18, pars. 1532ff.

208

etc. This is a natural fact demanding recognition, a question wanting an answer. It is a need that should be satisfied by a solemn act, characterizing the numinous moment with a combination of words and gestures of an archetypal, symbolic nature. *Rites* give satisfaction to the collective and numinous aspects of the moment, beyond their purely personal significance. This aspect of the rite is highly important. The pastor's personal prayer does not fill the need at all because the response should be collective and historical; it should evoke the "ancestral spirits" so as to unite the present with the historical and mythological past, and for that a re-presentation of the past is indispensable: rites should be *archaic* (in language and gesture). The proper kind of rite is not magically but psychologically efficacious. That is why a well-conducted Mass produces a powerful effect, particularly when the meaning of the ceremony can be followed. But once lost, lost forever! That is the tragedy of Protestantism. It has only one leg left. This lack may possibly be compensated by an artificial limb, but one never feels convinced that it is as good as the natural leg. The Protestant is restless, and something in him goes about looking for a solution. The wheel of time cannot be turned back. Things can, however, be destroyed and renewed. This is extremely dangerous, but the signs of our time are dangerous too. If there was ever a truly apocalyptic era, it is ours. God has put the means for a universal holocaust into the hands of men.

People hate the human soul, it is *nothing but* "psychological." They don't understand that it has needs, and they throw its treasures into the street without understanding them. That is what Protestantism started, the Encyclopedists continued, and *la Déesse Raison*[2] will finish off. Our rites will become solemn syntheses of hydrogen bombs.

Baptism, like the other sacraments, is really a mystery in so far as it represents an answer to the unconscious question put to us by the numinous moment. This question awaits a satisfactory reaction from our side. If there is no response, the lack of it augments the general dissatisfaction to the point of neurosis, and increases the disorientation to the point of mental blindness and collective psychosis which has characterized our time since 1933, or (in Russia) since the war of 1914–1918.

[2] The cult of the Goddess Reason was introduced in 1793 during the French Revolution at the instigation of Pierre-Gaspard Chaumette, public prosecutor of the Paris Commune. It lapsed with his execution in 1794.

I thank you very much for sending the book on baptism, which I am in the process of reading slowly. Perhaps I shall have still other reactions.

With my sincere regards, C. G. JUNG

To Mircea Eliade

Dear Professor Eliade,   19 January 1955

It is an honour to have been sent a copy of your book on yoga.[1] I greatly appreciate your kindness and generosity. I am now studying your work very carefully and profoundly enjoying its riches. It is certainly the best and most complete summary of yoga that I know of, and I am happy to possess such a mine of information. I was somewhat surprised, however, to find that you had not been able to grant me normal intelligence and scientific responsibility. As you know, I received my scientific education in the field of the natural sciences, whose principle is *nihil est in intellectu quod non antea fuerit in sensu*.[2] In any case, this is the fundamental credo of the medical alienist. So you can imagine my astonishment when I encountered associations of ideas, or rather "thought forms," among alienated and later among neurotics and normal persons, for which no models could apparently be found. Naturally this was particularly shocking to me because very recognizable models did exist, but entirely beyond the purview of my patients. There was not even the chance of cryptomnesia since the models did not exist in the patients' environment. I waited and explored all the possible explanations for fourteen years before I published the facts.[3] I went to the U.S.A. to study the dreams of Negroes in the southern states, and I found that their dreams contain the same archetypal motifs as ours.[4] Every

□ (Translated from French.) Mircea Eliade, Rumanian author and Orientalist, now professor of the history of religions at the University of Chicago; frequent lecturer at the Eranos meetings.

[1] *Yoga: Immortality and Freedom* (1958; orig. 1954).

[2] "There is nothing in the mind that was not previously in the senses." Leibniz, *New Essays on Human Understanding* (orig. 1703), Book II, ch. 1, sec. 2. The formula was scholastic in origin; cf. Duns Scotus, *Super universalibus Porphyrii*, qu. 3.

[3] In "Commentary on *The Secret of the Golden Flower*" (orig. 1929), CW 13; cf. pp. 3f.

[4] Cf. White, 10 Apr. 54, n. 22.

time that a patient spontaneously produced a mandala, I did my best to discover its origin. There were no models for them. We do not see such things around us, and, still more important, we do not know their use or their significance, nothing is taught us about them. It would even be difficult for us to find a scholar, like Tucci,[5] capable of giving us information about them. In India it is entirely different. There they *repeat and imitate* mandalas which are to be seen just about everywhere. If any "apish imitation"[6] occurs, no contrast is intended among the Tibetans and Hindus. But *the unconscious reacts instinctively, and instinct never imitates, it reproduces without a conscious model*, it follows its biological "behaviour pattern." This is exactly what happens with my individual mandalas: they are produced instinctively and automatically, without models or imitation.

Even my former teacher, Professor Freud, would never have admitted that the incest complex with its typical fantasies (what I call the "incest archetype") was nothing but an apish reaction, the imitation of a model. For him, incest was a biological affair, that is, a perverted sex instinct. The child who develops that sort of fantasies is not imitating adults. His own instinct is at the base of his fantasies. Every instinct generates its own forms and fantasies which are more or less identical everywhere, without having been spread by tradition, migration, imitation, or education. For example, the mandala seems originally to have been an apotropaic gesture for the purpose of concentration. That is why it reproduces a form which is the most primordial of infantile patterns. The statistics which Kellogg[7] compiled from the drawings of thousands of very young children are proof of this.

---

[5] Giuseppe Tucci, *The Theory and Practice of the Mandala* (tr., 1961; orig., 1949).

[6] On p. 230 of the French original, E. uses the words "simiesque" (apish) and "singer" (to ape). In his reply to this letter he expressed his regret about the misunderstanding, and he subsequently changed the words for the English edition of the book. The translation reads: "The spontaneous rediscovery of mandalas by the unconscious raises an important problem. We may well ask if the 'unconscious' is not in this case trying to imitate processes by which 'consciousness' (or, in some cases, the 'transconscious') seeks to obtain completeness and conquer freedom" (p. 226), and on p. 227 there is the phrase "mimicking imitation."

[7] Mrs. Rhoda Kellogg, a nursery-school teacher in San Francisco, had examined over a million scribblings of two- to five-year-olds from more than thirty countries for basic types and patterns. Her findings are published in *The Psychology of Children's Art* (1967).

211

To attribute the qualities of the conscious psyche to the unconscious is quite a serious error. I do not commit it, nor am I so stupidly ignorant that I cannot recognize the instinctive character of the unconscious. Above all, you have only to leaf through my works to assure yourself that I identify the archetype with the "pattern of behaviour." You have used the term "archetype" too, but without mentioning that you mean by this term only the repetition and imitation of a conscious image or idea. The real "ape" in us is consciousness; it is our consciousness that imitates and repeats. But the unconscious, being instinctive, is very conservative and difficult to influence. Nobody knows better than the psychiatrist how much the unconscious resists every effort to change it or influence it in the least. If it were "apish" it would be easy to make it forget its compulsions and its obstinate ideas—and, if it were imitative, it would not be creative. The lucky intuitions of the artist and the inventor are never imitations. Those gentlemen would be very much put out by such a thought.

There is a psychological problem here which I cannot explain. On the one hand, you make the very kind and generous gesture of sending me your book; on the other, you seem to consider me so idiotic as never even to have thought about the nature of the unconscious. How have I merited this ill-will? From the moment when I had the honour and pleasure of making your acquaintance personally, I have never felt anything other than admiration and esteem for your great work, and I would be distressed to have offended you without knowing it.

I hope that you will not be angry with me for writing you this long importunate letter, but I do not like to let a hidden sore fester. Needless to say how grateful I would be to you for a few words of explanation!

With admiration and lasting gratitude,

Very sincerely yours, C. G. JUNG

To Father Victor White

[ORIGINAL IN ENGLISH]

Dear Victor,   19 January 1955

It is now more than 2 months ago that I began to write a letter to you, but I could not continue it since I did not know what you were doing in California,[1] nor why you were sent there. From your recent letter I see that your stay in U.S.A. makes sense. No matter how little you can convey to your unprepared public, it contains at least some grains of the future.

I should have thanked you long ago for your kind messages and wishes for the New Year, but I hardly can keep up any more with all my obligations. There are many things I could or should tell you, but *desunt vires*.[2] It is nice to know that you come to Zurich in the end of April.

I know you will have some difficulties when my *Answer to Job* becomes public.[3] I am sorry. Already Philip Toynbee has reviewed it in an "abysmally stupid" way,[4] as R.F.C. Hull, the translator, rightly says (in a letter to me). It was to be expected. I have been up against the wall of stupidity for 50 years. That is just so and nothing can be done about it.

Your quotation from S. Thomas is a marvellous puzzle.[5] I have brooded over it for many hours and I can't make head or tail of it unless it is an attempt to give Evil some substantiality in recognition of the fact that we experience it as just as "substantial" as Good. What is Good then *in apprehensione animae*? He just does not carry through his argument, *cum malum sit privatio boni*, to which he sticks without looking at it from the other side. In ordinary logic, cold is the *carentia oppositi habitus, ergo* privation of warmth and vice versa, above–below, right–left, white–black, etc. In my "abysmal

---

[1] In Oct. 1954, W. had been sent to California without having been given any special assignment. He found, however, that there was a widespread interest in religion and psychiatry, and was soon invited to give a great many lectures to colleges, universities, social service agencies, seminaries, church halls, and he talked on television about Jung's psychology.

[2] = the strength is lacking.

[3] W. wrote that he was "frankly relieved that *Answer to Job* has not yet appeared in U.S.A." since it would have made it difficult for him to put over Jung's concepts to a rather naïve public. Cf. Priestley, 8 Nov. 54, n. 2.

[4] In the London *Observer*, 9 Jan. 1955. Cf. Hull, 24 Jan. 55.

[5] W. quoted a passage from the *Summa theologica*, I-II, 36, 1: "Malum enim . . . est privatio boni; privatio autem in rerum natura nihil est aliud quam carentia oppositi habitus. . . . In apprehensione autem ipsa privatio habet rationem cuiusdam entis, unde dicitur ens rationis. Et sic malum, cum sit privatio, se habet per modum contrarii." ("Evil is the privation of good; and privation is in reality nothing else than the lack of the contrary habit. . . . And even a privation, as apprehended, has the aspect of a being, wherefore it is called a being of reason. And in this way evil, being a privation, is regarded as a contrary." — Tr. Fathers of the English Dominican Province, 1947, vol. I, p. 747.) Jung's phrase "in apprehensione animae" ("as considered by the mind") occurs in a previous sentence.

stupidity" I can see nothing but a *petitio principii* if there ever was one. Why should an emotion be more concrete psychologically than the *ratio*? Does the *ratio* not affect the body?

There is a joke in your letter: after your argument, you write: "Well, I will weary you *now* more." You win, I have laboured for several days getting nowhere. Please don't get angry with me. I am obviously too dense. I hope you will be patient enough with my debility and explain the puzzle orally to me when I see you again in the flesh.

Although I cannot complain about my health, I am feeling the burden of my age. My last work, *Mysterium Coniunctionis*, is now with the printer, and I have no ideas any more—thank Heavens.

My best wishes for the New Year,

Cordially yours, C. G. JUNG

To Upton Sinclair

[ORIGINAL IN ENGLISH]

Dear Mr. Sinclair, 20 January 1955

Thank you ever so much for your awfully nice letter. You ought not to think that I shall be able to write you always such long letters in the future; it all depends on the button you push. It happens that your recent writings have touched off some electric charges. I am glad that my letter has pleased you and I have no objection whatever if you want to publish it in the *New Republic*. It is a great question to me whether the American public or at least some of its competent representatives can follow my argument. If the reduction to the simple human story would be the proper answer, the whole tradition of 2000 years would be wiped out together with the church that carries it. The disruption of tradition means the destruction of a culture. I am not sure that we ought to risk such a peril. If we want to maintain the spiritual contents of 2000 years of Christian tradition, we must understand what it is all about. One can do that only if one assumes that it makes sense. As religious assertions never make sense when understood concretely, they needs must be comprehended as a symbolic psychic phenomenon. That's the point I try to make clear to my contemporaries. It is an ambitious and perhaps hopeless enterprise, but I believe in the Roman principle *dulce et decorum est pro patria mori*; instead of *patria* you read *patrimonium christianum*.[1]

214

I have realized from your previous letter that you are already 76 years old; I hadn't realized that before. I am now in my 80th and I must say I am grateful to whomever administers my fate that I have met in you a kindred spirit interested in and talking of things that seem to be vital to you. I assure you there are not many. The *ecclesia spiritualis* is a very small concern, and pays little dividends. My best wishes for you,

Yours cordially, c. g. j u n g

P.S. Indeed I do remember Frederik van Eeden:[2] I may have seen him personally even, but I am not quite sure; it is so long ago, between 40 and 50 years. I remember him as a very sensitive and sweet nature, definitely without the stamina a pioneer needs. He was dangerously near the modern mind, but his weakness led him into the protection of the ecclesiastical walls. I don't know how he felt about his conversion. His was a way back, but not out.

[1] "It is sweet and fitting to die for your country" (Horace, *Odes*, II, 13). *Patrimonium christianum* = Christian heritage.
[2] Frederik van Eeden (1860–1932), leading Dutch writer, psychiatrist, and social reformer. He had been a friend of Sinclair's. After opening the first psychotherapeutic clinic in Holland in 1887, he founded in 1899 a semi-communistic settlement, and later started a colony of the same type in North Carolina. He was received into the Catholic Church in 1922.

To Michael Fordham

[ORIGINAL IN ENGLISH]

Dear Fordham,   24 January 1955

According to your wish and to my notoriously helpless state concerning higher mathematics, I have sent the galley proofs and your notes to Prof. Fierz.[1] You will find the other notes included in this letter. I am deeply obliged to you for all the trouble you have taken over this complicated matter.

An American pupil of mine, Dr. Progoff (New York), has tried to

[1] In collaboration with the editors of CW, Jung revised and rearranged portions of the material in "An Astrological Experiment" (ch. 2 of "Synchronicity"). Tabelle III in the German text is replaced by Figs. 2 and 3, and an appendix compiled by the editors on the basis of Fierz's mathematical argument has been added (CW 8, pp. 483f.). For other textual changes cf. Hull, 3 Aug. 53, n. 2. — Three letters to Markus Fierz concerning the statistics are included in CW 18, pars. 1193ff.

adapt and to explain synchronicity to the average reader,[2] but he landed his ship on the rocks because he could not free his mind from the deep-rooted belief in the Sanctissima Trinitas of the axiomata time, space, and causality. Funny how few people can draw the inevitable conclusion from causality being of statistical nature, that it must suffer exceptions. You can arbitrarily dismiss them as indispensable parts of the real world, if you like averages better than random facts. The latter are facts none the less and cannot be treated as non-existent. Moreover, since the real man is always an individual and unique event and as such merely "random," you have to label the whole of mankind in its essentials as "valueless." But on the other hand, only the individual carries life and consciousness of life, which seems to me rather a significant fact not to be lightly dismissed at least not by the physician. You can do such things in Nazi Germany or in Russia, but—God forbid—not with us. But wherever a philosophy based upon the sciences prevails (as in the USA), the individual man loses his foothold and becomes "vermasst," turned into a mass particle, because as an "exception" he is valueless, not very different from the Russian.

This is the reason and the motive of my essay. I am convinced that something ought to be done about this blind and dangerous belief in the security of the scientific Trinity. I don't expect that my contemporaries will accept my idea, but my book will be in existence and sooner or later somebody will draw the same conclusions.

By the way—do you know Brown's paper[3] about the Rhine experiments? I only know it in its French form (G. Spencer Brown: "De la récherche psychique considérée comme un test de la théorie des probabilités," *Revue métapsychique*, Mai-Août, 1954, p. 87 sqq.). The author cannot deny the validity of Rhine's results. But since it is "impossible" to look round corners and to know the future, the probability calculus must be basically wrong! This shows the impact of synchronicity upon the fanatical one-sidedness of scientific philosophy.

Thanking you again for your care and attention, I remain,

Yours sincerely, c. g. j u n g

[2] Ira Progoff, psychologist and therapist, now director of Dialogue House, New York. Cf. his *Jung, Synchronicity, and Human Destiny* (1973), containing the ms. referred to, with Jung's handwritten comments reproduced; also *Jung's Psychology and Its Social Meaning* (1953).
[3] Cf. Rhine, 25 Sept. 53, n. 3.

To R.F.C. Hull

[ORIGINAL IN ENGLISH]

Dear Hull,   24 January 1955

Thank you very much for your refreshing answer to Mr. Philip Toynbee. You have done it very well. No reason to believe you could not rectify such clumsy misunderstandings! I am obliged to you for your courageous answer.[1] There are damned few who have the guts to stand up for me. The latest comment about "Synchronicity" is that it cannot be accepted because it shakes the security of our scientific foundations, as if this were not exactly the goal I am aiming at and as if the merely statistical nature of causality had never been mentioned before. It is true however that it is the asses that make public opinion. 50 years of this stuff could have subdued me easily if I had not had the unshakable experience that my truth was good enough for myself and that I could live with it. If you like Camembert, you just like it, although the whole world would shout at you that it is very bad. Sooner or later, somebody else will also discover that nothing is quite secure, not even the SS. Trinitas, space, time, and causality.

I am sorry that I did not see you again.[2] Only once I saw you flitting by on your fiery chariot.[3] I am planning to come down to Ascona once more towards the end of February for about a fortnight.

Many thanks!

Yours cordially, C. G. JUNG

[1] Cf. White, 19 Jan. 55, n. 4. H.'s answer was never published.
[2] H. then lived in Ascona, in southern Switzerland, and Jung sometimes spent a vacation there.
[3] H. had had an attack of poliomyelitis in 1947 and went about in an electric-powered wheelchair.

To Hans A. Illing

Dear Dr. Illing,   26 January 1955

As a doctor, I consider any psychic disturbance, whether neurosis or psychosis, to be an individual illness, so the patient has to be

□ Psychotherapist, Los Angeles, California. — Illing, who together with George R. Bach was preparing a paper on group psychotherapy, asked for Jung's views on this form of therapy. Two letters of Illing's and this and the next letter of Jung's are

treated accordingly. The individual can be treated in the group only to the extent that he is a member of it. This is a great relief to begin with, since, being submerged in the group, he can escape from himself up to a point. The sense of security is increased and the sense of responsibility decreased when one is part of a group. Once I ran into a thick fog while crossing a treacherous glacier, full of crevasses, with a company of soldiers. The situation was so dangerous that everyone had to stop just where he happened to be. Yet there was no trace of panic, but rather the spirit of a public festival! Had one been alone, or had there only been two of us, the danger could not have been overlooked or laughed off. As it was, the brave and experienced had a chance to shine. The timid took heart from the plucky ones, and nobody said a word about the possibility of having to improvise a bivouac on the glacier, which could hardly have passed off without frostbite, etc., let alone about the perils of an attempted descent. This is typical of the mass mentality.

Young people in a group get up to tricks they would never do by themselves. During the war, compulsion neuroses among soldiers vanished overnight as a result of group activity. The group confessions of sects like the Oxford Movement are well known; also the cures at Lourdes, which would be unthinkable without an admiring public. Groups bring about not only astonishing cures but equally astonishing psychic changes and conversions precisely because *suggestibility is heightened*. This was recognized long ago by the totalitarian dictators; hence the mass parades, chanting, cheering, etc. Hitler inspired the most massive group experience of change in Germany since the Reformation and cost Europe millions of dead.

Heightened suggestibility means individual bondage, because the individual is at the mercy of environmental influences, be they good or bad. The discriminative capacity is weakened, and so is the sense of personal responsibility, which as in the Oxford Movement is left to "Lord Jesus." People have wondered belatedly about the psychology of the German Army—no wonder! Every single soldier and officer was just a particle in the mass, swayed by suggestion and stripped of moral responsibility.

Even a small group is ruled by a suggestive group spirit which, if it is good, can have very favourable social effects, though at the expense of mental and moral independence of the individual. The

published (in a different tr.) in Illing, "C. G. Jung on the Present Trends in Group Psychotherapy," *Human Relations*, X:1 (1957), 78ff.

group accentuates the *ego*; one becomes braver, more presumptuous, more cocky, more insolent, more reckless; but the *self* is diminished and gets pushed into the background in favour of the average. For this reason all weak and insecure persons belong to unions and organizations, and if possible to a nation of 80 million! Then one is a big shot, because he is identical with everybody else, but he loses his self (which is the soul the devil is after and wins!) and his individual judgment. The ego is pressed to the wall by the group only if in his judgment it is not in accord with the group. Hence the individual in the group always tends to assent as far as possible to the majority opinion, or else to impose his opinion on the group.

The levelling influence of the group on the individual is compensated by one member of it identifying with the group spirit and becoming the Leader. As a result, prestige and power conflicts are constantly arising due to the heightened egotism of the mass man. Social egocentricity increases in proportion to the numerical strength of the group.

I have no practical objections to group therapy any more than I have to Christian Science, the Oxford Movement, and other therapeutically effective sects. I myself founded a group nearly 40 years ago;[1] but it was composed of analysed persons and its purpose was to constellate the individual's social attitude. This group is still active today. The social attitude does not come into operation in the dialectical relationship between patient and doctor and may therefore remain in an unadapted state, as was the case with the majority of my patients. This drawback only became apparent when the group was formed and called for the mutual rubbing off of sharp edges.

In my opinion group therapy is only capable of educating the *social* human being. Attempts in this direction are being made in England, particularly with unanalysed persons, on the basis of psychological theories inaugurated by me. Mr. P. W. Martin,[2] Talboys, Oxted, Surrey, could give you further information. I rate these attempts very highly. However, in view of the foregoing critical remarks about group therapy, I do not believe that it can replace individual analysis, i.e., the dialectical process between two individuals and the subsequent intrapsychic discussion, the dialogue with the unconscious. Since the sole carrier of life and the quintessence of any kind of community is the individual, it follows that he and

[1] The Psychological Club, Zurich, founded 1916.
[2] Cf. Martin, 20 Aug. 37, n. □.

his quality are of paramount importance. The individual must be complete and must have substance, otherwise nothing has substance, for any number of zeros still do not amount to more than zero. A group of inferior people is never better than any one of them; it is just as inferior as they, and a State composed of nothing but sheep is never anything else but a herd of sheep, even though it is led by a shepherd with a vicious dog.

In our time, which puts so much weight on the socialization of the individual because a special capacity for adaptation is also needed, the formation of psychologically oriented groups is certainly more important than ever. But in view of the notorious tendency of people to lean on others and cling to various -isms instead of finding security and independence within themselves, which is the prime requisite, there is a danger that the individual will equate the group with father and mother and so remain just as dependent, insecure, and infantile as before. He may become adapted socially, but what of his individuality, which alone gives meaning to the social fabric? Sure, if society consisted of valuable individuals only, adaptation would be worthwhile; but in reality it is composed mainly of nincompoops and moral weaklings, and its level is far below that of its better representatives, in addition to which the mass as such stifles all individual values. When a hundred intelligent heads are united in a group the result is one big fathead. There used to be the quiz question: What are the three biggest organizations whose morality is the lowest? Answer: Standard Oil, the Catholic Church, and the German Army. It is precisely in a Christian organization that one might expect the highest morality, but the need to bring fractious factions into harmony requires compromises of the most questionable kind. (Jesuitical casuistry and perversion of the truth in the interests of the Church!) The worst examples to date are Naziism and Communism, where the *lie* has become the principal reason of State.

Conspicuous virtues are relatively rare and are mostly individual achievements. Mental and moral sloth, cowardice, bigotry, and unconsciousness dominate everything. I have 50 years of pioneer work behind me and could tell a pretty tale in this respect. Admittedly there has been scientific and technological progress, but no one has yet heard that people in general have become more intelligent let alone morally better.

Individuals can be improved because they present themselves for treatment. But societies only let themselves be deceived and misled, even if temporarily for their own good. For what we are dealing with is simply the passing and morally weakening effects of suggestion. (This is why medical psychotherapists, with few exceptions, have long since abandoned the use of suggestion therapy.) The good is never easy to reach; the more it costs the better it is. Socially good results have to be paid for too, usually later, but then with interest and compound interest (witness the Mussolini era in Italy and its catastrophic end).

To sum up, I have reached the following conclusions:

1. Group therapy is indispensable for the education of the social human being.

2. It is not a substitute for individual analysis.

3. The two forms of psychotherapy complement each other.

4. The danger of group therapy is getting stuck on the collective level.

5. The danger of individual analysis is the neglect of social adaptation.

Yours sincerely, C. G. JUNG

To Hans A. Illing

Dear Dr. Illing,   10 February 1955

I give the adaptation of the individual to society its full due.[1] But I still stand up for the inalienable rights of the individual since he alone is the carrier of life and is gravely threatened by the social levelling process today. Even in the smallest group he is acceptable only if he appears acceptable to the majority of its members. He has to resign himself to being tolerated. But mere toleration is no improvement; on the contrary, it fosters self-doubt, to which the isolated individual who has something to espouse is particularly prone. I am no preacher of "splendid isolation" and have the greatest difficulty in shielding myself from the crushing demands of people and human relationships. Without values of one's own even social relationships lack significance.

Yours sincerely, C. G. JUNG

[1] I. expressed his general agreement with Jung's statements but emphasized the value of the individual belonging to a constructive group. See the foregoing letter.

221

To A. M. Hubbard

[ORIGINAL IN ENGLISH]

Dear Sir,   15 February 1955

Thank you for your kind invitation to contribute to your mescalin scheme. Although I have never taken the drug myself nor given it to another individual, I have at least devoted 40 years of my life to the study of that psychic sphere which is disclosed by the said drug; that is the sphere of numinous experiences. Thirty years ago I became acquainted with Dr. Prinzhorn's mescalin experiments,[1] and thus I had ample opportunity to learn about the effects of the drug as well as about the nature of the psychic material involved in the experiment.

I cannot help agreeing with you that the said experiment is of the highest psychological interest in a theoretical way. But when it comes to the practical and more or less general application of mescalin, I have certain doubts and hesitations. The analytical method of psychotherapy (e.g., "active imagination") yields very similar results, viz. full realization of complexes and numinous dreams and visions. These phenomena occur at their proper time and place in the course of the treatment. Mescalin, however, uncovers such psychic facts at any time and place when and where it is by no means certain that the individual is mature enough to integrate them. Mescalin is a drug similar to hashish and opium in so far as it is a poison, paralysing the normal function of apperception and thus giving free rein to the psychic factors underlying sense perception. These aesthetic factors account for colours, sounds, forms, associations, and emotions attributed by the unconscious psyche to the mere stimulus provided by the objects. They are comparable in Hindu philosophy to the concept of the "thinker" of the thought, the "feeler" of feeling, the "sounder" of sound, etc. It is just as if mescalin were taking away the top layer of apperception, which produces the "accurate" picture of the object as it looks to us. If this layer is removed, we immediately discover the variants of conscious perception and apperception, viz. a rich display of contingent colours, forms, associations, etc., from which under normal conditions the process of apperception selects the correct quality. Perception and apperception result from a complicated process which transforms

□ Vancouver, British Columbia. — The letter was published in *Spring*, 1971.
[1] Hans Prinzhorn (1866–1933), German psychiatrist. Cf. his *Bildnerei der Geisteskranken* (1922).

the physical and physiological stimulus into a psychic image. In this way, the unconscious psyche adds colours, sounds, associations, meaning, etc. out of the treasure of its subliminal possibilities. These additions, if unchecked, would dissolve into or cover up the objective image by an infinite variety, a real "fantasia" or symphony of shades and nuances both of qualities as well as of meanings. But the normal process of conscious perception and apperception aims at the production of a "correct" representation of the object excluding all subliminal perceptional variants. Could we uncover the unconscious layer next to consciousness during the process of apperception, we would be confronted with an infinitely moving world riotous with colours, sounds, forms, emotions, meanings, etc. But out of all this emerges a relatively drab and banal picture devoid of emotion and poor in meaning.

In psychotherapy and psychopathology we have discovered the same variants (usually, however, in a less gorgeous array) through amplification of certain conscious images. Mescalin brusquely removes the veil of the selective process and reveals the underlying layer of perceptional variants, apparently a world of infinite wealth. Thus the individual gains an insight and a full view of psychic possibilities which he otherwise (f.i. through "active imagination") would reach only by assiduous work and a relatively long and difficult training. But if he reaches and experiences [them in this way], he has not only acquired them by legitimate endeavour but he has also arrived at the same time in a mental position where he can integrate the meaning of his experience. Mescalin is a short cut and therefore yields as a result oi a perhaps awe-inspiring aesthetic impression, which remains an isolated, unintegrated experience contributing very little to the development of human personality. I have seen some peyotees in New Mexico and they did not compare favourably with the ordinary Pueblo Indians. They gave me the impression of drug addicts. They would be an interesting object for a closer psychiatric investigation.

The idea that mescalin could produce a *transcendental* experience is shocking. The drug merely uncovers the normally unconscious functional layer of perceptional and emotional variants, which are only psychologically transcendent but by no means "transcendental," i.e., *metaphysical*. Such an experiment may be in practice good for people having a desire to convince themselves of the real existence of an unconscious psyche. It could give them a fair idea of its reality. But I never could accept mescalin as a means to convince people

223

of the possibility of spiritual experience over against their materialism. It is on the contrary an excellent demonstration of Marxist materialism: mescalin is the drug by which you can manipulate the brain so that it produces even so-called "spiritual" experiences. That is the ideal case for Bolshevik philosophy and its "brave new world." If that is all the Occident has to offer in the way of "transcendental" experience, we would but confirm the Marxist aspirations to prove that the "spiritual" experience can be just as well produced by chemical means.

. . .

There is finally a question which I am unable to answer, as I have no corresponding experience: it concerns the possibility that a drug opening the door to the unconscious could also *release a latent, potential psychosis*. As far as my experience goes, such latent dispositions are considerably more frequent than actual psychoses, and thus there exists a fair chance of hitting upon such a case during mescalin experiments. It would be a highly interesting though equally disagreeable experience, such cases being the bogey of psychotherapy.

Hoping you are not offended by the frankness of my critical opinion, I remain, dear Sir,

Yours very truly, c. g. jung

Anonymous

[ORIGINAL IN ENGLISH]

Dear N., 17 February 1955

Thank you very much for your kind letter which I have read with great interest. I only knew of the existence of a great alchemical library hidden in the London docks behind iron doors, but that there would be such an old fossil living in a secluded place still occupied with alembics and other alchemical apparatus is really news to me. But it wouldn't be helpful in any way to learn about his address, because such people, as I know from experience, are inaccessible to modern thought. There are fossils enough I have to deal with! Thank you anyhow for your interesting information. Cordial greetings,

Sincerely yours, c. g. jung

☐ To a woman in England.

To Pater Lucas Menz, O.S.B.

Dear Pater Lucas,   22 February 1955

I have read your draft with great interest. Considering the terrible time in which we are living, I am bound to agree. It reminds me of the beneficent work of the O.S.B.[1] in those dark centuries when the culture of antiquity was gradually falling into decay. Now once again we are in a time of decay and transition, as around 2000 B.C., when the Old Kingdom of Egypt collapsed, and at the beginning of the Christian era, when the New Kingdom finally came to an end and with it classical Greece. The vernal equinox is moving out of the sign of Pisces into the sign of Aquarius, just as it did out of Taurus (the old bull gods) into Aries (the ram-horned gods) and then out of Aries (the sacrificed lamb) into Pisces ('Ιχθῦς). It is to be hoped that the O.S.B. will succeed in launching another salvaging operation this time too. 1500 years ago St. Benedict could pour the new wine into new bottles; or rather, the seeds of a new culture germinating in the decay were bedded in the new spirit of Christianity. Our apocalyptic epoch likewise contains the seeds of a different, unprecedented, and still inconceivable future which could be bedded in the Christian spirit if only this would renew itself, as happened with the seeds that sprouted from the decay of classical culture.

But here, it seems to me, lies the great difficulty. The coming new age will be as vastly different from ours as the world of the 19th century was from that of the 20th with its atomic physics and its psychology of the unconscious. Never before has mankind been torn into two halves, and never before was the power of absolute destruction given into the hand of man himself. It is a "godlike" power that has fallen into human hands. The *dignitas humani generis* has swollen into a truly diabolical grandeur.

What answer will the genius of mankind give? Or what will God do about it? You answer with the historical spirit in which St. Benedict answered, but he spoke and acted with a new spirit that was a match for the anti-spirit of his age. Is that answer also equal to the present problem? And does it comprehend the terrible grandeur that has revealed itself in man?

It seems to me we haven't yet noticed that such a question has

☐ Ettal Abbey, Bavaria.
[1] Monastic Order of St. Benedict of Nursia, the Benedictines, or Black Monks.

been posed at all. We are still stuck in the fearful murk and confusion of unconsciousness. Christianity brought the world a new light, the *lux moderna*[2] (as the alchemists called their *lumen naturae*). Today this light flickers and wavers alarmingly, and the wheel of history cannot be turned back. Even the Emperor Augustus with all his power could not push through his attempts at repristination.

You have rightly guessed that I am as worried as you are and have every sympathy with your aspirations. But why do you turn to me, a dyed-in-the-wool Protestant? Presumably you are thinking of my psychology which, though born of the Christian spirit, seeks to give adequate answers to the spirit of this age: the voice of a doctor struggling to heal the psychic confusion of his time and thus compelled to use a language very different from yours. In all too many cases the old language is no longer understood, or is understood in the wrong way. If I have to make the meaning of the Christian message intelligible to a patient, I must *translate* it with a commentary. In fact this is one practical aim of my psychology, or rather psychotherapy. The theologian could hardly go along with this, although St. Paul himself spoke Greek to the Greeks and probably wouldn't have been deterred even if the head of the community at Jerusalem had forbidden it.

I am taking the liberty of sending you my book *Aion*, from which you will see that you are dealing with a heretic and could get your fingers burned. I would like to spare you this, for you can help many people even without modern psychology. I can only wish your endeavour every success, since I understand it perfectly although outsiders can't see that. For most people my Christian standpoint remains hidden, and because of the strangeness of my language and the incomprehensibility of my interests I am given a wide berth. With kind regards,

Yours sincerely, C. G. JUNG

[2] The term *lux moderna*, the new light, occurs for instance in an alchemical compilation by Johann Daniel Mylius, *Philosophia reformata* (1622), p. 244. Cf. *Mysterium Coniunctionis*, CW 14, par. 718 & n. 143.

To E. V. Tenney

[ORIGINAL IN ENGLISH]

Dear Dr. Tenney,   23 February 1955

It was a great pleasure to receive a letter from you. I often wondered how you were faring and how you digested all the difficult stuff you have devoured in Zurich. I see from your letter that the digestive process has made a great step forward, which is very satisfactory. There is no objection to your making extracts from the seminar notes, but I must warn you that I have never been able to go through them and correct minor errors of all descriptions found all over the texts. It is also expected that you wouldn't use them for quotations in printed papers without special permission. Now as to your questions:

1. Speaking with tongues (glōssōlalia)[1] is observed in cases of *ekstasis* (= *abaissement du niveau mental,* predominance of the unconscious). It is probable that the strangeness of the unconscious contents not yet integrated in consciousness demands an equally strange language. As it does demand strange pictures of an unheard-of character, it is also a traditional expectation that the spiritual demonic inspiration manifests itself either in hieratic or otherwise incomprehensible language. That is also the reason why primitives and civilized people still use archaic forms of language on ritual occasions (Sanskrit in India, Old Coptic in the Coptic church, Old Slavonic in the Greek Orthodox church, Latin in the Catholic church, and mediaeval German or English in the Protestant church). There are case reports about mediums that spoke foreign languages which were unknown to them in their waking state. Théodore Flournoy in Geneva reported such a case[2] in which he showed that it was a question of a cryptomnesic Sanskrit the medium had picked up in a Sanskrit grammar whose existence nobody was aware of. It is exceedingly difficult to establish the authenticity of these cases on account of cryptomnesia.

2. The healing function is not necessarily a characteristic of in-

---

□ Ph.D., analytical psychologist, professor of philosophy at the Fresno (California) State College.

[1] This passage on glossolalia ("speaking with tongues") is published in Morton T. Kelsey, *Tongue Speaking, An Experiment in Spiritual Experience* (1964).

[2] *From India to the Planet Mars* (1900). Jung read the book in the original French during his early years at the Burghölzli and suggested that Flournoy let him translate it into German. Cf. Jung and Jaffé, *Erinnerungen, Träume, Gedanken,* p. 378 (not in *Memories*).

dividuation; it is a thing in itself. It also doesn't work exclusively through transference; that is a Freudian prejudice. It is evident that healing presupposes a special kind and faculty of understanding and compassion.

3. You find visual images in the process of analysis chiefly with people of a visual type. The way the unconscious manifests itself depends very much upon your functional type. It can manifest itself in the most unexpectedly various ways. Your story of the Catholic priests is delightful;[3] they were obviously shielding themselves from the devil when he crept up in what you said. If you discuss religious problems and you bring in a psychological point of view, you instantly collide with the concretism of religious belief. You know the Virgin has been taken up to Heaven, and that ought to be believed quite concretely although no theologian can explain to me whether she has been taken up in her shirt or other pieces of clothing or naked, and what happened to her garments: did they become eternal too, or what happened to the microbes that are in every human body: did they become immortal too? You see, psychology takes into account all such heretical aspects, while the believers in concrete truth never think of such things.

You are quite right that you did not found any organization, things always become rigid.

I am very glad that *Time* has brought out a decent article;[4] I was afraid they would make a caricature of it as is usually the case.

Another aspect of this concretism is the rigidity of scholastic philosophy, through which Father White is wriggling as well as he can. He is at bottom an honest and sincere man who cannot but admit the importance of psychology, but the trouble is that he gets into an awful stew about it. Analytical psychology unfortunately just touches the vulnerable spot of the church, viz. the untenable concretism of its beliefs, and the syllogistic character of Thomistic philosophy. This is of course a terrific snag, but—one could almost say —fortunately people are unaware of the clashing contrasts. Father White, however, is by no means unconscious of those clashes; it is a very serious personal problem to him. But it is the same with Protestantism: there is the same difficulty between a concrete or historic

[3] Two Roman Catholic men closed their eyes and prayed during a lecture on "Psychology and Religion."

[4] *Time* (New York, LXV:7, 14 Feb. 1955) published a long article entitled "The Old Wise Man" (pp. 62–68) with a picture of Jung on its cover, "Psychiatrist Carl Jung."

belief and a symbolic understanding. One could well say it is a problem of our time whether our mind is capable of developing itself so that it can understand the symbolic point of view or not.

I had some correspondence recently with Upton Sinclair; he is going to publish my last letter in the *New Republic*.[5] You will see when you read that letter how I try to insinuate the symbolic point of view into a rationalistic attitude.

Now I think I have answered all your main questions. My best regards to Mrs. Tenney,

Yours sincerely, C. G. JUNG

[5] Cf. Sinclair, 7 Jan. and 20 Jan. 55.

To Adolf Keller

Dear friend,   25 February 1955

It was very kind of you to take the time and trouble to react at such length to the article in *Time*. Your interpretation of my strange-looking visage is excellent.[1] The photographer, who bored me excruciatingly with his many exposures, must have caught me in an absent-minded moment when I was sunk in my thoughts. My thoughts about "this world" were not—and are not—enjoyable. The drive of the unconscious towards mass murder on a global scale is not exactly a cheering prospect. Transitions between the aeons always seem to have been melancholy and despairing times, as for instance the collapse of the Old Kingdom in Egypt ("The Dialogue of a World-Weary Man with His Soul")[2] between Taurus and Aries, or the melancholy of the Augustinian age between Aries and Pisces. And now we are moving into Aquarius, of which the Sibylline Books say: *Luciferi vires accendit Aquarius acres* (Aquarius inflames the savage forces of Lucifer).[3] And we are only at the beginning of this apocalyptic development! Already I am a great-grandfather twice over and see those distant generations growing up who long after we are gone will spend

☐ (Handwritten.)

[1] For the photograph published in *Time* (cf. previous letter, n. 4), see pl. II.

[2] Cf. Klinckowstroem, 2 Sept. 53, n. 2.

[3] The so-called Sibylline Oracles, a collection of apocalyptic writings in Greek hexameters, composed by Jews in the late pre-Christian and early Christian era, mainly for purposes of propaganda, and by Christians in imitation of the pagan Sibylline Books. The quotation is from a Latin translation, *Oracula Sibyllina* (Amsterdam, 1689; in Jung's library).

their lives in that darkness. I would accuse myself of senile pessimism did I not know that the H-bomb is lying ready to hand—a fact that unfortunately can no longer be doubted. Only a Herostratus[4] in the Kremlin is needed to push the button. And if we are lucky enough to escape that, what about the overpopulation problem?

Best greetings, J U N G

[4] Cf. Pfäfflin, 22 Mar. 51, n. 4.

To Upton Sinclair

[ORIGINAL IN ENGLISH]

Dear Mr. Sinclair,   25 February 1955

Thank you very much for all you have sent me! You are really of an astounding fertility. I have read your drama[1] with the greatest interest. I could not help being deeply moved by the human aspect of this horrible problem. There is indeed no other answer to it but suicide. It is so because these inventions—the uranium and hydrogen bomb—are produced by the human mind, instigated by the great genocide the unconscious is planning in order to compensate the incessant and inevitable increase of populations, which must eventually lead to gigantic catastrophes if miraculous and unforeseen inventions do not intervene. But even then the conflagration would only be postponed. This is the sword of Damocles suspended on a thin thread above our heads. Your drama is certainly a thrust that goes home, at least in the case of a naïve spectator like myself, of whose literary incompetence I must warn you.

I have read your letter to *Time*[2] and I have added—with your permission—some further historical detail.

Thank you for the copy of *Time*![3] A. Keller was enthusiastic about my portrait. Needless to say I don't know myself from that side. The photographer must have caught me at something.

[1] "Dr. Fist," a modern Faust story in which Dr. Fist, a physicist, discovers the atom bomb after making a pact with the Chief Commissioner of Hell, Mephisto. In the end Dr. Fist commits suicide and the devil claims his soul. The play has never been published and is available only in typescript, as a promptbook, in the Theatre Collection of the New York Public Library, at Lincoln Center.
[2] *Time* (LXV:10, 7 Mar. 1955). S. points out that Freud could not be called the "discoverer" of the unconscious, since many books had been written about it before him. The letter was in answer to a statement in the article about Jung in *Time*, cited in Tenney, 23 Feb. 55, n. 4.
[3] Ibid.

I thank you also for your interesting *Mental Radio*.[4] Each time I read such reports I am reminded of the fact that our psyche has an aspect that defies space and time and incidentally causality, and this is just the thing our parapsychologists do not yet understand.

Your idea of a feminist revolt in Heaven is most amusing. Incidentally, this is the reason, viz. the Assumptio B.V. Mariae, why I enjoy a *relatively* decent press on the Catholic side, while the usual stuff I get is just the kind you have sent me. The incompetent and profoundly ignorant reviewers sneeze at me. On the average, I only get bad reviews, which ought to convince me that I am writing pretty good stuff. Sometimes it is hard to believe it. Yet in the same mail I received a very decent review of *Psychology and Alchemy* by an American, a Mr. Sykes.[5] He has to do with Salzburg and the American School there. But fortunately enough, to judge from the satisfactory sale of my books, the public does not heed such inadequate criticism.

You are quite right; with the dogma of the Assumptio the unconscious "wells into the Church," since Woman is its (the unconscious) representative on earth.

Concerning "Enemy in the Mouth,"[6] you might try the Bollingen Press. (. . .) Let me know and I shall recommend it to Barrett. Alcoholism is a terrible threat to a nation. *Look at France!*

My *Answer to Job* was left by the Bollingen Press to the English publishers,[7] since they were apparently afraid of something like "Unamerican activities"[8] and the loss of prestige presumably. It is a book for the few, yet—I am afraid—the many may read and misunderstand it. Yet even in this case I get most enthusiastic letters, but almost without exception from simple people. They seem to be the main readers of my books.

Now don't tease yourself—I am hardly respectable, but you are much better known in USA than I am. Please don't put yourself out for my little book. It will get on its way slowly as all my other work

[4] Pasadena and New York, 1930.
[5] Cf. Sykes, 21 Nov. 55, n. □.
[6] The MS "Enemy in the Mouth" was published as *The Cup of Fury* (Great Neck, New York, 1956; the same firm that published *Answer to Job*). It is a study of the destructive effects of alcoholism, the thesis being illustrated by the stories of eighty alcoholics, half of them well-known writers.
[7] Cf. Priestley, 8 Nov. 54, n. 2.
[8] A confusion with the witch-hunting activities of Sen. Joseph R. McCarthy's Permanent Subcommittee on Investigations.

has done. The ruler of my birth, old Saturnus, slowed down my maturation process to such an extent that I became aware of my own ideas only at the beginning of the second half of my life, i.e., exactly with 36 years.[9] I beg your pardon for using old astrological metaphors. "Astrology" is another of those "random phenomena" wiped off the desk by the idol of the average, which everybody believes to be reality itself while it is a mere abstract. Soon a little book of mine which I have published with the physicist Prof. W. Pauli will come out in English.[10] It is even more shocking than *Job*, but this time to the scientist, not the theologian. It deals with the "random phenomenon" of extrasensory perception, especially its theory, as far as my contribution goes. Pauli's part deals with the role the archetype plays in the formation of certain physical concepts. The public reaction will be even worse than in the case of *Job*.

The way in which the scientific world reacts reminds me strongly of those remote times when I stood up all alone for Freud against a world blindfolded by prejudice, and ever since I have been the subject of calumny, irritation, and contempt, although I have harvested a good deal of appreciation paradoxically enough just from universities (among them Oxford and Harvard).[11] I hardly dare to assume that they did not know what they were doing. Now who is right, my critics or the academies? In the meantime, I can say with Schopenhauer (whose fate was worse: of his first edition only 1 copy was sold![12]): *legor et legar!*[13]

I am sorry taking up your valuable time with such personal outpourings. I only wanted to explain why I take bad criticism as the thing to be expected, whereas a decent review is a rare exception and therefore an unpredictable "random phenomenon."

Hoping that I have answered every point in your letter, I remain,

Yours sincerely, c. g. j u n g

[9] The original version of *Symbols of Transformation* appeared in 1911/12 and marked the beginning of the break with Freud. The onset of the second half of life often marks a turning-point. Cf. "The Stages of Life," CW 8, par. 773.
[10] *The Interpretation of Nature and the Psyche* (1955). Jung's part, the essay on synchronicity, is in CW 8.
[11] Jung received, among others, honorary degrees from Harvard in 1936 and from Oxford in 1938. Cf. Künzli, 4 Feb. 43.
[12] The first edition of *The World as Will and Idea*.
[13] "I am read and I shall be read."

To Manfred Bleuler

Dear Colleague,   23 March 1955

My sincere thanks for your kind invitation to speak on schizophrenia at the International Congress for Psychiatry.[1] It would indeed
have been a great pleasure—quite apart from the honour—to give
such a lecture. Unfortunately I have become so antique by now that
it would be too difficult an undertaking. I am no longer up to the
effort of lecturing and must therefore decline your request. I do so
with all the livelier regret as it is now about 50 years since I first
pointed out the psychology of the illness that was then still known
as Dementia praecox.[2] Sometimes I seem an anachronism to myself.
Again with very best thanks,

Yours sincerely, C. G. JUNG

[1] The Second International Congress for Psychiatry was to take place in Zurich,
Sept. 1957. On the receipt of Jung's refusal B. suggested that he should send a
paper "summarizing your pioneer work on schizophrenia." This proposal was accepted, and Jung's paper "Schizophrenia" (CW 3) was read by his grandson, Dr.
Dieter Baumann.
[2] "The Psychology of Dementia Praecox" (orig. 1907), CW 3.

To Evelyn Thorne

[ORIGINAL IN ENGLISH]

Dear Miss Thorne,   23 March 1955

Thank you very much for your interesting letter. I can confirm
your observation[1] from my own experience. Time and again I have
observed that when I was busy with a special thought or a work of a
remote kind, I found that the theme was picked up in newspaper
articles or in letters I got from strangers as if it has been broadcasted.
Sometimes this observation was so striking that I myself thought of
the possibility that it might be a case of synchronicity. But your observation of the colours worn by people in a crowd shows that it must
be a matter of the accumulation phenomenon in chance series. You
can observe this fact easily when you watch the traffic on roads where
it is not continuous. You will notice that cars or pedestrians have a

☐ Lake Como, Florida.
[1] T. reported that she and a friend of hers, both editors of little magazines, had
observed that at some periods they received short stories with strikingly similar
plots and characters. They took this as an instance of synchronicity.

marked tendency to come in aperiodic batches interspersed with solitary pedestrians or cars. These accumulation phenomena are just chance occurrences. Thus we have to consider the coincidence of themes in manuscripts or newspaper articles in the first place as mere chance, although with a certain mental reservation. At the time of Immanuel Kant there were quite a number of philosophers with a very similar kind of mind, and also at the time of Charles Darwin there were at least three other minds at work to produce similar ideas independently of each other. In such cases one feels tempted to think of a peculiar *Zeitgeist* secretly at work and pushing forward certain instrumental individuals.

Unfortunately, this hypothesis is difficult to prove, yet it seems to me as if the latter phenomena were somewhere midway between mere chance occurrences and positive synchronistic phenomena.

By the way, my essay on synchronicity will soon be published in English translation by the Bollingen Press. Thanking you again, I remain,

Yours sincerely, C. G. JUNG

To Sylvester Schoening

[ORIGINAL IN ENGLISH]

Dear Mr. Schoening,   24 March 1955

Your question is difficult to answer, since Thomistic psychology is on a metaphysical basis, and the psychology of the unconscious on an empirical foundation. Through many talks with theologians, I have learnt that the greatest difficulty in discussing this matter consists in the difference of the *point de départ*. The theologian starts with philosophical concepts which have practically nothing to do with the merely nominalistic concepts of the empiricist. The theological terms contain what they are giving a name to, the empirical terms are just labels and don't contain what they are naming. The empirical emphasis is on facts, and names mean very little; also hypotheses mean just as little as they can easily be exchanged for a better point of view. The only possibility of a discussion I can see is the comparison of certain Thomistic statements with the statements of empirical psychology. If you have a chance to come to Zurich beginning of May, you will have an opportunity of meeting the Dominican Father Vic-

□ Theological student in Innsbruck.

tor White who is delivering a course of lectures at the C. G. Jung Institute. I have done a number of such comparisons with him, and he has a fair knowledge of my psychology, so that if you have a chance to talk with him it might be of considerable importance to you. If you should come to Zurich I am ready to see you and talk to you about this subject, but you must keep in mind that my knowledge of Thomistic psychology is almost nil since I have devoted all my available time to the study of facts and not of opinions.

Sincerely yours, c. g. JUNG

To Pater Lucas Menz

Dear Pater Lucas,   28 March 1955

Many thanks for your kind and illuminating letter. It affords me an invaluable glimpse into the process of becoming whole and holy. On the way back through the history of mankind[1] we integrate much that belongs to us and, deep down, also something of brother animal, who is actually holier than us since he cannot deviate from the divine will implanted in him because his dark consciousness shows him no other paths. On this way back—no matter where it is begun if only it is trodden in earnest—we fall into the fire or, as the logion says, come near to it: "He that is near me is near the fire. He that is far from me is far from the kingdom."[2]

The "taming of the beast," as you call it, is indeed a long process and coincides with the dissolution of *egohood*. What you call "deselving" I call "becoming a self": what previously seemed to be "ego" is taken up into a greater dimension which dwarfs and surrounds me on all sides, and which I cannot grasp in its totality. In this connection you, like me, rightly quote Paul,[3] who formulates the same experience.

This experience is a charisma on the one hand, for it is not vouchsafed to us *nisi Deo concedente*. On the other hand it is vouchsafed only if we give up the ego as the supreme authority and put ourselves wholly under the will of God.

---

[1] M. wrote that for him the process of becoming holy was a journey through the entire history of mankind, back to Adam.
[2] James, *The Apocryphal New Testament*, p. 35.
[3] "For in him we live, and move, and have our being" (Acts 17:28).

235

You yourself feel the need for a definition of "perfection." You define it as the "complete unfolding of nature on the level of holiness, brought about by surrendering to God." In so far as God is wholeness himself, himself whole and holy, man attains his wholeness only in God, that is, in self-completeness, which in turn he attains only by submitting to God's will. Since man in the state of wholeness and holiness is far from any kind of "perfection," the New Testament τέλειος[4] must surely be translated as "complete." For me the state of human wholeness is one of "completeness" and not of "perfection," an expression which, like "holiness," I tend to avoid.

You describe the ego (after the "taming of the beast") as being "in complete possession of itself." Here I would say that the resistance coming from the psychic depths ceases if we can give up our egohood, and the self (consciousness + unconscious) receives us into its greater dimension, where we are then "whole," and because of our relative wholeness we are near to that which is truly whole, namely God. (This is discussed in chs. IV and V of *Aion*.) Hence I would say that God is then "in complete possession of the ego and of myself" rather than stress the power of the ego.

I don't know whether it is permissible, in our incompetence, to think on things divine. I find that all my thoughts circle round God like the planets round the sun, and are as irresistibly attracted by him. I would feel it the most heinous sin were I to offer any resistance to this compelling force. I feel it is God's will that I should exercise the gift of thinking that has been vouchsafed me. Therefore I put my thinking at his service and so come into conflict with the traditional doctrine, above all with the doctrine of the *privatio boni*. Again, I have asked various theologians in vain what exactly is the relationship of Yahweh to the God of the Christians, since Yahweh, though a guardian of justice and morality, is himself unjust (hence Job 16:19ff.). And how is this paradoxical being related to the Summum Bonum? According to Isaiah 48:10–11 Yahweh torments mankind for his own sake: "Propter me, propter me faciam!"[5] This is understandable in terms of his paradoxical nature, but not in terms of the Summum Bonum, which by definition already has everything it needs for

---

[4] Cf. Matthew 5:48: "Be ye therefore perfect, even as your Father which is in heaven is perfect." The distinction between perfection and completeness plays an important role in Jung's psychology. *Psychology and Alchemy*, CW 12, par. 208: ". . . life calls not for perfection but for completeness." Cf. also *Aion*, CW 9, ii. pars. 123, 333.

[5] Isaiah 48:11: "For my own sake, even for my own sake will I do it."

perfection. Hence it has no need of man, unlike Yahweh. I must question the doctrine of the Summum Bonum because the non-existence of evil deprives evil of all substance and leaves over only the good or else nothing at all, which, since it is nothing, also effects nothing, i.e., cannot cause even the tiniest evil impulse. And since it is nothing, it cannot come from man either. Moreover the devil was there *before* man and was certainly not good. But the devil is not *nothing*. The opposite of the good is therefore not nothing but an equally real evil.

The depth of the psyche, the unconscious, is not made by man but is divinely created nature, which should on no account be reviled by man even though it causes him the greatest difficulties. Its fire, which "refines" us "in the furnace of affliction," is according to Isaiah 48:10 the divine will itself, i.e., the will of Yahweh, who *needs* man. Man's understanding and will are challenged and can help, but they can never pretend to have plumbed the depths of the spirit and to have quenched the fire raging within it. We can only hope that God, in his grace, will not compel us to go deeper and let ourselves be consumed by his fire.[6]

You have evidently offered him sacrifice enough by withstanding his fire until your egohood was sufficiently subdued. In reality your ego is by no means in complete possession of itself but has been practically reduced to ashes, so that you have become capable of a measure of selfless love. You could indeed rejoice over this did not your "joyfulness" crassly conflict with the suffering of the world and your fellow man. Even the Redeemer on the Cross uttered no joyful cry despite his having been credited with completely overcoming the world and himself. An "object" (as you put it), i.e., a *human being* who does not know that he has enkindled love in you does not feel loved but humiliated because he is simply subjected or exposed to your own psychic state in which he himself has no part. Being loved in that way would leave me cold. But you yourself say that inasmuch as one is oneself one is also the *other*. Then *his* suffering will also affect *you* and detract from your joyfulness. But when you go on to say that you "don't need Creation any more" you give your fellow man (who is also part of Creation) to understand that he is superfluous for you, even though you "joyfully acclaim God through him."

It falls to the lot of anyone who has overcome something or detached himself from something to bear in the same measure the bur-

---

[6] Most of this paragraph is quoted in Jaffé, *The Myth of Meaning* (orig. 1969; tr. 1971), p. 120.

dens of others. Generally they are so heavy that any shouts of joy die on one's lips. One is glad if only one can draw breath from time to time.

Much as I can go along with you in the process of "becoming whole and holy," or individuation, I cannot subscribe to your statements about the "ego in complete possession of itself" and unrelated universal love, although they bring you perilously close to the ideal of Yoga: *nirdvandva* (free from the opposites). I know these moments of liberation come flashing out of the process, but I shun them because I always feel at such a moment that I have thrown off the burden of being human and that it will fall back on me with redoubled weight.

You don't need to change your standpoint in any way in order to gain a knowledge of the archetypes. You are in the thick of it, even if you should take the view of the father confessor who told a student who came to him for advice on the study of psychology: "Don't study anything that upsets you."

As we have not yet reached the state of eternal bliss, we are still suspended on the Cross between ascent and descent, not only for our own but for God's sake and mankind's. With kind regards,

Yours sincerely, C. G. JUNG

To Father Victor White

[ORIGINAL IN ENGLISH]

Dear Victor,   2 April 1955

Thank you for your letter and all the criticism it contains.[1] As long as you do not identify yourself with the avenging angel, I can feel

[1] W. wrote a letter on 17 March on board the *Queen Mary* on his return from California. He admitted to being puzzled by Jung's being puzzled by the quotation from Thomas Aquinas (White, 19 Jan. 55, n. 5), thus showing the hopeless impasse into which the discussion of the *privatio boni* had run. Shortly before this he had published a highly critical review of "Answer to Job" in *Blackfriars* (Oxford), March 1955; a revised version appeared in his *Soul and Psyche* (1960), Appendix V: "Jung on Job." He refers to this review in his letter, saying: "I am very afraid indeed that you will think it unforgivable." But he goes on: "I just do not understand what is to be gained by the publication of such an outburst [referring to the book] . . . I can only see harm coming of it, not least to my own efforts to make analytical psychology acceptable to, and respected by, the Catholics and other Christians who need it so badly." This reaction, so very different from his enthusiasm three years earlier (White, Spring 1952, n. 6), reveals the gap that had opened out between the two men, a gap that both felt deeply and painfully.

your humanity and I can tell you that I am really sorry for my misdeeds and sore about God's ways with the poor anthropoids that were meant to have a brain enabling them to think critically. Just as I am grateful for the fact that you call me to order and that your judgment—be it correct or not—does not spare me, so I assume God will listen to a mortal voice, just as much as He has given His ear to Job when this little tortured worm complained about His paradoxical, amoral nature. Just as Job lifted his voice so that everybody could hear him, I have come to the conclusion that I had better risk my skin and do my worst or best to shake the unconsciousness of my contemporaries rather than allow my laxity to let things drift towards the impending world catastrophe. Man must know that he is man's worst enemy just as much as God had to learn from Job about His own antithetical nature. It is obvious that God's angel (having no will of his own) wanted to have his fight with Jacob and to kill him even if he would not defend himself. I bet the angel got some good knocking about before he succeeded in dislocating Jacob's hip. God surely expected Jacob to answer Him in kind. I am rather certain that Job's case was the same. As a matter of fact there is biblical authority on my side: (Isaiah 48: 10–11) "Behold, I have refined thee, but not with silver; I have chosen thee in the furnace of affliction. *For mine own sake, even for mine own sake* will I do it."[2]

Should I set the light of such an insight "under a bushel"? In peaceful and harmless conditions it would have been very unwise to *movere quieta*.[3] But in our time everything is at stake, and one should not mind the little disturbance I am causing. It is a mere fleabite on the immense body of Christendom. If I am causing trouble to the peace of mind of serious theologians, I am sorry, but I really do not see why their sleep is better than mine. They have no prerogative to hide from the great wind of the world and to leave uncomfortable things to themselves. The other day I got a letter from a student of (Catholic) theology who had asked his *directeur de conscience* for advice as to the study of modern psychology. Very aptly the rev. father said: "Don't study what troubles you!" I am afraid this is characteristic.

You should be glad that somebody thinks about God at all. The apostles and the early Fathers of the Church had no easy life and moreover no Christian is meant to go to sleep in a safe pew. Look at the world—the whole damn thing is rent from top to bottom, and so

---

[2] RSV has ". . . but not like silver; I have tried you . . ."
[3] Cf. White, 10 Apr. 54, n. 24.

is man in our infernal epoch. I hesitated and resisted long enough until I made up my mind to say what I think. The peace of the Church is one thing and getting behind the times another. I have asked four theologians (Prot.) about the modern position of the Church with reference to the question whether the God of the Old Testament is the same as that of the New. Two did not answer at all. One said that in the last 30 years theological literature does not speak of God any more. The last one said: "It is easy to answer your question. Yahweh is merely an archaic conception of God in comparison with the NT idea." I said: "This is exactly the kind of psychologism you accuse me of. When it suits you, God is suddenly nothing but a conception, but when you preach of Him, then it is the absolute truth." What did he say? Nothing. The old Jesuit father Nicolaus Caussinus had a better answer: In the OT God was like a raging rhinoceros, but in the NT He turned into a God of love conquered by the love of a pure virgin, having found peace in her lap at last.[4] This is at least a kind of answer. It is even a profound answer showing the importance of man in the divine drama of incarnation. It obviously began when God took on *personality* (in contradistinction to all other gods), i.e., *finiteness*. This was the first act of *kenosis* on the way to incarnation. This is the "Answer to Job": He had to give up being the victim of unreflected opposites.

You lose nothing and you even gain something in contemplating such thoughts. It affects your ecclesiastical position but not more than it disturbs my scientific position. The pope breaking through apostolic authority and the theological resistance of his own clergy got his share too. After *Ad Caeli Reginam* he got ill again. There must have been a terrific conflict in him, being the pope on the one hand and the religious innovator on the other. Should he have spared his clergy that could not agree with the new dogma?

I have no papal authority, only honest common sense and no power except the consensus of a very few thinking individuals. As you do not belong to the Church exclusively but also to humanity, it is not in the interest of the Church if you pay no tribute to our time. Even the pope did in his way.

Your sun in Libra demands undisturbed balance. You only get it *when either side carries equal weight*. Christ is crucified between the one going up and the other going down, i.e., between opposites. So

[4] Cf. Eysinga, 13 Feb. 54, n. 8.

do not try to escape your fate "written in the stars." I know, it is the mistake of Libra people: they are afraid of anything disturbing the balance. But they can maintain it only by "studying what troubles them."

Your criticism of my motive concerning *Job*[5] is certainly unjust and you know it. It is an expression of the mental torment you had to undergo in U.S.A.—and in Europe. Nobody has more sympathy with your predicament than I have, since more than 50 years of uphill work outside, and of the curtain rent inside, have taught me something. Having chosen the life of the monk you have separated yourself from this world and exposed yourself to the eternal fires of the other. Somewhere you have to pay the toll either to man or to God and in the end you will discover that both overcharge you. In this cruel suspension you will discover that redemption is to be found only on the middle ground, the centre of your self, which is just as much with as against God; with—inasmuch as God wills you; against—inasmuch as man's Luciferian autonomy exists outside of God. It is as a matter of fact a product of the opposites in God. That is exactly the problem I am treating in *Job* and that is why Job invokes the help of God against God. It would be a great mistake to think you can slip through such an ordeal without the most violent emotions. You yourself are profoundly emotional about it and you could not make anybody believe that you are not in a hell of suffering. There is no comfort and no consolation anywhere except in the submission to and the acceptance of the self, or you may call it the God that suffers in His own creation. "Excoxi te . . . et elegi te in camino paupertatis. Propter Me, propter Me faciam" (Isaiah 48:10–11).

My psychology unfortunately tries to be honest. It is certainly the hard way, neither an easy consolation nor a narcotic. Nobody touching it in earnest can avoid seeing the dark side and feeling it. Most certainly I shall never cover up the truth as I see it. The Church can take it as one of the diabolic temptations of the world, and the world can condemn it as foolishness. I shall stick to my conviction that my *Answer to Job* is a straightforward application of my psychological principles to certain central problems of our religion. They can take it or leave it. Moreover they will do what they please, without asking me.

[5] W. upbraided Jung for publishing this "cathartic outburst" and making "a public parade of splenetic shadow . . . so unlike the real you."

Somehow I can afford my independence, but I am fully aware that there are many who cannot do the same without risking their social existence. They must be able to live and to this end they have to protect themselves as well as they can. If I had not been able to live an independent life, I should have been far more cautious in expressing my opinions and many things would have gone another way, f.i., I would not even have stuck out my neck for Freud, who had become my first great indiscretion. *Primum vivere necesse est, deinde philosophari*[6]—this is the hard rule for everybody fed by an institution for services rendered. Only the free-lance can risk saying something beyond the conventional and thus cause discomfort to himself without endangering his very existence.

I fully understand therefore your critical outburst, but you must allow me nevertheless to call your attention to the fact that all the martyrs of your Church have been most unwise in this respect. I have discovered in my private life that a true Christian is not bedded upon roses and he is not meant for peace and tranquillity of mind but for war. And again I am realizing profoundly that not everybody's nature is as bellicose as mine, although I have attained—*Deo concedente*—a certain state of peace within, paid for by a rather uncomfortable state of war without. But even if a peaceful nature has reached a certain higher level of consciousness he cannot escape the raging conflict of opposites in his soul, as God wants to unite His opposites in man. As soon as a more honest and more complete consciousness beyond the collective level has been established, man is no more an end in himself, but becomes an instrument of God, and this is *really* so and no joke about it. I have not made this world nor have I put a human soul into it. This is His work and His responsibility and there is no judge above Him. That is why the story begins with Job on the human level and with the assumption of personality on the divine level. One can, like Job, lament about it, but it is to no purpose. It is just so. If turmoil and torment become too great, there is still the oneness of the self, the divine spark within its inviolable precincts, offering its extramundane peace. Please spend again some hours reading my *Answer to Job* with this comment in mind and see whether you still can maintain the idea that it is a case of mere spleen. Could we not apply the same qualification to your own bad temper?

[6] "It is necessary first to live, then to philosophize."

When you arrive in Zurich I shall be away in Bollingen; but when we return at the beginning of May, I should like you to stay with us in Küsnacht.[7]

Cordially yours, c. g.

[7] So far W. had always stayed at the Tower in Bollingen, where Jung used to see only his close friends. The invitation instead to Küsnacht, Jung's official residence, was something of a rebuff.

To Markus Fierz

Dear Professor Fierz,   5 April 1955

Very many thanks for kindly sending me your paper on Isaac Newton's theory of absolute space.[1] It is a subject that interests me very much, and I only hope my mental powers will be able to cope with Newton's thought processes.

I am about to pay a visit to your mother; it is wonderful how she endures her hopeless illness.[2]

With best thanks and kind regards,

Yours sincerely, c. g. jung

[1] "Ueber den Ursprung und die Bedeutung der Lehre Isaac Newtons vom absoluten Raum," *Gesnerus* (Aarau), II (1954).
[2] Linda Fierz-David (cf. Langenegger, 20 Nov. 30, n. 1). She died of cancer in May 1955.

To Ronald J. Horton

[ORIGINAL IN ENGLISH]

Dear Mr. Horton,   22 April 1955

The chance of seeing and enjoying the exquisite beauty of this unique piece of Greek sculpture[1] has been a boon I have to thank you for.

It is indeed a difficult task to identify the head. I am no archaeologist, and I cannot claim any competence in judging such a case.

☐ London.
[1] H. sent Jung photos of a Greek marble head and asked for his opinion. It is reproduced in *Man and His Symbols* (1964), p. 203.

My special interest besides my psychiatric work is research in the field of comparative psychology of religious symbolism.

Superficially looking at the head, one would be inclined to think of a relatively late date and one would be reminded of the Mithraic dadophors.[2] But as it is obviously a work of the highest Greek art, one has to go further back. The erotic element, the feminine sweetness of the face, the peculiar treatment of the hair on the one hand and the Phrygian *pileus*,[3] the juvenile masculinity on the other hand, suggest one of the early dying son-gods of the Near East. I think chiefly of Attis, the son and lover of Kybele. He is represented with the *pileus*. He has, like his analoga, viz. Adonis, Tammuz, and the Germanic Baldur, all the grace and charm of either sex. There is something of Demeter's serene beauty in his face. (The parallel is the Eleusinian Iacchus.)[4] As the cult of Attis is of considerable age, there is a certain possibility that it is an early representation of Attis.

That is about the nearest I can get to a diagnosis of the head and its truly bewitching beauty. At all events it expresses in a perfect way the feeling an Asiatic Greek would experience in worshipping Attis or one of his equivalents, one of the *pueri aeterni*, being the joy of men and women and dying early with the flowers of spring.

May I keep at least one of the photos? They have caught my fantasy thoroughly.[5]

I am sorry to give you such a meagre and tentative answer.

Sincerely yours, C. G. JUNG

[2] Mithras is frequently represented between two boys, or dadophors, carrying torches, the one raised, the other lowered. Cf. *Symbols of Transformation*, Plate XXb.

[3] The pointed hat which has been usurped by pixies and goblins.

[4] Son of Demeter or Persephone (Demeter's daughter) and Dionysus (with whom he is sometimes identified); depicted as celebrating the Eleusinian mysteries with a torch in his hand.

[5] Jung had the photo framed and kept it on his desk.

To Pater Raymond Hostie

Dear Pater,   25 April 1955

Unfortunately I am unable to thank you for sending me your book.[1] As you know through Father Bruno,[2] you criticize me as though I were a philosopher. But you know very well that I am an empiricist whose concepts have—as such—no content, since they are mere *nomina* that can be changed as convention requires. I have given you every opportunity in the past to discuss obscurities. You never came out with your criticism.

I have no doctrine and no philosophical system, but have presented new *facts* which you studiously ignore. It is as though one were to criticize the labels on the drawers of a collection of minerals without looking at their contents. It is not so much your fault that you do not appear to understand how it is that the psychic facts designated by my concepts possess an autonomy of their own. This is an empirical fact which is not understood by most people anyway, because they have never gone through the same experiences—quite understandably, since they take no notice of my method. *Si parva licet componere magnis*, the situation is the same as with Galileo, who discovered the hitherto unknown moons of Jupiter by means of a telescope. But no one wanted to look through it. So Jupiter had no moons. Mandala symbols, for instance, are seen not only in Zurich but also in Rio de Janeiro and San Francisco—naturally only by psychiatrists who get their patients to draw. These are the facts that count, not the names. You overlook the facts and then think that the name is the fact, and thus you reach the nonsensical conclusion that I hypostatize ideas and am therefore a "Gnostic." *It is your theological standpoint that is a gnosis, not my empiricism,* of which you obviously haven't the faintest inkling.

I must also express the conjecture that I may be doing injustice to *you personally* by taking your criticism as a perversion of the facts. You are, after all, the member of an Order whose principle is: *Quod oculis nostris apparet album, nigrum illa esse definierit, debemus itidem, quod nigrum sit, pronuntiare.*[3] Hence in any discussion there is no personal opponent with whom one could come to an understanding.

Yours truly, C. G. JUNG

□ S.J., Louvain. This letter is published without omissions at the specific request of H.

[1] *Du Mythe à la réligion* (1955; tr., *Religion and the Psychology of Jung*, 1957).

[2] Jung expressed his criticism of the book in a letter of 22 Dec. 54 to Father Bruno de Jésus-Marie (not in this selection). A long letter to Bruno is in CW 18, pars. 1518ff. Cf. below, 20 Nov. 56.

[3] "We have to pronounce as black what appears to our eyes white if she [the Church] calls it black." Ignatius of Loyola, *Exercitia Spiritualia*, in the 13th of the "Rules for the Unity of the Church."

To Karl Theens

Dear Herr Theens, 25 April 1955

I would gladly comply with your kind invitation to contribute something to the literature on *Faust* were it not that my old age sets definite and, unfortunately, narrow limits to my working capacity. *Faust II* has been my companion all my life,[1] but it was only 20 years ago that certain things began to dawn on me, especially when I read Christian Rosencreutz's *Chymical Wedding*, which Goethe also knew[2] but, interestingly enough, did not mention among the alchemical literature of his Leipzig days. This is what often happens with books or impressions which, piercing through the top layer of consciousness, sink down into the depths of the psyche and return to the surface only much later in altered form, bearing witness to their long-lasting effects. So far as we know, Goethe used only the relatively late alchemical literature, and it was the study of the classical and early medieval texts which first convinced me that *Faust I and II* is an *opus alchymicum* in the best sense. Recently Goethe as alchemist has been treated by the Englishman Ronald D. Gray (*Goethe the Alchemist*, Cambridge 1952), evidently under the stimulus of my own references to this subject. Unfortunately Gray's knowledge of alchemy is deficient so that he overlooks its main concern, the mystery of the *coniunctio*, or "chymical wedding," which runs through the whole of *Faust*. I have devoted a special work to this problem—*Mysterium Coniunctionis*, which is to appear shortly. It contains everything that forms the historical background —so far as this is alchemical—of *Faust*. These roots go very deep and seem to me to explain much of the numinous effect which emanates from Goethe's "main work." But for my feeling it is so vast that I would do better to say nothing at all, as it is quite impossible even to hint at the wealth of associations in a short essay, let alone make them intelligible. So it is not disinclination or indifference that checks my pen, but the insuperable difficulty of condensing such a profusion of material into a few words. Instead of a substantial contribution I can therefore offer nothing except these

☐ Stuttgart.

[1] *Memories*, pp. 6of./168f.

[2] Goethe, according to a letter of 28 June 1786 to his friend Frau von Stein, read the book in 1786. Cf. Bernoulli, 5 Oct. 44, n. 1.

skimpy references to researches and studies which, in my view at least, do shed some light on the problem of *Faust*.

Yours sincerely, C. G. JUNG

Anonymous

Dear Frau N.,   26 April 1955

I find your son's decision[1] very regrettable in the sense that it is hardly anything more than an evasion, though it is not as unusual as it may seem. When I was in Calcutta I met a whole lot of Europeans—Englishmen and Germans—who had joined the Ramakrishna Order there. With us this decision would be like entering a Catholic monastic order and would be more binding since it is more difficult to get out of the monastery or the Catholic priesthood than out of an exotic religious community. I know the patron saint of the Pramachari Order, Paramhansa Yogananda,[2] or rather I know his book. It is genuinely Indian and for our ears sounds utterly fantastic. As has often happened before, impressionable people living in India easily come under the influence of Indian ideas, which are admittedly impressive and at least quench in the Indian manner a thirst for knowledge which our theologians unfortunately cannot assuage. When these young people return to Europe they often find that they have to give up this fantastic-sounding philosophy simply because it does not fit our circumstances. Nobody can afford to go around every day with the begging bowl and sit in the street waiting for a pious soul to fill it with rice. This is a daily spectacle in India but with us the police and the traffic would render such an unusual religious exercise impossible. Missionaries here have to rely on a few gushing enthusiasts who, though they don't fill the rice bowl for them, occasionally drop a mild gift into their purse. For a young man with a strong but largely unrealized need for self-assertion this is a pretty dismal prospect in the long run.

☐ Switzerland.

[1] N. sent Jung a letter from her son, aged 24, in which he told her of his decision to join an Indian religious order and that he had changed his European name into an Indian one.

[2] The Pramachari Order or Yogoda Sat-Sanga Movement is known in the West as the Self-Realization Fellowship. Cf. Neumann, 28 Feb. 52, last par.

I therefore think you would be well advised not to put any difficulties in his way at present but to get him back to Europe sometime. There's no need to bother him emotionally, just ask him what he thinks of living on in the future: alms or earnings. If he has financial prospects which assure him a life free from care, he can safely keep to the Pramachari Mission as a way of passing the time. He will then discover soon enough that nothing comes out of it. Such ideas are suitable for countries where for 10 months it is so hot that you can hardly open your eyes for sweat. This is the great difference which Emile Zola pointed out when he said: "Mais chez nous, la misère a froid."

Yours sincerely, C. G. JUNG

Anonymous

Dear Herr N.,   28 April 1955

Your ideas[1] bring you up against a general cultural problem which is infinitely complicated. What is true in one place is untrue in another. "Suffering is the swiftest steed that bears you to perfection,"[2] and the contrary is also true. "Breaking in" can be discipline, and this is needed for the emotional chaos of man, though at the same time it can kill the living spirit, as we have seen only too often. In my opinion there is no magical word that could finally unravel this whole complex of questions; nor is there any method of thinking or living or acting which would eliminate suffering and unhappiness. If a man's life consists half of happiness and half of unhappiness, this is probably the optimum that can be reached, and it remains forever an unresolved question whether suffering is educative or demoralizing. In any case it would be wrong to give oneself up to relativism and indifferentism. Whatever can be bettered in a given place at a given time should certainly be done, for it would be sheer folly to do otherwise. Man's fate has always swung between day and night. There is nothing we can do to change this.

Yours sincerely, C. G. JUNG

☐ France.

[1] According to N., the general disorientation of our civilization, in particular the process of "breaking in," produces automatons.

[2] Untraced quotation from Meister Eckhart. Cf. Anon., 28 June 56, last par.

To Walter Robert Corti

Dear Herr Corti,   2 May 1955

At last I have found a quiet moment in which to finish reading your *Mythopoese*[1] and to append my answer. The reading has to be fresh in my mind so that I can react properly.

As always in such cases, it does not seem to me superfluous to begin with the constantly reiterated statement that I am neither a philosopher nor a theologian and so cannot deploy any artillery in the battle of arguments. While I was reading your book I felt myself transported back a century or more; at first, to be sure, only about 60 years, into those blossoming and springlike student days when, in enchanted inns in Markgrafenland,[2] amid a circle of friends (now, alas, almost extinct), one discussed the eternal verities with much earnest heating of the head, and never a thought to what Bismarck had started off in 1871 and what the fatally deluded Wilhelm II was then continuing. We were still living in the romantic age of Hegel, Schelling, and Schopenhauer. No wonder your words brought back the romantic mood. "Once more you hover near me, forms and faces / Seen long ago with troubled youthful gaze," I could say with Faust.[3]

The heaven-storming pretensions of the romantic intellect, sad to relate, have flown from me utterly. How can one decide the impossible? What in the world can one assert about God? Probably only antinomies, like *Deus est immobilis* and instigator of all motion, eternal source and goal, Creator uniting in himself genesis and decay, supreme light and gloomiest abyss, infinite as God, finite as personality (only this one and no other!), singular and plural, the unfolding and union of all opposites. There are some who, faced with these illimitabilities, can escape to the floating island of belief, take to the lifeboat of the graced, but I have never belonged to their number.

It seems to me that transcendental judgments of the intellect are absolutely impossible and therefore vacuous. But in spite of Kant and epistemology they crop up again and again and can evidently not be suppressed. This is probably because they represent emotional

☐ See Corti, 30 Apr. 29 (in vol. 1).

[1] *Die Mythopoese des werdenden Gottes* (1953).

[2] Usually Markgräflerland; district in southwestern Germany, adjacent to Basel, where Jung had been a student.

[3] *Faust, Part One* (tr. Wayne), p. 29.

needs and, as such, are psychological facts that cannot be eliminated, which is how they appear to the empirical mind. The assertions of the latter are not subjective confessions like your philosophical statements, but are empirical judgments which assert that a general consensus declares God to be *immobilis*, and that an equally general consensus says he is evolving. No philosopher knows who is right, and we don't know whether God himself knows.

So if you profess belief—with or without supporting arguments—in an evolving God, I can assure you on the basis of my mythological knowledge that you enjoy a greater consensus than the believers in a *Deus immobilis*. The biographical "metamorphosis of the gods"[4] is decidedly more popular than their static immutability. Even Yahweh, who lacked a personal biography, created a temporal world, allied himself to a people, begot a son and μορφὴν δοῦλον λαβών,[5] incarnated as a man, etc. In the New Testament he even changed his character. From an eternal he became an historical figure. Allah acts without being acted upon—a contradiction in terms—which is as it should be in view of the fact that he cannot be discussed.

It has yet to be explained why man makes transcendental statements, indeed must make them, it would seem (you are an example,[6] Herr Corti!). No doubt such statements have a primarily psychological cause, the exact nature of which is still controversial because it is connected with the unconscious. We only know that the primordial experience underlying mythological statements is highly numinous. This is a verifiable fact, as indisputable as my finding a particular picture beautiful or loving a particular person or smacking my lips over a particular dish. What is more, medical experience shows that it is advisable to take numinous experiences seriously, as they have a great deal to do with the fate of the individual. It also seems that the will to be taken seriously is implicit in the experience itself, since it comes upon us with the most vehement claim to truth. Your book bears witness to this.

I hear you are giving a lecture to theologians in Canton Bern (?).[7] I am sure you will learn a thing or two there about the efficacy of

---

[4] Allusion to a book of that name by Leopold Ziegler, *Gestaltwandel der Götter* (1920–22). Cf. Jacobi, 23 Dec. 32, n. 5.

[5] = took the form of a servant. (Phil. 2:6.)

[6] A misunderstanding on Jung's part. C. did not make any metaphysical or transcendental statements but spoke explicitly of mythopoesis, "myth-making," of God evolving ("werdend") as a pure hypothesis of the speculative, creative mind.

[7] "Das theogonische Denken Schellings," delivered 9 May 1955 to Swiss clergymen in Walkringen, Cant. Bern.

philosophical arguments. But that's the way it is: belief, even philosophical belief, demands avowals in order to banish doubt. But knowledge consists of nothing but doubts and so has nothing to avow. It partakes of the mystery of the known.

As you will have gathered from my answer, I have read your book with so much interest and involvement that I could not refrain from burdening you with a bit of my own biography.

Yours very sincerely, c. g. jung

To Father Victor White

[ORIGINAL IN ENGLISH]

Dear Victor,   6 May 1955

The serious illness of my wife has consumed all my spare time. She has undergone an operation so far successfully, but it has left her in a feeble state needing careful nursing for several weeks to come.

Since I am the cause of much discomfort to you,[1] I am not sure whether you care to see me or not. Please put conventionality aside and do not feel under any obligation. I can understand your true situation and I would prefer not to add to its spikes and thorns. A conventional call means nothing to me, and a straightforward talk may be painful and not desirable. Please decide according to your judgment. Needless to say, you can count upon my friendship.

Cordially yours, c. g.

P.S. I have just heard that you did not get a long letter[2] I sent to you (pr. adr. Blackfriars Oxford).

☐ (Handwritten.)
[1] Cf. White, 2 Apr. 55. W., then in Zurich for lectures at the C. G. Jung Institute, did not go to see Jung. Instead, he wrote three letters full of personal warmth but again expressing strong disagreement (one of them contained a long list of "problems arising from publication of 'Answer to Job' "). In a letter of 21 May he wrote: ". . . perhaps I may tell you how deeply I feel with you personally in this wrestle with the Divine Mysteries and with our Brother Death. I must leave the outcome trustingly to them and to your own fearless honesty and humility . . . For myself, it seems that our ways must, at least to some extent, part. I shall never forget, and please God I shall never lose, what I owe to your work and friendship."
— Although he wrote to Jung occasionally, Jung did not write back (though they met once more in June 1958), except for one short note in October 1959 when he heard from the Mother Prioress of a Carmelite Convent of W.'s serious illness, and the two last letters of 25 Mar. and 30 Apr. 60.
[2] The letter of 2 Apr. 55.

To B. A. Snowdon

[ORIGINAL IN ENGLISH]

Dear Mr. Snowdon, 7 May 1955

You were quite right in believing I would answer your letter. You are obviously a sincere man to whom one can give a straight answer. You want to know why you believe so confidently in the existence of God, and you mention your friends who believe they are able to explain the reason for our existence or who say that the world can just as well be accidental, or similar things. Nobody can answer such questions since there is no answer to them. Whether the world is accidental, or intended or planned, nobody can say. That I myself have a reasonable and provable cause is no news, but that man's existence in general has a definite and verifiable cause nobody can say, as little as we know the reasons why there are elephants, or trees, or amoebas, or anything else. Of course there are reasons why they exist, but they are all unpredictable facts, which means that in past geological ages nobody would have been in a position to predict the coming of mammals and incidentally of man. People who believe that they can explain these things are just a bit muddle-headed and victims of their own illusions. The only thing we can safely state is that all the said things do exist, for reasons unknown.

Now when you ask why you so confidently believe in the existence of God, nobody can tell you why. It is just a fact, a result or a fruit of your living mind. The mind is like a tree bringing forth its characteristic blossom and fruit; it is just so. As you call something that pleases you beautiful or good, so you confess to believe in God. As an apple tree that bears no fruit would be all wrong, so you would be all wrong if you didn't confess your truth. It just grows in and through you, and this great unknown thing that makes the universe tick at all, and incidentally causes ourselves to produce such thoughts and convictions, is what man since time immemorial has called "gods" or "God." It does not matter what he calls his God, whether he gives Him the name of "first cause," "matter," "ether," "will to be," "creative urge," etc. When somebody says that the thing he suggests is something new or other than God, he is a bit soft in the brain, i.e., he is incapable of thinking clearly. He still believes in the magic power of words as if he were able to change something in the world by saying: "This is not God, but something else." God

☐ Brighton, England.

is an immediate experience of a very primordial nature, one of the most natural products of our mental life, as the birds sing, as the wind whistles, like the thunder of the surf. If you find such a belief in you, you are just natural, and we know that your mind functions properly, but equally we are unable to say why there are different kinds of birds, or why there are birds at all; we cannot find the reasons why their song exists in its particular way. No scientist is able to tell you why we see a certain wave-length as green or red or blue, since all we can make out is only the length of the light waves, but it is a fact that we see these colours.

People who think that they know the reasons for everything are unaware of the obvious fact that the existence of the universe itself is one big unfathomable secret, and so is our human existence. You can just be glad to have such a conviction, like a man who is in a happy frame of mind, even if nobody else, not even himself, knows why, but certainly nobody could prove to him that he is unhappy or that his feeling happy is an illusion.

Sincerely yours, C. G. JUNG

To Hélène Kiener

Dear Fräulein Kiener,   14 May 1955

. . .

In the Christ symbol the conquest of evil is suggested by the descent into hell and the breaking open of its gates.[1] But nobody has ever heard that the devil departed this life afterwards; on the contrary, the authentic New Testament view is that after the thousand-year reign of Christ he shall be loosed again on earth in all his youthful freshness, in the form of Antichrist.[2] Also, as you rightly point out, a strong light is the best shadow-projector, provided that there is something to cast a shadow. Even the saints cast a shadow. We do not know whether there is more good than evil or whether the good is stronger. We can only hope that the good will predominate. If good is identified with constructiveness, there is

□ See Kiener, 6 Dec. 35 (in vol. 1).
[1] Cf. "Acts of Pilate" in James, *The Apocryphal New Testament*, p. 34.
[2] Rev. 20 : 2ff.

some probability that life will go on in a more or less endurable form; but if destructiveness were to prevail, the world would surely have done itself to death long ago. As that hasn't happened yet, we may suppose that the positive exceeds the negative. Hence the optimistic assumption of psychotherapy that conscious realization accentuates the good more than the overshadowing evil. Becoming conscious reconciles the opposites and thus creates a higher third.

. . .

With best regards,

Yours sincerely, c . g . j u n g

To Pastor Jakob Amstutz

Dear Pastor Amstutz,   Mammern, 23 May 1955

Meanwhile I have read your typescript, "Zum Verständnis der Lehre vom werdenden Gotte." It seems to me one more proof of the overweening gnostic tendency in philosophical thinking to ascribe to God qualities which are the product of our own anthropomorphic formulations. Every metaphysical judgment is *necessarily antinomian*, since it transcends experience and must therefore be complemented by its counterposition. If we describe God as "evolving," we must bear in mind at the same time that perhaps he is so vast that the process of cognition only moves along his contours, as it were, so that the attribute "evolving" applies more to it than to him. Moreover, "evolving" as a quality of human cognition is far more probable empirically than the presumptuous projection of this quality on to a Being whose nature and scope transcend by definition our human stature in every respect. Such projective statements are pure gnosticism.

I hold the contrary view that there are certain experiences (of the most varied kinds) which we characterize by the attribute "divine" without being able to offer the slightest proof that they are caused by a Being with any definite qualities. Were such a proof possible, the Being that caused them could only have a finite nature and so, by definition, could not be God. For me "God" is on the one hand a mystery that cannot be unveiled, and to which I must at-

□ Mammern (Cant. Thurgau) is a village on Lake Constance.

tribute only *one* quality: that it exists in the form of a particular psychic event which I feel to be numinous and cannot trace back to any sufficient cause lying within my field of experience.

On the other hand "God" is a verbal image, a predicate or mythologem founded on archetypal premises which underlie the structure of the psyche as images of the instincts ("instinctual patterns"). Like the instincts, these images possess a certain autonomy which enables them to break through, sometimes against the rational expectations of consciousness (thus accounting in part for their numinosity). "God" in this sense is a biological, instinctual and elemental "model," an archetypal "arrangement" of individual, contemporary and historical contents, which, despite its numinosity, is and must be exposed to intellectual and moral criticism, just like the image of the "evolving" God or of Yahweh or the Summum Bonum or the Trinity.

"God" as a mythologem dominates your discussion, which casts a deceptive veil over the religious reality. For the religious man it is an embarrassment to speak of the mystery which he can say nothing about anyway except paradoxes, and which he would rather conceal from profane eyes if he had anything in his hands at all that he could conceal from anybody. It is unfortunately true: he has and holds a mystery in his hands and at the same time is contained in its mystery. What can he proclaim? Himself or God? Or neither? The truth is that he doesn't know who he is talking of, God or himself.

All talk of God is mythology, an archetypal pronouncement of archetypal causation. Mythology as a vital psychic phenomenon is as necessary as it is unavoidable. Metaphysical speculations that keep within the bounds of reason (in the wider sense) are therefore quite in place so long as one is aware of their anthropomorphism and their epistemological limitations. The relatively autonomous life of the archetypes requires symbolic statements like the "evolving God" or the encyclicals *Munificentissimus Deus* and *Ad Caeli Reginam* or God as *complexio oppositorum*, etc., because collective psychic life is strongly influenced by changes in the "Pleroma" of the *mundus archetypus* (cf. Hitler's "saviour epidemic" and the worldwide Communist delusion of a Utopia peopled by human robots).

In this discussion, it seems to me, the gnostic danger of ousting the unknowable and incomprehensible and unutterable God by philosophems and mythologems must be clearly recognized, so that nothing is shoved in between human consciousness and the primordial numinous experience. The mythologem of the Incarnation seems to serve this purpose indirectly, because it is symbolic.

I hope you won't find my criticism of your discussion officious, but will take it rather as an expression of my sympathetic interest. For us psychotherapists, at any rate for those of them who have come to see how great is the importance of the religious attitude for psychic equilibrium, theological discussions are of the utmost practical value, because questions of this kind are directed to us more often than the layman imagines.

Yours sincerely, C. G. JUNG

To John J. Gruesen

[ORIGINAL IN ENGLISH]

Dear Dr. Gruesen, 4 June 1955

Thank you very much for your really interesting letter![1] The physiological approach to the most frequent and the most important archetype is indeed a major discovery, confirming in a way my suspicion that its localization could have to do with the brain-stem. But since my work is all on the biological and psychological side, I did not dare to speculate, having already the greatest trouble in convincing my contemporaries of the existence of original and basic patterns of psychic behaviour, i.e., of archetypes.

As you will readily understand, your communication is of the greatest value to me and I am most obliged to you for kindly giving me this information. Unfortunately my recent books are not yet published in English with the exception of *Psychology and Alchemy*, which first appeared more than 10 years ago. You could find a lot of corresponding material in my books.

The mandala motif, especially the *quadratura circuli*, is incidentally the most primitive form of infantile drawing, not ◎, but ⊕, for reasons unknown.

---

[1] G., a biologist at the Academy of Sciences in Washington, D.C., who was writing a thesis on the "Philosophical Implications of C. G. Jung's Individuation Process," mentioned a book by Wilder Penfield and Herbert Jasper, *Epilepsy and the Functional Anatomy of the Human Brain* (1954). They "succeeded in evoking an hallucinatory vision of coloured squares and circles by stimulating the occipital cortex" of an epileptic "who, as a prodromal symptom of the attack, always had a vision of a circle in a square" (Jung, "Schizophrenia," CW 3, par. 582).

It is somewhat unfortunate that some of my most advanced works, like the one with W. Pauli, are soon to appear without the intervening works leading up to them.[2]

Sincerely yours, C. G. JUNG

[2] The English tr. of "Synchronicity: An Acausal Connecting Principle" (CW 8) appeared in 1955, whereas *Aion* (CW 9, ii), one of Jung's most important books, was published in English only in 1959 (the first Swiss edition had appeared in 1946).

To Pastor Walter Bernet

Dear Pastor Bernet,   13 June 1955

At last I have got down to reading and studying your book[1] which you so kindly sent me. Please put the slowness of this procedure down to my old age! It was certainly not lack of interest that kept me reading so long, but rather a curiosity or—more accurately—a need to familiarize myself with and learn to understand the theological mode of thinking, which is so alien to me. I have been able to assimilate this thinking only very fragmentarily, if at all, in spite or perhaps because of the fact that I come from a theological milieu on my mother's side, and my father was himself a clergyman. It was the tragedy of my youth to see my father cracking up before my eyes on the problem of his faith and dying an early death.[2] This was the objective outer event that opened my eyes to the importance of religion. Subjective inner experiences prevented me from drawing negative conclusions about religion from my father's fate, much as I was tempted to do so. I grew up in the heyday of scientific materialism, studied natural science and medicine, and became a psychiatrist. My education offered me nothing but arguments against religion on the one hand, and on the other the charisma of faith was denied me. I was thrown back on experience alone. Always Paul's experience on the road to Damascus hovered before me, and I asked myself how his fate would have fallen out but for his vision. Yet this experience came upon him while he was blindly pursuing his own way. As a young man I drew the conclusion that you must obviously fulfill your destiny in order to get to the point where a *donum gratiae*

☐ Bern.
[1] *Inhalt und Grenze der religiösen Erfahrung* (1952).
[2] Cf. *Memories*, pp. 91ff./96ff.

257

might happen along. But I was far from certain, and always kept the possibility in mind that on this road I might end up in a black hole. I have remained true to this attitude all my life.

From this you can easily see the origin of my psychology: only by going my own way, integrating my capacities headlong (like Paul), and thus creating a foundation for myself, could something be vouchsafed to me or built upon it, no matter where it came from, and of which I could be reasonably sure that it was not merely one of my own neglected capacities.

The only way open to me was the experience of religious realities which I had to accept without regard to their truth. In this matter I have no criterion except the fact that they seem meaningful to me and harmonize with man's best utterances. I don't know whether the archetype is "true" or not. I only know that it lives and that I have not made it.

Since the number of possibilities is limited, one soon comes to a frontier, or rather to frontiers which recede behind one another presumably up to the point of death. The experience of these frontiers gradually brings the conviction that what is experienced is an endless approximation. The goal of this approximation seems to be anticipated by archetypal symbols which represent something like the circumambulation of a centre. With increasing approximation to the centre there is a corresponding depotentiation of the ego in favour of the influence of the "empty" centre, which is certainly not identical with the archetype but is the thing the archetype points to. As the Chinese would say, the archetype is only the *name* of Tao, not Tao itself. Just as the Jesuits translated Tao as "God," so we can describe the "emptiness"[3] of the centre as "God." Emptiness in this sense doesn't mean "absence" or "vacancy," but something unknowable which is endowed with the highest intensity. If I call this unknowable the "self," all that has happened is that the effects of the unknowable have been given an aggregate name, but its contents are not affected in any way. An indeterminably large part of my own being is included in it, but because this part is the unconscious I cannot indicate its limits or its extent. The self is therefore a *borderline concept*, not by any means filled out with the known psychic processes. On the one hand it includes the phenomena of synchronicity, on the other its archetype is embedded in the brain structure and

---

[3] For the Buddhist concept of *sunyata*, emptiness, cf. Evans-Wentz, 8 Dec. 38, n. 3. Also "Psychology and Religion," CW 11, par. 136.

258

is physiologically verifiable: through electrical stimulation of a certain area of the brain-stem of an epileptic it is possible to produce mandala visions (*quadratura circuli*). From synchronistic phenomena we learn that a peculiar feature of the psychoid[4] background is transgressivity[5] in space and time. This brings us directly to the frontier of transcendence, beyond which human statements can only be mythological.

The whole course of individuation is dialectical, and the so-called "end" is the confrontation of the ego with the "emptiness" of the centre. Here the limit of possible experience is reached: the ego dissolves as the reference-point of cognition. It cannot coincide with the centre, otherwise we would be insensible; that is to say, the extinction of the ego is at best an endless approximation. But if the ego usurps the centre it loses its object (inflation!).[6]

Even though you add to my "ultimate" an "absolute ultimate," you will hardly maintain that my "ultimate" is not as good an "ultimate" as yours. In any case all possibility of cognition and predication ceases for me at this frontier because of the extinction of the ego. The ego can merely affirm that something vitally important is happening to it. It may conjecture that it has come up against something greater, that it feels powerless against this greater power; that it can cognize nothing further; that in the course of the integration process it has become convinced of its finiteness, just as before it was compelled to take practical account of the existence of an ineluctable archetype. The ego has to acknowledge many gods before it attains the centre where no god helps it any longer against another god.

It now occurs to me—and I hope I am not deceiving myself— that from the point where you introduce the "absolute ultimate" which is meant to replace my descriptive concept of the self by an empty abstraction, the archetype is increasingly detached from its dynamic background and gradually turned into a purely intellectual formula. In this way it is neutralized, and you can then say "one can live with it quite well." But you overlook the fact that the self-constellating archetypes and the resultant situations steadily gain in numinosity, indeed are sometimes imbued with a positively eerie daemonism and bring the danger of psychosis threateningly close.

---

[4] Cf. Dr. H., 30 Aug. 51, n. 5.
[5] "Synchronicity," CW 8, par. 964.
[6] *Aion*, CW 9, ii, pars. 44f., 79.

The upsurging archetypal material is the stuff of which mental illnesses are made. In the individuation process the ego is brought face to face with an unknown superior power which is likely to cut the ground from under its feet and blow consciousness to bits. The archetype is not just the formal condition for mythological statements but an overwhelming force comparable to nothing I know. In view of the terrors of this confrontation I would never dream of addressing this menacing and fascinating opponent familiarly as "Thou," though paradoxically it also has this aspect. All talk of this opponent is mythology. All statements about and beyond the "ultimate" are anthropomorphisms and, if anyone should think that when he says "God" he has also predicated God, he is endowing his words with *magical power*. Like a primitive, he is incapable of distinguishing the verbal image from reality. In one breath he will endorse the statement *Deus est ineffabilis* without a thought, but in the next he will be speaking of God as though he could express him.

It seems to me—and I beg your pardon in advance if I am doing you an injustice—that something of the sort has happened to you. You write, apparently without any misgivings, that I equate God with the self. You seem not to have noticed that I speak of the *God-image and not of God* because it is quite beyond me to say anything about God at all. It is more than astonishing that you have failed to perceive this fundamental distinction, it is shattering. I don't know what you must take me for if you can impute such stupidities to me after you yourself have correctly presented my epistemological standpoint at the beginning of your book. I have in all conscience never supposed that in discussing the psychic structure of the God-image I have taken God himself in hand. I am not a word-magician or word-fetishist who thinks he can posit or call up a metaphysical reality with his incantations. Don't Protestant critics accuse the Catholic Mass of magic when it asserts that by pronouncing the words *Hoc est corpus meum* Christ is actually present?

In *Job* and elsewhere I am always explicitly speaking of the *God-image*. If my theologian critics choose to overlook this, the fault lies with them and not with me. They obviously think that the little word "God" conjures him up in reality, just as the Mass forces Christ to appear through the words of the Consecration. (Naturally I am aware of the dissident Catholic explanation of this.) I do not share your overvaluation of words, and have never regarded the equation Christ = Logos as anything else than an interesting symbol conditioned by its time.

This credulity and entrapment in words is becoming more and more striking nowadays. Proof of this is the rise of such a comical philosophy as existentialism, which labours to help being become being through the magical power of the word. People still believe that they can posit or replace reality by words, or that something has happened when a thing is given a different name. If I call the "ultimate" the self and you call it the "absolute ultimate," its ultimateness is not changed one whit. The name means far less to me than the view associated with it. You seem to think that I enjoy romping about in a circus of archetypal figures and that I take them for ultimate realities which block my view of the Ineffable. They guide but they also mislead; how much I reserve my criticism for them you can see in *Answer to Job*, where I subject archetypal statements to what you call "blasphemous" criticism. The very fact that you consider this critique of anthropomorphisms worthy of condemnation proves how strongly you are bound to these psychic products by word-magic. If theologians think that whenever they say "God" then God is, they are deifying anthropomorphisms, psychic structures and myths. This is exactly what I don't do, for, I must repeat, I speak exclusively of the *God-image* in *Job*. Who talks of divine knowledge and divine revelation? Certainly not me. "Ultimately" I have really reached the ultimate with my presumptuous anthropomorphisms which feign knowledge and revelation! I see many God-images of various kinds; I find myself compelled to make mythological statements, but I know that none of them expresses or captures the immeasurable Other, even if I were to assert it did.

However interesting or enthralling metaphysical statements may be, I must still criticize them as anthropomorphisms. But here the theologian buttonholes me, asseverating that *his* anthropomorphism is God and damning anyone who criticizes any anthropomorphic weaknesses, defects, and contradictions in it as a blasphemer. It is not God who is insulted by the worm but the theologian, who can't or won't admit that his concept is anthropomorphic. With this he puts an end to the much needed discussion and understanding of religious statements. Just as Bultmann's demythologizing procedure stops at the point where the demagicking of words no longer seems advisable to him, so the theologian treats exactly the same concept as mythological, i.e., anthropomorphic at one moment and as an inviolable taboo at the next.

I have begged four distinguished (academic) theologians to tell me what exactly is the attitude of modern Protestantism to the question of the identity of the God of the Old Testament with the God of the New, between whom the layman thinks he can spot quite a number of differences. The question is so harmless that it is like asking what the difference is between Freud's view of the unconscious and mine. Two didn't answer at all despite repeated requests. The third told me that there was no longer any talk of God in the theological literature of the last twenty years anyway. The fourth said the question was very easy to answer: Yahweh was simply a somewhat archaic God-concept in comparison with that of the New Testament. Whereupon I replied: "Look, my dear Professor, this is just the kind of psychologism the theologians accuse me of. Suddenly the divine revelation in the OT is nothing but an archaic *concept* and the revelation in the NT is simply a modern one. But the next moment this same revelation is God himself and no concept at all."

So you ride the hobby-horse of your choice. In order to do away with such tricks, I stick to my proposal that we take all talk of God as mythological and discuss these mythologems honestly. As soon as we open our mouths we speak in traditional verbal images, and even when we merely think we think in age-old psychic structures. If God were to reveal himself to us we have nothing except our psychic organs to register his revelation and could not express it except in the images of our everyday speech.

Let the Protestant theologian therefore abandon his hieratic word-magic and his alleged knowledge of God through faith and admit to the layman that he is mythologizing and is just as incapable as he is of expressing God himself. Let him not vilify and condemn and twist the arguments of others who are struggling just as earnestly to understand the mysteries of religion, even if he finds these arguments personally disagreeable or wrong in themselves. (I cannot exempt you, for one, from the obligation to give due regard to the epistemological premises of *Answer to Job* if you want to criticize it.)

So long as we are conscious of ourselves, we are supported by the psyche and its structures and at the same time imprisoned in them with no possibility of getting outside ourselves. We would not feel and be aware of ourselves at all were we not always confronted with the unknown power. Without this we would not be conscious of our separateness, just as there is no consciousness without an object.

We are not delivered from the "sin" of mythologizing by saying that we are "saved" or "redeemed" through the revelation of God in Christ, for this is simply another mythologem which does, however, contain a psychological truth. Consequently we can understand the "feeling of redemption" which is bound up with this mythologem; but the statement "revelation in Christ" merely affirms that a myth of this kind exists which evidently belongs to the symbolism of the self.

What impresses me most profoundly in discussions with theologians of both camps is that metaphysical statements are made apparently without the slightest awareness that they are talking in mythic images which pass directly as the "word of God." For this reason it is so often thoughtlessly assumed that I do the same thing, whereas quite to the contrary I am trained by my daily professional work to distinguish scrupulously between idea and reality. The recognition of projections is indeed one of the most important tasks of psychotherapy.

I have read your erudite book with great interest and profit and find it all the more regrettable that in spite of your admirably objective presentation of my standpoint at the beginning you nevertheless go off the rails at the end. You think I have deviated from my epistemological position in *Job*. Had you read the introduction you could never have pronounced this false judgment.

I can understand very well that you are shocked by the book; I was too, and by the original Job into the bargain. I feel that you have in general too poor an opinion of me when you charge me with the arrogance of wanting to write an *exegesis* of Job. I don't know a word of Hebrew. As a layman, I have only tried to read the translated text with psychological common sense, on the assumption, certainly, that I am dealing with anthropomorphisms and not with magical words that conjure up God himself. If in the Jewish commentaries the high priest takes the liberty of admonishing Adonai to remember his good rather than his bad qualities,[7] it is no longer so shocking if I avail myself of a similar criticism, especially as I am not even addressing Adonai, as the high priest did, but merely the anthropomorphic God-image, and expressly refrain from all metaphysical utterances, which the high priest did not. You will scarcely suppose that, despite my assurance to the contrary, the mere pronouncing of God's name conjures up God himself. At all events Adonai took the high priest's criticism and a number of other equally drastic observations without a murmur, thereby showing

[7] *Aion*, par. 110.

himself to be more tolerant than certain theologians. The reason why mythic statements invariably lead to word-magic is that the archetype possesses a numinous autonomy and has a psychic life of its own. I have dealt with this particular difficulty at some length in *Job*. Perhaps I may remark in conclusion that the theory of archetypes is more difficult, and I am not quite so stupid as you apparently think.

I cannot omit to thank you, all the same, for the great trouble you have taken in going into my proposition so thoroughly. It is obvious that this cannot be done without difficulties and misunderstandings, especially in view of the fact that our age is still for the most part trapped in its belief in words. Ancient Greece was on an even lower level, as the term *phrenes* with its psychic connotation shows.[8] The Pueblo Indians of New Mexico still think in the "heart" and not in the head.[9] Tantra Yoga gives the classic localizations of thought: *anahata*, thinking (or localization of consciousness) in the chest region (*phrenes*); *visuddha* (localized in the larynx), verbal thinking; and *ajna*,[10] vision, symbolized by an eye in the forehead, which is attained only when verbal image and object are no longer identical, i.e., when their *participation mystique*[11] is abolished.

I have this advance of human consciousness particularly at heart. It is a difficult task to which I have devoted all my life's work. This is the reason why I venture to plague you with such a long letter.[12]

Yours sincerely, C. G. JUNG

[8] The midriff or diaphragm; among the pre-Socratics, the seat of consciousness. In Homer, however, *phrenes* meant the lungs.

[9] *Memories*, p. 248/233.

[10] *Anahata, visuddha,* and *ajna* are three of the seven *chakras* in Kundalini Yoga. Cf. Kotschnig, 23 July 34, n. 2, and "The Realities of Practical Psychotherapy," CW 16 (2nd edn.), Appendix, par. 560.

[11] A term coined by Lévy-Bruhl for the "prelogical" mentality of primitives, but later abandoned by him. Jung made frequent use of it to denote the state of projection in which internal and external events are inextricably mixed up, resulting in an irrational and unconscious identity of inside and outside.

[12] A decade later, B. published extracts from Jung's letter with comments in an essay on Jung in *Tendenzen der Theologie im 20. Jahrhundert. Eine Geschichte in Porträts,* ed. H. J. Schulz (1966). He concluded: ". . . this outsider of theology has, with the relentless determination with which he demands experience of man, with his uncomfortable criticism of ecclesiastical talk of God, with his bold vision in particular of the Protestant Church, urged upon contemporary theological thought questions which in the interest of theology are absolutely necessary and which in their rigour show the way."

To Hélène Kiener

Dear Fräulein Kiener, 15 June 1955

"Thought transference" is a synchronistic phenomenon.

"Self" is something that can be verified psychologically. We experience "symbols of the self" which cannot be distinguished from "God symbols."[1] I cannot prove that the self and God are identical, although in practice they appear so. Individuation is ultimately a religious process which requires a corresponding religious attitude = the ego-will submits to God's will. To avoid unnecessary misunderstandings, I say "self" instead of God. It is also more correct empirically.

Analytical psychology helps us to recognize our religious potentialities.

I know the Jesuit X. Naturally he is afraid of the psychological truth. What a misfortune it would be for the Catholic Church if all religions could unite in a truly universal *Ecclesia spiritualis*! Then Père X would no longer be the only one who is right!

I have no ambitious power plans, but seek a passable way only for myself and a few others. I leave the will-to-power to the Churches, and the concomitant fear of losing power. I have nothing to lose in this respect.

All science is merely a tool and not an end in itself. Analytical psychology only helps us to find the way to the religious experience that makes us whole. It is not this experience itself, nor does it bring it about. But we do know that analytical psychology teaches us that *attitude* which meets a transcendent reality halfway.

Recently there appeared in Paris a book by another Jesuit, Père Hostie[2] (sic!), who criticizes my empirical concepts as though they were philosophical ones. The facts I report are largely ignored. Naturally this is an anxiety reaction which twists my findings as much as possible and imputes to me what these gentlemen do themselves. They see the mote in their brother's eye. Like drowning men they cling to a straw. Best greetings and wishes,

Yours sincerely, C. G. JUNG

[1] "Answer to Job," par. 757.
[2] Cf. Hostie, 25 Apr. 55, n. 1.

To Patricia Graecen

[ORIGINAL IN ENGLISH]

Dear Mrs. Graecen,   29 June 1955

In fulfilling your wishes I have corrected the pages of your MS here enclosed. The question of the letter to Joyce is mysterious. I am rather certain that I never wrote to him,[1] but the remark about Molly's monologue is definitely authentic, though where and to whom I made it is beyond the reach of my memory. I am sorry.

If you know anything of my anima theory, Joyce and his daughter are a classic example of it.[2] She was definitely his *femme inspiratrice*, which explains his obstinate reluctance to have her certified. His own anima, i.e., unconscious psyche, was so solidly identified with her that to have her certified would have been as much as an admission that he himself had a latent psychosis. It is therefore understandable that he could not give in. His "psychological" style is definitely schizophrenic, with the difference, however, that the ordinary patient cannot help talking and thinking in such a way, while Joyce willed it and moreover developed it with all his creative forces. Which incidentally explains why he himself did not go over the border. But his daughter did, because she was no genius like her father, but merely a victim of her disease. In any other time of the past Joyce's work would never have reached the printer, but in our blessed XXth century it is a message, though not yet understood.

Very truly yours, C. G. JUNG

☐ Patricia Graecen is the private name of Patricia Hutchins. The letter is published in part in Hutchins, *James Joyce's World* (1957), pp. 184f., and in Richard Ellmann, *James Joyce* (1959), p. 692.
[1] Jung's memory was clearly at fault; cf. Joyce, 27 Sept. 32.
[2] Jung had treated Joyce's daughter for schizophrenia. "When the psychologist pointed out schizoid elements in poems Lucia had written, Joyce, remembering Jung's comments on *Ulysses*, insisted they were anticipations of a new literature, and said his daughter was an innovator not yet understood. Jung granted that some of her portmanteau words and neologisms were remarkable, but said they were random; she and her father, he commented later, were like two people going to the bottom of a river, one falling and the other diving" (Ellmann, p. 692, based on an interview with Jung 1953). Jung was the twentieth doctor whom Joyce consulted for her. After some initial success he gave up the treatment (Ellmann, pp. 688ff.).

To Pastor William Lachat

Dear Pastor Lachat,   29 June 1955

Your letter of June 10th comes at the right moment, since I am in the hospital where I have time to answer it. I can subscribe to all the principal points made by Mr. Zacharias[1] with the exception of his metaphysical Christian interpretations and, above all, his identification of Christ, with the archetype of the self in the sense that Christ is himself the archetype. I cannot prove the identity of an historical personage with a psychological archetype. That is why I stop after establishing the fact that in the Occident this archetype, or this "God-image," is seen in Christ; in the Orient, in the Buddha, or in the form of Tao (which is not a personification but a metaphysical hypostasis). In these three concrete forms the archetype of the self has appeared to us. Since it represents the center of All, it can be called the *vas mysticum* filled with the *Spiritus Sancta servator mundi.*[2] This symbolic formula would be an entirely satisfactory characterization of the psychological nature of the archetype of the self if the paradoxical nature of the Holy Spirit, like that of the author of all things, could be admitted. Inasmuch as we attribute to the Holy Spirit *the faculty of procreating in matter,* we must unavoidably grant it a nature capable of contact with material existence, i.e., a chthonic aspect, as the alchemists did; otherwise it could not influence Physis. However, these are metaphysical considerations outside my empirical domain. But if you take them for what they are—that is, psychological qualifications—my formula seems perfectly applicable.

As for literature relevant to this subject, I would recommend my books *Aion* and *Symbolik des Geistes.* In the latter you will find a little essay on Mercurius[3] and the chthonic aspect of the Spirit.

I cannot share Zacharias' optimistic belief that the efficacy of the rites can be "repristinized." Unfortunately one must say: Once lost, lost forever! But I must also say that there will be psychological equivalents; the psychological work necessary for the realization of the individuation process is an *opus divinum* consisting of a series of symbolic acts, examples of which can be found in my book

---

☐ (Translated from French.)
[1] Cf. Zacharias, 24 Aug. 53.
[2] = the Holy Spirit, preserver of the world.
[3] "The Spirit Mercurius," CW 13.

Gestaltungen des Unbewussten ("Zur Empirie des Individuations-prozesses").[4]

Considering that the light of Christ is accompanied by the "dark night of the soul" that St. John of the Cross spoke about, and by what the Gnostics of Irenaeus called the *umbra Christi*, which is identical with the chthonic aspect mentioned above, the life of Christ is identical in us, from the psychological point of view, with the unconscious tendency toward individuation. That is what forces us to live life completely, an adventure which is often as heroic as it is tragic. Without error and sin there is no experience of grace, that is, no union of God and man. A complete life, unconditionally lived, is the work of the Holy Spirit.[5] It leads us into all dangers and defeats, and into the light of knowledge, which is to say, into maximal consciousness. This is the aim of the incarnation as well as the Creation, which wants each being to attain *its* perfection.

Very sincerely yours, c. g. jung

[4] Now "A Study in the Process of Individuation," CW 9, i.
[5] Cf. Lachat, *La Réception et l'action du Saint-Esprit dans la vie personnelle et communautaire* (1953).

To Pater Lucas Menz

Dear Pater,   29 June 1955

Many thanks for your detailed reply to my letter[1] and for telling me your sufferings and joys. One can well say that the experience of grace is paid for dearly. In an ordinary human life the opposites are not wrenched so far apart as in yours. The sufferings and joys are smaller and therefore don't clash so much. Light and shadow are complementary (Lao-tse!) and so are suffering and joy.

The question of the *privatio boni* is not so simple, for if evil = nonbeing then there's nothing there at all. But if I strike a person dead, something is there—a corpse—or if I steal 100 thalers from someone, I have them and he hasn't. Awkward though it is, evil is just as real as good, since both are facts which one person calls good and another evil. Evil = nonbeing means that I have done nothing evil, for I have literally done *nothing* and nothing is there, no corpse and no stolen money. Good and evil are relative human judgments

[1] Cf. 28 Mar. 55.

about what is but have no existence in themselves. Nor can you say that suffering is a privation of joy, for this means boredom at most, which is a long way from actual suffering.

Don't grow any more grey hairs on this account. You are, like the Babylonian hero Gilgamesh, a "woe-joyful man": both fall to your lot, happiness and unhappiness, one quarter joy and three quarters suffering, but your joy is such that it outweighs the excess of suffering. You could be an example to others of how to endure it. You also seem to have found in this your true calling. With best greetings and wishes,

Yours sincerely, c. g. j u n g

To Fritz Meerwein

Dear Colleague, [July 1955] 29 June 1956

Permit me, in memory of our meeting and your kind letter, to ask you a question which is still occupying my mind. As a psychiatrist, you are doubtless familiar with the phenomenon that can be paraphrased by the New Testament metaphor of the mote in one's brother's eye and the beam in one's own. The term "projection"[1] used for this, which I borrowed from Freud, has often been criticized in existentialist circles, but I have never understood what is wrong with it. It seems to me to designate quite correctly the illusion and unconscious assumption by which I ascribe to my fellow man what largely belongs to myself. I lodge it in him, so to speak. Since you also take exception to my concept of projection, I should be very grateful if you would kindly explain the true state of affairs. What sort of term do you use for it? Or do you deny the existence of this process altogether? For me it is simply a question of a more or less suitable designation for a group of empirical facts and not a philosophical problem, as it apparently is for the existentialists. One such philosopher asked me in all seriousness what would happen if all

☐ M.D., Psychiatric Clinic, Friedmatt, Basel. — This letter is dated 29 June 56 but was actually written July (or possibly June) 1955; owing to an illness of Jung's it got mislaid but was found again in 1956, when Jung sent it off. It is in answer to a question on the definition and justification of the term "projection," raised at a meeting between Jung and the staff of the Burghölzli Clinic at his house.

[1] *Psychological Types*, CW 6, Def. 43: "The expulsion of a subjective content into an object."

projections were withdrawn. Curiously enough he was dumbfounded when I replied that one would then have a better chance of recognizing reality. What sort of answer did he expect and what was it that flummoxed him? I grope as though in the dark and would be much obliged to you for enlightenment. With collegial regards and best thanks in advance,

Yours sincerely, c. g. j u n g

To Mary Bancroft

[o r i g i n a l   i n   e n g l i s h]

August 1955

A man's helplessness can be real, a woman's is one of her best stunts. As she is by birth and sex on better terms with nature, she is never quite helpless as long as there is no man in the vicinity.

Thank you for your refreshing and informative letter! The "boy friend" is amused. The article in *Time*[1] has done me a lot of good, more than all my books. I have appeared in the world, if that is good for me. My name enjoys an existence quasi independent of myself. My real self is actually chopping wood in Bollingen and cooking the meals, trying to forget the trial of an eightieth birthday. Many good wishes,

Yours cordially, c. g. j u n g

☐ U.S.A. — A handwritten note on a printed card of thanks issued on the occasion of Jung's 80th birthday. B. had sent her congratulations and asked if he had "ever known a helpless woman."
[1] Cf. Tenney, 23 Feb. 55, n. 4.

To Werner Kuhn

Vir Magnifice! 6 September 1955

Allow me to express to you and to the University of Basel my sincerest thanks for the great honour you have done me by participating in the festivities on my eightieth birthday. I would particularly like to thank you for the charter you presented me with on that occasion. It reminded me of the joy I felt when the University of my

☐ Then Rector of Basel U.

home town did me the honour of appointing me to a professorship,[1] and on the other hand of those bitter drops that fell into the beaker of joy when severe illness prevented the continuation of my teaching activity in Basel. But such is the fate of the pioneer: he himself is too early, and what he longs for comes too late. Nevertheless a kindly fate has allowed me to reach my eightieth year with an overflowing abundance of honours and rewards.

Accept, Vir Magnifice, the expression of my highest esteem and profound gratitude,

Yours sincerely, c . g . j u n g

[1] Cf. Keller, 21 Aug. 44, n. 3.

To Piero Cogo

Dear Signor Cogo,   21 September 1955

You cannot possibly imagine on the basis of a newspaper report[1] what it means when I say that one can know about God without having to make the often entirely fruitless effort to believe. As you are aware, I am a psychologist and am chiefly concerned with the investigation of the unconscious. The question of religion, among other things, also comes under this head. If you want to understand me correctly you should read my psychological findings. I can't communicate them to you in a letter. Without a thorough knowledge of the human psyche, remarks torn out of their context remain completely unintelligible. One cannot expect journalists to bother about the bases of our thinking.

From the psychological standpoint religion is a psychic phenomenon which irrationally exists, like the fact of our physiology or anatomy. If this function is lacking, man as an individual lacks balance, because religious experience is an expression of the existence and function of the unconscious. It is not true that we can manage

☐ Istituto Universitario di Architettura, Venice.
[1] C. had read the report of an interview with Jung in the Italian weekly *Oggi* and quoted Jung's statement that he did not *believe* in God because he *knew* of his existence. It is a translation of an interview with Frederick Sands, "Men, Women and God," published in the London *Daily Mail*, 25–29 Apr. 1955. The actual words (29 Apr.) are: "I only believe in what I know. And that eliminates believing. Therefore I do not take his existence on belief—I know that he exists." The interview is published in *C. G. Jung Speaking*.

with reason and will alone. We are on the contrary continually under the influence of disturbing forces that thwart our reason and our will because they are stronger. Hence it is that highly rational people suffer most of all from disturbances which they cannot get at either with their reason or their will. From time immemorial man has called anything he feels or experiences as stronger than he is "divine" or "daemonic." God is the Stronger in him. This psychological definition of God has nothing to do with Christian dogma, but it does describe the experience of the Other, often a very uncanny opponent, which coincides in the most impressive way with the historical "experiences of God." I once knew a professor of philosophy who thought he could get by with reason alone. But "God" forced a carcinoma-phobia[2] on him which he could not master and which made his life a torture. His misfortune was that he could not be simple enough to admit that this phobia was stronger than his reason. Had he been able to do so he would have found a way to submit rationally to the Stronger in him. But because of his arrogance he didn't understand his rationalistic superstition, or the danger that threatened him, or the meaning inherent in this threat. The working of the Divine is always overpowering, a sort of subjugation no matter what form it takes. Our reason is indeed a wonderful gift and an achievement not to be underestimated, but it covers only one aspect of reality which also consists of irrational factors. Natural laws are not axiomatic but are only statistical probabilities. Like reality, our psyche consists of irrational factors too. Therefore a mechanization of psychic life is impossible. We are like primitives in a dark world, at the mercy of unpredictables. Hence we need religion, which means a careful consideration of what happens (*religio* is derived from *religere* and not from *religare*)[3] and less sophistry, i.e., overvaluation of the rational intellect.

So I would advise you to concern yourself more with the psychology of the unconscious. All sorts of realizations might then dawn on you.

Yours sincerely, C. G. JUNG

---

[2] This case is discussed in "Psychology and Religion," CW 11, pars. 12, 19f.
[3] *Religere* = to go through again, think over, recollect; *religare* = to reconnect, link back, the latter being the derivation of *religio* given by the Church Fathers. Cf. *Symbols of Transformation*, CW 5, par. 669 & n. 71.

To Arnim Haemmerli

Dear Colleague,   25 October 1955

Now that the flood of letters on and around my eightieth birthday has abated somewhat, I can at last get down to thanking you for your card from Kos[1] and your highly appreciated letter of 4.VIII. Your letter from Kos moved me deeply, since your late brother,[2] who attended me when I had my cardiac infarct in 1944, was associated with Kos in a mysterious way. In my delirious states the image of your brother appeared to me, framed by the golden Hippocratic wreath, and announced—at that point I was already 2500 km. away from the earth and was about to enter a rock temple hollowed out of a meteorite—that I had no permission to go any further from the earth but had to return to it.[3]

From the moment of this vision I feared for the life of your brother, since I had seen him in his primal form as Prince of Kos, which signified his death. I discovered only afterwards that the great physicians of Kos styled themselves βασιλεῖς (kings). On 4 April 1944 I was allowed to sit up on the edge of the bed for the first time, and on that day your brother took to his bed, never to rise again.

With warm thanks and best wishes for a speedy recovery from your operation,

Ever sincerely yours, C. G. JUNG

☐ (Handwritten.) M.D., Zurich.
[1] Kos (or Cos), a Greek island in the Dodecanese. It was the birthplace of Hippocrates, the father of medicine (born ca. 460 B.C.). It was also famed for an important sanctuary of Asklepios, the god of healing, and the first school of scientific medicine.
[2] Cf. Keller, 21 Aug. 44, n. 2.
[3] There is a detailed report of this vision in *Memories*, pp. 292f./272f.

To Palmer A. Hilty

[ORIGINAL IN ENGLISH]

Dear Dr. Hilty,   25 October 1955

Your name "Hilty" is well known and even famous in Switzerland. I thank you for your frank questions, which I will try to answer—*hélas*—with much delay!

☐ Palmer A. Hilty, professor of English at the State College of Washington (Pullman), submitted the following questionnaire:

273

1. I am of the Swiss-Reformed branch. My father was parson. On my mother's side I had not less than 6 theologians in the family!

2. I consider myself a Protestant and very much so! I am even protesting against the backwardness of Protestantism.

3. I cannot say that I hold to church teachings, but I am considering them very seriously.

4. I don't *believe* [in a personal God], but I do *know* of a power of a very personal nature and an irresistible influence. I call it "God." I use this term because it has been used for this kind of experience since time immemorial. From this point of view any gods, Zeus,

---

"1. Are you of the Church background (Reformed Church of Zwingli)?

2. Do you still belong?

3. Do you still hold to the teachings of that or any church more or less *in toto*?

4. Do you believe in a personal God?

5. Do you believe in a God in any way over and above or outside or different from the totality of nature, nature being the complete biological and physical world or worlds?

6. Do you subsume the laws of nature under the heading of God (physicist's pantheism)?

7. Is the God, if any, you believe in, able to go against the laws of nature?

8. Does he?

9. Do you believe that miracles defined as events defying all laws of nature ever occurred? (E.g. A man ate fish and then went through a wood door, walked on water, and turned water into wine.)

10. Do you regard a feeling of sudden glory, of intense emotional satisfaction, of sudden insight sometimes called "inspiration" as proofs of a God?

11. Where do you think God exists?

12. Do you believe Jesus was a son of God more than Gautama, Socrates, Albert Schweitzer, Gandhi?

13. Do you believe Jesus arose from the dead?

14. That he ascended into heaven?

15. That the Virgin Mary ascended bodily into a heaven "above"?

16. Do you believe in personal immortality, i.e. conscious survival after death with memory of things that happened on earth?

17. Do you believe in the resurrection of the flesh as orthodox Christian creeds hold?

18. Do you believe that a resurrected body will ever go to heaven?

19. Or the "spirit" without the body go to heaven?

20. Do you believe in self-existent spirits coming down from eternity or having got started sometime millions of years ago?

21. Do you believe in devils?

22. Do you believe that man will, when dead, face a twofold hereafter, i.e., a heaven for the good and a hell for the bad?

23. Can non-Christians get to this heaven?

24. If they can, under what conditions?"

Wotan, Allah, Yahweh, the Summum Bonum etc., have their intrinsic truth. They are different and more or less differentiated expressions or aspects of one ineffable truth. (Cf. Foreword to *Answer to Job*[1] and "Psychology and Religion," Terry Lectures, 1937.)

5. As "God" is the overwhelming experience κατ᾽ ἐξοχήν,[2] He is an ἄρρητον, *ineffabile*, beyond which I would not dare to make any statements, although I fully accept the traditional inference of this absolute oneness (μονότης) and this *complexio oppositorum*. The use of such an image obviously includes Nature as an aspect of the Deity.

6. There are no natural laws, only statistical probabilities, included in "God."

7. As there are no axiomatic laws, any so-called "law" suffers exceptions. Nothing therefore is absolutely impossible except alogical contradiction (*contradictio in adiecto*).

8. I don't know whether God is doing improbable things.

9. Within the reach of my experience I have never encountered a miracle. Thus I don't know whether such things you mention are possible.

10. There is no proof of God's existence. I only know Him as a personal, subjective experience and indirectly through the *consensus gentium*.

11. This question is ridiculous. Time and space are epistemological categories indispensable for the description of moving bodies, but incommensurable with objects of inner experience.

12. As far as I can judge from the documents of Christian tradition, Jesus Christ was probably a definite human person, yet highly enveloped in archetypal projections, more so than other historical figures like Buddha, Confucius, Lao-tse, Pythagoras, etc. Inasmuch as Christ represents an archetypal image (viz. that of the ἄνθρωπος or υἱὸς τοῦ ἀνθρώπου), he is of divine nature and thus the "son of God." (Cf. *Answer to Job* and my disquisition about the psychology of the Christ-symbol in *Aion*, Ch. V.)

13. I know of resurrection only because it is a very important archetypal idea. I don't know whether it has ever occurred as physical fact. I see no point in believing something I don't know. The resurrection is a myth (like 14 and 15) and one of the characteristics of the hero (i.e., Anthropos), pointing to the extratemporal, i.e., transcendental, nature of the archetype. (Cf. my essay on the dogma of Trinity in *Symbolik des Geistes*, 1948.)

[1] Foreword = "Lectori Benevolo," CW 11, pars. 553ff.
[2] Cf. Baynes, 22 Jan. 42, n. 5.

16. I don't think that the human mind is eternal and therefore I don't assume that we can think eternal subjects like infinity, immortality, etc. We can only use such words. We just don't know what is going to happen after death. The only thing we know within reasonable certainty is that the psyche is *relatively* independent of time and space or that time and space (including causality) are *relatively* dependent upon the psyche. (*Vide:* Jung and Pauli, *The Interpretation of Nature and the Psyche*, 1955.) Further conclusions from this fact are very uncertain.

17–20. I do not deny the existence of things unknown and I do not presume to a belief in such matters.

21. "Devil" is a very apt name for certain autonomous powers in the structure of the human psyche. As such the devil seems to me to be a very real figure.

22–24. Unanswerable metaphysical problems beyond my reach.

As you have seen, I could not answer your questions with a simple yes or no, although I should have preferred it. The question of religion is unfortunately more complicated. It can't be reduced to mere belief or unbelief. This is only true for a confession or a church, but not for religion, the latter being chiefly a matter of experience. Since my answers are far from being complete I have added some books where you can get the necessary information.

Yours sincerely, C. G. JUNG

To Theodor Bovet

Dear Colleague,   9 November 1955

Very belatedly I am at last thanking you for your kind letter of congratulation on my 80th birthday. I was most surprised that you thought of me at all and even took the trouble to remember with goodwill the existence of my shadow. You may shake your head incredulously when I tell you that I would hardly have been able to form the concept of the shadow had not its existence become one of my greatest experiences, not just with regard to other people but with regard to myself. So I can gladly accept your allusions to Houdon's Voltaire[1] and to *Job*, though it is rather like carrying coals to New-

□ See Bovet, 25 Nov. 22. — This letter was published in *Spring*, 1971.
[1] Jung kept a reproduction of the bust of Voltaire by Jean-Antoine Houdon (1741–1828) in his waiting-room at Küsnacht. Dr. B. had said how disturbed he had

castle. I like to look at the mocking visage of the old cynic, who reminds me of the futility of my idealistic aspirations, the dubiousness of my morals, the baseness of my motives, of the human—alas!—all too human. That is why Monsieur Arouet de Voltaire still stands in the waiting room, lest my patients let themselves be deceived by the amiable doctor. My shadow is indeed so huge that I could not possibly overlook it in the plan of my life, in fact I had to see it as an essential part of my personality, accept the consequences of this realization, and take responsibility for them. Many bitter experiences have forced me to see that though the sin one has committed or is can be regretted, it is not cancelled out. I don't believe in the tiger who was finally converted to vegetarianism and ate only apples. My solace was always Paul, who did not deem it beneath his dignity to admit that he bore a thorn in the flesh.

My sin has become for me my most precious task. I would never leave it to anybody else in order to appear a saint in my own eyes, always knowing what is good for others.

The criticism and "understanding" I have had to endure at the hands of theologians (long before *Job*!) give me no cause to treat their theological concepts any more gently than they treated mine. The same is true of the Freudians.[2]

As for Trüb's "dialectics"[3] (which, if such they were, would require a partner), they consisted of a monologue in which I couldn't get a word in edgeways. Despite the honest efforts of my wife and myself even documented proofs were swept under the table without so much as a glance. His method was very like that of a theologian, as was his gross misunderstanding.

Protestantism is faced with questions which one day will have to be spoken out loud. For instance, the horrid sophism of the *privatio boni*, which even Protestant theologians are willing to endorse. Or the question of the relation between the Old and New Testament God

---

been by the contrast between the bust, "which receives you with its cynical-superior smile," and "the benevolent, warmly human doctor," as if the latter had "left his shadow in the waiting-room."

[2] B. expressed doubts about Jung's way of criticizing both theologians and Freudians.

[3] The Swiss physician Hans Trüb, originally a friend and follower of Jung, interpreted Jung's concept of individuation as too much "an end in itself" and this led to a growing estrangement. Cf. his *Vom Selbst zur Welt* (1947) and *Heilung aus der Begegnung* (1951).

(. . .).[4] When it suits them God is just an anthropomorphic idea, or they pretend they can conjure up God himself by naming him. But when I regard an anthropomorphic God-image as open to criticism, then it is "psychologism" or—worse still—"blasphemy"! Laymen to-day are no longer bamboozled by this kind of humbug, and Protestantism would do well to notice that someone is knocking on the door. I have knocked long and loud in order to rouse Protestant theology from its untimely slumbers, for I feel myself responsible as a "Protestant." I have delivered my message as clearly as I could, together with the relevant proofs. If the theologian, like Trüb, chooses to ignore it, that's his affair. I don't need to tell you what a troublesome spectacle this is.

Protestantism has long ceased to live its "protest." It draws its vitality from its encounter with the spirit of the age, of which psychology is now a part. If it fails in this task, it dries up. Actually the theologians should be grateful to me for the intense interest I take in them, and as a matter of fact a few of them are.

The length of my answer will be enough to show you that your educative efforts have fallen on thankful ground. I therefore allow myself to hope that you will raise this question of the shadow among your friends and cronies, the theologians and Freudians. With collegial regards,

Yours sincerely, C. G. JUNG

[4] Here follows the story of the four theologians which is told in Bernet, 13 June 55 and White, 2 Apr. 55.

Anonymous

[ORIGINAL IN ENGLISH]

Dear Mrs. N.,   19 November 1955

I am glad that you do understand the difficulty of your request. How can anybody be expected to be competent enough to give such advice? I feel utterly incompetent—yet I cannot deny the justification of your wish and I have no heart to refuse it. If your case were my own, I don't know what could happen to me, but I am rather certain that I would not plan a suicide ahead. I should rather hang on as

☐ The letter is addressed to a sick old lady in England. — Published in *Spring*, 1971, pp. 133f.

278

long as I can stand my fate or until sheer despair forces my hand. The reason for such an "unreasonable" attitude with me is that I am not at all sure what will happen to me after death. I have good reasons to assume that things are not finished with death. Life seems to be an interlude in a long story. It has been long before I was, and it will most probably continue after the conscious interval in a three-dimensional existence. I shall therefore hang on as long as it is humanly possible and I try to avoid all foregone conclusions, considering seriously the hints I got as to the *post mortem* events.

Therefore I cannot advise you to commit suicide for so-called reasonable considerations. It is murder and a corpse is left behind, no matter who has killed whom. Rightly the English Common Law punishes the perpetrator of the deed. Be sure first, whether it is really the will of God to kill yourself or merely your reason. The latter is positively not good enough. If it should be the act of sheer despair, it will not count against you, but a willfully planned act might weigh heavily against you.

This is my incompetent opinion. I have learned caution with the "perverse." I do not underestimate your truly terrible ordeal. In deepest sympathy,

Yours cordially, C. G. JUNG

To Gerald Sykes

[ORIGINAL IN ENGLISH]

Dear Mr. Sykes,   21 November 1955

I must apologize for being so late with my letter. My time since the summer has been much occupied by all sorts of things waiting my attention. Lately Mrs. Jung has been laid up with an illness that causes me much anxiety.

I have read your MS[1] with the greatest interest. It is rather difficult to judge its merits, because I am one of its objects. To myself personally its objective coming-from-the-outside style appeals strongly, as I

□ American writer and lecturer. In 1955 he was teaching English and American literature at the Salzburg Seminar in American Studies, an American school sponsored by the Ford Foundation. During his stay in Europe he spent a considerable time with Jung.

[1] Of *The Hidden Remnant* (New York, 1962), a collection of essays on psychology.

am always curious to learn about the different ways of approach people choose to acquire a firm standpoint in the shifting chaos of psychological opinions. Just before I could tackle your MS I had to finish reading a book concerned with the same subject, viz., Freud, Adler, and myself.[2] The author is a philosopher with independent psychological experience. His book is a sort of systematic presentation of the quintessence in each case and remarkably different from yours in every way. His words are written, yours are spoken. You talk argumentatively to an audience one can almost see. He is writing, or better, building up something like a suitable house with furniture, wallpapers, and pictures in the style and taste of its inmate. The American style, when it is alive, has the character of speech and when it is as it were impersonal, it is dead and drier than dust.

The dialectical method you have chosen is particularly apt in a case like Freud and Jung. It is only possible to bring out the many and often—to the layman invisible—subtle differences of the two different attitudes by a continuous exposition of the contrasting viewpoints. I have enjoyed following up your disquisition. I appreciate particularly your cultivated language. In how far you meet the taste and the mental capacity of the American public it is not for me to judge, since I have lost my contacts with the American postwar mind. The mental products of American brains that have reached my awareness are not particularly encouraging. But that is a matter for yourself to decide. I am not quite happy about your neologism "trialogue." The Greek word *dialogos* derives from the verb *dialegein* or *dialogizestai*, Germ. "sich auseinandersetzen," i.e., to talk *au fond* with a partner. The prefix *dia* has nothing to do with δύο (two). Thus *tria* being the neutr. plur. of *tris* (three) is wrong. There is the Greek word τριλογία (*trilogia* = trilogy), but it means an ensemble of three *tragedies* (!), which is hardly what you want to suggest. So you'd better say: a dialogue between three or [lacuna in text] = a *tripartite dialogue*.

Nov. 28. I cannot continue the letter. Yesterday I lost my wife after a serious illness lasting only 5 days. Please excuse me.

Yours sincerely, c. g. j u n g

[2] Probably Friedrich Seifert, *Tiefenpsychologie: Die Entwicklung der Lehre vom Unbewussten* (1955). Cf. Seifert, 31 July 35, n. □, and Nelson, 17 June 56.

To Simon Doniger

[ORIGINAL IN ENGLISH]

Dear Sir,   November 1955

In reply to your letter of October 13th, I send you a short biography and a list of the essential data in my life, which may be helpful for your purpose.

Your suggestion that I should tell you how *Answer to Job* came to be written sets me a difficult task, because the history of this book can hardly be told in a few words. I have been occupied with its central problem for years. Many different sources nourished the stream of its thoughts, until one day—and after long reflection—the time was ripe to put them into words.

The most immediate cause of the book being written is perhaps to be found in certain problems discussed in my book *Aion*, especially the problems of Christ as a symbolic figure and of the antagonism Christ-Antichrist, represented in the traditional zodiacal symbolism of the two fishes.

In connection with the discussion of these problems and of the doctrine of Redemption, I criticized the idea of the *privatio boni* as not agreeing with the psychological findings. Psychological experience shows that whatever we call "good" is balanced by an equally substantial "bad" or "evil." If "evil" is a μηὅν—nonexistent—then whatever there is must needs be "good." Dogmatically, neither "good" nor "evil" can be derived from man, since the "Evil One" existed before man as one of the "Sons of God."[1] The idea of the *privatio boni* began to play a role in the Church only after Mani. Before this heresy, Clement of Rome taught that God rules the world with a right and a left hand, the right being Christ, the left Satan. Clement's view is clearly *monotheistic*, as it unites the opposites in one God.

Later Christianity, however, is dualistic, inasmuch as it splits off one half of the opposites, personified in Satan, and he is *eternal* in his state of damnation. The crucial question of πόθεν τὸ κακόν;[2] (whence

---

□ D. was editor of the monthly journal *Pastoral Psychology* (Great Neck, N.Y.), whose associated Pastoral Psychology Book Club had undertaken to publish *Answer to Job* after the Bollingen Foundation had at first declined it. The letter was published as an article, "Why and How I Wrote my *Answer to Job*," in *Pastoral Psychology*, VI:60 (Jan. 1956), with the Book Club announcement. It appears as a Prefatory Note in CW 11, pp. 357f., and in Ges. Werke, XI, pp. 505f.

[1] Cf. Job 1:6: "Now there was a day when the sons of God came to present themselves before the Lord, and Satan came also among them."

[2] This very important phrase is, most unfortunately, omitted in the above-mentioned publications.

evil?) forms the *point de départ* of the Christian theory of Redemption. It is therefore of prime importance. If Christianity claims to be a monotheism, it becomes unavoidable to assume the opposites as being contained in God. But then we are confronted with a major religious problem: the problem of Job. It is the aim of my booklet to point out its historical evolution since the time of Job down through the centuries to the most recent symbolic phenomena like the *Assumptio Mariae,* etc.

Moreover the study of mediaeval natural philosophy—of the greatest importance to psychology—made me try to find an answer to the question: what image of God did those old philosophers have? Or rather: how should the symbols which supplement their image of God be understood? All this pointed to a *complexio oppositorum* and thus recalled again the story of Job to my mind: Job who expected help from God against God. This most peculiar fact presupposes a similar conception of the opposites in God.

On the other hand numerous questions, not only from my patients but from all over the world, brought up the problem of giving a more complete and explicit answer than I had given in *Aion.* For many years I hesitated to do this, because I was quite conscious of the probable consequences and knew what a storm would be raised. But I was gripped by the urgency and difficulty of the problem and was unable to throw this off. Therefore I found myself obliged to deal with the whole problem and did so in the form of describing a personal experience, carried by subjective emotions. I deliberately chose this form because I wanted to avoid the impression that I had any idea of announcing an "eternal truth." The book does not pretend to be anything but the voice or question of a single individual who hopes or expects to meet with thoughtfulness in the public.

Faithfully yours, C. G. JUNG

To Eugen Böhler

Dear Professor Böhler,   14 December 1955

Many thanks for your kind letters. The loss of my wife has taken it out of me, and at my age it is hard to recover.

☐ (1893–   ), professor of economics at the Swiss Federal Polytechnic (E.T.H.), Zurich, 1924–64. In July 1955 he was one of the speakers at a celebration when

Your suggestion that I should describe what one does with arche-types is very interesting.[1] In the first place it is they that do things with us and it is only afterwards that we learn what we can do with them. I have asked Dr. C. A. Meier to lend you my 1925 Seminar,[2] where I describe my first experiences in this field. I hope that in the meantime this Seminar report has reached you safely and will give you the information you want.

It is only of minimal importance what the individual does with archetypes. Infinitely more important is what the history of mankind has to tell us about them. Here we open the treasure-house of com-parative religion and mythology. It is from the Gnostic fragments in particular and from the Gnostic tradition of alchemical "philosophy" that we derive the most instruction. I have worked this field to the best of my ability and it has, I think, yielded all manner of fruit from which we can gain a more comprehensive insight than from the re-actions and labours of modern individuals, although it is precisely their experiences that prompted our historical researches. In practice, of course, the problem rests with the modern individual, who alone can give the modern answer. (The *lux moderna* is an alchemical term!) The answer, as always, depends on the contemporary concepts, i.e., it is psychologically scientific so far as the *theoria* is concerned. In practice it is the immemorial *religio*, i.e., careful consideration of the *numina*. (*Religio* comes from *religere* and not from the patristic *religare*.) In this way the unconscious data are integrated into con-scious life (as the "transcendent function"). Information on the em-pirical process can be found in "The Relations between the Ego and the Unconscious," in the dream series in *Psychology and Alchemy*, and in "A Study in the Process of Individuation."

Jung received an honorary degree in natural science at the Polytechnic. (Cf. Hug, Meier, Böhler, Schmid, *Carl Gustav Jung*, Kultur- und Staatswissenschaftliche Schriften, no. 91, 1955.) B.'s growing interest in the psychology of economics led to friendly personal relations between the two men. Cf. his "Conscience in Eco-nomic Life," in *Conscience* (Studies in Jungian Thought, 1970; orig. 1958), and "Die Grundgedanken der Psychologie von C. G. Jung," *Industrielle Organisation* (Zurich), no. 4, 1960.

[1] B. suggested that Jung write "a definitive work about your personal relation to archetypes" in order to help him overcome the paralyzing effect of the death of his wife.

[2] *Notes on the Seminar in Analytical Psychology* . . . *Mar. 23–July 6, 1925*, multi-graphed for private circulation. In it Jung gives a very personal account of the origin and development of his main concepts. Some of this material is incorpo-rated in *Memories*, ch. VI: "Confrontation with the Unconscious."

I would be glad to see you again soon. Please let me know what time would suit you. With kind regards,

Yours sincerely, c. g. jung

To Erich Neumann

Dear Neumann,   15 December 1955

Deepest thanks for your heartfelt letter. Let me in return express my condolences on the loss of your mother. I am sorry I can only set down these dry words, but the shock I have experienced is so great that I can neither concentrate nor recover my power of speech. I would have liked to tell the heart you have opened to me in friendship that two days before the death of my wife I had what one can only call a great illumination which, like a flash of lightning, lit up a centuries-old secret that was embodied in her and had exerted an unfathomable influence on my life. I can only suppose that the illumination came from my wife, who was then mostly in a coma, and that the tremendous lighting up and release of insight had a retroactive effect upon her, and was one reason why she could die such a painless and royal death.

The quick and painless end—only five days between the final diagnosis and death—and this experience have been a great comfort to me. But the stillness and the audible silence about me, the empty air and the infinite distance, are hard to bear.

With best greetings also to your wife and my warmest thanks,

Ever your devoted c. g. jung

□ (Handwritten.)

To Eugen Böhler

Dear Professor Böhler,   Bollingen, 8 January 1956

I want to thank you for your kind letter bearing the greetings of the season and to send you my wishes for the coming year. I also want to tell you once again how much your interest in my work means to me, and how much I appreciate this opportunity for fruitful discussion which you and a kindly fate have thrown my way. You will forgive me if I express the wish that you should give free rein to your

284

criticism, your observations, and questions regardless of personal considerations. As your letter[1] shows, you are rapidly approaching the problem of personal involvement beyond all intellectualistic themes, when the whole man speaks out of his unfathomable background. You strike this note with the idea of the *hero* and its inevitable consequences in personal and collective life. This brings you to the fictive personal ideal on the one hand, and on the other to the central figure of the Christian myth, who has guided us for the last eighteen hundred years and still does, albeit in an unconscious manner so long as there is no real awareness of this archetype. Actually "Anthropos" is a more suitable name than "hero" for this figure, since it expresses the psychic reality of the archetype in clearer and more specific form. Unlike the merely personal and fallible fiction of the hero, this formulation includes history and thus reproduces an image (Osiris!) that dates back to the fourth millennium before Christ and offers us a rich phenomenology of what, in psychological terms, I call the "self." The manifest career of this leading figure begins with the various types of gods, god-men, and kings. But quite early, at the time of Euhemeros, rationalism attempted to stop the projection of this symbolism, without realizing—and this is still true today—what happens when gods and kings are reduced to the proportions of the empirical man. Rationalism or Euhemerism merely subtracts and destroys, as did the old-fashioned excision of goitres, which while removing the tumour also takes away the thyroid and so produces a cretin. If it were creative it would have given us an equivalent or better symbol long ago. There are clear indications of this in primitive Christianity, namely in the Johannine gospel and the early Christian "Acts of John."[2] In spite of all this even the most modern Protestantism still insists on its archaic Christolatry, thus blocking the necessary advance which would assist the integration or conscious realization of this archetype. Instead, the Christian or halfway Christian culture of the West is threatened by the terrible regression of the East to the prehistoric level of Communist economy on the one hand and tribal tyranny on the other, an autocratic oligarchy which deprives the individual of social and political rights and enslaves him. The West stands there with empty

---

[1] B. cited a book by the Jewish philosopher Lazarus Ben David, *Versuch über das Vergnügen* (*ca.* 1795), in which he mentions under "spiritual pleasures" first of all "the pleasure derived from heroic deeds." B. wrote that David's remarks had given him a better understanding of the events in Italy, Germany, and Russia, and of their archetypal background.

[2] James, *The Apocryphal New Testament*, pp. 228ff.

hands and a few outmoded ideals and with its blind rationalism produces the very mentality that destroys its own roots. Increased production, improved social conditions, political peace, and the reign of Déesse Raison are the slogans to which West and East alike owe allegiance. But man and his soul, the individual, is the only real carrier of life, who doesn't just work, eat, sleep, reproduce, and die but also has a meaningful destiny reaching far beyond him. And for this we have no "myth" any more.

This was the question that raised its menacing head in 1912, when I put the full stop to my manuscript of *Wandlungen und Symbole der Libido*. The attempt to answer it led me straight into the unconscious, for only the psyche itself can provide the answer. Later, I welcomed with glee the alchemical dictum: *Rumpite libros, ne corda vestra rumpantur*.[3] But this sets us a task and imposes an opus of which the West has no inkling at present. Communism, at least for the dumb ones, has its chiliasm, the golden age of the future, where machines work for men, instead of like now, when man is chained to the workbench. But the Communist Utopia will never free him from his bondage, lack of rights, and the all-obstructing bureaucracy unless he finds his way back to himself. For this a relativation of rationalism is needed, but not an abandonment of reason, for the reasonable thing for us is to turn to the inner man and his vital needs.

Your dream[4] is especially interesting in this respect. The Romanesque arches are a stylistic pointer to that momentous period following the first millennium,[5] when the problems of our time had their real beginnings.

I look forward to seeing you next Wednesday. My secretary has told me of your kind consent.

Yours sincerely, C. G. JUNG

[3] "Rend the books, lest your heart be rent asunder." Cf. *Psychology and Alchemy*, CW 12, par. 564.
[4] In the dream the foundations of his study were completely demolished, and then rebuilt with two Romanesque arches.
[5] Cf. Wegmann, 12 Dec. 45, n. 1.

To Maud Oakes

[ORIGINAL IN ENGLISH]

Dear Miss Oakes, 31 January 1956

As you can imagine, I am quite astonished to hear about your project, although I am fully aware of the fact that an imaginative person could easily write not one but several volumes about my stone. All the volumes I have written are contained in it *in nuce*. The mandala itself is just a sort of hieroglyph, hinting at and trying to express a vast background in a most abbreviated form. Your method of realizing its contents through your subjective experience is unexceptionable, as a matter of fact the only correct way of reading its message. That is just the virtue of symbolic expression, that it can be read in many different ways by many different individuals. And if they are honest the reading will be correct. Thus, as you see, I am prepared for the shock of getting the MS about a thing most emphatically belonging to my innermost self. I only ask you to be patient with the slow ways of old age. *Deo concedente* you will get an answer. Inshallah!

Sincerely yours, c. g. j u n g

☐ American writer on Indian ethnology. Cf. her *Where the Two Came to Their Father: A Navaho War Ceremonial* (with Jeff King and Joseph Campbell; Bollingen Series I, 1944), *The Two Crosses of Todos Santos: Survivals of Mayan Religious Ritual* (1951), and *Beautyway: A Navaho Ceremonial* (with B. Haile and L. C. Wyman, 1957). — At the time she was working on a MS dealing with a block of stone which Jung had carved at his Tower in Bollingen. In *Memories* he describes the stone and says it expresses "what the Tower means to me" (pp. 226ff./214ff.). It has two sides with carved inscriptions and a third with a mandala, containing a tiny homunculus in the centre; the fourth side is blank. (See pl. viii.)

To E. L. Grant Watson

[ORIGINAL IN ENGLISH]

Dear Mr. Watson,   9 February 1956

You are surely touching upon a most important fact when you begin to question the coincidence of a purely mathematical deduction with physical facts, such as the *sectio aurea* (the Fibonacci series.[1] My source calls him Fibonacci, not -nicci. He lived 1180–1250) and in modern times the equations expressing the turbulence of gases. One has not marvelled enough about these parallelisms. It is quite obvious that there must exist a condition common to the moving

[1] G. W. submitted for comment the MS of a chapter on "Imaginative Fantasy" in a book he was working on: *The Mystery of Physical Life* (1964). Among other things he discusses the phenomenon of phyllotaxis, the arrangement of leaves on the stem of a plant. Their spiral arrangement follows a definite mathematical formula, that of the so-called Fibonacci series, discovered by the Italian mathematician Leonardo of Pisa (or Fibonacci) in the 13th cent.

body and the psychic "movement," more than a merely logical *corol-larium* or *consectarium*.[2] I should call it an *irrational* (acausal) *corol-lary* of synchronicity. The Fibonacci series is self-evident and a property of the series of whole numbers, and it exists independently of empirical facts, as on the other hand the periodicity of a biological spiral occurs without application of mathematical reasoning unless one assumes an equal arrangement in living matter as well as in the human mind, *ergo* a property of matter (or of "energy" or whatever you call the primordial principle) in general and consequently also of moving bodies in general, the psychic "movement" included.

If this argument stands to reason, the coincidence of physical and mental forms and also of physical and mental events (synchronicity) would needs be a regular occurrence, which, however, particularly with synchronicity, is not the case. This is a serious snag pointing, as it seems to me, to an indeterminate or at least indeterminable, apparently *arbitrary arrangement*. This is a much neglected but characteristic aspect of physical nature: the statistical truth is largely made up of *exceptions*. That is the aspect of reality the poet and artist would insist upon, and that is also the reason why a philosophy exclusively based upon natural science is nearly always flat, superficial, and vastly beside the point, as it misses all the colourful improbable exceptions, the real "salt of the earth"! It is not realistic, but rather an abstract half-truth, which, when applied to living man, destroys all individual values indispensable to human life.

The coincidence of the Fibonacci numbers[3] (or *sectio aurea*) with plant growth is a sort of analogy with synchronicity inasmuch as the latter consists in the coincidence of a psychic process with an external physical event of the same character or meaning. But whereas the *sectio aurea* is a static condition, synchronicity is a concidence in time, even of events that, in themselves, are not synchronous (f.i., a case of precognition). In the latter case one could assume that synchronicity is a property of energy, but in so far as energy is equal to matter it is a secondary effect of the primary concidence of mental and physical events (as in the Fibonacci series). The bridge seems to be formed by the *numbers*.[4] Numbers are just as much *invented* as

---

[2] *Corollarium* (corollary) denotes the practical consequence of a proposition; *consectarium* (consectary), a logical deduction or conclusion.

[3] This and the following paragraph are reprinted in W.'s book (p. 48) but with one serious mistake. He has ". . . the coincidence of a *physical* process with an external physical event . . . ," thus completely vitiating Jung's argument.

[4] The function and archetypal role of numbers is discussed at some length in "Flying Saucers," CW 10, pars. 776ff., and "Synchronicity," CW 8, par. 871.

they are *discovered* as natural facts, like all true archetypes. As far as I know, archetypes are perhaps the most important basis for synchronistic events.

I am afraid this is all rather involved and very difficult. I don't see my way yet out of the jungle. But I feel that the root of the enigma is to be found probably in the peculiar properties of whole numbers. The old Pythagorean postulate![5]

Mr. Cook[6] seems to have conceived his ideas about the same time I began to think about *archetypes* as unconscious *a priori* determinants of imagination and behaviour, reaching conscious apperception in the human mind chiefly in the form of so-called mythological images. I then spoke of "urtümliche Bilder" (primordial images, in *Wandlungen und Symbole der Libido*, 1912. Engl. tr. *Psychology of the Unconscious*, 1917).

Inasmuch as *karma* means either a personal or at least an individual inherited determinant of character and fate, it represents the individually differentiated manifestation of the instinctual behaviour pattern, i.e., the general archetypal disposition. *Karma* would express the individually modified archetypal inheritance represented by the collective unconscious in each individual. I avoid the term of *karma* because it includes metaphysical assumptions for which I have no evidence, f.i. that *karma* is a fate I have acquired in a previous existence or that it is the result of an individual life left over and by chance becoming my own. For such assumptions there is no empirical evidence I am aware of.

Well, your ideas move in the right direction. Good luck! — The interpretation of your dream[7] is more or less complete.

Sincerely yours, C. G. JUNG

[5] To the Pythagoreans the whole universe was explicable in terms of the relation of numbers to one another.

[6] Cf. Theodore Andrea Cook, *The Curves of Life* (New York, 1914), in which he gives "an elaborate description of spiral curves that enter into all forms of growth, from that of the minutest micro-organism to the great astro-nebulae of the heavens" (quoted in Watson's book, p. 41). Cook mentions the possibility of a "metaphysical determinant" which, properly understood, might be related to Jung's "*a priori* determinants," the archetypes. (The spiral structure of the "minutest microorganism" has been strikingly confirmed by the model of the DNA molecule, gene of heredity, as described by James D. Watson, *The Double Helix* (1968); a discovery for which he and his fellow researchers, Francis Crick and Maurice Wilkins, received the Nobel Prize for Medicine and Physiology in 1962.)

[7] W. sent the text of his dream together with the MS and added his own interpretation. For a previous dream of his, cf. Watson, 25 Jan. 54, n. 1.

To Maud Oakes

[ORIGINAL IN ENGLISH]

Dear Miss Oakes,   11 February 1956

I have read your meditation about the stone with much interest. Your method of reading its message is adequate and in this case the only one yielding positive results. You understand the stone as a statement about a more or less limitless world of thought-images. I quite agree with your view. One can read the symbols like that. When I hewed the stone I did not think, however. I just brought into shape what I saw on its face.

Sometimes you express yourself (in the MS) as if my symbols and my text were a sort of confession or a belief. Thus it looks as if I were moving in the vicinity of theosophy. In America especially one blames me for my so-called mysticism. Since I don't claim at all to be the happy proprietor of metaphysical truths, I should much prefer that you attribute to my symbols the same tentativeness which characterizes your explanatory attempt. You see, I have no religious or other convictions about my symbols. They can change tomorrow. They are mere allusions, they hint at something, they stammer and often they lose their way. They try only to point in a certain direction, viz. to those dim horizons beyond which lies the secret of existence. They are just no Gnosis, no metaphysical assertions. They are partly even futile or dubious attempts at pronouncing the ineffable. Their number therefore is infinite and the validity of each is to be doubted. They are nothing but humble attempts to formulate, to define, to shape the inexpressible. "Wo fass ich Dich, unendliche Natur?" (*Faust*).[1] It is not a doctrine but a mere expression of and a reaction to the experience of an ineffable mystery.

There is one point more I want to mention: the stone is not a product only of thought-images, but just as much of feeling and local atmosphere, i.e., of the specific *ambiente* of the place. The stone belongs to its secluded place between lake and hill, where it expresses the *beata solitudo* and the *genius loci*, the spell of the chosen and walled-in spot. It could be nowhere else and cannot be thought of or properly understood without the secret web of threads that relate it to its surroundings. Only there in its solitude it can say: *Orphanus sum*,[2] and only there it makes sense. It is there for its own sake and

---

[1] *Faust I*, Scene 1: "Where shall I grasp thee, infinite Nature?" (Cf. Wayne tr., p. 46; McNeice tr., p. 22.)

[2] "I am an orphan," beginning of the text carved on one side of the stone (*Mem-*

only seen by a few. Under such conditions only the stone will whisper its misty lore of ancient roots and ancestral lives.

Thank you for letting me see your typescript.

Sincerely yours, C. G. JUNG

P.S. When I saw you in Bollingen I did not realize that you are the author of *Todos Santos*,[3] a book which I have read with greatest interest and sympathy, otherwise I would have expressed my admiration of your careful study. I am doing it now with some delay.

---

ories, p. 227/215). For the philosophers' stone as orphan, cf. *Mysterium.* CW 14, par. 13.
[3] Cf. Oakes, 31 Jan. 56, n. □.

To Eugen Böhler

Dear Professor Böhler,   23 February 1956

I have just got back from the Tessin and found your letter. I look forward to seeing you next Tuesday 28.II. about 8 o'clock. Your dreams[1] are very interesting. As "contemporary" symbols of the opposites, the fishes have a tendency to devour each other if only they are left alone. In the end you have no alternative but to take the conflicts on yourself by ceasing to identify now with one side and now with the other. You become what happens in the middle. Then you are in the flow, and for this you need the high heart of the warrior. . . .

I have spent my free time making a thorough study of the *Evangelium veritatis*[2] of Valentinus. It is not exactly an easy problem. Meanwhile with kindest regards,

Very sincerely yours, C. G. JUNG

□ (Handwritten.)
[1] In the first dream a lake is covered all over by a pattern of opposing fishes. A revolution takes place which the dreamer can cope with only with great difficulty. He succeeds by letting the fishes devour each other. — In the second dream he finds himself on an old battlefield where he digs the heart of a fallen soldier out of the mud.
[2] Cf. White, 24 Nov. 53, n. 17.

To Laurens van der Post

[ORIGINAL IN ENGLISH]

Dear van der Post,   28 February 1956

Your amiable present from Africa[1] has reached me safely. The bow and the little arrows are just charming. I could not refrain from trying Cupid's weapon and I can confirm its efficiency. It shoots quite a distance. I am much obliged also for the maker's photograph. I have followed up your interesting trip through your reports published in the *Neue Zürcher Zeitung*,[2] and all my old longing to see Africa, God's unspoilt wilderness and its animal and human children once more [has returned]. Hélas—I have seen and tasted it once at least— *vita somnium breve*—so many things cannot be repeated and so many happy times cannot be called back. No wonder that the thoughts of old people dwell so much in the past, as if they were listening for a living echo that never comes. Time and again I have to make a vigorous effort to tear myself away from the things that have been in order to pay attention to things present, even to the future as if I were meant to be in it once.

I am deeply obliged to you for having remembered my fateful 80th

☐ (Handwritten.)

[1] A little bow, about 6 inches long, with a quiver containing correspondingly small arrows, which a Bushman uses to shoot at his chosen girl as a message of love. The photograph that v. d. P. sent, of a young Bushman in the act of shooting his bow and arrow, is this one:

[2] Six articles titled "Auf der Suche nach der ältesten Menschenrasse," published between Oct. 1955 and Jan. 1956. Extracts from the original *The Lost World of the Kalahari* (1958).

birthday. I am glad at last that I have been able (though not through my merit) to spare my wife what follows on the loss of a lifelong partner—the silence that has no answer.[3]

I thank you once more for your kindness. Please give my best regards to Mrs. van der Post. (. . .)

Yours cordially, c. g. jung

[3] In a letter of 29 Apr. 69 to the editor, v. d. P. wrote: "I think the concluding phrase 'the silence that has no answer' deserves a footnote, because three months later I had a much longer letter from Dr. Jung which arrived out of the blue . . . telling me that the silence had had an answer and that he had had that most wonderful dream . . . of how he entered a very dark empty theatre, and suddenly across the orchestra pit the stage was illuminated and in the centre of the stage sat Mrs. Jung in a wonderful light, looking more beautiful than ever . . ."

To Jolande Jacobi

Dear Dr. Jacobi,   13 March 1956

Forgive me for being so late with my report. I have read your essay[1] in the *Psyche* Festschrift with great interest. It is a very good presentation of my concepts, or rather of the names I use to express empirical facts. But I always stumble over the frequent use of the term "theory" or "system." Freud has a "theory," I have no "theory" but I describe facts. I do not theorize about how neuroses originate, I describe what you find in neuroses. Nor have I any theory of dreams, I only indicate what kind of method I use and what the possible results are. I must emphasize this because people always fail to see that I am talking about and naming facts, and that my concepts are mere names and not philosophical terms.

I still have to mention the following two points. On p. 269 you write that I apply Freud's "free" association to the personal context but not to archetypal material. I don't use free association at all,[2] since it is in any case an unreliable method of getting at the real dream material. On a journey through Russia, one of my psychiatric

□ (Handwritten.) See Jacobi (1890–1973), 20 Nov. 28 (in vol. 1). (See pl. iv.)
[1] "Versuch einer Abgrenzung der wichtigsten Konzeptionen C. G. Jungs von denen Freuds," *Psyche* (Stuttgart), IX:5 (Aug. 1955).
[2] Freud's free association proceeds at random away from the initial image or complex, whereas Jung developed a method of controlled or circular association (amplification or circumambulation) in which the image remains the centre of attention.

colleagues thoughtfully contemplated the Cyrillic notices in his sleeper, analysed himself by means of "free" association, and so discovered all his complexes. In this case you can be quite certain that the complexes of Herr X were not dreamt in the Cyrillic sleeper notices. That is to say, by means of "free" association you will *always* get at your complexes, but this does not mean at all that they are the material dreamt about. In dream analysis I proceed in a circumambulatory fashion, having regard to the wise Talmudic saying that the dream is its own interpretation.

P. 274: "The idea of the 'wholeness of the psyche,' which subsequently led Jung to the conception of the individuation process and to the methods of activating it, was from the beginning the determining factor in his psychological vision."

This sentence is incorrect. In the first place, the idea of wholeness did not lead me to the conception of the individuation process. The individuation process is not a "conception" at all, but designates a series of observed facts; and secondly, there is no method on earth that could "activate" it. The individuation process is the experience of a natural law and may or may not be perceived by consciousness.

The "idea of wholeness" is a word I have used—though only in later years—to describe the self. Concepts play no role whatever with me because I make no philosophical assumptions; hence I never started from an "idea of wholeness."

For the rest your work is good. I would only ask you to reconsider the two points I have mentioned, as they contain a fundamental misunderstanding. With best greetings,

Yours, C. G. JUNG

To Fowler McCormick

[ORIGINAL IN ENGLISH]

Dear Fowler,   20 March 1956

The book by Ruppelt about the Ufos[1] you have kindly sent me is just the thing I needed. It confirms the conclusions to which I came in my article in the *Weltwoche* 1954.[2] I said in the end of this article:

[1] Edward J. Ruppelt, *Report on Unidentified Flying Objects* (1956).
[2] Jung had replied in writing to some questions sent to him by Georg Gerster, of the Zurich weekly *Die Weltwoche*. His replies were incorporated in an article published in no. 1078 of this journal, 9 July 1954, entitled "C. G. Jung zu den Fliegenden Untertassen." The questions and replies are in CW 18, pars. 1431ff.

"Something is seen, but nobody knows what." That is precisely the conclusion Mr. R. also has reached. One does not even know for certain whether it is a natural phenomenon, or a contrivance invented by beings comparable to men, or rather a beastlike animal travelling in space, a sort of a huge space-bug, or—last but not least—a parapsychological phenomenon,—at all events a most tantalizing and disturbing phenomenon. I am most obliged to you for your kind attention. The book has given me not only great pleasure but also most valuable information.

We had an infernal winter over here, a kind of weather which I never experienced in my whole life before. It has caused no end of damage, but since yesterday we seem to be sailing into spring and nature begins to take on the blessed aspect of new life. Up to the present moment I got through this winter unscathed.

Hoping you are always in good health, I remain,

Yours cordially, C. G.

To Andrew R. Eickhoff

Dear Mr. Eickhoff,

[ORIGINAL IN ENGLISH]
7 May 1956

Thank you very much for sending your interesting MS about Freud and Religion.[1] The historical fact is that Freud's attitude towards religion in any form was a negative one, quite apart from the fact that he himself said so in his paper about this subject. Religious belief to him was indeed an illusion.[2] Whether this illusion is due to objective scientific argument or to personal bias does not matter when it comes to the question of actual facts. His negative attitude was one among a number of other points of litigation between us. No matter whether it was a Jewish or a Christian or any other belief, he was unable to admit anything beyond the horizon of his scientific materialism. I was most unsuccessful in my attempts to make him see that his standpoint was unscientifically prejudiced and his idea of religion was a foregone conclusion. In our many talks about this and similar subjects

---

☐ Methodist pastor and then professor of religion, Bradley University (Peoria, Illinois).
[1] E. had sent Jung a MS, "The Psychodynamics of Freud's Criticism of Religion," published in *Pastoral Psychology*, May 1960.
[2] Cf. *The Future of an Illusion* (1927), Standard Edn. 21.

he more than once quoted Voltaire's "écrasez l'infâme!"[3] and even went so far as to say that his doctrine of sexual repression, as the ultimate reason for all such foolish ideas as f.i. religion, should be counterweighted by making a dogma of his sex theory. Naturally he assumed that my more positive ideas about religion and its importance for our psychological life were nothing but an outcrop of my unrealized resistances against my clergyman father, whereas in reality my problem and my personal prejudice were never centred in my father but most emphatically in my mother. As you will doubtless have realized from the perusal of Freud's works, his father-complex sticks out everywhere, while the equally important mother-complex plays the most insignificant role. You might hold that, following the bias of my mother-complex, I have overrated the importance of religion—a criticism which I have considered seriously. In the case of a psychologist I don't consider it a particularly excusable mistake to allow personal bias to overrule one's own judgment. I have tried therefore, at least as well as I could, not to overlook the fact that my mother-complex might play me a trick, but if you should raise the point, I am sure you would find a willing ear to listen to your opinion.

I have always wondered how it comes that just the theologians are often so particularly fond of the Freudian theory, as one could hardly find anything more hostile to their alleged beliefs. This curious fact has given me much stuff for thinking.

Sincerely yours, C. G. JUNG

[3] The words were directed not against religion as such but against the system of privileged orthodoxy.

To Fowler McCormick

[ORIGINAL IN ENGLISH]

Dear Fowler,   8 May 1956

It was quite a shock for me to see from your letter that you suffer from an affection of the lungs. I seriously hope it wouldn't be too bad, since such things usually take time and demand care.

I am quite interested in the fact that you followed Prof. Hiltner's seminar. I had been pleasurably surprised reading his review of my

□ (Handwritten.)

Answer to Job;[1] it was remarkably understanding. I only wondered about his remark that I am, as he says, in certain places "esoteric." I wrote to him asking to give me examples of my esoterism. He answered that f.i. I used the term *hierosgamos*, which is a very usual term in comparative religion, and there is nothing esoteric about it. Thus I must conclude that the definition of "esoterism" in America differs widely from the European use of the word.

One of H.'s collaborators has told me that H. has received many reactions about *Job* and that he would tell me about it sometime. I am very curious indeed how his presentation of Job's case has been received.

I am glad to know that you are going to turn up in Switzerland again.

My very best wishes for a speedy recovery!

Yours sincerely, c. g. jung

[1] Seward Hiltner, professor of pastoral theology at the U. of Chicago, published a review in *Pastoral Psychology* (New York), VI:60, Jan. 1956. Jung wrote an article, "Why and How I wrote my *Answer to Job*," published in the same issue (and in CW 11, pp. 357f.). Cf. Doniger, Nov. 1955.

To Rudolf Jung

Dear Cousin,   11 May 1956

Your views on the origin of a carcinoma seem to me largely correct. I have in fact seen cases where the carcinoma broke out under the conditions you envisage, when a person comes to a halt at some essential point in his individuation or cannot get over an obstacle. Unhappily nobody can do it for him, and it cannot be forced. An inner process of growth must begin, and if this spontaneous creative activity is not performed by nature herself, the outcome can only be fatal. At any rate there is a profound disability, i.e., the constitution is at the end of its resources. Ultimately we all get stuck somewhere, for we are all mortal and remain but a part of what we are as a whole. The wholeness we can reach is very relative.

Just as carcinoma can develop for psychic reasons, it can also disappear for psychic reasons. Such cases are well authenticated. But

☐ Rudolf Jung von Pannwitz (1882–1958), opera singer; performed on German and Swiss stages.

297

this does not mean that it is amenable to psychotherapy, or that it could be prevented by a particular psychic development.

With best greetings, CARL

To Frau V.

Dear Frau V.,   12 May 1956

After your kindness in sending me these excellent bottles of Châteauneuf du Pâpe, I really did expect that some quite special favours had been piling up on your side. But if you are now in the dumps and up to your ears in the mire, you must tell yourself that you were obviously flying too high and that a dose of undiluted hellish blackness was indicated. The pickle you are in is certainly something you couldn't have brought on yourself. This shows that someone "out there" is surrounding you with provident thoughts and doing you the necessary wrong. You should regard your present situation as a mud bath from which after a while a small morning sun will burst forth again. "Patience be damned," says Faust, and you need it most of all. For your age and your circumstances you are still much too fractious. The devil can best be beaten with patience, having none himself. With best wishes,

Yours sincerely, C. G. JUNG

□ (Handwritten.) Switzerland.

To Eugen Böhler

Dear Professor Böhler,   16 May 1956

Best thanks for your friendly letter and my apologies for tearing the MS[1] away from you. All the copies have still to be corrected. I have already availed myself of your valuable suggestions, as you will see in the printed text.

Your remarks[2] obviously touch on something very essential in my

□ (Handwritten.)
[1] The MS of "Gegenwart und Zukunft," now "The Undiscovered Self," CW 10.
[2] B. wrote that his discussions with Jung had made him aware that he, Jung, "thanks to your sharp and extensive observation and your originality, have become accustomed to seeing things only for yourself," whereas he, Böhler, was still striving for communication and logical persuasion.

298

style, though I wasn't aware of it at all. For decades I have been either not understood or misunderstood, despite all the care I took to begin with in the matter of "communication and logical persuasion." But because of the novelty of my subject as well as of my thoughts I ran up everywhere against an impenetrable wall. This is probably why my style changed in the course of the years, since I only said what was relevant to the business in hand and wasted no more time and energy thinking about all the things that ill-will, prejudice, stupidity and whatnot can come up with. Bachofen, for example, took infinite pains to be persuasive. All in vain. His time had not yet come. I have resigned myself to being posthumous.

It is still much too early to speak to an educated public about "symbols of self-recollection." It would all be utterly incomprehensible since the foundations for any real understanding don't yet exist.

First and foremost it must be understood what the bell is tolling. Your dream tells us.[3] It begins high up in metaphysics. Already it stalks the earth. Your dream is an epilogue to my MS. With best greetings,

Yours sincerely, C. G. JUNG

[3] A figure, invisible at first, approached him from the left. When the figure uncovered its face, it was Satan.

To Romola Nijinsky

Dear Mrs. Nijinsky,   24 May 1956

Thank you for your letter of the 15th. I was interested to hear of your various activities.

The question of colours or rather absence of colours in dreams, depends on the relations between consciousness and the unconscious. In a situation where an approximation of the unconscious to consciousness is desirable, or vice versa, the unconscious acquires a special tone, which can express itself in the colourfulness of its images (dreams, visions, etc.) or in other impressive qualities (beauty, depth, intensity).

☐ Romola Nijinska, then in San Francisco; wife of the Russian dancer Vaslav Nijinsky (1890–1950); she had consulted Jung in 1919 on account of her husband's schizophrenia.

If on the other hand the attitude of consciousness to the unconscious is more or less neutral, or apprehensive, there is no marked need for the two to make contact, and the dreams remain colourless.

When Huxley says that a symbol is uncoloured,[1] this is an error. "Yellowing," "reddening," "whitening," the "blessed greenness,"[2] etc. play an important role in the highly symbolic language of the alchemists. You can also find the symbolism of colours in quite another field—that of Christian liturgy. You have only to think of the significance of the variously coloured garments used in the Mass.

The intense perception of colours in the mescalin experiment is due to the fact the lowering of consciousness by the drug offers no resistance to the unconscious. With kind regards,

Yours sincerely, C. G. JUNG

[1] Aldous Huxley, in *Heaven and Hell* (1956), states that "most dreams are without colour" and that "about two-thirds of all dreams are in black and white" (pp. 7–8; p. 6, Perennial Lib. edn.).
[2] These colours are stages in the alchemical opus for producing the philosophers' stone as well as denotations of inner psychic states which the alchemists experienced. Cf. *Psychology and Alchemy*, CW 12, pars. 333f.

To William Kinney

[ORIGINAL IN ENGLISH]

Dear Mr. Kinney,   26 May 1956

In answering your letter of May 7th I must tell you that there is neither an easy answer to the problem of ethics,[1] nor are there any books that would give you satisfactory guidance as far as my knowledge goes. Ethics depend upon the supreme decision of a Christian conscience, and conscience itself does not depend upon man alone, but as much upon the counterpart of man, namely God. The ethical question boils down to the relationship between man and God. Any other kind of ethical decision would be a conventional one, which means that it would depend upon a traditional and collective code of moral values. Since such values are general and not specific, they don't exactly apply to individual situations, as little as a schematic diagram expresses the variations of individual

[1] K., describing himself as "a freshman at Northwestern U., Evanston, Illinois, with the conscious purpose of finding some meaning in life," asked for an answer to the problem of ethics and value judgments. Later, a graduate student of philosophy at Ohio State U.

events. To follow a moral code would amount to the same as an intellectual judgment about an individual, viewed from the standpoint of anthropological statistics. Moreover, making a moral code the supreme arbiter of your ethical conduct would be a substitute for the will of a living God, since the moral code is made by man and declared to be a law given by God himself. The great difficulty of course is the "Will of God." Psychologically the "Will of God" appears in your inner experience in the form of a superior deciding power, to which you may give various names like instinct, fate, unconscious, faith, etc.

The psychological criterion of the "Will of God" is forever the dynamic superiority. It is the factor that finally decides when all is said and done. It is essentially something you cannot know beforehand. You only know it after the fact. You only learn it slowly in the course of your life. You have to live thoroughly and very consciously for many years in order to understand what your will is and what Its will is. If you learn about yourself and if eventually you discover more or less who you are, you also learn about God, and who He is. In applying a moral code (which in itself is a commendable thing), you can prevent even the divine decision, and then you go astray. So try to live as consciously, as conscientiously, and as completely as *possible* and learn who you are and who or what it is that ultimately decides.

I have discussed certain aspects of this problem in one of my books, called *Aion*.[2] As soon as the translation is ready, it will appear in my Collected Works, published by the Bollingen Press, in case you don't read German.

Sincerely yours, C. G. JUNG

[2] Pars. 48ff. Cf. also "A Psychological View of Conscience," CW 10, pars. 855f.

To Robert Dietrich

Dear Herr Dietrich,   27 May 1956

Best thanks for kindly telling me your interesting dream.[1]

. . .

☐ An engineer in Munich.
[1] A long and complicated dream about numbers, summarized in the P.S. to Kiener, 1 June 56. Jung's highly condensed comments on the significance of the various numbers have been omitted.

Mathematicians are not agreed whether numbers were *invented* or *discovered*.[2]

"In the Olympian host Number eternally reigns" (Jacobi).[3] Whole numbers may well be the discovery of God's "primal thoughts," as for instance the significant number *four*, which has distinctive qualities. But you ask in vain for speculations on my part concerning the "development of this principle of order." I cannot presume to say anything about this transcendental problem which is ingrained in the cosmos. The mere attempt to do so would strike me as intellectual inflation. After all, man cannot dissect God's primal thoughts. Why are whole numbers individuals? Why are there prime numbers? Why have numbers inalienable qualities? Why are there discontinuities like quanta, which Einstein would have liked to abolish?

Your dream seems to me a genuine revelation: God and Number as the principle of order belong together. Number, like Meaning, inheres in the nature of all things as an expression of God's dissolution in the world of appearances. This creative process is continued with the same symbolism in the Incarnation. (Cf. *Answer to Job*.)

Yours sincerely, C. G. JUNG

[2] Cf. Jung, "Ein astrologisches Experiment," *Zeitschrift für Parapsychologie und Grenzgebiete der Psychologie* (Bern), I:2/3 (1958), 88f.: "I must confess that I incline to the view that numbers were as much found as invented, and that in consequence they possess a relative autonomy analogous to that of the archetypes. They would then have, in common with the latter, the quality of being pre-existent to consciousness, and hence, on occasion, of conditioning it rather than being conditioned by it." ("An Astrological Experiment," CW 18, par. 1183.) Also cf. Watson, 9 Feb. 56, n. 4.
[3] Karl Jacobi (1804–51), German mathematician. Cf. "Synchronicity," CW 8, par. 942.

Anonymous

[ORIGINAL IN ENGLISH]

My dear N.,   May 1956

. . .

My conceptions are empirical and not at all speculative. If you understand them from a philosophical standpoint you go completely astray, since they are not rational but mere names of groups of irrational phenomena. The conceptions of Indian philosophy however

☐ A man from India, living in Europe.

are thoroughly philosophical and have the character of postulates and can therefore only be analogous to my terms but not identical with them at all. Take f.i. the concept of *nirdvandva*. Nobody has ever been entirely liberated from the opposites, because no living being could possibly attain to such a state, as nobody escapes pain and pleasure as long as he functions physiologically. He may have occasional ecstatic experiences when he gets the intuition of a complete liberation, f.i. in reaching the state of *sat-chit-ananda*.[1] But the word *ananda* shows that he experiences pleasure, and you cannot even be conscious of something if you don't discriminate between opposites, and thus participate in them.

My psychology deals with modern man in Europe, who is practically beyond the belief in philosophical postulates. They convey nothing to him any more. Whereas you are still a believer in orthodox philosophy; thus you can be compared to a staunch Christian, still convinced that he is redeemed through his Lord Jesus Christ, etc. He believes in postulates. It is quite obvious that such a man would neither have any use for a psychology of the unconscious nor would he understand such a psychology at all. He cannot imagine himself in the role of an unbeliever, moreover if he seriously tried to, he might get into a panic as he would feel the ground subsiding under his feet. He cannot admit or imagine that the idea of redemption through Christ's self-sacrifice could be an illusion, or at least a mere postulate of religious speculation, as you yourself would not dream of disbelieving the existence of the *atman*,[2] or the reality of *jivan-mukti*,[3] *samadhi*,[4] etc. This is in contradiction to the fact that a complete liberation from the opposites cannot be attained through *jivan-mukti*, the latter being a mere postulate and—as I told you above—not to be experienced in its totality.

Modern man in Europe has lost or given up—getting tired of them —his traditional beliefs and has to find out for himself what is going to happen to him in his impoverished state. Analytical psychology tells you the story of his adventures. Only if you are able to see the relativity, i.e., the uncertainty of all human postulates, can you ex-

---

[1] *Sat* = being, *chit* (or *cit*) = consciousness, *ananda* = bliss. This state denotes the attainment of Brahman, ultimate reality.

[2] The divine Self in every man, and as such identical with Brahman. The one eternal Self is also called Atman-Brahman.

[3] The state of being liberated from obstacles to union with the eternal Self; a *jivan-mukta* is "liberated while living," the divine man on earth.

[4] State of immersion in the eternal Self.

perience that state in which analytical psychology makes sense. But analytical psychology just makes no sense for you. Nothing of the things I describe comes to life unless you can accompany or sympathize understandingly with beings that are forced to base their life upon facts to be experienced and not upon transcendental postulates beyond human experience. Thus, inasmuch as you are a believer in postulates, you have no use for my psychology and you are not even able to understand why we shouldn't simply adopt Indian philosophy if we are dissatisfied with our religious philosophy. In other words, why study analytical psychology at all? It cannot make sense to you as it does not make sense to a Christian or any other believer. On the contrary the believer will translate the psychological terms into his metaphysical language. The Christian f.i. will call the self Christ and will not understand why I call the central symbol "self." He will not see why we need to know about the unconscious from A to Z, exactly like the Indian way. He is like you *in possession of the Truth*, while we psychologists are merely in search of something like the truth and our only source of information is the unconscious and its mythological products like archetypes, etc. We have no traditional beliefs or philosophical postulates. (. . .) Analytical psychology is an empirical science and (. . .) individuation is an empirical process and not a way of initiation at all.

. . .

Yours sincerely, C. G. JUNG

To Hélène Kiener

Dear Fräulein Kiener,   1 June 1956

I would answer your questions as follows:

The "Christ archetype" is a false concept, as you say. Christ is not an archetype but a personification of the archetype. This is reflected in the idea of the Anthropos, the *homo maximus* or Primordial Man (Adam Kadmon).[1] In India it is Purusha, and in China Chên-jên (the whole or true man) as a goal to be attained. Purusha as creator sacrifices himself in order to bring the world into being: God dissolves in his own creation. (This thought occurs in a

---

[1] The Original Man. In the Kabbalah (and Gnosis) he is the origin and spiritual substance of the world. Cf. *Mysterium Coniunctionis* (CW 14), index.

modern dream.)[2] The Incarnation results from Christ "emptying himself of divinity" and taking the form of a slave.[3] Thus he is in bondage to man as the demiurge is in bondage to the world. (Concerning the bondage of the creator to his creature, cf. *Answer to Job*, his identification with the two monsters[4] and his inability to understand man.)

The spiritual (as contrasted with the worldly) Messiah, Christ, Mithras, Osiris, Dionysos, Buddha are all visualizations or personifications of the irrepresentable archetype which, borrowing from Ezekiel and Daniel, I call the Anthropos.

Bernet's book[5] is illogical because he simply cannot understand that we are not speaking of God himself but only of an image we have of him. Through this epistemological slipperiness theology gets caught in its own toils. With best regards,

Yours sincerely, C. G. JUNG

P.S. The passage from the modern dream was as follows: There were "five unities" which represented "the whole creation of the universe. But then something happened . . . that shook me profoundly. . . . He, whose eternal existence I had never dared to doubt consciously, reduced the five unities to four unities by dissolving himself into Nothing."

[2] Cf. the P.S. and Dietrich, 27 May 56.
[3] Phil. 2:6f.
[4] Behemoth and Leviathan. "Answer to Job," CW 11, pars. 634ff.
[5] *Inhalt und Grenze der religiösen Erfahrung.*

To Warner S. McCullen

[ORIGINAL IN ENGLISH]

Dear Mr. McCullen,   4 June 1956

The loss of the mother in the early years of childhood[1] often leaves traces in the form of a mother-complex. If the influence of a living mother is too strong, it has the same effect as when she is absent. In either case it will be the cause of such a complex. One of the main features of a mother-complex is the fact that one is too

[1] M. described himself as a "theatrical hypnotist . . . long interested in depth psychologies." His mother died when he was 6 months old, and a Freudian analyst told him he was suffering from feelings of fear and guilt because he believed he had swallowed his mother (who had breast-fed him).

much under the influence of the unconscious. As the unconscious in a man's case has a female character,[2] it then looks, allegorically speaking, as if one had "swallowed" the mother. In fact, there is only an arrested development of the female side of a man's character. This shows either as too much femininity or too little. Not knowing your personal biography I would not be able to tell you which your case is. Fear and feelings of guilt, however, are characteristic of such a condition as a symptom of insufficient adaptation, as there is always something too much or too little, and moreover there is the feeling of a task to be fulfilled and not fulfilled yet. It is unimportant to know what the possible original cause of such a symptom is. The search for the cause is rather misleading, since the existence of the fear continues, not because it has been originally started in the remote past, but because a task is incumbent upon you in the present moment, and, inasmuch as it remains unfulfilled, every day produces fear and guilt anew.

The question is, of course, what do you feel to be your task? Where the fear, there is your task! You must study your fantasies and dreams in order to find out what you ought to do or where you can begin to do something. Our fantasies are always hovering on the point of our insufficiency where a defect ought to be compensated.

I thank you very much for your kind present of the Korean medal.[3] The representation of the Chinese Saturn period is particularly beautiful.

Faithfully yours, c. g. j u n g

[2] Owing to the presence of the anima.
[3] An old Korean coin, showing the points of the compass.

To Benjamin Nelson

[ORIGINAL IN ENGLISH]

Dear Professor Nelson,   17 June 1956

If I were younger I should take great pleasure in following your kind proposition to write a comprehensible essay about the confusing mass of opinions aroused by Freud's essential discovery:[1] the

[1] N. was editing for Meridian Books (New York) *Freud and the 20th Century* (1957) and asked Jung for a contribution. He suggested either a statement representing Jung's "ultimate verdict on Freud" or on Jung's "own approach to the understanding of the depth dimensions of man's society and culture." The con-

psychological *enchainement* of psychopathological phenomena and its consequences for normal psychology. But—hélas—in the meantime I have reached the age of 81 years with its inevitable reduction of efficiency, its fatigue, and its necessary restrictions. Moreover the stimulus of novelty so tempting to a writer has lost its charm, as I have done this kind of work already in an almost forgotten past, when even Freud was still a strange, unknown, or misunderstood figure. It is only within the last decade that his psychology was really taken notice of by academic minds and has penetrated the mental tenebrosities of the greater public. It was simply not to be expected that my criticism or my different point of view or even my attempt at a further development of psychological research should have been understood or been noticed at all. In the 18 or more volumes of my Collected Works I have said all I could possibly think of. Whatever I might be able to write now would neither be new nor in any way better than the stuff I produced 30 or 40 years ago. It is still neither read nor understood by my contemporaries. In full ignorance of my work one is satisfied with misconceptions, distortions, and prejudices. I cannot force people to take my work seriously and I cannot persuade them to study it really. The trouble is that I don't construct theories one can learn by heart. I collect facts which are not yet generally known or properly appreciated, and I give names to observations and experiences unfamiliar to the contemporary mind and objectionable to its prejudices.

Thus my chief contribution to the further development of the psychology of the unconscious, inaugurated by Freud, suffers from the considerable disadvantage that the doctors interested in psychotherapy have practically no knowledge of the general human mind as it expresses itself in history, archaeology, philology, philosophy, theology, etc., which demonstrate so many aspects of human psychology. It is the smallest part of the psyche, and in particular of the unconscious, that presents itself in the medical consulting room. On the other hand the specialists of the said disciplines are far

tribution was to be "as limpid an account as possible for the general reader," since "very few of your American readers are sufficiently familiar with . . . your thought on the subjects of religion, analytic psychology, psychoanalysis, and contemporary philosophy and theology." Evidently these remarks annoyed Jung, whose writings are full of explicit statements on all the subjects mentioned (CW 7, 12, 16, 17 had been available for several years). N.'s suggestion is all the more surprising since Meridian Books had just published a paperback edition of *Two Essays on Analytical Psychology* (CW 7).

from any psychological or psychopathological knowledge and the general public is blissfully unaware of all medical as well as any other kind of real and well-founded knowledge. The topics under discussion are of a highly complex nature. How can I popularize things so difficult, and demanding such an unusual amount of specific knowledge, to a public that does not or cannot take the trouble to settle down to a careful study of the facts collected in many volumes? How can anyone express the essentials of nuclear physics in two words? The comparison of modern psychology to modern physics is no idle talk. Both disciplines have, for all their diametrical opposition, one most important point in common, namely the fact that they both approach the hitherto "transcendental" region of the Invisible and Intangible, the world of merely analogous thought. The truth of physics can be convincingly demonstrated by the explosion of an H-bomb. The psychological truth is far less spectacular and only visible to a mind trained in Science as well as in many other often remote disciplines, that were never envisaged from a psychological point of view except in a most superficial and incompetent way. (Cf. f.i. Freud's *Totem and Taboo* and *The Future of an Illusion*.)[2] I don't claim any knowledge of modern physics myself, but I have worked together with the well-known physicist W. Pauli for a considerable time and as a result we were both satisfied with the fact that there is at least a very marked mutual *rapprochement* between the two most heterogeneous sciences in their epistemological preoccupations, i.e., in their antinomies (f.i. light = wave and corpuscle),[3] Heisenberg's "Unbestimmtheitsrelation,"[4] Bohr's complementarity,[5] not to speak of the archetypal models of representation. (Cf. Jung and Pauli: *Nature and Psyche*.)

The reader is by far better prepared to understand physics, whereas the psychology of the unconscious is to him a *terra incognita* populated by the most absurd misconceptions and prejudices—which is always the case where ignorance reigns supreme. The worst of ignorance is that it is never aware of how ignorant it is. Recently it happened that an academic theologian accused me of esoterism because

[2] Standard Edn. 13 and 21.

[3] The wave theory of light and the theory that light consists of minute corpuscles or particles in rapid motion are not contradictory but the result of two different ways of observing the same reality.

[4] = uncertainty principle.

[5] Cf. Whitmont, 4 March 50, n. 1.

I use the word *hierosgamos* (a well known technical term in comparative religion!!). With the same right he could accuse every other discipline of indulging in esoterics simply because he does not understand its concepts. That is the kind of thing I am up against. I should have to write a voluminous book for the sole purpose of explaining the fundamentals of my psychology of the unconscious. As a matter of fact I have written a good deal about elementary presuppositions. But the trouble is that Freud alone is already an indigestible lump that keeps them busy to the end of their days. Why bother about further complications? I remember the years when Freud first appeared on the scene and when I fought my first battles for him. What a mountain of prejudice, misunderstanding and mental inertia came down upon me! It took more than half a century to make him acceptable. He is not even yet so far understood that people would notice where something could be added or changed in his ideas, although there is no scientific truth that represents the last word. The problem nearest to Freud's heart was unquestionably the psychology of the unconscious, but none of his immediate followers has done anything about it. I happen to be the only one of his heirs that has carried out some further research along the lines he intuitively foresaw. As my modest attempts were judged to be almost blasphemous I have no earthly chance to write anything under my own name that would not be instantly branded with the mark of Cain. It must needs be somebody else that is willing to risk his skin. There is only one book that has seriously tried to tackle the thankless task of describing the development of depth psychology including my own contribution in its beginnings at least. My later and more important work (as it seems to me) is still left untouched in its primordial obscurity. The book is by Friedrich Seifert,[6] professor of philosophy (!) in Munich. As far as it goes it is a remarkably clear and objective piece of work and fills the bill of a fairly popular book. I can recommend it warmly to your attention. As far as I know, it is not translated yet.

Concerning my own writings I mention 3 articles about Freud:[7]

"Sigmund Freud in His Historical Setting" (*Character and Personality*, London, Vol. I, No. 1, Sept. 1932; German in: *Wirklichkeit der Seele*, 1932).

---

[6] *Tiefenpsychologie: Die Entwicklung der Lehre vom Unbewussten* (1955).
[7] The first and third are in CW 15, the second in CW 4.

"Freud and Jung: Contrasts" (in: *Modern Man in Search of a Soul*, Kegan Paul, London, 1933).

"Sigmund Freud" (in memoriam, *Basler Nachrichten*, 1 Oct. 1939).

The last of these articles might be of interest to you.

Sincerely yours, c. g. j u n g

Anonymous

Dear Dr. N.,   26 June 1956

It is only now that I can thank you for your letters and also for the book *Pan im Vaccarès*,[1] which I am saving for my holiday. At the moment my work allows me no such relaxation.

I was particularly interested in the dream[2] which, in mid August 1955, anticipated the death of my wife. It probably expresses the idea of life's perfection: the epitome of all fruits, rounded into a bullet, struck her like karma. The bullet represents death in perfect form; it is at the same time a symbol of the self. Death brought— and probably always brings—a confrontation with wholeness. But perhaps not always in such perfection. These are the thoughts I associated with your dream.

. . .

Yours very sincerely, c. g. j u n g

☐ A woman in Switzerland.
[1] Joseph d'Arbaud, *Pan im Vaccarès* (tr. from the French, 1954).
[2] The setting of the dream is in the south of France, with the Maquis around. Mrs. Jung is hit by a bullet made of fruit.

Anonymous

Dear Frau N.,   28 June 1956

It is hard to accept the fate you have described.[1] Quite apart from the moral achievement required, complete acceptance depends very much on the conception you have of fate. An exclusively causal view is permissible only in the realm of physical or inorganic proc-

☐ A woman in Switzerland.
[1] N. was the mother of an imbecile child.

310

esses. The teleological view is more important in the biological sphere and also in psychology, where the answer makes sense only if it explains the "why" of it. So it is pointless to cling on to the causes, since they cannot be altered anyway. It is more rewarding to know what is to be done with the consequences, and the kind of attitude one has—or should have—to them. Then the question at once arises: Does the event have a *meaning*? Did a hidden purpose of fate, or God's will, have a hand in it, or was it nothing but "chance," a "mishap"?

If it was God's purpose to try us, why then must an innocent child suffer? This question touches on a problem that is clearly answered in the Book of Job. Yahweh's amorality or notorious injustice changes only with the Incarnation into the exclusive goodness of God. This transformation is connected with his becoming man and therefore exists only if it is made real through the conscious fulfillment of God's will in man. If this realization does not occur, not only the Creator's amorality is revealed but also his unconsciousness. With no human consciousness to reflect themselves in, good and evil simply happen, or rather, there is no good and evil, but only a sequence of neutral events, or what the Buddhists call the Nidhana-chain, the uninterrupted causal concatenation leading to suffering, old age, sickness, and death. Buddha's insight and the Incarnation in Christ break the chain through the intervention of the enlightened human consciousness, which thereby acquires a metaphysical and cosmic significance.

In the light of this realization, the mishap changes into a happening which, if taken to heart, allows us to glimpse deeply into the cruel and pitiless imperfections of Creation and also into the mystery of the Incarnation. The happening then turns into that *felix culpa*[2] which Adam brought on himself by his disobedience. Suffering, Meister Eckhart says, is the "swiftest steed that bears you to perfection." The boon of increased self-awareness is the sufficient answer even to life's suffering, otherwise it would be meaningless and unendurable. Though the suffering of the Creation which God left imperfect cannot be done away with by the revelation of the good God's will to man, yet it can be mitigated and made meaningful.

Yours sincerely, C. G. JUNG

[2] = happy fault. Cf. Sinclair, 7 Jan. 55, n. 2.

JUNE 1956

To Elined Kotschnig

[ORIGINAL IN ENGLISH]

Dear Mrs. Kotschnig,   30 June 1956

It is not quite easy to answer your question[1] within the space of a letter. You know that we human beings are unable to explain anything that happens without or within ourselves otherwise than through the use of the intellectual means at our disposal. We always have to use mental elements similar to the facts we believe we have observed. Thus when we try to explain how God has created His world or how He behaves toward the world, the analogy we use is the way in which our creative spirit produces and behaves. When we consider the data of palaeontology with the view that a conscious creator has perhaps spent more than a thousand million years, and has made, as it seems to us, no end of detours to produce consciousness, we inevitably come to the conclusion that—if we want to explain His doings at all—His behaviour is strikingly similar to a being with an at least very limited consciousness. Although aware of the things that are and the next steps to take, He has apparently neither foresight of an ulterior goal nor any knowledge of a direct way to reach it. Thus it would not be an absolute unconsciousness but a rather dim consciousness. Such a consciousness would necessarily produce any amount of errors and impasses with the most cruel consequences, disease, mutilation, and horrible fights, i.e., just the thing that has happened and is still happening throughout all realms of life. Moreover it is impossible for us to assume that a Creator producing a universe out of nothingness can be conscious of anything, because each act of cognition is based upon a discrimination—for instance, I cannot be conscious of somebody else when I am identical with him. If there is nothing outside of God everything is God and in such a state there is simply no possibility of self-cognition.

Nobody can help admitting that the thought of a God creating any amount of errors and impasses is as good as a catastrophe. When the original Jewish conception of a purposeful and morally inclined God marked the end of the playful and rather purposeless existence of the polytheistic deities in the Mediterranean sphere, the result

□ See Kotschnig, 23 July 34 (in vol. 1).

[1] K. asked for an answer to the problem of an unconscious, ignorant creator-god and if this did not imply "some principle, some Ground of Being, beyond such a demiurge."

was a paradoxical conception of the supreme being, finding its expression in the idea of divine justice and injustice. The clear recognition of the fatal unreliability of the deity led Jewish prophecy to look for a sort of mediator or advocate, representing the claims of humanity before God. As you know, this figure is already announced in Ezekiel's vision of the Man and Son of Man.[2] The idea was carried on by Daniel[3] and then in the Apocryphal writings, particularly in the figure of the female Demiurge, viz. Sophia,[4] and in the male form of an administrator of justice, the Son of Man, in the Book of Enoch, written about 100 B.C. and very popular at the time of Christ. It must have been so well-known, indeed, that Christ called himself "Son of Man" with the evident presupposition of everybody knowing what he was talking about. Enoch is exactly what the Book of Job expects the advocate of man to be, over against the lawlessness and moral unreliability of Yahweh. The recently discovered scrolls of the Dead Sea mention a sort of legendary mystical figure, viz. "the Teacher of Justice."[5] I think he is parallel to or identical with Enoch. Christ obviously took up this idea, feeling that his task was to represent the role of the "Teacher of Justice" and thus of a Mediator; and he was up against an unpredictable and lawless God who would need a most drastic sacrifice to appease His wrath, viz. the slaughter of His own son. Curiously enough, as on the one hand his self-sacrifice means admission of the Father's amoral nature, he taught on the other hand a new image of God, namely that of a Loving Father in whom there is no darkness. This enormous antinomy needs some explanation. It needed the assertion that he was the Son of the Father, i.e., the incarnation of the Deity in man. As a consequence the sacrifice was a self-destruction of the amoral God, incarnated in a mortal body. Thus the sacrifice takes on the aspect of a highly moral deed, of a self-punishment, as it were.

Inasmuch as Christ is understood to be the second Person of the Trinity, the self-sacrifice is the evidence for God's goodness. At least so far as human beings are concerned. We don't know whether

[2] Ezekiel 1:16ff.
[3] Daniel 7:13ff.
[4] Proverbs 8:22ff.
[5] The Teacher of Justice, or of Righteousness, was the name given to the leader of a Jewish sect (probably the Essenes), parts of whose literature, the Dead Sea Scrolls, were found in 1947 (and after) near Qumran, northwest of the Dead Sea. The Essenes were an ascetic sect founded in the 2nd cent. B.C., living in communities in the Judaean desert.

there are other inhabited worlds where the same divine evolution also has taken place. It is thinkable that there are many inhabited worlds in different stages of development where God has not yet undergone the transformation through incarnation. However that may be, for us earthly beings the incarnation has taken place and we have become participants in the divine nature and presumably heirs of the tendency towards goodness and at the same time subject to the inevitable self-punishment. As Job was not a mere spectator of divine unconsciousness but fell a victim to this momentous manifestation, in the case of incarnation we also become involved in the consequences of this transformation. Inasmuch as God proves His goodness through self-sacrifice He is incarnated, but in view of His infinity and the presumably different stages of cosmic development we don't know of, how much of God—if this is not too human an argument—has been transformed? In this case it can be expected that we are going to contact spheres of a not yet transformed God when our consciousness begins to extend into the sphere of the unconscious. There is at all events a definite expectation of this kind expressed in the "Evangelium Aeternum" of the Revelations containing the message: Fear God![6]

Although the divine incarnation is a cosmic and absolute event, it only manifests empirically in those relatively few individuals capable of enough consciousness to make ethical decisions, i.e., to decide for the Good. Therefore God can be called good only inasmuch as He is able to manifest His goodness in individuals. His moral quality depends upon individuals. That is why He incarnates. Individuation and individual existence are indispensable for the transformation of God the Creator.

The knowledge of what is good is not given *a priori*; it needs discriminating consciousness. That is already the problem in Genesis, where Adam and Eve have to be enlightened first in order to recognize the Good and discriminate it from Evil. There is no such thing as the "Good" in general, because something that is definitely good can be as definitely evil in another case. Individuals are different from each other, their values are different and their situations vary to such an extent that they cannot be judged by general values and principles. For instance generosity is certainly a virtue, but it instantly becomes a vice when applied to an individual that misunderstands it. In this case one needs conscious discrimination.

[6] Rev. 14:6–7.

Your question concerning the relationship between the human being and an unconscious paradoxical God is indeed a major question, although we have the most impressive paradigm of Old Testament piety that could deal with the divine antinomy. The people of the Old Testament could address themselves to an unreliable God. By very overt attempts at propitiation I mean in particular the repeated assertion and invocation of God's justice and this in the face of indisputable injustice. They tried to avoid His wrath and to call forth His goodness. It is quite obvious that the old Hebrew theologians were continuously tormented by the fear of Yahweh's unpredictable acts of injustice.

For the Christian mentality, brought up in the conviction of an essentially good God, the situation is much more difficult. One cannot love and fear at the same time any more. Our consciousness has become too differentiated for such contradictions. We are therefore forced to take the fact of incarnation far more seriously than hitherto. We ought to remember that the Fathers of the Church have insisted upon the fact that God has given Himself to man's death on the Cross so that we may become gods. The Deity has taken its abode in man with the obvious intention of realizing Its Good in man. Thus we are the vessel or the children and the heirs of the Deity suffering in the body of the "slave."[7]

We are now in a position to understand the essential point of view of our brethren the Hindus. They are aware of the fact that the personal Atman is identical with the universal Atman and have evolved ways and means to express the psychological consequences of such a belief. In this respect we have to learn something from them. It saves us from spiritual pride when we humbly recognize that God can manifest Himself in many different ways. Christianity has envisaged the religious problem as a sequence of dramatic events, whereas the East holds a thoroughly static view, i.e., a cyclic view. The thought of evolution is Christian and—as I think—in a way a better truth to express the dynamic aspect of the Deity, although the eternal immovability also forms an important aspect of the Deity (in Aristotle and in the old scholastic philosophy). The religious spirit of the West is characterized by a change of God's image in the course of ages. Its history begins with the plurality of the Elohim, then it comes to the paradoxical Oneness and personality of Yahweh, then to the good Father of Christianity, followed by the

---

[7] Or "servant." Cf. Phil. 2:6.

315

second Person in the Trinity, Christ, i.e., God incarnated in man. The allusion to the Holy Ghost is a third form appearing at the beginning of the second half of the Christian age (Gioacchino da Fiore),[8] and finally we are confronted with the aspect revealed through the manifestations of the unconscious. The significance of man is enhanced by the incarnation. We have become participants of the divine life and we have to assume a new responsibility, viz. the continuation of the divine self-realization, which expresses itself in the task of our individuation. Individuation does not only mean that man has become truly human as distinct from animal, but that he is to become partially divine as well. This means practically that he becomes adult, responsible for his existence, knowing that he does not only depend on God but that God also depends on man. Man's relation to God probably has to undergo a certain important change: Instead of the propitiating praise to an unpredictable king or the child's prayer to a loving father, the responsible living and fulfilling of the divine will in us will be our form of worship of and commerce with God. His goodness means grace and light and His dark side the terrible temptation of power. Man has already received so much knowledge that he can destroy his own planet. Let us hope that God's good spirit will guide him in his decisions, because it will depend upon man's decision whether God's creation will continue. Nothing shows more drastically than this possibility how much of divine power has come within the reach of man.

If anything of the above should not be clear to you, I am quite ready for further explanation.

Sincerely yours, C. G. JUNG

[8] Cf. White, 24 Nov. 53, n. 10.

To Marianne Niehus-Jung

Dear Marianne,   Bollingen, 17 July 1956

Warmest thanks for your lovely letter, which was a great joy. I am glad you weren't bored with me. It was also a joy to be together with you for a while.

It is true that one cannot fully realize something that is not yet there, for one does not know what the pattern is which a still

☐ Cf. Marianne Jung, 1 July 19, n. ☐.

living person fills out. Mama's death has left a gap for me that cannot be filled. So it is good if you have something you want to carry out, and can turn to when the emptiness spreads about you too menacingly. The stone I am working on[1] (like the one I carved in the winter) gives me inner stability with its hardness and permanence, and its meaning governs my thoughts.

I will gladly read the MSS. I hope there's no hurry. The building is to start tomorrow[2] if the permit arrives. But I still have no news.

Will you be coming to Bollingen sometime? Ruth[3] sends best greetings,

Affectionately, YOUR FATHER

[1] This was a stone in memory of his wife; it was set up at Bollingen. The stone he carved in the winter of 1955/56 consisted of three stone tablets with the names of his ancestors. They were placed in the courtyard of the Tower (*Memories*, p. 232/220).
[2] In *Memories* (p. 225/213) Jung reports how after his wife's death he felt compelled to add an upper storey to the central section of the Tower, as a representation of his ego-personality: "Now it signified an extension of consciousness achieved in old age. With that the building was complete."
[3] Miss Ruth Bailey, an old friend of the family, who acted as Jung's housekeeper after his wife's death. Cf. Kuhn, 1 Jan. 26, n. 2.

To Enrique Butelman

[ORIGINAL IN ENGLISH]

Dear Sir,   July 1956

Concerning the Spanish translation of my book *Naturerklärung und Psyche*[1] I should advise you to make use of the English version. In comparison with the original German text there are quite a number of improvements in the English, which I think should be considered in the Spanish edition. I think also that the appendix added by the English editors[2] should form part of your edition.

I am very interested in the fact that you have taken up the subject of *synchronicity*. My ideas in this respect seem to be highly incomprehensible, to judge from the reactions I got. People seem to be

☐ Buenos Aires, Argentina. B. translated *Psychology and Religion* into Spanish (1949).
[1] Butelman's translation was not published, but the same publisher (Paidós) brought out a translation by Haraldo Kahnemann in 1964.
[2] "Synchronicity," CW 8, pp. 483f. Cf. Fordham, 24 Jan. 55, n. 1.

incapable of following my conclusions. It seems that they are particularly shocked by my using astrological statistics and that I believe that nothing is explained by the words telepathy, precognition, etc. . . . Physicists are even unable to accept the fact that the term *statistics* presupposes the existence of exceptions to the rule, as really existent as their averages. Causality as a *statistical truth* presupposes the existence of *acausality*, otherwise it cannot be a statistical truth. In other words, the exceptions to causality are real facts which I try to envisage from the standpoint of their *meaningful coincidence* or synchronicity. As a rule the improbability of a series of meaningful coincidences (i.e., of identical meaning) increases with the number of its individual occurrences. The question now is, where to find such a series. Astrology is—for the reasons indicated in my book—not a safe field for investigation. Rhine's chance-method has yielded the best results yet, but it remains sterile in view of a point of special interest. It concerns the question: what is the psychological condition in which a synchronistic phenomenon may be expected? Rhine's results have already shown that the test-person's lively interest is of paramount importance. When it slackens by the test-person getting accustomed the results quickly deteriorate. A certain affective condition seems to be indispensable. One has therefore to look for emotional conditions. We are actually investigating accidents, i.e., fractures with their preceding dreams and the corresponding results of other chance-methods of mediaeval origin as f.i. geomantics, horoscopy, playing cards, etc. We have some encouraging results. Owing to the traditional psychological nature of the said methods they permit a certain insight into the underlying unconscious constellations and their archetypal structure. I have observed personally quite a number of synchronistic events where I could establish the nature of the underlying archetype. The archetype itself (nota bene *not* the archetypal representation!) is psychoid,[3] i.e., transcendental and thus relatively beyond the categories of number, space, and time. That means, it approximates to oneness and immutability. Owing to the liberation from the categories of consciousness the archetype can be the basis of meaningful coincidence. It is quite logical therefore that you are interested in the effect of mescalin and similar drugs belonging to the adrenalin group. I am following up these investigations. It is true that mescalin uncovers

[3] Cf. Dr. H., 30 Aug. 51, n. 5.

the unconscious to a great extent by removing the inhibitory influence of apperception and by replacing the latter through the normally latent syndromous associations.[4] Thus we see the painter of colours, the inventor of forms, the thinker of thoughts actually at work.

. . .

Sincerely yours, c . g . j u n g

[4] This is a term not otherwise used by Jung. It characterizes "the associative variants that are excluded by normal apperception" but "can be observed . . . in intense fatigue and severe intoxication" ("Schizophrenia," CW 3, par. 569). The term "syndromous" would then indicate the concurrence of subliminal associations. Cf. Bender, 6 Mar. 58, n. 2.

To Ladis K. Kristof

Dear Herr Kristof,   July 1956

Since, as you know, I am not a philosopher but an empiricist, my concept of the collective unconscious is not a philosophical but an empirical one. I designate by this term all our experiences of "behaviour patterns" in so far as these support or cause the formation of certain ideas. By the latter I mean *mythic* ideas in the broadest sense of the word, such as can be observed in mythology and folklore as well as in the dreams, visions, and fantasies of normal and psychically ill persons. The existence and spontaneous emergence of such ideas independently of tradition and migration permit the inference that there is a universal psychic disposition, an instinct, which causes the formation of typical ideas. The disposition or instinctual "pattern" is inherited, but not the idea itself. This consists of recent, individually acquired elements.

While the inference of a universal psychic disposition of this kind is sufficiently assured by experience, I feel less certain when it comes to the question of hereditary "ramifications,"[1] i.e., specific differentiations conditioned by locality or race. It seems to me altogether possible and even probable that such differentiations really do exist (like the wingless insects of the Galápagos Islands) regardless of

☐ Chicago, Illinois.
[1] K. asked if, side by side with a universal collective unconscious, Jung recognized a "ramified" one which would explain individual differences in different peoples.

theoretical prejudices. But as yet I have found no certain proofs. In order to decide this question, one would have to undertake very extensive researches which would far exceed my capacities. I therefore regret that I can give you no clear answer on this point.

The problem of the *relation* of a people or culture with the collective unconscious has nothing to do with the question of its nature or with its differentiation. I have had ample opportunity to convince myself that the Indians and Chinese have just as little relation to the collective unconscious as Europeans. You find a better relation only among primitives. The development of consciousness proceeds at the cost of the relation to the unconscious. Primitives have evolved a number of techniques for making it conscious and in [Eastern] cultures these have reached a high degree of differentiation. In our highly developed modern cultures these techniques are dying out and the question of the relation to the collective unconscious is becoming obsolete. It is only modern psychology that has taken up the problem again. It should be added that the religions, so long as they are alive, have never ceased to foster the relation to the unconscious in one form or another.

Yours sincerely, C. G. JUNG

Anonymous

Dear N.,   10 August 1956

. . .

I was very pleased to hear that you now have house and land of your own. This is important for the chthonic powers. I hope you will find time to commit your plant counterparts to the earth and tend their growth, for the earth always wants children—houses, trees, flowers—to grow out of her and celebrate the marriage of the human psyche with the Great Mother, the best counter-magic against rootless extraversion!

With best regards to you and your dear husband,

Always your faithful C. G. JUNG

☐ U.S.A.

To H. J. Barrett

[ORIGINAL IN ENGLISH]

Dear Mr. Barrett,   August 1956

Sorry to be so late with my answer, but as I beat you by ten years I am presumably ten times slower than you.

Your letter[1] not only interested but also impressed me. The choice of your wives was characteristic. They were temporary incarnations of what I call your *anima*. I don't know whether you are so far acquainted with my writings that you know about the female archetype each man carries in his unconscious. The Middle Ages already knew about this peculiar psychic fact and said: *omnis vir feminam suam secum portat*.[2] In practice it means that the woman of your choice represents your own task you did not understand. There is a certain creative ability which apparently is not accompanied by a corresponding technical gift. Such people are pretty frequent and cannot understand that the creative man has to create and make visible in spite of the fact that he cannot do it properly. He may be a painter who cannot paint or a musician who cannot compose, not even play the piano. But he ought to do it nevertheless like the Jongleur de Notre Dame and *ad maiorem Dei gloriam*.

Your wives were "unfortunately" (for you) gifted enough to carry out what you should have done in an incompetent way, but you were too rational and also too intelligent to waste your time on an apparently thankless task. But there has always been the creative urge in you—at peace as long as the marriage functioned, as it was taken care of then, but appearing all by itself in a useless explosive form, namely as knockings and raps and such things after the death of your second wife. It then became urgent for you to realize the pressure of the unconscious and its desire to produce immediately with the humble means at your disposal. Never mind the imperfections of technique; the contents wanting to come to light are the thing that

_____

☐ Darien, Connecticut.

[1] The writer, describing himself as a man of 71, who had "survived life's struggle, successfully, financially, through capitalizing on a slight gift for writing," told of his three marriages: the first to a pianist who left him overnight after a happy marriage lasting 17 years; the second to a painter whose death in 1954 ended an "idyllic" marriage of 22 years; and the third to an actress. Ever since the death of his second wife he heard "raps and taps" in the bedroom (also heard by the third wife), doors swung open by themselves and mirrors tipped, the phenomena occurring about two or three times a week.

[2] "Each man carries his woman with him." Cf. Jacobi, 27 Sept. 46, n. 2.

matters. How psychic energy can transform itself into physically sound phenomena is a problem in itself. I don't know how it is done. We only know that it *is* done. This is the non-spiritualistic explanation which I prefer in such cases. It has to my mind the great advantage of bringing the problem home to the living individual.

Sincerely yours, C. G. JUNG

To Adolf Keller

Dear friend,   August 1956

My last letter[1] was not meant to be a letter of farewell; it merely gave vent to my annoyance that you have failed to see how much I have struggled to understand the dogmatic conception of Christ psychologically. Now as ever I am of the opinion that Protestant theologians would have every reason to take my views seriously, for otherwise the same thing could happen here as has already happened in China and will happen in India: that the traditional religious ideas die of literal-mindedness, or are spewed out en masse because of their indigestibility. In China, for instance, a philosopher like Hu Shih[2] is ashamed to know anything of the *I Ching*,[3] the profound significance of Tao has got lost, and instead people worship locomotives and aeroplanes. Nowadays there is only a handful of Protestant theologians who have the slightest idea of what psychology could mean for them.

. . .

With friendly greetings, CARL

[1] This letter has not been preserved.
[2] Chinese philosopher and diplomat (1891–1962); 1938–42 Chinese ambassador to the U.S.A.; often called the "Father of the Chinese Renaissance." Cf. *The Chinese Renaissance* (1934), and *The Development of the Logical Method in Ancient China* (2nd edn., 1963).
[3] See *Memories*, App. IV: "Richard Wilhelm," p. 374/343.

To Henry A. Murray

[ORIGINAL IN ENGLISH]

Dear Dr. Murray,   August 1956

Thank you ever so much for your kind letter. It is a great pleasure for me to hear of you after this long time. I thank you also for your good birthday wishes. — My correspondence with Freud will not be published in the near future. It must wait until I have left the premises for good.

I am very interested that you are lecturing about my psychology. I am glad to know how successful you have been in delivering your lectures. It seems to be an awfully difficult subject which I did not realize at all while writing my books.

It is true that the Bollingen Press was reluctant concerning the publication of my *Answer to Job*. They were afraid of its causing still more prejudice against and anger with my unconventional views. This is another of my books that demands some careful thinking.

I have always wished to make the acquaintance of Prof. Tillich,[1] but I have never found an opportunity.

Your questions concerning "individuation" and "individual" are highly philosophical and impressive. It is perfectly true that I never described an "individuated person" for the simple reason that nobody would understand why I describe such a case, and most of my readers would be bored to tears. I am also not such a great poet that I could produce a really worthwhile picture. A genius like Goethe or Shakespeare might hope to be able to describe the lordly beauty and the divine completeness of an individuated old oak-tree, or the unique grotesqueness of a cactus. But if a scientist risked doing the same, nobody would understand or appreciate it. Science is only concerned with the average idea of an oak or a horse or man but not with their uniqueness. Moreover an individuated human being is well-nigh impossible to describe as we have no standpoint outside the human sphere. Thus we don't know what man is. We only can say that he is no animal, nor a plant, nor a crystal, but what he is is impossible to say. We would need an intimate knowledge of the inhabitants of other planets, inasmuch as they can be compared with men, in order to enable us to form some idea of what man is. From the standpoint of science the individual is negligible or a mere curiosity. From the subjective standpoint, however, i.e., from the standpoint of the individual himself, the individual is all-important as he is the carrier of life, and his development and fulfillment are of paramount significance. It is vital for each living being to become its own *entelechia* and to grow into that which it was from the very beginning. This very

---

[1] Paul Johannes Tillich (1886–1965), German Protestant theologian; dismissed by the Nazis in 1933, afterwards in U.S.A. His most important work is *Systematic Theology* (I, 1953; II, 1957).

vital and indispensable need of each living being means very little or nothing from a statistical standpoint, and nobody outside can be seriously interested in the fact that Mr. X is to become a good businessman or that Mrs. Y is to get six children. The individuated human being is just ordinary and therefore almost invisible. Necessarily all criteria of individuation are subjective and outside the purpose of science.

You ask: what feeling does he have and what values, thoughts, activities and relations to his surroundings? Well, his feelings, thoughts, etc. are just anybody's feelings, thoughts, etc.—quite ordinary, as a matter of fact, and not interesting at all, unless you happen to be particularly interested in that individual and his welfare. He will be all right if he can fulfill himself as he was from the beginning. He will have no need to be exaggerated, hypocritical, neurotic, or any other nuisance. He will be "in modest harmony with nature." As Zen Buddhism says: first mountains are mountains and the sea is the sea. Then mountains are no more mountains, the sea is no more the sea, and in the end the mountains will be the mountains and the sea will be the sea.[2] Nobody can have a vision and not be changed by it. First he has no vision, and he is the man A, then he is himself plus a vision = the man B; and then it might be that the vision may influence his life, if he is not quite dull, and that is the man C. No matter whether people think they are individuated or not, they are just what they are: in the one case a man plus an unconscious nuisance disturbing to himself—or, without it, unconscious of himself; or in the other case, conscious. The criterion is consciousness.

The man with a neurosis who knows that he is neurotic is more individuated than the man without this consciousness. The man who is a damned nuisance to his surroundings and knows it is more individuated than the man who is blissfully unconscious of his nature, etc. — The scientific standpoint is good for many things. In the case of individuation—though it has a certain auxiliary significance—in the deciding issue it means nothing at all. If a man is contradicted by himself and does not know it, he is an illusionist, but if he knows that he contradicts himself, he is individuated. According to Schopenhauer man's only divine quality is his humour. If the Pope has humour, or if Albert Schweitzer knows that he ran away from the European problem, or Winston Churchill is aware of what an insupportable bully he can be, they are thus far individuated. But surely nobody is particularly interested in this highly subjective

2 "Foreword to Suzuki's *Introduction to Zen Buddhism*," CW 11, par. 884, n. 11.

finesse unless he is a psychologist, or somebody fed up with his unconsciousness.

Hoping you enjoy always good health I remain, with kind regards to Christiana,

Yours cordially, C. G. JUNG

To Patrick Evans □

[ORIGINAL IN ENGLISH]

Dear Mr. Evans, 1 September 1956

Thank you for telling me of your interesting dream.[1] The dream is quite remarkable in its simplicity. It is what the primitives would call a "great dream." Your attempt at an interpretation is not wrong, but it is a sort of sideline, though important in itself. The essential dream-image: the Man, the Tree, the Stone, looks quite inaccessible, but only to our modern consciousness which is, as a rule, unconscious of its historical roots. The first thing I would do in such a case is the following: I would try to establish the relationship of the symbolism to its historical antecedents, namely to the identical ideas that have played a role in the immediate or the remote past. Take the first item: the Man. The Man leads you straight to the Bible. There the Man is Adam, then there is the "Son of Man" who is Christ. Then you have the idea of the Primordial Man as it appears in the Kabbalah: Adam Kadmon, and the figure of the Anthropos who is described by Ezekiel, Daniel and in the Book of Enoch.

This idea of the Man played a considerable role during the whole of the Middle Ages as far as the 18th century in alchemical philosophy. The same is true of the two other items: the Tree and the Stone. The Stone is still alive in Freemasonry. For more information I should advise you to study my book *Psychology and Alchemy*, where you can find any amount of material for your three symbols. I also have devoted a special study to the Tree-symbol but it has not

---

□ Ruchwick, near Worcester, England.
[1] E., describing himself as a schoolmaster, happily married, aged 43, reported a dream in which he saw a book with the title "The Philosophy of Analogy and Symbolism." The book was "wise, deep and lucid," unlike a real book with that title which he felt was "silly and muddled." The dream book was open "somewhere in the last few pages" and he could see three parallel columns, not filled in, with the headings: "The Man," "The Tree," "The Stone." He identified man with the number 3, tree with 4, stone with 5, and added certain numerical speculations.

appeared in English yet.[2] The interesting fact is that quite independently of tradition these symbols are reproduced in dreams of
many modern individuals. They are expressions of latent archetypes
inherited from time immemorial. It is the most characteristic quality
of the archetype that it is numinous, i.e., it has a sort of emotional
charge that seizes consciousness whenever an archetypal image or
situation occurs. That explains the rather unusual impression the
dream made upon you.

The Man means Man as he has been in the beginning and/or
as he should be in the future, the complete or total Man.

The Tree expresses development, growth from the hidden roots.
The evolution towards totality.

The Stone means, particularly in the form of the Philosophers'
Stone, the attainment of totality and immutability for which the
Stone is a very apt symbol. As Adam, according to certain traditions,
was created in the form of a lifeless statue,[3] so the second Adam, i.e.,
the total Man, will become a stone, yet alive, as is said in the New
Testament: *transmutemini in vivos lapides*.[4]

The three symbols of your dream form the heads of columns like
titles, suggesting that the empty columns have yet to be filled out
by contents.

The general theme is clear. It can be formulated as the following
questions: what is Man? what is the way of his development? what is
his goal? — The psychology of the unconscious has much to say in
the way of answers. My book *Psychology and Alchemy* or my little
essay "Psychology and Religion" can give you hints in that direction.

You are quite right in assuming that these questions have somehow to do with mathematics, i.e., the theory of numbers, but in the
first place it will be the symbolism of numbers that has to be understood. You are quite right in identifying the Man with 3, or the Stone
with 5, if you think of the latter as a quincunx[5] and not as a series
of numerical units. The 4 as Tree means the unfolding of the One

---

[2] "The Philosophical Tree," CW 13.

[3] Cf. *Mysterium*, CW 14, pars. 559ff.

[4] The quotation is not directly from NT, which has at I Peter 2:5: "Be you also
as living stones built up" (DV). It is an amalgam of this and the saying of the
alchemist Gerhard Dorn: "transmutemini in vivos lapides philosophicos" (transform yourselves into living philosophical stones). Cf. *Psychology and Alchemy*,
CW 12 (1968 edn.), par. 378 & n. 76; "Psychology and Religion," CW 11, par.
154.

[5] An arrangement of the four points of the compass plus a fifth central point.

in 3, since the Man (Anthropos) is the visible manifestation of the original One, i.e., God.

The fact is that the numbers pre-existing in nature are presumably the most fundamental archetypes, being the very matrix of all others. Here Pythagoras was certainly on the right track and we modern men have forgotten this aspect of the pre-existing numbers because we were only busy manipulating numbers for the sake of counting and calculating. But Number is a factor pre-existent to man, with unforeseen qualities yet to be discovered by him.

Hoping this may shed some light on your dream, I remain,

Yours sincerely, C. G. JUNG

To Fritz Lerch

Dear Herr Lerch,   10 September 1956

Your question[1] concerns one of those problems that have intrigued me for years: the connection of the psychology of the unconscious with the properties of whole numbers on the one hand and the properties of matter on the other. I first approached this knotty problem from the purely epistemological angle. Here I must anticipate by saying that the term "epistemological" has a psychological flavour because I am obliged by my discipline to answer, or at least bear in mind, the question: What is happening psychologically if I either stop short at the epistemological barrier, or pronounce a transcendental judgment? Here psychological reactions take place which the epistemologist has hardly considered until now, if at all. The reason for this is that he does not know of the existence of an unconscious psyche. If, therefore, my cognitive process comes to a stop at one point or another, this does not mean that the underlying psychological process has also stopped. Experience shows that it continues regardless. When the physicist, for instance, can form no picture of the structure of the atom from the data at hand, something suddenly flashes into his mind—a model, perhaps the planetary model—as a product of unconscious associative activity. This flash or

☐ Zurich.
[1] "To what extent and in what way could psychic facts be used for the discovery of new realizations in physics, or vice versa. In other words: How strong and of what kind is the link between psyche and physis?"

327

"hunch" must be considered a psychic statement, which is ordinarily called intuition and is a common product of the external data and psychological apperception. Wherever the inquiring mind comes up against a darkness in which objects are only dimly discernible, it fills the gap with previous experiences or, if these are lacking, with imaginative, that is with archetypal or mythic, material. In the construction of physical theories you will therefore find the closest analogies with the psychology of the unconscious, since this too is up against the same difficulties. Our psychic foundations are shrouded in such great and inchoate darkness that, as soon as you peer into it, it is instantly compensated by mythic forms. When these compensations become too obvious, we naturally try to obviate them and replace them by "logical" concepts. But this is justified only when these concepts really do give adequate expression to what we have dimly discerned. Generally they don't. Hence the borderline concepts in both sciences are partly mythological. This would be a good reason for an epistemological-cum-psychological examination of their fundamental concepts.

Unfortunately I am not in a position to demonstrate, from the physical side, facts which have clearly discernible connections or analogies with the facts of psychology. I can do this only from the psychological side. Broadly speaking, atoms can be described as the elementary building blocks of physical nature. Here we have a still very problematical analogy in the psychology of the unconscious, namely in mandala symbolism, expressed in medieval terms as the *quadratura circuli*. The model for such configurations is based on the spontaneous self-representation of this archetype in pictorial form. It is a mathematical structure, which first made me hit on the idea that the unconscious somehow avails itself of the properties of whole numbers. In order to see my way more clearly, I tried to compile a list of the properties of whole numbers, beginning with the known, unquestionable mathematical properties. From this it appears that whole numbers are individuals, and that they possess properties which cannot be explained on the assumption that they are multiple units. The idea that numbers were invented for counting is obviously untenable, since they are not only pre-existent to judgment but possess properties which were discovered only in the course of the centuries, and presumably possess a number of others which will be brought to light only by the future development of mathematics. Like all the inner foundations of judgment, numbers are archetypal by nature and consequently partake of the psychic qualities of the archetype. This, as we know, possesses a certain degree of autonomy which enables it to influence consciousness spontaneously. The same must be said of numbers, which brings us back to Pythagoras. When we are confronted with this dark aspect of numbers, the unconscious gives an answer, that is, it compensates their darkness by statements which I call "indispensable" or "inescapable." The number 1 says that it is one among many. At the same time it says that it is "the One." Hence it is the smallest and the greatest, the part and the whole. I am only hinting at these statements; if you think through the first five numbers in this way you will come to the remarkable conclusion that we have here a sort of creation myth which is an integral part of the inalienable properties of whole numbers. In this respect Number proves to be a fundamental element not only of physics but also of the objective psyche.

It would be a worthy task for a mathematician to collect all the known properties of numbers and also all their "inescapable" statements—which should be quite possible up to 10—and in this way project a biological picture of whole numbers. For the psychologist it is not so simple. Apart from the above-mentioned question of epistemology, the possibilities open to him are still on the level of elementary experiences. They can be formulated as follows: What are the psychic compensations when a task confronts us with darkness? Here the necessary material on intuitions, visions, and dreams would first have to be collected.

I do not doubt that quite fundamental connections exist between physics and psychology, and that the objective psyche contains images that would elucidate the secret of matter. These connections are discernible in synchronistic phenomena and their acausality. Today these things are only pale phantoms and it remains for the future to collect, with much painstaking work, the experiences which could shed light on this darkness.

Yours sincerely, C. G. JUNG

P.S. I have just seen that Rob. Oppenheimer has published an article[2] in *The American Psychologist* (Vol. XI, 3, 1956) on the conceptual data in physics.

[2] J. Robert Oppenheimer (1904–67), American nuclear physicist; 1943–45 director of the Los Alamos Laboratory; 1946–52 chairman of the advisory committee to the U.S. Atomic Energy Commission. The article is "Analogy in Science," originally a lecture given to a meeting of the American Psychological Association in San Francisco, Sept. 1955.

To Adolf Keller

Dear friend,   September 1956

I was glad to hear you are well and as busy as ever. I wish you the best of luck in all your undertakings, especially the lectures on depth psychology. I entirely agree that for unprepared readers *Job* is a hard nut to crack. Anyone who finds in the problem of Job— which William James also tackled[1]—too much scorn, irony, and suchlike rubbish had better leave the book alone. Incidentally, the book club of the Pastoral Guild of Psychology has ordered 2500 copies at one go for its members. It looks as if a goodly number of American theologians have a mind to wrestle with the basic ideas in my *Answer to Job* for their own sake. Nothing is gained by simply dodging unpleasant questions.

With best greetings, CARL

[1] *The Varieties of Religious Experience*, Lecture XVIII: "It's a plain historic fact that they [post-Kantian idealists] never have converted anyone who has found in the moral conception of the world, as he experienced it, reasons for doubting that a good God can have framed it . . . No! the Book of Job went over this whole matter once for all and definitively."

To Melvin J. Lasky

Dear Mr. Lasky,   September 1956

Best thanks for sending me the three issues of *Der Monat* with James P. O'Donnell's article "Der Rattenfänger von Hameln"[1] and the replies by Hans Scholz[2] and Dr. E. Schmitz-Cliever.[3] I have read them with great interest and can fully concur with the views of the latter two writers. The historical facts reported by O'Donnell would never have sufficed to give rise to so strange and uncanny a legend.

In contributing—at your request—a few words to the discussion, I would like to lay stress on the reality around which the legend revolves. H. Scholz has done this too, and rightly warned against over-

☐ 1944–45, U.S. combat historian in France and Germany; 1948–58, editor of *Der Monat* (Berlin); after 1958, co-editor of *Encounter* (London). Jung's letter was published under the title "Wotan und der Rattenfänger, Bemerkungen eines Tiefenpsychologen," *Der Monat*, Oct. 1956.
[1] *Der Monat*, June 1956.
[2] "Ehrenrettung des Rattenfängers," ibid., July 1956.
[3] "Rattenfänger und Veitstanz," ibid., Aug. 1956.

looking it. As a psychiatrist, I give due weight to the reality at work here: to a power emanating from the unconscious, the nature of which I discussed years ago in my essay "Wotan"[4]—an essay which is not always read with pleasure. The psychic powers at whose mercy men found themselves were in former times called "gods," and this had the advantage of assuring them the necessary fear and devotion. Wotan is a restless wanderer, an ancient god of storm and wind, unleashing passion and frenzy. His name means literally "Lord and Maker of Fury." Adam of Bremen[5] wrote in 1070 or thereabouts: "Wodan id est furor." His essence is ecstasy; he is a turbulent spirit, a tempest that sets everything in motion and causes "movements." Among these were the orgiastic midsummer's day dances mentioned by Dr. Schmitz-Cliever; the religious movements of the Middle Ages named by H. Scholz also bore the mark of this perturbing spirit. The exodus of the children from Hamelin comes into this category. It should be noted that music is a primitive means of putting people into a state of frenzy; one has only to think of the drumming at the dances of shamans and medicine-men, or of the flute-playing at the Dionysian orgies.

Leibniz mentioned St. Vitus's dance as a possible cause of the events at Hamelin. In this connection I would like to draw attention to a related, though far more dangerous, manifestation of collective frenzy upon which Wotan has likewise left his mark. This is the "going berserk" of Wotan's followers, a regular seizure that drove them to madness and gave them supernatural strength. Not only single individuals were seized in this way, but whole crowds were swept along and infected with the "berserker rage." It was a mass frenzy, to which other people gave the expressive name *furor Teutonicus*. The exodus of the children from Hamelin may be conceived as a less brutal movement activated by the same "ecstatic" spirit. The rat-catching Pied Piper himself must have been possessed by the spirit of Wotan, which swept all those who were liable to such transports—in this case children—into a state of collective frenzy.

As to the disappearance of the children in the mountain, it should be remembered that legends often banish into a mountain certain heroes in whose death the populace cannot or will not believe, and whose return is expected, with fear or hope, in the distant future. For

[4] Jung's note: "In *Aufsätze zur Zeitgeschichte*, Zürich 1946 [*Essays on Contemporary Events*, London 1947]. Cf. also Martin Ninck, *Götter und Jenseitsglauben der Germanen*, Jena 1937, esp. the chapter "Wodan-Odin," pp. 159ff."
[5] A canon who wrote a Church History of Hamburg, containing valuable information about the people of northern Europe.

the psychologist this is an apt way of saying that though the forces represented by the banished and vanished children have momentarily disappeared from consciousness, they are still very much alive in the unconscious. The unconscious is perfectly symbolized by the dark, unknown interior of the mountain. It scarcely needs mentioning that a reawakening of these forces has actually taken place.

Another aspect of this disappearance is the state of "being lost to the world," which is frequently reported in connection with ecstasy and more particularly with "going berserk." According to legend, the hero becomes invisible or is transported to another place, or occasionally his double appears, as when he is seen in battle, while in reality he is sunk in trance-like slumber. That reports like these may have to do with parapsychological phenomena should not be dismissed out of hand, for such phenomena are associated to a great extent with highly emotional states. But as yet there is no possibility of a scientific explanation.

From a psychological point of view the motif of the rats, which seems to have been added afterwards, is an indication of Wotan's connection with the daemonic and chthonic realm, and with evil. Wotan was banished by Christianity to the realm of the devil, or identified with him, and the devil is the Lord of rats and flies.

The story of the Pied Piper, as well as the medieval movements mentioned by H. Scholz and Dr. Schmitz-Cliever, are symptoms of a pagan spirit working in the unconscious and not yet domesticated by Christianity. There are other such symptoms, of a more pacific nature —alchemy is one of them—which I have investigated at considerable length in my writings. This spirit the more readily takes possession of our consciousness the less our consciousness is willing to reflect upon its origins and roots. With kind regards,

Yours sincerely, C. G. JUNG

Anonymous

[ORIGINAL IN ENGLISH]

Dear Sir,   10 October 1956

I don't know where you picked up this rather childish yarn about directors of world affairs located in Tibetan lamaseries.[1] It would be

---

□ New York.

[1] N. wrote a rather fantastic letter about all sorts of esoteric groups "with their main headquarters in the trans-Himalayan mountains" running the fate of the world and claiming that Jung was one of them.

a difficult task if anybody should venture to ask you for the slightest evidence in this respect. At all events I can tell you that I am not a member of such a wholly fantastical organization. I have not even heard of its existence, and I would not be foolish enough to believe in it even if a dozen theosophical societies declared their faith in such an obvious swindle.

Have you ever seen even one true Tibetan *rimpoché*?[2] I have, and even one that has studied for 20 years in Lhasa. They know many interesting things, but they are miles from where we in the Western world think they are.

Yours sincerely, C. G. JUNG

[2] A *rimpoché* is the abbot of a Tibetan monastery. Jung mentions his conversation with the *rimpoché* Lingdam Gomchen in *Psychology and Alchemy*, CW 12, par. 123.

To H. J. Barrett

[ORIGINAL IN ENGLISH]

Dear Mr. Barrett, 12 October 1956

Although my time is short and my old age is a real fact, I would like to answer to your questions. They are not quite easy, f.i. the first question whether I believe in personal survival after death or not.[1] I could not say that I believe in it, since I have not the gift of belief. I only can say whether I know something or not. I do know that the psyche possesses certain qualities transcending the confinement in time and space. Or you might say, the psyche can make those categories as if elastic, i.e., 100 miles can be reduced to 1 yard and a year to a few seconds. This is a fact for which we have all the necessary proofs. There are moreover certain post-mortal phenomena which I am unable to reduce to subjective illusions. Thus I know that the psyche is capable of functioning unhampered by the categories of time and space. *Ergo* it is in itself an equally transcendental being and therefore relatively non-spatial and "eternal." This does not mean that I hold any kind of convictions as to the transcendental nature of the psyche. It may be anything.

2. There is no reason whatever to assume that all so-called psychic phenomena are illusory effects of our mental processes.

3. I don't think that all reports of so-called miraculous phenomena (such as precognition, telepathy, supranormal knowledge, etc.) are

[1] Cf. *Memories*, ch. XI: "On Life after Death."

doubtful. I know plenty of cases where there is no shadow of a doubt about their veracity.

4. I do not think that so-called personal messages from the dead can be dismissed *in globo* as self-deceptions.

Immanuel Kant once said that he would doubt all stories about spooks, etc., individually, but as a whole there was something in them, which reminds me fatally of a Professor of Catholic Theology who, treating the seven arguments about the existence of God, was made to admit that every one of them was a syllogism. But in the end he said: "Oh, I admit you can prove that every one taken singly may be at fault, but there are seven of them, that must mean something!" — I carefully sift my empirical material and I must say that among many most arbitrary assumptions there are some cases that made me sit up. I have made it a rule to apply Multatuli's[2] wise statement: There is nothing quite true, and even this is not quite true.

Hoping I have answered your questions to your satisfaction, I remain,

Yours sincerely, C. G. JUNG

[2] Pen-name of the Dutch writer Eduard Douwes Dekker (1820–87).

To the Rev. H. L. Philp

[ORIGINAL IN ENGLISH]

Dear Mr. Philp,   26 October 1956

Thank you very much for calling my attention to this new concoction *Christian Essays in Psychiatry*.[1] The idea that I convert people, as it were, to the new denomination "Jungianism" or better "Jungian Church" is sheer defamation. I know a considerable number of people that have converted to the Catholic Church after they were analysed by myself. A smaller number of Catholics that had become indifferent to the Church before felt completely out of it and adopted the standpoint more or less similar to mine, which I regard as a sort of left-wing Protestantism. I am definitely inside Christianity and, as far as I am capable of judging about myself, on the direct line of historical development. If the Pope adds a new and thoroughly unhistorical dogma to Catholicism, I add a symbolic interpretation of all Christian symbols. At least I am trying to. If the Reformation is a heresy, I am certainly a heretic too. There is nothing to be done about it, as once

☐ British psychologist and theologian.
[1] Edited by Philip Mairet (London, 1956).

334

it was a heresy even to suggest that the earth turns round the sun. It is of course a thorn in the flesh of the churches that I do not belong to any of the recognized sects. Looked at from a strictly Catholic point of view I make very heretical statements indeed; but there are plenty of reformers that have done the same thing, including the present Pope, declaring the dogma without the slightest apostolic authority and without the consent even of his own Church, which has emphatically resisted any such declaration during at least the 600 years of its early history. The absolute number of conversions having taken place under my direct or indirect influence is insignificant in comparison with that of the people returning to their original faith, including Parsees returning to their fire-temple, Jews appreciating again the deep significance of their own religion, Chinamen and Hindus understanding again the meaning of their forgotten Taoism and their religious philosophy. These facts have even prompted my critics to accuse me of a particular lack of character and even of betrayal of my Christian faith. They all want me therefore to confess my definite belief in certain metaphysical statements and complain bitterly that I do not comply with their wishes. The trouble with them is that they don't want to think about their own beliefs. Whereas I am insisting, with certain Fathers of the Church, that we ought to think about religious matters and that the way to the cognition of God begins with the cognition of oneself. As nearly everybody does, they also want to circumvent this odious task of self-cognition. But, I am afraid, we don't get anywhere by remaining blind in this respect. I consider it downright immoral to shut one's eyes to the truth about oneself. Thus far I am a Protestant in my soul and body, even if most of the Protestant theologians are just as childlishly prejudiced as the Catholic priests.

I am busy dictating answers to your questions,[2] but I am not yet through.

Sincerely yours, C. G. JUNG

[2] P. published a book on *Freud and Religious Belief* (1956) which aroused Jung's interest. Thus, when he planned to write a book with the suggested title "Jung and Religious Belief," Jung agreed to answer P.'s questions. This resulted in a lengthy correspondence in 1956 and 1957 consisting of P.'s questionnaires and Jung's answers (too long to be included in this selection). The whole correspondence, as well as some extensive answers Jung sent to the Rev. David Cox, who was also working on a book about the relation between Jung's psychology and religion (*Jung and St. Paul*, 1959), is published in Philp, *Jung and the Problem of Evil* (1958), although Jung strongly disagreed with its contents. His letters to Philp and Cox are in CW 18, pars. 1584ff.

To Jolande Jacobi

Dear Dr. Jacobi, 6 November 1956

In these terrible days,[1] when evil is once again inundating the world in every conceivable form, I want you to know that I am thinking of you and of your family in Hungary, and hope with you that the avenging angel will pass by their door. The fate of Hungary cries to heaven, and in the West stupidity and delusion have reached a fatal climax. *De profundis clamavi ad te Domine—*
In affection,

Sincerely yours, c. g. jung

☐ (Handwritten.)

[1] The Hungarian uprising of Oct. 1956, which was crushed on 4 Nov. by Russian forces. Two short public protests by Jung are included in CW 18, pars. 1456f.

To Père Bruno de Jésus-Marie

Dear Père Bruno, 20 November 1956

I have thought over our conversation[1] for a long time and have come to the conclusion that, just as it is the foremost task of the individual to become conscious of himself, it should also be the chiefest concern of a gathering of distinguished personalities to become conscious of their meaning within the greater society. As I have intimated to you, the spiritual scope of your Academy embraces the whole North, from the North Cape to the Alps, that is to say all those countries which were only partly Romanized, or not at all, and therefore had only indirect or sporadic contacts with the entirely different Mediterranean culture. In France there is a noticeable difference between the spiritually active North and the static life of the South, which it shares with Spain and Italy. Southern Europe remained stationary for many centuries after an initial contact had been made between the

☐ Paris. — Jung dictated the letter in German and had a French translation prepared, which was sent to B. Also cf. Jung's letter to B. of 5 Nov. 53, in CW 18, pars. 1518ff.

[1] B. had been offered the chancellorship of the Académie Septentrionale, founded in 1936 at Lille, with the aim of forming a cultural centre for the North of France and all countries bordering the North Sea. His plan was to organize a study of "Northern" mythology, and he asked Jung's advice. Jung invited him to Switzerland, where they met on 17 Nov.

peoples of the West and the then flourishing Islamic culture. But when the West had assimilated the remnants of classical culture that were still kept alive by Islam, a state of spiritual coexistence set in, and there were no more contacts between Islam and Christianity. Both cultures remained mutually isolated and cross-fertilization ceased. For the spiritually more mobile West, i.e., the Latin culture of the northern Mediterranean countries, had now found a different antagonist—the Teuton.

Not cast in the Latin mould, he confronted the civilized Latin peoples with all the diversity of a barbaric, tribally oriented social order. He brought with him a primitive tradition which had developed autochthonously within his tribes, presumably from the time of the Stone Age, and which despite the curiosity of the youthful barbarian never quite succumbed to the influence of Latin culture. Mediterranean culture is founded on a three- to four-thousand-year-old rule of order, both political and religious, which had long outgrown the locally conditioned, semi-barbarian forms of society. Thus the "esprit latin" has secure foundations guaranteeing a relatively unproblematical state of consciousness. The Teutonic man of the North, on the contrary, is driven around by the adventurous nomadic restlessness of those who have their roots in a different soil from the one they want to live on. Whether he will or no, there is a continual conflict in him over his foundations. He is always seeking his own, for what he usurped some 1500 years ago as a binding form of life would not harmonize with what he brought with him as a usurper. His polydaemonism had not yet reached the level and clarity of Mediterranean polytheism, and in this state he was suddenly confronted with a religion and view of the world that had sprung from the decay of Olympus and the transformation of the gods into philosophical and theological ideas. His still undifferentiated barbarian world, bursting with the vital seeds of possible future developments, sank down reviled but not explained. No bridge led from one to the other.

Here, it seems to me, is the source of that Teutonic turmoil which has more than once violently forced its way to the surface. Here is that tension of opposites which supplies the energy for physical and spiritual adventures. This is the man who, driven by his inner conflicts, was actually the first to discover the earth and take possession of it. At this centre of antagonistic forces lies your Academy, under whose auspices are united the most important representatives of Northern culture. It seems to me that its most urgent task is to create

337

a differentiated consciousness of this state of affairs and to publicize it. It would be rendering Western man a service of which he stands in the most urgent need at present—a knowledge of himself as he actually is, and who is the cause of the tremendous spiritual confusion of our time. As soon as I can I will send you a copy of my "Present and Future"[2] as a further illustration of my point of view. With best regards,

Yours sincerely, C. G. JUNG

[2] A literal translation of the German title ("Gegenwart und Zukunft") of the essay published as "The Undiscovered Self," CW 10.

To Frances G. Wickes

[ORIGINAL IN ENGLISH]

Dear Mrs. Wickes,   14 December 1956

I am sorry to hear that you have been laid up for a long time. Age is indeed a pleasure with a double face.[1] The decreasing of physical forces is a problem one is not quite adjusted to, and one only painfully learns to settle down to an ever-increasing restriction.

I got the picture you sent me and I thank you very much for it.[2] It is indeed very interesting and not at all orthodox, since the figure of the Anthropos is rising from the water and the earth and denotes its corporeality by the definitely fleshly aspect of the upper part of the body. It is also noteworthy that the head is cut off by the frame. Thus the emphasis is on the body. It is, though, quite understandable as the *spiritus Mercurialis*, the Anthropos of the alchemists. This spirit adds the chthonic reality of the creation to a purely spiritual conception in a way that would shake the very foundations of our medieval Christianity if people only would *think* about what they do. The picture could have been painted by someone who knew about the secret developments in our unconscious mind in the last 1000 years. Dali's genius translates the spiritual background of the concrete symbol of transmutation into visibility. This also explains the somewhat shocking and unorthodox representation of Christ as the blond Hero.

Thank you very much for sending me this tell-tale picture. It is quite on the line.

☐ Cf. Wickes, 9 Aug. 26 and pl. VI (in vol. 1).
[1] She was born in the same year as Jung (1875) and was one of his oldest friends and correspondents.
[2] See illustration.

338

Salvador Dali. *The Sacrament of the Last Supper*. Chester Dale Collection, The National Gallery of Art, Washington: see Wickes, 14 Dec. 56

Hoping your condition, whatever it is, will improve and that you will enjoy better health in the coming New Year, I remain,

Yours cordially, c. g. j u n g

P.S. I am reasonably well and I complain only of the increasing unreliability of my memory.

To H. J. Barrett

[ORIGINAL IN ENGLISH]

Dear Mr. Barrett,   27 December 1956

Thank you for your interesting letter. It is indeed an important question, the question of sleep and dream.[1] As far as my knowledge goes we are aware in dreams of our other life that consists in the first place of all the things we have not yet lived or experienced in the flesh. Beyond that material we are also aware of things we never can realize in the flesh and not in this life. Things belonging to the past of mankind and presumably to its future also. The latter can be realized only very rarely as future events, because we have no means, or very few, to recognize and identify future events before they have happened, as we also cannot understand thoughts we never had before. All the things which are not yet realized in our daylight experience are in a peculiar state, namely in the condition of living and autonomous figures, sometimes as if spirits of the dead, sometimes as if former incarnations. These formulations are probably auxiliary means supplied by our unconscious mind to express forms of psychic existence we do not really understand.

I am sorry my time does not allow me to comment in detail about your experiences. I hope my general observations will help you to a certain extent.

Sincerely yours, c. g. j u n g

[1] B. asked "where we are in sleep," mentioning a friend of his who had "achieved national fame as a poet through poems which she wrote as by dictation immediately upon awakening."

Anonymous

Dear Dr. N.,   2 January 1957

Many thanks for your detailed letter, the contents of which interested me very much. I was impressed above all by the fact that in the

☐ To a woman in Switzerland.

discussion between you and Frau X there is constant talk of "God" and of what he does or what he is. I miss any explicit recognition of the epistemological threshold. We cannot speak of "God" but only of a God-image which appears to us or which we make. If, for instance, we were to create a myth, we would say that "God" has two aspects, spiritual and chthonic, or rather: material. He appears to us as the world-moving spirit (= wind) and as the material of the world. That is the image we create for ourselves of the *prima causa*. But in reality we can say nothing at all about "God." We can only project a conception of him that corresponds to our own constitution: a body perceived by the senses and a spirit (= psyche) directly conscious of itself. After this model we build our God-image.

Coming now to cosmogony, we can assert nothing except that the body of the world and its psyche are a reflection of the God we imagine. The split in this image is an unavoidable trick of consciousness for making us aware of anything at all. But we cannot assert that this split actually exists in the objective world. Rather, we have every reason to suppose that there is only *one* world, where matter and psyche are the same thing, which we discriminate for the purpose of cognition.

As regards the Incarnation, the idea of God's descent into human nature is a true mythologem. What we can experience empirically as underlying this image is the individuation process, which gives us clear intimations of a greater "Man" than our ego. The unconscious itself characterizes this "Man" with the same symbols it applies to God, from which we can conclude that this figure corresponds to the Anthropos, in other words God's son, or God represented in the form of a man. The greater "Man" (the self) does not become identical with the empirical man in such wise that the ego is replaced by the self. The self becomes only a determining factor, and it is not bounded by its apparent entry into consciousness; in spite of this it remains an ideal, i.e., purely imagined, entity dwelling essentially in the background, just as we also imagine God existing in his original boundless totality in spite of the Creation and Incarnation.

So far as the integration of personality components are concerned, it must be borne in mind that the ego-personality as such does not include the archetypes but is only influenced by them; for the archetypes are universal and belong to the collective psyche over which the ego has no control. Thus animus and anima are images representing archetypal figures which mediate between consciousness and the unconscious. Though they can be made conscious they cannot be integrated into the ego-personality, since as archetypes they are also autonomous. They behave like the God-image, which while objectivating itself in the world nevertheless subsists of itself in the Unus Mundus.[1]

These are problems that cannot be discussed at all if epistemology is disregarded. They can be tackled only if you are constantly aware of epistemological criticism, in other words, if you do not forget that absolute reality can be conceived only in psychological terms. At the same time the psyche, or rather consciousness, introduces the prerequisites for cognition into the picture—the discrimination of particulars or qualities which are not necessarily separated in the self-subsistent world. We distinguish an organic and an inorganic world, for example. The one is alive, the other is dead; the one has psyche, the other not. But who can guarantee that the same vital principle which is at work in the organic body is not active in the crystal? It seems to me that due regard for the epistemological standpoint would make discussions with Frau X considerably easier. With best greetings,

Yours sincerely, c. g. jung

[1] This refers to the alchemical concept of the "one world" in which all opposites are united. Jung uses it as expressing the collective unconscious as the common background to microcosm (psyche) and macrocosm (physis). Cf. *Mysterium*, CW 14, index, s.v. world.

To Michael Fordham

[ORIGINAL IN ENGLISH]

Dear Fordham, 3 January 1957

I am glad to hear that your two books[1] are ready and going to press. My congratulations! I will write the introduction as soon as possible. For the time being I am nailed down to a revision of a paper I wrote in spring 1956, which should appear this month;[2] but as soon as I have finished this work I shall try to fulfil my promise. In view of my old age I don't trust my powers any more. I easily get tired and my creative ability, I am afraid, has become very faint indeed.

By the way, I have just read your paper on "Synchronicity."[3] I must

[1] *New Developments in Analytical Psychology* (1957) and *The Objective Psyche* (1958). Jung's foreword to the first is in CW 18, pars. 1168ff.

[2] "Gegenwart und Zukunft," which appeared in *Schweizer Monatshefte*, XXXVI: 12 (Mar. 1957).

[3] "Reflections on the Archetypes and Synchronicity," in *New Developments in Analytical Psychology*.

say, this is the most intelligent thing that has been said hitherto about this remote subject. I have enjoyed it very much. The experience you had with the *I Ching*, calling you to order when trying to tempt it a second time,[4] also happened to me in 1920 when I first experimented with it. It also gave me a wholesome shock and at the same time it opened wholly new vistas to me. I well understand that you prefer to emphasize the archetypal implication in synchronicity. This aspect is certainly most important from the psychological angle, but I must say that I am equally interested, at times even more so, in the metaphysical aspect of the phenomena, and in the question: how does it come that even inanimate objects are capable of behaving as if they were acquainted with my thoughts? This is, as the above formulation shows, a thoroughly paranoid speculation which one had better not ventilate in public, but I cannot deny my fervent interest in this aspect of the problem.

My best wishes for the New Year,

Cordially yours, C. G. JUNG

[4] As he recounts in *New Developments* (p. 49), F. had consulted the *I Ching* for clarification on a certain problem, and after getting an answer immediately consulted it again. He obtained Hexagram 4, "Youthful Folly," where The Judgment says:

> "the young fool seeks me.
> At the first oracle I inform him.
> If he asks two or three times, it is importunity.
> If he importunes, I give him no information."

To Karl Schmid

Dear Professor Schmid, 26 January 1957

Sincerest thanks for kindly sending me your rectoral address, *Neuere Aspekte der Geistesgeschichte*.[1] I had already got some idea of its con-

☐ Professor of German literature at the E.T.H. (Swiss Federal Polytechnic); 1969–72, president of the Schweizer Wissenschaftsrat. Cf. his *Aufsätze und Reden* (1957); *Hochmut und Angst* (1958); *Geheimnis der Ergänzung* (dedicated to Jung; 1960); *Europa zwischen Ideologie und Verwirklichung* (1966); *Zeitspuren* (1967). — He was Rector of the Polytechnic at the time of Jung's 80th birthday and played an active part on the occasion of Jung's honorary doctoral degree. Cf. Hug, Meier, Böhler, Schmid, *Carl Gustav Jung* (Kultur- und staatswissenschaftliche Schriften, E.T.H., no. 91, 1955).

[1] Kultur- und staatswissenschaftliche Schriften, E.T.H., no. 99 (1957). (= "Recent Aspects of Spiritual History.")

tent from the report in the *Neue Zürcher Zeitung,* but I missed the essential details. The complete copy of your address has now filled in all the gaps and confirmed my first impression of the very understanding way in which you have treated the social and spiritual implications of my basically medical and empirical work. I found your differential definition of the historical and psychological approach most illuminating, and I can only agree with what you say. I must add, however, that this applies only to a psychology which is still exclusively concerned with culture-promoting personalities and is therefore restricted to the sphere of individual phenomena. This is an aspect of psychology which affords us the greatest insight and is at the same time the unavoidable path leading down to the deeper levels from which those biological masterpieces we call personalities are produced. At these greater depths more general laws become discernible and more comprehensive figures stand out which eliminate the divisive factor of individual development and give psychology a homogeneity or inner coherence which raises it to the rank of a biological science.

By these deeper levels I mean the determining archetypes which are supraordinate to, or underlie, individual development and presumably are responsible for the supreme meaning of individual life. Seen from this level, not only is psychological experience a continuum, but the psychological approach also enables us to gain some knowledge of the inner connection between historical events. The archetypes have a life of their own which extends through the centuries and gives the aeons their peculiar stamp. Perhaps I may draw your attention to my historical contribution in *Aion,* where I have attempted to outline the evolutionary history of the Anthropos, which begins with the earliest Egyptian records. The material I have presented there may serve to illustrate these remarks of mine.

May I take this opportunity to express the modest wish to make your personal acquaintance?[2] I would very much like to discuss these far-reaching questions with you sometime. Thanking you again,

Yours sincerely, C. G. JUNG

[2] This letter led to the personal acquaintance of the two men and to numerous discussions between them.

Anonymous

[ORIGINAL IN ENGLISH]

Dear Mrs. N.,   8 February 1957

Thank you very much for your friendly letter with its kind advice. You can rest assured that having studied the Gospels for a life-time (I am nearly 83!) I am pretty well acquainted with the foundations of our Christianity. Surely the times of primitive Christianity were bad too, but not as bad as the world is now. Our plight is decidedly worse, and we have to learn about things the old Fathers of the Church did not even dream of. I am concerned with the world as it is today, namely godless and spiritually disoriented. In history there is never a way back. To be optimistic would mean to pull the wool over the eyes of the world. This would lead nowhere as it would confirm the childishness of people still more. They should realize in our days how much depends upon themselves and to what purpose they have been created. When you are still on the battlefield you cannot think of the good things that may come afterwards.

Sincerely yours, C. G. JUNG

☐ California.

To Ernst Hanhart

Dear Colleague,   18 February 1957

Very many thanks for kindly sending me your offprint, which I have read with great interest. The fate of children born of incest was most interesting and instructive. With regard to your questions, I much regret that I am no longer in a position to see you personally. Your letter arrived at the moment of my departure.

The question of the identity of psychological and physiological types is a complicated one. Kretschmer's types[1] are based primarily on

☐ M.D., (1891–   ), formerly lecturer at Zurich U. He asked whether Jung still regarded Freud as an extravert and Adler as an introvert, as which he had described them in CW 7, pars. 56ff. He also inquired about a possible relation between Jung's typology and that of E. Kretschmer.
[1] The German psychiatrist Ernst Kretschmer (1888–1964), in his *Physique and Character* (1925; orig., 1921), established a relationship between types of physique and certain neurotic and psychotic tendencies, distinguishing a leptosome (thin), pyknic (thick), and athletic type. (Concerning Kretschmer, cf. Schultz, 9 June 33, n. 2.)

somatic criteria. My typology is based exclusively on psychological premises which can hardly coincide with physiological or somatic qualities. Somatic characteristics are permanent and virtually unalterable facts, whereas psychological ones are subject to various alterations in the course of personality development and also to neurotic disturbances. Even though assignment to a particular type may in certain cases have lifelong validity, in other very frequent cases it is so dependent on so many external and internal factors that the diagnosis is valid only for certain periods of time. Freud was just such a case.[2] On the basis of an accurate knowledge of his character, I consider him to have been originally an introverted feeling type with inferior thinking. When I got to know him in 1907 this original type was already neurotically blurred. In observing a neurotic, one does not know at first whether one is observing the conscious or the unconscious character. Freud, then as later, presented the picture of an extraverted thinker and empiricist. His overvaluation of thinking coupled with his irresponsible manner of observation aroused my doubts as to his type. The subjective overvaluation of his thinking is illustrated by his dictum: "This must be correct because I have thought it."[3] His irresponsible manner of observation is demonstrated by the fact, for instance, that not one of his cases of "traumatic" hysteria was verified.[4] He relied on the veracity of his hysterical patients. When I analysed Freud a bit further in 1909 on account of a neurotic symptom, I discovered traces which led me to infer a marked injury to his feeling life. Experience shows that at such moments a feeling type switches over to thinking as the counterfunction, together

[2] The editor would not have felt justified in publishing the passage beginning with this sentence and ending with the conclusion of the paragraph had it not been published before (cf. *Katalog der Autographen-Auktion* (Marburg), no. 425 (23/24 May 1967); also *Tagesanzeiger für Stadt und Kanton Zürich*, 27 May 1967). Although the editor considers the previous publication an ill-advised indiscretion, it seems pointless to withhold the passage now. The indiscretion is all the more regrettable as Jung had communicated his observations confidentially as a medical secret (cf. Hanhart, 2 Mar. 57), and H. had in a letter of 6 Mar. 57 promised to keep Jung's words absolutely private. It may be of interest to add that the whole letter was expected to fetch DM 400 at the auction of autographs, but fetched in fact DM 1700 although it was not even handwritten.

[3] Presumably a remark made in conversation.

[4] Freud, in his *Studies on Hysteria* (1895; now in Standard Edn. 2), accepted the reports of his patients about early sexual seduction as facts. It was only in 1897 that he realized "the awful truth that most—not all—of the seductions in childhood which his patients had revealed, and about which he had built his whole theory of hysteria, had never occurred" (Jones, *Sigmund Freud*, I, p. 292).

with the compensatory overvaluation. The original auxiliary function —in this case intuition—is replaced by a somewhat deficient "fonction du réel."[5] This transformation has been described by the French as "simulation dans la charactère." Freud, when one got to know him better, was distinguished by a markedly differentiated feeling function. His "sense of values" showed itself in his love of precious stones, jade, malachite, etc. He also had considerable intuition. Yet the superficial picture he presented to the world was that of an extraverted thinker and empiricist who derived his philosophy of life from the man in the street, which is supposed to be modern.

This mutability of the psychological type makes the question of its relation to the somatic type an extremely complicated problem. And when we take the results of personality development into account, the crude features of introversion and extraversion are also reversed. The case of a man of 36 with a cardiac neurosis may serve as an example. He was an obviously extraverted type, and his wife was introverted to a pathological degree. They got a divorce. He then married an extremely extraverted woman, lost his cardiac neurosis, and became a typical introvert with the feeling that this was his true nature. He was a successful businessman who from humble beginnings had worked his way to the top. His originally introverted disposition was kept under by his hard struggle and energetic will, but had to be married in the form of an introverted wife and paid for with a cardiac neurosis.

I hope these few hints will show you why I regard the identity of somatic and psychological types, if not exactly as a question of incommensurables, then at least as a problem that at present remains completely unsolved. With collegial regards,

Yours sincerely, C. G. JUNG

[5] A term Jung sometimes used for the sensation function.

To Gus Clarites

[ORIGINAL IN ENGLISH]

Dear Sir,   23 February 1957

There is no objection to publishing my letter.[1] I draw your attention to the fact that there is no date on your copy of my letter to

[1] C., secretary of Leonard Albert, who was writing a book on Joyce (*Joyce and the New Psychology*, 1957), asked Jung for permission to include his letter to Joyce, 27 Sept. 32 (q.v.).

James Joyce. Perhaps you can find out in the original when the letter was written.

Please tell Dr. Albert that while Joyce lived in Zurich he became acquainted with Mrs. Edith McCormick,[2] whom I knew very well. She (. . .) had absorbed a great amount of psychological knowledge, and Joyce was one of her protégés. She had talked to him and, as she talked chiefly psychology being full of it, I am pretty certain that she didn't miss this opportunity to give him some lectures. There is however no definite evidence in this respect and I don't suppose that the points in *Ulysses* apparently referring to my psychology have anything to do with what he heard from Mrs. McCormick. Zurich however is a place where psychological talk is abundant and I cannot quite exclude the possibility of his having picked up certain ideas from other sources unknown to me. This is all I could contribute to Dr. Albert's researches.

Sincerely yours, c. g. j u n g

[2] Mrs. Edith Rockefeller McCormick had supported Joyce financially for a time but stopped this support suddenly. She had studied analytical psychology under Jung, and she and her husband had been members of the committee which planned the foundation of the Psychological Club, Zurich, in 1916.

To Ernst Hanhart

Dear Colleague,   2 March 1957

Best thanks for your explanatory remarks. With your permission, I will annotate your MS[1] in places. I should be glad if you would treat my analysis of Freud's character with discretion. I have communicated my views to you *sub secreto medici*.[2] Since my views spring from my intimate acquaintance with him, and in addition point to a rather delicate background for persons in the know, I would prefer discretion to prevail in this matter. People always assume anyway that my critical set-to with Freud was the result of a merely personal animosity on my part. Instead of using Freud and Adler as paradigms, you could use Nietzsche and Wagner as representing the Dionysian and Apollinian, or else Jordan's descriptions.[3] It should also be noted that my

[1] "Konstitution und Psychotherapie."
[2] The present letter was also offered for sale by auction on another occasion (cf. Hanhart, 18 Feb. 57, n. 2).
[3] *Psychological Types*, CW 6, chs. III and IV.

characterization of Adler and Freud as, respectively, introverted and extraverted does not refer to them personally but only to their outward demeanour. The question of the real personal type still remains open. I had little personal knowledge of Adler and so can say little about his real personality. Freud, on the other hand, I knew very well. He was unquestionably a neurotic. As I said before, I know from experience that in neurotic cases it is often extraordinarily difficult to make out the real type, because at first and for a long time afterwards you don't know what you are observing, the conscious or the unconscious behaviour. Freud's thinking had a definitely extraverted character, i.e., pleasure and unpleasure in the object. Adler's character, on the contrary, was introverted in so far as he gave paramount importance to the power of the ego.

As for your main question, the problem of small but decisive chance events, perhaps I may point out that I have not only never denied them but have even made them the subject of a special investigation (my essay in *The Interpretation of Nature and the Psyche* which I brought out with W. Pauli). Adler, by the way, once coined the nickname "iunctim"[4] for these phenomena. As meaningful coincidences, they present us with the quite special problem of "acausal arrangements"—if I may risk such a paradox.

As regards the tendency to self-punishment,[5] it would, for the sake of scientific accuracy, have to be divested of its ego character. Since it operates unconsciously, no participation by the ego can be proved. It is rather that objective processes not chosen by the ego take place, which in view of the one-sidedness of the ego have a complementary or compensatory character. The term "self-punishment" is therefore misleading on closer examination since it imputes to the ego an intention which in reality does not exist. What does in fact exist seems to be an objective psychic background, the unconscious, which predates consciousness and exists independently alongside it. With collegial regards,

Yours sincerely, C. G. JUNG

[4] From Lat. "iunctus," joined together. Cf. *The Freud/Jung Letters* (1974), 333J, n. 3.
[5] H. mentioned certain events in his life which he tried to explain as self-punishment.

To Aniela Jaffé

Dear Aniela,   18 March 1957

. . .

Here too the weather has been indescribably beautiful, and this
has most effectively prevented me from writing letters, but instead
I have finished painting the ceiling in Bollingen and done more work
on my inscription and—last but not least—rebricked the rivulets to
prevent seepage and cooked some good meals and found and bought
an excellent wine. All this has rested me and cured me of various
vexations. But I won't speak of that. Thank heavens I have no idea
how great is the disorder or order of my correspondence. My memory
has the most astonishing holes in it, so that I often catch myself
forgetting not only what I have done but more especially what I have
not done. It is therefore with a sigh of relief that I see from your
letter that, what with the good weather and the necessary rest, you
are gradually recuperating and hold out prospects of returning to
Küsnacht.

I have just got back from the timelessness of Bollingen and found
your letter and the very interesting article by Nowacki.[1] It is of great
importance. But I must give it a thorough thinking over.

I must stop now and say goodbye till Friday (hopefully).

Go on enjoying the spring in Tessin: here the weather has
changed. With cordial greetings and best wishes,

Yours, C. G.

☐ (Handwritten.)
[1] Cf. next letter, n. 1.

To Werner Nowacki

Dear Professor Nowacki,   22 March 1957

I don't want to miss the chance of thanking you for your thoughtfulness in sending me your interesting article.[1] Your ideas go back,

☐ (Handwritten.) Professor of mineralogy, Bern U.
[1] "Die Idee einer Struktur der Wirklichkeit," *Mitteilungen der Naturforschenden
Gesellschaft in Bern*, XIV (1957). In this paper N. interprets the elements of
symmetry in crystals as spiritual entities having a formative effect. He calls them
"primordial images" and regards them as "irrepresentable formal factors that arrange the planes of the crystal as the material datum in a meaningful way that

in modern form, to the familiar world of Plato's *Timaeus*, which was a sacrosanct authority for medieval science—and rightly so! Our modern attempts at a unitary view, to which your article makes very important contributions, do indeed lead to the question of the cosmic demiurge and the psychic aspect of whole numbers.

From the fact that matter has a mainly quantitative aspect and at the same time a qualitative one, even though this appears to be secondary, you draw the weighty conclusion, which I heartily applaud, that, besides its obviously qualitative nature, the psyche has an as yet hidden quantiative aspect. Matter and psyche are thus the terminal points of a polarity. The still largely unexplored area between them forms the *terra incognita* of future research. Here tremendous problems open out which you have approached from the physical side.

It seems to me that for the time being I have exhausted my psychological ammunition. I have got stuck, on the one hand, in the acausality (or "synchronicity") of certain phenomena of unconscious provenance and, on the other hand, in the qualitative statements of numbers, for here I set foot on territories where I cannot advance without the help and understanding of the other disciplines. In this respect your article is uncommonly valuable and stimulating. I am particularly grateful to you for your appreciation of the transcendent "arranger."

Yours sincerely, C. G. JUNG

---

conforms to law" (cf. Jaffé, *The Myth of Meaning*, pp. 29f.). He arrives at the conclusion that "the regions of matter and psyche are inseparably and unconditionally interconnected" and draws a parallel between the elements of symmetry and the archetypes.

To Eugen Böhler

Dear Professor Böhler,   25 March 1957

This is to thank you for kindly sending me your essay "Der Unternehmer in seiner persönlichen und staatspolitischen Verantwortung."[1] I found it particularly enjoyable because it closely parallels the essay I sent you,[2] though in a thoroughly original way that shows

[1] *Industrielle Organisation* (Zurich), I (1957).
[2] "The Undiscovered Self," CW 10.

how well you have absorbed and digested the psychological view of things. I was most impressed by the noble ethos that shines through everywhere and would doubtless look very odd in the rest of the literature. As you yourself have probably discovered to your disgust, the present time is content with intellectual solutions, or at least tries to master everything by force of reason without the slightest regard for man as he actually is, let alone for the whole man.

My secretary has read your essay with great interest and is dying to get a copy. I would like to lend this wish my ardent support provided that you still have some offprints. Since my secretary acts as a sort of clearing-house for psychological ideas, the gift would not be wasted or fall on stony ground.

I am taking the liberty of submitting to you by the same post an MS which I received from a candidate at Munich University dealing with the psychological aspect of money. I don't want to pass an opinion on it without first hearing a professional view. I would be most grateful if you could give it your attention. Excuse this attack on your valuable time, but I think you may have fellow workers who could help to lighten the task.

Could you come to see me on Saturday the 30th, in the evening, as usual? I plan to go to Bollingen on Monday, after a week brimful of work. With best greetings,

Yours sincerely, c. g. j u n g

To H. J. Barrett

[O R I G I N A L   I N   E N G L I S H]

Dear Mr. Barrett,   26 March 1957

Thank you for your interesting letter.[1] The probability of a very impressive parallelism between individuals is considerable inasmuch as the possibility of divergence and variations is rather limited owing to the fact that we belong to the species *Homo sapiens* and the subdivision of white man. Beside the enormous similarity or likeness the differences are so slight that to a complete outsider they almost disappear. So when you look at a crowd of Chinamen for the first time, they all look the same and you can only make out indi-

---

[1] B. reported a number of remarkable coincidences in his own life with that of an American writer, William Alexander Percy (1885–1942), whose autobiography, *Lanterns on the Levee* (1941), he had read. Both were born on the same day. He asked if Jung regarded this as an instance of a *Doppelgänger* or "double."

vidual characteristics by a careful scrutiny. If anybody is born on the same day and possibly in the same hour, he is like a grape of the same vineyard ripening at the same time. All the grapes of the same site produce about the same wine. This is the truth stated by astrology and experience since time immemorial. Thus it is very probable that you have quite a lot of things in common with Mr. Percy who was born on the same day as you. If you go critically through your list you will find a number of points in common not only with Mr. Percy but with any amount of other individuals (f.i. the Buddhist trend). There are many contributions to the *New Republic*, there are also many students at Harvard, and so on.

I regard such a case not at all as a *Doppelgänger*, which would be to me an unaccountable phenomenon, but rather as a peculiar synchronistic fact, if anything at all. I am not dense enough to overlook the curious fact of the considerable number of coincidences and particularly not the remarkable fact of swallowing a stone,[2] but I hold that there are quite a number of individuals born at the same time with an equally remarkable biographical likeness to you. I remember having read a case of a man born in the vicinity of Buckingham Palace on the same day and at the same hour as Edward VII. His life was the most ridiculous and close-fitting caricature of the King's life.

I don't want to offend you but I should like to call your attention to astrology, which has dealt with such phenomena for about 5000 years. I don't know whether you know the little book I have published with the physicist Prof. W. Pauli: *Nature and the Psyche*, where I make an attempt to cope with phenomena of this kind. I am afraid it is not quite simple apparently, but there are some physicists that seem to understand it.

In a Swiss journal recently an article appeared about an interesting case of coincidence: a man celebrating his birthday; his wife had given him a new pipe as a present. He took a walk, sitting down on a bench under a tree. Another elderly man came along and sat down beside him, smoking the same kind of pipe. Mr. A. drew Mr. B.'s attention to the fact that they both smoked the same pipe, whereupon Mr. B. told him that he was celebrating his birthday on the same date and had received the pipe from his wife. He introduced himself and it turned out that both had the same Christian name Fritz. — The rest is darkness! Mr. A. had the feeling that possibly

[2] He and Percy had both swallowed a fruit stone at the age of 13 and been convinced they would die of appendicitis.

a superior intelligence was at work. It would be most desirable to know a lot more about the psychology of the two fellows and what the possible reason was for this coincidence.

Sincerely yours, C. G. JUNG

To Robert Dietrich

Dear Herr Dietrich,   27 March 1957

If a person knows something, or thinks he does, he can and will speak of his knowledge regardless of whether the object of his knowledge is thereby devalued or not.

Compensatory contents rise up from the unconscious precisely because they possess healing power[1] and are necessary to consciousness.

There is no reason why whole numbers possess certain meanings or qualities, and no reason why elephants or men should exist. These arrangements are simply there as given facts, like the crystalline systems or the discontinuities of physics, even as the whole of creation is a "just-so story."

Your remark that "the real discoveries in the field of knowledge become ever fewer" astounds me. I have the impression that there are more and more of them, and that they become more and more difficult.

Where the determinants of all being come from is an unanswerable question before which I come to a halt, without pretending to know better or a feeling of sacred awe. Here epistemology sets us absolute limits. With best regards,

Yours sincerely, C. G. JUNG

[1] D. asked if making the deep contents of the psyche conscious did not deprive them of their healing power.

To Walter Cimbal

Dear Colleague,   28 March 1957

I was very glad to hear that you are following the developments in psychiatry with so much interest and attention. I see, however,

355

that you have been misled by newspaper reports.[1] I am sorry to tell you, first, that these reports were not put out into the world by me but by a person or persons unknown, and second, that they are not only mistaken but in part downright untrue. The facts underlying these rumours are as follows: Prof. Manfred Bleuler asked me to set down *my experiences* in the field of schizophrenia in a paper for the coming International Congress for Psychiatry in Zurich.[2] This I have done—so far as is possible in the framework of a paper—while confining myself to essentials. In it I have mentioned only in passing the extent to which the toxin hypothesis appears probable to me. The possibility of a toxin was already in the air 50 years ago, as you have set forth at such length. I well remember the cobra poison reaction,[3] which was often discussed at Bleuler's clinic. I cannot claim to be an authority on this matter. The question of the toxin itself interested me far less than its connection with the psychogenesis of schizophrenia. You will find all this discussed in the multigraph I am sending you by the same post.

I cannot regret that a false rumour has led you to write your long

☐ See Cimbal, 2 Mar. 34 (in vol. 1).

[1] C. cited an article by Gerhard Mauz in the German weekly *Die Welt*, 8 Mar. 1957, in which it was stated that Jung was going to read a paper on "Biochemistry or Psychology."

[2] Cf. Bleuler, 23 Mar. 55, n. 1. In his paper "Schizophrenia" (CW 3) Jung mentions the possibility of a toxic element (pars. 570, 583), a theory he had put forward fifty years earlier in "The Psychology of Dementia Praecox," CW 3, pars. 75f., 142, 195f.

[3] In answer to editorial inquiries, Prof. Manfred Bleuler has kindly supplied the following information. His letter (27 Apr. 71) is reproduced in full because of its historical and topical interest:

"I remember very well what Prof. Jung was referring to in the passage you quote from his letter: we heard in Burghölzli that acute psychoses set in after snakebites. Jung therefore raised the question whether his conjectural schizophrenia toxin might be identical with or similar to snake poison.

"The question was, in due course, answered in the negative sense. Above all, it was shown that in their symptomatology snake-bite psychoses are not schizophrenias but, like many other psychoses, are of the acute exogenous reaction type. In 1933 or 1934 cobra poison was experimentally introduced into medicine against neuritis and rheumatism and other ailments. (It was not a success.) Recalling Jung's conjectures, I often used it at that time in the treatment of rheumatism and neuritis among the mentally sound as well as among schizophrenics. The mentally sound and the schizophrenics reacted in exactly the same way.

"Jung's question about cobra poison is the exact counterpart of the modern question as to whether poisoning with LSD and mescalin produces a model of schizophrenia. It does not."

and painstaking letter, for it has brought back many old memories of that seminal time and also of our enjoyable collaboration.[4] So many things were going well until the political madness severed all continuity of meaning.

With cordial thanks and kindest regards,

Yours sincerely, C. G. JUNG

[4] C. was honorary secretary of the International General Medical Society for Psychotherapy and managing editor of its organ, the *Zentralblatt für Psychotherapie und ihre Grenzgebiete*, between 1926 and 1935.

To Traugott Egloff

Dear Herr Egloff,   3 April 1957

Many thanks for your kind letters, which I greatly enjoyed. It would indeed be desirable if my ideas could be expressed in a simple form everyone could understand. In conversation with certain individuals I can do this easily enough, but then it depends on the individual. Since my language is a reflection of my thinking and feeling, I cannot, when faced with a wider public, express myself otherwise than as I am, and I am anything but uncomplicated. I could never have published what I have discovered without a highly differentiated language, which I had to polish endlessly for this purpose, so much so that finally, when I try to express my ideas, I can no longer speak in any other way—unless, as I have said, it be to a particular individual with whom I can enter into an empathetic relationship. I can do this only up to a point with the general public, and then I always relapse into my generalizing and very differentiated conceptual terminology, which is the medium through which and into which I can translate my thoughts. Anyone who wanted to do what you propose would himself have to be on the same level and in the same medium as the general public.

You yourself are in an excellent position to do this, for from the letters you have written me I have never got the impression that language causes you any difficulties. I know of course that your language would not have come out as it did if it had not caused you the greatest trouble beforehand. But as Horace says in his *Ars Poetica*, the best poem is the one that does not make you aware of the

☐ Zurich.

357

difficulties of its composition, and this is also true of such writings of yours as I have seen, namely your letters. You express yourself very clearly and simply, and I believe you when you say that you are able to reach the ear and understanding of your fellows. I know very well that I could never do so myself, and that the man needed for this can only be found among people like you. Why then, I ask you, don't you take up your pen and try to bring to the many what I can communicate in complicated language only to the few? For me and people like me my language is simple and intelligible, but they are all people who have the same necessarily complicated assumptions. With such readers I can afford the luxury of describing things with bare hints and allusions which for other readers are bound to remain obscure for the simple reason that they have never heard of them. I see this even with my medical colleagues, for whom philosophical, historical, religious, etc. allusions are so much Chinese. It needs in fact people like you, who are inwardly gripped by the idea and have experienced its value, to find the form of expression which everyone can understand. I would therefore suggest in all seriousness that you make at least a tentative attempt to describe the essential features of my psychology. I am convinced that it would lie well within your powers. With best regards,

Yours sincerely, C. G. JUNG

To Edith Schröder

Dear Colleague,   April [?] 1957

In reply to your letter of the 26th inst. I must remark that many important things could be said about the theme you propose, "The Significance of Freud's Jewish Descent for the Origin, Content, and Acceptance of Psychoanalysis," if only the problem could be treated on a very high level. Racial theories and the like would be a most unsatisfactory foundation, quite apart from the futility of such speculations. For a real understanding of the Jewish component in Freud's outlook a thorough knowledge would be needed of the specifically Jewish assumptions in regard to history, culture and religion. Since Freud calls for an extremely serious assessment on all these levels, one would have to take a deep plunge into the history

☐ M.D., U. Policlinic, Würzburg.

of the Jewish mind. This would carry us beyond Jewish orthodoxy into the subterranean workings of Hasidism (e.g., the sects of Sabbatai Zwi[1]), and then into the intricacies of the Kabbalah, which still remains unexplored psychologically. The Mediterranean man, to whom the Jews also belong, is not exclusively characterized and moulded by Christianity and the Kabbalah, but still carries within him a living heritage of paganism which could not be stamped out by the Christian Reformation.

I had the privilege of knowing Freud personally and have realized that one must take all these facts into consideration in order to gain a real understanding of psychoanalysis in its Freudian form.

I do not know how far you are acquainted with these various sources, but I can assure you that I myself could carry out such a task only in collaboration with a Jewish scholar since unfortunately I have no knowledge of Hebrew.

In view of the blood-bespattered shadow that hangs over the so-called "Aryan understanding of the Jew," any assessment that fell below the level of these—as it may seem to you—high-falutin conditions would be nothing but a regrettable misunderstanding, especially on German soil.

Despite the blatant misjudgment I have suffered at Freud's hands, I cannot fail to recognize, even in the teeth of my resentment, his significance as a cultural critic and psychological pioneer. A true assessment of Freud's achievement would take us far afield, into dark areas of the mind which concern not only the Jew but European man in general, and which I have sought to illuminate in my writings. Without Freud's "psychoanalysis" I wouldn't have had a clue.

I am sorry that I have nothing but difficulties to offer you, but superficiality would be worse than silence. With collegial regards,

Yours sincerely, c. g. j u n g

[1] Sabbatai Zwi or Zevi (1625–76), of Anatolia, claimed to be the Messiah but later was forced to convert to Islam. Nevertheless the sect of the Sabbatians played for some time a considerable role in the development of Jewish mysticism. Cf. Gershom Scholem, *Sabbatai Ṣevi, The Mystical Messiah* (tr. 1973).

MAY 1957

To Eugen Böhler

Dear Professor Böhler, 12 May 1957

I have just finished reading your essay "Ethik und Wirtschaft"[1] and hasten to tell you how impressed I am. Above all it is the warmth —not to say fire—of your ethical commitment and reformative zeal that enkindles and sweeps one along. Your excellent formulations have lit a number of beacons for me, with regard for instance to the common market and social ethics in general. Thanks to your essay, the latter in particular, which until now has eked out a somewhat nebulous existence in my head, has taken on almost palpable form. Altogether, you are practising on me an extremely beneficial psychotherapy of a special kind, giving me the valuable experience of what I can only call "meaningful collaboration," a working together in spirit and in deed. My often painful isolation in time is thus brought to an end, and I begin to feel in what region of the social cosmos I belong.

For this I owe you my sincere thanks. I wish your essay every success and hope it will be very widely read. With cordial greetings,

Yours sincerely, c. g. j u n g

☐ (Handwritten.)
[1] *Industrielle Organisation*, IV (1957). (= "Ethics and Economy.")

Anonymous

Dear Sir, 20 May 1957

Please excuse the delay in my answer. I am a very busy man. Many thanks for so kindly sending me your drawings. This is one of those imaginative series which I always scrutinize in cases where an unconscious fantasy has been granted free expression. While you were, consciously, starting out on architectural problems you constellated a reaction of the unconscious, which is characteristic in such a case. Whenever and wherever you turn to some extent towards the unconscious it seldom or never answers as one would expect; it is rather as if nature itself were answering. Its answer does not necessarily refer to that piece of reality you have in mind, it is reacting to the whole man and brings into sight what the whole man should know, in other words, it compensates for an insight lacking in conscious-

☐ Switzerland. (Translated by Hildegard Nagel.)

360

ness. Since it has to do with the whole man, its answer also concerns the whole; something fundamentally important is being imparted. But this kind of answer is so personal and so often hits the weakest spot that no one, except during analytic treatment, can presume the right to comment upon it. So it is on these grounds that I do not go further into the nature of the reaction. I must leave the further exposition of the unconscious statement to your own best judgment and meditation. With the highest regards and best thanks,

Sincerely yours, c . g . j u n g

To Mrs. C.

[O R I G I N A L   I N   E N G L I S H]

Dear Mrs. C., 21 May 1957

Sorry to hear that you are having such a difficult time with X. Apparently you are not yet in such a state of simplicity that you could accept the helpful intentions of those knowing less than you. The more you know, the more you will grow out of the number of children needing parents. It seems to me as if there were something fateful about the so-called misunderstandings with X. (. . .) Such things usually occur when the time has come to give up the infantile way and to learn about the adult way, when one creates those people and those relationships one really needs. I am sure you have some amongst your [friends] to whom you might be able to talk and to explain yourself. One has no authority when one cannot risk it, and you will be quite astonished how very helpful people we might consider inferior can be. Even the Pope has a Father Confessor who is a simple priest and by no means one of the Cardinals. If you are all alone then it is because you isolate yourself; if you are humble enough you are never alone. Nothing isolates us more than power and prestige. Try to come down and be humble and you are never alone! I could easily contrive to be marvellously alone, because I never had the chance to get a superior Father Confessor. Not being able to get the necessary help from above, I need to fetch it from below, and what I was able to do you might do also. Try not to be tempted too much to draw help from me; it is so very much more useful to get it indirectly from yourself, from those who got it originally from yourself. My best wishes,

Yours, c . g . j u n g

☐ England.

To M. Esther Harding

[ORIGINAL IN ENGLISH]

Dear Dr. Harding,   30 May 1957

Your letter is a reminder that I have not written to you as I should have done about your book[1] and thanked you *expressis verbis* for your very kind dedication. As at least 90% of our sins are those of omission, I am no exception! As a matter of fact I began reading your book in December, but too much work of all sorts overwhelmed me and set me adrift. The deeper reason was that I was then occupied with the English translation of a paper of mine, "Present and Future." It has since appeared this spring in German (*Gegenwart und Zukunft*) and I am going to send you a copy. The English version is not yet out. Part of it should appear in *Atlantic Monthly*[2] and the whole afterwards.

The trouble is that I have to read so many manuscripts or offprints of my pupils that I simply can't keep up any more. The burden of 82 years is rather noticeable. After I had accomplished the task of writing the paper that was expected from me, I indulged in the vain hope that having fed the world of men by my paper, my own unconscious would spare me as it has done for about three years, spare me, namely, new ideas. As a matter of fact nothing new from within has happened, as it has done so often before, but somebody lifted the iron lid that has been clamped down over my head from without and in came the question: what do you think about the Flying Saucers?[3] — This is the thing that carried me away as soon as I had finished the other work, and again the already frightening pile of unanswered letters and unread manuscripts grew higher. Ever since I have been busy on this new errand. It is most adventurous and has carried me further than I ever expected. But please keep this news under the hat. Otherwise people get funny ideas about my senility.

I don't know why these unpopular things have this uncanny attraction for me. Now I hope, having come to an end with this new task, I shall be able to devote my available time to your book again.

---

[1] *Journey into Self* (1956).

[2] A section of "The Undiscovered Self" appeared under the title "God, the Devil, and the Human Soul" in *The Atlantic Monthly* (Boston), CC:5 (Nov. 1957).

[3] *Ein moderner Mythus: Von Dingen, die am Himmel gesehen werden* was published in 1958. The English translation, *Flying Saucers: A Modern Myth of Things Seen in the Skies*, appeared in 1959; now in CW 10.

For the time being there is nothing in sight that could lure me away from a quiet and friendly occupation.

I have heard quite a little about a certain awakening in theological circles in U.S.A. One could not say the same thing about theologians over here. They much prefer existentialist philosophy because it is very much up to date and entirely harmless. (. . .) Our Christianity with its Summum Bonum conception has entirely forgotten that one of the main aspects of real religion is fear. No charity in all the world can take away the divine terror. It could not even do away with the H-Bomb!

Please don't mind my negligence. The prerogative of old age is to be tolerated.

Please give my best regards to Eleanor Bertine, as well as my thanks for her book.[4] My best wishes to you both,

Cordially yours, c. g. j u n g

[4] *Human Relationships* (New York, 1958), with a foreword by Jung, now in CW 18, pars. 1259ff. Jung received a copy of the German original, *Menschliche Beziehungen: Eine psychologische Studie* (Zurich, 1957).

To Gustav Schmaltz

Dear Schmaltz,   30 May 1957

I understand your wish[1] very well, but must tell you at once that it does not fit in with my situation. I am now getting on for 82 and feel not only the weight of my years and the tiredness this brings, but, even more strongly, the need to live in harmony with the inner demands of my old age. Solitude is for me a fount of healing which makes my life worth living. Talking is often a torment for me, and I need many days of silence to recover from the futility of words. I have got my marching orders and only look back when there's nothing else to do. This journey is a great adventure in itself, but not one that can be talked about at great length. What you think of as a few days of spiritual communion would be unendurable for me with anyone, even with my closest friends. The rest is silence!

□ See Schmaltz, 9 Apr. 32 (in vol. 1).
[1] S., an old acquaintance of Jung's, asked if he could spend a few days with him at Bollingen for an exchange of ideas.

This realization becomes clearer every day as the need to communicate dwindles.

Naturally I should be glad to see you one afternoon for about 2 hours, preferably in Küsnacht, my door to the world. Around August 5th would suit me best, as I shall be at home then in any case. Meanwhile with best greetings,

Yours ever, JUNG

To Erich Neumann

Dear Neumann,   3 June 1957

I was very glad to hear from you again and to see that you have read my brochure.[1] It seems to have been a hit here for a 2nd edition is already on the way.

Basically we are in entire agreement about the so-called "New Ethic,"[2] but I would rather express this tricky problem in somewhat different terms. For it is not really a question of a "new" ethic. Evil is and remains what you know you shouldn't do. But unfortunately man overestimates himself in this respect: he thinks he is free to choose evil or good. He may imagine he can, but in reality, considering the magnitude of these opposites, he is too small and impotent to choose either the one or the other voluntarily and under all circumstances. It is rather that, for reasons stronger than himself, he does or does not do the good he would like, in exactly the same way that evil comes upon him as a misfortune.

An ethic is that which makes it impossible for him *deliberately* to do evil and urges him—often with scant success—to do good. That is to say, he can do good but cannot avoid evil even though his ethic impels him to test the strength of his will in this regard. In reality he is the victim of these powers. He is forced to admit that under no circumstances can he avoid evil absolutely, just as on the other side he may cherish the hope of being able to do good. Since evil is unavoidable, he never quite gets out of sinning and this is the fact that has to be recognized. It gives rise not to a new ethic but to differentiated ethical reflections such as the question: How do I relate to the fact that I cannot escape sin? The guidance

---

[1] "The Undiscovered Self," CW 10.
[2] *Depth Psychology and a New Ethic* (tr. 1969; orig. 1949). Jung's foreword is in CW 18, pars. 1408ff. Cf. Neumann, Dec. 48.

offered by Christ's logion, "If thou knowest what thou doest . . . ,"[3] points the way to the ethical solution of the problem: I know that I do not want to do evil yet do it just the same, not by my own choice but because it overpowers me. As a man I am a weakling and fallible, so that evil can overpower me. I know that I do it and know what I have done and know that all my life long I shall stand in the torment of this contradiction. I shall avoid evil when I can but shall always fall into this hole. But I shall try to live as if it were not so; I shall make the best of a bad job, like the unjust steward[4] who knowingly presented a false account. I shall do this not because I want to deceive myself, let alone the Lord, but so that I may not give public offence on account of the weakness of my brothers, and may preserve my moral attitude and some semblance of human dignity. I am therefore like a man who feels hellishly afraid in a dangerous situation and would have run for his life had he not pulled himself together on account of others, feigning courage in his own eyes and theirs in order to save the situation. I have not made my panic unreal but have got away with it by hiding behind the mask of courage. It is an act of supreme hypocrisy, just another sin without which we would all be lost. This is not a new ethic, merely a more differentiated one, disabused of illusion, but the same as it always was.

You can tell these subtle reflections to Zeus but not to an ox.[5] They are so subtle because they presuppose quite special conditions. They are valid only for a person who is really conscious of his shadow, but for anyone who treats his shadow as a passing inconvenience or, lacking all scruple and moral responsibility, brushes it off as irrelevant, they offer dangerous opportunities for aberrations of moral judgment, such as are characteristic of people with a moral defect who consequently suffer from an intellectual inflation. Many a conflict can be eased by winking the moral eye or by stretching a point or two, but one should know that it has to be paid for, since "every sin avenges itself on earth."[6]

---

[3] An uncanonical saying of Jesus, relating to Luke 6:4, in Codex Bezae Cantabrigiensis, a Greek New Testament MS of the 5th cent. The complete passage runs: "On the same day, seeing one working on the sabbath, he said unto him: Man, if indeed thou knowest what thou doest, thou are blessed: but if thou knowest not, thou art cursed, and a transgressor of the law." Cf. James, *The Apocryphal New Testament*, p. 33.

[4] Luke 16:1–13.

[5] "Quod licet Jovi non licet bovi."

[6] Goethe, *Wilhelm Meisters Lehrjahre*, Book II, ch. 13.

Just now I am engaged on a work with a quite different theme, but the discussion made it necessary for me to mention the ethical problem. I couldn't avoid repudiating the expression "new ethic," though I named no names.[7] This is yet another of those sins, a kind of disloyalty, which descends like doom the moment I have to protect the incomparably higher aspect of our psychology from the crudities of vulgar understanding, and to the general advantage at that. In this case the whole difficulty lies with the slipperiness of language. Hence one is forced to scatter sand, and occasionally it gets into the eyes of the reader.

I am looking forward to your extension of *Origins* to child psychology.[8] Plenty of illustrative material could be found there.

I feel very uncertain about the question of pessimism and optimism[9] and must leave the solution to fate. The only one who could decide this dilemma—God—has so far withheld his answer.

I hope all goes well with you in *ce meilleur des mondes possibles. Tout cela est bien dit, mais il faut cultiver notre jardin.* With best greetings,

Ever sincerely yours, JUNG

[7] The book Jung was working on was "Flying Saucers" (cf. Harding, 30 May 57, n. 3), where the ethical problem is discussed in pars. 676f. of the CW 10 version; par. 676 also cites the uncanonical saying and the parable of the unjust steward. There is, however, no reference to a "new ethic," so one must conclude that Jung later deleted his repudiation of the term.

[8] N. had planned for some time to extend certain concepts in his *The Origins and History of Consciousness* to the psychological development of the child. The plan remained uncompleted but the extant MS was posthumously edited by his widow, Julie Neumann, and appeared as *Das Kind* (1963; tr., *The Child*, 1973).

[9] N. thought that "The Undiscovered Self" might be regarded as too pessimistic, and that individuation, as a collective process, would be successful even if it took centuries (cf. esp. pars. 582–83).

To Ralf Winkler

Dear Herr Winkler,   5 June 1957

I am sorry you knocked at my door in vain, and that my secretary may not have made the true state of affairs sufficiently clear to you.[1] I understand your need for people very well, also your wish to

☐ Bassersdorf, Cant. Zurich.

[1] W. had appeared unannounced at Jung's door in Küsnacht in order to tell Jung

make contact with people who really have something to say. At the age of nearly 82 perhaps I may say without being presumptuous that in my long life I have seen so many people, and also helped them, that my present seclusion seems to me well earned and ought not to be grudged. The obligation to be there for others must now be taken over by others who have more strength. This has nothing to do with "lack of humanity" on my part, rather I appeal to your humanity to understand my situation.

Perhaps you also will one day understand that it is only the man who is really capable of being alone, and without bitterness, who attracts other people. Then he doesn't need to seek them any more, they come all by themselves, among them the very ones whom he himself needs. With my best wishes,

Yours, c. g. j u n g

---

his personal problems. Because Jung did not receive him, W. blamed him for want of humanity and left his address in the hope of receiving a letter.

To Bernhard Lang

Dear Colleague, 8 June 1957

Sincerest thanks for your kind letter.[1] An author is always delighted to learn that his voice has been heard. He could wish for nothing better.

. . .

I should be grateful if you would tell me again what you think Martin Buber was trying to prove to me. I could not decipher the word.[2] Buber is of the erroneous opinion that a metaphysical assertion is either true or untrue, and he doesn't understand that as a psychologist and psychiatrist I regard what is said and believed primarily as a statement which, though a fact in itself, cannot be asserted to be true or untrue. For instance, I can examine the state-

□ M.D., Langenthal, Cant. Bern.
[1] Expressing deep appreciation of "The Undiscovered Self."
[2] The word is "Immanentismus." In a letter in answer to Jung's question L., not being able to remember exactly what he had written, summed up the controversy between Buber and Jung as follows: "Is God a 'component' of the human psyche, i.e., something immanent, or a transcendental mystery, as Buber postulates?" Cf. Lang, 14 June 57, n. 1.

ment that Christ rose up at Easter in the body from the psychological standpoint without at the same time maintaining it is true or untrue. One can say of all metaphysical statements that their factuality consists in the fact of their being asserted, but none of them can be proved to be true or untrue. It does not come within the scope of a science like psychology to ascertain the truth or untruth of metaphysical assertions. It is a thoroughly outmoded standpoint, and has been so ever since the time of Immanuel Kant, to think that it lies within the power of man to assert a metaphysical truth. This is and remains the prerogative of belief. Belief in turn is a psychological fact, though it is far from being a proof. The most it tells us is that such a belief exists, and that the belief meets a psychological need. Since no human need is without a reason, we may also expect that the need for metaphysical assertions is based on a corresponding reason, even if we are not conscious of this reason. Nothing is thereby asserted, nothing denied, and this is just what Buber doesn't understand; for he is a theologian who naïvely thinks that what he believes must necessarily be so. We shall never be able to understand other philosophies or religions if everyone thinks his conviction is the only right one. Thus Buber blandly assumes that everyone thinks the same as he does when he says "God." But in reality Buber means Yahweh, the orthodox Christian means the Trinity, the Mohammedan Allah, the Buddhist Buddha, the Taoist Tao, and so on. Everyone insists on his standpoint and imagines he possesses the sole truth; therefore I counsel modesty, or rather the willingness to suppose that God can express himself in different languages. But it is the theologians of every variety who buttonhole God and prescribe to him what he has to be like in their estimation. This leads to no understanding between men, of which we stand in such dire need today. My apparent scepticism is only a recognition of the epistemological barrier, of which Buber doesn't seem to possess the ghost of an idea. When I say that God is first and foremost our conception, this is twisted into God is "nothing but our conception." In reality there is a background of existence which we can intuit at most but cannot transpose into the sphere of our knowledge. In any case a serious science should not succumb to this arrogance. The relation with transcendence is certainly a necessity for us, but gives us no power over it. With collegial regards,

Yours sincerely, C. G. JUNG

To the Rev. H. L. Philp

[ORIGINAL IN ENGLISH]

Dear Mr. Philp,   11 June 1957

The question about "sin" etc. you ask me[1] seems to me difficult to answer, as I don't understand where you see a difficulty in my way of using these "theological" terms. I beg your pardon, but speaking of "sin" or "evil" can be quite colloquial, at least this is the case with myself. I talk of them in a quite ordinary way so that everybody can understand what I mean. The same is the case when I mention the "Fall." It is Adam's story as we read it in Genesis. Thus I mean by "sin" an offence against our moral code, by "evil" the black fiend ever working in man's nature, and by "Fall" the disobedience against, and the deviation of the primordial Man from, God's command. These terms designate simple and recognizable psychological situations for ever repeating themselves in all human lives. The "Fall" f.i. covers the regular experience that I find myself deviating from the prescribed way from the very start. I am tempted and even possessed by evil forces (like St. Paul) time and again, and sin is *nolens volens* mingled with my daily bread. You find such statements moreover everywhere in all imaginable forms. It is f.i. bad and even evil to step on the chief's shadow or over a sleeping man. It is sinful to scrape a skin with an iron knife instead of a flint.[2] Whoever has bothered himself about the eternal problem πόθεν τὸ κακόν [whence evil?] has invented the story of a primordial awkwardness. A modern man with a yellow streak will explain himself f.i. by the fact that his grandfather's brother suffered from epilepsy and the alienist will nod his head: "I told you so."

The terms "sin" and "evil" are under no conditions "meaningless" and they are in no way in need of any particular framework, as little as the terms "good" and "bad," since they are merely emphatic expressions of an emotional, negative reaction in their colloquial or everyday use. However, where strong affects are in question we can expect unmistakable traces of a religious framework, i.e., a "theological" system of reference. But anybody, provided he is mad enough, can say "God damn it" without being conscious of a particular framework beyond colloquial habits.

When I speak of "original sin" I mean what the doctrine of the

---

[1] P.'s letter and this answer are published in Philp, *Jung and the Problem of Evil,* pp. 210ff.

[2] Cf. "A Psychological View of Conscience," CW 10, par. 836.

Church calls the *peccatum originale*, Adam's sin, i.e., man's disobedience clearly visible in everybody's life, his inevitable deviation from the state of grace, where there has been no sin yet. The latter begins with the dawn of consciousness, which implies "conscience," i.e., moral awareness and discrimination. Cases in which this function is absent are pathological (moral insanity).

Of course I am unable, as anybody is, to define what evil is in itself. There is nothing which at times cannot be called evil. It is a subjective qualification supported by a more or less general consent. Deviation from the numen seems to be universally understood as being the worst and the most original sin.

This is, as I hope, an elucidation of my approach to the matter in question. The early part of October would suit me perfectly.

Sincerely yours, C. G. JUNG

To Bernhard Lang

Dear Colleague,   14 June 1957

Your letter astounded me.[1] What Buber knows of me is based exclusively on my writings, or rather only on bits of them. He has completely misunderstood them because he has no conception of psychology. Psychology as I understand it is a science and not an opinion. So when we are dealing with a metaphysical statement we are dealing with the fact that the psyche makes such a statement. A descriptive science will therefore say: it is of the nature of the psyche to make such statements, no matter what their content may be. It doesn't matter whether it states a truth or not. Thus when I remain within the confines of my science, the established truth consists in my proof that such statements are made, but not that they are true or untrue in the philosophical or religious sense. Over and above this, psychology can establish in what relation these statements stand to the life of the psyche, and it will distinguish whether

---

[1] L. asked Jung to explain his statement in "The Undiscovered Self" (par. 509) that the life of the individual was determined by "a transcendent authority" and that there is "the incontrovertible experience of an intensely personal, reciprocal relationship between man and an extramundane authority which acts as a counterpoise to the 'world' and its 'reason.'" He wondered if an "extramundane authority" could be squared with Buber's criticism of Jung's alleged concept of an "immanent" God, i.e., God as a component of the human psyche.

they are merely individual opinions or collectively valid ideas. Taking the God-concept as an example, this is demonstrably grounded on archetypal premises corresponding essentially to the instincts. They are given and inherited structures, the instinctual bases of psychic behaviour as well as of thinking. These structures possess a natural numinosity (i.e., emotional value) and consequently a certain degree of autonomy. When, for instance, a so-called epiphany occurs, it is the projected appearance of this psychic structure, that is, of an image based on the archetypal structure. Owing to the autonomy and numinosity of the structure it appears as if it had a life of its own, different from my life. We then say: God has appeared. What can be established is not that God has appeared, but on closer examination the structure of an archetype. Thus far can science go. It cannot cross this threshold and assert that it was God himself. Only belief can do that. I do not appeal to this belief. In view of my human imperfection, I am satisfied with the statement that I have seen a divine image, but I am unable to make out whether it is God himself. Outside this image and its dynamic qualities, it is utterly impossible for me to make out anything about the nature of God. So when I say (in "The Undiscovered Self") that the social and political independence of the individual is guaranteed only by the feeling that he is "anchored in God," I mean that he divines the relationship through this intense inner experience. No one in his right senses would assert that the idea he has formed of a thing through his experience of it is identical with the nature of that thing. If he did, he would immediately collide with the fact that there are thousands of other opinions about this same thing, some of them like his own, others totally different, because no man can agree with another to the point where their respective ideas would be identical.

Buber completely overlooks the existence of the individual psyche. He also thinks he can override all other ideas of God by assuming that his God-image is *the* God-image.

I am far from denying the possibility that our psychic structure projects an image of *something*. But there is no reason whatever to suppose that the psychic image reflects the nature of its unknowable background either completely or in part or not at all; we cannot jump over our own heads since all we can ever assert is our own conception. No one can get round the self-limitation of human judgment; it is part of our human limitation in general. The psyche has

371

its own intrinsic reality which cannot be got rid of by believing in something. What I assert is not belief but knowledge, not of God himself but of the facts of the psyche. Apparently they are totally unknown to Buber, even though Plato has expounded this whole problem with unsurpassable clarity in his parable of the cave.[2]

To return to the psychic structure which projects the images or makes "metaphysical statements," we do not know what it itself rests on. We only know that something is there. From this we may postulate that beyond the psychic structure there is something—a substrate, an *ousia*—about which it is impossible in principle to make any assertion because it would only be yet another conception.

Hoping I have expressed myself with sufficient clarity, I remain, with collegial regards,

Yours sincerely, C. G. JUNG

[2] In the 7th book of *Republic* Plato tells his famous parable of the cave as an illustration of his theory of eternal Ideas or Forms: man is compared to a creature living in a cave, bound immovably hand and foot. At his back is the entrance to the cave, and all he can see are the shadows of the forms passing outside thrown on the wall in front of him; mistakenly he believes the shadows to be the real things.

To J. C. Vernon

Dear Sir,

[ORIGINAL IN ENGLISH]

18 June 1957

Since the archetypes are the instinctual forms of mental behaviour it is quite certain that, inasmuch as animals possess a "mind," their mind also follows archetypal patterns, and presumably the same that are operative in the human mind.[1] As we do not know the actual status of an archetype in the unconscious and only know it in that form in which it becomes conscious, it is impossible to describe the human archetype and to compare it to an animal archetype. But the hypothesis is that they are the same. This simply because there is no reason, or at least we don't see one, why it should be otherwise. If I say that we do not know "the ultimate derivation of the archetype," I mean that we are unable to observe and describe the archetype in its unconscious condition. When I say that

☐ Exmouth, England.
[1] V. asked: "Shall we not find the origin, or at least the development, of the archetypes by examining the family tree from which we trace our physical descent?"

archetypes evolve from instincts, I describe no facts. It is a mere hypothesis—albeit a likely one. But actually the facts of this origin are unknown in detail, although we may trace some lines leading into our animal ancestry. Thus f.i. the religious factor you mention. It is of course, as you say, an absurdity to isolate the human mind from nature in general. There is no difference in principle between the animal and the human psyche. The kinship of the two is too obvious.

Sincerely yours, C. G. JUNG

To Stephen I. Abrams

[ORIGINAL IN ENGLISH]

Dear Mr. Abrams,   20 June 1957

It is indeed a noteworthy fact that a young man of 18 is planning to work in parapsychology.[1] As you know, Prof. Rhine's work is a hitherto unique approach to the study of parapsychological phenomena. The statistical method demands an experimental arrangement of the simplest nature: its principle is the greatest material in the shortest time, since only very great numbers are of any conceivable value. This demands also suitable means and many collaborators. If you are able to invent a similarly simple question and a similar method you can continue this kind of research. But here is just the trouble. It is extremely difficult to find such a question. I must say that I gave much thought to it, but I have not yet succeeded in overcoming the difficulty. My approach to parapsychology has been of a different kind. Instead of asking myself the question of the general statistical truth of the phenomena, I have tried to find a psychological approach, namely to answer the question of the psychological conditions under which parapsychological phenomena occur. This approach, however, is equally difficult since it demands an unusual amount of psychological knowledge, particularly of the psychology of the unconscious. Such knowledge can only be acquired by practical work in this field. Since it is a matter of highly complex arrangements, one cannot produce ordinary statistical results, as you cannot

☐ Chicago, Illinois.
[1] A. was attending the Parapsychological Laboratory at Duke U. under J. B. Rhine. He planned a work on the experimental confirmation of Jung's theory of synchronicity and asked him for suggestions. In 1961 he became Director of the Parapsychological Laboratory at Oxford.

experiment with complex facts which are apt to be full of chance variations. To deal with such intricate facts you need certain hypothetical patterns serving as a means of comparison. I call them archetypes. To understand this concept you must have a fair knowledge of practical psychology in order to perceive these structures at work. If you look at my other writings you get an idea of what is needed in that respect. You would be entirely mistaken if you should assume that there is any kind of philosophy behind it. There are facts behind it, but for lack of psychological knowledge people don't see them. You must realize that parapsychology is one of the most difficult problems ever put to the human mind. Even nuclear physics can do better. The trouble with parapsychology is that the very framework of our understanding and explanation, namely time, space, and causality, becomes questionable. That is the reason why I went back to the problem of Geulincx and Leibniz[2] in order to find a possible principle of connection other than causality. The principle of synchronicity represents the essential particularity of a non-statistical world, where facts are not measured by numbers but by their psychological significance.

I would not say that it is impossible to deal with problems of synchronicity by experimental means. Rhine's method shows the contrary, but any step beyond Rhine will complicate the question of probability and will become correspondingly unwieldy. The approach from the side of psychology, on the other hand, demands a thorough revolution of our scientific thinking, namely the recognition of all the chance or random material excluded by statistics, i.e., just the things that fall under the table when you apply the statistical principle. But since improbable facts do exist—otherwise there would be no statistical mean—we are still on the firm foundation of facts, however improbable they are. It has been my endeavour to complement the obvious insufficiency of statistical truth through a description of improbable facts and their nature, within the confines of psychology at least. I soon understood that parapsychological facts are interwoven with psychic conditions and cannot be really understood without psychology. It is, of course, in our days still the most important problem to show that they really exist, and it is an ulterior problem *how* they exist. This is the task of the psychology of the unconscious.

As far as I can see, there are only two ways of approach to para-

[2] Arnold Geulincx (1624–99), Flemish philosopher. Concerning the problem of Geulincx and Leibniz cf. "Synchronicity," par. 937, n. 58.

psychology: the one is the experimental way without psychology, and the other the psychological approach without hope of a statistical method.

Hoping I have given you a fair picture of the actual situation, I remain,

Yours, c. g. jung

To Bernhard Lang

Dear Colleague, June 1957

Many thanks for your friendly letter, which shows that the Buber-Jung controversy is a serious matter for you.[1] And so indeed it is, for here that threshold which separates two epochs plays the principal role. I mean by that threshold the theory of knowledge whose starting-point is Kant. On that threshold minds go their separate ways: those that have understood Kant, and the others that cannot follow him. I will not enter here into the *Critique of Pure Reason*, but will try to make things clear to you from a different, more human standpoint.

Let us take as an example the believing person who has Buber's attitude to belief. He lives in the same world as me and appears to be a human being like me. But when I express doubts about the absolute validity of his statements, he expostulates that he is the happy possessor of a "receiver," an organ by means of which he can know or tune in the Transcendent. This information obliges me to reflect on myself and ask myself whether I also possess a like receiver which can make the Transcendent, i.e., something that transcends consciousness and is by definition unknowable, knowable. But I find in myself nothing of the sort. I find I am incapable of knowing the infinite and eternal or paradoxical; it is beyond my powers. I may *say* that I know what is infinite and eternal; I may even assert that I have experienced it; but that one could actually *know* it is impossible because man is neither an infinite nor an eternal being. He can know only the part but not the whole, not the infinite and eternal. So when the believer assures me that I do not possess the organ he possesses, he makes me aware of my humanity, of my limita-

---

[1] L. asked: "Do you regard yourself as a believing person and is your statement 'modern consciousness abhors belief' simply the legitimate, descriptive statement of a scientist about the present state of consciousness, or do you identify yourself personally with this attitude?"

tion which he allegedly does not have. He is the superior one, who regretfully points out my deformity or mutilation. Therefore I speak of the *beati possidentes* of belief, and this is what I reproach them with: that they exalt themselves above our human stature and our human limitation and won't admit to pluming themselves on a possession which distinguishes them from the ordinary mortal. I start with the confession of not knowing and not being able to know; believers start with the assertion of knowing and being able to know. There is now only one truth, and when we ask the believers what this truth is they give us a number of very different answers with regard to which the one sure thing is that each believer announces his own particular truth. Instead of saying: To me personally it seems so, he says: It is so, thus putting everybody else automatically in the wrong.

Now in my estimation it would be more human, more decent, and altogether more appropriate if we carefully inquired beforehand what other people think and if we expressed ourselves less categorically. It would be more becoming to do this than to believe subjective opinions and to damn the opinions of others as fallacies. If we do not do this, the inevitable consequence is that only my subjective opinion is valid, I alone possess the true receiver, and everyone else is deformed who lacks such an important organ as belief is considered to be. Buber is unconscious of the fact that when he says "God" he is expressing his subjective belief and imagining by "God" something other people could not sanction. What, for instance, would a Buddhist say about Buber's conception of God? My human limitation does not permit me to assert that I know God, hence I cannot but regard all assertions about God as relative because subjectively conditioned—and this out of respect for my brothers, whose other conceptions and beliefs have as much to justify them as mine. If I am a psychologist I shall try to take these differences seriously and to understand them. But under no circumstances shall I assume that if the other person doesn't share my opinion it is due to a deformity or lack of an organ. How could I have any communication at all with a person if I approached him with the absolutist claims of the believer? Though I am sure of my subjective experience, I must impose on myself every conceivable restriction in interpreting it. I must guard against identifying with my subjective experience. I consider all such identifications as serious psychological mistakes indicative of total lack of criticism. For what purpose am I endowed with a modicum of intelligence if I do not apply it in these decisive matters? Instead of being delighted with the fact of my inner experience, I am then using it merely to exalt myself, through my subjective belief, above all those who do not accept my interpretation of the experience. The experience itself is not in question, only the absolutizing interpretation of it. If I have a vision of Christ, this is far from proving that it was Christ, as we know only too well from our psychiatric practice. I therefore treat all confessions of faith with extreme reserve. I am ready at any time to confess to the inner experience but not to my metaphysical interpretation, otherwise I am implicitly laying claim to universal recognition. On the contrary, I must confess that I cannot interpret the inner experience in its metaphysical reality, since its essential core is of a transcendental nature and beyond my human grasp. Naturally I am free to believe something about it, but that is my subjective prejudice which I don't want to thrust on other people, nor can I ever prove that it is universally valid. As a matter of fact we have every reason to suppose that it is not.

I am sorry to say that everything men assert about God is twaddle, for no man can know God. Knowing means seeing a thing in such a way that all can know it, and for me it means absolutely nothing if I profess a knowledge which I alone possess. Such people are found in the lunatic asylum. I therefore regard the proposition that belief is knowledge as absolutely misleading. What has really happened to these people is that they have been overpowered by an inner experience. They then make an interpretation which is as subjective as possible and believe it, instead of remaining true to the original experience. Take as an example our national saint Nicholas von der Flüe: he sees an overwhelmingly terrifying face which he involuntarily interprets as God and then twiddles it around until it turns into the image of the Trinity, which still hangs today in the church at Sachseln.[2] This image has nothing to do with the original experience, but represents the Summum Bonum and divine love, which are miles away from God's Yahwistic terrors or the "wrath fire" of Boehme. Actually after this vision Nicholas should have preached: "God is terrible." But he believed his own interpretation instead of the immediate experience.

This is a typical phenomenon of belief and one sees from it how such confessions of faith come about. Because this so-called knowledge is illegitimate, inner uncertainty makes it fanatical and gen-

[2] Nicholas von der Flüe was baptized and buried in the church of Sachseln, Cant. Unterwalden. Cf. Jung, "Brother Klaus," and Blanke, 2 May 45, n. 12.

erates missionary zeal, so that through the concurrence of the multitude the subjective interpretation, precarious enough as it is, may not be shaken still further. But the certitude of inner experience generates greater certainty than the interpretation we have imposed upon it. Buber fails to see that when he says "My experience is God" he is interpreting it in such a way as to force everyone into believing his opinion—because he himself is uncertain; for confronted with the great mystery no mortal man can aver that he has given a reliable interpretation, otherwise it would no longer be a mystery. It is only too plain to see that such people have no mysteries any more, like those Oxfordites who think they can call up God on the telephone.

When you ask me if I am a believer I must answer "no." I am loyal to my inner experience and have *pistis* in the Pauline sense,[3] but I do not presume to believe in my subjective interpretation, which would seem to me highly obnoxious when I consider my human brothers. I "abhor" the belief that I or anybody else could be in possession of an absolute truth. As I have said, I regard this unseemliness as a psychological mistake, a hidden inflation. If you have inner experiences you are always in danger of identifying with them and imagining that you are specially favoured, or are a special species of man who possesses one organ more than others. I know only too well how difficult it is for people to stand off from their own experience far enough to see the difference between the authentic experience and what they have made of it. For if they stood by it, they would reach very weighty conclusions which could severely shake their interpretation. Obviously they want to avoid these consequences, and my critical psychology is therefore a thorn in their flesh. I can also confirm that I regard all declarations of faith, which Buber for instance has in mind, as an object of psychological research, since they are subjective human statements about actual experiences whose real nature cannot be fathomed by man in any case. These experiences contain a real mystery, but the statements made about them don't. Thus it remained a real mystery to Brother Klaus what that terrifying countenance of God actually meant.

Incidentally, I would like to remark that the concept "transcendent" is relative. Transcendence is simply that which is unconscious

[3] Cf. "Psychology and Religion," par. 9: "*pistis*, that is to say, trust or loyalty, faith and confidence in a certain experience of a numinous nature. . . . The conversion of Paul is a striking example of this." Also I Cor. 12:9: "To another faith by the same Spirit . . ."

to us, and it cannot be established whether this is permanently inaccessible or only at present. In the past many things were transcendent that are now the subject-matter of science. This should make one cautious—especially when dealing with ultimate things man cannot know about. We cannot, after all, assert that belief enables us to attain godlike knowledge. We merely believe we can become godlike, but we must modestly accept the fact that we cannot thrust this belief on anybody else. We could never prove that this would not be an unbelievable presumption. I for one am convinced that it is.

All that I have written you is Kantian epistemology expressed in everyday psychological language. I hope by this means to have gained your ear.

In case my idea of interpretation should seem unintelligible to you, I would like to add a few words more. Interpretation by faith seeks to represent the experienced content of a vision, for instance, as the visible manifestation of a transcendental Being, and it invariably does so in terms of a traditional system and then asserts that this representation is the absolute truth. Opposed to this is my view, which also interprets, in a sense. It interprets by comparing *all* traditional assumptions and does not assert that Transcendence itself has been perceived; it insists only on the reality of the fact that an experience has taken place, and that this is exactly the form it took. I compare this experience with all other experiences of the kind and conclude that a process is going on in the unconscious which expresses itself in various forms. I am aware that this process is actually going on, but I do not know what its nature is, whether it is psychic, whether it comes from an angel or from God himself. We must leave these questions open, and no belief will help us over the hurdle, for we do not know and can never know. With collegial regards,

Yours sincerely, C. G. JUNG

To Aniela Jaffé

Dear Aniela,   Bollingen, 9 July 1957

. . .

Unlike me, you torment yourself with the ethical problem. I am tormented *by* it. It is a problem that cannot be caught in any

□ (Handwritten.)

formula, twist and turn it as I may; for what we are dealing with here is the living will of God. Since it is always stronger than mine, I find it always confronting me; I do not hurl myself upon it, it hurls itself upon me; I put up no resistance yet am compelled to fight against it, for God's power is greater than my will. I can only be its servant, but a servant with knowledge who can make infinitesimal corrections for better or worse. I am dependent on God's verdict, not he on mine. Therefore I cannot reason about ethics. I feel it unethical because it is a presumption. God presents me with facts I have to get along with. If he doesn't reject them, I cannot. I can only modify them the tiniest bit.

Good holidays!

Yours, c. g. j.

To J. G. Thompson

[ORIGINAL IN ENGLISH]

Dear Mr. Thompson, 23 July 1957

If somebody has a vision it doesn't mean that he is necessarily insane. Perfectly normal people can have visions in certain moments. St. Paul was definitely not insane nor was his vision extraordinary. I know quite a number of cases of visions of Christ or auditions of a voice from within. Being a highly religious man St. Paul was almost expected to have such experiences, as he had also received his Gospel through immediate revelation. As experience shows, the figure one sees is not necessarily identical with the person one identifies with it, just as the picture by an artist is not identical with the original; but it is obvious that the vision of Christ was a most important religious experience to St. Paul.

Being a rather old man I am not capable of answering any letters. If you should have some more questions important to your spiritual welfare, my secretary will be answering them.

. . .

Faithfully yours, c. g. j u n g

☐ Grand Cayman, British West Indies.

380

To Meggie Reichstein

Dear Dr. Reichstein,   2 August 1957

Thank you very much for the great trouble you have taken in working through Sumantri Hardjo Rakosa's book on "The Conception of Man in Indonesian Religion as a Basis for Psychotherapy,"[1] and for furnishing such a clear report of its contents. Your résumé of his remarks on my psychology was most helpful. They paint a picture of the limitations of his understanding.

You are right in supposing that the author hasn't grasped much of my thinking. In his ideas he remains stuck in the traditional outlook of the East. He mistakes me for a philosopher, which I am quite definitely not. I am a psychologist and empiricist, and for me the meaning of life does not lie in annulling it for the sake of an alleged "possibility of transcendental existence" which nobody knows how to envisage. We are men and not gods. The meaning of human development is to be found in the fulfilment of *this* life. It is rich enough in marvels. And not in detachment from this world. How can I fulfil the meaning of my life if the goal I set myself is the "disappearance of individual consciousness"? What am I without this individual consciousness of mine? Even what I have called the "self" functions only by virtue of an ego which hears the voice of that greater being.

I fear I have saddled you with a thankless task in working through this book. That you have discharged it with such patience and lucidity was a very great help. With best regards,

Yours sincerely, C. G. JUNG

☐ Zurich.
[1] Diss., U. of Leiden, 1956; in Dutch.

To Ellen Gregori

Dear Fräulein Gregori,   3 August 1957

I have read with much interest your essay on "Rilke's Psychological Knowledge in the Light of Jungian Theory."[1] Your argument and the beautiful quotations make it very clear that Rilke drew from the

☐ Marquartstein, Bavaria.
[1] The essay was never published.

same deep springs as I did—the collective unconscious. He as a poet or visionary, I as a psychologist and empiricist.

I hope you will allow me—as a token of my esteem for your work—to add a few remarks that came into my head as I was reading. I cannot escape the feeling that for all his high poetic gifts and intuition Rilke was never quite a contemporary. Of course poets are timeless phenomena, and the lack of modernity in Rilke is a badge of genuine poetry-craft. Often he reminds me of a medieval man: half troubadour, half monk. His language and the form he gave his images have something transparent about them, like the windows of Gothic cathedrals. But he doesn't have what it takes to make a man complete: body, weight, shadow. His high ethos, his capacity for abnegation, and perhaps also his physical frailty naturally led him towards a goal of completeness, but not of perfection. Perfection, it seems to me, would have broken him.

I wish somebody could be found who would set the inner and outer data of this life in order and interpret it with the necessary psychological understanding. It would certainly be well worth doing.

Again with best thanks for your essay and kind regards,

Yours sincerely, c. g. j u n g

To Betty Grover Eisner

[ORIGINAL IN ENGLISH]

Dear Mrs. Eisner,   12 August 1957

Thank you for your kind letter.[1] Experiments along the line of mescalin and related drugs are certainly most interesting, since such drugs lay bare a level of the unconscious that is otherwise accessible only under peculiar psychic conditions. It is a fact that you get certain perceptions and experiences of things appearing either in mystical states or in the analysis of unconscious phenomena, just like the primitives in their orgiastic or intoxicated conditions. I don't feel happy about these things, since you merely fall into such experiences without being able to integrate them. The result is a sort of theosophy, but it is not a moral and mental acquisition. It is the eternally primitive man having experience of his ghost-land, but it is not an achievement of your cultural development. To have so-called reli-

☐ Clinical psychologist, Los Angeles, California.
[1] E. stated that for her LSD was "almost a religious drug."

gious visions of this kind has more to do with physiology but nothing with religion. It is only that mental phenomena are observed which one can compare to similar images in ecstatic conditions. Religion is a way of life and a devotion and submission to certain superior facts—a state of mind which cannot be injected by a syringe or swallowed in the form of a pill. It is to my mind a helpful method to the barbarous Peyotee, but a regrettable regression for a cultivated individual, a dangerously simple "Ersatz" and substitute for a true religion.

Sincerely yours, C. G. JUNG

To Roswitha N.

Dear Miss Roswitha,   17 August 1957

Many thanks for the kind letter you sent me on my birthday. I have heard with great sorrow of your father's illness and can only hope that it will soon take a turn for the better.

I was very interested to hear of the success of your lecture. My little book on Job is naturally meant for older people, and especially for those who have some knowledge of my psychology. They must also have pondered a good deal on religious questions in order to understand it properly. Because there are very few people who meet these conditions, my book has been widely misunderstood. They should also know something about the unconscious. As an introduction to this I would recommend another little book of mine, "On the Psychology of the Unconscious," and, on the religious problem, "Psychology and Religion." *Symbolik des Geistes* and *Von den Wurzeln des Bewusstseins* probe rather more deeply into these matters.

You are undoubtedly right to tackle the problem of society first. There you learn the ways of other people and are forced to find a common basis of understanding.

The question of the young architect as to what it might mean for God if he demands Christianity of us: first one must understand what Christianity means. This is obviously the psychology of the Christian and that is a complicated phenomenon which cannot be taken for granted. And what something might mean for God we

□ The recipient was a young Swiss girl about 20 years old.

cannot know at all, for we are not God. One must always remember that God is a mystery, and everything we say about it is said and believed by human beings. We make images and concepts, and when I speak of God I always mean the image man has made of him. But no one knows what he is like, or he would be a god himself. Looking at it in one way, however, we do indeed partake of divinity, as Christ himself pointed out when he said: "Ye are gods."[1] You will find a lot about this in *Answer to Job*.

Your question why it is more difficult for us to do good than to do evil is not quite rightly put, because doing good is as a rule easier than doing evil. True, it is not always easy to do good, but the consequences of doing good are so much more pleasant than those of doing evil that if only for practical reasons one eventually learns to do good and eschew evil. Of course evil thwarts our good intentions and, to our sorrow, cannot always be avoided. The task is then to understand why this is so and how it can be endured. In the end good and evil are human judgments, and what is good for one man is evil for another. But good and evil are not thereby abolished; this conflict is always going on everywhere and is bound up with the will of God. It is really a question of recognizing God's will and wanting to do it.

The other question of what meaning the Bible ascribes to society is of great importance, for the solidarity and communal life of mankind go to the roots of existence. But the question is complicated by the fact that the individual should also be able to maintain his independence, and this is possible only if society is accorded a relative value. Otherwise it swamps and eventually destroys the individual, and then there is no longer any society either. In other words: a genuine society must be composed of independent individuals, who can be social beings only up to a certain point. They alone can fulfil the divine will implanted in each of us.

The paths leading to a common truth are many. Therefore each of us has first to stand by his own truth, which is then gradually reduced to a common truth by mutual discussion. All this requires psychological understanding and empathy with the other's point of view. A common task for every group in quest of a common truth. With best greetings,

Yours sincerely, C . G . J U N G

[1] John 10:34.

To J. Vijayatunga

[ORIGINAL IN ENGLISH]

Dear Sir,   August 1957

I have looked in your interesting little book *Yoga—the Way of Self-Fulfilment*.[1] I also have read your letter with attention. Your spiritual situation in India, where I have been nearly 20 years ago, before she got home rule, is practically the same as it is with us, although our history is very different. We are both at the cross-ways: in a time when the old-established meaningful ways have become obsolete, no matter whether it is welcome or unwelcome, right or wrong, true or false, it is so, as it is. We are confronted with the onslaught of disrupting powers, either from this or from the other side. The two poles, the pairs of opposites, are represented by America and Russia. They are not the true agents but the main victims of the separation of opposites in the man of today. He has gradually come down from the unity of being he had reached on the summit of his medieval culture, and fascinated by the ten thousand things he has fallen into the opposites. He is no more *nirdvandva* but torn between the opposites by his desirousness. Thus he is split into two halves, the one is conscious of the one thing, and the other of the other thing, and they do not see their other side any more. The trend of the time is one-sidedness and disagreement, and thus the dissociation and separation of the two worlds will be accomplished. Nothing will prevent this fact. We have no answer yet that would appeal to the general mind, nothing that could function as a bridge. You are naturally reaching back to Yoga in the proper understanding that it has once been the right way which should still be the right way for our time. But the world has become wrong and nobody listens to the old ways any more, in spite of the fact that the underlying truth is still true. The same is the case in the West, where one makes futile attempts to give life to our Christian tenets; but they have gone to sleep. Yet in Buddhism as well as in Christianity there is at the basis of both a valid truth, but its modern application has not been understood yet.

"By whatsoever consciousness, whatsoever compounds, whatsoever individuality he may be denoted—all that is finished, cut off at the root, made like a baseless palmtree, made non-becoming, of a nature

☐ New Delhi, India.
[1] London, 1953.

to arise no more in the future. Freed from consciousness, from the compounds, from individuality is the Tathāgata."[2]

"Tathāgata" literally translated means the "thus going-one." This passage describes the effect we shall undergo in order to be liberated from our illusions. Over against our consciousness we must learn to live as it were unconsciously, only thus are able to fulfil the superior will, following the path of a Tathāgata. If you are consciously the one and unconsciously the other, you don't know any more who you are. But you are nevertheless, and you are Tathāgata. Thus there is no question whether women have children or not, whether you have a car or not, whether you are this or that—you are the self, which is greater than yourself. Circumstances will teach us this truth without fail.

My greeting to you!

Yours sincerely, c. g. jung

[2] Quotation from V.'s book. The Tathāgata is the Buddha. H. Zimmer, *Philosophies of India* (p. 133, n. 49), translates it as "he who has come in truth."

To Attila Fáj

Dear Doctor Fáj: September 1957

My best thanks for your kindness in sending me your article[1] on the Madách question in *Osservatore letterario* and the German abstract "Word and Truth" in the *Monatsschrift für Religion und Kultur*. I do not know Madách's work "The Tragedy of Man," and your statements regarding its contents have enabled me to understand what these visions mean to the Hungarian people. The fact is that real poets create out of an inner vision which, being timeless, also unveils the future, if not in actualities at least symbolically. It is interesting that such an urgently warning voice was raised just when, in the middle of the last century, the "age of technology" really began. As in Goethe's *Faust*, here too it is the feminine element (Eve) that knows about the secret which can work against the total destruction of mankind, or man's despair in the face of such a de-

☐ (Translated by Hildegard Nagel.) — Dr. Attila Fáj, a refugee from Communist Hungary; lecturer on the Hungarian language at the U. of Genoa.
[1] F. had sent Jung an article of his on the Hungarian dramatist Imre Madách (1823–64), whose chief work is *The Tragedy of Man* (1860; tr. 1964). In it Adam and Eve dream the future history of mankind and its final downfall.

velopment. Perhaps some day there will appear a poet courageous enough to give expression to the voices of the "mothers." So far only one has come within my sight—to be sure, not to whom one can ascribe world-dimension—namely the Austrian emigrant Hermann Broch.[2]

Yours sincerely, C. G. JUNG

[2] Cf. Jacobi, 23 Dec. 32, n. 6.

To A. Gerstner-Hirzel

Dear Herr Gerstner-Hirzel,   September 1957

Unfortunately it is impossible for me to answer your questions[1] in a few words; the problem is too complicated. First of all I must emphasize that patterns of this kind always seem to occur where meditation and other such exercises are practised. Psychologically, these can be summed up under the concept "concentration of attention" (in plain English, "devotion"). Concentration is necessary whenever there is the possibility or threat of psychic chaos, i.e., when there is no central control by a strong ego or dominant idea. This situation is frequently met with in primitive or barbarous societies, and also on a higher level when the hitherto existing order is about to decay and a new order has to be firmly centred. The new dominant idea is then depicted in the form of a symbol, and the chaotic currents and cross-currents are tamed, we might say, by rhythmical ornamentation. There are beautiful examples of this in the Arabian art which went hand in hand with the psychic reorientation of a primitive society under the influence of Islam. In Buddhist art, as in the Celtic illuminated manuscripts and sculptures, the complicated designs and intricate rhythms of the border pattern serve to coax the frightening, pullulating chaos of a disorganized psyche into harmonious forms. The same purpose is served by the often very complicated mandalas of neurotics and psychotics, or of normal persons who have collided headlong with the fatal disorientation of our time. You will find examples in the book I brought out with Richard Wilhelm, *The Secret of the Golden Flower*, and in my *Gestaltungen des*

□ Basel.
[1] Concerning the possible connections between the interlaced patterns in pre-Christian and early Christian Celtic art (e.g., the 8th-cent. Lindisfarne Gospels) and Indian mandalas.

387

Unbewussten.[2] I would also draw your attention to H. Zimmer's *Kunstform und Yoga im indischen Kultbild* (Berlin, 1926).

I have observed especially the skein motif among modern people, and it always signifies an intense effort to concentrate or else to suppress and transform violent emotions. In all such cases I found it was an effective method of self-therapy. The same may also be true of the mentality of the Irish monks. Equally, the complicated ornamentation of ritual mandalas in Buddhism could be regarded as a sort of psychic "tranquillizer," though this way of looking at it is admittedly one-sided. On the other hand it should be noted that the harmonization of the swirling lines is arranged round an ideal centre, or represents it directly in the symbolic form, for instance, of a richly ornamental cross. In primitive societies even objects of daily use are often thought of as animated and numinous in themselves; they are receptacles for the projection of emotional processes and, as such, are elaborately ornamented. They represent household gods, i.e., autonomous psychic dominants.

We may think of the Irish monk as a man who still has one foot in the animistic world of nature-demons with its intense passions, and the other in the new Christian order symbolized by the Cross, which condenses the primordial chaos into the unity of the personality.

In the hope that these few hints may have answered your questions, I remain,

Yours sincerely, C. G. JUNG

[2] Cf. the mandalas in "A Study in the Process of Individuation" and "Concerning Mandala Symbolism," CW 9, i, and the commentary on "The Secret of the Golden Flower," CW 13.

To Karl Oftinger

Dear Professor Oftinger, September 1957

Unfortunately I am so old and tired that I am no longer able to comply with your wish.[1] You may be assured, however, that I have every sympathy with your project and understand it only too well. I personally detest noise and flee it whenever and wherever possible,

[1] O., professor of law at the U. of Zurich, had founded an association to combat noise ("Liga gegen den Lärm") and asked Jung for a contribution to be published in a reputable newspaper.

because it not only disturbs the concentration needed for my work but forces me to make the additional psychic effort of shutting it out. You may get habituated to it as to over-indulgence in alcohol, but just as you pay for this with a cirrhosis of the liver, so in the end you pay for nervous stress with a premature depletion of your vital substance. Noise is certainly only one of the evils of our time, though perhaps the most obtrusive. The others are the gramophone, the radio, and now the blight of television. I was once asked by an organization of teachers why, in spite of the better food in elementary schools, the curriculum could no longer be completed nowadays. The answer is: lack of concentration, too many distractions. Many children do their work to the accompaniment of the radio. So much is fed into them from outside that they no longer have to think of something they could do from inside themselves, which requires concentration. Their infantile dependence on the outside is thereby increased and prolonged into later life, when it becomes fixed in the well-known attitude that every inconvenience should be abolished by order of the State. *Panem et circenses*—this is the degenerative symptom of urban civilization, to which we must now add the nerve-shattering din of our technological gadgetry. The alarming pollution of our water supplies, the steady increase of radioactivity, and the sombre threat of overpopulation with its genocidal tendencies have already led to a widespread though not generally conscious *fear* which *loves noise* because it stops the fear from being heard. Noise is welcome because it drowns the inner instinctive warning. Fear seeks noisy company and pandemonium to scare away the demons. (The primitive equivalents are yells, bull-roarers, drums, fire-crackers, bells, etc.) Noise, like crowds, gives a feeling of security; therefore people love it and avoid doing anything about it as they instinctively feel the apotropaic magic it sends out. Noise protects us from painful reflection, it scatters our anxious dreams, it assures us that we are all in the same boat and creating such a racket that nobody will dare to attack us. Noise is so insistent, so overwhelmingly real, that everything else becomes a pale phantom. It relieves us of the effort to say or do anything, for the very air reverberates with the invincible power of our modernity.

The dark side of the picture is that we wouldn't have noise if we didn't secretly want it. Noise is not merely inconvenient or harmful, it is an unadmitted and uncomprehended means to an end: compensation of the fear which is only too well founded. If there were

389

silence, their fear would make people reflect, and there's no knowing what might then come to consciousness. Most people are afraid of silence; hence, whenever the everlasting chit-chat at a party suddenly stops, they are impelled to say something, do something, and start fidgeting, whistling, humming, coughing, whispering. The need for noise is almost insatiable, even though it becomes unbearable at times. Still, it is better than nothing. "Deathly silence"—telling phrase!—strikes us as uncanny. Why? Ghosts walking about? Well, hardly. The real fear is what might come up from one's own depths—all the things that have been held at bay by noise.

You have taken on a difficult task with this much needed noise-abatement, for the more you attack noise the closer you come to the taboo territory of silence, which is so much dreaded. You will be depriving all those nobodies whom nobody ever listens to of their sole joy in life and of the incomparable satisfaction they feel when they shatter the stillness of the night with their clattering motor-bikes, disturbing everyone's sleep with their hellish din. At that moment they amount to something. Noise is their *raison d'être* and a confirmation of their existence. There are far more people than one supposes who are not disturbed by noise, for they have nothing in them that could be disturbed; on the contrary, noise gives them something to live for.

Between this stratum of the population and the inertia of the authorities there is an unconscious *contrat social*[2] giving rise to a vicious circle: what the one doesn't want is welcomed by the other.

Modern noise is an integral component of modern "civilization," which is predominantly extraverted and abhors all inwardness. It is an evil with deep roots. The existing regulations could do much to improve things but they are not enforced. Why not? It's a question of morality. But this is shaken to its foundations and it all goes together with the spiritual disorientation of our time. Real improvement can be hoped for only if there is a radical change of consciousness. I fear all other measures will remain unreliable palliatives since they do not penetrate to the depths where the evil is rooted and constantly renewed.

Zola once aptly remarked that the big cities are "holocaustes de l'humanité," but the general trend is set in that direction because destruction is an unconscious goal of the collective unconscious at

---

[2] In his *Contrat social* (1762) Rousseau tried to show that all government should be based on the consent of the governed.

the present time: it is terrified by the snowballing population figures and uses every means to contrive an attenuated and inconspicuous form of genocide. Another, easily overlooked weapon is the destruction of the ability to concentrate—the prime requisite for operating our highly differentiated machines and equipment. The life of the masses is inconceivable without them and yet it is constantly threatened by superficiality, inattention, and slovenliness. The nervous exhaustion caused by the tempo leads to addiction (alcohol, tranquillizers, and other poisons) and thus to an even poorer performance and the premature wastage of the vital substance—another effective weapon for inconspicuous depopulation.

Excuse this somewhat pessimistic contribution to one of the less delectable questions of our time. As a doctor I naturally see more than others of the dark side of human existence and am therefore more inclined to make the menacing aspects the object of my reflections than to advance grounds for optimistic forecasts. In my view there are more than enough people catering to this already.

Yours sincerely, c. g. jung

To Pastor Hans Wegmann

Dear Pastor Wegmann, September 1957

For a long time I have been meaning to answer your letter and thank you for your sermon,[1] but this summer has been so brimful of work that I simply haven't got round to it. I hope you will make allowances for my old age.

I am glad that you pointed out in your sermon how necessary it is to disregard the ego and its will, and that you go back to St. Paul as a great example. But, by your leave, exactly how do your flock set about distinguishing the ego from the non-ego—especially in such matters of daily importance as those you mention? It cannot be assumed that everyone possesses the religious genius of Paul. I, at any rate, know from my medical practice that nothing is more difficult than to make this subtle distinction. It cannot be done by extinguishing the ego, and anyone who reflects at all constantly finds himself in the difficult position of having to safeguard his ego and at

☐ Zurich. See Wegmann, 5 Mar. 37 (in vol. 1).
[1] The sermon has not been preserved.

the same time lend an ear to the non-ego. It is just in this conflict that he proves his humanity, or so it seems to me.

I am glad you have taken up *The Secret of the Golden Flower* again. The East often knows the answer to questions which appear insoluble to us Christians.

Again with thanks and best greetings,

Yours sincerely, C. G. JUNG

To Maud Oakes

[ORIGINAL IN ENGLISH]

Dear Miss Oakes,   3 October 1957

Since you want to hear my opinion about your essay on the stone,[1] I should say that I find it a bit too intellectual, as it considers the thought-images only, but as I have already called your attention to its *ambiente* I miss the all-important feeling-tone of the phenomenon. . . . If you want to do justice to the stone you have to pay particular attention to the way in which it is embedded in its surroundings: the water, the hills, the view, the peculiar atmosphere of the buildings, the nights and days, the seasons, sun, wind, and rain, and man living close to the earth and yet remaining conscious in daily meditation of everything being just so. The air round the stone is filled with harmonies and disharmonies, with memories of times long ago, of vistas into the dim future with reverberations of a faraway, yet so-called real world into which the stone has fallen out of nowhere. A strange revelation and admonition. Try to dwell in this wholeness for a while and see what happens to you.

Sincerely yours, C. G. JUNG

[1] Cf. Oakes, 31 Jan. 56, 11 Feb. 56.

To John Trinick

[ORIGINAL IN ENGLISH]

Dear Mr. Trinick,   15 October 1957

First of all I must ask your forgiveness for having caused this long delay of my reaction. My plan was to study your MS[1] in my summer

☐ Cliftonville, Thanet, England.

[1] "Signum atque Signatum" (The Sign and the Signed), an interpretation of alchemy, published as *The Fire-Tried Stone* (1967). Jung's letter (and an earlier

vacation with the necessary leisure. But the god of chance had another idea and crammed any amount of disturbances and obligations into my holidays and on top of everything I had to finish a little book[2] and I was forced to lose a certain amount of time with the International Psychiatric Congress in Zurich.[3]

Thanks to your generous permission to keep your MS for the time being, I have been able to read it with attention not only once but in several parts twice. Such a continuous argument as your "enquiry" demands some concentration, as in certain places at least it is no easy reading. This is of course only an external difficulty. The real reason for the inevitable slowing down of the reading process is the controversial and enigmatic nature of the subject itself. While reading one must pay close attention not only to what you say but also to the disturbing upsurge of unconscious reactions in one's self.

Just as some alchemists had to admit that they never succeeded in producing the gold or the Stone, I cannot confess to have solved the riddle of the *coniunctio* mystery. On the contrary I am darkly aware of things lurking in the background of the problem—things too big for our horizons. This background begins to stir when one reads your paper. Your erudite disquisition has taught me quite a few things, especially your careful analysis of Eirenaeus Philalethes,[4] who indeed deserves special treatment. It would have been within the scope of my book[5] to pay special attention to his work but he is a problem in himself, like Andreae and *Die Chymische Hochzeit*[6] (the model for *Faust II*, insufficiently treated by Mr. Gray in his book: *Goethe the Alchemist*).[7] I am glad you have taken up the challenge of Philalethes. He is remarkable, and your analysis does justice to him. I was deeply impressed by your care and tactful handling of the material and by

---

one of 13 Oct. 56, not in this selection) are printed as a preface to the book, which is dedicated to T.'s wife and to Jung.

[2] "Flying Saucers," CW 10.

[3] Cf. Bleuler, 23 Mar. 55, n. 1.

[4] Eirenaeus Philalethes, pseudonym ("peaceful lover of truth") of a 17th-cent. English alchemist, believed by some to be identical with the mystic and alchemist Thomas Vaughan (1622–66). Several treatises ascribed to him are contained in the *Musaeum hermeticum* (1678), tr. Waite, *The Hermetic Museum, Restored and Enlarged* (1893; repr. 1953).

[5] *Psychology and Alchemy*, CW 12. Cf. index, s.v. Philalethes.

[6] Cf. Boner, 8 Dec. 38, n. 2.

[7] Ronald D. Gray, *Goethe the Alchemist. A Study of Alchemical Symbolism in Goethe's Literary and Scientific Works* (1952).

your unusual knowledge of, and your profound insight into, the significance, implications and innuendos of this central alchemical problem. It is astounding how a young man like Philalethes succeeded in producing such an extraordinary presentation of the problem; yet we encounter a similar miracle in Andreae's case and to a certain extent in Goethe's too, viz. the main parts of *Faust*. For the explanation of this fact, I have to point out the archetypal nature of the *coniunctio* on the one hand and the youthful intuition of archetypes on the other. The younger an individual is, the nearer he is to the primordial unconscious with its collective contents. This becomes particularly impressive when one studies those dreams of earliest childhood that are still remembered in adult age. They yield most astounding results, as they show an apparent knowledge of archetypes quite inexplicable in the individual case. I think that something along that line explains Philalethes' and Andreae's precocity. The archetype is ageless and ever-present.

To deal with the *coniunctio* in human words is a disconcerting task, since you are forced to express and formulate a process taking place "in Mercurio"[8] and not on the level of human thought and human language, i.e., not within the sphere of discriminating consciousness. On this side of the epistemological barrier we have to separate the opposites in order to produce comprehensible speech. You have to state that *a* is not *b*, that above is not below, that the perfume of the Spiritus Sanctus is not the *malus odor sepulchrorum sive inferni*[9] and that the *nuptiae spirituales* are not the carnal union of bodies. Yet in the archetypal unimaginable event that forms the basis of conscious apperception, *a* is *b*, stench is perfume, sex is *amor Dei*, as inevitably as the conclusion that God is the *complexio oppositorum*. The alchemists were more or less aware of this shocking state of affairs, although rarely explicitly so. Usually, whether consciously or not, they tried not to commit themselves, yet they also did not avoid symbolic allusions or pictures of an alluring kind. They expressed f.i. shock at the idea of *incest*, yet they could not refrain from using the term, just as little as undoubtedly Christian poets did, f.i. Chrêtien de Troyes: "Dieu qui fit de sa fille sa mère."[10]

The fact is that the figures behind the epistemological curtain, i.e.,

---

[8] Jung's meaning is that the *coniunctio*, or *hierosgamos*, takes place on a symbolic, archetypal level above and beyond logical definition. Cf. Anon., 20 July 42, n. 2.
[9] The "sweet odour" of the Holy Ghost is a frequent image in ecclesiastical and alchemical language; its counterpart is the "stench of the graves or of hell."
[10] Cf. Birnie, 14 May 48, n. 2.

the archetypes, are "impossible" unions of opposites, transcendental beings which can only be apperceived by contrasts. Good can only be understood by "not bad," "day" by "not night," etc. Alchemy tries to express the Good, the Splendid, the Light, the Gold, the *Incorruptibile et Aeternum* by the *materia vilis*[11] and is therefore forced to speak of Death, *Putredo, Incineratio, Nigredo, Venenum, Draco, Malus Odor, Pestilentia, Leprositas*, etc.[12]

Since the *coniunctio* is an essentially transcendental, i.e., archetypal process and since our mental attitude is still essentially Christian we emphasize the Spirit, the Good, the Light, the Above, the spiritualized, i.e., subtle body, purity, chastity, etc. and separate all that from the contrary, which we have to mention nevertheless, even by explicitly denying, disregarding and condemning it. It will be there, because it belongs inevitably to the transcendental, archetypal reality. Good cannot exist without Evil, nor *luminositas sine nigredine*.[13] *Mysteria revelata vilescunt*.[14] In trying to reveal that which no mortal being is able to conceive, we distort and say the wrong things. Instead of creating light, we conceal in darkness, instead of lifting up, we expose the treasure to ridicule and contempt. Instead of opening a way, we barricade it by an inextricable snarl of paradoxes. "In Mercurio" spirit and matter are one. This is a mystery nobody is ever going to solve. It is real, but we are unable to express its reality. An alchemist very wisely said: *Artifex non est magister Lapidi sed potius ejus minister*.[15] When the artifex speaks, he will always say the wrong things, or at least things that are also wrong. It is *neti-neti*,[16] in other words: beyond our grasp, although it is a definite experience. It is said of the Stone: *habet mille nomina*,[17] which means that there is not one name

[11] = lowly matter, a synonym for the *prima materia*.

[12] All these terms are alchemical similes expressing the contrast between the goal to be attained (the philosophers' stone) and the difficulties of the opus leading to the goal. (*Leprositas* = leprous condition of metals = verdigris.)

[13] = luminosity [cannot exist] without darkness.

[14] Cf. Rosencreutz's motto to his *Chymische Hochzeit*: "Arcana publicata vilescunt et gratiam profanata amittunt" (Mysteries profaned and made public fade and lose their grace).

[15] "The artifex is not the master of the stone but rather its minister." Cf. "The Psychology of the Transference," CW 16, par. 531 & n. 16.

[16] Cf. *Brihadaranyaka Upanishad*, 3.9.26 (in R. E. Hume, *The Thirteen Principal Upanishads*, p. 125): "That Soul (*Atman*) is not this, it is not that (*neti, neti*). It is unseizable, for it is not seized. . . . It is unattached, for it does not attach itself . . ."

[17] = it has a thousand names.

expressing the Mystery. Your attempts to formulate it are not vain or futile; on the contrary, our labours are witnesses to the living Mystery, honest attempts to find words for the *Ineffabile*.

The "way" is not an upward-going straight line, f.i. from earth to heaven or from matter to spirit, but rather a *circumabulatio* of and an approximation to the Centrum. We are not liberated by leaving something behind but only by fulfilling our task as *mixta composita*,[18] i.e., human beings between the opposites. The spiritualism of a Berdyaev[19] and others is only the contrary of materialism, one half of the truth. There is not God alone but also His creation, i.e., the will of God in Christian terminology. *Homo sapiens* has to envisage both. That was the great discovery of *Mater Alchimia*.

Your opus ought to be published, as it is a link in the *Aurea Catena*[20] reaching through twenty centuries down to our benighted present. With all my good wishes,

Yours sincerely, C. G. JUNG

[18] = mixed entities.
[19] Nikolas Berdyaev (1874–1948), Russian idealist philosopher, originally an ardent supporter of Marx and the Revolution; later his spiritual ideals clashed with State Communism. Emigrated to Berlin, then to Paris, where he founded an academy of the philosophy of religion. T. had mentioned him as one of his sources, and a chapter of his book is dedicated to Berdyaev.
[20] Cf. Bernoulli, 5 Oct. 44, n. 3.

To Martin Flinker

Dear Herr Flinker,   17 October 1957

You have been kind enough to ask me what I am working on now and what questions and problems concern me most. Well, at the moment, thank God, I have no new work in view. The works I completed this year have cost me energy and time enough, and I hope I may now be granted a longish spell of leisure without any new questions forcing me to new answers.

Within the political and social sphere it is the role of the individual that especially concerns me. Improbable as this may sound, it is only the individual who is qualified to fight against the threat today of international mass-mindedness. In this very unequal-looking struggle the individual does not by any means occupy a lost outpost if he succeeds in seriously getting down to the old Christian injunction to see the beam in his own eye and not worry about the mote in his brother's. My views on the problem of the individual and the mass, with all its political and religious implications, are set forth in my essay "The Undiscovered Self."

In my proper field of work, psychiatry, I have dealt with the theory of schizophrenia and the still unresolved question of its aetiology in a long report to the International Congress for Psychiatry, Zurich 1957.[1] Here the recent researches into the possible influence of a toxin seem to me just as interesting and important as the continued investigation of the images and visions appearing in the fantasies of schizophrenics.

As I have always been intrigued by what is off the beaten track and is usually ridiculed or simply shrugged off with a joke, I have, after studying the available literature for many years, undertaken to interpret the myths that have grown up around the reports of "flying saucers." This inquiry is now in the press, with the title *Ein moderner Mythus von Dingen, die am Himmel gesehen werden.*[2]

This, too, is an expression of something that has always claimed my deepest interest and my greatest attention: the manifestation of archetypes, or archetypal forms, in all the phenomena of life: in biology, physics, history, folklore, and art, in theology and mythology, in parapsychology, as well as in the symptoms of insane patients and neurotics, and finally in the dreams and life of every individual man and woman. The intimation of forms hovering in a background not in itself knowable gives life the depth which, it seems to me, makes it worth living.

Please would you let me know whether these lines will be published in German or French in your Almanac. If in French, I would be glad of an opportunity to review the translation.

Yours sincerely, C. G. JUNG

☐ F., head of the Librairie Française et Etrangère, Paris, asked Jung for his answers to the following questions: What are you working on now? What new work have you in view? What are the questions and problems that concern you most? Jung's letter was published in the *Flinker Almanac 1958* (Paris, 1957), pp. 52ff., along with replies from other literary personalities, including Thomas Mann, Hermann Hesse, Hermann Broch, and Robert Musil. For a statement in the *Flinker Almanac 1961*, on bilingualism, see CW 18, pars. 1770ff.

[1] "Schizophrenia," CW 3.
[2] "A Modern Myth of Things Seen in the Sky" = "Flying Saucers," CW 10.

To Stephen Abrams

[ORIGINAL IN ENGLISH]

Dear Mr. Abrams,   21 October 1957

Your letter leads into the centre of a very complicated problem.[1] Being a scientist I am rather shy of philosophical operations, particularly of conclusions reaching beyond the limits of experience. F.i. I would not go as far as to say that the categories of space and time are definitely non-objective. I would rather ask, on which level or in which world are space and time not valid? In our three-dimensional world they are certainly and inexorably objective, but we have the definite experience that occasionally—presumably under certain conditions—they behave as if they were relatively subjective, that is relatively non-objective. We are not sure how far the relativity can go, so we do not know whether there is a level or a world on or in which space and time are absolutely abolished; but we remain within the limits of human experience when we accept the fact that it is the psyche which is able to relativize the apparent objectivity of time and space. This conclusion is fairly safe as we have, to my knowledge, no known reasons to assume that it is the action of time and space which enables the psyche to perform an act of precognition. They are in our experience, apart f.i. from parapsychology, unchangeable. However, Einstein's relativity theory[2] shows that they are not necessarily identical with our idea of them, f.i. that space may be curved and that time necessarily depends upon the stand-point and the speed of the observer. Such considerations support the idea of their relative validity. Parapsychological experience definitely shows their uncertain behaviour under psychic influence.

We conclude therefore that we have to expect a factor in the psyche that is not subject to the laws of time and space, as it is on the contrary capable of suppressing them to a certain extent. In other words: this factor is expected to manifest the qualities of time- and spacelessness, i.e., "eternity" and "ubiquity." Psychological experience knows of such a factor; it is what I call the archetype, which is ubiquitous in space and time, of course relatively speaking. It is

[1] A. stated that "parapsychology can only be approached from the psychology of the unconscious." He asked if he was "correct in assuming that space and time do not have any objective existence in your view?"

[2] Einstein, in his theory of relativity, recognized that it is impossible to determine absolute motion, and that we have to assume a four-dimensional space-time continuum. This general theory of relativity leads to a new concept in which space is caused to curve by the presence of matter in space, thus setting up a gravitational field.

398

Jung at Bollingen, about 1950

I

II   The photograph published in *Time*, 1955

With Herbert Read at Küsnacht, 1949

With Emma Jung at Bollingen, 1954

III

IV

(*left, from top*) Toni Wolff;
Jolande Jacobi; Erich
Neumann; (*above and
right*) Fowler McCormick;
R.F.C. Hull; Karl Kerényi

M. Esther Harding

VI

(*clockwise*) Beatrice M. Hinkle, 1917;
Kristine Mann, 1932; Eleanor Bertine

The Stone

VIII

a structural element of the psyche we find everywhere and at all times; and it is that in which all individual psyches are identical with each other, and where they function as if they were the one undivided Psyche the ancients called *anima mundi* or the *psyche tou kosmou*.[3] This is no metaphysical speculation but an observable fact, and therefore the key to innumerable mythologies, that is, to the manifestations of unconscious fantasy. From *this* observation it does not follow that this factor is one and the same thing [inside] and outside the psyche, as it were. It may be, from a psychological point of view, a mere similarity and not a unity in essence. This question cannot be decided by ordinary psychology, but here parapsychology comes in, with its psi-phenomena that unmistakably show an essential identity of two separate events, as f.i. the act of prevision and the objective precognized fact. These experiences show that the factor in question is one and the same inside and outside the psyche. Or in other words: there is no outside to the collective psyche. In our ordinary mind we are in the worlds of time and space and within the separate individual psyche. In the state of the archetype we are in the collective psyche, in a world-system whose space-time categories are relatively or absolutely abolished.

This is about as far as we can go safely. I see no way beyond, since we are not capable of functioning in a four-dimensional system at will; it only can happen to us. Our intellectual means reach only as far as archetypal experiences, but within that sphere we are not the motors, we are the moved objects. Experiment in the ordinary sense therefore becomes impossible. We can only hope for occasional observations. From this argument it follows that we should expect an operative archetype. I have carefully analysed many parapsychological cases and I have been satisfied with the fact that there are indeed operative archetypes in many cases. I could not say: in all cases, I call them exceptions because they are very curious indeed. I don't want to enter into this point here. I only want to state my general experience: perhaps in most of the cases there is an archetype present, yet there are many other archetypal situations in which no parapsychological phenomenon is observable, and there are also cases of psi-phenomena where no archetypal condition can be demonstrated. There is no regularity between archetype and synchronistic effect. The probability of such a relation is presumably the same as that of the Rhine results.

I think you are correct in assuming that synchronicity, though in

---

[3] = cosmic psyche.

practice a relatively rare phenomenon, is an all-pervading factor or principle in the universe, i.e., in the Unus Mundus,[4] where there is no incommensurability between so-called matter and so-called psyche. Here one gets into deep waters, at least I myself must confess that I am far from having sounded these abysmal depths.

In this connection I always come upon the enigma of the *natural number*. I have a distinct feeling that Number is a key to the mystery, since it is just as much discovered as it is invented. It is quantity as well as meaning. For the latter I refer to the arithmetical qualities of the fundamental archetype of the self (monad, microcosm, etc.) and its historically and empirically well-documented variants of the Four, the $3 + 1$ and the $4 - 1$.[5]

It seems that I am too old to solve such riddles, but I do hope that a young mind will take up the challenge. It would be worth while.[6]

I have already heard some rumours about the foundation of a Parapsychology Club at the University of Chicago. I accept with pleasure and gratitude the honour of honorary membership. It is none too early that somebody in the West takes notice of synchronicity. As I have been informed, the Russians have already caught hold of my paper.[7]

Sincerely yours, C. G. JUNG

[4] Cf. Anon., 2 Jan. 57, n. 1.

[5] Cf. Wylie, 22 Dec. 57, n. 1.

[6] Since then, this subject has been taken up by M.-L. von Franz in her *Zahl und Zeit. Psychologische Überlegungen zu einer Annäherung von Tiefenpsychologie und Physik* (1970; tr., *Number and Time*, 1974).

[7] Jung had been told by a physicist who attended a congress in Japan, in either 1953 or 1954, that Russian physicists had expressed to him their interest in synchronicity. As a matter of fact they were working on problems of telepathy. According to a communication from A., Prof. Vasiliev of the Physiological Institute of Leningrad U. spoke in 1963 of his interest in synchronicity.

To John Trinick

[ORIGINAL IN ENGLISH]

Dear Mr. Trinick,   26 October 1957

Thank you ever so much for your very kind letter. It has left a certain question in my mind which I think is of some importance, as it seems that you naturally prefer a so-called Christian interpretation of alchemistic thought, understanding it as an attempt at a spiritualization of chthonic forces. This interpretation is certainly in accord with the general character of medieval alchemy.

The very existence of alchemistic philosophy proves that the spiritualization process within Christian psychology did not yield satisfactory results. Hence it is understandable that alchemy had to take up this problem and add its special method in order to obtain the result devised by the Christian mind. In doing this, alchemy reached a result which does not really coincide with the Christian goal. Therefore the Christian symbol was left more or less as an analogy of the stone, or the stone an equivalent of Christ. The method to this end was a *coniunctio oppositorum*, which is not exactly a Christian idea, since historical Christian psychology thinks rather of suppression of evil than of a *complexio boni et mali*.[1] Thus alchemy tried the idea of a certain transformation of evil with a view to its future integration. In this way it was rather a continuation of Origen's thought that even the devil may be ultimately redeemed, a thought discouraged by the Church. If, therefore, alchemistic thought essentially coincides with the general Christian idea, one does not see exactly what the purpose of transformation of the Christian thought into alchemistic symbols would be, and why the alchemistic goal is the Lapis and not Christ. Why should it speak of the Lapis at all? But the fact that the Lapis is an existence different from Christ shows that alchemy really had a different goal in mind. This is obvious inasmuch as the Lapis derives from a synthesis of the opposites, which the dogmatic Christ is definitely not. For these reasons I cannot agree with the Christian interpretation of the alchemistic procedure. On the contrary, I see in alchemy the attempt at a different solution, namely to bring about the union of opposites which is lacking in the historical Christian doctrine. In accordance with this the ruling spirit of alchemy is *Mercurius utriusque capax*[2] and not the third Person of the Trinity, i.e., of the Summum Bonum. It is a problem of modern times foreshadowed since the beginning of the new millennium.

I think that alchemy has left us with a difficult task.

Please consider my views in this respect as my subjective contribution.

Sincerely yours, C. G. JUNG

[1] = synthesis of good and evil.
[2] = Mercurius, capable of both.

401

Anonymous

[ORIGINAL IN ENGLISH]

Dear Dr. N.,   12 November 1957

What you told me is a typical story of what I call the projection of the anima into a woman and of the animus into a man. Anima is the soul-image of a man, represented in dreams or fantasies by a feminine figure. It symbolizes the function of relationship. The animus is the image of spiritual forces in a woman, symbolized by a masculine figure. If a man or a woman is unconscious of these inner forces, they appear in a projection.

The psychiatrist calls you "his equal," and that feeling of relationship shows that you carry the image of his soul. Since he is unable to see you as a real woman behind his projection, you seem to be a "sphinx." In reality his soul is his sphinx, and he should try to solve the riddle.

You are wrong in assuming that he alone needs help. You need help as well. You call yourself a woman of a "very ordinary intellectual capacity" who has "never delved very deep into any metaphysical subject." As your story shows, the projection of the animus into a "psychiatrist of international repute" happened because you should get more psychological knowledge. Knowing more about the soul and its mysteries you could free yourself from the fascination which makes you suffer. In the second half of life one should begin to get acquainted with the inner world. That is a general problem.

Your world seemed to be a happy one. But the strange happenings showed that something ought to be changed.

The projection of anima and animus causes mutual fascination. Phenomena which you describe as "telepathic" happen when one gets emotional, i.e., when the unconscious has an opportunity to enter consciousness. You really ought to know a bit more about the psychology of the unconscious. It would help you to understand the situation, which—by the way—should be understood. There is a little book by Frieda Fordham: *Introduction to Jung's Psychology* (Pelican Books), which I recommend to you.

Faithfully yours, C. G JUNG

☐ A woman, M.D., in England.

To Charles B. Harnett

[ORIGINAL IN ENGLISH]

Dear Sir,   12 December 1957

Your interest in the hitherto unquenchable lore of Ufos meets with my full approval. The story is a most fascinating mental symptom of our time—if anything. I answer your questions[1] in the following way:—

1. I do not believe and do not disbelieve in the existence of Ufos. I simply do not know what to think about their alleged physical existence.

2. The information at the disposition of the public is so scant that one just does not know enough to decide with certainty about the physical existence of Ufos. The only tangible fact seems to be the radar echo, but I am informed by experts on radar that such observations are not beyond reasonable doubt. It is very difficult in spite of all the reported visual observations to obtain reliable photos. To my knowledge it has never been seriously attempted to examine the psychology of the Ufo-witnesses thoroughly, i.e., with all the modern means of personality analysis. The question whether those witnesses are under the influence of certain unconscious contents has not even been raised.

3. As it is questionable in how far Ufos are physical facts, it is indubitable that they are psychological facts. They have a definite and very meaningful psychology. I have made it the object of a psychological research, the results of which I have laid down in a little book that is soon to appear. Its German title is: *Ein moderner Mythus von Dingen, die am Himmel gesehen werden* (Rascher Verlag, Zurich). An English translation is forthcoming in 1958.[2]

I am utterly unable to explain the Ufos' physical nature. I am not even sure that it is a matter of machines; they could be anything, even animals, but I would not dare to contradict statements as to their physical reality.

4. This question is answered by the above.

5. As concerns the physical reality, many people are already too eager to confirm it by every available means. I am only competent to advise on the psychic side. There I think it would be a definite step forward if a competent psychologist would take the trouble to

☐ Springfield, Illinois.
[1] The questionnaire has not been preserved.
[2] It appeared in 1959 ("Flying Saucers," CW 10).

examine the conscious and unconscious mentality of Ufo-witnesses, in order to learn something about the possibility of the Ufos being psychic projections of unconscious contents.

6. No special comment.

Yours sincerely, c. g. j u n g

To Philip Wylie

[O R I G I N A L   I N   E N G L I S H]

Dear Mr. Wylie,   22 December 1957

Despite your protestation I will write to you if only to tell you how grateful I am for your kind letter. I have got so much human disregard that I began to understand—finally—that it was a just punishment for my own faults in the same respects. It has taken me too long to discover the greatest thing, i.e., Man and what he means and why. Thus there is no need at all for you to feel yourself as exceptional. Like every one of us you were part of the great dimness overshadowing the greater part of mankind, in the first place the western socalled Christian man. To discover Man is a great adventure. I am glad and grateful that people like yourself begin to see the dawn.

Don't worry about my mathematics. I never dreamt of adding anything to mathematics, being myself utterly "amathematikós." My affiliation to it consists only in the equation $3 + 1 = 4$,[1] which is a psychological fact indicating the fundamental relation between psychology and mathematics. This is—it may seem ridiculous to a

---

□ See Wylie, 19 Feb. 47 (addenda in vol. 2). — W. told Jung of the great impression "God, the Devil, and the Human Soul" had made upon him (cf. Harding, 30 May 57, n. 2). He also mentioned his lasting admiration for Jung's work and how much his ideas had influenced him in his latest book *An Essay on Morals* (1947), of which he sent Jung a copy.

[1] W. expressed doubts concerning Jung's use of quantum mechanics and mathematics in elucidating some of his psychological concepts. — The "equation $3 + 1 = 4$" refers to the three differentiated and the one undifferentiated (unconscious) function in the psychology of the individual, the "4" representing the totality of the personality as the goal of the process of individuation. — In the psychology of religion the "4" represents to Jung the necessary complement to the Christian Trinity, as the "dark," feminine element completing the Trinity to the quaternity as totality. Cf. Jung, *Psychology and Alchemy*, CW 12, pars. 192, 209f., et al., and "A Psychological Approach to the Dogma of the Trinity," CW 11; also letter to Dr. H., 17 Mar. 51, n. 4. — Finally, Jung's concept of synchronicity complements the three categories of time, space, and causality, again in sense of the "3 + 1" formula.

mathematician—the mystery of the psychologist. To the former, number is a means of counting; to the latter, it is a discovered entity capable of making individual statements if it is given a chance. In other words: in the former case number is a servant, in the latter case an autonomous being. It is the same difference as between the general, the professor, the stockbroker on the one hand and the human being on the other.

Well, I thank you, because you are the only one who admits that I am the *petra scandali*. From this fact I have formerly concluded that I am an exceptionally unpleasant person. In my later years (I am now in my 83rd) I became doubtful, since I have received so much love and consideration that I have no reason to grumble. I have not "eaten of the herb of bitterness,"[2] but I am astonished at the power of prejudice and superficiality of the "clercs."

My best regards to Mrs. Wylie and my cordial wishes for a happy New Year, I remain,

Yours gratefully, c. g. j.

[2] Cf. Exod. 12:8.

To T. Yagisawa

[ORIGINAL IN ENGLISH]

Dear Sir,   24 December 1957

Thank you ever so much for your kind letter. You are the first representative of the Japanese nation from whom I hear that he has read my books. So your letter is a memorable fact in my life. It shows how slow mental travelling is: it took me more than 30 years to reach Japan but I have not even arrived yet at the University of my own town. It is indeed most gratifying and encouraging to me to know that I have readers in Japan, since I know how specifically European most of my works are. It is true, however, that I have tried to demonstrate the universal character of the psyche as well as I could. But it is an almost superhuman task: "Art is long, and our life is short."[1] I am now in my 83rd year and my creative work has come to an end. I am watching the setting sun.

Many thanks and my best wishes for a happy New Year,

Yours sincerely, c. g. jung

☐ Tokyo.
[1] Cf. *Faust*, Part One (tr. Wayne), p. 50.

To Gustav Steiner

Dear friend,   30 December 1957

Your assumption that I already have more than enough to occupy me is only too true. I drown in floods of paper. You are quite right. When we are old, we are drawn back, both from within and from without, to memories of youth. Once before, some thirty years ago, my pupils asked me for an account of how I arrived at my conception of the unconscious. I fulfilled this request by giving a seminar.[1] During the last years the suggestion has come to me from various quarters that I should do something akin to an autobiography. I have been unable to conceive of my doing anything of the sort. I know too many autobiographies, with their self-deceptions and downright lies, and I know too much about the impossibility of self-portrayal, to want to venture on any such attempt.

Recently I was asked for autobiographical information, and in the course of answering some questions I discovered hidden in my memories certain objective problems which seem to call for closer examination. I have therefore weighed the matter and come to the conclusion that I shall fend off my other obligations long enough to take up at least the very first beginnings of my life and consider them in an objective fashion. This task[2] has proved so difficult and singular that in order to go ahead with it, I have had to promise myself that the results would not be published in my lifetime. Such a promise seemed to me essential in order to assure for myself the necessary detachment and calm. It became clear that all the memories which have remained vivid to me had to do with emotional experiences that stir up turmoil and passion in the mind—scarcely the best condition for an objective account! Your letter "naturally" came at the very moment when I had virtually resolved to take the plunge.

Fate will have it—and this has always been the case with me—that all the "outer" aspects of my life should be accidental. Only what is interior has proved to have substance and determining value. As a re-

□ (1878–1967) of Basel. He was a friend from Jung's student days; both belonged to the same student fraternity, "Zofingia," at Basel U. — Except for the two opening sentences and the ending, the letter is published in A. Jaffé's introduction to *Memories*, and the whole letter in an article by S., "Erinnerungen an Carl Gustav Jung. Zur Entstehung der Autobiographie," *Basler Stadtbuch* 1965 (1964), pp. 125f.

[1] Cf. Böhler, 14 Dec. 55, n. 2.

[2] Jung had begun to write down his recollections of childhood and youth, which formed the first three chapters of *Memories*.

sult, all memory of outer events has faded, and perhaps these "outer" experiences were never so very essential anyhow, or were so only in that they coincided with phases of my inner development. An enormous part of these "outer" manifestations of my life has vanished from my memory—for the very reason, I now realize, that I was never really "in" them, although it seemed to me then that I was participating with all my powers. Yet these are the very things that make up a sensible biography: persons one has met, travels, adventures, entanglements, blows of destiny, and so on. But with few exceptions they have become phantasms which I barely recollect, for they no longer lend wings to my imagination.

On the other hand, my memories of the "inner" experiences have grown all the more vivid and colourful. This poses a problem of description which I scarcely feel able to cope with, at least for the present. Unfortunately I cannot, for these reasons, fulfil your request, very much to my regret.

With best wishes for the New Year,

Your old fellow Zofinger,[3] CARL

[3] See □ supra.

Anonymous

[ORIGINAL IN ENGLISH]

Dear N.,   2 January 1958

. . .

Ever since my paper about the Ufos I feel queer and distracted, as if something were going on in my unconscious. Now I know there is something. I just found a book by Fred Hoyle.[1] He got the Ufo problem all right! The title is *The Black Cloud*—a cosmic cloud with a diameter equal to the sun-earth distance—containing intelligence. The book is highly worth while, as it describes how the collective unconscious is coming to an astronomer. Very exciting!

Cordially, C. G.

[1] Cf. the epilogue to "Flying Saucers," CW 10, which Jung wrote when a book by Orfeo Angelucci, *The Secret of the Flying Saucers* (1955), came into his hands. After finishing his commentary on this book he happened on a novel by the English astronomer Fred Hoyle, *The Black Cloud* (1967), and he added another lengthy passage to the epilogue (pars. 810–20). Still later, he added for the English edition a short comment on John Wyndham's *The Midwich Cuckoos* (1957), pars. 821ff.

To Aniela Jaffé

Dear Aniela,   4 January 1958

Hearty thanks for the News Letter and best wishes for the New Year! I am glad you have done your best for X. It really is a problem: why the suffering? Why the torment of dying? Why does anything good have such difficulty in appearing? Why the painful separation from the dead? Occasionally a gleam of goodness breaks through. Thus on New Year's Eve I had a great dream about my wife, which I will tell you sometime. It seems that individuation is a ruthlessly important task to which everything else should take second place. Evidently I still don't know this well enough, even now.

Hoyle's book has arrived and I've finished it already. It is extraordinarily interesting to see how an astronomer collides with the unconscious and especially with the Ufo problem. What a pity my little book is already in print! Hoyle has the *rotundum*, the doctrine of the Anthropos, the cosmic wisdom of matter, which he naturally confuses with consciousness, and so fails to do justice to the problem of suffering. But it is extremely stimulating!

I am a bit less tired, but it's slow going. All the best!

Your faithful C. G.

☐ (Handwritten.)

Anonymous

[ORIGINAL IN ENGLISH]

Dear N.,   9 January 1958

You must bear with my peculiar mental state. These days my thoughts were caught in a circumambulation of an entirely new proportion to me, namely an order from within to write up my earliest recollections. This command made necessary a new attitude of mind, consisting in an acceptance of a sort of autobiographical interest violently resisted hitherto.

While I am writing this I observe a little demon trying to abscond my words and even my thoughts and turning them over into the rapidly flowing river of images, surging from the mists of the past, portraits of a little boy, bewildered and wondering at an incomprehensibly beautiful and hideously profane and deceitful world.

Yours affectionately, C. G.

To L. Kling

Dear Colleague,   14 January 1958

Your question concerning synchronicity and ideas of reference[1] is very interesting indeed. I have often found that synchronistic experiences were interpreted by schizophrenics as delusions. Since archetypal situations are not uncommon in schizophrenia, we must also suppose that corresponding synchronistic phenomena will occur which follow exactly the same course as with so-called normal persons. The difference lies simply and solely in the interpretation. The schizophrenic's interpretation is morbidly narrow because it is mostly restricted to the intentions of other people and to his own ego-importance. The normal interpretation, so far as this is possible at all, is based on the philosophic premise of the sympathy of all things,[2] or something of that kind. Your patient is obviously someone who would need either to pay his tribute to Nature or to make some correspondingly meaningful sacrifice. What this might be is provisionally indicated by the dreams. We certainly shouldn't think we know what good advice to offer or what, if anything, ought to be done. On the contrary we must endeavour to find out what the unconscious thinks and adjust our attitude accordingly. If synchronicities occur in these cases it is because an archetypal situation is present, for whenever archetypes are constellated we find manifestations of the primordial unity. Thus the synchronistic effect should be understood not as a psychotic but as a normal phenomenon.

Ideas of reference arise as a concomitant symptom of the patient's wrong understanding, and consequent repression, of his psychic situation. Then what should normally have been an expression of the sympathy of all things turns into a pseudo-rationalistic attempt to explain the missing sympathy, so in place of the uniting Eros he feels a divisive fear or a hatred which is its opposite. The pathological factor is that the original participation in all things is perverted into a negation on rational or other plausible grounds which seem obvious

☐ M.D., analytical psychologist, of Strasbourg.

[1] Ideas of reference frequently occur in schizophrenia when the patient interprets quite ordinary events as having some special reference to him.

[2] The "sympathy of all things," the harmonious interdependence and interaction of the elements of the universe, is a concept largely developed by the Stoic philosophers Chrysippus (*ca.* 280–207 B.C.) and Poseidonius (*ca.* 135–50 B.C.). It greatly influenced the thought of the Middle Ages (cf. "Synchronicity," CW 8, pars. 924ff.).

enough to the average intelligence. Not only is no account taken of the significance of this sympathy, but the religious attitude is also lacking which sees in it a divine will that has to be served accordingly. Thus the erotic relationship, no matter how unconventional it may be, would have to be understood as an *opus divinum*, and the perhaps necessary sacrifice of this relationship as a *thysia*, a "ritual slaughter."[3]

Naturally these things can hardly be instilled into unintelligent people. An adequate capacity to understand is essential, for without a considerable degree of subtler intelligence they will only be misunderstood. Unfortunately one must abandon from the start any attempt to make such things clear to one's scientifically minded colleagues. A scientific education does not by any means go hand in hand with higher intelligence.

The therapeutic possibilities are consequently limited and the whole operation remains a difficult and delicate affair. You would do best to adapt to the level of the patient's understanding. How much you can expect of him is shown by the dreams. In such cases I always carefully feel my way along by the dreams and assiduously avoid having better ideas about them. The only important thing is that *he* should understand and not *I*.

In the hope that I have clarified the situation, I remain, with collegial regards,

Yours sincerely, c. g. jung

[3] The symbolic meaning of the *thysia* is discussed in "Transformation Symbolism in the Mass," CW 11, pars. 302ff., 324f., 345f.

To Cary F. Baynes

[ORIGINAL IN ENGLISH]

Dear Cary, 24 January 1958

Thank you very much for your kind and beautiful letter. As I am continuously in doubt about my subjective material,[1] it has given me a bit more confidence in my actual work: it consists in the most peculiar and to me unexpected fact that I try to work out the history

□ M.D., (1883–), then living in Connecticut. Translator, with H. G. Baynes, of Jung, *Contributions to Analytical Psychology* and *Two Essays on Analytical Psychology* (both 1928); alone, of R. Wilhelm and Jung, *The Secret of the Golden Flower* (1931) and Wilhelm's tr. of the *I Ching*. She was an old acquaintance of Jung's.
[1] Jung, who was working on his *Memories*, had sent the MS to B. for comment.

of my early days, seen as I have seen it in my youth without knowing what it meant and unable then to express it in words. Now I have the memories and the words but I am continuously disturbed by my own subjectivity. It is curious how one has an absolutely certain feeling of value on the one side and on the other an equally certain doubt about its value.

. . .

Hoping you all right, I remain,

Yours very cordially, c . g .

To Max Imboden

Dear Professor Imboden,   30 January 1958

First of all, I must thank you very much for giving me the opportunity to study your essay "Die Struktur des Staates als Symbol und als Wirklichkeit."[1] I must apologize for the delay in returning it to you, together with my answer. At my age, unfortunately, everything goes rather slowly, and I always have to wait for a favourable moment amid the flux of my intensive work in order to collect the thoughts that come to me after my reading.

Your essay is uncommonly stimulating and leads down into the depths. I entirely agree with your conception of the symbolic character of the threefold structure of the State. Seen in historical perspective, this does in fact have its origin in the trinity motif. But since I, as a psychologist, am mainly concerned with the trinitarian archetype,[2] it seems to me that the historical sequence of events merely gives the appearance of a causal nexus and that in reality the trini-

□ (1915–1969), from 1952 professor of civil law at the U. of Basel; from 1965 president of the Schweizerische Wissenschaftsrat.

[1] MS of a lecture given to the Psychological Club, Zurich, under the title "Die Symbolik der Staatsstruktur," 30 Nov. 1957. I. discussed the classical concept of sociology according to which there exist three modes of political structure (monocracy, aristocracy, democracy), whose combination alone results in a stable political organization. He suggested "an archetypal origin of the modern concept of the division of political authorities" as a "secularized trinity." He also mentioned the teachings of the German sociologist Max Weber (1864–1920), who held that "political authority has a threefold legitimization: rational, charismatic, and traditional government." (Quotations from I.'s résumé in the annual report of the Psychological Club, 1957/58.)

[2] Cf. "Dogma of the Trinity," CW 11, pars. 196f., 209, 223f., 281.

tarian archetype is always present everywhere and consequently forms the basis of every triad that manifests itself in human constructs. Originally it may well be that the triad was at the same time a religious as well as a political configuration. We can still see this in the ancient Egyptian idea of the triunity of God, *ka-mutef*, and Pharaoh.[3] Historically, too, this configuration was the model for God the Father, the Holy Ghost or procreator, and the Son = man on the religious level. On other levels it underlies all trinitarian doctrines. The trinitarian archetype seems to characterize all man's conscious constructs, in strange contrast to the fact that this archetype is really a quaternity which historically is very often represented as $3 + 1$, three equal elements being conjoined with an unequal Fourth. (In alchemy this is known as the "Axiom of Maria,"[4] where the fourth element signifies at the same time the unity of them all.)

As a human construct it is only natural that the political structure should take on a trinitarian form intended and created by man. But from the standpoint of the natural psyche this structure is not a totality, since it lacks a Fourth. As a triad it is not a natural form but is artificially carved out of Nature. Something is missing. In the case of the religious triad the Fourth is obviously the devil, a metaphysical figure missing in the Trinity. If a totality of sorts can be ascribed to the triad, the same is also true of the Fourth. That is to say, the so-called "upper," bright, conscious triad is opposed by another, "lower" triad,[5] examples of which would be the three-headed Hecate or Dante's Satan.[6] The Fourth therefore appears as an inversion of the Three—an inversion of God's or the State's sovereignty.

In the purely psychological domain, four functions characterize the

---

[3] *Ka-mutef* is the divine procreator, the "bull of his mother," the vital force of the Pharaoh who after his death becomes the father-god again. The triunity is thus compounded of the father-god (of whom Pharaoh is the incarnation), *ka-mutef* (procreative power), and Pharoah (the son). Cf. ibid., pars. 177, 197, and *Mysterium*, CW 14, pars. 350ff.

[4] Maria Prophetissa, also called Mary the Jewess, was in all likelihood an historical alchemist of the Alexandrian period (4th cent. B.C. to 7th cent. A.D.). Her axiom, one of the most influential in alchemy, runs: "One becomes two, two becomes three, and out of the third comes the one as the fourth" (*Psychology and Alchemy*, pars. 26, 209).

[5] Cf. "The Phenomenology of the Spirit in Fairytales," CW 9, i, par. 426; also 427: "If one imagines the quaternity as a square divided into two halves by a diagonal, one gets two triangles whose apices point in opposite directions." The Fourth corresponds to the lower triangle or triad.

[6] *Inferno*, Canto XXXIV, 38. Cf. "Dogma of the Trinity," par. 252; "The Spirit Mercurius," CW 13, par. 283.

orientation of consciousness. We know from experience that these functions are variously differentiated in the individual. Dream symbolism shows that three of them are capable of becoming conscious, but the fourth function remains torpid in the darkness and eludes conscious differentiation, or else it offers the greatest resistance. In its unconscious condition it is contaminated with the collective unconscious, and if, in order to put it to some conscious use, one tries to drag it out of its unconsciousness, the whole archaic background of the psyche is pulled up along with it, since the two cannot be separated. This reminds one of the myth of Hercules who went down to the underworld to free Theseus. But Theseus had grown fast to the rocks, so that when Hercules tried to wrench him free he caused a mighty earthquake. This myth, it seems to me, describes the world situation today. With the Fourth it's always the whole that's at stake. To the world as a whole one can only hold out a unitary view of the world, and that's what we lack today. The result is the great schism between West and East. The West has its trinitarian, constitutional State, the East its archaic lawlessness under a chieftain.

I was quite particularly interested to see that you substitute the "people" for the Fourth. In psychological parlance, this would correspond to the collective unconscious, and the political situation in Russia would mean an invasion by the collective unconscious. In psychopathology this means a psychosis. Your inclusion of the people, as you rightly emphasize, logically involves the necessity of integrating the whole within the individual. Without this the people would be nothing but an amorphous mass, like the inarticulate plebs of Russia. You know how deeply we are agreed on this point.

Again with best thanks and kindest regards,

Yours sincerely, C. G. JUNG

To Kurt Wolff

Dear Mr. Wolff,   1 February 1958

Best thanks for your kind letter. Frau Jaffé has told me that she has written to you that I am engaged in setting down the memories of my

□ (1887–1963), founder of the Kurt Wolff Verlag, Leipzig; emigrated to U.S.A., director of Pantheon Books, New York, which published the Bollingen Series 1946–60 and distributed it until 1967. Jung's *Memories* is his brain-child (cf. ibid., p. v/9).

early childhood. It is indeed true that while I was recounting my memories to her I myself got the desire to delve more deeply into them sometime. Often we do not sufficiently appreciate what we are carrying around in us. I realize that in a certain sense I am coming into collision with Frau Jaffé's work, but I think this difficulty can be obviated by our entering into a collaborative relationship. I would contribute my bit, so to speak. Since the whole thing is still in a fluid state at present, any technical publishing problems have not yet become acute. These will arise only when the general make-up of the book has to be considered. I myself don't know how far my preoccupation with my early memories will lead me. At the moment I feel I would like to carry my account of them only up to the point where they join up with my scientific work. For me every book is a kind of fate, and for this reason I cannot say with any certainty where the boundary line will set itself.

You may rest assured, however, that I have no desire to publicize my present activities unnecessarily. I have always observed this principle whenever I was preparing a book. While it is in the making I forbid myself all speculations about its future.

So if you want to discuss the situation with me sometime, your next visit to Europe will be soon enough. For the time being there is no need for a definitive arrangement on my side.

I had a very amiable letter from Cary in which she expressed a very positive opinion on what she had read, and I have already answered her.

Meanwhile I remain, with best greetings,

Very sincerely yours, C. G. JUNG

To Hans Bender

Dear Colleague,   . 12 February 1958

Your prefatory note[1] on synchronicity is perfectly adequate up to the point where you speak of the "synchronistic effect that was

☐ Professor of psychology, U. of Freiburg im Breslau, Germany. Director of the Institut für Grenzgebiete der Psychologie und Psychohygiene and editor of the *Zeitschrift für Parapsychologie und Grenzgebiete der Psychologie* (Bern).
[1] B. had drafted a prefatory note to Jung's "Ein astrologisches Experiment," later published in the above *Zeitschrift*, I:2/3 (May 1958), 81–92. (In CW 18.) The note appeared together with Jung's letter. The article was written as a

sought." This effect was, if I may be permitted the remark, not sought at all but found, and it was found probably because the experiment was so arranged that the restrictions were reduced to a minimum; in other words, wide room was left for the play of chance. If you give the "synchronistic arrangement" the smallest possible play, the play of chance is obviously restricted and the synchronistic "effect" thereby hindered. The synchronistic phenomenon in my experiment consists in the fact that the classical expectations of astrology were confirmed in all three batches [of marriage horoscopes], which is extremely improbable although taken individually the figures are not significant. Such a result has in principle nothing whatever to do with astrology, but could occur just as well in any other set of statistics. The astrological experiment is by its very nature a lucky hit; were it not so it would have to be casual. But presumably it is causal only in the most minimal degree. You could therefore dismiss it as a mere *lusus naturae* if nobody wondered about the so-called chance. The psychologist, who is concerned with the processes in the unconscious, knows that these remarkable "chances" happen chiefly when archetypal conditions are present, and it often looks as if the inner psychic disposition were reflected either in another person or in an animal or in circumstances generally, thanks to a simultaneous and causally independent parallel disposition. Hence the accompanying phenomena in cases of death: the clock stops, a picture falls off the wall, a glass cracks, etc. Until now such phenomena were furnished with *ad hoc* explanations and with names like telepathy, clairvoyance, precognition, psychokinesis, and so on. But that explains nothing, even when certain of these phenomena are compared with radar. I have never yet heard of a radar beam that could pick up a point in the future. It is probably better, therefore, not to put forward any such *ad hoc* analogies or special fantasy hypotheses of this kind, but to lump together all these phenomena, which exceed the range of physical probability, under the uniform aspect of the meaningful "lucky hit" and to investigate under what emotional conditions these coincidences occur; and then, following Rhine, to demonstrate the existence of these phenomena with the largest possible numbers. My line of inquiry aimed at the psychic conditions of their occurrence, and I rejected any semi-physicistic explanations in terms of energy.

---

simplified explanation of ch. 2 of "Synchronicity," CW 8. This chapter had led to many misunderstandings, as if it were meant to confirm astrological causality. Cf. Metman, 27 Mar. 54, n. 2.

I hope I have expressed myself clearly. There is, if I may be permitted the further remark, no particular meaning in investigating marriages. You could just as well observe a beehive and then, under a particular psychic condition, statistically determine the number of bees flying in and out, or watch a stony slope and see how many pebbles roll down. It is obvious that, if you choose an experimental set-up that allows chance the least possible play, you will, if you conduct it skilfully, also get the least possible chances out of it; that is, you have effectively prevented a synchronistic "effect" from taking place.

It seems to be very difficult to form a picture of the Geulincx-Leibniz lateral connection of events[2] and to rid oneself of the causal hypothesis. Chance is an event, too, and if it didn't exist causality would be axiomatic. Meaningful coincidences present a tremendous problem which it is impossible to overestimate. Leibniz as well as Schopenhauer[3] had inklings of it, but they gave a false answer because they started with an axiomatic causality.

With friendly greetings and best thanks,

Yours sincerely, C. G. JUNG

[2] The lateral connection of events refers to Leibniz's "System of Communication between Substances" according to which "From the beginning God has made each of these two substances [body and soul] of such a nature that merely by following its own peculiar laws, received with its being, it nevertheless accords with the other. . . ." He compares body and soul to two synchronized clocks, an idea Leibniz may have taken over from Geulincx. Cf. "Synchronicity," par. 937 & n. 58, also par. 948.
[3] Cf. Bender, 10 Apr. 58, n. 2.

To Baroness Vera von der Heydt

Dear Baroness,   13 February 1958

My remark about the Resurrection[1] is simply an allusion to the kind of popular phraseology that goes: Christ has proved to us by

□ Analytical psychologist, London.
[1] "The Undiscovered Self," CW 10, par. 521: "But if . . . the statement that Christ rose from the dead is to be understood not literally but symbolically, then it is capable of various interpretations that do not conflict with knowledge and do not impair the meaning of the statement." v.d.H. asked why this statement had been understood only literally and not symbolically.

his Resurrection that we also shall rise again. And so he has shown us that the hope of immortality is a justified belief—as though nobody had believed in immortality before. This is surely a layman's view which can easily be swept away with theological arguments. But for that very reason it still persists with the public, just like the Marxist theory which has been refuted hundreds of times, though this still doesn't prevent so-and-so many hundreds of millions of people from holding Communist views. It is also the general view that the event at Easter has a general significance and is not merely the local opinion that the disciples had to be given an ocular demonstration of the Lord's continued existence. Taken in its biblical context this opinion is certainly correct but it doesn't reflect the general view at all. As psychologists we are not concerned with the question of truth, with whether something is historically correct, but with living forces, living opinions which determine human behaviour. Whether these opinions are right or wrong is another matter altogether. One critic, for instance, has taken me to task for having chosen to comment on such an inferior text as the *Amitayur-Dhyana-Sutra;*[2] there were much better Pali texts[3] for elucidating the essence of Buddhism. But in Japan and the Mongolian areas of Buddhism this *Sutra* enjoys the highest authority and is far better known than the Pali Canon. For me, therefore, it was much more important to comment on this *Sutra* than on the undoubtedly more correct views of the Canon. It is the same with the Christian doctrine: if we wish to discuss it in its present form we can only do so in terms of the current opinions and not on the basis of the best textual editions and the best possible theological explanations. Otherwise we would be theologizing and that is decidedly off my beat. I am concerned with the real man here and now, quite particularly so in an essay like "The Undiscovered Self." With best greetings,

Yours sincerely, C. G. JUNG

[2] Commented on in "The Psychology of Eastern Meditation," CW 11.

[3] Pali is a dialect related to Sanskrit; the Pali Canon is a collection of Hinayana Buddhist texts, preserved in Ceylon. (Hinayana, "the Small Vehicle," is an early form of Buddhism, largely replaced by Mahayana, "the Great Vehicle.")

417

To Karl Schmid

Dear Professor Schmid,   25 February 1958

Please excuse my long silence! Meanwhile I have submitted your two kind gifts[1] to an attentive reading. You can scarcely imagine what an encouragement it is for me to see someone making a sensible use of my ideas. Forgive me for stressing this egocentric viewpoint. The truth is that I have not been exactly spoiled in this respect and have often had to ask myself whether I have any "contemporaries" at all.

I was especially interested in your "Versuch über die schweizerische Nationalität," a subject to which I have devoted some thought. This by way of necessity, since I have knocked about a bit in the world and so could not help becoming conscious of myself as a Swiss. True to my nature-loving bias, I have followed the call of the wild, the age-old trail through secluded wildernesses where a primitive human community may be found. In my youth I made a discovery which was confirmed for me many years later by the inhabitants of the savannahs of Mt. Elgon.[2] There we came across people who had never seen any white men before. We had to communicate with them through three languages. We asked them what they were called. They named their individual names—most unexpectedly, because all the tribes we had met till then had, without being asked, called themselves by the name of their tribe. With visible effort and much hemming and hawing the Elgonyis came out with an obviously embarrassed answer which sent my black bearers into fits of laughter. My headman, a long thin Somali, told me the "natives" were so stupid that they didn't even know what they were called. They said they were called "the people who are there." I found this very enlightening.

In my youth I "got at" Switzerland from four different directions: from Germany, from the Franche Comté, the Vorarlberg, and the Plain of Lombardy. From the heights of the Black Forest you look across the Rhine into a wide bowl between the Jura Mountains and the Alps; from France you wander through gently rolling hills up to

---

☐ (Handwritten.)

[1] Schmid, *Neuere Aspekte der Geistesgeschichte*, Kultur- und Staatswissenschaftliche Schriften (Zurich), no. 99 (1957); "Versuch über die schweizerische Nationalität," *Aufsätze und Reden* (1957).

[2] Cf. *Memories*, pp. 253ff./238ff.

the steep precipices descending into this bowl. From Italy you climb over the high Alpine crest which forms, as it were, the hinge of the mussel-shell, and from the Vorarlberg the Lake of Constance and the deep valleys of the Rhine and the Landquart[3] finish off the oval. The people who sit in the shell and round its rim are the Swiss, and that's me. Having to speak a different language depending on the locality becomes second nature and is a trifle compared with the overwhelming fact of the mussel-shell we are housed in. We are "the people who are there" and need no name. They are called "Swiss" only by accident. Even the earlier name "Helvetii" did not sit with them naturally. No other people could live here as they would then have the wrong ancestral spirits, who dwell in the earth and are authentic Swiss.

This feeling of primordiality seems to me the beginning of all things. Everything that happens "outside" is echoed in the "resonant" Swiss who is my neighbour or even lives in the same house. Usually I hear through him what is happening outside. Strange or incomprehensible it may be, but not hatefully antagonistic. One can talk with him about it, for as a Swiss, a fellow inhabitant of the mussel-shell, he is only half besotted by it and only fooled up to a point. He may even be my cousin or brother-in-law and "in our family," etc. So everything that comes from outside is divided by 2 or 3 and is always balanced by an "on the other hand." For this reason we are a constant stumbling-block to all the tomfooleries and excesses of the outside. Sitting in the central mussel-shell, we are the "sons of the mother." Hence the old astrological tradition says that our zodiacal sign is Virgo (♍). However, there is no unanimity on this score, since the other version says that our sign is Taurus (♉). It is a virile, creative sign, but *earthly* like Virgo. This ancient psychological insight expresses the fact that what is enclosed in the mother is a germinating seed that will one day burst through, as you have shown with other words and convincing examples. The stolidity, inaccessibility, obstinacy and whatever else of the kind the Swiss are accused of are all marks of the feminine element Virgo. The union of ♂ and ♀ alludes to the *principium individuationis* as a supreme union of opposites, as you too have proclaimed in the confusion of the present, at least for those that have ears to hear. For this I am especially grateful to you. It is all so exceedingly delicate and yet so important that I cannot refrain from wishing

---

[3] Tributary of the Rhine, in Canton Graubünden.

it might yet be discussed by us Swiss, anyway under our breath, and an incontestable monument to the *esprit Helvetien* be erected, which would serve as a far-shining beacon to the rudderless Western world and would above all else enlighten our own darkness. From those "outside" we should not expect too much at present. After all, they have no nephews and nieces who speak a different language, nor do they live in the mussel-shell of the παμμήτωρ,[4] the *genetrix omnium*.

I have reaped a rich harvest from your essay and I hope your book will find many eager readers. Again with best thanks,

Very sincerely yours, c. g. j u n g

[4] = Mother of All, equivalent of *genetrix omnium*.

To Hans Bender

Dear Colleague,   6 March 1958

I have looked through the galleys[1] as requested. I quite agree with you that the word "effect" should really always be put in quotation marks or, better, avoided altogether.

Everything that can be repeated experimentally is necessarily causal, for the whole concept of causality is based on this statistical result. If, for instance, we examine Rhine's experiments critically, we cannot avoid the conclusion that they include a causal factor in so far as they are repeatable. We think this causal factor is to be found in the known emotional condition, i.e., in the archetypal situation. The experimental activation of an archetypal situation has to be explained causally, since there is no possibility of explaining it otherwise and no reason to do so. In this emotional condition a syndrome[2] occurs which has no causal explanation, but it does not occur of necessity and does not occur regularly, only with a certain frequency that exceeds mere probability. How it comes about that space and time are reduced by these meaningful chance occurrences cannot be understood in terms of causality. This is most obviously the case with precognitions. If we succeed in producing an archetypal situa-

[1] Cf. Bender, 12 Feb. 58, n. 1.
[2] "Syndrome" is used here in the literal sense of a set of concurrent events (the usual meaning is the concurrence of symptoms in disease).

420

tion experimentally, we create an opportunity for such occurrences to produce themselves, though they need not. According to Leibniz and Schopenhauer these lateral connections of events are necessary events, i.e., they must occur under certain conditions. But this is not borne out by experience. Nevertheless, Rhine's experiments prove that their probability is lower than the mathematical probability. The situation is undoubtedly complicated and at every step one risks falling back into the causal view again. There is also—and this point must always be kept in mind—the possibility of certain physical factors which we simply know nothing about at present. In the existing state of our knowledge, anyway, it seems utterly impossible to reverse causality, as in precognition, where a future event, apparently not yet in existence, causes an event in the present. Even so it should be noted that Heisenberg considers a reversal of the time-flow in the microcosm thinkable.[3] The microcosm, however, coincides with the unconscious. The hypothesis of a fabric of order would fit the Leibniz-Schopenhauer theory[4] perfectly, according to which correspondences must occur at the points of intersection between the meridians and the parallels. But for this, as I have said, there is no evidence. Everything, at least so far as my experience goes, indicates that undeniable correspondences do *occasionally* occur, which I call "synchronistic" just because of their temporal simultaneity, i.e., their *coincidentia*.

With regard to the horoscope I have serious doubts whether it can be understood as a purely synchronistic phenomenon, for there are unquestionable causal connections between the planetary aspects and the powerful effects of proton radiation,[5] though we are still very much in the dark as to what its physiological effects might be.

Regarding my secretary's letter I would like expressly to authorize the publication of my first letter as well as any use you might care to make of this one.

Yours sincerely, C. G. JUNG

[3] The proposition that any physical situation should be reversible in time, the so-called "time and reflection symmetry."
[4] Cf. Bender, 10 Apr. 58, n. 2.
[5] Cf. Jaffé, 8 Sept. 51, n. 2.

To the Rev. H. L. Philp

[ORIGINAL IN ENGLISH]

Dear Mr. Philp,   10 March 1958

I am bewildered by your questions.[1] It is surely obvious to everybody why I am concerned with theology: I am asked a hundred theological questions by my patients, anxious to get an answer they were unable to obtain from their priest or parson. I myself, as you know, could not get an answer to the question about the identity of the Old Testament and New Testament conception of God.

The archetype is the psychological interpretation of the theologoumenon "God" and this has obviously to do with theology. I am very much concerned with theological teaching, since I am seriously occupied with the urgent questions of my patients and—last but not least—of myself. Our Christian theology is obviously *not* based "on the total religious experience." It does not even consider the ambivalent experience of the Old Testament God. Being based on faith, it is only remotely conditioned by the immediate archetypal experience. If it were acquainted with it, theologians would not have the least difficulty in understanding my argument.

You know better than I do through how many discussions and through what labour pains the dogma of Trinity came into existence. There is no evangelical or apostolic evidence for this dogma with the exception of the τρισάγιον formula.[2] One can only say that it was an archetypal experience inasmuch as it was a pre-Christian, pagan image, the famous ὁμοουσία[3] of father God, Ka-mutef, and Pharaoh.[4] This was the age-old Egyptian model of the Trinity, not to mention the numerous pagan triads.[5] If I remember correctly, the term ὁμοούσιος appears first with the Egyptian Gnostic, Basilides.

It is indeed the Trinity dogma where one can see clearly the influence of the archetype on theological formulation. Another most

---

[1] P. submitted questions on the following topics in connection with his forthcoming *Jung and the Problem of Evil* (cf. Philp, 26 Oct. 56, n. 2): 1. the relationship between the archetypal God-image and the God of theology; 2. Jung's concern with theology; 3. the relationship of "the total religious experience" to the archetype of God. He also stated that the doctrine of the Trinity did not "come into existence mainly as a theological structure but was based on what the early Christians believed was an experience of God."

[2] The Trishagion ("thrice holy"), the threefold invocation of God as "Holy, Holy, Holy" in the Gallican (Old French) Mass. Cf. Isaiah 6:3.

[3] Cf. Niederer, 23 June 47, n. 6.

[4] Cf. Imboden, 30 Jan. 58, n. 3.

[5] Such triads are discussed in "Dogma of the Trinity," CW 11, pars. 172ff.

striking example is Artemis,[6] the Ephesian Magna Mater, resurrecting as θεοτόκος at the Concilium of Ephesus,[7] and glorified as *regina coeli* and *domina omnium rerum creatarum*,[8] as a real *Dea Natura*, in the Assumptio B.V.

On the other hand it is just the Trinity dogma, as it stands, that is the classical example of an artificial structure and an intellectual product, so much so that no theologian has yet recognized or admitted its origin in Egyptian theology. It is by no means an original Christian experience, but presumably a dim reminiscence. We don't know when the knowledge of the hieroglyphs completely vanished, but it is quite likely that it lasted down to Ptolemaean times[9] and even later.

I must admit that I do not understand the purpose of your questions. Why—indeed—do we discuss theological questions at all?

Sincerely yours, C. G. JUNG

[6] Artemis (the Roman Diana), the virgin huntress. She was worshipped in Ephesus as the goddess of fertility: the many-breasted Diana. Cf. *Symbols of Transformation*, CW 5, Pl. XXIVb.

[7] Theotokos, "God-bearer." The Council of Ephesus (A.D. 431) affirmed Mary's status as "God-bearer" in opposition to the Nestorians, who accorded her merely the title of Anthropotokos, "Man-bearer." Cf. "Dogma of the Trinity," CW 11, par. 194, and *Mysterium*, CW 14, par. 237.

[8] = Queen of Heaven and Mistress of All Created Things.

[9] The Ptolemies, Macedonian kings of Egypt, ruled between 323 and 30 B.C.

Anonymous

Dear Herr N.,   13 March 1958

Thank you for your kind letter of 7.2.58. You have rightly recognized that the encounter with the anima logically leads to a great expansion of our sphere of experience. The anima is a representative of the unconscious and hence a mediatrix, just as the Beata Virgo is called "mediatrix" in the dogma of the Assumption. On the one hand the anima is an allurement to an intensification of life, but on the other she opens our eyes to its religious aspect. Here you are confronted with the whole problem of the present and, in particular, with the question you raise concerning the nature of religious experience. The greater part of modern humanity is satisfied with the Church and with belief in the ecclesiastical sense. Another part

□ Switzerland.

demands the convincing primordial experience. Theology, precisely because it is ecclesiastical, naturally knows very little of this and has developed an understandable resistance to it. The primordial experience is not concerned with the historical bases of Christianity but consists in an immediate experience of God (as was had by Moses, Job, Hosea, Ezekiel among others) which "con-vinces" because it is "overpowering." But this is something you can't easily talk about. One can only say that somehow one has to reach the rim of the world or get to the end of one's tether in order to partake of the terror or grace of such an experience at all. Its nature is such that it is readily understandable why the Church is actually a place of refuge or protection for those who cannot endure the fire of the divine presence. A logion says: "He that is near me is near the fire. He that is far from me is far from the kingdom."[1] I think I understand ecclesiastical Christianity but the theologians do not understand me. Their *raison d'être* consists in the very fact of belonging to a Church, and mine in coming to terms with that indefinable Being we call "God." Probably no compromise is possible except that of "coexistence," each allowing the other his say. At any rate, again and again the allegory is repeated of the strait and steep path trodden by the few and the broad path trodden by the many, though with no guarantee that the few will necessarily get to heaven and the many go down to hell.

Wherever our need for knowledge may turn we stumble upon opposites, which ultimately determine the structure of existence. The centre is the indivisible monad of the self, the unity and wholeness of the experiencing subject. With best regards,

Yours sincerely, c. g. j u n g

[1] Cf. Corti, 30 Apr. 29, n. 4.

To Daniel Brody

Dear Dr. Brody,   18 March 1958

I feel the need to recommend the collected papers of Toni Wolff[1] to your attention. As president of the Psychological Club in Zurich for many years, she had a unique opportunity to get to know the

☐ (1883–1969), Hungarian journalist, later in Switzerland as proprietor of Rhein Verlag (Zurich), whose publications included the *Eranos-Jahrbücher* and Joyce's *Ulysses* in German.

424

ambience of analytical psychology from all sides as well as a host of its representatives from practically all the nations of Europe and all Anglo-Saxon countries. Her circle of friends and acquaintances extended over continents and, as an assiduous correspondent, she maintained the liveliest contacts with them all her life. Her activity as a practising psychologist, however, left her little time for literary work, only a small part of which has been printed and become known to a wider public. All her papers have been collected in this volume. They are distinguished not only by their intellectual content but by the fact that the author had personally experienced the development of analytical psychology from the fateful year 1912[2] right up to the recent past and was thus in a position to record her reactions and sympathetic interest from the first. Her papers therefore also have a documentary value. Even those who did not know the author personally will glean from them an impression of the versatility and depth of her spiritual personality. I am sure that her collected papers will be welcomed not only by the numerous friends who mourn her death but by many other people who are interested in the problems of analytical psychology.

Please remember me to your wife!

Very sincerely yours, C. G. JUNG

[1] Cf. Kirsch, 28 May 53, n. 1.
[2] Marking the break with Freud.

To F. Fischer

Dear Herr Fischer,   23 March 1958

In reply to your letter of March 18th I can only tell you that though Prof. Pauli has informed me of his collaboration with Heisenberg he did not—for understandable reasons—give me the details of this collaboration. Unfortunately I am unable to express an opinion on Heisenberg's formula[1] because, firstly, as said, I don't know

☐ Electrical engineer, Zurich.
[1] The formulation of the unified field theory in 1958 which, if it had been verified, would have abolished the "uncertainty (or indeterminacy) principle" (cf. Nelson, 17 June 56, n. 4) formulated by Heisenberg himself in 1927. A unified field theory would combine the electromagnetic and gravitational fields in one set of equations. Einstein worked on it in his later years, but without success, nor has Heisenberg's formula been satisfactorily proved.

the details, and secondly, I would not be in a position to follow the mathematical argument. I deduce the fact that acausal phenomena must exist from the purely statistical nature of causality, since statistics are only possible anyway if there are also exceptions. This relationship of the expected to the unexpected can be considered compensatory on heuristic grounds. It is not improbable that a unitary formula would recognizably include the quaternity principle, but because of my ignorance of the actual state of affairs I would not venture any statements on this subject. On the other hand, it is obvious to me that synchronicity is the indispensable counterpart to causality[2] and to that extent could be considered compensatory. By far the greatest number of polarities that occur in nature are compensatory in this sense. This "world model" would indeed mean an incalculable upheaval in our understanding of the cosmos. The upheaval has begun in any case with the posing of this question, even though it cannot yet be answered with certainty.

Yours sincerely, c. g. j u n g

[2] F. asked Jung if he thought it possible that causality and synchronicity might stand in a relationship of complementarity.

To Cottie A. Burland

[O R I G I N A L   I N   E N G L I S H]

Dear Mr. Burland,   7 April 1958

I am most obliged to you for sending me your interesting account of the Fejérváry-Mayer time-mandala.[1] As I am unfortunately a complete layman *in rebus Mexicanis* I can only admire your insight into old Mexican symbolism. My general and non-specific knowledge of symbolism enables me however to appreciate the remarkable paral-

☐ British writer on pre-Columbian Mexico, alchemy, etc.

[1] B. was writing a commentary on the Mexican Codex Laud which, together with the Codex Fejérváry-Mayer (Mayer Collection, Free Public Museum, Liverpool), is one of the oldest Mexican MSS, predating A.D. 1350. The Codex opens up with a page showing the four directions of time in the form of a mandala (see illus., from *Symbols of Transformation*, CW 5, fig. 38; cf. Burland, *The Gods of Mexico*, 1967, Pl. 8). The pattern is found also in the Aztec "Great Calendar Stone" (*Psychology and Alchemy*, CW 12, fig. 41). Cf. Burland, *Introduction to Codex Laud* (Graz, 1966).

lelism between old Mexico and the rest of the world, including the unconscious of modern European man. The underlying scheme, the *quaternio*, i.e., the psychological equation of primordial dynamis (*prima causa*) with gods and their mythology, time and space, is a psychological problem of the first order. I have tried to deal with it many a time and particularly in my book *Aion* (not yet translated into English). The first steps in this direction you will find in *The Secret of the Golden Flower*. It is a difficult subject, I admit, but it is the basic phenomenon in many religions.

I am glad to know that you appreciate the *I Ching*. The European mind often finds it difficult to follow the movements of Tao. In this respect dream analysis has helped me very much, as it has taught me to consider the psyche as an objective entity and not only as a willful product of my consciousness. The summit of European hybris is the French phrase: "faire un rêve." But in reality we seem rather to be the dream of somebody or something independent of our conscious ego, at least in all fateful moments.

Sincerely yours, C. G. JUNG

Aztec mandala (world plan), from a codex: see Burland, 7 Apr. 58

To Hans Bender

Dear Colleague,   10 April 1958

Very many thanks for so thoughtfully sending me your report on Ufo observation.[1] I shall read it soon and will then return it to you.

It is indeed very difficult to explain the astrological phenomenon. I am not in the least disposed to an either-or explanation. I always say that with a psychological explanation there is only the alternative: either *and* or! This seems to me to be the case with astrology too. The readiest explanation, as you quite rightly point out, would seem to be the parallelistic view. It is in line with the Geulincx-Leibniz theory of collateral correspondences which you will find formulated most clearly in Schopenhauer.[2]

My objection to this theory is that it presupposes a strict causality, or rather, is founded on an axiomatic causality. Accordingly, the correspondence would have to conform to law. This is to some extent so with very large numbers, as Rhine has shown; but nevertheless so seldom that the limits of mathematical probability are exceeded only by a little. From this we could conclude that in the realm of smaller numbers the correspondence lies within the limits of probability and so cannot be rated a phenomenon that conforms to law, as your clock and watch simile demonstrates.[3] You set your watch by the clock, and this amounts to a causal dependence, just as in Leibniz's monadology all the monadic watches were originally wound up by the same creator.

The synchronicity concept discards this *harmonia praestabilita*, or parallelism, because if this principle operated there would necessarily be a far greater and more regular number of correspondences than is the case in reality. Making due allowance for errors, one gets the impression that these "lucky hits" occur relatively seldom. Although

---

[1] B. sent Jung the transcript of a tape recording in which several people, whom B. considered reliable witnesses, reported Ufo sightings.

[2] Schopenhauer, in his "Transcendent Speculations on the Apparent Design in the Fate of the Individual," *Parerga und Paralipomena*, I (1891), employs a geographical analogy to illustrate the simultaneity of causally unconnected events, where the parallels of latitude intersect the meridians of longitude, which are thought of as causal chains; by virtue of this cross-connection even simultaneous events are linked to causality. Cf. "Synchronicity," par. 828.

[3] B. spoke of "a structure of order which would probably have to be understood in a parallelistic sense, as in the oft-quoted relationship between clock and watch, where the directing *tertium* [third] remains open."

we cannot conceive of a causal law and hence necessary connection between an event and its determination in time (horoscope), it nevertheless looks as though such a connection did exist; for on it is based the traditional interpretation of the horoscope, which presupposes and establishes a certain regularity of events. So even if we ascribe only a limited meaning to the horoscope, we are already assuming a necessary connection between the event and the heavenly constellation.

The fact, however, is that our whole astrological determination of time does not correspond to any actual constellation in the heavens because the vernal equinox has long since moved out of Aries into Pisces and from the time of Hipparchus has been artificially set at o° Aries. Consequently the correlations with the planetary houses are purely fictitious, and this rules out the possibility of a causal connection with the actual positions of the stars, so that the astrological determination of time is purely symbolic. Even so, the rough correlation with the actual seasons remains unimpaired, and this is of great significance so far as the horoscope is concerned. There are, for instance, spring births and autumn births, which play an especially important role in the animal world. Then, besides the seasonal influences there are also the fluctuations of proton radiation, which have been proved to exert a considerable influence on human life. These are all causally explicable influences and argue in favour of astrological correlations that conform to law. To that extent, therefore, I would be inclined to rank astrology among the natural sciences.

On the other hand, astrological observation yields cases where one hesitates to maintain the validity of a purely causalistic explanation. Cases of astonishing predictions, for instance, give me at any rate the feeling of a meaningful "lucky hit," a meaningful coincidence, since they seem to me to make excessive demands on a causal explanation by their extreme improbability, and to that extent I would rather adduce synchronicity as an explanatory principle. An historical example of this kind is the reputed coincidence of Christ's birth with the triple royal conjunction in Pisces in the year 7 B.C.[4]

As I have said, astrology seems to require differing hypotheses, and I am unable to opt for an either-or. We shall probably have to

---

[4] The conjunction of Jupiter and Saturn, the astrological signs of life and death, signifies the union of extreme opposites. This conjunction occurred three times in the year 7 B.C. (*Aion*, CW 9, ii, par. 130).

resort to a mixed explanation, for nature does not give a fig for the sanitary neatness of the intellectual categories of thought.

Should you care to make use of these remarks you are quite free to do so. Hoping I have made my perplexity clear to you, I remain,

Yours very sincerely, C. G. JUNG

P.S. I am taking the liberty of sending you by the same post a copy of my little book *Ein moderner Mythus*.[5]

[5] See Flinker, 17 Oct. 57, n. 2.

To F. v. Tischendorf

Dear Colleague, 19 April 1958

You have posed a rather ticklish question,[1] for where "national character" is concerned the most unlikely people become sensitive and sometimes even go to the length of asserting that no such thing exists.

Just as a person refuses to recognize his own shadow side, so, but all the more strongly, he hates recognizing the shadow side of the nation behind which he is so fond of concealing himself. At any rate, remarks on national character, particularly when they are to the point, are the least appreciated and are fought tooth and nail. Furthermore, a psychology that takes its stand on nationality does not yet exist, or is only in its most tentative beginnings. For this a mind is required that is not only not blinded by national prejudice but is also capable of seeing other nationalities objectively, that is, not in terms of its own national bias. This prerequisite is most exacting and is seldom if ever met with.

As a Swiss, my situation is such that by nature my heart is divided into four,[2] and because of the smallness of our country I can count on coming into contact at least with the four surrounding nations or cultural complexes. In so far as I am to some extent international

□ Bad Godesberg, Germany.

[1] T. asked Jung for an article on "National Character and Road Behaviour." Jung felt unprepared for such a task, but his letter was published as an article, "Nationalcharakter und Verkehrsverhalten," in the *Zentralblatt für Verkehrs-Medizin, Verkehrs-Psychologie und angrenzende Gebiete* (Alfeld), IV:3 (1958).

[2] Corresponding to the four components of the Swiss population: German, French, Italian, Romansch.

and well acquainted with the Anglo-Saxon world, and have also learned a thing or two about Oriental cultures, I might almost fancy myself capable of saying something almost to the point. But on the other hand I must admit that the limited horizon of the Swiss can be effectively preserved only thanks to a national prejudice. We experience nationality as a peculiar factor that differs essentially from the national feeling of other peoples. The strength of the prejudice depends very much on whether one belongs to a numerically small or large nation. These prejudices are unavoidable and, I would say, of almost superhuman proportions. That is why no useful work has yet been done on the psychology of nations.

With special regard to "road behaviour," a psychological approach to this problem would first of all have to concern itself with the psychology of the persons suffering and causing accidents, and only then seek to establish the more general conditions to which individual modes of behaviour can be reduced. The primarily personal causes of negligence or recklessness derive from a whole series of more or less typical attitudes which are well known to the characterologist. Less known are those causes which are not traits of character or behaviour but derive from general assumptions. Here we enter the realm of assumptions underlying national psychology, general consciousness of the law, religious ideas, etc. Investigation of these conditions then necessarily leads to observations on national differences.

One of the most important points in this respect is one's attitude towards emotionality, and to what extent an affect is held to be controllable or not. The English believe in controlling emotions and bring up their children accordingly. Having emotions is "bad taste" and proof of "bad upbringing." The Italians cultivate their emotions and admire them, for which reason they become relatively harmless and at most absorb too much time and attention. The Germans feel entitled to their manly anger, the French adore analysing their emotions rationally so as not to have to take them seriously. The Swiss, if they are well brought up, do not trust themselves to give vent to their emotions. The Indians, if influenced by Buddhism, habitually depotentiate their emotions by reciting a *mantra*. Thus, in Ceylon, I once saw two peasants get their carts stuck together, which in any other part of the world would have led to endless vituperation. But they settled the matter by murmuring the *mantra* "aduca anatman" (passing disturbance—no soul).

The high figures for motoring accidents, relatively the same in all countries, show that none of these attitudes is an adequate palliative.

Only the way in which accidents come about or are dealt with displays certain differences.

With the exception of the English and the Buddhists, nobody is aware that an affect is in itself a morbid condition. The well-known fact that the Englishman feels at home everywhere comes out in the story of the Austrian and the Englishman. The Austrian says to him: "I see you're a stranger here." The Englishman replies: "Of course not, I'm British!" This kind of prejudice can make a motorist very careless and reckless. The German feels a stranger everywhere because he suffers from a national feeling of inferiority. Consequently, he lets himself be far too much impressed by foreign ways and habits, and at the same time feels obliged to protest against them, thus making himself thoroughly unpopular. The Italian will tell you a lie because he doesn't want to make a disagreeable impression. The well-brought-up Frenchman is extremely polite in order to keep you at a distance. The American is a problem in himself. It is his national prejudice to be as harmless as possible, or at least to appear so. He has the unpleasant task of having to assimilate primitive cultures in his midst, and to do this he has to believe pre-eminently in himself in order to escape infection. As a result, he is always animated by the best motives and is profoundly unconscious of his own shadow.

You see from these examples that all sorts of *aperçus* can be arrived at, but they lack any kind of system because the subject is too large. National prejudice is something bigger than the individual and is answered by compensations coming from the collective unconscious. This causes almost insuperable difficulties for the rational intellect. Hence, too, the old idea that every country or people has its own angel, just as the earth has a soul. And in the same way that nations lead lives of their own, the unconscious compensation has an existence of its own which manifests itself in a special development of symbols. It can be seen in religious and political developments as well—for instance, loss of monarchy and difficulties in establishing a democracy; or, as in England, retention of monarchy and a correspondingly smoother course of democratic development. The French have never got over the murder of their king. For France as well as Germany democracy is not a uniting bond but an unleashing of regional interests having all the marks of an infantile condition. The fact that one can go on with these *aperçus* ad infinitum demonstrates the unwieldiness of the problem.

Thanks to my profession and my clients, I have an intimate knowledge of modern man in his national setting. But for that very reason

I could in no circumstances muster up the courage to tackle this problem. If the psychology of individuals is still only in its beginnings, how much more so is the psychology of nations—not to mention the psychology of mankind. We are still a long way from being able to frame generally valid theories, let alone construct a system. Even if, undeterred by age, I tried to fulfill the task you have set me, this *tour de force* would nonetheless be impossible to bring off because the difficulty of the problem far exceeds my powers. All the same, I am extremely interested that you have recognized its existence so clearly. I feel rather like old Moses, who was permitted to cast but a fleeting glance into the land of ethnopsychological problems.

Yours sincerely, C. G. JUNG

To James Kirsch

Dear Kirsch,   29 April 1958

Thank you for your letter and the additional information about the Guatemala Ufo![1] I am glad at least to have made an understatement and not the contrary. (Here I notice that I am quite needlessly answering you in English, due to the fact that by now I have come to speak more English than German.)[2] O *quae mutatio rerum!*

It is characteristic that in your dream it is the Russians who send the Ufos (white discs), for Russia represents the other side which complements the West.

I wish you good luck and patience for your theological talks. I know only a few theologians who understand the difference between *image* and *original* and take it seriously. Too little *humilitas* and too much *hybris*! And what about the psychologists? V*ae scientibus!*[3]

☐ (Handwritten.) Published (in K.'s tr.) in *Psychological Perspectives*, III:2 (fall 1972).

[1] In Dec. 1956 while in Guatemala, K. had observed a Ufo, "a shining small sphere in the sky which remained in the same place for many hours." He went home and immediately wrote to Jung about his observation. — The "additional information" was that "our two Guatemalan women servants had continued observing the Ufo outside" and that "the Ufo had suddenly moved, and very swiftly, to another place." The two women described to K. exactly where it was but he could not see it although they went on seeing it for some time. Cf. "Flying Saucers: A Modern Myth," CW 10, par. 613.

[2] This sentence and the rest of the letter are written in German.

[3] = Woe to the scientists!

433

I am getting along fairly well, growing older all the time. With best regards,

Yours ever, C. G. JUNG

To the Rev. Morton T. Kelsey

[ORIGINAL IN ENGLISH]

Dear Mr. Kelsey, 3 May 1958

Thank you very much for your kind letter.[1] I appreciate it indeed, since it is the first and only one I got from a Protestant theologian [in the U.S.A.] who has read *Job*. I can't help feeling that I am beneath consideration. All the more I value your kind effort to write to me. The psychology of the Book of Job seems to be of the highest importance concerning the inner motivation of Christianity. The fact that none—as far as I am able to see—of the existing commentaries has drawn the necessary conclusions has long since been a cause of wonder to me. Occasional outbursts of shortsighted wrath didn't surprise me. The almost total apathy and indifference of the theologians was more astonishing.

As you realize, I am discussing the admittedly anthropomorphic image of Yahweh and I do not apply metaphysical judgments. From this methodological standpoint I gain the necessary freedom of criticism. The absence of human morality in Yahweh is a stumbling block which cannot be overlooked, as little as the fact that Nature, i.e., God's creation, does not give us enough reason to believe it to be purposive or reasonable in the human sense. We miss reason and moral values, that is, two main characteristics of a mature human mind. It is therefore obvious that the Yahwistic image or conception of the deity is less than [that of] certain human specimens: the image of a personified brutal force and of an unethical and non-spiritual mind, yet inconsistent enough to exhibit traits of kindness and generosity besides a violent power-drive. It is the picture of a sort of nature-demon and at the same time of a primitive chieftain aggrandized to a colossal size, just the sort of conception one could expect of a more or less barbarous society—*cum grano salis*.

---

[1] K., rector of St. Luke's Episcopal Church, Monrovia (near Los Angeles), California, wrote a highly appreciative letter about *Answer to Job*: "How can I thank you enough for this book? It has served as a catalyst enabling a fusion to take place between my theological thinking and the experience of life, which my analytical work has stimulated . . ."

This image owes its existence certainly not to an invention or intellectual formulation, but rather to a spontaneous manifestation, i.e., to religious experience of men like Samuel[2] and Job and thus it retains its validity to this day. People still ask: Is it possible that God allows such things? Even the Christian God may be asked: Why do you let your only son suffer for the imperfection of your creation?

The image of God corresponds to its manifestation, i.e., such religious experience produces such an image. There is no better image anywhere in the world. For this reason Buddha has placed the "enlightened" man higher than the highest Brahman gods.

This most shocking defectuosity of the God-image ought to be explained or understood. The nearest analogy to it is our experience of the unconscious: it is a psyche whose nature can only be described by paradoxes: it is personal as well as impersonal, moral and amoral, just and unjust, ethical and unethical, of cunning intelligence and at the same time blind, immensely strong and extremely weak, etc. This is the psychic foundation which produces the raw material for our conceptual structures. The unconscious is a piece of Nature our mind cannot comprehend. It can only sketch models of a possible and partial understanding. The result is most imperfect, although we pride ourselves on having "penetrated" the innermost secrets of Nature.

The real nature of the objects of human experience is still shrouded in darkness. The scientist cannot concede a higher intelligence to theology than to any other branch of human cognition. We know as little of a supreme being as of matter. But there is as little doubt of the existence of a supreme being as of matter. *The world beyond is a reality*, an experiential fact. We only don't understand it.[3]

Under these circumstances it is permissible to assume that the Summum Bonum is so good, so high, so perfect, but so remote that it is entirely beyond our grasp. But it is equally permissible to assume that the ultimate reality is a being representing all the qualities of its creation, virtue, reason, intelligence, kindness, consciousness, *and their opposites*, to our mind a complete paradox. The latter view fits the facts of human experience, whereas the former cannot explain away the obvious existence of evil and suffering. Πόθεν τὸ κακόν;[4]—this age-old question is not answered unless you assume the existence of a [supreme] being *who is in the main unconscious*. Such a model would

---

[2] Cf. I Sam. 3.

[3] This paragraph is published in Kelsey, *Tongue Speaking: An Experiment in Spiritual Experience* (1964), pp. 192f.

[4] = Whence evil?

explain why God has created a man gifted with consciousness and why He seeks His goal in him. In this the Old Testament, the New Testament, and Buddhism agree. Master Eckhart said it: "God is not blessed in His Godhead, He must be born in man forever."[5] This is what happens in Job: *The creator sees himself through the eyes of man's consciousness* and this is the reason why God had to become man, and why man is progressively gifted with the dangerous prerogative of the divine "mind." You have it in the saying: "Ye are gods,"[6] and man has not even begun yet to know himself. He would need it to be prepared to meet the dangers of the *incarnatio continua*,[7] which began with Christ and the distribution of the "Holy Ghost" to poor, almost unconscious beings. We are still looking back to the pentecostal events in a dazed way instead of looking forward to the goal the Spirit is leading us to. Therefore mankind is wholly unprepared for the things to come. Man is compelled by divine forces to go forward to increasing consciousness and cognition, developing further and further away from his religious background because he does not understand it any more. His religious teachers and leaders are still hypnotized by the beginnings of a then new aeon of consciousness instead of understanding them and their implications. What one once called the "Holy Ghost" is an impelling force, creating wider consciousness and responsibility and thus enriched cognition. The real history of the world seems to be the progressive incarnation of the deity.

Here I must stop, although I should like to continue my argument. I feel tired and that means something in old age.

Thank you again for your kind letter!

Yours sincerely, c. g. jung

[5] Cf. *Psychological Types*, CW 6, par. 418.
[6] John 10:34.
[7] Continuing incarnation, resulting from the past, present, and future indwelling of the Holy Ghost in man. Cf. Evans, 17 Feb. 54, n. 5.

To H. Rossteutscher

Dear Herr Rossteutscher,   3 May 1958

Your reflections are eminently philosophical.[1] I myself do not belong to this fraternity, being a mere empiricist who is content with makeshift models. But I do expect such a model to take adequate account of the nature of the phenomenon in question. One characteristic that leaps to the eye is the absence of any demonstrable causation, or rather the impossibility of a causal hypothesis. Hence the concept of "effect" falls to the ground, and its place is taken by the simple postulate of coincidence, which need not in itself have any causal connotation.

A second characteristic is the equivalence of meaning, which gives mere coincidence the appearance of an interconnection. Accordingly I chose the name synchronicity, as it brings out the relative simultaneity of such phenomena and supplements it with the conjecture of meaningful coincidence.

As you see, my hypothesis is not an explanation but only a designation. It does however take due account of the fact that causality is a statistical truth which necessarily allows for exceptions. The term "synchronicity" is first and foremost a proposed name which at the same time stresses the empirical fact of meaningful coincidence. For the empiricist it is only a makeshift model, but it does not rule out the possibility of other hypotheses such as your "reciprocal effect." I would object at most to the term "effect" since it carries a causal flavour. I am ready at any time to accept the idea of a reciprocal effect if anyone can demonstrate by empirical methods how this effect comes about.

You mention the archetype as a basis, and as a matter of fact an archetypal basis can be demonstrated in most cases of meaningful coincidence. But no causal nexus is thereby expressed, since from what we know of the archetype it is a psychoid content which cannot with certainty be said to exert a simultaneous effect on external events. We have only a very remote conjecture that psychic patterns fall in with the fundamental forms of the physical process in general. ("Psychoid" archetype!) But this is a possibility that must remain open.

Yours sincerely, C. G. JUNG

☐ Berlin.
[1] R., a student of philosophy, speculated that the concept of "reciprocal effect" or interaction might provide a hypothetical basis for further research into the problem of synchronicity. He quoted Pauli's remark on the "uncontrollable interaction between observer and system observed" which "invalidates the deterministic conception of the phenomena assumed in classical physics" (*Interpretation of Nature and the Psyche*, tr. 1955, p. 211).

To Karl Kötschau

Dear Colleague, 16 May 1958

There is no psychology worthy of this name in East Asia,[1] but instead a philosophy consisting entirely of what we would call psychology. Hence there is no psychoanalysis either, for what Freudian analysis endeavours to unearth is already included in the totalistic thinking of the East. Your conjecture that the totalistic order has largely been abandoned in the West is in best agreement with the facts. Accordingly everything must needs be for the best in the East. But this is by no means so, because the totalistic attitude, which is of the greatest importance for us, imposes upon the East the immense burden of totality. This can be seen even in the smallest details. For instance I once had a talk with Hu Shih,[2] then the ambassador of the Kuomintang in Washington, and the foremost modern Chinese philosopher. I noticed that he was completely exhausted after two hours although I had confined myself to a few simple questions concerning specific points. But I saw that this form of questioning was extraordinarily difficult for him; it was as though I had asked him to bring me a blade of grass and each time he had dragged along a whole meadow for me, which of course made his exhaustion perfectly comprehensible. Each time I had to extract the detail for him from an irreducible totality.

For us this totalistic view of things naturally has something very wonderful about it. But for the Oriental it results in a curious detachment from the world of concrete particulars we call reality. He is so weighed down by the totality that he can scarcely get hold of the details. Therefore—and this explains the tremendous upheaval going on in the East—he has a profound need for mastery over the concrete, with the result that America's gadget-mania works on him like a devastating bacillus. Our childish passion for ever faster cars and aeroplanes is for him a dream of bliss. No wonder the old Chinese wisdom is dying out even more rapidly than the philosophical apathy of yoga in India. It has happened to me more than once that educated East Asians rediscovered the meaning of their philosophy or religion only through reading my books. Perhaps the profoundest insights into the

---

□ M.D., Bad Harzburg, Germany.

[1] K. asked whether the Far East had developed its own psychology or psychoanalysis, and argued that the West needed them because it had relinquished the idea of a totalistic order.

[2] Cf. Keller, Aug. 56, n. 2.

peculiarities of the East Asian mind come from Zen, which tries to solve the Eastern problem on the level of our Scholasticism.

The dialogue with the East is therefore extraordinarily important for us as well as for them. In this respect Lily Abegg's book[3] is one of the most instructive I know. With collegial regards,

Yours very sincerely, C. G. JUNG

[3] *Ostasien denkt anders* (1949). Jung's foreword is in CW 18, pars. 1483ff.

To H. Rossteutscher

Dear Herr Rossteutscher,   20 May 1958

My remarks about the concept of "reciprocal effect" as a causalistic premise naturally do not imply that the reciprocal effect and/or causality is absolutely out of the question in the realm of parapsychological phenomena. The explanation depends entirely on the experience itself. It is altogether possible that cases which we today explain as synchronistic will tomorrow turn out to be causal in a manner that cannot yet be foreseen. I must confess, however, that I wouldn't expect such a surprise in the case of precognition. The classic example of reciprocal effect is surely complementarity. Should it turn out that the majority of synchronistic phenomena are by their very nature reciprocal effects, then the term synchronicity would become manifestly superfluous. But this proof has still not been furnished at present and, as I have said, in the case of precognition it is even more improbable. On the other hand, we know with sufficient certainty that the so-called causal law is a statistical truth, and accordingly there must be exceptions for which a causal explanation is, shall we say, valid for only 40% of them, the remaining 60% coming into the category of acausality, just like precognitive phenomena.

Obviously there would be no parapsychological phenomena whose very nature presupposes a reciprocal effect if such an effect were to be ruled out from the start. But at present we have—and this is my premise—no sufficient empirical grounds for assuming that parapsychological phenomena are in all cases based on reciprocal effect. This is not to say that there is no reciprocal effect whatever, but merely that this is not the decisive factor. Here you have the justification for my hypothesis of a principle which is based not on causality but on the equivalence of the meaning of events. This whole question should be thoroughly immunized against philosophical speculations. Experience alone can help us forward.

Yours sincerely, c. g. jung

To Ceri Richards

[ORIGINAL IN ENGLISH]

Dear Sir, 21 May 1958

Mrs. F. has kindly brought me your picture, for which I owe you many thanks. It came as a great surprise to me. I must confess, however, that I have no relation whatever to modern art unless I understand a picture. This is occasionally the case and is also the case with your picture. Purely aesthetically I appreciate the delicacy of the colours. The background (wood) points to matter and thus to the medium in which the round thing is to be found and with which it contrasts. The round thing is one of many. It is astonishingly filled with compressed corruption, abomination, and explosiveness. It is pure black substance, which the old alchemists called *nigredo*, that is: blackness, and understood as night, chaos, evil and the essence of corruption, yet the *prima materia* of gold, sun, and eternal incorruptibility. I understand your picture as a confession of the secret of our time.

Many thanks,

Yours sincerely, c. g. jung

□ (1903–71), Welsh painter, in London. He gave Jung a chalk and watercolour study for an oil painting, entitled "Afal Du Brogŵyr" (Black Apple of Gower)—Gower is a Welsh seigniory with very old historical connections and figures in the Arthurian Romances. According to a communication from R., the picture expresses "the great richness, the fruitfulness and great cyclic movement and rhythms of the poems of Dylan Thomas. The circular image . . . is the metaphor expressing the sombre germinating force of nature—surrounded by the petals of a flower, and seated within earth and sea." (See illustration.)

To J. E. Schulte

Dear Colleague, 24 May 1958

It is not in my line to make statements about things that I cannot prove. There are weighty reasons why a large number of the so-called

□ M.D., Maastricht, Netherlands.

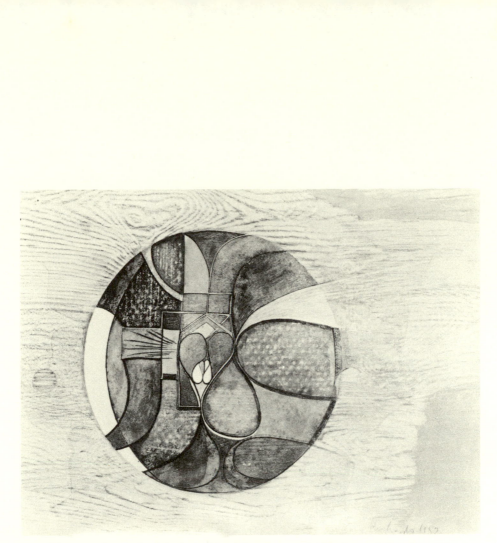

Ceri Richards. Study for *Black Apple of Gower*: see Richards, 21 May 58

Ufo sightings can be explained as projections. In my book I leave the question open as to whether this is a sufficient explanation for all the sightings, or whether some of them might be based on an inexplicable reality. It is obvious enough that such a reality would also attract projections. I always say that if there is a projection there must also be a corresponding hook on which to hang it.

The "miraculous appearance" of Ufos—if such it should be—is however of a very different kind from the miraculous cures at Lourdes. Although I have never been to Lourdes I cast no doubts on them. So far as they are medically verifiable I do not consider them "projections" in any sense. Anyway projection is not the right term to use in explaining these cures. "Suggestive effect" would be more appropriate. Suggestive effects are not acts of cognition in the sense that Ufo projections are.

Since in the case of Ufos there are no actual facts at hand that could be investigated more closely, their verification is an open and still unanswered question. In my view they are not technological achievements of human provenience. With collegial regards,

Yours sincerely, c. g. j u n g

To Gerhard Adler

Dear Dr. Adler,   3 June 1958

It was very kind and equally responsible of you to have reached for your pen and given the proper answer to this unscrupulous chatterer.[1] I appreciate it all the more that for once one of my pupils has broken a lance for me, and moreover in such a venomous affair. My task of having to say unpopular things is difficult enough as it is, so that it is truly not necessary to add to the pile of prejudices.

The weariness that comes with old age and my forgetfulness are increasing slowly but surely and I feel *procul negotiis*[2] for this and other

☐ (Handwritten.)
[1] The London *New Statesman* of 17 May 58 had published a long letter by an American, A. D. Parelhoff, in which he spoke of "the long-known aberrations of Jung" and attacked him for his "anti-semitic theories," using misquotations and distortions of meaning. A. wrote a detailed reply, published in the same journal on 24 May, pointing out Parelhoff's falsifications and mistranslations, and giving at the same time a true picture of Jung's highly critical attitude to Nazi Germany.
[2] = far from the business of this world.

reasons, while the world does everything it can to begrudge me *otium cum* or *sine dignitate*.[3] Fortunately since my "Modern Myth"[4] I have not been plagued by any more new ideas. Incidentally, John Wyndham's *The Midwich Cuckoos* (1957)[5] is a good saucer story and introduces a new version of the Holy Ghost.

With many thanks and cordial greetings,

Yours ever, C. G. JUNG

[3] = leisure with or without dignity. Cf. von Pelet, 6 Jan. 60, n. 1.
[4] See Harding, 30 May 57, n. 3.
[5] See Anon., 2 Jan. 58, n. 1.

To Edward J. Steiner

[ORIGINAL IN ENGLISH]

Dear Dr. Steiner, 5 June 1958

No doubt it would be an excellent scheme to have a machine for recording the voices of spirits. Unfortunately there are no cases on record where spirits had the good grace to present themselves as test-persons. Whatever else we can produce as spirit voices are those of mediums, and there the great trouble is to establish whether the communicated contents derive from ghosts or from unconscious fantasies of the medium or of any other member of the circle. I would not go so far as to deny the possibility that a medium can transmit a ghostly communication, but I don't know in which way one can prove it, as such a proof is outside of our human possibility. Your idea that any kind of phenomenon needs must represent a certain quantity of energy is—as far as our energy-concept goes—perfectly correct. It is certainly true for the world of causal connections; but suppose, for the sake of the argument, an acausal arrangement of events, which is equally possible, since even causality is a statistical truth and not an axiom. In that case we will try in vain to catch as much as a quantum of energy. This whole question of so-called "occult phenomena" is nothing one could be naïve about. It is an awful challenge for the human mind.

Sincerely yours, C. G. JUNG

□ M.D., Cincinnati, Ohio.

To Mrs. Otto Milbrand

[ORIGINAL IN ENGLISH]

Dear Mrs. Milbrand,   6 June 1958

I have often been asked the question you put to me: whether I have any reason to believe in a survival. As it means very little to me when somebody says "I believe this or that," I assume that it would be pretty futile to say "Yes, I believe in survival." I dislike belief in every respect, because I want to know a thing, and then I don't have to believe it if I know it. If I don't know it, it looks to me like an usurpation to say "I believe it," or the contrary. I think one ought to have at least some more or less tangible reasons for our beliefs. One should have some knowledge at least that makes a hypothesis probable. Your experience[1] f.i. is not a convincing reason, since we have no means of establishing whether it is a hallucinated piece of memory or a real ghost. In other words, I would dismiss neither the one nor the other possibility.

The only scientific approach to the question of survival is the recognition of the fact that the psyche is capable of extrasensory perceptions, namely of telepathy and of precognition, particularly the latter. This fact proves a relative independence of the psyche from time and space. This means that the two elements of time and space, indispensable for change, are relatively without importance for the psyche. In other words: the psyche is up to a certain point not subject to corruptibility. That's all we know. Of course one can have experiences of a very convincing subjective nature which need no support through scientific possibilities. But for those people not possessing the gift of belief it may be helpful to remember that science itself points to the possibility of survival.

I remain, dear Mrs. Milbrand,

Yours sincerely, C. G. JUNG

□ Pompano Beach, Florida.

[1] M. reported that she "met" a friend of her husband's who had been killed in a motoring accident two weeks before. He smiled at her and vanished.

To Karl Schmid

Dear Professor Schmid,   11 June 1958

Frau Jaffé has laid before me the questions[1] you have raised in your very kind letter to her. Your questions are of such a nature that

I have to answer them myself, so I must apologize for officiously intervening in the discussion.

The difficulty you are up against has to do with the real nature of empirical thinking. For instance, when you ask about the "organizing archetype," this is a philosophical and speculative question far removed from empirical thinking, which is primarily concerned with facts, though the empiricist too is an inquisitive fellow with a bent for speculation. I forbid myself to ask such a question because it is not underpinned by a sufficient number of facts for us to be able to answer it. First of all we have to ascertain the facts of the so-called "organization" or arrangement. We have taken the first tentative steps in this direction by setting up the hypothesis that in very many cases there exist recognizable archetypal models upon which the whole arrangement appears to be constructed. This is a formal statement of the same kind as the characterization "synchronicity." Nothing substantive has been said about the nature of this arrangement; in other words, no theological or any other speculative hypostasis has been made. I can also say, therefore, that in itself the archetype is an irrepresentable configuration whose existence can be established empirically in a multitude of forms. The archetype of the "mother," for instance, manifests itself in infinitely many forms and yet the one common characteristic of the mother-idea always remains intact. The same is true of the "father." At the same time the archetype is always of an objective nature since it is an *a priori* ideational pattern which is everywhere identical with itself. Thus it can appear as the image of the real mother but also as Sophia, or matter, which, as the name shows, also contains the mother-idea although it refers to a scientific concept.

The archetype, then, is a modality that represents visual forms, and synchronicity is another modality representing events. The concept "event" cannot be included under the concept "form," since form and event cannot be made to coincide. Hence you cannot describe synchronicity as an archetype but only as a modality *sui generis*. The concept of synchronicity says that a connection exists which is not of a causal nature. The connection consists firstly in the fact of coincidence and secondly in the fact of parallel meaning. It

---

[1] The questions were mainly concerned with the nature of the "organizing archetype" (cf. "On the Nature of the Psyche," CW 8, par. 440), with synchronicity in general and the possibility of an "archetype of synchronicity" in particular.

is a question of meaningful coincidences. Therefore it would only be confusing to throw together two entirely different concepts.

The empiricist only speaks of data that can be determined with sufficient certainty, and from these data he tries to crystallize out characteristics of the as yet unknown. Starting from the equation the unconscious = the unknown, he can determine that one aspect of it is the archetype. With regard to the dynamic processes of the unconscious, he can also determine that the further characteristic of synchronicity exists; in other words, that archetypes have something to do with synchronicity. These two aspects are joined together by the hypothesis that synchronistic phenomena are very often connected with archetypal constellations. This much can be determined by experience.

In so far as both modalities, archetype and synchronicity, belong primarily to the realm of the psychic, we are justified in concluding that they are psychic phenomena. In so far, however, as synchronistic events include not only psychic but also physical forms of manifestation, the conclusion is justified that both modalities transcend the realm of the psychic and somehow also belong to the physical realm. This can be expressed in other words by saying that there is a relativity of the psychic and physical categories—a relativity of being and of the seemingly axiomatic existence of time and space.

The expression "type" is applicable only to the archetypes, since they are in fact typical. It cannot be applied to synchronicity, since the only typical thing that can be determined about it is the meaningful coincidence. So far as our experience goes, all that can be determined about synchronicity at present is a boundless variety of phenomena even though a number of synchronistic events could be characterized as typical. Typical characterizations have therefore been chosen, for instance telepathy, precognition, clairvoyance, etc. But these characterizations are not types of meaning such as the archetypes are.

So your question concerning the "freedom" of the unconscious is easily answered: the freedom appears in the non-predictability of synchronistic phenomena. It is possible only where no causal nexus is present, as is by definition the case with synchronicity.

Time and space are present for the empiricist, and causality likewise, which is not possible without them. For the empiricist it is unthinkable that they are mere categories of understanding and would not exist at all outside it. But he knows that causality is only a statistical truth and accordingly there must be exceptions, i.e., legitimate instances of acausality where time and space are relative or absent and something nevertheless occurs. Research has shown that such unconditioned or absolute events do occur within the field of archetypal constellations and in the form of meaningful coincidences.

It is unthinkable that a world could have existed before time and space, for whatever world we can imagine is always bound to time and space and hence to causality. The most we can imagine is that there are statistical exceptions to such a world.

Synchronicity is not a name that characterizes an "organizing principle," but, like the word "archetype," it characterizes a modality. It is not meant as anything substantive, for what the psyche is, or what matter is, eludes our understanding. Modern physics is in a similar situation, as it can make no valid statements about what is substantive. Not, at any rate, to the extent that it can about those modalities which are expressible in equations, whereas we have no means of visualizing the nature of light, or can grasp it only by means of a paradox, i.e., as wave and particle.

No more than we can determine what psyche or matter is can we recognize what the "organizing principle" is. Naturally we can postulate that there is "something" hidden behind these phenomena, but this gets us no forrader since it is impossible for us to conceive what that "something" would have to be like in order to appear now as causality and now as synchronicity. I have just read that modern physicists have coined a name for it: the terrifying expression "universon," which is at the same time "cosmon" and "anti-cosmon." Such extravaganzas get us nowhere. This is where mythology begins. I therefore stop speculating when I have no more possibilities of ideas and wait on events, no matter of what kind, for instance dreams in which possibilities of ideas are presented to me but do not come this time from my biased speculation but rather from the unfathomable law of nature herself. The result is a legitimate mythology and not an arbitrary universon-fantasy. It is legitimate to ask yourself what it is that carries the qualities of the archetypal and synchronistic, and to pose the question, for instance, of the intrinsic nature of the psyche or of matter. This natural need is a legitimate occasion for further conceptualizations which, precisely because the question is all-embracing, cannot be the product merely of the conscious intellect but must necessarily proceed from the total man, i.e., from the co-participation of the unconscious. Thus, starting from the principle *unus est lapis*,[2] the medieval alchemists inferred the unity of human nature, and for them the synthesis of the stone harmonized with the synthesis of our human components; hence they equated the *Vir Unus*[3] with the *Unus Mundus*.[4] (Microcosm = macrocosm. In India: personal atman-purusha = suprapersonal atman-purusha.) This far-reaching speculation is a psychic need which is part of our mental hygiene, but in the realm of scientific verification it must be counted sheer mythology.

Although there is a psychic need to postulate things like "universon," "matter," "anti-matter," etc., no scientifically responsible knowledge is gained thereby. So if I occasionally speak of an "organizer," this is sheer mythology since at present I have no means of going beyond the bare fact that synchronistic phenomena are "just-so." The same is true of the inherent "knownness" of things (there are many examples of this in biology!). "The 'absolute knowledge' which is characteristic of synchronistic phenomena, a knowledge not mediated by the sense organs, supports the hypothesis of a self-subsistent meaning, or even expresses its existence. Such a form of existence can only be transcendental, since, as the knowledge of future or spatially distant events shows, it is contained in a psychically relative space and time, that is to say in an irrepresentable space-time continuum."[5] This statement, too, is mythology, like all transcendental postulates. But this particular statement is a psychic phenomenon which also underlies the "subjectless" consciousness in yoga philosophy.

Hoping I have given some sort of answer to these difficult questions,

Yours sincerely, C. G. JUNG

[2] = the stone is one (or: unity).
[3] = the one (integrated) man.
[4] Cf. Anon., 2 Jan. 57, n. 1.
[5] "Synchronicity," CW 8, par. 948.

To K. Neukirch

Dear Frau Neukirch,   13 June 1958

Of course you can dream of the sun! Here is an example: a lady I was treating dreamt that she saw a sunrise. She saw the sun rising up, half hidden behind the roof of my house. Above it, as though written in the sky, was the Latin word *exorietur*: "It will rise."

The point is that a great light had dawned on her during the treatment. The only odd thing is how anybody could get the idea that you can't dream of the sun!

Yours sincerely, C. G. JUNG

☐ Zwickau, East Germany.

To Michael Fordham

[ORIGINAL IN ENGLISH]

Dear Fordham,   14 June 1958

I don't flatter myself on having a theory of heredity. I share the ordinary views about it. I am convinced that individual acquisitions under experimental conditions are not inherited. I don't believe that this statement could be generalized, since changes in individual cases must have been inherited, otherwise no change would have come about in phylogenesis; or we would be forced to assume that a new variety, or a new species, was shaped by the creator on the spot without inheritance. Concerning archetypes, migration and verbal transmission are self-evident, except in those cases where individuals reproduce archetypal forms outside of all possible external influences (good examples in childhood dreams!). Since archetypes are instinctual forms, they follow a universal pattern, as do the functions of the body. It would be highly miraculous if that were not so. Why should the psyche be the only living thing that is outside laws of determination? We follow archetypal patterns as the weaver-bird does. This assumption is far more probable than the mystical idea of absolute freedom.

It is true that I have set aside hitherto general biology. This for good reasons! We still know far too little about the human psychology to be able to establish a biological basis for our views. In order to do that, we ought to know far more about the psychology of the unconscious and what we know about consciousness cannot be connected with biological viewpoints directly. Most attempts in this direction are rather futile speculations. The real connections with biology are only in the sphere of the unconscious, i.e., in the realm of instinctive activities. We gain the necessary material on the one hand from the explanation of individual cases and on the other hand from historical and comparative research. Only by this work we can establish the existence of certain instinctual patterns that allow a comparison with the facts of biology. For our purposes it is highly indifferent whether archetypes are handed down by tradition and migration or by inheritance. It is an entirely secondary question, since comparable biological facts, i.e., instinctual patterns with animals, are obviously inherited. I see no reason to assume that man should be an exception. The assumption, therefore, that the (psychoid) archetypes are inherited is for many reasons far more probable than that they are handed down by tradition. Instincts are not taught, as a rule. The childish prejudice against inherited archetypes is mostly due to the fact that one thinks archetypes are representations; but in reality they are preferences or "penchants," likes and dislikes.[1]

As a matter of fact we have practically no evidence for inherited representations (although even this statement is not quite safe), but we have plenty of proof that archetypal patterns exist in the human mind. How do you explain f.i. the fact of a little child dreaming that God is partitioned into four?[2] The child belongs to a little bourgeois family in a little town and certainly she has never had the slightest possibility of hearing and understanding the name "Barbelo," meaning: "in the four is God."[3]

The doubt in the existence of archetypes is merely an affair of ignorance and therefore a lamentable prejudice. For many scientific reasons it is far more probable that there are such forms than that there are not. My reasons are not philosophical ones, they are statistical.

Hoping that I have explained myself satisfactorily, I remain,

Yours cordially, C. G. JUNG

[1] Cf. Devatmananda, 9 Feb. 37, n. 1.
[2] Jung discusses the dream in "Approaching the Unconscious," *Man and His Symbols* (1964), pp. 73ff.; also in CW 18, pars. 525ff.
[3] Barbelo = B'arbhe Eloha. Various Gnostic sects were called Barbelo-Gnostics because of the importance they attached to that formula.

To Kurt Wolff

Dear Mr. Wolff,   17 June 1958

Best thanks for your letter of June 3rd.

Your wish that I should expatiate at greater length on psychotherapy seems to me unfulfillable because I have already written a whole lot on this subject from the scientific standpoint and none of it is suitable for a biography. I would have to expose a mass of empirical material which was very important to me personally, but unfortunately medical discretion forbids me to make use of it. Some of the patients are still alive, and if dead they have relatives who could easily recognize from my account, if it were reliable, whom it concerned. I have to be extremely careful in these matters.

As for my meeting with William James, you must remember that I saw him only twice and talked with him for a little over an hour, but there was no correspondence between us. Apart from the personal impression he made on me, I am indebted to him chiefly for his books. We talked mostly about his experiments with Mrs. Piper,[1] which are well enough known, and did not speak of his philosophy at all. I was particularly interested to see what his attitude was to so-called "occult phenomena." I admired his European culture and the openness of his nature. He was a distinguished personality and conversation with him was extremely pleasant. He was quite naturally without affectation and pomposity and answered my questions and interjections as though speaking to an equal. Unfortunately he was already ailing at the time so I could not press him too hard. Aside from Theodore Flournoy[2] he was the only outstanding mind with whom I could conduct an uncomplicated conversation. I therefore honour his memory and have always remembered the example he set me.

Incidentally I have discussed James at some length in my book on types.[3] If I were to write an appreciation of James from my present standpoint it would require an essay in itself, since it is impossible to sketch a figure of such stature in a few words. It would be an unpardonable exercise in superficiality if I presumed to do so.

I regret that my biography, as I envisage it, is in many respects unlike other biographies. It is utterly impossible for me, without expressing value judgments, to remember the millions of personal details and then have such a conceit of them in retrospect as to tell them again in all seriousness. I know there are people who live in their own biography during their lifetime and act as though they were already in a book. For me life was something that had to be lived and not talked about. Also, my interest was always riveted only by a few but important things which I couldn't speak of anyway, or

[1] Cf. Künkel, 10 July 46, nn. 3, 4.
[2] Cf. Flournoy, 29 Mar. 49, n. □.
[3] *Psychological Types*, CW 6, ch. VIII.

452

had to carry around with me for a long time until they were ripe for the speaking. In addition I have been so consistently misunderstood that I have lost all desire to recall "significant conversations." God help me, when I read Eckermann's *Conversations* even Goethe seemed to me like a strutting turkey-cock. I am what I am—a thankless autobiographer! With friendly greetings,

Very sincerely yours, C. G. JUNG

To Herbert E. Bowman

[ORIGINAL IN ENGLISH]

Dear Dr. Bowman, 18 June 1958

Thank you ever so much for your kind and refreshing letter.[1] Believe me: there are rather few of this kind in my mail-bag. As to your question "Why has the Self gone undiscovered?" I must tell you that my American publisher had the grace to invent this title. I would never have thought of it, as the self is not really undiscovered, it is merely ignored or misunderstood; but for the American public it seems to have been the right term. The self is known in ancient and modern Eastern philosophy. Zen philosophy is even fundamentally based on the cognition of the self. In Europe, as far as I can make out, Meister Eckhart is about the first where the self begins to play a noticeable role. After him some of the great German alchemists took up the idea and handed it down to Jacob Boehme and Angelus Silesius and kindred spirits.

Goethe's Faust almost reached the goal of classical alchemy, but unfortunately the ultimate *coniunctio* did not come off, so that Faust and Mephistopheles could not attain their oneness.

The second attempt, Nietzsche's *Zarathustra*, remained a meteor that never reached the earth, as the *coniunctio oppositorum* had not and could not have taken place. In the course of my psychiatric and psychological studies I could not help stumbling upon this very obvious fact and I therefore began to speak of the self again.

For about 1900 years we have been admonished and taught to project the self into Christ, and in this very simple way it was re-

---

□ Professor of Slavic language and literature, U. of Oregon (Eugene); now at U. of Toronto.

[1] B. wrote that *The Undiscovered Self* is "the book I would have liked to have written, on the subject that seems to me the only really important one in our day."

moved from empirical man, much to the relief of the latter, since he was thus spared the experience of the self, namely the *unio oppositorum*. He blissfully does not know the meaning of the term. If you are interested in the secret peripeteia of the spiritual development of Western man, I might mention to you my volume *Aion* (Rascher Verlag, Zurich, 1951), in which you find two essays, the one by M.-L. von Franz,[2] concerning the transition of the antique mind into Christian form, and an essay of mine in which I deal with the transmutation of the Christian mind towards the end of the Christian aeon. (The English version is on the way and is going to be printed by the Bollingen Press, New York.)

Thanking you again for your kind interest, I remain,

Yours sincerely, C. G. JUNG

[2] "Die Passio Perpetuae," a record of the visions of St. Perpetua (martyred A.D. 257) and her friends, and an account, attributed to Tertullian, of their death. (Tr. in *Spring*, 1949.)

To Carol Jeffrey

[ORIGINAL IN ENGLISH]

Dear Mrs. Jeffrey,   18 June 1958

I understand that you are worried by this peculiar fact that so many women are frigid. I have noticed the same fact, and I must say I have been duly impressed by it. I would never have expected such a frequency of the said phenomenon. My colleagues in the field of psychotherapy have been busy, as you know, in explaining it out of their experience of the consulting room. I have looked at the question from a somewhat different angle, although I have been concerned enough with such cases in my practice. I have tried during my voyages abroad in exotic countries to gather as much information as possible, and I reached the conclusion that mostly orgasm is connected with the expectation and even fear of conception, but in a not too inconsiderable number of cases orgasm is connected with a peculiar kind of relationship quite apart from the question of conception. One could characterize these two types of woman as the "married mothers" and as the "friends and concubines." The representatives of the latter class would be normally dissatisfied in marriage and vice versa. Thus far prostitution is a normal phenomenon, which is perfectly visible in primitive tribes where marriage law is strict and its circumvention therefore a particular pleasure. Nearly every wife has not only the opportunity but also the satisfaction of having illicit intercourse.

I myself have experienced such a telltale fact: a settlement of about 400 souls was thoroughly infected with syphilis within 3 weeks, after one woman of the tribe had gone to a distant market-place where she got infected. When you looked at that tribe outwardly, you would have been impressed by its respectability. Partout comme chez nous! That is what already St. Augustine—if I am right—said, that only three out of a hundred virgins entered marriage in the virginal state. Marriage, statistically considered, increases the need of licentiousness, not only because matrimony gets stale, but also because of a certain psychic need which is associated with the hetaira-nature of the sex-object.

It is unfortunately true that when you are wife and mother you can hardly be the hetaira too, just as it is the secret suffering of the hetaira that she is not a mother.[1] There are women who are not meant to bear physical children, but they are those that give rebirth to a man in a spiritual sense, which is a highly important function. Man is a very paradoxical structure with two main trends, namely the biological and animal instincts of propagation and the cultural instinct of psychic development. Therefore prostitution in not a few places has been an important constituent of religious service, viz. the institution of hierodules. This is by no means a perversity but is continued in the still existing institution of the French "salon." This is an entirely refined affair of a highly social importance.

From my experience I can recommend to you an attitude towards sex which avoids prejudices as much as possible. I forbid myself thinking in statistical numbers because it impairs your judgment. I treat every case as individually as possible, as the solution of the problem is only possible in individual cases and never through general laws and methods. Nowhere else than in these delicate matters does the Latin proverb *quod licet Jovi non licet bovi* come more into its own. It remains eternally true! What is healing medicine for the one is poison for the other. Healthy and complete life is not to be

---

[1] Toni Wolff (*Studien zu C. G. Jungs Psychologie*, 1959) developed a structural scheme of the feminine psyche, in which the mother and the hetaira are opposite poles, the other two being the Amazon and the mediumistic type.

455

attained by general principles and regulations, because it is always the individual who carries it. The solution begins with oneself, and if you know how to do the thing in your own case, you know how to do it in another case. There is no general principle that would be valid throughout, and the psychological statement is only true when you also can turn it round into its contrary. Thus a kind of solution that would be simply impossible for myself may be just the right thing for somebody else. I am not the *arbiter mundi* and I leave it to the Creator himself to start reflections about the varieties and the paradoxes of his creation.

Sincerely yours, C. G. JUNG

To Frau V.

Dear Frau V.,   28 June 1958

When you say that an experience of wholeness is the same as a "dynamic irruption of the collective unconscious," this is an in- dubitable error. The experience of wholeness is, quite to the contrary, an extremely simple matter of feeling yourself in harmony with the world within and without. If you have attained this simplicity, you will not let yourself be upset either by your son's awkward family circumstances or by the loss of your "book of voices." You don't have your roots in this book of voices nor are you your son, who must and will have a life of his own despite the fact of your clinging to him. Everything that is necessary can be lived if only you will stand by yourself and endure things as they are without grumbling. You should always tell yourself: that's how it is, and there's nothing I can do about it. Everything that will or must be comes without your doing, and you have only to hold your own in order to come through the darknesses of human existence. Too strong a dependence on the outside and too dynamic a view of the inside stem essentially from your desire, intention, and will, which you should push into the background a little for the sake of what really concerns you: holding your own in the chaos of this world.

With best wishes,

Yours sincerely, C. G. JUNG

☐ Written to a psychologically endangered personality (Switzerland).

456

To Wilhelm Bitter

Dear Colleague, 12 July 1958

The concept of Freud's super-ego[1] is complicated by the fact that no proper distinction is made between conscious ethical decision and the customary, virtually unconscious, reaction on the part of our conscience. What Freud calls the super-ego is the operation of a complex which from ancient times has found expression in the moral code, and therefore surely appertains to the general and traditional consciousness. When he seeks the origins of the moral reaction in man's hereditary disposition, this contradicts his assumption that such reactions stem from the experiences of the primal horde, when the primal father created the Oedipus situation through his own willfulness. Either it was the tyranny of the primal father which created morality, or, if it was already implanted in human nature, it was also present in the primal father, who by his very constitution bore the moral law within him. The question cannot be resolved empirically because it is in the highest degree improbable that a primal father ever existed and, furthermore, we ourselves were not around when the first moral reactions took place. "Age-old phylogenetic experience"—this is approximately what I have termed the collective unconscious. Freud, as you know, rejected my view, and this complicates the situation still further.[2] For him conscience is a human acquisition. I, on the contrary, maintain that even animals have a conscience—dogs, for instance—and empirically there is much to be said for this, since instinctual conflicts are not altogether unknown on the animal level.

The inheritance of instincts is a known fact, whereas the inheritance of acquired characteristics is controversial. Freud's view that conscious experiences are inherited[3] flies in the face of common knowledge and also contradicts his own hypothesis that conscience

---

□ (1893–1974), M.D., Ph.D., specialist in nervous diseases, analytical psychologist; founder of the Stuttgarter Gemeinschaft "Arzt und Seelsorge." Cf. his *Die Angstneurose* (2nd edn., Berlin, 1971), *Der Verlust der Seele* (1969). The first two paragraphs of this letter are published (with one short omission) in Bitter (ed.), *Gut und Böse in der Psychotherapie* (1959), pp. 56f.

[1] The super-ego is the unconscious authority built up by early experiences, principally of the child's relation to his parents. It functions as a kind of conscience checking the tendency of the ego to gratify primitive impulses.

[2] Cf. *Totem and Taboo*, Standard Edn. 13, p. 146.

[3] Cf. Jones, *Sigmund Freud* (London edn.), I, p. 381.

is made up of ancestral experiences. Of course you can maintain that morality, as the word "mores" shows, derives from conscious memories handed down by tradition. But then it cannot at the same time be an inherited instinct. If it is an inherited instinct, then the experiences in question do not represent a beginning but are the outcome of that instinct.

I seem to remember that I mentioned the example from Zschokke's *Selbstschau*[4] because it demonstrates the infectiousness of guilt feelings. I do not know whether it evoked a feeling of guilt in Zschokke himself. Some psychological truths can be established by scientific methods, others not. Although the assertion of immortality is in itself a fact, it is no more proof of immortality than are any other mythological statements. The only sure thing is that man does make such statements. This is the only validity they possess and the only possibility we have of approaching them scientifically. We can only establish that the animal Man makes them and that they have considerable psychological value. These statements are anthropomorphic, and it cannot be established whether they give grounds for a possible metaphysical reality. We shall never be able to jump over the epistemological barrier.

I hope we shall meet again at the coming Congress.[5] With collegial greetings,

Very sincerely yours, C. G. JUNG

[4] In "A Psychological View of Conscience" (CW 10, par. 850) Jung cites the case described by the Swiss writer Heinrich Zschokke (1771–1848) in his *Eine Selbstschau* (1843): he saw with his mind's eye, while sitting in an inn, how a young man, who in reality sat opposite him, committed a burglary. He challenged the young man, who then admitted the crime.
[5] The First International Congress for Analytical Psychology in Zurich, 7–12 August 1958.

To K. R. Eissler

[ORIGINAL IN ENGLISH]

Dear Dr. Eissler, 20 July 1958

As you know I have stipulated that my correspondence with Freud[1] ought not to be published before 30 years have elapsed after my

☐ M.D., psychoanalyst, secretary of the Sigmund Freud Archives, New York. The letter, with E.'s reply, is published in *The Freud/Jung Letters*, introduction, pp. xxvii f.

death, but lately I have been asked from different sides to permit—inasmuch as I am competent—an earlier publication of the whole correspondence.

Such a change of my will is not a simple matter. First of all I don't know how you feel about such a proposition and secondly I couldn't permit an earlier publication without a necessary revision of my letters. My letters were never written with any thought that they might become broadcast. As a matter of fact many of them contain unchecked and highly objectionable materials as they are produced in the course of an analysis[2] and shed a most onesided and dubious light on a number of persons whom I don't want to offend in any manner whatever. Such material enjoys the protection of the *secretum medici*. These people or their descendants are still alive.

I should be deeply obliged to you if you would kindly inform me of your feelings in this matter, especially if you would agree with an earlier publication under strict observation of the rule of discretion and the risk of libel.

Faithfully yours, C. G. JUNG

[1] See introduction to the present vol., pp. xi f.
[2] The Germanic construction of this passage renders it ambiguous in English: "materials as they are produced" means "such as are produced" (the German would be "wie sie produziert sind"). The reader unfamiliar with the use of "wie" might mistake "as" for "because" and refer "they" back to "many of them," i.e., to the letters. The letters were not produced during the course of an analysis with Freud or anybody else.

To Edward Thornton

[ORIGINAL IN ENGLISH]

Dear Thornton,   20 July 1958

The question[1] you ask me is—I am afraid—beyond my competence. It is a question of fate in which you should not be influenced by any arbitrary outer influence. As a rule I am all for walking in two worlds at once since we are gifted with two legs, remembering that spirit is pneuma which means "moving air." It is a wind that all too easily can lift you up from the solid earth and can carry you away

☐ Bradford, Yorkshire.
[1] T. asked whether he should accept the implications of certain coincidences and retire from his business in order to concentrate on his spiritual interests. Cf. his *The Diary of a Mystic* (1967).

on uncertain waves. It is good therefore, as a rule, to keep at least one foot upon *terra firma*. We are still in the body and thus under the rule of heavy matter. Also it is equally true that matter not moved by the spirit is dead and empty. Over against this general truth one has to be flexible enough to admit all sorts of exceptions, as they are the unavoidable accompaniments of all rules. The spirit is no merit in itself and it has a peculiarly irrealizing effect if not counter-balanced by its material opposite. Thus think again and if you feel enough solid ground under your feet, follow the call of the spirit.

My best wishes,

Yours cordially, c. g. jung

To R.F.C. Hull

[ORIGINAL IN ENGLISH]

Dear Hull, 15 August 1958

The question of "representation" and "idea" with reference to the German "Vorstellung" and "Idee"[1] is indeed a serious trouble. Roughly speaking: what the English call an "idea" would be in German "Vorstellung." But the English word "representation" contains nothing that could be expressed by "Idee." The latter term in German has retained the original meaning of a transcendental *eidos*, respectively of *eidolon*,[2] when it becomes manifest. In most cases, where I use the word "Vorstellung" the English "idea" would be the equivalent. Where I speak of "Idee," it always means something similar to Kant and Plato. At all events, when I speak of "Vorstellung" I mean about the contrary of what the German "Idee" is. It might therefore be advisable to explain by a special note that the German "Idee" is meant in the Platonic or Kantian way and not in its colloquial English meaning. Thus the term "representation" would become somewhat redundant and could be more or less avoided. It is more important to produce a readable and easily understandable English text than to complicate it by too many philological or philosophical finesses. The German word "Idee" can often be rendered by "imago," if the latter is understood, or defined as a

---

[1] H. was at the time preparing the translation of CW 8, where these two terms occur very frequently.

[2] *Eidos* = Platonic idea or form, transcendental because it is an *a priori* condition of experience; *eidolon* = immaterial image.

thought-form, which, as an archetypal "Idee," can easily be inherited, although the perceptible archetypal image is not identical with the inherited thought-form, which allows an indefinite number of empirical expressions. I must leave it to your tact and judgment to create an equivalent rendering of the intention of my German text.

Sincerely yours, C. G. JUNG

To James Gibb

[ORIGINAL IN ENGLISH]

Dear Mr. Gibb,   1 October 1958

Thank you for your interesting letter.[1] It is indeed as you say: one could speak of a pool of good and a pool of evil. But this statement is a bit too simple, because good and evil are human opinions and therefore relative. What is good for me can be bad for somebody else and the same with evil. In spite of the fact that good and evil are relative and therefore not generally valid, the contrast exists and they are a pair of opposites basic to the structure of our mind. The opposition good – evil is universal in our experience, but one must always ask to whom? This is a great difficulty. Otherwise the situation would be quite simple if you could make general statements about good and evil. You could then clearly designate the things that are good and the things that are evil. As this is not the case, the question is the human individual, namely, the latter is the decisive factor because it is the individual that declares something good and something evil. It is not for you or for anybody else to judge, it is only the individual in question that decides whether something is good for him or bad. Thus our attention must be given to the individual that decides and not to the question of good or evil, which we cannot make out for other people. That is the reason why you cannot tell whole nations what is good for them. You only can encourage the individual to make ethical decisions, with the hope for general consent. What a whole nation does is always the result of what so many individuals have done. You also cannot educate a nation. You only can teach or change the heart of an individual. It

☐ Corinth, Ontario.

[1] G., who described himself as "only a labourer" and asked Jung to "overlook his shortcomings," told him of his idea of two pools of good and evil. Was there any way to counteract the power of evil?

is true that a nation can be converted to good or bad things, but in this case the individual is merely acting under a suggestion or under the influence of imitation and his actions are therefore without ethical value. If the individual is not really changed, nothing is changed. This is unwelcome news and because it is so, the helpful attitude, I do suggest, is not perceived by the ear of a nation. Therefore one says it is not popular. In other words: it does not agree with people. They will do it when everybody else is doing it. And everybody is waiting for everybody to do it. So nobody begins. One is either too modest or too lazy, or too irresponsible to think that one can be the first to do the right thing. If everybody felt the same thing, there would be at least a vast majority of people thinking responsibility a good thing. Under those circumstances the major evils of mankind would have been dealt with long ago.

I call your attention to a little book I have written not long ago, where you will find some considerations about the same subject. It is *Answer to Job*. You will find it either in *Psychology and Religion* (Bollingen Series, New York) or as a small volume published in England (Routledge and Kegan Paul, London).

Sincerely yours, C. G. JUNG

To Charles H. Tobias

[ORIGINAL IN ENGLISH]

Dear Sir,   27 October 1958

A bird has whistled to me[1] and told me that you have reached your 70th year of life. Although I do not know you, I assume you are quite satisfied with this achievement. It is something. I can talk with some authority, as I am in my 84th and still in passably good form and—looking back, as you probably do on this day of celebration and congratulation—I see following behind myself the long chain of 5 children, 19 grandchildren, and about 8 or 9 great-grandchildren. (The latter number is not quite safe as at frequent intervals a new one drops from heaven.) Mature youth begins, as one says, at seventy and it is in certain respects not so nice and in others more beautiful

---

□ Boston.

[1] T.'s son, completely unknown to Jung, asked him to write a congratulatory letter for his father's 70th birthday, since Jung was "one of the famous men and women whose accomplishments he [the father] has always admired."

than childhood. Let us hope that in your case the latter part of the sentence will confirm itself.

My best wishes,

Yours cordially, c. g. jung

To Mrs. C.

[ORIGINAL IN ENGLISH]

Dear Mrs. C. 3 November 1958

If power symptoms creep into the work that is done round you, then diminish your own power and let others have more responsibility. It will teach you a very sound lesson. They will learn that more power and more influence bring more suffering, as you yourself are learning under the present conditions.

One should not assert one's power as long as the situation is not so dangerous that it needs violence. Power that is constantly asserted works against itself, and it is asserted when one is afraid of losing it. One should not be afraid of losing it. One gains more peace through losing power.

Cordially yours, c. g. jung

□ England.

To Robert L. Kroon

[ORIGINAL IN ENGLISH]

15 November 1958

Astrology is one of the intuitive methods like the *I Ching*, geomantics, and other divinatory procedures. It is based upon the synchronicity principle, i.e., meaningful coincidence. I have explored experimentally three intuitive methods: the method of the *I Ching*, geomantics, and astrology.

Astrology is a naïvely projected psychology in which the different attitudes and temperaments of man are represented as gods and identified with planets and zodiacal constellations. While studying astrology I have applied it to concrete cases many times.

There are remarkable coincidences, e.g., the position of Mars in

□ Correspondent in Geneva for the American periodicals *Time* and *Life*. No evidence of the publication of this communication could be found.

the zenith in the famous horoscope of Wilhelm II, the so-called "Friedenskaiser." This position is said already in a medieval treatise to mean always a *casus ab alto,* a fall from the height.

The experiment is most suggestive to a versatile mind, unreliable in the hands of the unimaginative, and dangerous in the hands of a fool, as those intuitive methods always are. If intelligently used the experiment is useful in cases where it is a matter of an opaque structure. It often provides surprising insights. The most definite limit of the experiment is lack of intelligence and literal-mindedness of the observer. It is an intelligent *aperçu* like the shape of the hand or the expression of the face—things of which a stupid and unimaginative mind can make nothing and from which a superstitious mind draws the wrong conclusions.

Astrological "truths" as statistical results are questionable or even unlikely. (Cf. my paper "Synchronicity: An Acausal Connecting Principle" in Jung-Pauli: *The Interpretation of Nature and the Psyche,* Bollingen Series LI, New York 1952. Pag. 83 ff.)[1]

The superstitious use (prediction of the future or statement of facts beyond psychological possibilities) is false.

Astrology differs very much from alchemy, as its historical literature consists merely of different methods of casting a horoscope and of interpretation, and not of philosophical texts as is the case in alchemy.

There is no psychological exposition of astrology yet, on account of the fact that the empirical foundation in the sense of a science has not yet been laid. The reason for this is that astrology does not follow the principle of causality, but depends, like all intuitive methods, on acausality. Undoubtedly astrology today is flourishing as never before in the past, but it is still most unsatisfactorily explored despite very frequent use. It is an apt tool only when used intelligently. It is not at all foolproof and when used by a rationalistic and narrow mind it is a definite nuisance.

[1] "Synchronicity," CW 8, pars. 904ff.

To Harold Lloyd Long

[ORIGINAL IN ENGLISH]

Dear Sir,   15 November 1958

The derogatory interpretations of the unconscious are usually due to the fact that the observer projects his primitivity and his blindness into the unconscious. He thereby pursues the secret goal of protecting himself against the inexorable demands of nature in the widest sense of the word.

As the term "unconscious" denotes, we don't know it. It is the unknown, of which we can say anything we like. Not one of our statements will be necessarily true. The reason why the unconscious appears to us in such a disagreeable form is because we are afraid of it, and we revile it because we hope that by this method we can free ourselves from its attractions. It is a puzzler—I admit—to anybody who occasionally indulges in thinking.

Sincerely yours, c. g. j u n g

☐ Chicago.

To Karl Schmid

Dear Professor Schmid,   8 December 1958

Having been prevented by various circumstances I am thanking you only today for your book *Hochmut und Angst*[1] now that I have perused its contents. I am still under the impact of the treasures displayed in it, which are indeed so vast that an effort is needed to grasp their profusion.

I own the first English edition of Böhme's *40 Questions Concerning the Soul*, 1647. In it as a mandala or "Eye of ye Wonders of Eternity, or Looking-Glass of Wisdom,"[2] comprising Man, God, Heaven, World, and Hell. Your book is another such looking glass of wisdom. Not only does it mirror the countless facets of our contemporary world, it is also an intelligent and interpretive magnifying glass which brings the barely comprehensible into sharp focus. You hold a mirror up to the world in which it can recognize its own image, or rather could do so did not the well-intentioned reader usually think: "Yes, that's what people—other people—are like." Only a very few readers seem to know that they themselves are also the others. What then is to be said of the ill-intentioned? A good many will admit that self-knowledge and reflection are needed, but very few indeed will consider such necessities binding upon themselves.

☐ (Handwritten.)
[1] Zurich, 1958.
[2] The mandala is reproduced in "A Study in the Process of Individuation," CW 9, i, p. 297.

465

As a critique of European culture your book goes very deep, as pages 139/140 show.[3] A lot more could be said about that. What is the question that the world-shaking phenomenon of Naziism answered, and what does it mean for the German psyche, and not for it alone but also for the psyche of humanity, particularly that of the West? The East has been churned up by it to its very foundations. But what is the reaction of the West? Here it is not even realized that the answer has not been given. Ostensibly it is the Russians who leave us no time for it. We have got brainlessly stuck on the defensive. Your book is therefore extremely timely. One can only wish that it will be widely read and that somebody will start drawing conclusions. This used to be the preserve of the Germans, but today Germany regards herself as an American colony and there is little hope in this respect.

In my old age the three-dimensional world is slipping away from me, and I perceive only from afar what in the year 1958 is being said and done in this one of the possible worlds. It is an interesting historical process which—fundamentally—no longer affects me. But I am thankful to hear another voice that has taken over the function of one crying in the wilderness.

Very cordially, C. G. JUNG

[3] These pages give an analysis of the irrationality of Naziism as a revolution against the rule of reason, bound to be destructive because of the vacuity of its own images and its daemonism, leading not to a union of rational and irrational values but to their mutual extinction.

To James Kirsch

Dear Colleague,   10 December 1958

Best thanks for your kind and interesting letter of December 2nd. The satori experience of your friend, Dr. K., is a typical mandala vision. If there are people in the East who claim to have had an imageless experience, you must always remember that the report is as a rule highly unpsychological. It is the tradition that a satori experience is imageless and they therefore say it was imageless. That it cannot possibly have been imageless is proved by the fact that they

☐ Published (in K.'s tr.) in *Psychological Perspectives*, III:2 (fall 1972).

remember something definite. Had it been totally imageless they could never say they remember something, since the memory is an image of something that has been. But this simple reflection does not come to the Oriental, and for the same reason he can assert that he passed into an imageless condition when he received an illumination. He knows it was an imageless condition and this in itself is already an image, but these people can't see that. I have never really succeeded in convincing an Indian that if no conscious ego is present there can be no conscious memory either. The comparison they always make with deep sleep when all memory is extinguished is a condition in which no memory whatever can come into existence precisely because nothing is perceived. But in the satori experience something *is* perceived, namely that an illumination or something of the sort has occurred. This is a definite image which can even be compared with the tradition and brought into harmony with it. I therefore regard this assertion of an imageless condition as an uncritical and unpsychological statement due to lack of psychological differentiation. This lack also explains why it is so difficult for us to have any real contact with such people, and it is no accident that the only person who was able to give you a satisfactory answer is himself an observant psychologist.[1] It is simply not to be comprehended how an experience can be established as having happened if nobody is there who has had it. This "nobody" who establishes it is always an ego. If no ego is present nothing whatever can be perceived. Even with us there are people who make such assertions; for instance a Christian can assert that he has been redeemed by Christ, although it is easy enough to prove to him that in reality he has been redeemed from nothing. He has merely experienced a change of mind and sees certain things differently from before. But the situation is fundamentally the same as it always was.

. . .

With my best wishes for the New Year,

Yours sincerely, C. G. JUNG

[1] Dr. K., mentioned at the beginning of the letter, a Japanese psychiatrist who had been in analysis for four years with a well-known psychoanalyst in New York.

To K. W. Bash

Dear Colleague,   12 December 1958

Best thanks for your exposé.[1] I fully agree with it, only I would ask you to state explicitly that in my psychology the "mythological" aspect means "religious attitude." You will surely have noticed in reading my writings that I do not mince my words and clearly and expressly point out that the regard for mythological parallels is conducive to a religious attitude. The absence of a unitary view of the world is just what is deplored by many people today and is said to be a sad loss, unlike earlier times when people had a general *Anschauung* that was a bulwark against the difficulties of life. It was the Enlightenment which destroyed this bulwark by reducing the unitary view to nothing but mythology. In its modern usage mythology simply means "it is nothing," since myths are unrealistic. My whole endeavour has been to show that myth is something very real because it connects us with the instinctive bases of our existence.

The astronomer Hoyle[2] offers an instructive example in this respect: he emphasizes that astronomy can't find any God and that therefore there isn't one, yet writes a novel in which a cosmic cloud represents this very God.

One has to be extremely careful in using the word "mythology" as it brings you into head-on collision with the all-pervading infantile arguments of the Enlightenment. With cordial greetings,

Yours sincerely, C. G. JUNG

☐ M.D., analytical psychologist; then a medical officer of the World Health Organization in Cairo, afterward professor of psychology in Bern.
[1] B. had written a contribution to a discussion on "The Mental Health Problems of Ageing and the Aged" from the viewpoint of analytical psychology, organized by the Expert Committee on Mental Health of WHO, which he sent to Jung. The paper was published in the *Bulletin of the World Health Organization*, no. 21 (1959), 563ff.
[2] Cf. Anon., 2 Jan. 58, n. 1.

To Baroness Vera von der Heydt

Dear Baroness,   22 December 1958

Your question evidently emanates from an atmosphere in which many words are buzzing about.[1] The real situation cannot, however, be clarified by mere concepts but only by the inner experience that corresponds to them. With concepts you invariably miss the mark because they are not philosophical ideas but merely names for experiences. That is why things that previously seemed all confused suddenly become clear when one lets experience speak. What I have called "active imagination" can become necessary at any stage of the analysis. It is obvious that not every analysis leads to individuation, or rather, every analysis is on the way to the distant goal of individuation. It is equally obvious that every insight into what I have called the "shadow" is a step along the road of individuation without one's being obliged to call this an individuation process.[2] Here it is plain to see how a concept like individuation becomes either much too narrow or much too broad, and then muddles arise which in reality do not exist.

Because of this conceptual hair-splitting everybody is both right and wrong. Thus X.'s view that active imagination begins when the transference has been fully analysed is an incorrect statement.

From such discussions we see what awaits me once I have become posthumous. Then everything that was once fire and wind will be bottled in spirit and reduced to dead nostrums. Thus are the gods interred in gold and marble and ordinary mortals like me in paper.

My best wishes for Christmas and the New Year,

Very sincerely yours, c. g. j u n g

[1] Her question concerned the controversial views on the role of active imagination.

[2] By "individuation" Jung understands here the natural development of the individual, whereas the "process of individuation" denotes the same development where it is observed and furthered by consciousness, as for example in analysis.

To R.F.C. Hull

[ORIGINAL IN ENGLISH]

Dear Hull,   27 December 1958

Your suggestion to translate the subtitle of the *Mysterium Coniunctionis* as "An Inquiry into the Fission and Fusion of Psychic Opposites in Alchemy" is indeed very clever. It is audacious and in a way profoundly right. This idea is so creative that I cannot assume responsibility for it. So I should make the further suggestion that in a translator's note you explain your translation of my bland terminology "Trennung und Zusammensetzung." I congratulate you on this very successful interpretation of my understatement. I myself am deeply convinced of the basic analogy between physical and psychological discoveries. I have often discussed this problem with the late Prof. Pauli, who was also fascinated by what he called the mirror-reflection, causing the existence of two worlds which are really united in the *speculum,* the mirror, that is lying in the middle. As Prof. Fierz in his speech at Pauli's funeral has mentioned: speculation comes from *speculum.* Thus "speculation," a very typical form of consciousness, becomes the real centre of the world, the basis of the Unus Mundus. On this ground your translation is warrantable. It has my full approval on condition that you write a translator's preface in which you defend your interpretative translation. You have to submit your innovation probably also to the editorial Olympos, I don't feel quite competent.[1]

The idea of a fourth part of the *Mysterium Coniunctionis*[2] is not at all a bad one, but I am afraid it has been already anticipated by the bulk of Freudian psychology. He was fascinated by the dark side of man, i.e., by all those things that make up the contents of the "Mysterium Iniquitatis," the mystery of the shadow. Without his emphasis on the dark side of man and the chaos of his chthonic desires, I could not have found access to the "Mysterium Coniunctionis." The "Mysterium Iniquitatis" is represented in modern literature by a whole library of Psychopathologia Sexualis,[3] criminology, detective stories, etc. and on top the whole Freudian literature. It needs no further elucidation. The only trouble with this literary production is that nobody seems aware of a mysterium. My chance was that I saw it was a mysterium.

On this occasion let me express to you all my good wishes for

---

[1] A fortnight later Jung changed his mind and wrote on 11 Jan. 59: ". . . I had to think about your proposition. It is very witty indeed and I felt tempted to adopt it. But 'fission and fusion' are too specific to express the very general meaning of the logical terms 'analysis and synthesis.' I do not mean more than that which the latter signify. I particularly wish to avoid allusions of this kind, because they would certainly be interpreted in a detrimental way. I am sorry but I have to reckon with a usually hostile critique."

[2] A joking suggestion that Jung should write a fourth volume to the Swiss edition of *Mysterium Coniunctionis* consisting entirely of lurid case histories: a "Mysterium Iniquitatis," mystery of iniquity. Cf. II Thess. 2:7.

[3] An allusion to *Psychopathia Sexualis* (1886), a famous textbook on sexual perversions by the Viennese psychiatrist Richard von Krafft-Ebing (1840–1902).

Christmas and a happy New Year and also my gratitude for the immense work you have put into your translations. Your brilliant suggestion has shown me once more that your participation in your work is more than professional. It is alive.

Yours cordially, c. g. j u n g

To the Rev. Morton T. Kelsey

[ORIGINAL IN ENGLISH]

Dear Mr. Kelsey,   27 December 1958

Thank you for your kind letter. My comment on it begins with the last phrase of your dream:[1]

> "It is easier for a minister"
> *It is easier for a camel*
> "To be committed to religion"
> *To go through the eye of a needle*
> "Than a doctor. . . ."
> *Than a rich man. . . .*

The question that gave cause for this remark is: Why did your means of transportation fail? Why did you need transportation? To get with Mr. X. to hear my lecture. Why do you have me over in California? In order to talk to me about yourself rather than about religion, "as it is easier for a minister," etc. The doctor's way then seems to be the hard one, since his worldly riches pave the way to Hell for him, to remain within the frame of your parable.

This is something of a puzzle. You know I am the unbelieving outsider who asks naïve questions, f.i. why would you need or prefer to talk to a doctor since you are totally committed to a Sōter,[2] the greatest of all healers? You say of your experience that it was one of

---

[1] K., who had visited Jung in October in Küsnacht, reported a dream in which he meets a fellow clergyman, X., who is going to hear Jung lecture in Los Angeles. He offers X. transportation, but it breaks down. Finally he decides that he wants to talk to Jung about himself, not about religion. When he sees Jung, who is dressed in a white doctor's coat, Jung asks him why his transportation failed. They then have a talk and the gist of Jung's conversation "is that it is easier for a minister to be committed to religion than a doctor."

[2] For K. the most valuable experience of God had not been of him as the *summum bonum,* the highest good, but as the *soter,* the saviour.

"salvation, of being saved by something with enough power to save and sufficient will to do the same. This all I know and all I need to know." Why should the one who can slip through the eye of a needle consult with the rich man who goes down the broad way? Of course it is just a dream. But did you make it, or who gave it to you?

You know that I believe I have some good reasons for paying attention to dreams no matter how small and unimportant they seem to be. I would conclude from your dream that somewhere something is amiss.

I don't know whether you realize or not how singularly alike the formulation of your experience is to the Christocentric tenet of modern Protestantism? To the psychologist it is a most noteworthy fact that the religious emphasis has shifted from the triune *patēr pantōn*[3] to the Son and Sōter and historical man, who was originally one third of the Godhead and is now the central and almost unique feature of the Protestant's religion. Protestantism has stripped off almost the whole of the original dogma and ritual and concentrated solely upon Christ, the Saviour. This is, in my humble opinion, just as it ought to be, because it expresses the fact that the Protestant has had the experience of a saving or guiding principle which manifests itself in the human psyche. It has been called instinct, intuition, and unconscious. "Name is sound and smoke," says Goethe's Faust. Nevertheless these names point to something basic, to a mysterious agency that is concerned with the whole of man. Therefore science, proceeding from without to within, from the known to the unknown, has called it the self in contradistinction to the ego, which represents the centre of consciousness only.

Owing to His human nature, Christ is the accessible part of the Godhead, and His empirical essence expresses the aforesaid experience. The doctor says: "Christ is another name for the self" and the minister says: "What you call the self is in reality Christ in everybody. *Christus intra nos.*[4] To Him you can leave all your perplexities. He will take care of them." — "This is all very nice," says the doctor, "but what is causing all the jams and fixes from which we need to be saved? And moreover your Christ is all light and no darkness, while the self manifests in two colours, white and black. As subtly

[3] = father of all things.
[4] = Christ within us. Cf. *Psychology and Alchemy*, par. 8.

472

as you are led into the right path, you are also misled into the mire, and just as often. Good as a rule is not followed by better but by worse. There is no chance to get out of sin. Where is the world after 2000 years of Christianity?"

We don't need to point to the world in general; it is enough to consider one's own case. Who could say in earnest that he is *saved?* By an act of grace he got for once out of a hole. But he will fall into the swamp again. It even looks as if there were a secret liaison between sin and grace and as if each sin had also the aspect of a *felix culpa.* As I said, the self casts a shadow. Christ does not. He cannot be identified with the whole self, only with its light side.

Yahweh gives life and death. Christ gives life, even eternal life and no death. He is a definite improvement on Yahweh. He owes this to the fact that He is suffering man as well as God. Through His approximation to man, the *auctor rerum* improves in moral character. Christ appears as a guarantee of God's benevolence. He is our advocate in Heaven, Job's "God against God."

This means that man has learned that if he chooses the side of the Good, he avoids many consequences which would be disastrous if he had not warded them off by his conscious moral decision. He has acquired enough conscience to decide freely and to choose accordingly. Where unconsciousness prevails, there is no freedom and man remains a victim of the opposites. This is the great teaching of Christ: as He has chosen the light and denied the darkness, man can do likewise and escape the opposites—*up to a certain point.* And this is the problem that is raised in our days: where do we land if we believe in the almightiness of our will and in the absolute freedom of our choice? These divine gifts are apt to get us too far away from our earthly bondage and from our inexorable reality. God is light *and* darkness, the *auctor rerum* is love *and* wrath. We still pray: "Lead us not into temptation." (The French Catholic version of the Vulgate has: "Ne nous laisse pas tomber dans la tentation"!)[5]

The consequence is that we moderns are dissociated and unaware of our roots. That is the reason why the good Christian still needs the doctor, and why his dreams advise a consultation.

Excuse this long letter! I just wanted to give you an idea about the way in which I would undertake an interpretation.

Sincerely yours, C. G. JUNG

[5] "Let us not *fall* into temptation."

473

To A. Tjoa and R.H.C. Janssen

[ORIGINAL IN ENGLISH]

Dear Sirs,   27 December 1958

Your questions[1] remind me of a very wonderful discussion I once attended at a joint session of the Mind Association and the Aristotelian Society in London[2] about the question: are the individual minds contained in God or not? I must call your attention to the fact that I cannot possibly tell you what a man who has enjoyed complete self-realization looks like, and what becomes of him. I never have seen one, and if I did see one I could not understand him because I myself would not be completely integrated. Thus far your question is a scholastic one, rather like the famous "how many angels can stand on the point of a needle?" Integration in the empirical sense of this word means completion and not perfection. Being a doctor I have seen much of the profound misery of man in our days and of his dissociation. I had to help innumerable people to get a bit more conscious about themselves and to consider the fact that they consist of many different components, light and dark. That's what one calls integration: to become explicitly the one one has been originally. As Japanese Zen says: "Show me thine original face."

To get integrated or complete is such a formidable task that one does not dare to set people farther goals like perfection. As f.i. the ordinary physician neither imagines nor hopes to make of his patient an ideal athlete, so the psychological doctor does not dream of being able to produce saints. He is highly content if he brings forth—in himself as well as in others—a fairly balanced and mentally more or less sound individual, no matter how far from the state of perfection. Before we strive after perfection, we ought to be able to live the ordinary man without self-mutilation. If anybody should find himself after his humble completion still left with a sufficient amount

☐ Leiden, Netherlands.

[1] T. and J., both students of psychology, asked about the nature of integration: whether it would imply a saint-like quality expressed in "moral dominance over one's fellow men," or "only the inner freedom and firmness of structure . . . without any moral and characterological content . . . so that it would be possible even for a criminal to be integrated and individuated."

[2] The conference was held at Bedford College, London U., in 1914, at a joint meeting of the Aristotelian Society, the Mind Association, and the British Psychological Society. Cf. "Basic Postulates of Analytical Psychology," CW 8, par. 660.

of energy, then he may begin his career as a saint. I never thought that I might be able to help him along far enough on this way. — In a case of criminality, I am sure that the process of completion would bring it to daylight that he is a wrong one, but these cases don't come to the doctor. They find their way all by themselves. But it is quite possible that a fellow wrongly believes he is a criminal and analysis makes it clear to him that he is no such thing. He would seek the doctor's help, but not the real criminal.

May I give you some advice? Don't get caught by words, only by facts.

Sincerely yours, c . g . j u n g

To Claire Scheuter

Dear Fräulein Scheuter,   10 January 1959

Your question regarding the unconscious reactions which might influence the referendum[1] on February 1st is complicated and not easy to answer in a few words. As a basis for prediction we really need statistics showing the frequency and intensity of male resistance to greater emancipation for women. Unfortunately it is impossible to obtain such statistics without a Gallup poll of large numbers of men. We therefore have to make do with vague estimates which, in their turn, are subject to our own prejudices.

Judging by our medical experience of marriage psychology and of the relations between the sexes in general, one can count on a considerable amount of resistance. The so-called objective judgment of many men is influenced to a large extent by unconscious resentments, prejudices, and resistances, so much so that the crucial factor in this referendum is: how many men will look into themselves and seriously reflect whether their vote is an objective one or is swayed by their mood? Since self-knowledge is one of the more difficult arts, it is scarcely to be hoped that many men will take the trouble to search their conscience and consider how much their decision depends on their subjective relations with women. Male prestige on the one hand, which is of the utmost value in the struggle for existence, is a

[1] S., editor of the "woman's page" of the Zurich daily *Die Tat*, circularized a number of psychologists and psychiatrists for their opinion on the extent to which unconscious reactions would influence the referendum on giving women the vote. The letter was published in *Die Tat*, 23 Jan. 1959.

sensitive thing, and on the other hand a man's weakness, his emotional susceptibility, his proneness to feminine influence are sometimes so great that it is difficult for him to estimate the true importance of these factors. What is more, in planning this referendum far too little stress was laid on how eminently psychological the whole thing is. All honour to rational arguments! But in this question, I should say, it is just the irrational imponderables of a psychological nature that have to be taken into account.

Yours sincerely, c. g. j u n g

To H.A.F.

Dear Dr. F.,   16 January 1959

Many thanks for kindly sending me your very interesting dream.[1] I found it especially worthy of note that you obviously felt this dream to be highly significant right from the start. And so indeed it is, in so far as it pictures a phenomenon that is constantly recurring these days all over the world. The motif of being "carried off," for instance, occurs in widely believed reports in which the occupants of Ufos invite people to climb aboard in the friendliest manner and to make a round trip round the moon or to fly to Venus or Mars. The occupants of these contraptions are either very beautiful "higher" men or else spiritual beings or angels. These fairytale reports have the character of dreams of the same kind, such as yours. The bird signifies the aerial, volatile spirit (in the chemical sense "spirit" is volatile, but it also designates the Spiritus Sanctus), whose physical and spiritual meanings are united in the alchemical *spiritus Mercurialis*. The bird is a messenger of the gods, an *angelus*. This image hints at some activity "in the Beyond" relating to your consciousness, which is thereby to be raised to a "higher" level, transported from the banal sphere of everyday life and wafted away from the

□ Switzerland.
[1] H.A.F. reported a dream in which he saw a large bird he wanted to photograph. But suddenly the bird—a swan—crashed to the ground, leaving a plume of smoke like an aeroplane. In the next scene an aeroplane appeared through clouds of smoke or fog. Then a contraption like a helicopter descended towards the dreamer to fetch him. He saw shadowy figures which he knew to be higher types of men, with greater knowledge and absolutely just, visitors from another world.

476

rational world of the intellect. In parallel dreams one is fetched into the Beyond,[2] the "world of spirits," or experiences an illumination akin to a *metanoia* through the intervention of "higher beings."

I myself recently dreamed that a Ufo came speeding towards me which turned out to be the lens of a magic lantern whose projected image was myself;[3] this suggested to me that I was the figure, himself deep in meditation, who is produced by a meditating yogi. The yogi would be a transcendental figure comparable to the meditant in the Chinese text of *The Secret of the Golden Flower*.[4]

The crash is an indication that something coming down to earth from heaven, from the "Beyond," is felt as a catastrophe. According to other parallels this is the fire which descends to earth, like the outpouring of the Holy Ghost in the form of tongues of fire. It produces smoke or fog, i.e., a "fogging" and obfuscation of consciousness, a disturbance of our orientation, turning eventually into panic and collective psychosis, a fall of the angels with apocalyptic consequences. These symbolisms, which are cropping up everywhere nowadays, paint a picture of the end of time with its eschatological conceptions: destruction of the world, coming of the Kingdom of Heaven or of the world redeemer.

Finally a question: would you allow me to publish your dream[5] in the event of a second edition of my Ufo book?

With kind regards and again many thanks,

Yours sincerely, C. G. JUNG

[2] Cf. "Flying Saucers," CW 10, pars. 697ff. & Pl. I, at p. 404.
[3] As a matter of fact the images of the magic lantern and the yogi appeared in two different dreams; both are reported in *Memories*, p. 323/298.
[4] Cf. CW 13, pp. 30–33.
[5] The dream was never published.

To Verena Ballmer-Suter

Dear Frau Ballmer-Suter,   24 January 1959

I find it incomprehensible how anybody can credit me with being opposed to female suffrage out of fear that it might lead to the danger of "masculinization." My experience has impressed the tenacity and toughness of the female nature, which nothing has changed for

☐ Basel.

thousands of years, far too deeply upon me for me to suppose that the right to vote could bring such a wonder to pass. If a woman becomes "masculinized" this happens for quite other reasons than political activity. Naturally political activity can masculinize a woman, but so can all other activities; for instance, wives and mothers who in the common estimation could have a satisfying fate in their feminine role tyrannize over husbands and families with a masculine animus who can throw his weight about without any need on their part to have the right to vote as well. In an utterly feminine way a woman can have a—from her point of view—well-founded opinion without suffering the slightest injury to her nature. The fact that she can have convictions and insights is a generally human characteristic and one that is not peculiar only to men. At all times there have been wise and shrewd women to whom even clever men have gone for advice. There are countless women who succeed in public life without losing their femininity. On the contrary, they succeeded precisely because of it. The unpleasant power-complex of the female animus is encountered only when a woman does not allow her feeling to express itself naturally or handles it in an inferior way. But this, as said, can happen in all situations of life and has nothing whatever to do with the right to vote. With best regards,

Yours sincerely, c . g . j u n g

To Traugott Egloff

Dear Herr Egloff,   26 January 1959

Many thanks for your kind New Year's letter, which I am rather late in answering. Your remarks about the shadow[1] are very true and are based on sound observation. The numinosity of the shadow reposes ultimately on the dark aspect of God, the *deus absconditus*, who is making himself distinctly heard these days.

Recently I have sometimes found my thoughts turning in your direction and have wondered how you are getting on. So I was very glad to have such a long letter from you.

With best wishes for the New Year,

Yours sincerely, c . g . j u n g

[1] E. wrote that the confrontation with the shadow—the inferior side of the personality—filled him with fear mingled with admiration amounting to a feeling of reverence in spite of its evil and threatening nature.

To Dieter Meyer

Dear Herr Meyer, 26 January 1959

The symptom you describe[1] is a particularly pronounced instance of the *sentiment du déjà-vu*. It is usually explained as a sort of memory hallucination. It is true that such cases do occur in states of fatigue, but considering the nature of the symptom, and especially when it happens habitually, it seems to me to be something else, namely an actual fore-vision, whether in a dream or simply when one is asleep, of situations which in themselves are completely trivial and which one no longer remembers afterwards although one has a *sentiment du déjà-vu*. This interpretation seems to me particularly appropriate where an actual and conscious fore-vision has occurred. These ESP (Extra-Sensory Perception) phenomena are much more common than is generally assumed. They point to a quality of the unconscious which is outside the categories of time and space. Rhine's experiments, conducted with large numbers of people, offer irrefutable proof of this. There is nothing uncanny about it, since experiences like yours come within the range of the normal.

Yours sincerely, c . g . j u n g

☐ Wiesbaden, Germany.
[1] M., a singer of 24, described experiences in which he "recognized" as known things and experiences which he had never before come across.

Anonymous

Dear Herr N., 26 January 1959

Best thanks for telling me about the progress of your *opus*.[1] It does indeed, as you say, make considerable demands on our constitution. It goes to the very limit, but no further. Most people cannot reach their destinies anyway without a streak of craziness, and so long as they haven't it is better not to exorcize their demons. For if one did succeed in doing so it would merely be a successful amputation.

Your dream of 6.I.1959:[2] "Dirt" is always related to greatness. It

☐ Switzerland.
[1] N. had illustrated his "individuation process with about 400 pictures," and said that it "needed the constitution of an elephant."
[2] The setting was a bare room in a slummy apartment with dirty walls.

is a necessary compensation. Because we are so small, contact with greatness always carries with it the danger of inflation. Then our dreams speak of dirt and squalor, so that we shall remain down below and not be swept into the distance by the great world-wind. It is only from the purely human standpoint that the divine game is seen as a sickness, a leprosy, a perilous threat to the bond with human society. It is therefore advisable not to rant about it but to carry on the work in secret.

Wishing you continued good luck and a stout constitution,

Yours sincerely, c . g . j u n g

Anonymous

Dear Frau N.,   26 January 1959

I gather from your letter that you have a desire and a plan to do something.[1] This is very understandable and also very useful inasmuch as you learn most of all about yourself. You say you would "like to get the archetype of the daughter to speak." This you can do any time by playing the role of the daughter who in your view is the counterpart of the Regina Coeli,[2] and in that capacity say what you have to say through your identification with this daughter. It is not altogether clear to me what you mean when you say that you are "looking for the right place." There is no sense in your expecting to be expected anywhere. Rather you can be quite certain that you are not expected and can say it nevertheless. If you wish to speak of these things you must also be able to talk to your stove,[3] which cannot even give an understanding nod. Above all you cannot hope to "collaborate" in some way, for where in our time and our society would you find a person who knew how to express what your uniqueness alone can express? This is the jewel that must not get lost. But collaboration and especially "teamwork" are the quickest possible

☐ Germany.

[1] As a result of her intensive study of Jung's books she wanted to "do" something to help solve the problems of the world.

[2] Queen of Heaven. N. regarded the "archetype of the daughter as the Protestant counterpart of the Catholic cult of Mary" and wanted to get Mary "to speak through" her.

[3] In Grimm's fairytale "The Goose Girl," the princess whose place has been taken by an evil maidservant pours out her grief to an iron stove.

480

way of losing it. You can guard it only by enduring the solitude that is its due. This is the achievement for which the whole world, in its heart of hearts, is expectantly waiting. With friendly greetings,

Yours sincerely, C. G. JUNG

To Traugott Egloff

Dear Herr Egloff,   9 February 1959

Very many thanks for your kind letter. It instructed, soothed, and did not bore me in the least, for I am always interested to see how a man makes out with his anima. Recognizing the shadow is what I call the apprenticepiece, but making out with the anima is the masterpiece which not many can bring off. With best greetings,

Yours sincerely, C. G. JUNG

To Gertrud Rohde-Heussner

Dear Frau Rohde-Heussner,   11 February 1959

Best thanks for your kind letter. I was very interested to hear that you can make something of my way of looking at things and thinking about them. The difference between the two kinds of thinking[1] struck me a long time ago, and for my domestic use I have described the first kind as two-dimensional and the second kind as three-dimensional. Its "round" form is due to the fact that the thinking always circumambulates round the essential in an endless approximation to the centre. Paradoxically, as you rightly point out, this centre has to be created although it has always been there.

Thank you for telling me about Ringbom's book.[2] For several years now it has been in my wife's library; she was engaged in a study of the Grail up to her death in 1955. Her work has been brought

---

□ Berlin.

[1] N. found there were two ways of thinking, a logical and an alogical one. She described the latter as a "round, ontological form of thought," which she found confirmed in Jung's writings. Cf. *Symbols of Transformation*, CW 5, Part I, ch. II: "Two Kinds of Thinking" (also in the 1911 original; cf. *Psychology of the Unconscious*).

[2] Lars-Ivar Ringbom, *Graltempel und Paradies* (Stockholm, 1951).

to completion by one of my pupils and is to be published in the near future by Rascher in Zurich.[3]

Yours sincerely, C. G. JUNG

[3] Emma Jung and M.-L. von Franz, *The Grail Legend* (tr. 1971; orig. 1960).

To Pastor Tanner

Dear Pastor Tanner,   12 February 1959

Before going into the question[1] you have asked me I would like to thank you for the sympathetic interest you have taken in my opinions.

As you rightly remark, it is difficult to discuss the question of "faith without religion" because we must first establish what exactly we mean by "religion." Naturally I can define this concept only in psychological terms, and this definition is fundamental to everything I say about religion. I distinguish between "religion" and "creed"; the one is generic, the other specific. The ancients derived *religio* from *relegere* or *religere*, to ponder, to take account of, to observe (e.g., in prayer). Cicero: *religiosus ex relegendo*;[2] *religens* = god-fearing. A *conscientias scrupulus*[3] has *religio*. *Religio* is *iustitia erga deos*[4] (Cicero). *Divum religio i.e. religio erga deos*[5] (Lucretius). *Conficere sacra Cereris summa religione*[6] (Cicero). The Church Fathers, among them St. Augustine, derive it from *religare*, to bind, to reconnect: *Religio ex eo dicta est, quod nos religat Deo*,[7] and:

☐ Kronbühl, Canton St. Gallen. First name not obtained.
[1] T. asked Jung's opinion on the teachings of certain theologians, in particular the followers of Dietrich Bonhoeffer (1906–45), according to which modern man needs a "faith without religion."
[2] "Those who carefully . . . retraced everything which concerned the worship of the gods were called religious from *relegere*." Cicero, *De natura deorum*, 2, 28.
[3] = scruples of conscience.
[4] "Religion (is) that which gives due reverence [lit. does justice] to the gods." Cicero, *De partitione oratoriae*, 78.
[5] "*Divum religio* here means reverence towards the gods." Lucretius, *De rerum natura*, 6, 1276.
[6] "To perform the sacred rites of Ceres with the strictest reverence." Cicero, *Pro Balbo*, 24.
[7] "The word religion is derived from what binds us to God." Augustine, *Retractiones*, 1.13.9.

Religio vera ea est, qua se uni Deo anima, unde se peccato velut abruperat, reconcilatione religat.[8]

The latter interpretation derives on the one hand from the Jewish idea of marriage with God,[9] to which man can be unfaithful, and on the other hand from the character of Yahweh, i.e., from his injustice, which in Hellenistic times led to the conception of an *advocate*, foreshadowed in the Book of Job, who represents man at the heavenly court, as in Daniel and especially in the Book of Enoch (1st cent.). The distance between God and man is so great that Yahweh sees himself obliged to set up an embassy among men—the ambassador is his own son—and to deliver a missive to them (the gospel). At the same time Christ is the mediator with the title of *filius hominis*, Son of Man, as in Daniel and Enoch, and, as such, also an advocate.

The Jewish conception of the religious relationship with God as a legal contract (covenant!) gives way in the Christian conception to a love relationship, which is equally an aspect of the marriage with God. The bond of love can also be severed by estrangement and adultery.

As a contrast to this Judaeo-Christian conception we have the totally alien views current in pagan antiquity: the gods are exalted men and embodiments of ever-present powers whose will and whose moods must be complied with. Their *numina*[10] must be carefully studied, they must be propitiated by sacrifices just as the favour of archaic princes is won by gifts. Here religion means a watchful, wary, thoughtful, careful, prudent, expedient, and calculating attitude towards the powers-that-be, with not a trace of that legal and emotional contract which can be broken like a marriage.

Obviously the idea of marriage with God is a later and special development, whereas the original form of *religio* is, without question, aptly characterized by the implications of *relegere*. I prefer this interpretation of *religio* because it is in better accord with the general psychological findings.

By "religion," then, I mean a kind of attitude which takes careful

---

[8] "True religion is that by which the soul binds itself to the One God by reconciliation, whence by sin in the same manner it has severed itself." Augustine, *De quantitate animae*, 36.

[9] Hosea 2:19: "And I will betroth thee unto me for ever."

[10] *Numen* (whence *numinosum*) means "nod" (of the head); in a narrower sense, the god showing his will by nodding his head. Cf. *Aion*, CW 9, ii, par. 110, quoted passage.

and conscientious account of certain numinous feelings, ideas, and events and reflects upon them; and by "belief" or "creed" I mean an organized community which collectively professes a specific belief or a specific ethos and mode of behaviour. "Faith without religion" could therefore be translated as "(non-denominational) religion without creed," manifestly an unorganized, non-collective, entirely individual exercise of the "religious function." (By the latter I mean the allegiance, surrender, or submission to a supraordinate factor or to a "con-vincing" [= overpowering!] principle: *religio erga principium.*[11]) This trend is characteristic of present-day humanity, especially the young. The reason for this singular phenomenon, as I see it, is that people have grown rather *tired of believing* and are worn out by the effort of having to cling on to ideas which seem incomprehensible to them and are therefore quite literally *unbelievable.* This doubt is only reinforced by contemporary events. Things are going on in the world which make the public ask: Is it possible that a world in which such things happen is ruled by a good God, by a Summum Bonum? Our world is actually riven in two by an Iron Curtain, and in one half all religious activity is discouraged or suppressed, and the "Prince of Lies," the devil, who in our half has lost all substance by evaporating into a mere *privatio boni,* has for reasons of state been elevated into the supreme principle of political action. These facts have a highly suggestive effect on Christians who profess the collective belief. Whenever *belief* is stressed, demanded or expected, *doubt* infallibly increases and so does the vulnerability of belief in particular tenets.

In consequence, the tenets of belief have to be purified, or made easier, by being relieved of their principal encumbrances, which for the rationalist are their particularly obnoxious "mythological" components. Bultmann's endeavours are obviously intended to serve this purpose. Where they should or could stop is highly questionable. Christ as "Redeemer," for instance, is a mythologem of the first order, and so too is the "Son of God," the "Son of Man," the "Son of the Virgin," etc. "Faith without religion" or "religion without creed" is simply a logical consequence which has got out of Bultmann's control.

But if the believer without religion now thinks that he has got rid of mythology he is deceiving himself: he cannot get by without "myth." *Religio* is by its very nature always an *erga,* a "towards," no matter whether the following accusative be "God," "Redeemer," a philosophical idea or an ethical principle; it is always a "mythic" or

[11] = religion (due reverence) towards a principle.

transcendental statement. This is naturally also the case when the ultimate principle is called "matter." Only the totally naïve think this is the opposite of "myth." *Materia* is in the end simply a chthonic mother goddess, and the late Pope seems to have had an inkling of this. (Cf. the second Encyclical[12] to the dogma of the Assumption!)

Clearly the anti-mythological trend is due to the difficulties we have in clinging on to our previous mythological tenets of belief. Nowadays they demand too much of the effort to believe. This was not so in earlier centuries, with their very limited knowledge of nature. It needed no *sacrificium intellectus* to believe in miracles, and the report of the birth, life, death, and resurrection of the Redeemer could still pass as biography. All this has radically changed in recent times under the compelling influence of scientific rationalism, and the aversion of the younger generation for mythology seems the natural outcome of the premise: we are tired of the excessive effort of having to believe, because the object of belief is no longer inherently convincing. The dogma of the Trinity, the divine nature of the Redeemer, the Incarnation through the Holy Ghost, Christ's miraculous deeds and resurrection, are more conducive to doubt than to belief. One dogma after another falls. The "message of the Crucified and Risen Christ" is just not understood any more, but is, at most, felt as a well-meant object lesson in ethics that is conceded to have some practical utility. From here it is but a short step to the view that certain ethical principles can be acquired without the mythological trimmings.

But for people with religious sensibilities this rationalism is not enough; they have a dim suspicion that ethics needs a different foundation from the one which Janus-faced reason grants it. "Reason" is, notoriously, not necessarily ethical any more than intelligence is. These people sense in religion an indispensable I-Thou relationship which is not at hand in any rational decisions based on ego-conditioned judgments. They therefore reserve for themselves a personal relationship to Christ, as can plainly be seen in the Christocentric trend of recent developments in Protestantism. This conception of belief presupposes only *one* mythologem: the continuing, living presence of the Risen Christ. For many religious people today even this concession to myth is dropped and they content themselves with a bashfully veiled theism[13] which has a minimum of the traditional mythic en-

---

12 *Ad Caeli Reginam.* Cf. Sinclair, 7 Jan. 55, n. 7.
13 Belief in a god, but with denial of revelation.

cumbrances. Beyond that there are only surrogates like exotic theosophical ideas or other regressive -isms, all of which culminate in materialism, where one succumbs to the illusion of having finally escaped each and every mythological bugbear.

With this radical "demythologization" *religious communication* comes to a dead end too. Myth is pre-eminently a social phenomenon: it is told by the many and heard by the many. It gives the ultimately unimaginable religious experience an image, a form in which to express itself, and thus makes community life possible, whereas a merely subjective religious experience lacking the traditional mythic imagery remains inarticulate and asocial, and, if it does anything at all, it fosters a spiritually *anchoritic life*.

Although the anchorite does not represent a model for living, the solitude of religious experience can be, and will be, an unavoidable and necessary transitional phase for everyone who seeks the essential experience, that is to say the *primordial* religious experience. This alone forms the true and unshakable foundation of his inner life of belief. But once he has attained this certitude, he will in the normal course of things be unable to remain alone with it. His fulfilment spills over in communication, and communication requires language. But what language shall he choose? Obviously one that is generally understood. So for practical reasons he will not invent a new idiom, which would merely do him a bad service by branding him as an unintelligible eccentric, but will be bound to make use of the immemorial myth, in this case the Christian myth, even at the risk of being accused of pouring new wine into old bottles. If his individual experience is a living thing, it will share the quality of all life, which does not stagnate but, being in continual flux, brings ever new aspects to light. The old myth, which always holds within it something yet older and more aboriginal, remains the same, this being an essential quality of all forms of religion; it only undergoes a new interpretation. Thus the Reformation was no more a repristination of the early Church than the Renaissance was a mere revival of antiquity, but a new exposition which could not throw off its own historical evolution.

The imageless and unbiased experience modern man strives for will —unless he aspires to the role of the prophet—lead to the modest conclusion that notwithstanding its numinosity it was after all only his own subjective experience. If he has the necessary knowledge at his disposal, he will also come to see that it was not unique in its substance but has been observed in many other cases as well. Furthermore, he will have no difficulty in understanding that experiences of this kind are inherent in the nature of the psyche at all times, no matter to what causative God they may be attributed. We can in imagination and belief go beyond the psyche, just as in fantasy we can go beyond the three-dimensional world. But we can have immediate *knowledge* only of the psychic, even though we may be *sure* that our imageless experience was an "objective" fact—a fact, however, that can never be proved.

Nowadays one very often hears people asserting that something or other is "only" psychic, as though there were anything that is *not* psychic. When we assert that something is present, we must necessarily have "re-presentation," i.e., an image of it. If we had none, it would at the very least be unconscious to us. But then we would not be able to assert, let alone prove, anything about it either. The presence of objects is entirely dependent on our powers of representation, and "representation" is a psychic act. But these days "only psychic" simply means "nothing." Outside psychology only modern physics has had to acknowledge that no science can be carried on without the psyche.[14]

For more than a hundred years the world has been confronted with the concept of an unconscious,[15] and for more than fifty years with the empirical investigation of it, but only a very few people have drawn the necessary conclusions. Nobody seems to have noticed that without a reflecting psyche the world might as well not exist, and that, in consequence, consciousness is a second world-creator, and also that the cosmogonic myths do not describe the absolute beginning of the world but rather the dawning of consciousness as the second Creation.

Myths are descriptions of psychic processes and developments, therefore. Since these, so long and so far as they are still in the unconscious state, prove to be inaccessible to any arbitrary alteration, they exert a compelling influence on consciousness as pre-existent conditioning factors. This influence is neither abolished nor corrected by any environmental conditions. From ancient times, therefore, it has been deemed a *daemonium*.[16] No amount of reason can conjure this empirical fact out of existence.

Now whether these archetypes, as I have called these pre-existent

[14] Cf. Whitmont, 4 Mar. 50, n. 1.
[15] For instance C. G. Carus, *Psyche* (1846). The book opens with the sentence: "The key to knowledge of the nature of conscious psychic life lies in the realm of the unconscious."
[16] The intermediate realm of supernatural powers between gods and men.

and pre-forming psychic factors, are regarded as "mere" instincts or as daemons and gods makes no difference at all to their dynamic effect. But it often makes a mighty difference whether they are undervalued as "mere" instincts or overvalued as gods.

These new insights enable us to gain a new understanding of mythology and of its importance as an expression of intrapsychic processes. And from this in turn we gain a new understanding of the Christian myth, and more particularly of its apparently obnoxious statements that are contrary to all reason. If the Christian myth is not to become obsolete—which would be a sell-out with quite unpredictable consequences—the need for a more psychologically oriented interpretation that would salvage its meaning and guarantee its continuance forces itself upon us. The danger of its final destruction is considerable when even the theologians start to demolish the classic world of mythological ideas without putting a new medium of expression in its place.

———

I must apologize, my dear Pastor, for the unusual prolixity of my letter. Considering the importance of your question my exertions are small enough. At the age of 84 I am somewhat tired, but I am concerned about our culture, which would be in danger of losing its roots if the continuity of tradition were broken. For close on sixty years I have felt the pulse of modern man from all continents of the earth, and have experienced far too much of the woes of our time not to take the gravity of your question profoundly to heart.

Yours sincerely, C. G. JUNG

To Cleome C. Wadsworth

Dear Mrs. Wadsworth,

[ORIGINAL IN ENGLISH]

14 February 1959

Thank you very much for sending me the draft of your interview[1] and particularly for the beautiful arrangement of flowers. They brought the whole spring into my house.

As a rule I don't like subsequent reports about interviews. As the doctor is pledged to silence and discretion, so is the patient, even if he feels very innocent about it. It is like painting a portrait. You always put yourself into it. If you want to use it at all, please refrain from

☐ Washington, D.C.

[1] The résumé of an interview she had with Jung.

488

any too public use. With very good friends of whose discretion you are sure, you may show it with the comment that it is a portrait *you* have painted. There is a certain subtle undertone in it for which I am hardly responsible.

Hoping you are always in the best of spirits, I remain,

Yours sincerely, C. G. JUNG

To Stephen I. Abrams

[ORIGINAL IN ENGLISH]

Dear Mr. Abrams,   5 March 1959

Thank you very much for your interesting news. I was quite impressed by the fact, unknown to me, that Kammerer committed suicide shortly after his remarkable book.[1] It was obviously a case like Silberer,[2] who put his foot into a new dimension and committed suicide. I must say: I sympathize with them. I always marvelled that I could fight my way through the inimical jungle.

I should be very interested in the thesis you mention about my astrological experiment.[3] I am rather astonished that these people have not thought of sending me a copy, which would be a common usage in scientific circles.

The nature of ESP is a really difficult problem. The ESP experiments are in a way repeatable and in another way not. This shows that one has not to do with a constant quality of the psychic process. Under a certain condition the quality appears as if out of nowhere, and under a certain other condition it is as if it were not there at all. Even people with habitual clairvoyance are under the law of this restriction inasmuch as they cannot use it for their own purposes.

We have obviously to realize that we are confronted here with an

☐ Writing as a member of the Parapsychology Society, U. of Chicago.

[1] Paul Kammerer (1880–1926) committed suicide after the publication of his book *Die Vererbung erworbener Eigenschaften* ("The Inheritance of Acquired Characteristics"; 1924), when it was discovered that one of his assistants had produced faked experimental results in order to prove the theory of the French naturalist Lamarck (1744–1829). Jung's reference here, however, is to Kammerer's *Das Gesetz der Serie* (1919), discussed in "Synchronicity," CW 8, pars. 824f. Cf. also Arthur Koestler, *The Case of the Midwife Toad* (1971).

[2] Cf. Neumann, 22 Dec. 35, n. 1.

[3] Reference to a M.Sc. thesis (U. of Chicago) submitted by an acquaintance of A. in 1957, which contained an analysis of Jung's synchronicity statistics and came to the conclusion that they were valid.

entirely new and strange behaviour of facts. The question of the conditioning factor occupies me the most. The only definite contribution I can make in this respect is the observation that in most synchronistic cases it is a matter of a constellated archetype.[4] That is the nearest I can get to the psychology of synchronicity. The archetype shares its peculiar nature with the natural numbers, i.e., they are subjective psychological phenomena on the one hand and have objective existence on the other. As there are equations that coincide *a posteriori* with physical facts,[5] so there are physical facts that coincide *a posteriori* with archetypal representations.

It seems to me that any experimental arrangement disregarding the presence of this archetypal disposition, or assuming ESP to be a constant quality, would be more or less sterile. There is however a certain chance of demonstrating by such experiments what ESP is not. Undeniably a *per exclusionem* method has its merits. The question of learning and unlearning has, as it seems to me, much to do with the said autonomous condition. The facts underlying synchronistic phenomena seem to have a certain behaviour, expressing itself in subjective psychic and at the same time in objective physical conditions. This is indeed a great puzzle.

. . .

Sincerely yours, C. G. JUNG

P.S. I was under the obviously erroneous impression that I had answered the paper you sent to me. It happens occasionally that when I have thought about something it leaves me with the impression that the question has been dealt with. Your paper, even in its second edition, is indeed very difficult. Hearing it, I should not have been able to follow its content. One of the difficulties is that your audience could not possibly understand what I mean by "archetype." One feels that you yourself are not too clear about it and your audience knows just nothing about it. To understand the peculiar phenomenon of the archetype one needs a lot of practical experience, f.i. the numinous quality, so indispensable to the recognition of an archetype, is an indefinable imponderable like the expression of the human eye, which is indubitable yet indescribable. As the archetypal representa-

---

[4] This term describes an emotionally charged situation, frequently a psychological impasse, in which an archetype is activated or "constellated"; cf. "Synchronicity," CW 8, par. 847.

[5] Cf. Watson, 9 Feb. 56, n. 1; also *Aion*, CW 9, ii, par. 413.

tion, which is not identical with the archetype itself, is the symbolic formulation of the instinct itself, it is our only means of recognizing the manifestation of an instinctual situation. It is a piece of man's instinctual life, and as such it functions in a sphere that is mainly unconscious and possesses therefore all the qualities of a psyche outside of all categories that make consciousness possible at all. It is neither here nor there, neither now nor past nor future. It is not localized at all, which explains why it appears outside (ectopsychic) as well as inside (endopsychic).[6] It is one and the same, yet divided in two or more independent events manifesting the same meaning. One is dealing with something obviously beyond all traditional expectations of our rational thinking. A careful experimental study of the *I Ching* as a rule yields most instructive material.

[6] "What I understand by the *ectopsyche* is a system of relationship between the contents of consciousness and facts and data coming in from the environment. . . . The *endopsyche*, on the other hand, is a system of relationship between the contents of consciousness and postulated processes in the unconscious." *Analytical Psychology: Its Theory and Practice*, p. 11, and fig. 4, p. 49 (= "The Tavistock Lectures," CW 18, par. 20 and fig. 4 at par. 88).

Anonymous

[ORIGINAL IN ENGLISH]

Dear Mrs. N.,   5 March 1959

I cannot tell you how deeply I have been moved by the appalling news of your son's premature death. . . . Yes, life is a mysterious affair. Sometimes it starts with a profound *no* to its own existence, and its only goal seems to be that it ends. In such a case one can only ask: what was before? and what comes afterwards? Sometimes one has a dream which answers our question. But mostly we are left in utter darkness about motive and meaning of an individual life; even our own life seems to consist of a long chain of events, of which only a certain stretch is illuminated by consciousness, but darkness covers that which has been before the beginning and that which is after its end.

My deep sympathy!

Yours sincerely, c . g . j u n g

☐ U.S.A.

491

Anonymous

Dear Frau N., 6 March 1959

Many thanks for kindly telling me your Ufo dreams. Understood as a psychological phenomenon, Ufos compensate our insecurity in this world. They are like an assurance that we have a connection with the extramundane.

As a general rule it may be taken as axiomatic that the patient always gets stuck just where the analyst can make no further progress himself, so your conjecture is probably right. Your son has, of course, a considerable mother complex that prohibits him from leaving the maternal magic circle and standing on his own feet. One must in the end be able to withstand one's own panic. For your part, you need the inner certainty of instinct which an animal has: when the time has come, it bites its young away from the feeding trough. It is quite clear that your son should risk taking his exam, but he can only do that if he gives up his infantile dependence for good and all. He handles himself with imitated maternal feelings and kid gloves when he should summon up the courage to give himself a cruel pinch or two. Too much of that kind of handling has an anaesthetizing effect and undermines his morale. He needs more of a cold water treatment. Tender solicitude saps his strength.

This is roughly what I would tell you or your son in a consultation. With friendly greetings,

Yours sincerely, C. G. JUNG

☐ Switzerland.

Anonymous

Dear N., 9 March 1959

I am sorry you are so miserable. "Depression" means literally "being forced downwards." This can happen even when you don't consciously have any feeling at all of being "on top." So I wouldn't dismiss this hypothesis out of hand. If I had to live in a foreign country, I would seek out one or two people who seemed amiable and would make myself useful to them, so that libido came to me from outside, even though in a somewhat primitive form, say of a

☐ U.S.A. (a woman).

dog wagging its tail. I would raise animals and plants and find joy in their thriving. I would surround myself with beauty—no matter how primitive and artless—objects, colours, sounds. I would eat and drink well. When the darkness grows denser, I would penetrate to its very core and ground, and would not rest until amid the pain a light appeared to me, for *in excessu affectus*[1] Nature reverses herself. I would turn in rage against myself and with the heat of my rage I would melt my lead. I would renounce everything and engage in the lowest activities should my depression drive me to violence. I would wrestle with the dark angel until he dislocated my hip. For he is also the light and the blue sky which he withholds from me.

Anyway that is what I would do. What others would do is another question, which I cannot answer. But for you too there is an instinct either to back out of it or to go down to the depths. But no half-measures or half-heartedness.

. . .

With cordial wishes,

As ever, c. g. jung

[1] = in an excess of affect or passion. Cf. "Synchronicity," par. 859.

To Erich Neumann

Dear friend,   10 March 1959

Best thanks for your long and discursive letter of 18.II. What Frau Jaffé sent you was a first, as yet unrevised draft,[1] an attempt to pin down my volatile thoughts. Unfortunately the fatigue of old age prevents me from writing a letter as discursive as yours.

I

The question: *an creator sibi consciens est?*[2] is not a "pet idea" but an exceedingly painful experience with well-nigh incalculable consequences, which it is not easy to argue about. For instance, if

□ Parts of this letter were published in Jung and Jaffé, *Erinnerungen, Träume, Gedanken*, pp. 376ff. (not in *Memories*). The whole letter, together with Neumann's of 18 Feb., is in Jaffé, *Der Mythus vom Sinn im Werk von C. G. Jung* (1967), pp. 179ff. (not in tr., *The Myth of Meaning*).
[1] The first draft of ch. XII, "Late Thoughts," in *Memories*.
[2] = is the creator conscious of himself?

somebody projects the self this is an unconscious act, for we know from experience that projection results only from unconsciousness.

Incarnatio means first and foremost God's birth in Christ, hence psychologically the realization of the self as something new, not present before. The man who was created before that is a "creature," albeit "made in the likeness" of God, and this implies the idea of the *filiatio* and the *sacrificium divinum*. Incarnation is, as you say, a "new experience."

"It has happened almost by accident and casually . . ."[3] This sentence might well characterize the whole process of creation. The archetype is no exception. The initial event was the arrangement of indistinct masses in spherical form. Hence this primordial archetype [mandala] appears as the first form of amorphous gases, for anything amorphous can manifest itself only in some specific form or order.

The concept of "order" is not identical with the concept of "meaning." Even an organic being is, in spite of the meaningful design implicit within it, not necessarily meaningful in the total nexus. For instance, if the world had come to an end at the Oligocene period, it would have had no meaning for man. Without the reflecting consciousness of man the world is a gigantic meaningless machine, for in our experience man is the only creature who is capable of ascertaining any meaning at all.

We still have no idea where the constructive factor in biological development is to be found. But we do know that warmbloodedness and a differentiated brain were necessary for the inception of consciousness, and thus also for the revelation of meaning. It staggers the mind even to begin to imagine the accidents and hazards that, over millions of years, transformed a lemurlike tree-dweller into a man. In this chaos of chance, synchronistic phenomena were probably at work, operating both with and against the known laws of nature to produce, in archetypal moments, syntheses which appear to

---

[3] Paraphrase of a passage in *Memories* (which N. had read in MS form): "Natural history tells us of a haphazard and casual transformation of species over hundreds of millions of years of devouring and being devoured" (p. 339/312). He objected to the "Darwinistic residue" in "haphazard and casual transformation" and suggested a different theory "in which your concept of the archetype and of absolute and extraneous knowledge will play a part." Concerning N.'s concept of extraneous knowledge—a knowledge steering the life process and in which the division between inner and outer reality, psyche and world, is transcended in a "unitary reality"—cf. his "Die Psyche und die Wandlung der Wirklichkeitsebenen," *Eranos Jahrbuch* 1952.

us miraculous. Causality and teleology fail us here, because synchronistic phenomena manifest themselves as pure chance. The essential thing about these phenomena is that an objective event coincides meaningfully with a psychic process; that is to say, a physical event and an endopsychic one have a common meaning. This presupposes not only an all-pervading, latent meaning which can be recognized by consciousness, but, during that preconscious time, a psychoid process with which a physical event meaningfully coincides. Here the meaning cannot be recognized because there is as yet no consciousness. It is through the archetype that we come closest to this early, "irrepresentable," psychoid stage of conscious development; indeed, the archetype itself gives us direct intimations of it. Unconscious synchronicities are, as we know from experience, altogether possible, since in many cases we are unconscious of their happening, or have to have our attention drawn to the coincidence by an outsider.

II

Since the laws of probability give no ground for assuming that higher syntheses such as the psyche could arise by chance alone, there is nothing for it but to postulate a latent meaning in order to explain not only the synchronistic phenomena but also the higher syntheses. Meaningfulness always appears to be unconscious at first, and can therefore only be discovered *post hoc*; hence there is always the danger that meaning will be read into things where actually there is nothing of the sort. Synchronistic experiences serve our turn here. They point to a latent meaning which is independent of consciousness.

Since a creation without the reflecting consciousness of man has no discernible meaning, the hypothesis of a latent meaning endows man with a cosmogonic significance, a true *raison d'être*. If on the other hand the latent meaning is attributed to the Creator as part of a conscious plan of creation, the question arises: Why should the Creator stage-manage this whole phenomenal world since he already knows what he can reflect himself in, and why should he reflect himself at all since he is already conscious of himself? Why should he create alongside his own omniscience a second, inferior consciousness—millions of dreary little mirrors when he knows in advance just what the image they reflect will look like?

After thinking all this over I have come to the conclusion that being "made in the likeness" applies not only to man but also to the

Creator: he resembles man or is his likeness, which is to say that he is just as unconscious as man or even more unconscious, since according to the myth of the *incarnatio* he actually felt obliged to become man and offer himself to man as a sacrifice.

Here I must close, aware as I am that I have only touched on the main points (so it seems to me) in your letter, which I found very difficult to understand in parts. It is not levity but my *molesta senectus*[4] that forces economy on me. With best greetings,

Sincerely yours, c. g. jung

[4] = burdensome old age.

To Cary F. Baynes

[ORIGINAL IN ENGLISH]

Dear Cary,   12 April 1959

. . .

X.'s shyness in touching upon the psychological problem is a fact well known to me. I have seen it in many cases. You rarely find a similar attitude in women though. It is just as if women knew less of its implications, as they know psychology chiefly as a means to an end, while a man has an incomparably more complete intuition about it although he knows very much less of it than a woman. A woman thinks she is moving in a sphere of more or less known factors, while a man is terrified by the certainty of having to deal with the well-known "Unknowns," as Wagner says in *Faust*: "Berufe nicht die wohlbekannte Schar!"[1] The "Unknowns" are a very definite factor in a man's life. He knows them quite well, so well in fact that he keeps on assuring himself and others that there is no such thing. He even builds up a lamentable superiority in this respect. This is the average man, and he is right in his anxiousness, because it is a matter of the fathers and mothers of all the terrors he is bringing to this world in the form of Communism and H-bombs, and last but not least by his fertility and the inevitable overpopulation. He still thinks in terms of mass-hygiene and has nightmares about mass-killing. Why should he learn about the unconscious, the mother of the future?! Man still hopes, in a primitive way, that not knowing, not naming, not seeing a danger would remove it. Why should he

[1] "O summon not that well-known throng!" (Cf. Wayne tr., p. 68; MacNeice tr., p. 40.)

bother with psychology, that is meant to help him in a situation which is declared to be invisible? X.'s psychology in this respect is just every man's behaviour, and I am the fool speaking about bad weather while the sun shines.

. . .

Cordially yours, C. G.

To Werner Bruecher

[ORIGINAL IN ENGLISH]

Dear Mr. Bruecher,   12 April 1959

Your kind letter[1] has come as a great surprise to me, as it contains a message from a group of people of whose existence I had not an inkling. It gives me the enjoyable thought that there may be similar groups in other remote places of the world interested in my psychology. I have often asked myself where my books go and how they are received. The only thing I know definitely is that they have a tolerable sale, if compared to others treating similarly difficult subjects.

Moreover, I always have been impressed by the apparently general opinion that my books are difficult to read and I have seen myself from so many unfavourable critiques that there must be something in them which does not go down easily. All the more I have been surprised by your so very positive and friendly welcome and understanding. It is now over half a century ago that I tried to reach the ear of my contemporaries, with an astonishingly small echo. I cannot complain, though, about academic honours bestowed upon me in Europe, America and even in remote India,[2] but I am more than doubtful about the effect my books had upon those who were responsible for the bestowal of such honours. I suppose that my books expect a human understanding of which the intellectual world or the world of intellect is afraid, although I can easily understand

☐ Tucson, Arizona.
[1] B., together with several other people in the same city, expressed their deep appreciation of Jung's work. He described the "group of friends who live in central Arizona as the types of souls whose main urge it is to try to understand themselves, the world around them, and the relation between the two," calling Jung "one of the great souls who help to usher in a new age when its time has come."
[2] Cf. Künzli, 4 Feb. 43.

497

why that is so. It is a great satisfaction to know that such an understanding does exist, because I know from the work with my patients, as well as pupils, how much the modern mind is in need of some guidance and how helpless people are in envisaging and dealing with the enormities the present time and still more the immediate future will present us with. I cannot help believing that the real problem will be from now on until a dim future a psychological one. The soul is father and mother of all the apparently unanswerable difficulties that are building themselves up into the heavens before our eyes. We are thoroughly in need of a new orientation, and I hope that my small effort and yours will be a contribution to the solving of the great riddle.

I thank you and your friends warmly for the kindness and generosity which have inspired your letter.

Sincerely yours, C. G. JUNG

To Wilhelm Bitter

Dear Colleague, 17 April 1959

Best thanks for your news concerning the publication of the report of the meeting.[1]

As you can imagine, your question about miracle cures[2] cannot be answered in a few words. The best way to answer it would probably be in the form of case histories, as it is very difficult to lay down any general principles in regard to this strange material. The first thing is to distinguish between apparent cures, i.e., those which appear miraculous to the layman, and cures which appear miraculous also to the initiate. I would guess that a high percentage of so-called miracle cures are due to psychic associations which have nothing miraculous about them for us. I remember the case of a woman of 60 who had been walking on crutches for 17 years because of an inexplicable pain in her left knee.[3] This was at the time I conducted Forel's clinic

---

[1] Bitter (ed.), *Gut und Böse in der Psychotherapie* (1959), report of a meeting in Zurich, autumn 1958. Jung's contribution, "Good and Evil in Analytical Psychology," is in CW 10.

[2] B. was editing the report of two other meetings held in Stuttgart in May and October 1958, published as *Magie und Wunder in der Heilkunde* (1959). Jung's letter was printed (with minor omissions) as the first contribution.

[3] The case is described in "Crucial Points in Psychoanalysis," CW 4, par. 581,

for treatment by hypnosis and suggestion, before the first World War. When I told her I was going to hypnotize her, she fell without any assistance from me into an hypnotic somnambulism from which I had the greatest difficulty in awakening her. As soon as she came to, she leapt up and cried, "I am cured!" When her female companion handed her the crutches, she waved them away and marched home in triumph without any support. My students were deeply impressed by this "miracle." The basis of the cure was that she had a son on whom she set all her ambitious hopes, but who had become mentally ill and was actually in the clinic in my department, though I didn't know this because in the meantime she had remarried and bore another name. For her I represented the successful son and her transference therefore fastened on me. The cure was a demonstration in my favour *ad maiorem gloriam filii*. She was able to give up her neurotic pains in exchange for this blissful transference.

Much the same thing happens in church, where it is well worth one's while to be cured directly by the mother of God and be publicly admired for this privilege. But it is a very different matter in the case of some organic disease, tuberculosis for instance, when by all medical standards no sudden curative processes can be expected to supervene and yet a cure is effected. I have treated a number of cases of chronic pulmonary tuberculosis which necessitated annual visits to Davos, and observed that the lesion healed up in a few weeks so that no further visits were needed. For the layman this is miraculous, but for the doctor it is something that can nevertheless be understood. The same is true of tumours. I have seen several cases where some psychic event, or psychological treatment, caused not only proliferating metastases to vanish but the primary tumour as well. Not that these observations would be enough to make me believe in the possibility of a psychotherapeutic cure for tumours. In some cases of psychotherapeutic treatment, contact with the sphere of the archetypes can produce the kind of constellation that underlies synchronicity. Naturally in these circumstances anything that borders on the miraculous, or actually is miraculous, may be expected, because for the life of us we cannot discover exactly how a synchronistic result comes about. Obviously the greatest caution is indicated, since cures that are psychically understandable in themselves

---

and more fully in *Memories*, pp. 118f./119. (The patient's age in the two reports differs, but the case is obviously the same.)

can come about in such ultra-refined ways that very great experience is needed in order to recognize them as such. Even so, there are instances of cures which by our standards were just as unthinkable as that connection between the dream and the real scarab.[4] At whatever point we enter the sphere of the archetypal, synchronistic events may be expected with some degree of probability; and, as you rightly point out, they happen to believers and unbelievers alike. These phenomena are relatively rare, and they occur on a plane beyond belief and disbelief. It is clear that such things do not happen only under inner psychic conditions; very often they also need an external ambience to happen in, for instance a numinous spot. At Lourdes, where Mary appears as a kind of rebirth-giving Earth Mother, it is the cave and the underground spring. The latter is actually one of Mary's appellatives: *page pagon*.[5]

These are roughly the thoughts that have come to me on the subject of "miracle cures." With best greetings,

Yours sincerely, C. G. JUNG

[4] Cf. "Synchronicity," CW 8, par. 843, and appendix, par. 982: while a patient was reporting a dream in which she was given a golden scarab a scarabeid beetle flew into the room.
[5] = source of sources.

To Joseph F. Rychlak

[ORIGINAL IN ENGLISH]

Dear Mr. Rychlak,   27 April 1959

The philosophical influence that has prevailed in my education dates from Plato, Kant, Schopenhauer, Ed. v. Hartmann,[1] and Nietz-

□ M.D., then director of a mental health clinic connected with Washington State U., now professor of psychology at Purdue U., Indiana. — According to a letter from R., 16 Jan. 70, quoted with his kind permission, "the 'question' was essentially 'what role did Hegelian philosophy play in your education?' and then more indirectly 'what are your thoughts on the dialectic?' . . . It is my thesis that both Freud and Jung were instrumental in retaining the dialectical side of man (as metaconstruct) in this century of Lockean images of man (cybernetics, S-R psychology, etc.). As with most dialecticians in history Jung has had to bear the unfounded criticisms of being vague, mystical, and even sophistical—precisely because we have no appreciation of dialectical reasoning today." Jung's letter and R.'s thesis are published in his *A Philosophy of Science for Personality Theory* (1968).
[1] Eduard von Hartmann (1842–1906), German philosopher. His most important work is *Die Philosophie des Unbewussten* (1869).

500

sche. These names at least characterize my main studies in philosophy. Aristotle's point of view had never particularly appealed to me; nor Hegel, who in my very incompetent opinion is not even a proper philosopher but a misfired psychologist. His impossible language,[2] which he shares with his blood-brother Heidegger, denotes that his philosophy is a highly rationalized and lavishly decorated confession of his unconscious. The fact that I use the term "dialectical procedure"[3] or something of this sort exposes me to the misunderstanding that I envisage an intellectual procedure, which is not the case, but in truth a practical method of dealing with the very concrete propositions the unconscious presents us with. This is a very important chapter of psychotherapy. Since neurosis consists in a dissociation of personality, one is always confronted with an opposite or a *vis-à-vis* you have to reckon with; a fact which is unknown only to people who know of nothing else but the contents of their consciousness. Moreover the science of all moving as well as living bodies is based upon the concept of energy. Energy itself is a tension between opposites. Our psychology is no exception to the principle that embraces about the whole of natural science.

In the intellectual world in which I grew up, Hegelian thought played no role at all; on the contrary, it was Kant and his epistemology on the one hand, and on the other straight materialism, which I never shared, knowing too much about its ridiculous mythology. Hegel's dialectics, I can safely say, had no influence at all, as far as I know myself. The German term "Auseinandersetzung" was used by me in its colloquial sense. Being an empiricist and not a philosophical thinker, the terms I chose have their real source in experience; thus when I speak of "Auseinandersetzung" it could be just as well the discussion between Mr. A. and his wife. Another common misunderstanding is that I derive my idea of "archetypes" from Philo or Dionysius Areopagita, or St. Augustine. It is based solely upon empirical data, viz. upon the astonishing fact that products of the unconscious in modern individuals can almost literally coincide with symbols occurring in all peoples and all times, beyond the possibil-

---

[2] There is an anecdote according to which Hegel is supposed to have said: "Only one man has understood me, and even he has not."

[3] Cf. "General Problems of Psychotherapy," CW 16, pars. 1 & 7, where Jung describes psychotherapy as "a kind of dialectical process, a dialogue or discussion between two persons," and "the dialectical procedure as the latest phase of psychotherapeutic development." His practical therapeutic use of the term "dialectic" is completely different from Hegel's, to whom the dialectical method was a purely philosophical and abstract law of thought.

ity of tradition or migration, for which I have given numerous proofs.

I have never studied Hegel properly, that means his original works. There is no possibility of inferring a direct dependence, but, as I said above, Hegel confesses the main trends of the unconscious and can be called "un psychologue raté." There is, of course, a remarkable coincidence between certain tenets of Hegelian philosophy and my findings concerning the collective unconscious.

Hoping that I have answered your question satisfactorily, I remain,

Yours faithfully, C. G. JUNG

To G. Krönert

Dear Dr. Krönert,   28 April 1959

If the father's intention were a unique and isolated factor—as one usually imagines it is—it would indeed be miraculous if the embryo noticed it and consequently had a feeling of resentment.[1] But the father's intention is never a unique and isolated thing; it is an act with an antecedent history and a consciousness which extends over many years right up to the present. The father has not *done* it but himself *was* it for the greater part of his life. No act drops out of the blue or can be wiped out. It is part of his substance. That is what the child reacts to—to the quiddity of the father, without knowing that this quiddity once exemplified itself in an act. Nothing is in us that was not there before, and nothing that has once been can vanish.

If you should come to Switzerland sometime I would be happy to make your acquaintance.

Yours sincerely, C. G. JUNG

☐ Oberfischach, Württemberg, Germany.
[1] K. asked if an embryo could be affected by the father's demand that the mother get an abortion.

To Jean Vontobel-Ruosch

Dear Herr Vontobel-Ruosch,   28 April 1959

You are quite right: I also ask myself why I do not use the means that appear to be at my disposal to do my bit in combatting the atrocities that are going on in the world.[1] I can give no rational reasons for this. In such matters I usually wait for an order from within. I have heard nothing of the kind. The world situation has got so hopelessly out of hand that even the most stirring words signify nothing. It would be more to the point, or so it seems to me, if each of us were sure of his own attitude. But an individual who thinks that his voice is heard afar merely exposes himself to the suspicion that he is one of that band who have said something in order to prove to themselves that they have done something whereas in reality they have done nothing at all. Words have become much too cheap. Being is more difficult and is therefore fondly replaced by verbalizing. Unfortunately this is all I have to say on the matter.

Yours sincerely, C. G. JUNG

□ Winterthur.

[1] V.-R. asked why Jung didn't protest against the injustice done to Tibet by the Chinese occupation and its consequences.

To Sándor Török

Dear Sir,   29 April 1959

Your question about homesickness is one that I can answer only from the standpoint of an empirical psychologist. Homesickness in this sense is a special phenomenon, possibly a symptom, that has two aspects: either one is still clinging on to the memory of the original homeland, or one thinks one is still clinging to this memory-image but has unconsciously projected into it the conception of a longed-for goal. This is so with all those people who, when they return to their homeland, or come back to the situations for which they are homesick, are bitterly disappointed. There are people who because of their homesickness cannot accustom themselves to any new situation. But then they would never have accustomed themselves to their homeland either. Others, who identify with their homeland, youth, and origins, regard them as a kind of lost paradise and yearn to get back again. A Kabbalist has said that after the Fall God removed paradise into the future.[1] They long to get back but don't know that it is the future they long for. Others, again, have reversed their homesickness and labour under the delusion that things will be much better in the

□ Budapest.

[1] *Mysterium*, par. 338, n. 676.

future than they are in the present. But all of them share the same illusion that the goal is somewhere to be found in outward things and conditions, without realizing that psychologically they already carry it within them and always have. If they knew that, the question of homesickness would be answered once and for all.

Yours sincerely, C. G. JUNG

Anonymous

Dear Herr N.,   9 May 1959

While thanking you for your interesting offprints[1] I would also like to try to answer your questions to the best of my ability in writing.

A transference in the clinical sense does not always need a personal relationship as a bridge, but can take place via a book, a piece of hearsay, or a legend. In your case it is obvious that unconscious contents have forced themselves on you which have put you in the situation, so well known in the East, for instance in India, of the pupil who receives the necessary guidance from a guru (teacher). Since I was the nearest to hand, I have been assimilated to the East by this archetype.

It seems that one essential point at least—the concept of the archetype—has transferred itself to you. It may be a prejudice to think that the world of human ideas is conditioned by archetypes, but it is also a means of grasping something of the psychology of another organism. In this way a man can learn a good deal about the differences between this organism and himself, although in theory he will never succeed in forming a picture of the *Weltanschauung* of a salamander. "Teachings" are tools not truths; points of view that are laid aside once they have served their purpose. All systemizations are to be avoided. We would be going round every teaching in an endless circle if we did not constantly find new ways of escaping from it. Thus the environment delivers us from the power of the archetypes, and the archetypes deliver us from the crushing influence of the environment.

Just like the animal, man too is caught up in the conflict between

□ Switzerland.
[1] Of some of his zoological writings. N. was at the time a student.

504

archetypal drives and environmental conditions. The solution is always a compromise. I am chary of all anticipatory generalizations. For me the archetype means: an image of a probable sequence of events, an habitual current of psychic energy. To this extent it can be equated with the biological pattern of behaviour. If exact observation—of the fright pattern, for instance—shows that the human and the animal pattern are identical, we have, in accordance with the principle *principia explicandi non sunt multiplicanda praeter necessitatem,*[2] no grounds for assuming (errors always excepted!) that another principle must be at work simply because we are dealing with an animal and not with a human being. It would be a prejudice to assume that the behaviour of a fish, for instance, necessarily cannot be compared with that of another organism. Cogent reasons would have to be offered for this.

If you isolate any way of looking at things, even one that has proved in practice to be the best, and then extend it to infinity you will end up with nonsense. This is a piece of morbid intellectualism which at most a philosopher can afford, but not an empiricist, who knows full well that all his views are provisional and cannot be valid for all eternity. It is therefore pointless to speculate about what would happen if all projections were withdrawn. Withdrawal of projections is obviously a truth whose validity is only of limited application. It is pretty certain that they can be withdrawn only to the extent that one is conscious. How far a man can become conscious nobody knows. We have as a matter of fact been able to correct a number of projections. Whether this amounts to much or little, and whether it is a real advance or only an apparent one, is known only to the angels. As to what absolute consciousness might be, this is something we cannot imagine even in our wildest dreams.

My remarks about the translation of the figurative language of alchemy into modern scientific terminology, and about this being yet another figurative language, were made partly *ad hoc* and partly as an expression of my doubt whether we have really conquered the final peak with our present achievements, which is highly unlikely. As a rule it so happens that what passes for the profoundest knowledge and the ultimate truth on the first level is understood and derided as ridiculous ignorance on the next, and it is thought that now at last we have arrived at the right insights. When we reach the third level the same thing happens as before. We cannot see how

[2] Cf. Frischknecht, 7 Apr. 45, n. 2.

we could ever attain to a universally valid view of the world in this way. You can, if you like, call these views an intellectual game with nature, but nature has the uncomfortable quality of occasionally playing a game with us, though we would scarcely have the nerve to call it a "game" any more.

Notwithstanding these doubts it would, however, be quite wrong to relapse into an impatient nihilism and, intellectually anticipating the worst, to write off all man's scientific achievements as nugatory. With science you really do get somewhere, even if you don't attain the ultimate philosophical insights. We don't attain any "ultimate truths" at all, but on the way to them we discover a whole lot of astonishing partial truths. You can call this progress, which indeed it is within the limited area of the drive for human knowledge. If we knew the meaning of the whole, we would know how much or how little progress we have made. But as we do not possess this knowledge we must be content with the feeling of satisfaction which is our reward for every increase in knowledge, even the smallest. With best greetings,

Yours sincerely, C. G. JUNG

To Carleton Smith

[ORIGINAL IN ENGLISH]

Dear Mr. President,   12 May 1959

In reply to your letter I should like to suggest a topic that concerns everybody in all ways of his life:[1]

Who or what is hindering man from living peacefully on this earth? The most disparate names you have mentioned as guests of the symposium are certainly difficult to unite under one capital question, but I think that the question I propose is the one that can go to the heart of every one of them.

Hoping that you and your family are in the best of health, I remain, dear Mr. President,

Yours sincerely, C. G. JUNG

---

[1] S., president of the National Arts Foundation (U.S.A.), asked Jung to suggest a subject for a symposium to be held under its auspices. Among the names he mentioned as possible participants were those of Adlai Stevenson, Mrs. Eleanor Roosevelt, Nelson Rockefeller, Ernest Hemingway, J. Robert Oppenheimer, and André Malraux. The symposium did not take place.

To Ignaz Tauber

Dear Colleague, 22 May 1959

Dr. Jacobsohn's criticism[1] is certainly a fatal blow but was to be foreseen. I am sorry I was the bird of ill omen who had to convey to you this negative experience. Even without Jacobsohn I could have told you that you were making an improper use of the amplification method, but I didn't want to keep back the expert opinion of a scientifically trained Egyptologist who is in a better position than I am to pick holes in the material. I am thoroughly aware of my incompetence in the field of Egyptology, in obvious contrast to yourself. You are too quick to brush aside any positive knowledge of Egyptology with fallacious reasoning. Your use of the amplification method is uncritical because you do not amplify from the knowledge proper to an Egyptologist but just as you please, that is to say from your knowledge of the medieval and modern mind. When we amplify a modern dream whose content we do not at first understand, the amplifications are not chosen at random, but are supported either by the associative material of the dreamer himself or by the tradition available to him, or, going further afield, by the tradition of his historical milieu, and finally by fundamental conceptions of a more general nature, as for instance the Trinity, the quaternity, and other universal myth-motifs. In dealing with a definitely historical text it is absolutely essential to know the language and the whole available tradition of the milieu in question and not to adduce amplifications from a later cultural milieu. This can be done when, and only when, the meaning has been sufficiently well established with the help of methods warranted by the historical milieu itself. Only then may we adduce for comparison amplifications from other times and places, but under no circumstances can we use them to explain the text. One cannot be cautious enough in this regard.

Now for your dreams. The dream of the silver wires tangled up with the teeth may be interpreted as follows: the teeth, understood as organs for gripping, for instance in the predators, here represent the concepts by which things are grasped[2] and dissected, i.e., discriminated, but are needlessly impeded by "silver wires" which have no business to be in the mouth. These wires are alien and irrelevant

[1] T. had sent Jung a work on Egyptian mythology which he, with T.'s consent, passed on to Dr. J. for an expert opinion.
[2] Cf. Kotschnig, 16 Apr. 36.

appendages that do not belong to the natural function of the teeth and have been improperly introduced from outside. This is precisely what I have to criticize about your method.

The other dream points to the coming shock, a complete shattering of your view of the world, as a result of which you and your anima fall into the depths—the catacombs. These, like the pagan temples, stand for the origins of Christianity, whose two church towers remain unshaken. With this fall into the depths you come to the firm historical foundations upon which Christianity is built. Once you have this solid ground under your feet, you can regain the historical continuity from which you have evidently cut yourself off, misled by your intuition. It has inveigled you into a bottomless edifice of speculation which again and again will collapse about your ears.

So if you want to work your dissertation up into a poem I can raise no objections, for then poetic licence will stand you in good stead and you can give free rein to your intuition since it no longer lays claim to scientific validity. Intuition is a dangerous gift, tempting us over and over again into groundless speculation. An intuition needs an uncommonly large dose of sobering criticism, otherwise it exposes us only too easily to the kind of catastrophic experience that has befallen you.

The dream of the catacombs ends on a hopeful note, and I hope very much that this negative and painful experience will turn out to your advantage. With friendly greetings,

Yours sincerely, C. G. JUNG

To Traugott Egloff

Dear Herr Egloff,   8 June 1959

I am very much obliged to you for your kind gift.[1] It has awakened old memories of my youth, when I read Kügelgen's book. The little book you have given me is a valuable document from an age when the newer psychology was putting forth its first tender shoots.

You are quite right when you say that the "truth" is actually star-

---

[1] A book by W. Kunz, *Johann Georg Schröpfer, ein Magier des 18. Jahrhunderts* (1957). Schröpfer was a German Freemason and spiritualist (1730–74). His personality is described in Wilhelm von Kügelgen, *Jugenderinnerungen eines alten Mannes* (1870).

ing us in the face but that often we are as though smitten with blindness so that we cannot see it. Everything could be said much more simply, but this simplicity is just what we ourselves and others lack, with the result that it is more trouble for us to speak really simply than to speak in a rather complicated and roundabout way. The simplest is the most difficult of all, because, in the process of reaching consciousness, it breaks up into many individual aspects in which the mind gets entangled and cannot find a suitably simple expression. The trouble may lie in language itself, which is just as much lacking in that needful simplicity as are our powers of conception. Only numinous experiences retain their original simplicity or oneness which still gives us intimations of the Unus Mundus.²

The androgyny of the anima³ may appear in the anima herself at a certain stage, but it derives at a higher level from unity of the self. Just as our masculine consciousness is a concretized aspect of the masculine, so the anima is a concretized aspect of the feminine. Her masculine aspect is expressed very clearly in the anima figure in the Song of Songs: "terrible as an army with banners."⁴ These opposites are in reality united in the irrepresentable because transcendent self, which in the process of becoming conscious divides into opposites again through progressive dichotomy.

Again with best thanks,

Yours sincerely, C. G. JUNG

² Cf. Anon., 2 Jan. 57, n. 1.
³ A reference to some unconscious material reported by E.
⁴ Song of Songs 6:10.

To Peter de Brant

[ORIGINAL IN ENGLISH]

Dear Sir,   20 June 1959

In dealing with space,¹ man has produced—since time immemorial —the circle and the square, which are connected with the idea of shelter and protection, place of the hearth, concentration of the family and small animals, and on a higher level the symbol of the *quadratura circuli*, as the dwelling place of the "inner man," the

□ London.
¹ B., a student of architecture, asked about "the psychology of man's reaction to space created by architectural planning" and about the possible existence of "archetypal space forms."

abode of the gods, etc. This original conception has undergone many changes since man has found himself removed from the unity with nature and himself separated from the gods, thus shaping temples of elongated form, the gods at one end and the human public at the other end. Most pronounced in the Christian churches, except the old Baptisteria,[2] in which man's original identity with God is reasserted. Any development that leads further away from the round and the square becomes increasingly neurotic and unsatisfactory, particularly so when the elements of the building, i.e., the rooms, lose their approximation to the round or the square. A certain interplay of round and square seems to be indispensable.

This is about all I can tell you about "architectural archetypes."

Sincerely yours, C. G. JUNG

[2] The ground plan of most baptisteria is a mandala with the baptismal font as its centre.

To E. A. Bennet

[ORIGINAL IN ENGLISH]

Dear Bennet,   28 June 1959

I have chosen the title *Aion* because the contents of the German edition are chiefly connected with the psychological changes characteristic of the transition from one historical aeon, i.e., era, or segment of historical time, to another. The other essay is M.-L. von Franz's "Passio S. Perpetuae," describing the psychological phenomena which accompanied the transformation of the pagan antique world into the early Christian mentality. My contribution to the book concerns the peculiar historical transformations that took place within Christianity up to modern times. It is evident, of course, that history takes on a new aspect when considered not only from the standpoint of our conscious reason, but also from that of the phenomena due to unconscious processes which never fail to accompany the *peripeteia* of consciousness.

As Dr. von Franz is chiefly concerned with the Christian transformation of paganism, my work deals in the main with the transformation of Christian tenets within the Christian era. As we are profoundly influenced in our practical life by our historical Christian education, we are also exposed to secular changes in the basic Christian dominants, e.g., the schism of the Christian Church and the

510

development of anti-Christian traits. Developments on such a scale are only possible when the individual, i.e., many individuals, are transforming themselves in their personal psychological life, a fact which cannot take place without a profound shaking up of one's mental peace. The same happens today and here the alienist comes in. That is the reason why I try to explain the bewildering situation of the modern mind by showing its own anamnesis.

I am grateful to you that you are willing to say a few useful words in the *British Medical Journal*.[1]

Hoping that my answer is sufficient, I remain,

Yours sincerely, c. g. jung

P.S. I just got a letter from Dr. Fordham[2] telling me that he has asked you to review *Aion* for the *Journal of Analytical Psychology*. I do not need to tell you how much I would appreciate that a balanced mind should write a review about this book, which has chiefly aroused subjective emotions but hardly any objective evaluation. I know how much you have to do, and I hate to burden you with such a cumbersome task.

[1] Cf. Bennet, 22 May 60, n. 1.
[2] Dr. Fordham was at the time the editor of *The Journal of Analytical Psychology* (London). B.'s review appeared in vol. V, No. 2 (July 1960).

To Lloyd W. Wulf

[ORIGINAL IN ENGLISH]

Dear Sir, 25 July 1959

I can understand that people find it rather difficult to answer your propositions. You use terms which in themselves are most controversial.

1. So f.i. "God," then "magic," "religious," etc. I would propose the term "numinous" instead of "magic" or "religious," which are prejudiced in a very definite way.

2. Any convinced Christian of today would contest your assumption that his religion is not dynamic. Though I think that such a statement, namely the feebleness of our religion, is not unfair.

3. It is rather conspicuous that the creators of modern art are unconscious about the meaning of their creations.

□ American Embassy, Quito, Ecuador.

4. What modern art-forms represent is questionable. It is certainly something which transcends any hitherto valid form of understanding.

Your general conclusion that contemporary Western artists unconsciously depict God's image is questionable, as it is by no means certain that any inconceivability could be called "God," unless one calls everything "God," as everything ends in inconceivability. But when one calls everything which is inconceivable "God," then the term "God" loses all sense. According to my view, one should rather say that the term "God" should only be applied in case of numinous inconceivability. Since the term "God" always includes the meaning of an insurmountably strong affect of collective nature, I am not convinced that every piece of modern art is living up to such a postulate. Very often indeed it is easy to see that very inferior factors have been at work.

Excuse the long delay of my answer.

Sincerely yours, C. G. JUNG

To H. Richard Mades

[ORIGINAL IN ENGLISH]

Dear Sir,   3 August 1959

Thank you for your interesting letter.[1] I quite agree with you that the best thing would be if we could all get together and say: "Now, let us be reasonable." But unfortunately that is precisely the thing that does not happen, and I cannot see how such an event could be brought about by artificial means. The sad fact is that men of today are not reasonable. Knowing this, it would not be reasonable to hope for a reasonable solution which we know cannot be brought about in a reasonable way. Try by all means!

I don't believe that man, as he is today, is capable of evading the vicious circle in which he moves, as long as he is as immature as he actually is. The only thing I can do is to try at least to be as reasonable as possible in my own life and to help a few others to be also reasonable. Even if the great disaster should overtake us, there may

☐ Lexington, Massachusetts.

[1] M. suggested that the function of the State is to "govern in a manner which will allow the greatest degree of individual freedom of movement, education, and expression which is possible."

512

survive a few who have learned to be reasonable and who were helped by the serious attempt to get a bit more conscious than their somnambulistic entourage. I think it is even better to make ready for the great catastrophe than to hope that it will not take place and that we are allowed to continue the dream-state of our immaturity. Maybe I am too pessimistic, but it does not look too nice, does it?

Sincerely yours, c. g. jung

To Susan M. Margulies

[ORIGINAL IN ENGLISH]

Dear Madam,   15 August 1959

Being a scientist I prefer not to be a prophet if I can help it. I am in no position to ascertain facts of the future.[1]

Faithfully yours, c. g. jung

[1] The American magazine *Esquire* (of whose editorial staff M. was a member) was preparing "a survey among prominent men . . . with the idea of attempting to pinpoint the most dramatic developments of the coming decade" and asked for comment on such developments in the field of psychology.

To Wilhelm Bitter

Dear Colleague,   23 August 1959

I return herewith your manuscript[1] with the marginal comments you requested. The archetypality of Communism is on the one hand the common ownership of goods, as in primitive societies, and on the other hand the unlimited power of the tribal chieftain. Ostensibly all goods belong to all. Everybody has his share. But since all are represented by one man, the chieftain, only one man has control of everything. Practically every revolution seeks refuge in these two primordial images because man's belief that everything was once paradisal seems to be ineradicable. With cordial greetings,

Yours sincerely, c. g. jung

[1] "Das Gewissen in der Tiefenpsychologie," subsequently published in *Gut und Böse in der Psychotherapie*. B. asked for comment on that part of the essay which dealt with conscience in economics and politics.

513

To J. O. Pearson

[ORIGINAL IN ENGLISH]

Dear Dr. Pearson,   29 August 1959

The lack of dreams has different reasons: the ordinary reason is that one is not interested in the mental life within and one does not pay attention to anything of this kind. Another reason is that one has not dealt enough with one's conscious problem and waits for dreams so that the unconscious would do something about it; and the third reason is that the dreams have—as it were—emigrated into a person in our surroundings, who then is dreaming in an inordinate way.[1] A fourth reason, finally, can be a mental condition, in which dreams are redundant, inasmuch as compensations for the conscious attitude are not needed. A light sleep is certainly a favourable condition for the remembrance of dreams.

There is certainly a great difference between dreams. According to a primitive classification there are big dreams and small ones. The example you describe[2] is obviously a big dream of very particular importance. The small dreams are the ordinary stuff of unconscious fantasies which become perceptible particularly in light sleep.

Sincerely yours, C. G. JUNG

☐ Constantia (Cape Province), South Africa.
[1] Cf. the example of an 8-year-old boy "who dreamt the whole erotic and religious problem of his father," in CW 16, par. 106. "The father could remember no dreams at all, so for some time I analysed the father through the dreams of his eight-year-old son."
[2] P. described a dream of "terrific intensity . . . one was everything, time, space, it was like being the hall, the audience, the players, the music, i.e., as if one could be each and every member of an orchestra at the same time. Marvellous, exciting, terrifying in that one felt what an atom must feel like before it is split." He asked why there appeared to be a dearth of such intense dreams.

Anonymous

Dear N.,   Bollingen, August 1959

As promised, I will try to sketch my "reaction":[1] I was drawn into the dream which oneself is, and in which there is no I and no You any more. It begins with the great parents, the King and Queen, who own many forests, fields, meadows, and vineyards. Late in life some-

☐ To a Swiss woman.
[1] A paraphrase of a fantasy story sent by N. about a vine shoot.

one finds his inheritance, a tiny little bit of land, where he grows his vine and tree of life (*vita* = life, *vitis* = vine, *vinum* = wine). He has to acquire it for himself because he has been expelled from paradise and has nothing more, or rather he has but doesn't know it. It is walled round like a holy place. There he sees everything that has ever happened to him: sun and rain, heat and cold, sickness, wounds, tears and pain, but also fruitfulness and increase, sweetness and drunkenness, and therewith access to the All, the Whole. Though he doesn't know it, somebody else is there, an old man who knows but doesn't tell. When one has looked and laboured for a long time, one knows oneself and has grown old. — The "secret of life" is my life, which is enacted round about me, my life and my death; for when the vine has grown old it is torn up by the roots. All the tendrils that would not bear grapes are pruned away. Its life is remorselessly cut down to its essence, and the sweetness of the grape is turned into wine, dry and heady, a son of the earth who serves his blood to the multitude and causes the drunkenness which unites the divided and brings back the memory of possessing all and of the kingship, a time of loosening, and a time of peace.

There is much more to follow, but it can no longer be told.

Ever yours, C . G .

To Mrs. C.

[O R I G I N A L   I N   E N G L I S H]

Dear Mrs. C.,   24 September 1959

. . .

The dream of X. means chiefly that it would be advisable to you to give yourself that kind of loving attention as well as whatever X. means for you in yourself. In other words: worry about yourself more than about others; see and understand what you do more than what you assume other people do. Otherwise you will be accused of a meddling power drive. The latter would be a compensation for a troublesome feeling of inferiority. Therefore be kind, patient, and understanding with yourself. If you don't feel self-sufficient, give yourself the chance to take yourself as self-sufficient even if you don't believe it, but make an effort to allow such kindness to yourself. You cannot apply kindness and understanding to others if you have not applied it to yourself. This is quite serious. We are never sufficient to

☐ England.

ourselves. This is the burden everybody has to carry: to live the life we have got to live. So be kind to the least of your sisters who is yourself.

Sincerely yours, C. G. JUNG

To the Mother Prioress of a Contemplative Order

[ORIGINAL IN ENGLISH]

Rev. Mother Prioress, September 1959

I hope you will forgive the long delay of my answer to your kind letter of July 24. It came at a time when I was very tired and ever since I was waiting for a propitious moment. I am very old and there are too many people who want to see me.

I am very grateful for the spiritual help you extend to me. I am in need of it with this gigantic misunderstanding which surrounds me. All the riches I seem to possess are also my poverty, my lonesomeness in the world. The more I seem to possess, the more I stand to lose, when I get ready to approach the dark gate. I did not seek my life with its failures and accomplishments. It came on me with a power not my own. Whatever I have acquired serves a purpose I have not foreseen. Everything has to be shed and nothing remains my own. I quite agree with you: it is not easy to reach utmost poverty and simplicity. But it meets you, unbidden, on the way to the end of this existence.

I am glad that you gave me some news about Father White's activity. Thus I know that he does not fully disapprove of my work.[1] I have heard of his terrible accident.[2] But I have no news since and I would be very grateful if I had some further information of his state of health.

I thank you for the unasked-for kindness of your letter. There is so much evil and bitterness in this world that one cannot be too grateful for the one good thing which happens from time to time.

Yours devotedly, C. G. JUNG

□ The Mother Prioress had known Father White for a number of years and he had been in close contact with her convent. She sent Jung her birthday greetings and told him of the great influence that his writings, communicated through Father White, had had on herself and her community.

[1] Cf. White, 31 Dec. 49, n. 11, and 2 Apr. 55, n. 1.

[2] W. had had a serious accident on his motorcycle in Apr. 1959.

To Günter Wittwer

Dear Herr Wittwer,   10 October 1959

Your question is legitimate: who actually is behind the books I have written?[1]

It is much more difficult to answer this question than you might think. To answer it satisfactorily, I would need to know exactly who I am, give you a picture of myself to match, and finally prove to you that my report is not a mere tinkling of words. Even if you were to confine your question to my "religion" or "outlook on life" it would still affect the whole of my personality, for I am convinced that one's "outlook on life" can claim to be genuine only when it springs from the encounter of the whole man with his world. If it doesn't, it's so much twaddle. But because my consciousness is narrow, and incapable of grasping the whole in all its parts, every statement is but patchwork. We are, unfortunately, always only parts of a whole, although glimmerings of it are possible.

I cannot allow myself arbitrarily to believe something about things I don't know. I would regard this as impertinent and unwarranted. Anyone whom I believed, just like that, to be a liar and a thief would take my attitude very badly indeed, just as he would laugh at me pityingly if I believed him to be a saint. You can easily find out from my books what I think about religion (e.g., "Psychology and Religion"). I profess no "belief." I *know* that there are experiences one *must* pay "religious" attention to. There are many varieties of such experiences. At first glance the only thing they have in common is their *numinosity*, that is to say their gripping emotionality. But on closer inspection one also discovers a *common meaning*. The word *religio* comes from *religere*, according to the ancient view, and not from the patristic *religare*. The former means "to consider or observe carefully." This derivation gives *religio* the right empirical basis, namely the religious *conduct of life*, as distinct from mere credulity and imitation, which are either religion at second hand or substitutes for religion. This view is a most inconvenient one for the "theologian," and he suspects it of psychologism, though actually it turns out that he has a very poor opinion of the psyche, this centre-piece

□ Bern.

[1] W., still at school, had read several of Jung's books and was deeply impressed by them. He wanted to know "who is behind these words, what conviction drives you on?"

517

of religious experience. That is also why he is much fonder of Freud's view than of mine, since it does him the service of sweeping all inconvenient experiences under the table by intellectualizing them. I myself feel committed to such experiences both intellectually and ethically. They are of many kinds, as I have said. My books give detailed information about them. You can also see from my writings that I am not playing any intellectual or aesthetic or otherwise edifying game with the religious problem.

Yours sincerely, C. G. JUNG

To Father Victor White

[ORIGINAL IN ENGLISH]

Dear Victor,   21 October 1959

From your letter I see with great satisfaction that you are up and active again.[1] I sincerely hope that no irreparable damage has been done.

Concerning my doubts about your general attitude I must mention in self-defence that you expressed yourself publicly[2] in such a negative way about my work that I really did not know what your real attitude would be.

Thank you for your kind letter.

Hoping and wishing for a complete recovery, I remain,

Yours, C. G.

[1] On 18 Oct., W. thanked Jung for a message to the Mother Prioress wishing him a speedy recovery from his accident. He mentioned that on account of his approval of Jung's work his future had become uncertain and added: "But I think you will agree that your work itself will be moribund if there is not some disagreement about it, and some *Auseinandersetzung* from those with different backgrounds and experiences—and perhaps different typologies!"
[2] Cf. White, 24 Apr. 55, n. 1, and 25 Mar. 60, n. 3.

To Charles E. Scanlan

[ORIGINAL IN ENGLISH]

Dear Sir,   5 November 1959

Thank you very much for your informative letter.[1] It is evident that my standpoint is not a theological one. I make no metaphysical asser-

□ Cambridge, Massachusetts.
[1] S. objected to some of Jung's statements, particularly about the nature of original sin, from the standpoint of the Catholic Church. He upheld the

tions. My standpoint is purely empirical and deals with the psychology of such assertions.

I agree fully with the statement that God is not limited, because if He were limited He would not be God. The lack of limitation is a logical consequence of the assumption of a supreme being, of which man cannot judge really. He can make more or less founded statements answering to certain needs in his nature. We would be naturally inclined to assume that God also knows the future. But if we make such a statement, then everything is tending towards the future. In other words: it is necessary and inevitable. Therewith we declare that the world-process contains no problems, as everything is on its predestined way, and we are in full contradiction with the assumption of free will.

The *peccatum originale* has brought about a considerable change in the human status, so that man before the Fall is something different from man after the Fall. Therefore Christ and His mother belong to another order of things than man after the Fall. When you call them human, your term has a double meaning. As most of my patients are as ignorant *in theologicis* as I myself, we try in the first place to understand theological tenets as psychological statements and we also try to avoid flagrant contradictions like the above-mentioned.

We know that metaphysical assertions are indisputable, because no human being can know beyond himself, only God can know the truth.

Since there is no end of evil in this world, and since evil is the indispensable counterpart of the antithesis good–evil, it would be an arbitrary limitation of the concept of God to assume that He is only good and so deprive evil of real being. If God is only good, everything is good. There is not a shadow anywhere. Evil just would not exist, even man would be good and could not produce anything evil. This is another paradox which psychology has to straighten out for our sake, because the flagrant sophisms connected with the discussion of things like the *privatio boni* spoil the understanding and acceptance of religious tenets. Since metaphysical concepts are nowhere touched by psychological argument—because they are indisputable—I remain within the frame of disputable things.

Sincerely yours, c. g. j u n g

"Catholic position . . . that God is not limited, but infinite and all-powerful, and all good."

To James Kirsch

Dear Kirsch,   12 November 1959

I am glad to hear of your activity on the radio.[1] Nowadays this is the way to get at the public. I personally am opposed to it, but then I belong increasingly to the past and can no longer adapt to the restlessness and superficiality of modern life. It surpasses my comprehension how anyone can talk about "Job" on the radio without provoking misunderstandings—especially if such a banal thinker as X. precedes you as a speaker—since its argument is one of the subtlest that can be imagined. I therefore wish you the very best of luck in this unpredictable undertaking. However, there is one thing I do not underestimate, and that is the—to me—amazing and unexpected *intuition* of the American public, of which I was given an impressive sample on the occasion of my lectures at Yale University.[2] The little book[3] has a steady if limited sale in the U.S.A. I am eager to hear of your experiences. Possibly you may start a "war," which will certainly break out one day the more darkly the political sky becomes overcast. My appearance on the British television[4] seems to have been a considerable and unexpected success. My best wishes,

Ever sincerely yours, C. G. JUNG

☐ Published (in K.'s tr.) in *Psychological Perspectives*, III:2 (fall 1972).
[1] In Oct. and Nov. 1959 K. had tape-recorded a series of four lectures on "Psychology and Religion," the last of which, entitled "Job," was an extensive discussion of Jung's *Answer to Job*. The lectures were broadcast in Apr. and May 1960 on radio station KPFK, Los Angeles.
[2] The Terry Lectures, published as *Psychology and Religion* (1937); revised and augmented version now in CW 11.
[3] Presumably the Yale U. Press edition of the Terry Lectures, though the 1956 U.S. edition of *Answer to Job* may be intended.
[4] Cf. Brooke, 16 Nov. 59, n. 1.

To Valentine Brooke

[ORIGINAL IN ENGLISH]

Dear Sir,   16 November 1959

As you have learned from Mr. Richardson's account,[1] I am an irritating person. I am dealing with doubts and views which puzzle the

☐ Worthing, Sussex.
[1] On 22 Oct., the British Broadcasting Corporation broadcast a television inter-

modern mind consciously as well as unconsciously. I am treading on corns right and left. As a consequence I have to spend a great amount of my time in handing out apologies and explanations for saying things which allude to facts and ideas unknown to the reader. Moreover the reader is handicapped by his positivistic premise that the truth is simple and can be expressed by one short sentence. Yet "nothing is quite true and even this is not quite true," as Multatuli says. A psychologist concerned with the treatment of mental disturbances is constantly reminded of the fallacies in our verbal formulations. In spite of all the difficulties besetting my way, I will try to explain my standpoint.

Whatever I perceive from without or within is a representation or image, a psychic entity caused, as I rightly or wrongly assume, by a corresponding "real" object. But I have to admit that my subjective image is only *grosso modo* identical with the object. Any portrait painter will agree with this statement and the physicist will add that what we call "colours" are really wave-lengths. The difference between image and real object shows that the psyche, apperceiving an object, alters it by adding or excluding certain details. The image therefore is not entirely caused by the object; it is also influenced by certain pre-existent psychic conditions which we can correct only partially. (We cannot remove colour perception, f.i.) Moreover we know from experience that all acts of apperception are influenced by pre-existent patterns of perceiving objects (f.i., the premise of causality), particularly obvious in pathological cases (being exaggerations or distortions of so-called "normal" behaviour). They are presuppositions pertaining to the whole of humanity. The history of the human mind offers no end of examples (f.i., folklore, fairy tales, religious symbolism, etc.). To explain the spontaneous origin of such parallelisms, the theory of migration[2] is insufficient. I call them archetypes, i.e., instinctual forms of mental functioning. *They are not inherited ideas, but mentally expressed instincts*, forms and not contents.

---

view with Jung conducted by John Freeman in the series "Face to Face." In the course of the interview Freeman asked: "Do you believe in God?" to which Jung answered after a long pause: "I don't need to believe, I know." These words gave rise to considerable argument, and B. sent Jung a rather derogatory review of the broadcast by Maurice Richardson in the London *Observer*, 25 Oct. 1959, as well as some of the correspondence published in the same paper about Jung's words. B. asked for their exact meaning. The interview with Freeman is published in *C. G. Jung Speaking*.

[2] Cf. Flournoy, 29 Mar. 49, n. 3.

They influence our image-formation. As experience shows, archetypes are equipped with a specific energy without which they could not have causal effects. Thus when we try to form an image of the fact one calls "God" we depend largely upon innate, pre-existent ways of perceiving, all the more so as it is a perception from within, unaided by the observation of physical facts which might lend their visible forms to our God-image (though there are plenty cases of the sort).

"God" therefore is *in the first place* a mental image equipped with instinctual "numinosity," i.e., an emotional value bestowing the characteristic autonomy of the affect on the image.

This is my chief statement. Now people unaccustomed to proper thinking assume that it is a final statement. No scientific statement is final: it is a likely formulation of observation and analysis. It goes as far as a scientific statement can go. But it does not and cannot say what "God" is; it only can define what He is in our mind. The mind is neither the world in itself nor does it reproduce its accurate image. The fact that we have an image of the world does not mean that there is only an image and no world. But this is exactly the argument of those who assume that when I speak of the God-image I mean that God does not exist, *as He is only an image.*

Our images are, as a rule, *of something,* and even delusions are "images" of something, as modern psychology has amply shown. If f.i. I imagine an animal which does not exist in reality as we know it, I form the picture of a mythological entity, following the age-old activity of our ancestors in imagining fairy beasts and "doctor animals." I am functioning within the frame of an archetype. I am in this case strongly influenced by it. (The archetype has efficacy.) But although we can be fairly certain that no such animal exists in physical reality, there is nevertheless a real cause which has suggested the creation of the dragon. The dragon-image is its expression.

The God-image is the expression of an underlying *experience of something* which I cannot attain to by intellectual means, i.e., by scientific cognition, unless I commit an unwarrantable transgression.

When I say that I don't need to believe in God because I "know," I mean I know of the existence of God-images in general and in particular. I know it is matter of a universal experience and, in so far as I am no exception, I know that I have such experience also, which I call God. It is the experience of my will over against another and very often stronger will, crossing my path often with seemingly disastrous results, putting strange ideas into my head and maneuvering my fate

sometimes into most undesirable corners or giving it unexpected favourable twists, outside my knowledge and my intention. The strange
force against or for my conscious tendencies is well known to me. So I
say: "I know Him." But why should you call this something "God"?
I would ask: "Why not?" It has always been called "God." An excellent and very suitable name indeed. Who could say in earnest that his
fate and life have been the result of his conscious planning alone?
Have we a complete picture of the world? Millions of conditions are
in reality beyond our control. On innumerable occasions our lives
could have taken an entirely different turn. Individuals who believe
they are masters of their fate are as a rule the slaves of destiny. A
Hitler or Mussolini could believe they were such masterminds.
Respice finem! I know what I want, but I am doubtful and hesitant
whether the Something is of the same opinion or not.[3]

Hoping I have succeeded in elucidating the puzzle,

Sincerely yours, c. g. j u n g

[3] Most of this paragraph is reproduced in Jaffé, *The Myth of Meaning* (1971),
p. 53.

To M. Sickesz

Dear Colleague,   19 November 1959

Best thanks for your friendly letter. Unfortunately I can answer
only one central question, that concerning consciousness and self. By
definition, the self is a combination of consciousness and the unconscious and is therefore more comprehensive than the ego. Only what
is associated with the ego can become conscious. But since the ego is
only a part of the whole, I can become conscious only of a part. The
whole can be comprehended only by a whole. Therefore, when the
self *qua* whole grasps something, it grasps the whole. But this whole
is much too big for the ego to grasp. It can only be divined, but this
is not cognition. I can become conscious neither of the whole of myself nor of the whole of the world. I know that the East believes in a
consciousness without a subject and says that the personal *atman* is
capable of encompassing the knowledge of the whole. Nevertheless
the East also says that dreamless sleep is the highest stage of cogni-

☐ Amsterdam (a woman physician).

tion. For us this is an inconceivable paradox because dreamless sleep is, for us, the epitome of an unconscious state in which no consciousness exists, as we understand it. Empirically, we do not know what happens in this state, since there is no subject to cognize it, at least for us. Perhaps there is a transcendental consciousness of the self which cognizes the whole. But since I am a mere mortal and an empiricist to boot, I cannot assert that I am this self which is capable of such cognition. On the contrary, I must admit that all my cognition is piecemeal and that my ego is far from being able to cognize a whole. Also, I have never discovered, either in the literature or in conversation with an Oriental, any cognition that could be said to be a cognition of the whole. It is merely said to be so, just as we Christians say that we are redeemed of our sins by Christ. Unfortunately I haven't yet noticed anything of the sort, any more than I have noticed a cognition of the self as subject.

Hoping I have made my standpoint clear, and with collegial regards,

Yours sincerely, C. G. JUNG

To Hugh Burnett

[ORIGINAL IN ENGLISH]

Dear Mr. Burnett,   5 December 1959

So many letters I have received have emphasized my statement about "knowing" (God) that I have written an answer to a man whose letter was particularly articulate in this respect.[1] (You will find a copy enclosed.) I explained what my opinion is about a "knowledge of God." I know it is an unconventional way of thinking and I quite understand if it should suggest that I am no Christian. Yet I think of myself as a Christian, since I am entirely based upon Christian concepts. I only try to escape their internal contradictions by introducing a more modest attitude which takes into consideration the immense darkness of the human mind. The Christian idea proves its vitality by a continuous evolution, just like Buddhism. Our time certainly demands some new thoughts in this respect, as we cannot continue to think in an antique or medieval way when we enter the sphere of religious experience.

◻ BBC producer of the Freeman interview.
[1] Cf. following letter. A letter published in *The Listener* (London), 21 Jan. 1960, is a combination of the letters to Burnett and Leonard and for this reason has been omitted.

Thank you very much for the nice photos. It is good for one's self-education to see some undeniable evidence for the stupidity of facial expression.

Yours sincerely, C. G. JUNG

To M. Leonard

[ORIGINAL IN ENGLISH]

Dear Sir,   5 December 1959

Mr. Freeman in his characteristic manner fired the question you allude to at me in a somewhat surprising way,[1] so that I was perplexed and had to say the next thing which came into my mind. As soon as the answer had left the "edge of my teeth" I knew I had said something controversial, puzzling, or even ambiguous. I was therefore just waiting for letters like yours. Mind you, I didn't say "there is a God." I said: "I don't need to believe in God, *I know*." Which does not mean: I do know a certain God (Zeus, Yahweh, Allah, the Trinitarian God, etc.) but rather: I do know that I am obviously confronted with a factor unknown in itself, which I call "God" in *consensu omnium (quod semper, quod ubique, quod ab omnibus creditur)*.[2] I remember Him, I evoke Him, whenever I use His name, overcome by anger or by fear, whenever I involuntarily say: "Oh God." That happens when I meet somebody or something stronger than myself. It is an apt name given to all overpowering emotions in my own psychic system, subduing my conscious will and usurping control over myself. This is the name by which I designate all things which cross my wilful path violently and recklessly, all things which upset my subjective views, plans, and intentions and change the course of my life for better or worse. In accordance with tradition I call the power of fate in this positive as well as negative aspect, and inasmuch as its origin is beyond my control, "God," a "personal God," since my fate means very much myself, particularly when it approaches me in the form of conscience as a *vox Dei* with which I can even converse and argue. (We do and, at the same time, we know that we do. One is subject as well as object.)

Yet I should consider it an intellectual immorality to indulge in the

☐ King's College, Newcastle upon Tyne.
[1] Cf. Brooke, 16 Nov. 59, n. 1.
[2] "What is believed always, everywhere, and by everybody." Cf. Anon., 6 Jan. 43, n. 3.

belief that my view of a God is the universal, metaphysical Being of the confessions or "philosophies." I commit the impertinence neither of a *hypostasis* nor of an arrogant qualification such as: "God can only be good." Only my experience can be good or evil, but I know that the superior will is based upon a foundation which transcends human imagination. Since I *know* of my collision with a superior will in my own psychic system, *I know of God*, and if I should venture the illegitimate hypostasis of my image, I would say, of *a God beyond Good and Evil*, just as much dwelling in myself as everywhere else: *Deus est circulus cuius centrum est ubique, cuius circumferentia vero nusquam.*[3]

Hoping I have answered your question, I remain, dear Sir,

Yours sincerely, C. G. JUNG

[3] Cf. Frischknecht, 8 Feb. 46, n. 13.

To Mary Louise Ainsworth

[ORIGINAL IN ENGLISH]

Dear Miss Ainsworth,   23 December 1959

I have read your friendly letter with interest.[1] I have been particularly interested in what you say about the book of *Job*, i.e., the divine omniscience. While reading this little book you must be constantly aware of the fact that whatever I say in it does not refer to God himself, but rather to the idea or opinion man makes of God. When I use the term "the omniscience of God" it means: this is what man says about God and not that God *is* omniscient. Man always uses that knowledge he finds in himself to characterize his metaphysical figures. Thus you could make an analogy between the obliviousness of the human being and a similar state of his God. But this is not permissible in so far as man himself has made the dogmatic statement that God's omniscience is absolute and not subject to man's shortcomings. Thus God's omniscience means really a perfect presence of mind, and then only it becomes a blatant contradiction that He does not consult it or seems to be unaware of it. In this sense "God" is very paradoxical and I call my reader's attention to such and other contradictions

☐ Berkeley, California.

[1] A. wrote: "If we apply to God the same psychological processes as to ourselves, what would it mean for God to consult his omniscience? . . . The great wholeness of God . . . would presuppose the perfect balance of doing and knowing. . . . So, if God did not consult his omniscience, he was not whole."

to wake him up, so that he gets aware of the insufficiency of his representations and indirectly of the need to revise them.

This is the point which is regularly misunderstood: people assume that I am talking about God himself. In reality I am talking about human representations. So if anybody should talk to you about my *Job*, you had better refer him to this passage.

With my best wishes for Xmas and the New Year, I remain,

Yours sincerely, C. G. JUNG

To Hugo Charteris

[ORIGINAL IN ENGLISH]

My dear Charteris,   23 December 1959

Have I been too aggravating? I should be sorry indeed, since you were so charmingly unassuming and so properly impressed with the mallard[1] and you did not even fail to notice the stone[2] with the Greek inscription. The three photos are excellent. As a portrait[3] I should prefer the half-length with the pipe in my hand. It is one of the best pictures taken of me.

My best Xmas wishes!

Yours cordially, C. G. JUNG

☐ English author (1928–1970); had visited Jung at Bollingen in Aug. 1959 and had written an article about their talk for the *Daily Telegraph* (London). He sent the MS to Jung for comments, and Jung suggested many cuts and changes. The article appeared 21 Jan. 60.
[1] C. had found Jung sitting near the lake with a mallard at his feet.
[2] Cf. Oakes, 31 Jan. 56, and pl. VIII.
[3] The photograph was published with the article. See frontispiece of the present vol.

To Ewald Jung

Dear Cousin,   30 December 1959

Now at last I can pay off my long overdue debt of gratitude. Very many thanks for the two photos of the portrait of my great-grandfather;[1] they show a distinct family likeness, in my opinion anyway.

☐ See E. Jung, 31 July 35.
[1] Franz Ignaz Jung (1759–1831), German physician.

527

In strong contrast to my grandfather C. G. Jung,[2] he seems to have been an introvert, which would obviously account for the discord between father and son and probably also for the marital problem between Sophie *née* Ziegler[3] and Franz Ignaz. My grandfather's conversion under Schleiermacher's influence[4] seems to have had a hand in it. Best thanks also for the photo of Reimer-Jung.[5] Aunt Anna kept her beauty into old age. She had an aristocratic air, a most vivacious temperament and intelligence, and flashing blue eyes. She always embellished my Christmases with "Pfefferkuchen" (English: gingerbread). I visited her as late as 1900 in Stuttgart and also got to know Uncle Reimer, a psychiatrist.

I have been reading the book about G. A. Reimer[6] with great interest. Sophie Ziegler-Jung's mental illness has absorbed me again. The only documents relating to this are some letters of hers in my possession. The handwriting shows no schizophrenic traits, but rather, for all its character, an emotional ravagement such as can be observed in psychogenic melancholias. My grandfather's fervid relationship with her is a complete contra-indication of schizophrenia. It is indicative rather of a strong mother-son relationship, which in turn would be an occasion for dissension with her husband. The Ziegler sisters were lively artistic personalities who did a great deal for the Mannheim theatre at the time of the memorable première of Schiller's *Räuber*.[7] At that time, too, a transference to Goethe would not have been impossible; it might even have prejudiced her marriage with Franz Ignaz

[2] Cf. Corbin, 4 May 53, n. 3.

[3] Cf. *Memories*, p. 35/47, n. 1: "The wife of my great-grandfather . . . Sophie Ziegler, and her sister were associated with the Mannheim Theater and were friends of many writers. The story goes that Sophie Ziegler had an illegitimate child by Goethe, and that this child was my grandfather, Carl Gustav Jung. . . . Sophie Ziegler Jung was later friendly with Lotte Kestner, a niece of Goethe's 'Lottchen.' This Lotte frequently came to see my grandfather—as, incidentally, did Franz Liszt."

[4] Carl Gustav Jung left the Roman Catholic Church and became a Protestant. Cf. Corbin, 4 May 53, n. 2.

[5] Anna Reimer-Jung, daughter of Carl Gustav Jung's first wife Virginia, *née* de Lassaulx (1804–1840). She married the psychiatrist Hermann Reimer, son of the Berlin publisher and bookseller Georg Andreas Reimer.

[6] Hermann Reimer, *Georg Andreas Reimer. Erinnerungen aus seinem Leben* (1900).

[7] Schiller's tragedy, *Die Räuber*, was one of the most successful plays of the Sturm und Drang period and received an enthusiastic welcome at its première in 1782.

and given rise to all kinds of rumours,[8] unless there is a contamination with Marianne Willemer,[9] *née* Jung. Certainly a study of the portrait of Franz Ignaz makes his ancestorship seem likely. I am returning the Reimer-Jung photo but would like to keep the book about G. A. Reimer a while longer, as I want to have a copy made of some passages concerning my grandfather.

I am slowly recovering from too much work and the aggravations of the Föhn,[10] which has got me down more than ever this time.

Again with best thanks and all good wishes to you and your wife for the New Year,

Your devoted cousin, CARL

[8] See n. 3 supra.
[9] Marianne von Willemer (1774–1860), friend of Goethe's; she inspired many of his poems in *West-östlicher Divan* (1819), where she appears as Suleika.
[10] A strong warm and dry wind of the Northern Alps, frequently causing headaches and other psychic irritations.

To Eugen Böhler

Dear Dr. Böhler,   Bollingen, 1 January 1960

My first letter in this New Year, which opens a new decade, shall be to you, dear friend. It brings you my very cordial wishes not only for the coming year but also for this dawning decade 1960–70, in whose lap the black and white cards of our uncertain fate await us. The past decade dealt me heavy blows—the death of dear friends and the even more painful loss of my wife, the end of my scientific activity and the burdens of old age, but also all sorts of honours and above all your friendship, which I value the more highly because it appears that men cannot stand me in the long run. Since I do not deem myself god-almighty enough to have made them other than they are, I must put it down entirely to my own account and lengthen my shadow accordingly. Your understanding and your interest have done much to restore my self-confidence, severely shaken by my incessant struggle with difficult contemporaries. It is indeed no trifling thing to be granted the happy proof that somehow one is "possible" and has achieved something whose meaning someone else, apart from

☐ (Handwritten.)

myself, is able to see. Being well-known not to say "famous" means little when one realizes that those who mouth my name have fundamentally no idea of what it's all about. The gratification of knowing that one is essentially posthumous is short-lived. That is why your friendship is all the dearer to me in my grey old age, since it gives me living proof that I have not dropped out of the human setting into the shadowy realm of historical curiosities. Please accept this letter as a poor expression of my gratitude for the many kindnesses you have done me. Although the years hasten away more swiftly than ever, I still hope the New Year may bring a little more light and warmth.

Yours ever, C. G. JUNG

To Walther and Marianne Niehus-Jung

Dear Walther, dear Marianne, [Bollingen] 3 January 1960

On the occasion of the New Year and at the beginning of a new decade I can collect my thoughts together in the peace of Bollingen and bring to mind all the things you have done for me in the past year. I would therefore not like to miss this opportunity of expressing my heartiest thanks and letting you both know what a deep impression your helpful attitude has left behind. In the turmoil of Küsnacht I can seldom or never turn my thoughts upon myself, much less express them in writing. Scarcely is one thing finished than another has already taken its place. But here it is as it was in the years of my youth, when time was still so long that one could ask oneself, What can I do now? Now there is so much leisure that I can remember myself and let the past unroll before my eyes.

Besides the heavy burdens which the dark twists of fate have destined for us, friendly and joyful images emerge which instil into me a warm feeling of gratitude towards you. This is what I wanted you to know.

With best wishes for the New Year,

Your Father

☐ (Handwritten.) Küsnacht. — W. Niehus, architect, husband of Jung's daughter Marianne (d. 1965). Cf. Marianne Jung, 1 July 19, and Niehus, 5 Apr. 60.

To Emma von Pelet

Dear Frau von Pelet,   6 January 1960

Many thanks for your kind letter, which reminds me of how long it is since I have heard from you.

My congratulations on the success you have had with your interesting tasks!

As for myself, I am not planning any further publications and have nothing of the sort in hand. It seems rumours have reached you that I am writing my biography. I have always vowed I would never write an autobiography and in this case have only wetted my feet a little; its is rather Frau Jaffé who is writing a biography to which I have made a few contributions. So I have nothing more to do with it and am in the fortunate position of leaving the headaches to others and indulging in *otium cum dignitate*,[1] as befits my old age. If my luck holds, I won't be plagued by any new ideas either, but can withdraw with untroubled heart into the lands behung with dream-clouds.

Best wishes for the New Year, also to Frau von Keller,

Yours sincerely, c. g. jung

☐ See Pelet, 15 Jan. 44 (in vol. 1).
[1] = leisure and dignity (Cicero, *Pro sestio*, XLV, 98).

To Hugo Charteris

[ORIGINAL IN ENGLISH]

Dear Mr. Charteris,   Bollingen, 9 January 1960

You surely have hit the bull's eye by mentioning the "music-practising Socrates."[1] The story starts with his *daimonion* whispering into his ear: "Thou shouldst make more music, Socrates!" Whereupon dear old well-meaning Socrates went to buy a flute and began lamentable exercises. He obviously misunderstood the advice, but in a characteristic way, reminding me of his elder brother in spirit Confucius, who in his commentary emphatically declares: "Great is the I *Ching!*" It is always right, but once only it said something of which Confucius

☐ (Handwritten.)
[1] In Plato's *Phaedo*, dealing with the last hours of Socrates, Phaedo reports how Socrates told those present a recurrent dream urging him to compose and practise music.

531

could not make head or tail. It produced the hexagram "Gentleness or Charm."[2] This, Confucius thought, was wholly out of gear. He was obscured by his pedagogics and could not pay attention in spite of his knowing that "spiritual agencies move the stalks."[3] But Socrates was greater, he listened to his *daimonion* and bought a flute. Notwithstanding his *maieutikē*[4] ("art of the midwife"), he humbly obeyed the small voice from within, understanding it literally and technically as if he were a modern man. The *daimonion* meant "music," the art of feeling in contrast to his perpetual preoccupation with the "ratio" of the adolescent age, the worry of his homosexual Plato. Where was his anima? Obviously in Xantippe[5] and concealed in his *daimonion*, an apparent neuter. He also met her once in Diotima,[6] without drawing conclusions except the wrong ones. Hélas—he lived at a time when the wobbly *polis* still needed the homosexual glue. But at least he has shown us the one precious thing: "To hell with the Ego-world! Listen to the voice of your *daimonion*. It has a say now, not you."

With existentialism our words come to an end in complete meaninglessness and our art in total inexpressivity, and our world has acquired the means to blast us into cosmic dust. But who is listening to the *daimonion*? We talk but *it* says nothing, it does not even exist, and if it should exist it would be a merely pathological mistake. Socrates' "naïveté" is his greatness, still greater than ours. His humbleness is the ideal we have not reached yet. We still consider his *daimonion* as an individual peculiarity if not worse. Such people, says Buddha, "after their death reach the wrong way, the bad track, down

---

[2] That is, *I Ching*, Hexagram 22: "Grace." Cf. "Foreword to the *I Ching*," CW 11, par. 995. R. Wilhelm appended a footnote to this hexagram (*I Ching*, 1967, p. 91, n. 1): "This hexagram shows . . . the tranquillity of pure contemplation . . . removed from the struggle for existence. This is the world of art. . . . Hence this is still not the true way of redemption. For this reason Confucius felt very uncomfortable when once . . . he obtained the hexagram of Grace."

[3] Yarrow stalks are used for consulting the oracle of the *I Ching*.

[4] In Plato's *Theaetetus*, Socrates compared his cross-questioning method, by which he brought out the truth in his pupils, to the art of the midwife (his mother Phainarete had in fact been a midwife).

[5] The wife of Socrates who has, unjustly, become notorious for her bad temper and shrewishness.

[6] Diotima, a priestess, was the legendary teacher of Socrates. In the *Symposium*, Plato makes her the mouthpiece of his metaphysics of Eros.

532

to the depth, into an infernal world." Well, we are not very far from it.
Cordial greetings!

Yours sincerely, C. G. JUNG

P.S. If your way should lead you once again to Switzerland I should
be pleased to see you.

To J.A.F. Swoboda

Dear Dr. Swoboda,   23 January 1960

Very early on, at the time of my association experiments, I became
interested in tuberculosis as a possible psychic disease,[1] having observed that reactions due to complexes frequently cause a long-lasting
reduction in the volume of breathing.[2] This inhibition causes defec-
tive ventilation of the apices of the lungs and may eventually give
rise to an infection. The shallow breathing due to complexes is often
characterized by repeated deep expirations (sighs). I also observed that
a large number of my neurotic patients who were tubercular were
"freed" from their complexes under psychotherapeutic treatment,
learnt to breathe properly again and in the end were cured. As a result I jokingly called tuberculosis a "pneumatic disease,"[3] seeing that
psychic relief brings about a radical change of mental attitude. I am
therefore entirely of your opinion that a salutary dose of psychology
should be administered not only to tubercular patients but to many
others as well, and also to so-called normal people. Just *how* this
could be done is a problem with horns, since there is a shortage of
staff and doctors who would be capable of performing such an operation. By and large the universities are against it and they don't encourage young people to acquire any psychological knowledge since
the professors have none themselves. This is very understandable,
since such knowledge cannot be acquired if one assiduously avoids

☐ M.D., director of a London chest clinic.
[1] S. had written of his observations on tuberculosis patients which had led him
to accept the psychological factor in this disease.
[2] Cf. CW 2: "Psychophysical Investigations with the Galvanometer and Pneu-
mograph in Normal and Insane Individuals" (with F. Peterson) and "Further
Investigations on the Galvanic Phenomenon and Respiration in Normal and
Insane Individuals" (with C. Ricksher), originally published in 1907–8.
[3] The Greek *pneuma* means both wind and spirit.

knowing oneself. In medicine every conceivable method can be employed without one's being affected by it in any way. This is not possible in psychology, where everything depends on the dialectical process between two personalities. Holding lectures, giving instruction, pumping in knowledge, all these current university procedures are no use at all here. The only thing that really helps is self-knowledge and the change of mental and moral attitude it brings about. There are only a very few people who are minded to take such an apparently thankless task upon themselves for the good of their fellow men, and besides that they meet with the bigotry and mistrust of official organizations and institutions. What people would like best is the pursuit of science without man, completely oblivious of the fact that the individual psyche is the source of all science. Under these circumstances any organization that proposes collective methods[4] seems to me unsuitable, because it would be sawing off the branch on which the psychotherapist sits. In the last resort, the salutary effect can only come from one man's influence on another. However, much would be gained if intellectualism and rationalism were at least purged of their prejudices, so that a more favourable climate could be created for the psychological approach. I have done my utmost in this respect and now, at 85, am no longer the right man to shoulder such a Herculean task.

Yours sincerely, c. g. jung

[4] S. asked Jung to sponsor an international research organization on tuberculosis.

To Vaun Gillmor

[ORIGINAL IN ENGLISH]

Dear Miss Gillmor, 3 February 1960

The "Introitus apertus ad occlusum Regis palatium"[1] is certainly a work deserving the highest attention of any student interested in the deeper understanding of alchemy. Mr. Trinick[2] is a connoisseur of

☐ Vaun Gillmor (Mrs. Hector McNeile) was assistant editor of Bollingen Series and vice-president of the Bollingen Foundation, which sponsored the publication of the Collected Works.
[1] An alchemical treatise attributed to Eirenaeus Philalethes (cf. Trinick, 15 Oct. 57, n. 4). Tr. in Waite, *The Hermetic Museum*, II, ch. V: "An Open Entrance to the Closed Palace of the King."
[2] Trinick had sent his MS to the Bollingen Foundation in the hope of having it

Hermetic philosophy, and the results of his far-reaching investigation should be accessible to the scholars at least. As you know, I have re-opened the discussion about alchemical philosophy, i.e., I have at least shown a way which allows a new interpretation of its essential thoughts. The public which is capable of understanding this research is exceedingly small. Nobody except the very few have paid attention yet to the problems raised by my *Mysterium Coniunctionis*. The reason for this attitude is that there are very few capable of following up the problems of the collective unconscious on the one hand and the problems of Hermetic philosophy on the other. As far as my knowledge goes, some advanced physicists, like the late Professor Pauli and through him Professor Heisenberg, have become acquainted with the parallel developments in the psychic field. To understand this implication it needed the extraordinary mental capacity of a man like Pauli, and following him Heisenberg, to appreciate the importance of the problem of the complementarity of opposites, symmetry and asymmetry, raised by nuclear physics on the one hand and the psychology of the unconscious on the other. The physical side of the problem is a well-known matter, whereas the psychological and Hermetic side of this problem is accessible only to a very few, on account of the fact that the subject of unconscious phenomena is studied only by a very few and the study of alchemy is—if possible—still more unknown. On the side of physics it was Pauli alone who appreciated alchemical thought very highly.

Trinick's book is a contribution to a better knowledge of alchemy, helped along by psychological understanding. It would have been a book appreciated by Pauli as much as by myself. If it should be published, it would encounter the same stony incomprehension which my *Mysterium Coniunctionis* has received—at least for the time being. It is most unfortunate that Pauli died so early, as he was a physicist who had the ear of his time, more so than a psychologist like myself. There is a chance, however, that the future may develop a better understanding of the psychology of the unconscious and its far-reaching problems, and through it even its medieval pre-stages may become fertile ground for the further growth of the common problems raised by nuclear physics and the psychology of the unconscious.

This is the chance I can see for Trinick's very special investigation.

---

published in Bollingen Series, but without success. It was published in England in 1967 (cf. Trinick, 15 Oct. 57, n. 1).

Ours is surely the hard way, but everything that begins is small and meets with the unwillingness and the conservatism of established thought, which is no valid reason why the ever-changing further development of scientific understanding should come to a standstill. I think, therefore, if you consider the possibility of a later publication of Mr. Trinick's book, it would be a meritorious act.

Sincerely yours, C. G. JUNG

To the Mother Prioress of a Contemplative Order

[ORIGINAL IN ENGLISH]

Reverend Mother Prioress,   6 February 1960

It is very kind of you to give me news about Victor White, although it is much worse than I expected. I assume that a malignant tumour has been revealed through the operation. Let us hope that by the Grace of God and the aid of a human physician the ordeal of his passing away will be mitigated.

My dreams have warned me of this unexpected development. The last news I got from him was of a rather cheerful nature, so that I was not expecting a deterioration of his state. I am very grateful to you that you let me know the truth about him. You have cleared up several points of what I have recently observed and experienced. As there are so few men capable of understanding the deeper implications of our psychology, I had nursed the apparently vain hope that Father Victor would carry on the *opus magnum*.[1] But it is the curious fact that most of the intelligent men I became acquainted with and who began to develop an uncommon understanding have come to an unexpected, early end.[2] It looks as if only those who are relatively close to death are serious or mature enough to grasp some of the essentials in our psychology, as a man who wants to get over an obstacle grasps a handy ladder.

Well, it is a sad truth that we know very little about the most important aspects of life.

[1] The alchemists used this term to describe their work; Jung took it over to describe the process of individuation. In the context of this letter it may be an allusion to his past hopes that Father White would carry on his work.
[2] Richard Wilhelm, Heinrich Zimmer, Erich Neumann, and Wolfgang Pauli had all died at a relatively young age.

If Father Victor is still in a condition of enough consciousness, please give him my message that I know and think of him.

Yours devotedly, C. G. JUNG

To A. D. Cornell

Dear Mr. Cornell,   9 February 1960

Your interest in the origin of Psi-activity brings you face to face with a problem of the first order. The only thing we know positively in this respect is that experimentally verifiable Psi-phenomena are conditioned by a psychological factor, namely the stimulus of *novelty*, which is responsible for the good results obtained in the beginning of Rhine's laboratory experiments and their decrease upon repetition. It is important to remember that novelty represents an emotional situation (beginner's luck).

Outside the laboratory, too, synchronistic phenomena occur for the most part in emotional situations; for instance, in cases of death, sickness, accident, and so on. During the psychotherapeutic treatment of neuroses and psychoses we observe them relatively frequently at moments of heightened emotional tension, which need not however be conscious. Emotions have a typical "pattern" (fear, anger, sorrow, hatred, etc.); that is, they follow an inborn archetype which is universally human and arouses the same ideas and feelings in everyone. These "patterns" appear as archetypal motifs chiefly in dreams. The majority of synchronistic phenomena thus occur in *archetypal situations* such as are connected with risks, dangers, fateful developments, etc., and they manifest themselves in the form of telepathy, clairvoyance, precognition, and so forth.

In Rhine's case the experimental set-up is influenced by the expectation of a *miracle*. A miracle is an archetypal situation which is accompanied by a corresponding emotion.

☐ President, Cambridge U. Society for Research in Parapsychology. — The original English version of this letter was translated into German by H. Bender (cf. Bender, 12 Jan. 58) for publication in his *Zeitschrift für Parapsychologie* and appeared in V:1 (1961), with corrections and additions by Jung. The German version was subsequently translated into English by Hildegard Nagel and was published in *Spring*, 1961, which version is reproduced here with minor modifications.

The investigation of a great number of synchronistic phenomena has convinced me that at least one of their most frequent prerequisites is the presence of an active archetype. An archetypal dream may follow the critical event or even precede it (without being its cause in the latter case). In cases of telepathy it might be possible under some circumstances to give a causal explanation, but in the case of precognition this is out of the question. "Telepathy," "precognition," etc. are mere concepts (words) and explain nothing. The only explanatory factor we can establish with some certainty is the almost regular, or at least very frequent, simultaneous emergence of an archetype, or rather, of an emotion corresponding to it. One of the commonest symptoms of the presence of an archetype is its connection with religious ideas and convictions.

Two roads for further investigation exist: 1. experiment, and 2. the study of case material.

1. Under certain conditions it is possible to experiment with archetypes, as my "astrological experiment" has shown.[1] As a matter of fact we had begun such experiments at the C. G. Jung Institute in Zurich, using the historically known intuitive, i.e., synchronistic methods (astrology, geomancy, Tarot cards, and the I Ching). But we had too few co-workers and too little means, so we could not go on and had to stop.

2. This would require the observation of individual cases of death, severe illness, and serious accidents, together with a careful analysis of the concomitant psychological situations. Some work along these lines has already been done in Zurich but it is far from sufficient.

Research of this kind requires teamwork and money, and we have neither at present. Above all, superior intelligence and psychological competence are needed. Both are hard to find.

Paranormal psychic phenomena have interested me all my life. Usually, as I have said, they occur in acute psychological states (emotionality, depression, shock, etc.), or, more frequently, with individuals characterized by a peculiar or pathological personality structure, where the threshold to the collective unconscious is habitually lowered. People with a creative genius also belong to this type.

Experience has shown that the so-called Psi-faculty occurs as a spontaneous phenomenon and is not a regular function or quality of the psyche. One can count on its "regularity" only when the observations are based on very large numbers of cases, as in Rhine's experi-

[1] "Synchronicity," CW 8, ch. 2.

538

ments. In Psi-phenomena the psyche apperceives definite impressions through the usual channels of the senses: seeing, hearing, touch, and endopsychic perception (intuition). The "miracle" does not consist in the process of perception itself but rather in the event perceived. In other words, I perceive with my normal senses and the object of my perception is an objective event. Nevertheless it is an inexplicable event, for within the framework of our physical premises we could not have counted upon its happening. The problem has already been posed in this form by Geulincx, Leibniz, and Schopenhauer.

What I mean is that a telepathically perceived event—a vision, let us say—is not the product of a telepathic faculty but rather that the outer event *occurs simultaneously inside the psyche* and reaches consciousness by the usual pathways of inner perception. However, it is not always possible to determine whether a primary inner process is accompanied by an outer one or whether, conversely, a primary outer event is being reflected in a secondary inner process.

To give an example: Two English society ladies, sisters, were sitting by the fire one evening. Both were indignant and filled with hatred because of an inheritance which, contrary to their expectations, had not been left to them. It was a matter of an old family mansion with a title attached and a large landed estate. The inheritance had gone instead to a distant cousin, and both sisters were convinced that this was unjust. Suddenly one of them proposed that they should make an "image" of the heir. This they did together. They shaped it like a wax doll and then, in accordance with ancient custom, threw it into the fire. That same night the mansion was burned to the ground. If we disregard the hypothesis that this was "chance" (which explains nothing), we have here an example of synchronicity in which the *inner* image was probably primary, though it could easily be the other way round. But in either case there was no observable causality. Hence the "magical" hypothesis arises: Either the doll set fire to the mansion (but how?), or the fire kindled the fantasy of the sisters (but how?)

My emphasis—as in all such cases—lies on the *reality of the event*, not on its having been perceived. This point of view accords with the hypothesis of an *acausal connection*, i.e., a non-spatial and non-temporal conditioning of events.

Since causality is not an axiomatic but a statistical truth, there must be exceptions in which time and space appear to be relative, otherwise the truth would not be statistical. On this epistemological basis one *must* conclude that the possibility does exist of observing

539

non-spatial and non-temporal events—the very phenomena which we actually do observe contrary to all expectations and which we are now discussing.

In my view, therefore, it is not our perception which is necessarily para- or supranormal but the *event itself*. This, however, is not "miraculous" but merely "extra-ordinary" and unexpected, and then only from our biased standpoint which takes causality as axiomatic. From the statistical standpoint, of course, it is simply a matter of random phenomena, but from a truly realistic standpoint they are actual and significant facts. Exceptions are just as real as probabilities. The premise of probability simultaneously postulates the existence of the improbable.

Wherever and whenever the collective unconscious (the basis of our psyche) comes into play, the possibility arises that something will happen which contradicts our rationalistic prejudices. Our consciousness performs a selective function and is itself the product of selection, whereas the collective unconscious is simply Nature—and since Nature contains everything it also contains the unknown. It is beyond truth and error, independent of the interference of consciousness, and therefore often completely at odds with the intentions and attitudes of the ego.

So far as we can see, the collective unconscious is identical with Nature to the extent that Nature herself, including matter, is unknown to us. I have nothing against the assumption that the psyche is a quality of matter or matter the concrete aspect of the psyche, provided that "psyche" is defined as the collective unconscious. In my opinion the collective unconscious is the preconscious aspect of things on the "animal" or instinctive level of the psyche. Everything that is stated or manifested by the psyche is an expression of the nature of things, whereof man is a part.

Just as in physics we cannot observe nuclear processes directly, so there can be no direct observation of the contents of the collective unconscious. In both cases their actual nature can be inferred only from their effects—just as the trajectory of a nuclear particle in a Wilson chamber[2] can be traced only by observing the condensation trail that follows its movement and thus makes it visible.

In practice we observe the archetypal "traces" primarily in dreams,

---

[2] The "cloud chamber," developed by the English physicist C.T.R. Wilson, is an apparatus for observing the tracks made by electrically charged particles. For this discovery he received the Nobel Prize for Physics in 1927.

540

where they become perceptible as psychic forms. But this is not the only way they reach perception: they can appear objectively and concretely in the form of physical facts just as well. In this case the observation is not an endopsychic perception (fantasy, intuition, vision, hallucination, etc.) but a real outer object which behaves as if it were motivated or evoked by, or as if it were expressing, a thought corresponding to the archetype. Take for instance my case of the scarab: at the moment my patient was telling me her dream a real "scarab" tried to get into the room, as if it had understood that it must play its mythological role as a symbol of rebirth.[3] Even inanimate objects behave occasionally in the same way—meteorological phenomena, for instance.

Since I assume that our instincts (i.e., archetypes) are biological facts and not arbitrary opinions, I do not believe that synchronistic (or Psi-) phenomena are due to any supranormal (psychic) faculties but rather that they are *bound to occur* under certain conditions if space, time, and causality are not axiomatic but merely statistical truths. They occur spontaneously and not because we think we possess a special faculty for perceiving them. For this reason I do not think in terms of concepts like "telepathy," "precognition," or "psychokinesis."

In the same way, the archetype is not evoked by a conscious act of the will; experience shows that it is activated, independently of the will, in a psychic situation that needs compensating by an archetype. One might even speak of a spontaneous archetypal intervention. The language of religion calls these happenings "God's will"—quite correctly in so far as this refers to the peculiar behaviour of the archetype, its spontaneity and its functional relation to the actual situation.

The situation may be indicative of illness or danger to life, for instance. Consciousness feels such a situation to be overwhelming in so far as it knows no way of meeting it effectively. In this predicament, even people who can boast of no particular religious belief find themselves compelled by fear to utter a fervent prayer: the archetype of a "helpful divine being" is constellated by their submission and may eventually intervene with an unexpected influx of strength, or an unforeseen saving impulse, producing at the last moment a turn in the threatening situation which is felt to be miraculous. Such crises have occurred countless times in human history. They are the lot of

[3] "Synchronicity," par. 843, and Appendix, par. 982.

man, who is exposed to the vicissitudes of Nature and constantly gets into situations where he must call on instinct because his reason fails. Instinct appears in myths and in dreams as the motif of the helpful animal, the guardian spirit, the good angel, the helper in need, the saint, saviour, etc. "God is nearest where the need is greatest." An "instinct" warns birds and quadrupeds of impending catastrophes, and even humans are sometimes gifted with second sight. Emergencies of other kinds, as we know from experience, evoke the archetypes that correspond to them.

Hence the archetype has a compensatory effect, as do most of our more important dreams. Because of its ubiquity, the archetype can by its very nature manifest itself not only in the individual directly concerned but in another person or even in several people at once—for instance in parallel dreams, the "transmission" of which should be regarded more as a Psi-phenomenon than anything else. Similarly, collective psychoses are based on a constellated archetype, though of course this fact is not taken into account at all. In this respect our attitude is still characterized by a prodigious unconsciousness.

I must add, however, that I have observed and also partially analysed people who seemed to possess a supranormal faculty and were able to make use of it at will. But the apparently supranormal faculty consisted in their already being in, or voluntarily putting themselves into, a state corresponding to an archetypal constellation—a state of numinous possession in which synchronistic phenomena become possible and even, to some extent, probable. This faculty was clearly coupled with a religious attitude which enabled them to give suitable expression to their sense of the ego's subordination to the archetype. In one such case I predicted a catastrophic end if the patient abandoned this attitude. He did and he actually lost his life.[4] The religious tendency is obvious enough in nearly all serious-minded mediums. As a rule they cannot exploit their "art" for egoistic purposes; and this proves that their faculty is not subject to the will of the ego but owes its existence rather to the overriding dominance of the unconscious.

I therefore think it would be advisable to consider Psi-phenomena in the first place as *sua sponte* facts and not as supranormal perceptions. The uncertainty of their relation to time and space does not necessarily depend on a supranormality of our perceptions but rather

[4] The case of the mountaineer dreaming of stepping off into empty space, described in "Child Development and Education," CW 17, pars. 117ff., and in "The Practical Use of Dream Analysis," CW 16, pars. 323f.

on the relativity and only partial validity of time and space categories. Most of the cases of Psi-perception are due to the presence of a constellated archetype, which produces an *abaissement du niveau mental* (numinosity, emotion). Under such a condition unconscious contents become manifest, i.e., can be perceived by the normal sense organs. Thus, for example, psychokinesis or extrusions of ectoplasm are objective facts and not intuitions or hallucinations. The medium producing these effects is in a markedly passive state (trance), which shows that an *abaissement*—the elimination of consciously controlled psychic activity—is needed in order to give spontaneous phenomena a chance. Hence the universal belief that "spiritual agencies" are at work—agents that do not coincide with the conscious psyche. The phenomena may be purely psychic or of a material nature too. This latter fact is an indication that "psyche" and "matter" are not basically incommensurable, but may perhaps be qualities of one and the same existential being.

Hoping I have made myself understandable, I remain,

Yours sincerely, c. g. j u n g

To Karl Schmid

Dear Professor Schmid, 9 February 1960

Best thanks for your kind letter.

It is indeed a great honour that you wish to dedicate your essays on Goethe and Schiller to me.[1] Thank you very much. I am looking forward to seeing what you mean by "completion."

You are too modest! In reality you create images and viewpoints which have only been helped along by some of my ideas. This gives me great satisfaction, because what alone has always mattered to me was to find out whether my way of looking at things is in accord with life or not. If it is, then it will live on and express something alive. If there's one thing that terrified me, it was dead conceptualism.

Again with best thanks,

Yours sincerely, c. g. j u n g

[1] *Geheimnis der Ergänzung* (1960).

To Eugen Böhler

Dear friend, 25 February 1960

It is time I gave you some news of my existence. I am now well enough to write letters again. On Jan. 23rd I had a slight embolism followed by not too severe heart cramps. I was under house arrest for a month, forbidden all mental activity, i.e., active concentration. However, it didn't stop me from my long planned (renewed) reading of Buddhist texts, whose content I am leaving to simmer inside me. Thanks to my isolation I have been slipping away from the world and holding converse not with the men of today but with voices long past. On my return to the 20th century I discovered that I have heard nothing from you. Therefore I wanted to notify myself that it was I who was fetched out of the present and transported into the neighbourhood of the Bardo,[1] which always happens when I hear such a distinct *memento mori*.

I am sufficiently restored to health to go, with luck, to Lugano this Saturday in the hope of heedless and deedless days in the blessed sun.

Hoping to see you again when I get back,

Yours ever, C. G JUNG

☐ (Handwritten.)
[1] Cf. Bertine, 9 Jan. 39, n. 1.

To Father Victor White

[ORIGINAL IN ENGLISH]

My dear Victor, 25 March 1960

Since you are very much in the situation of the suffering Job[1] I shall not play the role of his friends, not even that of the wise Elihu.[2] I humbly submit the suggestion that you might apply your personalistic point of view to your own person and to your own case instead of to the unknown person of the individual Job. You can see then what it does to yourself as well as to myself—if I may introduce myself as an individual.

Job is very much the respectable Hebrew of his time. He observes

☐ (Handwritten.)
[1] On 18 March W. wrote telling Jung of a "serious operation to the intestines for a malignant growth." Cf. Mother Prioress, 6 Feb. 60.
[2] Job 32–37.

544

the law and—by force of the covenant—his God ought to do the same. Now let us assume that Job is neurotic, as one can easily make out from the textual allusions: he suffers from a regrettable lack of insight into his own dissociation. He undergoes an analysis of a sort, f.i. by following Elihu's wise counsel; what he will hear and what he will be aware of are the discarded contents of his personal subconscious mind, of his shadow, but not the divine voice, as Elihu intends. You faintly insinuate that I am committing Elihu's error too, in appealing to archetypes first and omitting the shadow.[3] *One cannot avoid the shadow* unless one remains neurotic, and as long as one is neurotic one has omitted the shadow. The shadow is the block which separates us most effectively from the divine voice. Therefore Elihu in spite of his fundamental truth belongs to those foolish Jungians, who, as you suggest, avoid the shadow and make for the archetypes, i.e., the "divine equivalents," which by the way are nothing but escape camouflage according to the personalistic theory.

If Job succeeds in swallowing his shadow he will be deeply ashamed of the things which happened. He will see that he has only to accuse himself, for it is his complacency, his righteousness, his literal-mindedness, etc. which have brought all the evil down upon him. He has not seen his own shortcomings but has accused God. He will certainly fall into an abyss of despair and inferiority-feeling, followed, if he survives, by profound repentance. He will even doubt his mental sanity: that he, by his vanity, has caused such an emotional turmoil, even a delusion of divine interference—obviously a case of megalomania.

After such an analysis he will be less inclined than ever before [to think] that he has heard the voice of God. Or has Freud with all his experience ever reached such a conclusion? If Job is to be considered as a neurotic and interpreted from the personalistic point of view, then he will end where psychoanalysis ends, viz. in disillusionment and resignation, where its creator most emphatically ended too.

Since I thought this outcome a bit unsatisfactory and also empirically not quite justifiable, I have suggested the hypothesis of archetypes as an answer to the problem raised by the shadow. This

[3] In his review of *Psychology and Religion* (CW 11) for the *Journal of Analytical Psychology*, IV:1 (Jan. 1959), W. asked: "Can we legitimately transfer our personal splits and ills to our Gods and archetypes, and put the blame on them? . . . Or are the critics right who consider that Jungians have become so possessed by archetypes that they are in danger of abandoning elementary psychology altogether?"

545

apparently inordinate idea, also favoured but produced at the wrong moment by the wise Elihu, is a *petra scandali* of the worst kind. In my naïveté I had imagined it to be something better than sheer despair and resignation, also something more true than mere rationalism and thoughtlessness. Your aggressive critique has got me in the rear. That's all.

Don't worry! I think of you in everlasting friendship. *Ultra posse nemo obligatur.*[4] Thus I ask for your forgiveness, as is incumbent on one who has given cause for scandal and vexation. It is difficult not to be crushed by the inexorable truth: *Le Vray en forme brute est plus faux que le faux,*[5] or the mountain you have heaped up is your burial mound.

My best wishes in every respect!

Yours ever, C. G.

Postscriptum. I had a light embolism in the heart, the consequences of which kept me in the house for 4 weeks. I see from your letter that you have published a new book *Soul and Psyche,*[6] but neither my secretary nor I myself have seen a copy. I would be very interested indeed to learn your views about the intricacies of psychological terminology in this field disputed by empiricism on the one hand and metaphysics on the other.

If you had seen Mr. X's wife (as I have) you would know *everything* about him. When Johannes Hus[7] bound to the stake saw a little old woman adding her last bundle of sticks to the pile, he said: *O sancta simplicitas!*

[4] = Nobody is obliged to do more than he can.
[5] "Truth in brute form is falser than falsity."
[6] London, 1960.
[7] Bohemian religious reformer, b. 1369. He was influenced by the writings of the English reformer John Wycliffe (*ca.* 1320–84) and criticized clerical abuses. He was excommunicated 1410 and burnt at the stake in Constance 1415.

To the Mother Prioress of a Contemplative Order

[ORIGINAL IN ENGLISH]

Reverend Mother,   26 March 1960

Many thanks for your kind report about Father Victor! I am still shaken by this stroke of fate which has felled him. According to the

□ (Handwritten.)

experience and knowledge of medical science the verdict seems to be absolute, yet, in order to do justice to your faith, I must say that I know (and have seen myself) of certain similar cases where an apparently miraculous recovery took place. There is a 1:x probability of an unaccountable cure.

I would share your standpoint of undaunted faith if I were not disturbed by the thought that this earthly life is not supreme, but subject to the decrees of a superior economy. I try to accept life *and* death. Where I find myself unwilling to accept the one or the other I should question myself as to my personal motives. . . . Is it the divine will? Or is it the wish of the human heart which shrinks from the Void of death?

. . .

We should not only have a more or less complete understanding of ourselves but also of the way in which we are related to our fellow-beings and of their nature. Our moral freedom reaches as far as our consciousness, and thus our liberation from compulsion and captivity. In ultimate situations of life and death complete understanding and insight are of paramount importance, as it is indispensable for our decision to go or to stay and let go or to let stay.

Since I had your letter, I have heard that the truth has been told to Victor White (which I hoped for fervently) and, as far as I know, the effect has been all to the good.

There is such a thing as *tempus maturum mortis* and it is up to our understanding to fulfill its conditions.

Sincerely yours, C. G. JUNG

To Margaret Sittler

Dear Frau Sittler,   29 March 1960

I was naturally overjoyed to have such interesting news from you.[1] As with every author, one does not live from air and bread alone but now and then needs a bit of moral encouragement.

Unfortunately I am not very well up in English *belles lettres*, because I got the hang of English at a time when science had already taken possession of me. In my youth French literature was much closer, and English far away and strange. People from England came

☐ New York City.
[1] *Answer to Job* had made a deep impression on her.

to us from across the sea and so were quite different from the French! They consisted of nothing but Lords or eccentrics.

Faust and Nietzsche occupied me very much more than anything I knew of English literature. I have never read Shelley's "Prometheus Unbound"² in the original, but shall hasten to make good this omission at your behest.

Although I do not doubt that *Job* has become a burning question for other people too, it seems that in our own blessed day their numbers are pretty limited, judging by what I know of the reactions to my little book. What I have heard from the theological side has readied me for a special compartment in hell. Other people seem to have little interest in it. You, dear lady, are an exception, and your letter is truly a red letter day for me.

Yours sincerely, c. g. j u n g

² She was writing a thesis on this work (1819), generally regarded as Shelley's masterpiece. She drew Jung's attention to the profound symbolic and mythological content of the poem.

Anonymous

[O R I G I N A L   I N   E N G L I S H]

Dear Mrs. N.,   30 March 1960

Thank you very much for your kind attention!¹ The book will interest me very much, also what you told me about the Buddhist Society came quite *à propos*, since I have been studying Buddha's sermons in the Middle Collection of the Pali-Canon for several months.²

I am trying to get nearer to the remarkable psychology of the Buddha himself, or at least of that which his contemporaries assumed him to be.

It is chiefly the question of karma and rebirth which has renewed my interest in Buddha.

With my very best thanks I remain,

Yours cordially, c. g. j u n g

□ England.

¹ N.'s letter has not been preserved.

² The Middle Collection, *Majjhimanikaya*, comprises 152 pieces of the Buddha's conversations with his disciples. Tr. by T. W. Rhys Davids in *Sacred Books of the Buddhists*, II–IV. For Jung's interest in the Buddha's teachings cf. "Zu Die Reden Gotamo Buddhos," Ges. Werke, XI, pp. 690–93 (not in CW 11, but published in CW 18, pars. 1575ff.).

548

To Miguel Serrano

[ORIGINAL IN ENGLISH]

Dear Mr. Serrano,   31 March 1960

Thank you for your interesting letter.[1] I quite agree with you that those people in our world who have insight and good will enough should concern themselves with their own "souls" more than with preaching to the masses or trying to find out the best way for them. They only do that because they don't know themselves. But alas, it is a sad truth that usually those who know nothing for themselves take to teaching others, in spite of the fact that they know the best method of education is the good example.

Surely modern art is trying its best to make man acquainted with a world full of darkness, but alas, the artists themselves are unconscious of what they are doing.[2]

The very thought that mankind ought to make a step forward and extend and refine consciousness of the human being seems to be so difficult that nobody can understand it, or so abhorrent that nobody can pluck up his courage. All steps forward in the improvement of the human psyche have been paid for by blood.

I am filled with sorrow and fear when I think of the means of self-destruction which are heaped up by the important powers of the world. Meanwhile everybody teaches everybody, and nobody seems to realize the necessity that the way to improvement begins right in himself. It is almost too simple a truth. Everybody is on the lookout for organizations and techniques where one can follow the other and where things can be done safely in company.

I would like to ask Mr. Toynbee:[3] Where is your civilization and what is your religion? What he says to the masses will remain—I am afraid—sterile, unless it has become true and real in himself. Mere

□ Then Chilean ambassador in New Delhi, later ambassador in Belgrade; student of mythology and yoga, Antarctic explorer. — The letter is published in S.'s *C. G. Jung and Hermann Hesse: A Record of Two Friendships* (1966), pp. 74f. Cf. also his *The Visits of the Queen of Sheba* (Bombay, 1960), with part of a letter by Jung, 14 Jan. 60, as foreword (published in CW 18, pars. 1769ff.).

[1] S. had written Jung 24 Feb. 60: "it would probably be better for the Westerners to recede into the background now and leave others to do the world's business, since the most urgent task for the Christian world today is to try to preserve Individuality . . ." (*Jung and Hesse*, p. 73).

[2] Cf. Jung, "Picasso," CW 15.

[3] The British historian Arnold Toynbee, whose visit S. had mentioned, had been lecturing in India on "A World Civilization," "A World Religion," and related subjects.

words have lost their spell to an extraordinary extent. They have been twisted and misused for too long a time.

I am looking forward to your new book[4] with great interest!

Hoping you are always in good health, I remain

Yours sincerely, C. G. JUNG

[4] *The Visits of the Queen of Sheba.*

To Walther Niehus-Jung

Dear Walther,   5 April 1960

I want to thank you for your efforts on behalf of my so-called "Autobiography" and to reaffirm that I do not regard this book as my undertaking but expressly as a book which Frau A. Jaffé has written. The chapters in it that are written by me[1] I regard as a contribution to Frau Jaffé's work. The book should appear under her name and not under mine, since it does not represent an autobiography that I myself have composed.[2]

With cordial regards,

Your father-in-law, C. G. JUNG

[1] Cf. Aniela Jaffé's introduction to *Memories, Dreams, Reflections*, pp. vi–vii/ 10–11.

[2] In view of the genesis of the book, A. Jaffé chose, with Jung's approval, the present, neutral title for the Swiss edition: *Erinnerungen, Träume, Gedanken von C. G. Jung*, aufgezeichnet und herausgegeben von Aniela Jaffé (= recorded and edited by A. J.). The title of the London edn., *C. G. Jung: Memories, Dreams, Reflections* misses Jung's intention, which is expressed more suitably as *Memories, Dreams, Reflections by C. G. Jung* in the New York edn.

To Erich A. von Fange

[ORIGINAL IN ENGLISH]

Dear Mr. von Fange,   8 April 1960

I have read your letter with great interest and I congratulate you on your attempt at further investigation in the field of typology.[1]

It is a line of thought which I have not pursued any further, since

[1] F., dean of students at Concordia College, Edmonton, Alberta (Canada), was writing a thesis on the statistical evaluation of types and asked for Jung's comments.

my original tendency was not the classification of normal or pathological individuals but rather the discovery of conceptual means
deriving from experience, namely the ways and means by which I
could express in a comprehensible way the peculiarities of an individual psyche and the functional interplay of its elements. As I have
been chiefly interested in psychotherapy I was always mostly concerned with individuals needing explanation of themselves and
knowledge of their fellow-beings. My entirely empirical concepts
were meant to form a sort of language by which such explanations
could be communicated. In my book about types I have given a
number of examples illustrating my *modus operandi*. Classification
did not interest me very much. It is a side-issue with only indirect
importance to the therapist.

My book, as a matter of fact, was written to demonstrate the
structural and functional aspect of certain typical elements of the
psyche. That such a means of communication and explanation
could be used also as a means of classification was an aspect which I
was rather afraid of, since the intellectually detached classifying point
of view is just the thing to be avoided by the therapist. But the classifying application was—I almost regret to say—the first and almost
exclusive way in which my book was understood, and everybody
wondered why I had not put the description of the types right at
the beginning of the book instead of relegating it to a later chapter.
Obviously the tendency of my book has been misunderstood, which
is easily understandable if one takes into account that the number
of those people who would be interested in its practical psychotherapeutic application is infinitely small in comparison with the number
of academic students.

I admit that your statistical line of research is perfectly legitimate
but it certainly does not coincide with the purpose of my book,
which in my humble opinion aims at something far more vital than
classification. Though I have expressed my therapeutic views most
emphatically only very few of my readers noticed them. The possibility of classification seems to be far more attractive.

By this rather longwinded peroration I am trying to explain to
you why I am more or less unable to give you any helpful suggestions
in your specific enterprise, since my thoughts do not move on this
line at all. I am even sceptical in this respect.

I hold the conviction that for the purpose of any classification one
should start with fundamental and indubitable principles and not

with empirical notions, i.e., with almost colloquial terms based upon mere rules of thumb. My concepts are merely meant to serve as a means of communication through colloquial language. As principles however I should say that they are in themselves immensely complicated structures which can hardly fulfil the role of scientific principles. Much more important are the contents conveyed by language than their terms.

Sincerely yours, c. g. jung

To the Mother Prioress of a Contemplative Order

[ORIGINAL IN ENGLISH]

Reverend Mother, 29 April 1960

I am very sorry indeed that the news about Victor White is so bad and the end apparently so near. If you have any chance to let him know about myself I should be much obliged if you would tell him that I am at peace with him and that he should not worry any more. I am quite convinced of his sincere and human loyalty. I am sorry if I should have upset him by my attempt to explain to him the reason for a certain critique I had to make. In my letter to him which contains the explanation, I also told him that it did not matter and he should not worry about it. I don't know what more I could tell him to reassure him of my feeling. If I were young and could trust my physique I would certainly come over to England and reassure him of my personal feeling. Unfortunately, however, extravagances are out of the question. So I would be most obliged if you would kindly let him know of my letter to you.

He has sent his new book to me which I am going to read just now (having had to finish another book[1] first). I am very interested in it and it was my intention to write to him only after having gone through his book as carefully as possible. I am afraid the reading will take some time. Under these circumstances I would perhaps do better if I wrote to him soon.

Sincerely yours, c. g. jung

[1] See following letter, n. 1.

To Josef Rudin

Dear Dr. Rudin,   30 April 1960

I have just finished reading your book.[1] I read it from beginning to end with great interest, for it has long been my dearest wish to build a bridge—or at least try to—between the two disciplines which accept practical responsibility for the *cura animarum*: theology on the one hand and medical psychology on the other. However different their *point de départ* may be, they both converge in the empirical psyche of the human individual. On the Protestant side I have succeeded in bridging the gap with Professor Hans Schär, of Bern; on the Catholic side I have met with extraordinary understanding from you, for which I am heartily grateful. By skilfully negotiating the epistemological reef you have given empirical psychology its due place in Catholic thinking, in commendable contrast to those Anglo-Saxon and French theologians who are unconscious of the epistemological problem and consequently deny empirical psychology the right to exist. Your work has performed the inestimable service of making it possible for us to go a further stretch of the way together—I hope to our mutual advantage. We are both convinced that our imperilled epoch is in need of psychological enlightenment, and that *someone* has to make a beginning, although he cannot do it unaided. Your positive attitude is therefore an important step forward and a great encouragement not only for me but, above all, for the good cause we both serve.

The difference between our *points de départ*, our clients and their spiritual needs, presupposes an "external" difference of aim. Your theological orientation revolves round its ecclesiastical axis, whereas I see myself compelled to follow the guidelines of the way of individuation and its symbolism wherever they may lead. Where you speak specifically of Christ, I as a mere empiricist must avail myself of the more cautious term Anthropos, since the Anthropos is an archetype with a history more than 5,000 years old. This term is less specific and therefore more suitable for general use. I have in the main to do with people who have either lost their Christianity or never had any, or with adherents of other religions who nevertheless belong to the human family. It is impossible for me to subscribe to the view of a theo-

□ Zurich. — In a different tr., published in the English version of Rudin's book, *Psychotherapy and Religion* (1968).
[1] *Psychotherapie und Religion* (1960).

logical friend who said: "Buddhists are no concern of ours." In the doctor's consulting-room they are very much our concern and deserve to be addressed in a language common to all men.

I understand perfectly, therefore, that the individuation process and its symbolism have to come up for discussion much less often with you than with me.

One more question! Is it in a tone of mild reproach that you say (with reference to *Answer to Job*) I take no account of "Bible theology"? Had I done so I would have written from the theological standpoint, and you would have every right to accuse me of blasphemy. A similar accusation has been made from the Protestant side, that I disregard the higher textual criticism. But why haven't these gentlemen edited Job in such a way that it reads as it should, according to their view? I am a layman, and I have only the (translated) Job before me that has been served up to the lay public *cum consensu autoritatis*. It is about this Job that the layman thinks and not about the speculations of textual criticism, which he never gets a sight of anyway and which contribute nothing relevant to the spirit of this book.

This only by the way! I am genuinely glad that we find ourselves so far in accord and I wish your book every possible success.

My best thanks!

Yours very sincerely, C. G. JUNG

To Father Victor White

[ORIGINAL IN ENGLISH]

My dear Victor,   30 April 1960

I have heard of your illness[1] and I should have liked to come to England to see you, but I have to be careful with my own health and I must avoid all exertions. As I am completing my 85th year, I am really old and my forces are definitely limited. In February I had a bit of a heart embolism and my doctor is strict.

I have to thank you for the kind gift of your book *Soul and Psyche*. It is certainly a theme worthy of a lengthy discussion in the "Auseinandersetzung" between theology and psychology. I just began to read it. I had to finish first the book *Psychotherapie und Religion* by Dr. Josef Rudin, S.J. The bit I have read in your book is most interesting and promising and I certainly shall go on studying it carefully.

☐ (Handwritten.)
[1] Cf. White, 25 Mar. 60, n. 1.

In the meantime I hope you don't worry about my letter.[2] I want to assure you of my loyal friendship. I shall not forget all the useful things I have learned through our many talks and through your forbearance with me. I was often sorry to be a *petra scandali*. It is my fate however, not my choice, and I had to fulfill this unbecoming role. Things had to be moved in the great crisis of our time. New wine needs new skins. We need no further outbursts on a grand scale or so it seems to me. The "iron curtain" is quite sufficient to me to demonstrate the enormous split in the "soul" (or $\psi\nu\chi\acute{\eta}$)[3] of modern man, but we are mostly asleep. It needs some noise to wake the sleepers.[4]

Many greetings and cordial wishes!

Yours ever, C. G.

[2] Ibid.
[3] A pun on the title of W.'s *Soul and Psyche*.
[4] W. dictated an answer on 8 May, thanking Jung for his "wonderful and comforting letter." He enclosed a letter written on 6 May in answer to Jung's of 25 March, in which he tried once more to clear up "some strange misunderstanding—or non-understanding—which has arisen between us," adding: "And such are our several conditions that it seems unlikely that we shall be able to meet and talk again in this world." The letter of 8 May ends: "May I add that I pray with all my heart for your well-being, whatever that may be in the eyes of God. Ever yours cordially and affectionately, Victor White." He died on 22 May. The Mother Prioress wrote on the same day to Jung: "My dear Dr. Jung, Father Victor's beloved soul has returned to God. He died this morning between 11–12 a.m. from a sudden thrombosis. He was fully awake, and praying before he became unconscious, and they say he had no great pain . . ."

To Mrs. C.

[ORIGINAL IN ENGLISH]

Dear Mrs. C.,   3 May 1960

I have read your letter with great interest. It is true that a certain kind of resistance has an almost murderous effect, as if it were a physical assault. It is even as if the vehemence of the attack were not wholly in the consciousness of the aggressor, but rather in the air round him. Thus it is not properly directed, and therefore anybody getting into this atmosphere will undergo its violent effect. If he happens to be weakened he will get injured, while the stronger one will be able to deflect the blow, which he can do more successfully if

☐ England.

555

somebody is present who offers a sort of safety-valve by which the intensity of the evil force can escape. Such an event points to your strength, which seems to me enough to cope with unusual situations. If wisely used, it will be a strong defence, but don't assume that it is your personal property, being rather a grace than anything else.

My best wishes,

Yours sincerely, C. G. JUNG

Anonymous

[ORIGINAL IN ENGLISH]

Dear Sir,   7 May 1960

As your friendly letter has brought not only much amusement but also illumination to me, it deserves special consideration.[1] It is a model for the intelligent reader of today. It follows the excellent rule: Never read prefaces or introductions or footnotes as they are useless embellishments. Best begin reading in the end or at the most in the middle of the book. Then you see all there is about the twaddle. What an ass I have been not to see how simple things are: *God is Love,* that is the thing, and the whole of theology can go into the dust-bin. Mineralogy is just stones, zoology simply animals, technology only how things are made to work, and mythology old fables of no consequence at all. I did not know that things are as simple to a joyous Christian. That is indeed an evangel, a Glad Tidings. To hell with all -logies. Why should anybody fuss with the history of symbols when everything is quite clear and can be summed up in the short formula "God is Love"? You seem to know it. I know much less about God, since whatever I might say about the supreme Unknown is arrogant anthropomorphism to me.

If you had cast a look into my preface and introduction you might have discovered that my little book is not interested in the least in what you or I believe about God, but solely and modestly in what the history of symbols has to say about it. Not having noticed this little difference you misunderstand the whole of my argument, as if I had

☐ Chicago, Illinois.

[1] N. wrote a long letter setting forth his reaction to *Answer to Job.* In his concluding paragraph he said: "The whole situation would be aired and simplified if we could stop imputing human characteristics to God, and accept the idea that God is Love."

discussed the nature of God. In reality I am dealing with anthropo-morphic representations of the deity and thus walking through the dough at the bottom of the sea, as you aptly put it. This dough how-ever is the human mind, as it has been for several thousand years. Being a physician I am concerned with the woes of the world and their causes, and I at least try to do something about them. But you are a joyous Christian way above the doughy bottom and you exult in your marvellous confession that God is Love, to which nobody listens. You are so little concerned with the "dough" that you do not even notice what I am preoccupied with. I have to help man, who sticks in the dough. In order to help his suffering I must understand his "dough." To me there is no high-handed dismissal of man's folly. It is your prerogative not to be interested in man but in your Love, which is God according to your statement.

Now, what about it? Since Love is your highest value, how do you apply it? It does not even reach as far as a compassionate interest in this insufferable dough, in which man is caught and suffering accord-ingly. The joyous Christian tells us how things ought to be, but he is careful not to touch things as they are. They are merely deplorable. This admirable superiority is almost enviable: one can leave things to themselves and let man wriggle in his comfortable mud.

Yes, what about your Love? On p. 2 of your letter you say: "What right had Job to go crying to God about his loss of mere things?" In case you should be married, please ask your wife how she feels about being considered as a "mere thing," a piece of furniture, f.i., some-body has smashed. She will certainly esteem such lovely appreciation. Your involuntary use of language throws a telltale light on the way in which your "Love" functions. Isn't it charming?

You deny the right of crying out to God. Does pain ever ask whether it has a right to cry out in its need and despair or not? Has the joyous Christian no right to cry out to his loving father or to the "God of Love" or "Love-God" for a certain amount of consideration or patience or at least of mere justice?

The "no right" for Job shows up your superior legalistic standpoint, but no human feeling.

I am weak and stupid enough to consider a certain amount of com-passion, humility, love, and feeling as indispensable for the under-standing of the human soul and its woeful dough, i.e., the slime and mud at its bottom, which seems to disappear when you look away from the old fables to the pleasant vistas of a simplified "reality."

557

I am much obliged to you for your benevolent honesty, which has allowed me to understand more and better why my *Answer to Job* is so thoroughly misunderstood. Please consider my letter as a further attempt to clarify the position of Job.

Sincerely yours, C. G. JUNG

To E. A. Bennet

[ORIGINAL IN ENGLISH]

My dear Bennet,   22 May 1960

Thank you very much for your kind review of my *Aion*.[1] There is only one remark I do not quite understand.

Speaking of the hypothesis of archetypes, you say that there is no scientific proof of them yet.[2] A scientific hypothesis is never proved absolutely in so far as an improvement is always possible. The only proof is its *applicability*. You yourself attest that the idea of the archetype explains more than any other theory, which proves its applicability. I wonder therefore which better proof you are envisaging. When you assume the existence of an instinct of migration you can't do better than to apply it f.i. to birds and demonstrate that there are actually birds which migrate. The archetype points out that there are thought-formations of a parallel or identical nature distributed all over the world (f.i., holy communion in Europe and Teoqualo[3] in ancient Mexico), and furthermore that they can be found in individuals who have never heard of such parallels. I have given ample evidence of such parallels and therewith have given evidence of the applicability of my viewpoint. Somebody has to prove now that my idea is *not* applicable and to show which other viewpoint is more applicable. I wonder now, how you would proceed in providing evidence for the existence of archetypes other than their applicability?

---

[1] "Archetype and Aion," *British Medical Journal*, 14 May 1960.

[2] "Jung's hypothesis of the collective (impersonal, objective) unconscious and its mode of functioning, the archetypes, is a bold theory. . . . The hypothesis, though lacking scientific foundation, none the less provides a more satisfactory explanation for certain psychological facts than any other at present available." Jung's letter is the first in a long correspondence on this point, all of it published in Bennet, *C. G. Jung*, pp. 95–103.

[3] Teoqualo, or "god-eating," was an Aztec rite in which the figure of Huitzilopochtli, the god of war and storms, was moulded out of poppy seeds and eaten. For the parallel with the Christian Communion cf. "Transformation Symbolism in the Mass," CW 11, pars. 339ff.

What is better proof of a hypothesis than its applicability? Or can you show that the idea of "archetype" is a nonsense in itself? Please enlighten my darkness.

Yours cordially, C. G. JUNG

To Elisabeth Herbrich

Dear Dr. Herbrich,   30 May 1960

Your letter brings me the unexpected and painful news of the death of Prof. Betschart,[1] to whom I am bound by many fond memories. I first became acquainted with him at the Paracelsus celebrations in Einsiedeln, and I remember the many talks we had about the philosophy and psychology of the old master. Later, unfortunately, we did not see each other any more, after he became a professor in Salzburg. Only a few letters were exchanged. So I had heard nothing of his death.

At that time the main subject of discussion was the philosophical views of Paracelsus and his relation to Hermetic philosophy; these emerge with particular clarity in the treatise *De Vita Longa* of Adam von Bodenstein, to which I have devoted a major study.[2] In this connection, inevitably, further psychological themes were discussed, especially the archetypes, which are so often misunderstood. Pater Betschart lent an attentive ear, and I admired the openness of mind with which he followed my arguments. Platonic philosophy afforded welcome common ground where we could agree relatively easily on the ideal side of the problem. From there we could pass on with some success to a discussion of its scientific aspect. The main difficulty here is that the eternal ideas have been dragged down from their "supracelestial place"[3] into the biological sphere, and this is somewhat confusing for the trained philosopher and may even come to him as a shock. Actually this needn't be so, because Plato's heavenly proto-

□ Salzburg. — Published in *Der Mensch als Persönlichkeit und Problem*, Gedenkenschrift für Ildefond Betschart, ed. Elisabeth Herbrich (1963).

[1] P. Ildefond Betschart, O.S.B. (d. 1959), professor of psychology, metaphysics, and the history of philosophy at the U. of Salzburg.

[2] Pupil of Paracelsus and editor of his *Liber de Vita Longa*. Jung discusses this book at length in "Paracelsus as a Spiritual Phenomenon," CW 13, pars. 169ff., 213ff., the lecture he gave in 1941 on the 400th anniversary of the death of Paracelsus at Einsiedeln, his birthplace.

[3] Cf. *Psychological Types*, CW 6, par. 56 & n. 23.

types extend through all spheres of the cosmos down to the most concrete level. Hence it is not in the least surprising that one also encounters them—one might even say, more particularly—in the biological realm. Here they appear, perhaps rather unexpectedly, in the form of the "behaviour pattern," i.e., in the typical and hereditary instincts such as the migratory or nest-building instinct. The Platonic "Idea" is in this case no longer intellectual but a psychic, instinctual pattern. Instinctual patterns can be found in human beings too. They illustrate man's specifically human modes of behaviour. Naturally these do not express themselves only in unconsciously motivated, instinctive activities but also in patterns of thought and perception which present themselves to him involuntarily and unconsciously and whose numerous parallels can be observed all over the earth. Were this not so, human beings could not communicate with one another at all. These patterns are the precondition for the inner affinity of all races of men. They express themselves chiefly in mythological motifs whose existence is substantiated not merely by the fact that they may have been disseminated by tradition and migration, but that—quite apart from this—they reappear spontaneously again and again in the unconscious products of modern individuals. This phenomenon is naturally of no small concern to theologians and philosophers and would merit their highest interest did not a host of prejudices stand in the way. However, Pater Betschart did not allow himself to be held up by them but followed my argument with keen attention.

When one considers that for over 50 years there has been a definite conception of the unconscious which is supported by empirically demonstrable facts, it is little short of amazing that philosophers still haven't found the time to do anything but pooh-pooh it. Professor Betschart was a great and praiseworthy exception. He was one of the first and the few to look at the problem in a positive way. In Switzerland, at any rate, he was the first philosopher with whom I could talk sense in these matters, and for this I am everlastingly grateful to him.

Since my time and working capacity are very limited as a result of old age, I would ask you to make use of this letter, perhaps, if you are going to publish a memorial volume for Professor Betschart.[4] I shall seldom be at home this summer, as I have to escape the menacing flood of visitors. They sap too much of my time and energy—forgive me.

Yours sincerely, C. G. JUNG

4 Cf. n. □.

Anonymous

Dear Frau N.,   30 May 1960

My old age and the need for rest make me fight shy of too many visitors, so I have to confine myself as far as possible to written answers.

I can answer your question about life after death just as well by letter as by word of mouth. Actually this question exceeds the capacity of the human mind, which cannot assert anything beyond itself. Furthermore, all scientific statements are merely probable. So we can only ask: is there a probability of life after death? The point is that, like all our concepts, time and space are not axiomatic but are statistical truths. This is proved by the fact that the psyche does not fit entirely into these categories. It is capable of telepathic and precognitive perceptions. To that extent it exists in a continuum outside time and space. We may therefore expect postmortal phenomena to occur which must be regarded as authentic. Nothing can be ascertained about existence outside time. The comparative rarity of such phenomena suggests at all events that the forms of existence inside and outside time are so sharply divided that crossing this boundary presents the greatest difficulties. But this does not exclude the possibility that there is an existence outside time which runs parallel with existence inside time. Yes, we ourselves may simultaneously exist in both worlds, and occasionally we do have intimations of a twofold existence. But what is outside time is, according to our understanding, outside change. It possesses relative eternity.

Perhaps you know my essay "The Soul and Death."[1] For its scientific foundation I would draw your attention to my "Synchronicity: An Acausal Connecting Principle," in Jung and Pauli, *The Interpretation of Nature and the Psyche*.

These are my essential thoughts, and I would not express them otherwise in a talk with you.

Yours sincerely, C. G. JUNG

☐ Luxembourg.
[1] In CW 8. Cf. also *Memories*, ch. XI: "On Life after Death."

To E. A. Bennet

[ORIGINAL IN ENGLISH]

My dear Bennet,   3 June 1960

Thank you very much for your kind reply and your interesting article about "Individualism in Psychotherapy"[1]—a very useful paper in the actual circumstances.

There seems to be some misunderstanding of terms: by "applicability of a theory" I don't mean its practical application in therapy, f.i., but its application as a principle of understanding and heuristic means to an end as a characteristic of every scientific theory.

There is no such thing as an "absolute proof"; not even the mathematical proof is absolute as it only concerns the *quantum* and not the *quale*, which is just as important if not more so. I wondered therefore about your statement that scientific proof of the conception of the archetypes is lacking, and I thought you had something special up your sleeve when you made it. As there is no such thing as "absolute proof" I wondered where you draw a line between the applicability of a theory and what you call "scientific proof."

As far as I can see the only proof of a theoretical viewpoint is its applicability in a sense mentioned above, namely that it gives an adequate or satisfactory explanation and has a heuristic value.

. . .

If this is not scientific evidence then I must expect of you that you show me what scientific evidence would be in this case. In other words: what proof is it in your mind that is lacking? It cannot be an "absolute proof" because there is no such thing. It must be what you call "scientific proof," a special kind of proving of which you know since you are able to state that it is lacking.

. . .

I cannot be satisfied with the statement that something is lacking, because it is too vague. I know that there is always something lacking. Therefore I should be most indebted if you could tell me what is lacking, as you must have some definite idea of how such a thing should be proved otherwise than by the observation of relevant facts.

Please don't be impatient with me. It is not hair-splitting but it has much to do with what I call "psychic reality," a concept very often not understood.

I appreciate your answer highly since I am always eager to improve on whatever I have thought hitherto.

Cordially yours, C. G. JUNG

[1] *The British Journal of Medical Psychology*, XVII:3/4 (1938).

To C. K. Ginsberg

Dear Mrs. Ginsberg,   3 June 1960

Thank you for kindly telling me the news of Father White's end. It forms a valuable supplement to the thoughts that have moved me from the moment when I saw that we had come to the parting of the ways. I was at the end of my resources and had to leave him *nolens volens* to the decree of his fate. I saw that his arguments were valid for him and allowed of no other development. I accepted this in silence, for one can only respect such reasons even though one is convinced that—had the circumstances been favourable—one might yet have reached out beyond them. In such cases I usually tell my patients: here only fate can decide. For me personally it is, every time, a matter of life and death, where only the person concerned can speak the word. For it depends entirely on him and his decision what will happen. Knowing how much depended on whether Father White could understand my arguments or not, I still tried to point out the difficulties in my second-last letter to him.[1] With the feeling, however, that it would not be granted me to pierce through to his understanding.

It was then that I sinned against my better insight, but at least it served as a pretext for my asking his forgiveness and offering him a touch of human feeling in the hope that this would afford him some small relief.

As I have so earnestly shared in his life and inner development, his death has become another tragic experience for me. To us limits are set which we cannot overstep, not in our time. Perhaps what has evolved in the course of the centuries will not cease to be active for just as long a span. It may take many hundreds of years for certain insights to mature.

I am glad and grateful that you looked after him so kindly. It was always my fear that he would have to spend his last days in the professional chill of a hospital or in the atmosphere of a monastery cell. Thank God that was spared him. One must also be grateful for the merciful intervention of the embolism.

I thank you for your kind offer to let me see the drawings.[2] I hope you will understand that I prefer to let the images of the living man steadfastly gazing ahead live on in my memory. In gratitude,

Yours sincerely, C. G. JUNG

☐ London.
[1] Cf. White, 25 Mar. 60.
[2] Copies of drawings made of Father White on his deathbed.

To Kurt Hoffmann

Dear Herr Hoffmann,   3 June 1960

Your question as to who invented the legends of the stars naturally cannot be answered. All sources are lacking. But from time immemorial, that is to say from the time of the ancient Egyptians and Babylonians, the stars and constellations have had their names. One is inclined to assume, not without reason, that this knowledge may go back to the megalithic age.

From what we know of genuine primitives today, the stars play an astonishingly small role in their lives, a fact which may justify the assumption that the projection of the constellations and their interpretation coincided with the beginnings of a reflecting consciousness, i.e., with the first steps in civilization. These beginnings are naturally shrouded in deep darkness. We must bear in mind that we do not *make* projections, rather they *happen* to us. This fact permits the conclusion that we originally read our first physical, and particularly psychological, insights in the stars. In other words, what is farthest is actually nearest. Somehow, as the Gnostics surmised, we have "collected" ourselves from out of the cosmos. That is why the idea of "gathering the seeds of light"[1] played such an important role in their systems and in Manichaeism.

I enclose some literary references which may be of use to you.

Yours sincerely, C. G. JUNG

☐ Stuttgart.

[1] Cf. "On the Nature of the Psyche," CW 8, par. 388, n. 56.

To Robert L. Kroon

[ORIGINAL IN ENGLISH]

Dear Sir,   9 June 1960

There is hardly a psychological statement of which you cannot prove the contrary. Such a statement as Dr. Eysenck's can be true,[1] but *grosso modo*, as it is sometimes very difficult to establish the diagnosis with certainty. As soon as there are symptoms of a neurosis the diagno-

[1] K. sent a clipping from *Newsweek*, 30 May 1960, reporting the findings of the London psychologist H. J. Eysenck (a protagonist of behaviour therapy) that extraverts tend to smoke cigarettes and introverts pipes.

564

sis becomes uncertain, as one does not know *prima vista* whether you are confronted with the picture of the true character or of the opposite compensating character. Moreover there are not a few introverts who are so painfully aware of the shortcomings of their attitude that they have learned to imitate the extraverts and behave accordingly, and vice versa there are extraverts who like to give themselves the air of the introvert because they think they are then more interesting. Although I have never made a statistique of this kind I have always been impressed by the fact that pipe-smokers are usually introverted. The typical extravert is too much of a busybody to bother and fuss with the pipe which demands infinitely more nursing than a cigarette that can be lighted or thrown away in a second. That does not prevent me from having found heavy cigarette-smokers among my introverts and not a few pipe-smokers among the extraverts, but normally with empty pipes. Pipe-smoking was in their case one of the cherished introverted mannerisms. I cannot omit to remark that the diagnosis is not rarely hampered by the fact that it is chiefly extraverts who resent being called extraverts, as if it were a derogatory designation. I even know of a case where a famous extravert, having been called an extravert, challenged his opponent to a duel.

Faithfully yours, C. G. JUNG

To E. A. Bennet

Dear Bennet,

[ORIGINAL IN ENGLISH]
11 June 1960

Thank you very much for your illuminating letter. I see from it that you understand by "scientific evidence" something like a chemical or physical proof. But what about evidence in a Law Court? The concept of scientific proof is hardly applicable there, and yet the Court knows of evidence which suffices to cut a man's head off, which means a good deal more than the mere universality of a symbol. I think that there is such a thing as "commensurability of evidence." Obviously the way of proving a fact is not the same and cannot be the same in the different branches of knowledge. For instance, the mathematical method is not applicable either in psychology or in philosophy and vice versa. The question ought to be formulated: what is physical, biological, psychological, legal, and philosophical evidence? By which principle could one show that physical evidence is superior to any other evidence? Or how could anybody say that there is no psychological evidence for the existence of a quantum or a proton? Obviously no branch of knowledge can be expressed in terms of another branch, just as one cannot measure weight by kilometres or length by litres or ohms by volts. There is also no "scientific proof" of the existence of the migration instinct, for instance, yet nobody doubts it. It would be too much to expect chemical proof in a murder case, yet the case can be proved by a legal method quite satisfactorily. Why should psychology be measured against physics—if one is not a member of the Leningrad Academy?

Many thanks,

Yours cordially, C. G. JUNG

To the Rev. Kenneth Gordon Lafleur

[ORIGINAL IN ENGLISH]

Dear Sir, 11 June 1960

Thank you very much for your friendly letter. I am glad to know that my ideas met an echo in yourself.

One sentence in your letter has puzzled me. You write: "I hope that you will not be too discouraged concerning the possibility of religion's part in the necessary process of individuation of personality."

I don't see where you get the impression that I might be discouraged in this respect, since I was the first to emphasize the enormous role religion plays particularly in the individuation process, as I was the first to raise the question of the relation between psychotherapy and religion in its practical aspects. As a matter of fact I have so frequently dealt with the problem of religion that I have been alternately accused of agnosticism, atheism, materialism, and mysticism. I should hardly risk all these misunderstandings if I had been discouraged. I can tell you moreover that it needed some courage to deal with the religious question at all. I should appreciate it therefore all the more if you could kindly enlighten me about the meaning of the sentence quoted above.

Yours sincerely, C. G. JUNG

☐ Castine, Maine.

To E. A. Bennet

[ORIGINAL IN ENGLISH]

Dear Bennet,   23 June 1960

I can entirely subscribe to your statement in "Methodology in Psychological Medicine,"[1] p. 3: "Its (the scientific method's) tool is the objective observation of phenomena. Then comes the classification of the phenomena and lastly the deriving of mutual relations and sequences between the observed data, thereby making it possible to predict future occurrences, which, in turn, must be tested by observation and experiment," if, I must add, the experiment is possible. (You cannot experiment with geological strata for example!)

What you state is exactly what I do and always have done. Psychic events are observable facts and can be dealt with in a "scientific" way. Nobody has even shown me in how far my method has not been scientific. One was satisfied with shouting "unscientific." Under these circumstances I do make the claim of being "scientific" because I do exactly what you describe as the "scientific method." I observe, I classify, I establish relations and sequences between the observed data, and I even show the possibility of prediction. If I speak of the collective unconscious I don't assume it as a principle, I only give a name to the totality of observable facts, i.e., archetypes. I derive nothing from it as it is merely a *nomen*.

The crux is the term "scientific," which in the Anglo-Saxon realm means, it seems, physical, chemical, and mathematical evidence only. On the continent, however, any kind of adequate logical and systematic approach is called "scientific"; thus historical and comparative methods are scientific. History, mythology, anthropology, ethnology, are "sciences" as are geology, zoology, botany, etc.

It is evident that psychology has the claim of being "scientific" even when it is not concerned only with (most inadequate) physical or physiological methods. Psyche is the mother of all our attempts to understand Nature, but in contradistinction to all others it tries to understand itself by itself, a great disadvantage in one way and an equally great prerogative in the other!

Thanking you again for all the trouble I have caused and you took, I remain,

Yours sincerely, C. G. JUNG

---

[1] *Journal of Mental Science*, LXXXVI:361 (Mar. 1960).

To Cornelia Brunner

Dear Frau Brunner, 28 June 1960

Now that the splendid celebration at the Dolder[1] is over, I would like to thank you for everything you have done to make the festivities a success. It was an extraordinarily fine affair, and I was able to enjoy every minute of it. In particular, I was of course profoundly surprised by the stage performance of Elsie Attenhofer,[2] whose art I have admired for many a long decade.

Above all, however, I would like to express my very special thanks to you, and also to the Club, for the astonishing and sumptuous gift[3] you have made me, evidently on the psychologically correct assumption that my ever-alert imagination will be instantly at hand to convert the concentrated energy into the most variegated forms of fireworks, which will indeed be the case.

Please convey my cordial thanks to the Club for this gift.

I hope the great success of the festivities has afforded you some satisfaction also. With the very best greetings,

Gratefully, C. G. JUNG

☐ Since 1953, president of the Psychological Club, Zurich. Cf. her *Die Anima als Schicksalsproblem des Mannes* (Studien aus dem C. G. Jung-Institut XIV, Zurich, 1963). Jung's foreword is in CW 18, pars. 1276ff.
[1] A celebration in honour of Jung's 85th birthday, held on 25 June 1960 at the Grand Hotel Dolder, Zurich.
[2] Swiss cabaret artist.
[3] The Psychological Club had presented Jung with a sum of money with which to buy anything he particularly wanted.

To Olga Fröbe-Kapteyn

Dear Frau Fröbe, 28 June 1960

With great regret I have heard that you have had to undergo an operation for cataract. I am now greatly relieved to know that the operation has been a success.

As you know, physical events of this kind are always at the same time psychic ones, and what the doctors not unjustly consider to be post-operative shock is in reality the release of concomitant psychic

☐ See Fröbe-Kapteyn, 29 Jan. 34 (in vol. 1).

phenomena that are already present. In so far as cataract causes blindness, it represents psychologically an unconsciousness of those contents which then appear in the shock. The more of these contents there are and the stronger they are, the more closely does the conscious perception of them approximate to a delirious state.

The medicaments in the prescription you mention do not in themselves cause delirium, but they can bring about an *abaissement du niveau mental* which helps to make the unconscious contents visible.

The first vision[1] depicts what comes to consciousness in the night of blindness. The cathedral is an expression of the collective Christianity in which you as a Christian are crucified (*imitatio Christi*). This vision indicates that you, as a contemporary, whole human being, are still nailed fast in the Christian form. The cathedral, however, is in ruins. Consequently—one might say—you get into the cellar, i.e., from high up aloft down into a depth in which you appear to be locked up. The presence of the nurse[2] shows that this is the post-operative period, the time of the so-called shock, when you still cannot make out where you are locked up, or at least are afraid of being locked up. There you feel so absolutely alone with yourself that you have anxiously to assure yourself that the nurse is still there. This is a clear indication that the unconscious is manifesting a strong tendency to lock you up with yourself, so that you are deprived of any form of communication with the outside world.

Anyone who falls down from the roof or ceiling of the Christian cathedral falls into himself. Think of the situation of the historical Jesus who felt himself abandoned by God on the Cross and was nothing more than himself alone! We have believed this for so long and have asserted that sometime it must become a reality.

---

[1] In a letter to Jung dated 24 June 1960 Frau Fröbe described the following vision: "Somewhere in an endless night, dimly illuminated, stood the ruins of an old cathedral . . . High up there was a sort of wooden scaffolding beneath the ruins of the roof. On this scaffolding I was fastened crosswise, facing downwards . . . I knew that I was going to be pierced through the heart with a lance from behind . . ."

[2] Second vision: "I was in my bed in the clinic in Bellinzona. Around me were the 'little nurses' . . . One of the nurses was supposed to sleep on a pile of mattresses beside my bed. I was afraid because the matron said she was going to lock us in until she returned at 11 o'clock. Then I grew frightened and the room changed into a cellar in which my bed stood. . . . The nurse slept beside my bed . . . and I touched her head to assure myself that she was still there. . . . I spent the whole night in terror of being locked in."

Now the reconstruction has begun.[3] We must build ourselves up again with all the means at our command (the temple that is built again on the third day). You have to do this yourself, and I would therefore advise you to carry on with your attempts to create form and at least to build up in pictures what you can build up out of yourself. If you do that you are wholly on the right track. From that which you do it will be seen who you are. In your newest attempts the very oldest things of all, the most primordial, become visible. With best wishes,

Sincerely yours, C. G. JUNG

[3] The letter says: "Now [a month after the operation] I do not see any more visions, but try every day to reconstruct something [from them]."

To Robert C. Smith

[ORIGINAL IN ENGLISH]

Dear Mr. Smith,   29 June 1960

Buber and I[1] start from an entirely different basis: I make no transcendental statements. I am essentially empirical, as I have stated more than once. I am dealing with psychic phenomena and not with metaphysical assertions. Within the frame of psychic events I find the fact of the belief in God. It *says*: "God is." This is the fact I am concerned with. I am not concerned with the truth or untruth of God's existence. *I am concerned with the statement only*, and I am interested in its structure and behaviour. It is an emotionally "toned" complex like the father- or mother-complex or the Oedipus complex. It is obvious that if man does not exist, no such statement can exist either, nor can anybody prove that the statement "God" exists in a non-human sphere.

What Buber misunderstands as Gnosticism is *psychiatric observation*, of which he obviously knows nothing. It is certainly not my

□ Then in Villanova, Pennsylvania. Now assistant professor of philosophy and religion, Trenton State College (New Jersey). At the time of writing S. was preparing as a thesis "A Critical Analysis of Religious and Philosophical Issues between Buber and Jung." Cf. Neumann, 28 Feb. 52, n. 9.
[1] In his letter S. had reported a conversation with Buber in which the latter had accused Jung of being a "monologist," having reduced God to an object, and maintaining that Jung's statement that without man no God would be possible was an ontological denial of God.

invention. Buber has been led astray by a poem in Gnostic style I made 44 years ago for a friend's birthday celebration[2] (a private print!), a poetic paraphrase of the psychology of the unconscious.

"Every pioneer is a monologist" until other people have tried out his method and confirmed his results. Would you call all the great minds which were not popular among their contemporaries, monologists, even that "voice of one crying in the wilderness"?

Buber, having no practical experience in depth psychology, does not know of the *autonomy of complexes,* a most easily observable fact however. Thus God, as an autonomous complex,[3] is a *subject* confronting me. One must be really blind if one cannot get that from my books. Likewise the *self* is a redoubtable reality, as everybody learns who has tried or was compelled to do something about it. Yet I define the Self as a *borderline concept.* This must be a puzzler for people like Buber, who are unacquainted with the empiricist's epistemology.

Why cannot Buber get into his head that I deal with psychic facts and not with metaphysical assertions? Buber is a theologian and has far more information about God's true existence and other of His qualities than I could ever dream of acquiring. My ambitions are not soaring to theological heights. I am merely concerned with the practical and theoretical problem of how-do-complexes-behave? F.i. how does a mother-complex behave in a child and in an adult? How does the God-complex behave in different individuals and societies? How does the self-complex compare with the *Lapis Philosophorum* in Hermetic philosophy and with the Christ-figure in patristic allegories, with Al Chadir in Islamic tradition, with Tifereth in the Kabbalah, with Mithras, Attis, Odin, Krishna, and so on?

As you see, I am concerned with *images,* human phenomena, of which only the ignorant can assume that they are within our control or that they can be reduced to mere "objects." Every psychiatrist and psychotherapist can tell you to what an enormous degree man is delivered over to the terrific power of a complex which has assumed superiority over his mind. (*Vide* compulsion neurosis, schizophrenia, drugs, political and private nonsense, etc.) Mental possessions are just as good as ghosts, demons, and gods.

It is the task of the psychologist to investigate these matters. The

[2] *Septem Sermones ad Mortuos.* Cf. Maeder, 19 Jan. 17, n. 1.
[3] Cf. White, 5 Oct. 45, n. 2.

theologian certainly has not done it yet. I am afraid it is sheer prejudice against science which hinders theologians from understanding my empirical standpoint. Seen from this standpoint the "experience of God" is *nolens volens* the psychic fact that I find myself confronted with, a factor in myself (more or less represented also by external circumstances) which proves to me to be of insurmountable power. F.i. a most rational professor of philosophy is entirely possessed by the fear of cancer which he knows does not exist. Try to liberate such an unfortunate fellow from his predicament and you will get an idea of "psychic autonomy."

I am sorry if X. bothers about the question of the basis upon which "religion rests." This is a metaphysical question the solution of which I do not know. I am concerned with *phenomenal religion*, with its observable facts, to which I try to add a few psychological observations about basic events in the collective unconscious, the existence of which I can prove. Beyond this I know nothing and I have never made any assertions about it.

How does Buber know of something he cannot "experience psychologically"? How is such a thing possible at all? If not in the psyche, then where else? You see, it is always the same matter: *the complete misunderstanding of the psychological argument*: "God" within the frame of psychology is an *autonomous complex, a dynamic image, and that is all psychology is ever able to state*. It cannot know more about God. It cannot prove or disprove God's actual existence, but it does know how fallible images in the human mind are.

If Niels Bohr compares the model of atomic structure with a planetary system, he knows it is merely a model of a transcendent and unknown reality, and if I talk of the God-image I do not deny a transcendental reality. I merely insist on the psychic reality of the God-complex or the God-image, as Niels Bohr proposes the analogy of a planetary system. He would not be as dumb as to believe that his model is an exact and true replica of the atom. No empiricist in his senses would believe his models to be the eternal truth itself. He knows too well how many changes any kind of reality undergoes in becoming a conscious representation.

All my ideas are names, models, and hypotheses for a better understanding of observable facts. I never dreamt that intelligent people could misunderstand them as theological statements, i.e., hypostases. I was obviously too naïve in this regard and that is the reason why I was sometimes not careful enough to repeat time and again: "But what I mean is only the psychic image of a *noumenon*"[4] (Kant's thing-in-itself, which is not a negation as you know).

My empirical standpoint is so disappointingly simple that it needs only an average intelligence and a bit of common sense to understand it, but it needs an uncommon amount of prejudice or even ill-will to misunderstand it, as it seems to me. I am sorry if I bore you with my commonplaces. But you asked for it. You can find them in most of my books, beginning with the year 1912,[5] almost half a century ago and not yet noticed by authorities like Buber. I have spent a lifetime of work on psychological and psychopathological investigations. Buber criticizes me in a field in which he is incompetent and which he does not even understand.

Sincerely yours, C. G. JUNG

[4] "An object of purely intellectual intuition, devoid of all phenomenal attributes" (*Shorter Oxford Dict.*). The term was introduced by Kant to distinguish between "noumenon" and "phenomenon" as "an immediate object of perception."
[5] Date of publication of *Wandlungen und Symbole der Libido* (orig. version of *Symbols of Transformation*).

To Hugh Burnett

[ORIGINAL IN ENGLISH]

Dear Mr. Burnett,   30 June 1960

Your letter and invitation[1] have arrived at a moment when I find it hard to make up my mind at all. I am tired by the work of a whole year and I could not envisage the possibility of further exertions. I don't want to say "no" definitely, but I should like to postpone my answer to a time when I have had my due rest. My wish is that you would take up the problem once more in September, when I am more sure of my capacity again.

Your quite understandable proposition to confront me with an interlocutor whom I do not know personally does not simplify the situation, as I am rather frightened of my colleagues on account of so many unfortunate experiences, i.e., unnecessary misunderstandings and prejudices. I will mention only a few of them: archetypes are metaphysical ideas, are mystical, do not exist, I am a philosopher,

[1] The "Face to Face" interview with John Freeman (cf. Brooke, 16 Nov. 59, n. 1) had been such a success that the BBC requested another interview, this time with a psychiatrist about medical problems. It did not take place.

573

have a father-complex against Freud, and so on. It is unsatisfactory and fatiguing to deal with people who neither have read my books nor have the slightest notion of the methods I am applying and their justification. I cannot deal any more with people who are unacquainted with the world of problems I am concerned with. I avoid as much as possible interviews with those of my colleagues who are in need of basic information. I also avoid people with an antagonistic attitude from the start, who only want to know their own ideas but not mine. I consider a certain amount of open-mindedness as indispensable for an interview. I can explain my standpoint but I refuse to fight uphill. Such gladiator-games are good for so-called scientific congresses but are the worst obstacle to real understanding. I have no patience any more with sheer ignorance. If you are sure your man is open-minded, fair and willing to weigh my argument objectively, and capable of doing so, I can look forward more easily to such an interview.

I must ask for your forgiveness for these measures of precaution, because my old age has left me with a sorry remnant of my former energies. I cannot explain and fight at the same time against ignorance and incompetence. I have, for the sake of my health, to ask my partner first: Have you read a book I have written within the last 30 years? And did you understand it? — If not, I shut up. I am sick of talking to people who do not even know the psychological ABC. There are so many people who either designate themselves as my pupils or aver that they know my "system" that I am always a bit scared when I have to meet an unknown person. I trust you are aware of this serious question. The whole interview depends on it. A few years ago (. . .) University got an interview out of me to which they sent a Professor of Psychology who was completely ignorant and to whom one could not talk intelligently. I had then been still strong enough to push him aside and give a free talk about some basic aspects. I could not do that any more. At all events I should be much obliged to you if you would give me the chance to see my psychiatric partner before we start, so that I can get an idea of the level on which a talk would be possible.

Many apologies for my hesitations and anxieties! I remain,

Yours sincerely, C. G. JUNG

To Pastor Oscar Nisse

Dear Pastor Nisse,   2 July 1960

It was actually through my therapeutic work that I began to understand the essence of the Christian faith. It became clear to me that the preoccupation with anxiety in psychoanalysis, where as you know it plays a considerable part, is not to be explained by the presence of religious teaching but rather by its absence.

With Freud personally—as I saw clearly over a period of years— anxiety played a great part. It is not hard to see that in him its source was the fear of Yahweh which is always present in the unconscious, particularly of Jews. In the Jewish mentality this imprint is so deep that the individual Jew can rarely get away from it. That is because he is Jewish, because he belongs and has belonged for thousands of years to a people characterized by their intimate connection with Yahweh.

With the Christian this anxiety is less important thanks to the fact that it was not until the day before yesterday that he rid himself of the gods, who represented the numinous aspects of the transcendent being as a plurality.

I assure you it was precisely through my analytic work that I arrived at an understanding not only of the Christian religion but, I may say, of all religions.

The Freudian idea that religion is nothing more than a system of prohibitions is very limited and out of touch with what is known about different religions.

To be exact, I must say that, although I profess myself a Christian, I am at the same time convinced that the chaotic contemporary situation shows that present-day Christianity is not the final truth. Further progress is an absolute necessity since the present state of affairs seems to me insupportable. As I see it, the contributions of the psychology of the unconscious should be taken into account.

□ (Translated from French.) Brussels. — In a letter of 16 June 60 N. had reported a lecture by a psychoanalyst who had maintained that anxiety (*Angst*) had to be regarded as the true root of religion and, in the discussion following, that Jung's writings did not allow the conclusion that Jung regarded himself as a Christian. N. had, on the contrary, formed the opinion that it was exactly through his psychological researches that Jung had arrived at his positive attitude to religion.

But naturally it is impossible for me to argue that point in a letter. With your permission, let me recommend my little book, *Psychologie et Religion* (Edition Corréa, Paris, 1958) or the introduction to my book *Psychologie und Alchemie* (Zurich, 1952, not yet translated into French).[1]

With highest regards, I am,

Yours sincerely, C. G. JUNG

[1] Tr. Henry Pernet and Roland Cahen (Paris, 1970).

To Stephen I. Abrams

[ORIGINAL IN ENGLISH]

Dear Mr. Abrams,   11 July 1960

Cases with a continuous output of positive ESP or other paranormal effects are very interesting indeed. They were puzzling to me inasmuch as archetypal constellations are usually more or less momentary and don't extend over longer periods. I have followed up a case of a man who was practically invulnerable even to rapier thrusts through kidney and liver. His remarkable achievement lasted over several years. It was accompanied by a pious and devoted attitude. He was unselfish and idealistic. Two bad friends succeeded in persuading him that there was money in it. The next experiment killed him. In this case it was quite obvious that he owed his invulnerability to an intensely religious attitude which is an archetypal constellation. It is possible also that other conditions like physical traumata, diseases and physiological constellations can maintain an *abaissement* of consciousness which enables unconscious effects to cross the threshold. I should not wonder at all if synchronistic phenomena would manifest in the form of physiological effects. I don't feel particularly optimistic with reference to the possibility of control and predictability.

The mathematical theory of information[1] is beyond the reach of my understanding, but it sounds interesting nevertheless. It is quite possible, even probable, that man has a much greater amount of ESP at his disposal than one generally supposes. This must be so if

[1] Information theory is a branch of cybernetics, the theory of communication. A. had used this theory in his work on ESP and believed he had found that "subjects have available much more ESP than they actually use."

576

it is true that synchronicity belongs to the basic qualities of existence (or being, ὄν, οὐσία).

. . .

Good luck to your adventure,

Sincerely yours, C. G. JUNG

To B. von Fischer

Sir,   11 July 1960

Please accept my most cordial thanks for your kind birthday letter, which it was both an honour and a pleasure to receive. I am particularly sensible of the appreciative words you have written on my life's work, for they are a melody which one does not often hear in our dear Fatherland.

. . .

A man's lifework is like a ship he has built and equipped himself, launched down the ramp and entrusted to the sea, steered towards a distant goal and then left like a passenger, in order to sit on the shore and gaze after it till it is out of sight. Like all three-dimensional things it gradually sinks below the horizon. What remains is what has been.

I am, Sir, respectfully and gratefully yours,

C. G. JUNG

☐ Then Swiss Ambassador in Vienna.

To Cornelia Brunner

Dear Frau Präsidentin,   2 August 1960

I still owe you my express thanks for the wonderful, spirit-infused gift that flew into the house on my birthday. You have endowed this birthday of mine with incredible generosity, so that I stand there quite ashamed beside all the magnificence, with the painful feeling that I can no longer give the Club what would otherwise be given so willingly.

I have to adapt myself with considerable effort to the role of recip-

☐ (Handwritten.)

ient in which I have been living for nearly fifteen years. In this respect the wine is a great tonic, and I am very grateful for the bountiful selection.

Please give my best thanks to the Club members as well!

Very sincerely yours, C. G. JUNG

To E. L. Grant Watson

[ORIGINAL IN ENGLISH]

Dear Watson,   8 August 1960

Thank you very much for the amazing flood of material you have inundated me with. You know, an 85-year-old ruin of a formerly capable man cannot live up to it any more. Have mercy on us!

The interesting pictures of labyrinths are known to me. They have presumably the fundamental significance of mandalas, i.e., places of refuge, sanctuary, rebirth, renewal, initiation, etc. like the Neolithic stone-circles. You find very good comparative material in the book by John Layard:[1] Stone Men of Malekula (London, 1942). It is clear that such formations, particularly under primitive circumstances, are more of anatomical than geometrical nature, i.e., organic cavities like uterus or brain or cranium, very much later also heart.

Please don't mix me up with your unconscious, which projects itself into everything obscure and unreasonable. It is exceedingly difficult to find out how that unconscious looks which is really in the object. First of all one has to consider every kind of impression as of subjective origin. Only then can one hope to be able to discover what belongs to oneself and what is objectively universal. If you don't discriminate enough I am on the best way to becoming a real Museum of Metaphysical Monsters. Consider please that in the year 1960 we are still far from being out of the primitive woods. There are very few beings yet capable of making a difference between mental image and the thing itself. This primitivity is poisoning our human world and is so dense a mist that very few people have discovered its existence yet.

My richly celebrated 85th birthday has left me a wreck, and this

---

[1] D.Sc., (1891–1974), British anthropologist and analytical psychologist. Cf. his The Virgin Archetype (Spring Publs., New York, 1972).

miserable summer we enjoy does not exactly support one's optimism, not to speak of the political situation of the world which reminds me of the tower of Babel and its fate. I think of the German poet Hölderlin, one of Goethe's contemporaries:

"But we are fated
To find no foothold, no rest,
And suffering mortals
Dwindle and fall
Headlong from one
Hour to the next,
Hurled like water
From ledge to ledge
Downward for years to the vague abyss."[2]

Sincerely yours, c. g. j u n g

[2] Hölderlin's "Hyperion's Song of Fate," last stanza (tr. Michael Hamburger, *Poems and Fragments*, 1967; by permission of Routledge & Kegan Paul Ltd. and the University of Michigan Press).

To the Earl of Sandwich

[ORIGINAL IN ENGLISH]

Dear Lord Sandwich,   10 August 1960

It was a great pleasure to receive your kind letter and congratulations on my 85th birthday.

It is indeed quite a number of years since our interview in 1938, when I received an Honorary Degree at Oxford, while lecturing there at a Congress of Psychotherapists.[1] It was on the eve of war and I remember the air filled with forebodings and anxious anticipations. I remember vividly looking at the delightful buildings and lawns of the Universitas Oxonensis as if seeing them for the first and last time. Although Oxford has been spared barbarous destruction I *had* seen it for the first and last time. I have not been there again al-

□ George Charles Montagu (1874–1962), of Huntingdon; member of the Committee of the British Council, Arts Section. — The letter was published in *Spring*, 1971.
[1] The 10th International Medical Congress for Psychotherapy, of which Jung was president. His presidential address is in CW 10, Appendix, pars. 1069ff.

though I always dreamt and hoped to delve more deeply into the treasures of alchemistic manuscripts at the Bodleian. Fate has decreed otherwise.

I had to follow the ineradicable foolishness which furnishes the steps to true wisdom. Since man's nature is temperamentally set against wisdom, it is incumbent upon us to pay its price by what seems foolish to us.

Old age is only half as funny as one is inclined to think. It is at all events the gradual breaking down of the bodily machine, with which foolishness identifies ourselves. It is indeed a major effort—the *magnum opus* in fact—to escape in time from the narrowness of its embrace and to liberate our mind to the vision of the immensity of the world, of which we form an infinitesimal part. In spite of the enormity of our scientific cognition we are yet hardly at the bottom of the ladder, but we are at least so far that we are able to recognize the smallness of our knowledge.

The older I grow the more impressed I am by the frailty and uncertainty of our understanding, and all the more I take recourse to the simplicity of immediate experience so as not to lose contact with the essentials, namely the dominants which rule human existence throughout the millenniums.

There are two sciences in our days which are at immediate grips with the basic problems: nuclear physics and the psychology of the unconscious. There things begin to look really tough, as those who have an inkling of understanding of the one thing are singularly incapable of grasping the other thing; and here, so it looks, the great confusion of languages begins, which once already has destroyed a tower of Babel.

I am trying to hold those two worlds together as long as my machinery allows the effort, but it seems to be a condition which is desperately similar to that of the political world, the solution of which nobody yet can foresee. It is quite possible that we look at the world from the wrong side and that we might find the right answer by changing our point of view and looking at it from the other side, i.e., not from outside, but from inside.

Thanking you once more for your kind letter, I remain, dear Lord Sandwich,

Yours very sincerely, C. G. JUNG

To the Mother Prioress
of a Contemplative Order

[ORIGINAL IN ENGLISH]

Dear Mother Prioress,   12 August 1960

Thank you ever so much for your letter with all its information about Fr. Victor's end.

I am most gratful to you for sending me the picture you mention. The living mystery of life is always hidden between Two, and it is the true mystery which cannot be betrayed by words and depleted by arguments.

Sincerely yours, C. G. JUNG

To Pastor Werner Niederer

Dear Pastor Niederer,   13 August 1960

It is clear from your manuscript that your recommendation raises a very delicate problem.[1] You are risking difficulties not only with your own colleagues but—and this is more serious—also with the medical faculty.

Naturally one cannot avoid taking risks, for nothing new would happen without them. But one must ask oneself in all seriousness whether the difficulties would jeopardize the whole project, or can really be overcome. It is quite inconceivable that all theologians, to a man, would go in for a training analysis, as you rightly demand that they should. Nor is a training analysis the end of it, for in addition they would have to acquire a whole lot of technical knowledge, for which purpose, as you know, the C. G. Jung Institute was founded. A diploma from this Institute is the minimal preparation needed for the activity you have in mind. The mental and moral maturity you also require of the trainee is indeed commendable, but it is a postulate that cannot be carried out in practice. Hence there are good reasons for combining psychotherapy, as a rule, either with a study of medicine, which is long and expensive and therefore offers some guarantee of the perseverance, reliability, and responsibleness of those who take up such a profession, or with a completed course of academic studies which at least ensures an all-round education.

[1] N. recommended greater consideration of Jung's psychology in the training of clergymen and proposed that they undergo a training analysis.

But lay psychologists, too, are necessarily obliged to work together with doctors because the neuroses are frequently and unavoidably complicated by dangerous psychotic phenomena to which only a man who is protected by a medical diploma can and should expose himself.

So if you were to attempt such a radical breakthrough it is 1000:1 that you will fail. One has to be content with tentative, self-sacrificing efforts gradually to alter the marked aversion of the theological mind for psychology and transform its prejudices against the human psyche into a positive interest. Unfortunately hardly a beginning has been made with this work in the world of theology. The first step would be to sweep away all the various prejudices that hamper understanding. Secondly, large numbers of theologians would have to acquire a deeper knowledge of psychology, which would be possible at first only in the realm of theory. But nothing is gained by encouraging unprepared, prejudiced persons, however well-intentioned they may be, to take up a practical activity of whose scope, meaning, and risks they haven't the glimmering of an idea. They would endanger not only themselves but also the "patients" entrusted to their care. One should first educate the educator and not hand the pupil over to an incompetent who, if he is honest, only gets his education from the pupil. It would, however, be a delusion to assume that everyone can meet the demand for moral maturity. In my experience the opposite is generally the case.

In my opinion, therefore, it would be much more suitable if a serious attempt were made in the theological faculty, the breeding-ground of theologians, to come to terms with the facts of psychology on the basis of real knowledge, and to give the student some conception of the contemporary problems he will meet with in his parish. I would even advise you to ask a leading member of the theological faculty to give you a candid opinion of your proposal after a thorough study of your manuscript. His reactions would show you what your chances are, and how a further *modus procedendi* might be worked out. You will probably find it pretty difficult to convince any authority at all that your project is worth taking seriously. It would then be up to you to prove that it is.

. . .

With kind regards,

Yours sincerely, c. g. j u n g

To Robert C. Smith

[ORIGINAL IN ENGLISH]

Dear Mr. Smith,   16 August 1960

Why can't you understand that the therapeutic performance is a vital process,[1] which I call the "process of individuation"? It takes place objectively and it is this experience which helps the patient and not the more or less competent or foolish interpretation of the analyst.

The best the analyst can do is not to disturb the natural evolution of this process. My so-called views about it are only poor means of representing the very mysterious process of transformation in the form of words, which serve no other purpose than to describe its nature.

The process consists in becoming whole or integrated, and that is never produced by words or interpretations but wholly by the nature of Psyche itself. When I say "Psyche" I mean something unknown, to which I give the name "Psyche." There is a difference between hypothesis and hypostasis. My hypothesis is that all psychic products referring to religious views are comparable on the basis of a fundamental similarity of the human mind. This is a scientific hypothesis. The Gnostic, which Buber accuses me of being, makes no hypothesis, but a hypostasis in making metaphysical statements.

When I try to establish a fundamental similarity of individual psychic products and alchemistic or otherwise Gnostic noumena, I carefully avoid making a hypostasis, remaining well within the boundaries of the scientific hypothesis.

The fact that I try to make you see my standpoint could show to you that I don't mind the criticism. I only want to defend myself against wrong premises. If I could not stand criticism I would have been dead long ago, since I have had nothing but criticism for 60 years. Moreover I cannot understand what my alleged incapacity to stand criticism has to do with the reproach that I am a Gnostic. You simply add to the arbitrary assumption that I am a Gnostic the blame of moral inferiority, and you don't realize that one could make the same subjective reproach against you.

I have accused nobody and if I am attacked I have the right to

---

[1] In reply to Jung's letter of 29 June 60, S. said "there are many times when a therapist's theory affects the conceptions of his patients," and posed the question whether faith or knowledge was the more effective healing agent.

defend myself in explaining my point of view. There is no need at all to blame me under those circumstances for being intolerant.

Sincerely yours, C. G. JUNG

To the Rev. W. P. Witcutt

[ORIGINAL IN ENGLISH]

Dear Sir,   24 August 1960

I must apologize for not having answered your letter[1] of July 18th. I hasten therefore to answer this time at once. I was very interested in your letter, as you can imagine. Since 1924 I have done much work with the *I Ching* and I have discussed it with my late friend Richard Wilhelm, who had first-hand knowledge of its workings.

As you have found out for yourself, the *I Ching* consists of readable archetypes, and it very often presents not only a picture of the actual situation but also of the future, exactly like dreams. One could even define the *I Ching* oracle as an experimental dream, just as one can define a dream as an experiment of a four-dimensional nature. I have never tried even to describe this aspect of dreams, not to speak of the hexagrams, because I have found that our public today is incapable of understanding. I considered it therefore my first duty to talk and write of the things that might be understandable and would thus prepare the ground upon which one could later on explain the more complicated things. I quite agree that the *I Ching* symbolism can be interpreted like that of dreams.

By the way: I must call your attention to the fact that I have no theory that God is a quaternity. The whole question of quaternity is not a theory at all, it is a Phenomenon. There are plenty of quaternary symbolizations of the Deity and that is a fact, not a theory. I would not commit such a crime against epistemology. This is the stumbling block over which Father Victor White has fallen and many others. I am in no way responsible for the fact that there are quaternity formulas.

Now, as to your new book,[2] to which I am looking forward with great interest: unfortunately my doctor is strictly against too much mental work, since it increases my blood pressure. Thus I have to

☐ Southend, England.
[1] The letter deals mainly with the relationship between the *I Ching* oracle and dreams.
[2] An unpublished MS titled "The Prophetic Dream."

584

omit all mental efforts. I would have liked to write a preface to your indubitably meritorious book, but I could not do it without a careful study and digestion of your MS—not to mention the formulation of my own standpoint in these highly complicated matters. *Sunt certe denique fines*³—that is precisely the situation in which I find myself now. I cannot fight the battle any more and I refuse to produce superficial and cheap stuff. I hope you will understand this painful confession of *non possumus*. Nobody regrets this defeat through old age more than I myself.

Yours very sincerely, C. G. JUNG

³ "There are fixed limits" (Horace, *Satires*, I, 106).

To Jolande Jacobi

Dear Dr. Jacobi,   25 August 1960

I was very impressed and pleased to hear that my autobiographical sketches have conveyed to you something of what my outer side has hitherto kept hidden. It had to remain hidden because it could not have survived the brutalities of the outside world. But now I am grown so old that I can let go my grip on the world, and its raucous cries fade in the distance.

The dream¹ you have called back to my memory anticipates the content and setting of the analysis in a miraculous way. Who knew that and who arranged it? Who envisioned and grasped it, and forcibly expressed it in a great dream-image? He who has insight into this question knows whereof he speaks when he tries to interpret the psyche. With cordial greetings,

Yours sincerely, C. G. JUNG

☐ (Handwritten.)
¹ J. retold a "big dream" of hers in 1927 which had the character of an initiation. It is reported in her *The Way of Individuation* (1967), pp. 76f.

To Heinrich Berann

Dear Herr Berann,   27 August 1960

Thank you very much for the samples you have sent me of your paintings.

Although you may not know it, I find it very difficult, both as a psychologist and a human being, to establish any relationship with modern abstract art. Since one's feelings seem to be a highly unsuitable organ for judging this kind of art, one is forced to appeal to the intellect or to intuition in order to gain any access to it. But even then most of the little signs and signals by which human beings relate to one another seem to be absent. The reason for this, it seems to me, is that in those depths from which the statements of the modern artist come the individual factor plays so small a role that human communication is abolished. "I remain I and you remain you"—the final expression of the alienation and incompatibility of individuals.

These strange messages are well suited to our time, marked as it is by mass-mindedness and the extinction of the individual. In this respect our art has an important role to play: it compensates a vital deficiency and anticipates the illimitable loneliness of man.

The question that forces itself upon me when contemplating a modern picture is always the same: what *can't* it express?

Yours sincerely, c. g. JUNG

☐ Innsbruck.

To Herbert Read

[ORIGINAL IN ENGLISH]

Dear Sir Herbert,   2 September 1960

I have just read the words of a *Man*, that is, the statement of your views about my work.[1] Courage and honesty have won out, two qualities the absence of which in my critics hitherto has hindered every form of understanding. Your blessed words are the rays of a new sun over a dark sluggish swamp in which I felt buried. I often thought of Meister Eckhart who was entombed for 600 years. I asked myself time and again why there are no men in our epoch who could see at least what I was wrestling with. I think it is not mere vanity and desire for recognition on my part, but a genuine concern for my fellow-beings. It is presumably the ancient functional

☐ See Read, 17 Oct. 48 (in vol. 1). See pl. III.
[1] An essay published as a pamphlet in honour of Jung's 85th birthday, *Zum 85. Geburtstag von Professor Carl Gustav Jung, 26. Juli 1960* (Zurich, 1960). The original English version appeared in Read, *The Art of Art Criticism* (London, 1957).

Sept 2ᵈ 1960

Dear Sir Herbert,

I have just read the words of a <u>Man</u>, that is. the statement of your views about my work. Courage and honesty have won out, the two qualities, the absence of which in my hitherto critics has hindered every form of understanding. Your blessed words are the rays of a new sun over a dark sluggish swamp, in which I felt being buried. I often thought of Master Eckart who was entombed for 600 years. I asked myself time and again, why there are no men in our epoch, who could see at least, what I was wrestling with. I think it is not mere vanity and desire for recognition on my part, but a genuine concern for my fellow beings. It is presumably the ancient functional relationship of the medicine man to his tribe, the "participation mystique" and the essence of the physician's ethos. I see the suffering of mankind in the individual's predicament and vice-versa.

As a medical psychologist I do not merely assume, but I am thoroughly convinced, that

Herbert Read, 2 Sept. 60, first page only

587

relationship of the medicine-man to his tribe, the *participation mystique* and the essence of the physician's ethos. I see the suffering of mankind in the individual's predicament and vice versa.

As a medical psychologist I do not merely assume, but I am thoroughly convinced, that *nil humanum a me alienum esse*[2] is even my duty. I am including "modern art"—and passionately— though I see you indulgently smiling. I have regretted very much not to have had the opportunity of a real talk with you about your book,[3] which has brought back to me all my thoughts about art. I have never been explicit about them because I was hampered by my increasing awareness of the universal misunderstanding I encountered. As the problem is subtle, its solution demands subtlety of mind and real experience of the mind's functioning. After 60 solid years of field-work I may be supposed to know at least something about my job. But even the most incompetent ass knew better and I received no encouragement. On the contrary I was misunderstood or completely ignored. Under those circumstances I even grew afraid to increase the chaos of opinion by adding considerations which could not be understood. I have given a good deal of attention to two great initiators: Joyce and Picasso.[4] Both are masters of the fragmentation of aesthetic contents and accumulators of ingenious shards. I knew, as it seems to me, what that crumpled piece of paper meant that went out down the Liffey in spite of Joyce.[5] I knew his pain, which had strangled itself by its own strength. Hadn't I seen this tragedy time and again with my schizophrenic patients? In *Ulysses* a world comes down in an almost endless, breathless stream of débris, a "catholic" world, i.e., a universe with moanings and outcries unheard and tears unshed, because suffering had extinguished itself, and an immense field of shards began to reveal its aesthetic "values." But no tongue will tell you what has happened in his soul.

I saw the same process evolving in Picasso, a very different man. Here was strength which brought about the dissolution of a work. He saw and understood what the surge of depth meant. Almost consciously he accepted the challenge of the all-powerful spirit of the time. He transformed his "Können" ("Kunst" derives from "kön-

[2] "Nothing human is alien to me." Cf. Terence, *Heauton Timorumenos*, I.1.25: "Homo sum; humani nil a me alienum puto."
[3] Read, *The Form of Things Unknown* (1960).
[4] Cf. "Ulysses" and "Picasso," CW 15.
[5] Concerning the "light crumpled throwaway" drifting down the Liffey cf. "Ulysses," pars. 186ff.

nen") into the art of ingenious fragmentation: "It shall go this way, if it doesn't go the other way." I bestowed the honour upon Picasso of viewing him as I did Joyce. I could easily have done worse by emphasizing his falsity. He was just catering to the morbidity of his time, as he himself admits. I am far from diagnosing him a schizophrenic. I only emphasize the analogy to the schizophrenic process, as I understand it. I find no signs of real schizophrenia in his work except the analogy, which however has no diagnostic value, since there are plenty of cases of this kind yet no proof that they are schizophrenics.

Picasso is ruthless strength, seizing the unconscious urge and voicing it resoundingly, even using it for monetary reasons. By this regrettable digression he shows how little he understands the primordial urge, which does not mean a field of ever so attractive-looking and alluring shards, but a new world after the old one has crumpled up. Nature has a *horror vacui* and does not believe in shard-heaps and decay, but grass and flowers cover all ruins inasmuch as the rains of heaven reach them.

The great problem of our time is that we don't understand what is happening to the world. We are confronted with the darkness of our soul, the unconscious. It sends up its dark and unrecognizable urges. It hollows out and hacks up the shapes of our culture and its historical dominants. We have no dominants any more, they are in the future. Our values are shifting, everything loses its certainty, even *sanctissima causalitas* has descended from the throne of the axioma and has become a mere field of probability. Who is the awe-inspiring guest who knocks at our door portentously?[6] Fear precedes him, showing that ultimate values already flow towards him. Our hitherto believed values decay accordingly and our only certainly is that the new world will be something different from what we were used to. If any of his urges show some inclination to incarnate in a known shape, the creative artist will not trust it. He will say: "Thou art not what thou sayest" and he will hollow them out and hack them up. That is where we are now. They have not yet learned to discriminate between their wilful mind and the objective manifestation of the

---

[6] Perhaps the fantasy figure personifying the dark aspect of the unconscious, destructive and creative at once, described in Jung's earliest childhood dream (*Memories*, pp. 11ff./25ff., esp. p. 15/29). Many years later he encountered a parallel figure, "the pilgrim of eternity," in *The Candle of Vision* (1920) by the Irish poet "A.E." (George W. Russell), which impressed him profoundly.

psyche. They have not yet learned to be objective with their own psyche, i.e., [to discriminate] between the thing which you do and the thing that happens to you. When somebody has a happy hunch, he thinks that *he* is clever, or that something which he does not know does not exist. We are still in a shockingly primitive state of mind, and this is the main reason why we cannot become objective in psychic matters. If the artist of today could only see what the psyche is spontaneously producing and what he, as a consciousness, is inventing, he would notice that the dream f.i. or the object is pronouncing (through his psyche) a reality from which he will never escape, because nobody will ever transcend the structure of the psyche.

We have simply got to listen to what the psyche spontaneously says to us. What the dream, which is not manufactured by us, says is *just so*. Say it again as well as you can. *Quod Natura relinquit imperfectum, Ars perficit.*[7] It is the great dream which has always spoken through the artist as a mouthpiece. All his love and passion (his "values") flow towards the coming guest to proclaim his arrival.

The negative aspects of modern art[8] show the intensity of our prejudice against the future, which we obstinately want to be as we expect it. *We* decide, as if we knew. We only know what we know, but there is plenty more of which we might know if only we could give up insisting upon what we do know. But the Dream would tell us more, therefore we despise the Dream and we are going on to dissolve *ad infinitum*.

What is the great Dream? It consists of the many small dreams and the many acts of humility and submission to their hints. It is the future and the picture of the new world, which we do not understand

---

[7] = What Nature left imperfect, the [alchemical] Arts perfects.

[8] Sir Herbert Read replied to Jung's letter on 19 Oct. 1960. With regard to fragmentation (par. 2 at n. 4) he said: "The whole process of fragmentation, as you rightly call it, is not, in my opinion, wilfully destructive: the motive has always been (since the beginning of the century) to destroy the conscious image of perfection (the classical ideal of objectivity) in order to release new forces from the unconscious. This 'turning inwards' . . . is precisely a longing to be put in touch with the Dream, that is to say (as you say) the future. But in the attempt the artist has his 'dark and unrecognizable urges,' and they have overwhelmed him. He struggles like a man overwhelmed by a flood. He clutches at fragments, at driftwood and floating rubbish of all kinds. But he has to release this flood in order to get nearer to the Dream. My defence of modern art has always been based on this realization: that art must die in order to live, that new sources of life must be tapped under the crust of tradition."

yet. We cannot know better than the unconscious and its intimations. *There* is a fair chance of finding what we seek in vain in our conscious world. Where else could it be?

I am afraid I never find the language which would convey such simple arguments to my contemporaries. Apologies for the length of my letter!

Sincerely yours, C. G. JUNG

To Miguel Serrano

[ORIGINAL IN ENGLISH]

Dear Sir, 14 September 1960

Your letter of May 7th, 1960, is so vast that I don't know where to begin answering it.[1] The way towards a solution of our contemporary problems I seem to propose is in reality the process I have been forced into as a modern individual confronted with the social, moral, intellectual, and religious insufficiencies of our time. I recognize the fact that I can give only one answer, namely mine, which is certainly not valid universally, but may be sufficient for a restricted number of contemporary individuals inasmuch as my main tenet contains nothing more than: Follow that will and that way which experience confirms to be your own, i.e., the true expression of your individuality. As nobody can become aware of his individuality unless he is closely and responsibly related to his fellow beings, he is not withdrawing to an egoistic desert when he tries to find himself. He can only discover himself when he is deeply and unconditionally related to some, and generally related to a great many, individuals with whom he has a chance to compare and from whom he is able to discriminate himself. If somebody in supreme egoism should withdraw to the solitude of Mt. Everest, he would discover a good deal about the amenities of his lofty abode but as good as nothing about himself, i.e., nothing he could not have known before. Man in general is in such a situation in so far as he is an animal gifted with self-reflection but without the possibility of comparing himself to another species of animal equally equipped with consciousness. He is a top animal exiled on a tiny speck of planet in the Milky Way. That

[1] S.'s letter of 7 May 60 and this letter are published in S., *C. G. Jung and Hermann Hesse* (1966), pp. 79ff. (Present text from the original.)

592

is the reason why he does not know himself; he is cosmically isolated. He can only state with certainty that he is no monkey, no bird, no fish, and no tree. But what he positively is, remains obscure.

Mankind today is dreaming of interstellar communications. Could we contact the population of another star, we might find a means to learn something essential about ourselves. Incidentally we are just living in a time when *homo homini lupus*[2] threatens to become an awful reality, and when we are in dire need to know beyond ourselves. The science fiction about travelling to the moon or to Venus and Mars and the lore about Flying Saucers are effects of our dimly felt but none the less intense need to reach a new physical as well as spiritual basis beyond our actual conscious world. Philosophers and psychologists of the XIXth and XXth centuries have tried to provide a *terra nova* in ourselves, that is, the *unconscious*. This is indeed a discovery which could give us a new orientation in many respects. Whereas our fictions about Martians and Venusians are based upon nothing but mere speculations, the unconscious is within the reach of human experience. It is almost tangible and thus more or less familiar to us, but on the other hand a strange existence difficult to understand. If we may assume that what I call archetypes is a verifiable hypothesis, then we are confronted with autonomous *animalia* gifted with a sort of consciousness and psychic life of their own, which we can observe, at least partially, not only in living men but also in the historic course of many centuries. Whether we call them gods, demons, or illusions, they exist and function and are born anew with every generation. They have an enormous influence on individual as well as collective life, and despite their familiarity they are curiously non-human. This latter characteristic is the reason why they were called gods and demons in the past and why they are understood in our "scientific" age as the psychic manifestations of the instincts, inasmuch as they represent habitual and universally occurring attitudes and thought-forms. They are basic forms, but not the manifest, personified, or otherwise concretized images. They have a high degree of autonomy, which does not disappear when the manifest images change. When f.i. the belief in the god Wotan vanishes and nobody thinks of him any more, the phenomenon,

---

[2] "Man is wolf to man." With these words Thomas Hobbes (1588–1679), in his *Leviathan*, characterized the presocial and premoral state of man leading to a "condition of war of everyone against everyone."

called Wotan originally, remains; nothing changes but its name, as National Socialism has demonstrated on a grand scale.[3] A collective movement consists of millions of individuals, each of whom shows the symptoms of Wotanism and proves thereby that Wotan in reality never died but has retained his original vitality and autonomy. Our consciousness only imagines that it has lost its gods; in reality they are still there and it only needs a certain general condition in order to bring them back in full force. This condition is a situation in which a new orientation and adaptation are needed. If this question is not clearly understood and no proper answer given, the archetype which expresses this situation steps in and brings back the reaction which has always characterized such times, in this case Wotan. As only certain individuals are capable of listening and of accepting good advice, it is most unlikely that anybody would pay attention to the statement of a warning voice that Wotan is here again. They would rather fall headlong into the trap.

As we have largely lost our gods and the actual condition of our religion does not offer an efficacious answer to the world situation in general and to the "religion" of Communism in particular, we are very much in the same predicament as the pre-National-Socialistic Germany of the twenties, i.e., we are apt to undergo the risk of a further but this time worldwide Wotanistic experiment. This means mental epidemics and war.

One does not realize yet that when an archetype is unconsciously constellated and not consciously understood, one is *possessed by it* and forced to its fatal goal. Wotan then represents and formulates our ultimate principle of behaviour, but this obviously does not solve our problem.

The fact that an archaic god formulates and expresses the dominant of our behaviour means that we ought to find a new religious attitude, a new realization of our dependence upon superior dominants. I don't know how this could be possible without a renewed self-understanding of man, which unavoidably has to begin with the individual. We have the means to compare man with other psychic *animalia* and to give him a new setting which throws an objective light upon his existence, namely as a being operated and manoeuvred by archetypal forces instead of his "free will," that is, his arbitrary egoism and his limited consciousness. He should learn that he is not the master in his own house and that he should carefully study

[3] Cf. "Wotan," CW 10.

the other side of his psychic world which seems to be the true ruler of his fate.

I know this is merely a "pious wish" the fulfillment of which demands centuries, but in each aeon there are at least a few individuals who understand what man's real task consists of, and keep its tradition for future generations and a time when insight has reached a deeper and more general level. First the way of a few will be changed and in a few generations there will be more. It is most unlikely that the general mind in this or even in the next generation will undergo a noticeable change, as at present man seems to be quite incapable of realizing that under a certain aspect he is a stranger to himself. But whoever is capable of such insight, no matter how isolated he is, should be aware of the law of synchronicity. As the old Chinese saying goes: "The right man sitting in his house and thinking the right thought will be heard a 100 miles away."[4]

Neither propaganda nor exhibitionist confessions[5] are needed. If the archetype, which is universal, i.e., identical with itself always and anywhere, is properly dealt with in one place only, it is influenced as a whole, i.e., simultaneously and everywhere. Thus an old alchemist gave the following consolation to one of his disciples: "No matter how isolated you are and how lonely you feel, if you do your work truly and conscientiously, unknown friends will come and seek you."

It seems to me that nothing essential has ever been lost, because its matrix is ever-present within us and from this it can and will be reproduced if needed. But only those can recover it who have learned the art of averting their eyes from the blinding light of current opinions, and close their ears to the noise of ephemeral slogans.

You rightly say with Multatuli, the Dutch philosopher: "Nothing is quite true" and should add with him: "And even this is not quite true." The intellect can make its profound statement that there is no absolute Truth. But if somebody loses his money, his money is lost and this is as good as an absolute Truth, which means that he will not be consoled by intellectual profundity. There is a thing like convincing Truth but we have lost sight of it, owing the loss mostly to our gambling intellect, to which we sacrifice our moral certainty

---

[4] Cf. *I Ching* (3rd edn., 1967), p. 305: "The Master said: The superior man abides in his room. If his words are well spoken, he meets with assent at a distance of more than a thousand miles."

[5] As practised by the Oxford Movement.

and gain thereby nothing but an inferiority-complex, which—by the way—characterizes Western politics.

To be is to do and to make. But as our existence does not depend solely upon our ego-will, so our doing and making depend largely upon the dominants[6] of the unconscious. I am not only willing out of my ego, but I am also made to be creative and active, and to be quiet is only good for someone who has been too—or perversely—active. Otherwise it is an unnatural artifice which unnecessarily interferes with our nature. We grow up, we blossom and we wilt, and death is ultimate quietude—or so it seems. But much depends upon the spirit, i.e., the meaning or significance, in which we do and make or—in another word—live. This spirit expresses itself or manifests itself in a Truth, which is indubitably and absolutely convincing to the whole of my being in spite of the fact that the intellect in its endless ramblings will continue forever with its "But, ifs," which however should not be suppressed but rather welcomed as occasions to improve the Truth.

You have chosen two good representatives of East and West. Krishnamurti[7] is all irrational, leaving solutions to quietude, i.e., to themselves as a part of Mother Nature. Toynbee on the other hand believes in making and moulding opinions. Neither believes in the blossoming and unfolding of the individual as the experimental, doubtful and bewildering work of the living God, to whom we have to lend our eyes and ears and our discriminating mind, to which end they were incubated for millions of years and brought to light about 6000 years ago, viz. at the moment when the historical continuity of consciousness became visible through the invention of script.

We are sorely in need of a Truth or a self-understanding similar to that of Ancient Egypt, which I have found still living with the Taos Pueblos. Their chief of ceremonies, old Ochwiäh Biano (Mountain Lake)[8] said to me: "We are the people who live on the roof of the world, we are the sons of the Sun, who is our father. We help him daily to rise and to cross over the sky. We do this not only for ourselves, but for the Americans also. Therefore they should not interfere with our religion. But if they continue to do so [by mis-

---

[6] Cf. Schmid-Ernsthausen, 25 Apr. 52, n. 1.

[7] Jiddu Krishnamurti (1895–), a leading Indian theosophist, later in California. He was discovered by Annie Besant (1847–1933), an English pupil of Helena Blavatsky (1831–91), and declared by her in 1925 to be the Messiah, a claim which he himself later renounced.

[8] Cf. Mirabal, 21 Oct. 32; also *Memories*, pp. 250ff./235ff.

sionaries] and hinder us, then they will see that in ten years the Sun will rise no more."

He correctly assumes that their day, their light, their consciousness, and their meaning will die when destroyed by the narrow-mindedness of American rationalism, and the same will happen to the whole world when subjected to such treatment. That is the reason why I tried to find the best truth and the clearest light I could attain to, and since I have reached my highest point I can't transcend any more, I am guarding my light and my treasure, convinced that nobody would gain and I myself would be badly, even hopelessly injured, if I should lose it. It is most precious not only to me, but above all to the darkness of the creator, who needs man to illuminate His creation. If God had foreseen his world, it would be a mere senseless machine and man's existence a useless freak.

My intellect can envisage the latter possibility, but the whole of my being says "No" to it.

Sincerely yours, C. G. JUNG

To Patrick Whitaker

[ORIGINAL IN ENGLISH]

Dear Sir,   8 October 1960

Thank you very much for your kind letter of August 21st. Unfortunately my answer is late. I have been ill in the meantime and unable to take care of my correspondence.

I have studied your "proposal"[1] with much interest. Frankly, such a plan would be quite impossible in Europe, but with reference to the "land of unlimited possibilities" one feels differently.

Your basic assumption that a Museum of Sanctuary is needed for the preservation of religious phenomena is quite correct. Our present state of civilization becomes more and more unable to understand what a religion means. Europe has already lost half of its population to a mental state worse than ancient paganism. There is however a grave doubt in my mind: just as the accumulation of masterworks of art threatens to kill each individual work, so the accumulation of religions in the manner of a spiritual zoo seems to be very dangerous

---

☐ Patrick Andrew Whitaker, artist of New York City.

[1] W. submitted to many prominent persons a proposal for developing Ellis Island (in New York Bay) into a world sanctuary for religion, a "museum of living religious shrines." It did not materialize.

for the spiritual life of each religion. Without it, it is a mere curiosity. Religions are like plants which belong to a particular soil and a particular climate. Outside of their vital conditions their existence can be maintained only artificially. Nearly all confessions are afraid of anthropology and psychology and rightly so. I am sure they would feel most uncomfortable finding themselves neatly classified along with Mahayana Buddhism, Zen, Voodoo, and Australian *alcheringe mijinas*.[2] But even under such conditions Ellis Island would be one of the most remarkable Museums of the World.

I should be indeed quite interested to learn about the further progress of your initiative.

Sincerely yours, C. G. JUNG

[2] The ancestral souls which are reactivated in the religious rites of certain aboriginal Australian tribes. *Alcheringa* is the mythical time in which these half-animal ancestors lived. It is also the dream-world.

To Hans Seifert

Dear Herr Seifert,   14 October 1960

Best thanks for telling me about your interesting experience.[1] It is a type of experience that has become very rare nowadays. It may have appeared again because the time was favourable.

Possibly the vision was caused by the sudden appearance of a deer. There usually is some such cause, but the important thing is what the cause triggers off. Here it is the archetypal motif of two animals fighting. You often find it in illuminated manuscripts of the 11th and 12th centuries, and also in the capitals and friezes of Romanesque churches, where it can take the form of a man fighting an animal, or of a man between two animals.

It is not difficult to see that the stag of your vision is related to

☐ Schaffhausen.
[1] S. described "a collectively experienced animal encounter" in which he, his wife, his daughter (aged 13), and his son (aged 8) had participated. He saw what he at first believed to be a wild sow; his wife saw it as a wolf, his daughter as a stag. The animal then turned into a white stag behind which appeared a black dog, servile but treacherous. After a short time both animals disappeared in the forest. The son noticed only the brown back of an animal.

the stag of St. Hubert[2] and St. Eustace,[3] which is an allegory of Christ because it tramples˜ on the serpent. (The Celtic stag-god Kerunnus[4] holds a serpent by the neck.) Conversely, Christ himself is the serpent hung on a pole[5]—an indication of the identity of opposites. The dog, or whatever it is that threatens the stag, is its opposite—white stag opposed by black dog, quarry by wolf.

The two together represent a supernatural, unitary being at war with itself. The animal form shows that the conflict, symbolized by this paradisal being, is largely unconscious. That is to say, you see your conflict as something personal, whereas in the vision it is produced by an extra-personal pair of opposites. You do not produce your conflict, you are rather its unconscious victim or exponent. The vision is more or less collective because it expresses the collective situation and not the individual will. Your little son, who you say was furthest from the conflict, sees only something light brown, which was probably the real cause of the vision. Despite their powers of imagination, children often observe things much more accurately than grown-ups. They are naturally and instinctively adapted to reality; their next task is to find their way about in it. Grown-ups, on the other hand, especially those approaching middle life, get around to feeling that there is still a psychic reality about which our culture knows much too little and cares less. People would rather hang on to the old dogmas than let experience speak.

According to your vision, the stag is rather dejected and worn out. He also seems to have rubbed his horns down to stumps. By contrast, the black dog is uncanny but much more alive.

I do not know how far you are acquainted with the psychology of the unconscious. I won't go into details, but would only point out that a collective vision is a phenomenon of the time, depicting the great problem of our day in individual form.

Yours sincerely, C. G. JUNG

[2] The patron saint of huntsmen; he is supposed to have met a stag with a crucifix between its antlers.

[3] A soldier in the service of the Emperor Trajan, also supposed to have seen a vision of a stag with the crucifix.

[4] The horned god of the Celts, represented as three-headed and connected with the underworld and with fertility.

[5] John 3:14. Cf. *Psychology and Alchemy*, CW 12, Fig. 217.

To Melvin J. Lasky

Dear Mr. Lasky,   19 October 1960

I don't feel happy about the reaction to Koestler which you received from Zurich through the medium of my secretary. I am recovering from a serious illness and I was unable to take care of my correspondence for several weeks. The impression you got from my message must have been confusing. This unfortunate effect can hardly be avoided when one has to deal with such a paradoxical phenomenon as Zen (and the less complicated Yoga).

In the main I fully agree with Koestler's rather unfavourable opinion. His is a meritorious as well as a needful act of debunking for which he deserves our gratitude. The picture he draws of Yoga and Zen, as seen by the Western mind, is rational, distant, and—as it were—unprejudiced and correct. As far as this kind of mind reaches and can be called valid, Koestler's judgment is true.

But the question that must be asked is this: Is the Western point of view really unprejudiced? What about its rationalism and its habit of opinionating from without, viz., its extraversion? Rationality is only one aspect of the world and does not cover the whole field of experience. Psychic events are not caused merely from without and mental contents are not mere derivatives of sense-perceptions. There is an irrational mental life within, a so-called "spiritual life," of which almost nobody knows or wants to know except a few "mystics." This "life within" is generally considered nonsense and has therefore to be eliminated—curiously enough in the East as well as in the West. Yet it is the origin and the still-flowing source of Yoga, Zen, and many other spiritual endeavours, not only in the East but in the West too.

But just as Buddhism in its many differentiations overlaid the original spiritual adventure, so Christian rationalism has overlaid medieval alchemistic philosophy, which has been forgotten for about 200 years. This philosophy is as completely lost to us as the *I Ching* is to China. Alchemy also developed the symbolism of aiming, shoot-

□ This letter is in reaction to two articles by Arthur Koestler, "Yoga Unexpurgated" and "A Stink of Zen," in *Encounter* (London), nos. 83 (Aug.) and 85 (Oct. 1960), which form part of Koestler's book *The Lotus and the Robot* (1960). Jung's letter was published in *Encounter*, no. 89 (Feb. 1961), and as an epilogue to the German translation of Koestler's book (*Von Heiligen und Automaten*, 1961) but not in the English original.

600

ing, and hitting the target,[1] not with the bow but with the crossbow, and not as a real practice but as a purely pictorial metaphor. It used this symbolism in order to express the idea that its procedure had a purpose, a goal, and a target, though it never concretized the symbol to the extent of making a ritual of shooting with crossbows—it remained a metaphor. But the actual chemistry attempted in alchemy was an obvious result of the literal-mindedness of the adept, who tried to cook, melt, and distil "symbolic" substances.

Even a genuine and original inner life has a tendency to succumb again and again to the sensualism and rationalism of consciousness, i.e., to literal-mindedness. The result is that one tries to repeat a spontaneous, irrational event by a deliberate, imitative arrangement of the analogous circumstances which had apparently led to the original event. The immense hope, the liberating *ekstasis* of the primordial experience, soon turns into the pertinacity of an intellectual pursuit which tries, through the application of a method, to attain the effect of the primordial experience, namely, a kind of spiritual transformation. The depth and intensity of the original emotion become a passionate longing, an enduring effort that may last for hundreds of years, to restore the original situation. Curiously enough, one does not realize that this was a state of spontaneous, natural emotion or *ekstasis*, and thus the complete opposite of a methodically construed imitation.

When the old Chinese master asked the pupil, with whom he was walking at the time of the blossoming laurel: "Do you smell it?" and the pupil experienced *satori*, we can still guess and understand the beauty and the fullness of the moment of illumination. It is overwhelmingly clear that such a *kairos*[2] can never be brought back by a wilful effort, however painstaking and methodical. There is no doubt that patient and pertinacious application does produce effects of a kind, but it is more than doubtful whether they represent the original *satori* or not.

An even greater distance seems to separate the *satori* of meaningful *koans*[3] from Zen archery. It is comparable to the difference between

---

[1] Cf. *Psychology and Alchemy*, CW 12, Fig. 48.

[2] Cf. Dr. H., 30 Aug. 51, n. 12.

[3] A problem given by the Zen Master to his pupil, usually a highly irrational question to which no rational answer is possible (e.g., "What is the sound of one hand clapping?"). Cf. "Foreword to Suzuki's *Introduction to Zen Buddhism*," CW 11, pars. 894f.

the events depicted in the gospels, or the illumination of St. Paul, and the *Exercitia Spiritualia* of St. Ignatius of Loyola.

The original Gnostic conception of alchemy is still visible in Zosimos of Panopolis (3rd cent. A.D.) and one can understand, from the depth and power of these ideas, the subsequent obstinacy of the alchemical quest, which for 1700 years could not give up its hope of producing the panacea or the artificial gold in spite of all disenchantments and all "debunking" through the centuries.

I quite agree with Koestler when he puts his finger on the impressive mass of nonsense in Zen, just as I agree with all the former critiques of alchemy. But I want to point out at the same time that, just as the obviously absurd chemistry of alchemy was a half-conscious blind for a very real spiritual longing, the secret passion which keeps Zen and other spiritual techniques alive through the centuries is connected with an original experience of wholeness—perhaps the most important and unique of all spiritual experiences. Since there are apparently no external, rational, controllable, and repeatable conditions to prove or justify the existence or validity of an inner life, one is inclined to think that such an unusual amount of absurdities would have killed any spiritual movement in no time, or would kill it at least in our more enlightened days. This very understandable Western expectation does not come off, because it envisages only the non-essential, but not the essential, which is omitted in our judgment. We in our Western ignorance do not see, or have forgotten, that man has or is visited by subjective inner experiences of an irrational nature which cannot be successfully dealt with by rational argument, scientific evidence, and depreciative diagnosis.

Because the West has deprived itself of its own original irrational methods and yet needs them so badly, and because the inner life can only be repressed but not helped by rationalism, it tries to adopt Yoga and Zen. It is just pathetic to see a man like Herrigel acquiring the art of Zen archery,[4] a non-essential if ever there was one, with the utmost devotion—but, thank God, it has obviously nothing to do with the inner life of man!

We are even afraid of admitting the existence of such a thing because it might be "pathological." This is the poisonous dart in the bow of the sceptic, the suicidal doubt in a weak mind! Curiously

[4] Eugen Herrigel, *Zen in the Art of Archery* (tr., 1953). — Herrigel was teaching philosophy at Tokyo U. between the wars. He returned to Germany in 1930 and became an active member of the Nazi party.

enough, one does not realize that the only living existence we immediately contact is our spontaneous subjective life and not our opinionated life, which is one step removed from reality. The opinionated life should perhaps be a happy one according to our standards, yet it is not; and vice versa. We are unexpectedly happy when we are doing uphill work, like Till Eulenspiegel,[5] and should be gloomy, at least by all reasonable expectations. We hate and fear the irrationality of the things within, and thus never learn the art of living with things as they are. We prefer opinions to real life and believe in words rather than facts, with the result that our experience is two- rather than three-dimensional.

The more this is the case, the more the longing for wholeness intensifies. But instead of considering one's own irrationality one eagerly studies Zen and Yoga, if possible the more obvious and tangible parts of both. If one is patient enough (e.g., to spend years and years in learning Zen archery) one is rewarded, as one always is, when one does something disagreeable with the utmost patience and discipline. These in themselves are reward enough, but not more.

Yours sincerely, C. G. JUNG

[5] A popular figure in German folklore, representing the superiority of the wily peasant over the towndwellers and tradesmen. The first collection of his jests and practical jokes was published in 1515. In one story Till Eulenspiegel, unlike his companions, rejoices when walking uphill in anticipation of the coming easy descent.

To the Mother Prioress of a Contemplative Order

[ORIGINAL IN ENGLISH]

Dear Reverend Mother,   19 October 1960

According to your wish[1] I wrote, as soon as I got your letter, to Dr. Rudin, S.J. (the director of the Institutum Apologeticum in Zurich), who knew Victor White, asking for his cooperation. Thus I hope your wish will be granted.

It was perhaps just as well that my message[2] did not reach V.W.

[1] The Mother Prioress asked if a Roman Catholic priest in Zurich would offer Mass for Victor White's soul on the occasion of what would have been his 58th birthday, 21 Oct.
[2] Cf. Mother Prioress, 29 Apr. 60. Not knowing that Victor White's end was so near, and also on the advice of friends, she did not deliver the message.

603

any more. It might have worried him. When I wrote my explanation[3] I was not yet informed of the seriousness of his condition, and from his reaction I only saw that he did not understand what I meant, which was not astonishing under the circumstances. On the whole I prefer people knowing all they can about themselves when *in conspectu mortis*. But the moment was ill chosen. Don't worry too much about it, as V.W. received my real message and was not able to understand it any more. My message to you was only an attempt to pacify his mind about my intentions. I was afraid he might be unduly worried about the letter he could not understand.

I have now seen quite a number of people die in the time of a great transition, reaching as it were the end of their pilgrimage in sight of the Gates, where the way bifurcates to the land of Hereafter and to the future of mankind and its spiritual adventure. You had a glimpse of the Mysterium Magnum.

Yours sincerely, c. g. jung

P.S. I have just received Dr. Rudin's answer. He himself will celebrate the mass.

[3] Cf. White, 25 Mar. 60.

To René A. Kipfer

Dear Herr Kipfer,   21 October 1960

It is very kind of you to have made me a present of your interesting picture.[1]

Contemplation of an abstract painting always starts me off on the following train of thought: it is not an object of experience in the outer world, nor is it meant to be. If nevertheless there are hints of something recognizable, this is an unintentional lapse or an unavoidable concession to the understanding of the beholder, or to a desire to communicate.

Experience of the inner world has for its object the phenomena of the psychic background, which in itself is so indefinite or so multifaceted that it can be expressed in an infinite variety of forms. We will disregard trashy and commercial daubs and consider only those paintings which display a serious purpose. Such paintings are

[1] K., a young artist of Bern, had sent Jung an abstract oil painting as a sign of gratitude for Jung's work. It could be interpreted as the figure of a dragon.

usually under the spell of a classic archetype, such as can be found not only in dreams but in the myths and folklore of all times and places. Your painting comes under the sign of the dragon motif. Blue signifies air and water, and from it one could easily construct the image of a Chinese dragon. But any such concretizing intention is thwarted by your technique: the dragon is all hollowed out and has a ribbonlike appearance. This loss of substance shows that the dragon is not material but "spiritual." In Chinese, *tao* is described as the "valley spirit"[2] and is depicted as a dragon, i.e., as a winding watercourse.

When Henry Moore[3] sculpts human figures he hollows them out as much as possible in order to show that they are not concrete human beings but substanceless, sacred divinities, for instance King and Queen. Another archetype is expressed by Mother and Child.

Your dragon comes into the category of the great animals in the background who seem to regulate the world. Hence the mainly theriomorphic symbols for the signs of the zodiac as dominants of the psychic process.

Naturally the phenomena observed in the background are not always archetypes; they can also be personal complexes which have acquired excessive importance. Father and mother are not only personal entities but also have a suprapersonal meaning and are frequently used as symbols for the deity. In this way the religious view of the world, thrown out at the front door, creeps in again by the back, albeit in strangely altered form—so altered that nobody has yet noticed it. Thus does modern art celebrate the great carnival of God. With best greetings,

Yours sincerely, C. G. JUNG

---

[2] Cf. *Psychological Types*, CW 6, par. 362, quoting the *Tao Te Ching*, ch. 6.
[3] For a psychological interpretation of Moore's work cf. Neumann, *The Archetypal World of Henry Moore* (1959).

To Herbert Read

[ORIGINAL IN ENGLISH]

Dear Sir Herbert,   22 October 1960

I ask your pardon for bothering you again with a letter. I have just read the review of your book *The Form of Things Unknown* in *The Listener* of September 22nd, 1960.[1]

Alloway asks the silly question "what do the archetypes communicate?" In case you should like to answer him I should like you to
point out his remarkable ignorance. One knows a great deal about
what archetypes communicate even if one has never been inside a
Catholic Church. It is really a bit too much that an educated person of today does not even know what an archetype communicates.
It is only yesterday that I wrote to a young artist who has sent me
one of his abstract pictures, which very clearly suggests the archetype
of the Dragon, though a bit distorted and hollowed out to make it
unrecognizable. Thus obviously the religious views which were eject-
ed through the front door into the street return through the back
door.

Archetypes are forms of different aspects expressing the creative
psychic background. They are and always have been numinous and
therefore "divine." In a very generalizing way we can therefore
define them as attributes of the creator. That would explain the
compelling character of such inner perceptions. The pictures themselves would have the significance of ikons.

It is just that. No answer needed.

Cordially yours, C. G. JUNG

---

[1] In a very critical review of R.'s book in *The Listener*, Lawrence Alloway wrote:
"It is by means of Jung's theory of archetypes that Sir Herbert invests the unique
product of the artist with this high general significance to express the profoundest
truths about reality. . . . However, Sir Herbert leaves unanswered a crucial question: *what* do the archetypes communicate?"

To Peter Birkhäuser

Dear Herr Birkhäuser,   2 November 1960

I want to tell you that your horse-boar-monster has had its after-
effects in me.[1] As a prelude to my latest illness I had the following
dream:

☐ Swiss artist (1911–　），married to Albert Oeri's daughter Sibylle. Cf. Birk-
häuser-Oeri, 13 July 50. Jung reproduced a painting of his in "Flying Saucers," CW
10, pl. III.
[1] This monster had appeared in several of B.'s dreams and he had painted two
pictures of it. One of them is reproduced in *Man and His Symbols*, ed. Jung
(New York and London, 1964), p. 199. Jung had discussed the dreams and
pictures with him.

In an unknown place and at an unknown time, as though standing in the air, I am with a primitive chieftain who might just as well have lived 50,000 years ago. We both know that now at last *the* great event has occurred: the primeval boar, a gigantic mythological beast, has finally been hunted down and killed. It has been skinned, its head cut off, the body is divided lengthwise like a slaughtered pig, the two halves only just hanging together at the neck.

We are occupied with the task of bringing the huge mass of meat to our tribe. The task is difficult. Once the meat fell into a roaring torrent that swept it into the sea. We had to fetch it back again. Finally we reach our tribe.

The camp, or settlement, is laid out in a rectangle, either in the middle of a primeval forest or on an island in the sea. A great ritual feast is going to be celebrated.

The background of this dream is as follows: At the beginning of our *Kalpa* (cosmic age) Vishnu created the new world in the form of a beautiful maiden lying on the waters. But the great serpent succeeded in dragging the new creation down into the sea, from which Vishnu retrieved it, diving down in the shape of a boar. (A parallel to this dream is the Cabbalistic idea that at the end of days Yahweh will slay the Leviathan and serve it up as a meal for the righteous.)[2]

At the end of this cosmic age Vishnu will change into a white horse and create a new world. This refers to Pegasus, who ushers in the Aquarian Age.[3]

I wanted to let you know of this development. With best regards,

Yours sincerely, C. G. JUNG

[2] Cf. *Mysterium Coniunctionis*, CW 14, par. 338. — Jung added this sentence by hand.
[3] Cf. Tauber, 13 Dec. 60.

Anonymous

Dear Herr N.,   2 November 1960

Although I don't like analysing dreams by post, I will make an exception in your case as the dream[1] is particularly clear.

☐ Switzerland.
[1] The dreamer was doing an experiment on the right side of a church with a

The church stands for your religious situation. The right is the conscious side, the left the unconscious. You are therefore conscious of possessing a vessel that contains water and some kind of plant. This plant is an inner, spiritual growth, the development of a tree of life and knowledge which played a great role in alchemy.

The priest is the orthodox Catholic in you who interrupts this process of growth by emptying the water out on the left. In other words, he puts the process back into the unconscious again because for understandable reasons he cannot approve of it.

In general it is advisable to watch these inner developments and not let them slip back into the unconscious, lest they get stuck in the physiological sphere, or rather in the realm of the [psychoid] unconscious which merges with the body, where they give rise to pathological formations which a wise man carefully avoids.

Yours sincerely, C. G. JUNG

---

green glass vessel containing water and a plant. A priest took the vessel away and emptied the water into a stone basin on the left side of the church.

To Leo P. Holliday

[ORIGINAL IN ENGLISH]

Dear Sir,   6 November 1960

You are obviously deeply impressed by the present non-political moral and psychological situation.[1] As far as I can see, it is a psychological problem *par excellence*. Man is confronted with powers apparently created by himself but which he cannot control.

This is *au fond* a primitive situation, with the difference only that the primitive does not imagine himself to be the author of his demons.

The very objects and methods which have led civilized man out of the jungle have now attained to an autonomy which terrifies him, all the more so as he sees no ways and means to cope with them. Since he knows that his ogres are man-made, he lives under the illusion that he could and should control them and he does not understand why this is not so. He is like Goethe's sorcerer's ap-

☐ Hackensack, New Jersey.
[1] H. put forward the idea of establishing "an international research and advisory organization for the purpose of joining together various fields of knowledge and advancing on a common front."

prentice who, using his master's magic, vivified his broom and could not stop it any more. This prejudice increases the difficulties, of course. In a way it would be a much more manageable situation if man could understand his unruly monsters in the primitive way, as autonomous demons. But they are indeed not objective demons, they are mere rational structures which simply and inexplicably escape our control. Yet we are still, as a matter of fact, in the same old jungle, where the individual is still threatened by dangerous factors—by machines, methods, organizations, etc., even more dangerous than the wild animals.

Something has not apparently changed at all: we have carried the old jungle with us, and this is what nobody seems to understand. The jungle is in us, in our unconscious, and we have succeeded in projecting it into the outside world, where now the saurians are lustily playing about again in the form of cars, airplanes, and rockets.

Now, if a psychologist should participate in your world organization, he would be up against the thankless task of making his colleagues from other disciplines see where they have the blind spot. Do you think that such a thing would be possible? I have already tried it for about 60 years, and there are relatively few individuals who were inclined to listen to me. The human mind, still an adolescent boy, will sacrifice everything for a new gadget but will carefully refrain from a look into himself.

You must judge for yourself whether my view is pessimistic or optimistic, but I am rather certain that something drastic will have to happen to wake up the dreamers who are already on the way to the moon.

Sincerely yours, C. G. JUNG

To Robert M. Rock

[ORIGINAL IN ENGLISH]

Dear Sir,   11 November 1960

I quite agree with you: without relatedness individuation is hardly possible. Relatedness begins with conversation mostly. Therefore communication is indubitably important.

For 60 years I have practised this simple truth. I also agree with you that a religious experience depends upon human relatedness to

☐ St. Louis, Missouri.

a certain extent. I don't know to what extent. There is f.i. the apocryphal logion: "When there are two together, they are not without God, and when there is one alone, I am with him."[1] And what about the hermits?

If you seek, I feel sure that you will find a suitable interlocutor. It is always important to have something to bring into a relationship, and solitude is often the means by which you acquire it.

Sincerely yours, C. G. JUNG

[1] James, *The Apocryphal New Testament*, p. 27, x.

To Eugene Rolfe

[ORIGINAL IN ENGLISH]

Dear Sir,   19 November 1960

Having finished reading your book[1] from cover to cover, I am now better prepared to give you my impressions or rather some of them. The theme itself is so rich that one cannot hope to explain it. I have discovered quite a number of old friends in your book and I admire your wisdom and caution in not connecting them with my name of ill omen. I can say: you have fulfilled your task of demonstrating the approach to Christianity to a Christian-minded agnostic. But if the latter should not be "Christian-minded," but thoroughly blackened by the fires of Hell which have broken through in Europe for 20 years now, what then? It is beautiful to hear of the Love of God again, but what about the Fear of God, the ominous message of Evangelium Aeternum? πόθεν τὸ κακόν; [whence evil?], in a word.[2] The agnostics of our days are by no means all Christian-minded. There is a terror which goes much deeper. You call up again Tertullian's Christian anima of the first Roman centuries, which claimed to be the light that shineth in the darkness. What about the anima of our benighted days? Let us hope that your readers will find the way back to the path of the centuries, the beautiful and spirit-filled baptisteria with their mysteria, the Eucharist and its first emotions, the παντοκράτωρες,[3] rul-

[1] *The Intelligent Agnostic's Introduction to Christianity* (1959).
[2] The "everlasting gospel," Rev. 14:6–7. Jung associates the everlasting gospel with the ambivalent image of God as both good and evil. Cf. "Answer to Job," CW 11, par. 733.
[3] = The Pantocrator, creator of all things.

610

ing the spiritual universe. But here the ominous history of the world will begin again with the fearful question of the unredeemed darkness which comprehendeth not. The sophism of the *privatio boni* is too obviously thin.

By the way, you seek the enigmatic oracle *Vocatus atque non vocatus deus aderit*[4] in vain in Delphi: it is cut in stone over the door of my house in Küsnacht near Zurich and otherwise found in Erasmus's collection of *Adagia*[5] (XVIth cent.). It is a Delphic oracle though. It says: yes, the god will be on the spot, but in what form and to what purpose? I have put the inscription there to remind my patients and myself: *Timor dei initium sapientiae*.[6] Here another not less important road begins, not the approach to "Christianity" but to God himself and this seems to be the ultimate question.

Sincerely yours, C. G. JUNG

[4] "Called or not called, the god will be present."
[5] The *Collectanea adagiorum* of Erasmus (1466–1536) is a collection of analects from classical authors. Jung had acquired a 1563 edn. when he was 19.
[6] "The fear of the Lord is the beginning of wisdom" (Psalms 111:10; cf. Proverbs 1:7).

To Olga von Koenig-Fachsenfeld

Dear Dr. von Koenig-Fachsenfeld,   30 November 1960

Best thanks for your letter with its ghostly tidings.[1] One is naturally inclined to explain such visionary experiences in a rational way. But long experience has forced me to realize that these attempts are usually unsatisfying. Certain factors are involved which fly in the face of reason and make a mockery of our explanatory theories.

This applies above all to the wish-fulfillment theory, but also to the possibility of an historical explanation; the idea, for instance, that a residue of past lives still attaches to things is equally unsatisfying. Take the hordes of children in these visions. In spite of their antique costume, they don't fit into the historical picture; and the fact that they all wear little brown caps shows that they are of the same nature

☐ See Koenig-Fachsenfeld, 5 May 41 (in vol. 1).
[1] Visionary experiences of her mother in her last (83rd) year in which she saw many children in antique costume and brown caps.

and points in quite another direction. They are elfin beings, and I don't dare to think about what they might mean.

The fact, too, that the subject of these visions is very old and *in confinio mortis* suggests that a glance has been cast beyond the border, or that something from the other side has seeped through into our three-dimensional world.

This might have a functional significance in that what appears to be nothingness and emptiness is compensated by fullness (comparable to the "wild hunt" or the "blessed people"[2] led by Wotan).

It is one of the self-delusions of our time to think that the spirits do not ride again or that the "wild hunt" gallops no more. We are removed only from the place of such happenings, carried away by our madness. Those of us who are still there, or have found their way back again, will be smitten by the same experience, now as before.

I would like to recommend to you the book by M.-L. von Franz, *Die Visionen des Niklaus von Flüe* (Zurich, 1959) and A. Jaffé's *Geister-erscheinungen und Vorzeichen*[3] (Rascher, 1958). There you can see very clearly the nature of these experiences. With best greetings,

Yours sincerely, C. G. JUNG

[2] In German mythology, the "wild hunt" is led by Wotan, who is also the leader of the dead souls, the "blessed people." Cf. "Flying Saucers," CW 10, par. 701.
[3] *Apparitions and Precognition* (tr., 1963).

To Edward Thornton

[ORIGINAL IN ENGLISH]

Dear Mr. Thornton,   1 December 1960

Thank you for your interesting letter.[1] Things seem to come your way. Writing is a difficult question, since it is not only a blessing but also a bad temptation because it tickles the devil of self-importance. If you want to write something, you have to be quite sure that the whole of your being wants this kind of expression. If it is really the whole, then it is the thing itself, namely the theme and the object of your effort, and it will become obvious that you mean your object and not your own ambition. This needs some self-exami-

[1] T. planned to write a book which was eventually published under the title *The Diary of a Mystic* (1967). Jung's letter is printed in the preface.

nation and careful consideration of your dreams. Therefore don't hurry and better wait until the thing begins to grow out of itself.

. . .

Sincerely yours, C. G. JUNG

To Ronald W. Weddell

[ORIGINAL IN ENGLISH]

Dear Mr. Weddell,   6 December 1960

Your experience with the Eastern magic method is not uncommon.[1] People in the West are peculiarly severed from their unconscious, so that the latter cannot participate any more in conscious life and causes a state of dissociation. The East on the other hand is not dissociated in the same way and to the same extent as the West. The connection is maintained and the East has developed a number of methods to restore this connection when it has been severed.

Subud is such a method. Thus you are filled with a new power of life when you can respond to such a method. It is something like hypnotism which can also heal certain dissociations through the intervention of the hypnotist. In such a case healing comes to you like a gift. A door is opened and you do not know how, and something comes in and you do not know what. The danger is naturally that some day something walks in through the door which is less welcome. Our Western endeavour therefore is to learn about the thing we are dealing with. We try to know what that open door means and what is waiting behind it. Thus we learn how to deal with and how to control the powers we invite. This is a much needed safeguard against the unknown contents and powers of the unconscious which might overwhelm consciousness. These Eastern methods don't enrich consciousness and they don't increase our real knowledge and our self-criticism, and that is the thing we need, namely a consciousness with a wider horizon and a better understanding. That at least is what I am trying to do for the patient: to make him independent and conscious of the influences of the unconscious. Just as we, in the West, are separated too much from the unconscious, the East is apt to be

---

□ Swanbourne, West Australia.

[1] W. described his beneficial experiences with Subud, a mystical movement founded by an Indonesian, Pak Subuh. In his initiation he felt a tremendous access of power "almost like a great flow of electricity flowing through my body." He asked if the practice of Subud could be dangerous for a Westerner.

too much identical with it. Therefore most of the Eastern methods are invented to fetter and suppress the unconscious powers, which are too strong for them. One certainly has a better chance to control things when you know them than when you simply open a door to them.

What you have read in *The Secret of the Golden Flower* gives you a glimpse of such methods.

Sincerely yours, C. G. JUNG

To Wilhelm Bitter

Dear Colleague, 7 December 1960

Best thanks for kindly sending me the extract from your introduction to the report of the meeting.[1] As you rightly conjecture, I was particularly interested in the Dominican reaction to your question. You have poked into a sleeping hornets' nest, but we cannot be sure that the hornets have woken up.

I have taken special note of Augustine's gem: *Aufer meretrices de rebus humanis, turbaveris omnia libidinibus.*[2] St. Thomas, as usual, gets out of it by begging the question. I would like to ask: If God is so powerful and so good that he can make good out of evil, what does he make evil out of?

The world may have been perfect "sortant des mains de l'Auteur des choses,"[3] but it fell into an almighty suffering because of the division into particulars. Who was responsible for this division? It is the cause of all those *mala et defectus*[4] which afflict the whole of creation.

In view of the *omnipotentia Dei* the world cannot have fallen away from God. He could easily have kept it in his hands, but according to the creation story, things were created in their differences by God himself, each "after his kind," which even St. Thomas cannot deny.

Even the venerable Church Fathers had to admit that evil is not only unavoidable but actually necessary in order to avert a greater evil.

---

[1] Bitter, "Einleitung" to the report of the 1960 "Arzt und Seelsorger" meeting, *Zur Rettung des Menschlichen in unserer Zeit* (1961).

[2] "Banish whores from the human realm and you will have confounded everything with lust."

[3] The famous opening words of Rousseau's *Emile*: "Everything as it leaves the hands of the Author of things is good; everything degenerates under the hands of man."

[4] = evils and defects.

The modern approach to this question is one they would applaud. There is no clear dividing line between prostitution and crime. The one is an evil like the other and is in some degree necessary, for a crimeless society would speedily go to rack and ruin.

In this respect our criminal justice stands on a weak footing; it punishes something that is a social necessity. Understandably enough, such a dilemma is an occasion for syllogistic acrobatics, judicial as well as ecclesiastical. Punishment is also an evil and just as much a transgression as crime. It is simply the crime of society against the crime of the individual. And this evil, too, is unavoidable and necessary.

Psychology has the invidious task of rubbing the world's nose into these truths. No wonder nobody takes to it or loses a wink of sleep over it. And it never ceases to amaze me that theologians are incapable of drawing conclusions from their own premises.

With cordial greetings and best wishes for your health,

Yours sincerely, C. G. J U N G

To Ignaz Tauber

Dear Dr. Tauber,   13 December 1960

Many thanks for your kind suggestion that I write a commentary on my Bollingen symbols.[1] Nobody is more uncertain about their meaning than the author himself. They are their own representation of the way they came into being.

The first thing I saw in the rough stone was the figure of the worshipping woman, and behind her the silhouette of the old king sitting on his throne. As I was carving her out, the old king vanished from view. Instead I suddenly saw that the unworked surface in front of her clearly revealed the hindquarters of a horse, and a mare at that, for whose milk the primitive woman was stretching out her hands. The woman is obviously my anima in the guise of a millennia-old ancestress.

Milk, as *lac virginis*, virgin's milk, is a synonym for the *aqua doctrinae*,[2] one of the aspects of Mercurius, who had already bedevilled the Bollingen stones in the form of the trickster.[3]

[1] The figures Jung carved in bas-relief on the outside wall of his Tower (see illus., p. 617). Cf. Jaffé, *From the Life and Work of C. G. Jung* (tr. 1971), p. 133.
[2] The water of doctrine, originally a Christian concept for the store of pure wisdom of the Church.

615

The mare descending from above reminded me of Pegasus. Pegasus is the constellation above the second fish in Pisces; it precedes Aquarius in the precession of the equinoxes. I have represented it in its feminine aspect, the milk taking the place of the spout of water in the sign for Aquarius. This feminine attribute indicates the unconscious nature of the milk. Evidently the milk has first to come into the hands of the anima, thus charging her with special energy.

This afflux of anima energy immediately released in me the idea of a she-bear, approaching the back of the anima from the left. The bear stands for the savage energy and power of Artemis. In front of the bear's forward-striding paws I saw, adumbrated in the stone, a ball, for a ball is often given to bears to play with in the bear-pit. Obviously this ball is being brought to the worshipper as a symbol of individuation. It points to the meaning or content of the milk.

The whole thing, it seems to me, expresses coming events that are still hidden in the archetypal realm. The anima, clearly, has her mind on spiritual contents. But the bear, the emblem of Russia, sets the ball rolling. Hence the inscription: *Ursa movet molem.*[4]

There's not much more I can tell you, but as a sign of the times I would like to cite the opinion of one of my critics. He accuses me of being so uneducated that I don't even know that the sun moves into Pisces from Aquarius and not the other way round! Such is the level of my public. With best greetings to you and your wife,

Yours sincerely, C. G. JUNG

[3] Cf. Hull, 3 Aug. 53, and illustration; also Jung, "On the Psychology of the Trickster Figure," CW 9, i.

[4] "the she-bear moves the mass." Next to the female figure with the horse Jung carved two inscriptions: "Exoriatur lumen quod gestavi in alvo" (let the light that I have carried in my womb shine forth) and πήγασος πηγάζων ὑδροφόρου χοή (Pegasus leaping forth—a consecrating gush of the water-carrier). The latter involves a pun on the meaning of the name Pegasus, lit. "fount-horse."

To Albert Jung

Dear Colleague,   21 December 1960

Thank you for kindly sending me your lecture,[1] which has given me a valuable glimpse into your research work. Your equation of certain

[1] "Ueber vegetative Neurosen," given to the Annual Meeting of the Swiss Society for Analytical Psychology, Oct. 1960. It formed the basis for another

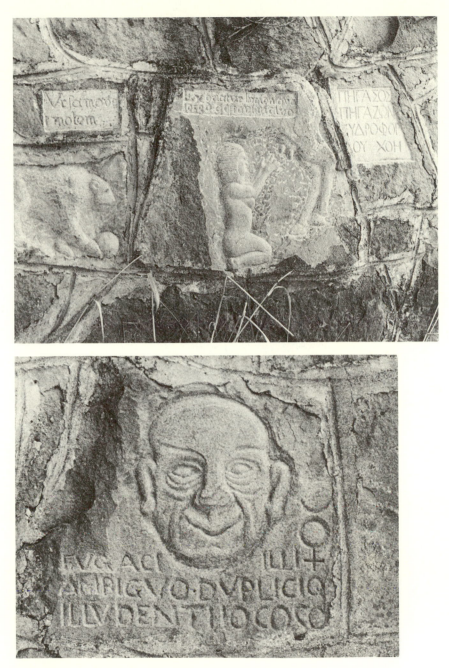

Reliefs on the Tower wall at Bollingen; the "trickster" is at the bottom:
see Tauber, 13 Dec. 60

archetypal ideas with fundamental physiological processes has my undivided applause. It is only the limitation to my subject and to the resulting method that has prevented me from dilating on this aspect of the unconscious except in a few individual instances. I am reluctant to express any views, let alone convictions, in domains where I do not feel fairly competent.

The division of the sympathicus[2] seems to me particularly important psychologically. So I am not in the least surprised when you say that the alchemical pairs of opposites can be correlated with the endophylactic-trophotropic and the ergotrop-dynamic systems.[3]

It goes without saying that it is hardly possible for consciousness to establish a conscious relationship with the Anthropos, i.e., the natural self. For, as you rightly point out, it would mean extending ego-consciousness into the realm of the transcendent, which by definition as well as on empirical grounds is beyond the reach of consciousness.

I do not doubt that the alchemical Mercurius was, for the medieval mind, compensatory to the Christ figure. Admittedly my attempt to outline the historical situation[4] is unsatisfactory in one respect, since neither of these figures nor their synthesis can be presented in a purely abstract and intellectual way; they form a living totality which cannot be represented by any conscious means. This requires for its representation not merely all our capacities for experience, all our descriptive powers; it also needs the active participation of the Mercurius/Christ figure itself, or, to put it symbolically, an *influxus divinus* that grips our very life and not just our so-called spiritual faculties, which al-

---

lecture, "Psychologie vegetativer Neurosen," read at the Second International Congress for Analytical Psychology, Aug. 1962, and published in Adolf Guggenbühl-Craig (ed.), *Der Archetyp/The Archetype* (Proceedings of the Second International Congress for Analytical Psychology, Basel/New York, 1964).

[2] Originally the whole autonomic-vegetative system was called the sympathetic nervous system. Later it was subdivided into the sympathetic and parasympathetic systems.

[3] In his lecture A. made use of the researches of the Swiss physiologist Walter Rudolf Hess (1881–   ), who received the Nobel Prize for Medicine in 1949. He introduced the distinction between the ergotrop-dynamic (or dynamogene) and the endophylactic-trophotropic (or economic) functional systems, the first directed towards the production of energy (movement, sexual function, warmth), the latter towards protecting the vital organic functions (growth, restitution). A. related these two systems to the alchemical polarities Sal/Luna and Sulphur/Sol.

[4] Cf. "The Spirit Mercurius," CW 13, pars. 271, 289ff.

619

ways remain caught in the toils of the intellect, intuition, and feeling. As the alchemists rightly say: *Ars requirit totum hominem.*[5] But our consciousness is never the whole.

Only this gripping of consciousness can be regarded as an approximation to totality. Abstract thinking can lead us no further than to intellectual sophistries, which are invariably used as shields and subterfuges and are calculated to prevent the realization of the whole.

When we ourselves cannot go ahead actively any more, we *suffer* the activity, and then we are no longer the hand that wields the hammer but the hammer that is wielded, or some kind of tool that has got out of control. Since man is relatively free to choose the way he will go, he is also free to go the wrong way and, instead of coming to grips with the reality of his unconscious, to speculate about it and cut himself off from the truth of nature. I therefore cherish no philosophical hopes. One half of the truth lies in the hand of man, the other half in the hand of that which is greater than we. In the first case we can be active, in the second we are bound to be passive, which means: to suffer. No philosophy can help us here, it can only deceive us; and the lamentable spiritual void we are living in today cannot be filled with words but only by our total commitment, or, in mythological terms, by our voluntary self-sacrifice, or at least our readiness for it. We are not even in a position to decide the nature of this self-sacrifice, for this decision depends on the other side.

The process of individuation, of becoming whole, includes by definition the totality of the phenomenon Man and the totality of the riddle of Nature, whose division into physical and spiritual aspects is merely an act of discrimination in the interests of human cognition. With collegial regards and best thanks,

Yours sincerely, C. G. JUNG

[5] = The [alchemical] Art requires the whole man.

To Fowler McCormick

[ORIGINAL IN ENGLISH]

Dear Fowler, [December] 1960

Just a few words and greetings for Xmas and New Year! Thank you for the promised book I have not yet received. My health is better

☐ (Handwritten.)

but the recovery took me a long time and it was a very obstinate and deep-reaching infection. I have been down in Lugano for a fortnight with Walter and Marianne,[1] but the food in the Villa Castagnola was lamentable. I did not enjoy my stay there, though we have seen many new places, among them the cathedral at Monza with the famous Iron Crown of Lombardy of the VI century.

Hoping you are in flourishing health.

Officia peragere iucundum[2]—don't forget!

Yours cordially, c. g.

[1] See Niehus, 3 Jan. 60.
[2] M. wrote in explanation of this letter:

"This note is of interest for two reasons. In the first place it was written in the holiday season which lay between the severe illness we lived through in 1960 and C. G.'s death in 1961.

"Secondly, in the last line it contains the Latin motto which C. G. originated in connection with ITCRA. ITCRA—International Touring and Culinary Research Association—was the name which I gave to our group of three as we went on our drives. [Cf. McCormick, 22 Feb. 51.]

"The Latin motto arose from the following sequence of events: One afternoon when I took C. G. and Ruth [Bailey] for a drive, I could see that the old man was very tired. Under such circumstances I would say nothing, and in this case, after being silent for about half an hour, C. G. suddenly declared: 'It is always a pleasure to carry out the duties of this association.' You can understand how delightful this utterance was in its spontaneity, wit and happiness.

"Some weeks later I said to C. G. that I thought we should make this utterance the motto of our association, but that I thought it was only appropriate to put it into Latin. After some thought, C. G. came out with 'Officia peragere iucundum' . . ."

To the Rev. Arthur W. Rudolph

[ORIGINAL IN ENGLISH]

Dear Sir,   5 January 1961

It would be too ambitious a task to give you a detailed account of the influence of Nietzsche's thoughts on my own development. As a matter of fact, living in the same town where Nietzsche spent his life as a professor of philosophy,[1] I grew up in an atmosphere still vibrat-

☐ Writing a Ph.D. diss., U. of Southern California, on Nietzsche's influence on Jung; the work was published in various articles. Now lecturer on humanities, Arizona State U., and Episcopal priest.
[1] At the age of 11, Jung went to school in Basel, and later studied at the U. 1895–1900 for his medical degree before taking up a post as assistant physician

621

ing from the impact of his teachings, although it was chiefly resistance which met his onslaught. I could not help being deeply impressed by his indubitable inspiration ("Ergriffenheit").[2] He was sincere, which cannot be said of so many academic teachers to whom career and vanity mean infinitely more than the truth. The fact that impressed me the most was his encounter with Zarathustra and then his "religious" critique, which gives a legitimate place in philosophy to passion as the very real motive of philosophizing. The *Unzeitgemässe Betrachtungen* were to me an eye-opener, less so the *Genealogy of Morals* or his idea of the "Eternal Return" of all things. His all-pervading psychological penetration has given me a deep understanding of what psychology is able to do.

All in all Nietzsche was to me the only man of that time who gave some adequate answers to certain urgent questions which then were more felt than thought.

Max Stirner,[3] whom I read at the same time, gave me the impression of a man who was trying to express an infinitely important truth with inadequate means. Over against him the figure of Zarathustra seems to me the better formulation. Those are the main points I could mention about Nietzsche and his influence on my own development.

If you have any further questions and if their answer is within my reach, I am quite ready to cope with them.

Sincerely yours, C. G. JUNG

P.S. I may call the attention to the existence of notes that have been taken of my Seminars about Nietzsche's *Zarathustra*.[4] They would be accessible to you in California.

---

at the Burghölzli Clinic in Zurich. Nietzsche was professor of classical philology at the U. 1869–79.

[2] Cf. Keyserling, 21 Jan. 28, n. 1.

[3] Max Stirner (pseudonym of Kaspar Schmidt; 1806–56), German anarchist writer. In his main work, *Der Einzige und sein Eigentum* (1912; orig. 1845; tr., *The Case of the Individual Against Authority*, 1918), he advocated complete revolt against the State and the full liberation of the individual from all social and moral restraints. The individual is the only reality; everything has to serve his purpose.

[4] Cf. Körner, 22 Mar. 35, n. 1.

To Michael A. Ledeen

[ORIGINAL IN ENGLISH]

Dear Mr. Ledeen,   19 January 1961

I gather from your letter that your immediate wish is to have some suggestions for your forthcoming sermon on the problem of Job.[1] As you yourself realize, one hour is hardly enough to deal with such a big problem satisfactorily.

I would suggest a reduction of your programme, namely that you deal with its important aspect. It would be the fundamental fact of the pair of opposites united in the image of God, i.e., Yahweh. The two are Love and Fear, which presuppose an apparently irreconcilable contradiction. Yet such an opposition must be expected wherever we are confronted with an immense energy. There is no dynamic manifestation without a corresponding initial tension which provided the necessary energy. If we suppose the deity to be a dynamic phenomenon in our experience, its origin must be an opposition or a paradox.

Job obviously is confronted with this problem and he even expresses his conviction that God will help him against God. As the monotheistic tendency always tries to postulate or to construct an anthropomorphic unity of the God-image, it is strange and painful to us to admit a paradoxical or a contradictory God-image. If we try to realize what the full acceptance of such an image means, we will soon discover why most people are afraid of it. This problem is so difficult that its discussion will fill an hour easily. This in spite of the fact that it is an old truth.

I was quite interested to learn from your letter that my ideas have appealed to you.

. . .

Sincerely yours, C. G. JUNG

☐ Claremont, California.
[1] L., a medical student of 19 with a liberal Jewish background, had, after reading *Answer to Job*, asked his rabbi to give a sermon on the book. The rabbi suggested that L. deliver the sermon himself, and L. asked Jung how to approach the problem and what should be the point of departure.

To William G. Wilson

[ORIGINAL IN ENGLISH]

Dear Mr. Wilson,   30 January 1961

Your letter was very welcome indeed. I had no news from Roland H. any more and often wondered what has been his fate. Our conversation which he has adequately reported to you had an aspect of which he did not know. The reason was that I could not tell him everything. In those days I had to be exceedingly careful of what I said. I had found out that I was misunderstood in every possible way. Thus I was very careful when I talked to Roland H. But what I really thought about was the result of many experiences with men of his kind.

His craving for alcohol was the equivalent on a low level of the spiritual thirst of our being for wholeness, expressed in medieval language: the union with God.*

How could one formulate such an insight in a language that is not misunderstood in our days?

The only right and legitimate way to such an experience is that it happens to you in reality, and it can only happen to you when you walk on a path which leads you to higher understanding. You might be led to that goal by an act of grace or through a personal and honest contact with friends or through a high education of the mind beyond the confines of mere rationalism. I see from your letter that Roland H. has chosen the second way, which was, under the circumstances, obviously the best one.

I am strongly convinced that the evil principle prevailing in this world leads the unrecognized spiritual need into perdition, if it is not counteracted either by a real religious insight or by the protective wall of human community. An ordinary man, not protected by an action from above and isolated in society, cannot resist the power of evil, which is called very aptly the Devil. But the use of such words arouses so many mistakes that one can only keep aloof from them as much as possible.

These are the reasons why I could not give a full and sufficient explanation to Roland H. But I am risking it with you because I conclude from your very decent and honest letter that you have acquired a point of view about the misleading platitudes one usually hears about alcoholism.

☐ (1896–1971), co-founder of Alcoholics Anonymous; he was known as "Bill W." His letter, dated 23 Jan. 61, and Jung's reply were published in the Jan. 1963 issue of *AA Grapevine* (monthly journal of Alcoholics Anonymous) and again in Jan. 1968. In his letter W. recounts how Jung's remark in 1931 to Roland H. (whom he was treating for chronic alcoholism), that his situation was hopeless unless "he could become the subject of a spiritual or religious experience—in short a genuine conversion," was instrumental in his own conversion and cure, and how as a result he came to found the organization in 1934.

You see, alcohol in Latin is *spiritus* and you use the same word for the highest religious experience as well as for the most depraving poison. The helpful formula therefore is: *spiritus contra spiritum.* Thanking you again for your kind letter, I remain,

Yours sincerely, C. G. JUNG

* "As the hart panteth after the water brooks, so panteth my soul after thee, O God" (Psalm 42:1).

To Father David

[ORIGINAL IN ENGLISH]

Dear Father David,   11 February 1961

After 60 years of experience I can wholeheartedly confirm my former dictum about the healing of neurosis.[1]

As a neurosis starts from a fragmentary state of human consciousness, it can only be cured by an approximative totality of the human being. Religious ideas and convictions from the beginning of history had the aspect of the mental *pharmakon*. They represent the world of wholeness in which fragments can be gathered and put together again. Such a cure cannot be effected by pills and injections.

I thank you for your kind letter, which I appreciate all the more as I am not very popular either with theologians or my own guild. It is astonishing and not astonishing.

I remain, dear Father David,

Yours very sincerely, C. G. JUNG

☐ Capuchin Franciscan Friary, Cashelmore (Co. Donegal), Ireland.
[1] D. asked if Jung still adhered to his words in "Psychotherapists or the Clergy" (orig. 1932) that "among all my patients in the second half of life . . . none . . . has been really healed who did not regain his religious outlook" (CW 11, par. 509).

To Roger Lass

[ORIGINAL IN ENGLISH]

Dear Mr. Lass,   11 February 1961

It seems to me—to judge from your exposé[1]—that you have a correct idea of my leading thoughts. Only, in par. 6, I would like to

☐ Brooklyn, New York.

emphasize that it very often does not depend upon the use one makes of an image, but rather upon the use the archetypes make of ourselves, which decides the question whether it will be artistic creation or a change of religious attitude. I find that this "choice" is in many cases rather a fate than a voluntary decision. I see that many of my pupils indulge in a superstitious belief in our so-called "free will" and pay little attention to the fact that the archetypes are, as a rule, autonomous entities, and not only material subject to our choice. They are, as a matter of fact, dominants up to a certain point. That is the reason why one is confronted with an archetype, because we cannot undo it by merely making it conscious. It has to be taken into account and that is the main task of any prolonged analysis.

The deviation from the dominants causes a certain dissociation, i.e., a loss of vitality, what the primitives call "a loss of soul." The primitive has a very keen realization in this respect. I would mention the story of a primitive Negro who had been invited to be driven in a car. After half an hour he asked the people to stop. He stepped out and stretched himself on the ground. They asked him whether he was sick, and he said "no," he felt all right, but he had just to wait for his soul that had remained behind, as they went too fast for it. I had to think of my American visitors who fly over in six hours and are still in America for several days, without noticing it.

Your exposé is perfectly clear otherwise and it can serve you well in your further investigations.

Sincerely yours, C. G. JUNG

¹ L. submitted an exposé of his ideas on the "dynamics of the creative process" which he hoped to make the subject of his graduate studies in literature. His par. 6 contains the formulation that "the differentiation between artistic and religious expression . . . depends on the use to which the [archetypal] image is put."

Anonymous

[ORIGINAL IN ENGLISH]

Dear Sir,   14 February 1961

It is very difficult to answer your question.¹ I should give you the same answer as Shri Ramana Maharshi,² but I see too much the difficulty of the practical application.

If you want to do something useful, it only can be there where you

☐ California.

live, where you know the people and circumstances. In nosing around among them you will find a possibility to help. It is certain that you will find one, but not rarely the unconscious blindfolds you, because it does not want you to find an application of your energies to external circumstances. The reason for such a resistance lies in the fact that you need some reconstruction in yourself which you would gladly apply to others. Many things should be put right in oneself first, before we apply our imperfections to our fellow-beings.

Thus, if you should find no obvious possibility, it means that you have to cultivate your own garden first. It is like water in a valley. It cannot flow and it stagnates, but if you have a lake on a hill you cannot keep it from overflowing. It may be that you need to raise your own level.

Sincerely yours, C. G. JUNG

[1] N., a man of "near sixty," asked if "there were some spot where I could make use of my knowledge in helping the world."
[2] Cf. Mees, 15 Sept. 47 & n. 2. N. quoted the Maharshi's answer to the same question he had asked Jung: "Help yourself and you help the world, for you are the world."

To Walter Schaffner

Dear Herr Schaffner,   16 February 1961

In reply to your question about levitation,[1] I myself have never observed the levitation of a living body. But apparently such things do happen.

On the other hand I have seen objects moving that were not directly touched and moreover under absolutely satisfactory scientific conditions. One could describe these movements as levitation if one assumes that the objects moved by themselves. But this does not seem to have been the case, since all the objects that apparently moved by themselves moved as though lifted, shaken, or thrown by a hand.

In this series of experiments I, together with other observers, saw a hand and felt its pressure—apparently the hand that caused all the other phenomena of this kind.

These phenomena have nothing to do with the "will," since they occurred only when the medium was in a trance and precisely not in

☐ Wettingen, Switzerland.
[1] S., a young seminarian, asked about the phenomenon of levitation and its possible connection with Ufos.

control of his will. They seem to fall into the category of poltergeist manifestations.

The experiments here mentioned[2] were conducted in the Psychiatric Clinic at the Burghölzli in Zurich and not at the Federal Polytechnic.

Frankly, I see no connection between these phenomena and Ufos. Unfortunately the latter phenomenon, if it exists at all, is complicated in the highest degree by fantasies and downright fraud. I must caution you against people like Desmond Leslie and George Adamski.[3]

Although I have been studying the Ufo phenomenon for about 12 years now and have read practically all the relevant literature, I am still unable to form a satisfactory picture of it or to assert that anything adequate is known about the nature of Ufos. I cannot even say whether they exist or not.

Whether so-called levitation is in some way connected with anti-gravity is an unanswerable question. With best regards,

Yours sincerely, C. G. JUNG

[2] This refers to experiments with the medium Rudi Schneider which took place in the presence of the parapsychologist Baron Albert Schrenck-Notzing and Prof. Eugen Bleuler. — In the early thirties Jung and Bleuler were present at similar seances with the medium O. Schl. at the house of Prof. Rudolf Bernoulli. Fanny Moser, in her book *Der Okkultismus—Täuschung und Tatsachen* (1935), reported on these seances on the basis of the protocols taken at them. Cf. also *Memories*, p. 255/239.
[3] Authors of *Flying Saucers Have Landed* (1953). Cf. "Flying Saucers," CW 10, par. 612.

To G. Krüger

Dear Sir,   17 February 1961

Please excuse my delay in answering your letter. At my age I can no longer hurry. I can answer it only with unsatisfactory brevity. A detailed answer would go far beyond the framework of a letter. I must therefore confine myself to your direct questions.

Your first question is: what do I regard as my specific contribution to modern psychology? I consider it senseless to air my views in this matter. I have set it all down in my books, and if anyone finds something commendable in them, he can form his own judgment.

□ Berlin.

Your second question is: how do I evaluate my works, and are they out of date, etc.? To this I can only reply that every single book was written with all the responsibility I could muster, that I was honest, and have presented facts which in themselves are not out of date. I wouldn't wish any of my publications undone and I stand by everything I have said.

Not being a philosopher, I have no general conception of the psyche. I am an empiricist, as anyone can discover for himself if he takes the trouble to study my writings. The many aspects I have worked out have naturally given rise to various changes in my formulations; these are not contradictory in themselves but are perfectly understandable if one knows the material.

Your third question concerns the use of foreign words. You won't find any scientific study that is not obliged to make use of foreign words, not only in its technical terminology, where no equivalent concepts existed before, but also in its style, which for unavoidable reasons has to be a specialist language and is not meant to serve the aesthetic purposes of a literary presentation.

It is untrue that I and my pupils have no clue as to the meaning of modern art.[1] But there is no point in discussing our views because the psychological facts involved are still not understood by the public. Nobody bothers to devote serious study to my contributions to scientific psychology. The medical man lacks the time and training, and the philosophical or academic psychologist lacks practical knowledge of the material. The theologian, the only person besides the psychotherapist to declare himself responsible for the *cura animarum*, is afraid of having to think psychologically about the objects of his belief. He prefers simple childlike faith and backs out of every discussion.

Thus I stand isolated between the faculties and can only hope that someone seriously follows up this line of research, which until now has happened in only a very few cases. The theologians who have come to grips with my ideas are Prof. Haendler[2] and Prof. Hans Schär.[3] Both are Protestants. In general, Catholic theologians are much more interested than the Protestant ones in the psychological approach.

---

[1] Cf. Neumann, *The Archetypal World of Henry Moore* (tr., 1959), and his *Art and the Creative Unconscious* (tr., 1959); Jaffé, "Symbolism in the Visual Arts," *Man and his Symbols* (1964), also her *The Myth of Meaning* (tr., 1971), pp. 61ff.; Jacobi, *Vom Bilderreich der Seele* (1969).

[2] Friedrich Haendler, German Protestant theologian, professor of theology at the Free Berlin U. Cf. his *Grundriss der praktischen Theologie* (1957).

[3] Cf. Schär, 16 Sept. 51, and Neumann, 5 Aug. 46, n. 2.

629

There are a number of Anglo-Saxon publications,[4] most of which, however, misunderstand the empirical viewpoint for lack of the necessary epistemological premises.

Klee's work is well known to me. We psychotherapists can gain access to this kind of painting because for decades we have been familiar with the pictures our patients have produced of the contents of the unconscious, as I showed long ago in my essay on Picasso.

Sincerely yours, C. G. JUNG

[4] Cf. Philp, *Jung and the Problem of Evil* (1958); Cox, *Jung and St. Paul* (1969).

To the Rev. John A. Sanford

[ORIGINAL IN ENGLISH]

Dear Mr. Sanford,   10 March 1961

Thank you very much for kindly sending me your sermon.[1] I have read it with interest and pleasure. It is a historical event, as you are— so far as my knowledge goes—the first one who has called the attention of the Christian congregation to the fact that the Voice of God can still be heard if you are only humble enough.

The example you give is very beautiful and meaningful, as it shows the benevolent intention and the meaningful allusion to a continuation of our existence—two important postulates of the Christian creed.

The understanding of dreams should indeed be taken seriously by the Church, since the *cura animarum* is one of its duties, which has been sadly neglected by the Protestants. Even if confession is a relatively poor version of the *cura*, the Catholic Church knows at least the function of the *directeur de conscience*, a highly important function which is unknown to the Protestants.

I admire your courage and sincerely hope that you will not become too unpopular for mentioning a topic so heartily hated and despised by most of the theologians. This is so at least over here. There are only single individuals who risk the fight for survival. The pilgrim's way is spiked with thorns everywhere, even if he is a good Christian, or just therefore.

My best wishes!

Yours sincerely, C. G. JUNG

□ Los Angeles.

[1] The sermon was on the importance of dreams. Cf. his *Dreams: God's Forgotten Language* (1968).

630

The Collected Works of C. G. JUNG

The Collected Works of C. G. JUNG

Editors: Sir Herbert Read (d. 1968), Michael Fordham, and Gerhard Adler; executive editor, William McGuire. Translated by R.F.C. Hull (d. 1974), except vol. 2; cf. vol. 6.

(continued)

* Published 1957; 2nd edn., 1970.   † Published 1973.

---

* Published 1960.   † Published 1961.
‡ Published 1956; 2nd edn., 1967.

*6. PSYCHOLOGICAL TYPES (1921)
   A *Revision by R.F.C. Hull of the Translation by H. G. Baynes*
   With Four Papers on Psychological Typology (1913, 1925, 1931, 1936)

†7. TWO ESSAYS ON ANALYTICAL PSYCHOLOGY
   On the Psychology of the Unconscious (1917/1926/1943)
   The Relations between the Ego and the Unconscious (1928)
   Appendix: New Paths in Psychology (1912); The Structure of the Un-
      conscious (1916) (new versions, with variants, 1966)

‡8. THE STRUCTURE AND DYNAMICS OF THE PSYCHE
   On Psychic Energy (1928)
   The Transcendent Function ([1916]/1957)
   A Review of the Complex Theory (1934) ·
   The Significance of Constitution and Heredity in Psychology (1929)
   Psychological Factors Determining Human Behaviour (1937)
   Instinct and the Unconscious (1919)
   The Structure of the Psyche (1927/1931)
   On the Nature of the Psyche (1947/1954)
   General Aspects of Dream Psychology (1916/1948)
   On the Nature of Dreams (1945/1948)
   The Psychological Foundations of Belief in Spirits (1920/1948)
   Spirit and Life (1926)
   Basic Postulates of Analytical Psychology (1931)
   Analytical Psychology and *Weltanschauung* (1928/1931)
   The Real and the Surreal (1933)
   The Stages of Life (1930–1931)
   The Soul and Death (1934)
   Synchronicity: An Acausal Connecting Principle (1952)
   Appendix: On Synchronicity (1951)

**9. PART I. THE ARCHETYPES AND THE
   COLLECTIVE UNCONSCIOUS
   Archetypes of the Collective Unconscious (1934/1954)
   The Concept of the Collective Unconscious (1936)
   Concerning the Archetypes, with Special Reference to the Anima Concept
      (1936/1954)
   Psychological Aspects of the Mother Archetype (1938/1954)
   Concerning Rebirth (1940/1950)
   The Psychology of the Child Archetype (1940)
   The Psychological Aspects of the Kore (1941)
   The Phenomenology of the Spirit in Fairytales (1945/1948)
   On the Psychology of the Trickster-Figure (1954)
   Conscious, Unconscious, and Individuation (1939)
   A Study in the Process of Individuation (1934/1950)
   Concerning Mandala Symbolism (1950)
   Appendix: Mandalas (1955)

(continued)

* Published 1971.   † Published 1953; 2nd edn., 1966.
‡ Published 1960; 2nd edn., 1969.   ** Published 1959; 2nd edn., 1968.

635

* Published 1959; 2nd edn., 1968.   † Published 1964; 2nd edn., 1970.
‡ Published 1958; 2nd edn., 1969.

636

The Psychology of Eastern Meditation (1943)
The Holy Men of India: Introduction to Zimmer's "Der Weg zum Selbst"
(1944)
Foreword to the "I Ching" (1950)

*12. PSYCHOLOGY AND ALCHEMY (1944)
Prefatory note to the English Edition ([1951?] added 1967)
Introduction to the Religious and Psychological Problems of Alchemy
Individual Dream Symbolism in Relation to Alchemy (1936)
Religious Ideas in Alchemy (1937)
Epilogue

†13. ALCHEMICAL STUDIES
Commentary on "The Secret of the Golden Flower" (1929)
The Visions of Zosimos (1938/1954)
Paracelsus as a Spiritual Phenomenon (1942)
The Spirit Mercurius (1943/1948)
The Philosophical Tree (1945/1954)

‡14. MYSTERIUM CONIUNCTIONIS (1955–56)
AN INQUIRY INTO THE SEPARATION AND
SYNTHESIS OF PSYCHIC OPPOSITES IN ALCHEMY
The Components of the Coniunctio
The Paradoxa
The Personification of the Opposites
Rex and Regina
Adam and Eve
The Conjunction

**15. THE SPIRIT IN MAN, ART, AND LITERATURE
Paracelsus (1929)
Paracelsus the Physician (1941)
Sigmund Freud in His Historical Setting (1932)
In Memory of Sigmund Freud (1939)
Richard Wilhelm: In Memoriam (1930)
On the Relation of Analytical Psychology to Poetry (1922)
Psychology and Literature (1930/1950)
"Ulysses": A Monologue (1932)
Picasso (1932)

§16. THE PRACTICE OF PSYCHOTHERAPY
GENERAL PROBLEMS OF PSYCHOTHERAPY
Principles of Practical Psychotherapy (1935)
What Is Psychotherapy? (1935)

(continued)

---

* Published 1953; 2nd edn., completely revised, 1968.
† Published 1968.   ‡ Published 1963; 2nd edn., 1970.
** Published 1966.
§ Published 1954; 2nd edn., revised and augmented, 1966.

* Published 1954.

INDEX TO VOLUMES 1 AND 2

INDEX TO VOLUMES 1 AND 2

VOLUME numbers are in superscript position. Names of addressees are in capitals and small capitals. Under the names, letters are arranged by year, with general references separated from the letters by a dash. References to the preliminaries (roman numerals) of vol. 1 usually apply also to vol. 2, where the introduction and chronology are repeated.

A

abaissement du niveau mental, [1]433; [2]543, 569, 576

ABEGG, CARL JULIUS, [1]1941, 296–97; Johanna, ein Schicksal, [1]296n

Abegg, Lily, Ostasien denkt anders, [2]439 & n

Abel, [2]117n, 156n

Abraham, [2]33n

Abraham, H. C., and Ernst L. Freud, A Psycho-Analytic Dialogue, [1]5n

ABRAHAM, KARL, [1]1908, 4–6, 6–7, facsim. facing p. 4 — 10n, 11, 167n; "The Psychosexual Differences between Hysteria and Dementia Praecox," [1]6n

Abraham ben Meier ibn Ezra, [2]60n, 117

ABRAMS, STEPHEN I., [2]1957, 373–75, 398–400; 1959, 489–91; 1960, 576–77

Abraxas, [1]574n

abreaction, [1]4

absconditum, [1]400

absolute knowledge, [2]18, 449

absolute truth, [2]595

absolute ultimate, [2]259, 261

Académie Septentrionale, Lille, [2]336 & n, 337

Academy of German Scientists and Physicians, [1]329

Academy of Sciences, Washington, D.C., [2]256n

acausal correspondences, [2]46, 539

acausal phenomena, [2]426, 448

accumulation phenomena, [2]233–34

achurayim, [1]513

Actaeon, [1]376

Acta Psychosomatica, [1]379n

active imagination, [1]xxii, 83n, 416n, 458, 459, 500, 561; [2]222, 233, 469

Acts of John, [1]416, 417n; [2]285

Acts of Pilate, [2]253n

Acts of the Apostles, [1]229, 261n, 488n, 492n; [2]199 & n, 235n

Acts of Thomas, [1]416, 417n

Adam, [1]462; [2]165, 235n, 311, 314, 325, 326, 386; Second (Christ), [1]414 & n; sin of, [2]369, 370

Adam Kadmon, [2]304, 325

Adam of Bremen, [2]331

Adam von Bodenstein, [2]559 & n

Adamski, George, [2]627n, 628

Ad Caeli Reginam, encyclical, see Pius XII

Adirondacks, [1]532

Adler, Alfred, [1]13 & n, 19, 27n, 77, 131n, 172, 184, 211, 215, 430n, 557; [2]280, 346n; Freud compared with, [1]301–2; [2]349–50; separation from Freud, [1]557

ADLER, GERHARD, [1]1932, 93–94; 1934,

complex, ^{2}211; inherited, ^{2}450–51; instinct and, ^{1}526, 547; ^{2}152, 255; Lamb's use of word, ^{2}131n; mandalas as, ^{2}xlvi; in mathematics, ^{2}22–23, 328–29; mother, ^{1}432, 499; ^{2}446; *mundus archetypus*, ^{2}22 & n, 31n; music and, ^{1}542; neuroses and, ^{1}299; ^{2}160–61; organizing, ^{2}446 & n; parental, ^{1}52, 499; *per se*, ^{1}226n, 313n; physiological basis of, ^{2}159–61; in primitive beliefs, ^{1}320; psi phenomena and, ^{2}537, 538, 541, 542; psychoid nature of, ^{1}226n; ^{2}22 & n, 259, 318, 437, 451; in quantum theory, ^{2}22; regression and, ^{2}148, 149; ritual amnesis in rebirth mysteries, ^{1}413, 414; of sacrifice, ^{1}467; of self, ^{1}418, 507, 533; ^{2}267; space as, ^{1}454; in spiritualism, ^{1}432, 433; synchronicity and, ^{1}395; ^{2}289, 437, 446n, 447, 490; uses of, ^{2}626 & n; "what do they communicate?" ^{2}606 & n; Wise Old Man, ^{1}499

architectural space, ^{2}509–10

Archiv für genetische Philosophie, ^{1}64n

Archives de psychologie, ^{1}22n, 524n

Aries, ^{1}138 & n, 139; ^{2}167, 225, 229, 429

Aristarchus of Samos, ^{2}72–73n

Aristotelian Society, ^{2}474 & n

Aristotle (Aristotelianism), ^{1}250n, 317, 318, 454n, 458, 492n; ^{2}158n, 315, 501

Arius of Alexandria (Arianism), ^{2}xxxvi & n

Arizona, ^{1}101n, 320n; ^{2}497n

art: educative purpose of, ^{1}108; modern, ^{1}107–8, 225–26, 286, 316, 469; ^{2}81–83, 440, 511–12, 549, 586, 589–91, 604–5, 629, 630; neurosis and, ^{1}333; of patients, *see* drawing and painting; psychology of, ^{1}388

Artemidorus Daldianus, ^{1}547; *Oneirokritika*, ^{1}547n

Artemis, ^{1}343n, 376n; ^{2}423n, 616

artificial insemination, ^{2}110–11

artists: creative, ^{1}77; mother complex of, ^{1}266–67, psychology of, ^{1}107–8,

173 & n, 225–26, 388; Renaissance, ^{1}226

Aryans, ^{1}157, 159, 219n, 233, 242

ARZ, PASTOR W., ^{1}1933, 117–18, 119

ASBECK, ERNA, ^{1}1947, 460–61

Aschaffenburg, Gustav, ^{1}3 & n, 4, 210 & n

ASCHNER, BERNARD, ^{2}1951, 14–15; *Lehrbuch der Konstitutionstherapie*, ^{2}15n

Ascona, ^{1}139n, 284n, 298, 304, 320n, 341n, 374, 376, 420, 441, 453, 505, 527n; ^{2}217 & n

Ashmole, Elias, ^{2}47 & n; dreams, ^{2}47–50, 51, 62–63; *Fasciculus Chemicus*, ^{2}63; *Theatrum Chemicum Britannicum* (ed.), ^{2}50, 51, 63

Asia, ^{1}252n

Asia Institute, New York, ^{1}560n

Asklepios, ^{1}342n, 343n, 360n, 376n; ^{2}273n

Assagioli, R., ^{1}22 & n

Assisi, ^{1}499

association: free, ^{2}293 & n, 294; Jung's technique, ^{2}293; syndromous, ^{2}319 & n

association test, ^{1}210

Assumption of the Virgin, dogma of, ^{1}499n, 566n, 567–68; ^{2}7–8, 32, 65, 67, 73, 92, 137, 203 & n, 206, 228, 231, 282, 334, 335, 423, 485

Astrological Magazine, ^{1}475

Astrologie Moderne, ^{2}175n

astrology, ^{1}24, 56, 138–39, 475–76; ^{2}23–24, 38, 107n, 162 & n, 232, 318, 354, 415, 428–29, 463–64, 538; historical periods, ^{1}69–70n, 138n; psychology and, ^{2}175–77

Athanasius, St., ^{2}203 & n

Atharva Veda, ^{1}223n

atheism, ^{1}123, 361, 409; ^{2}168

athletic type, ^{2}346n

Atlantic Monthly, ^{2}362 & n

Atlantis, ^{1}204, 208; ^{2}4

Atman, ^{1}247 & n, 281; ^{2}33, 146, 303 & n, 315, 395n

atomic bombs, ^{1}378, 402, 407, 505; ^{2}209, 230; *see also* hydrogen bombs

atomic physics, *see* physics

647

D

659

Guild of Pastoral Psychology, [1]501*n*; [2]155*n*

Guisan, Henri, General, [1]290*n*

Gurdjieff, George Ivanovitch, [2]180 & *n*; *All and Everything*, [2]180*n*; *Meetings with Remarkable Men*, [2]180*n*

Gurney, E., F.W.H. Myers, and F. Podmore, *Phantasms of the Living*, [2]126 & *n*

guru, [1]172, 235*n*, 237, 491, 492; [2]504

Gyógyászat, [1]13*n*

H

H., Dr., [2]1951, 6–9, 21–23

HABERLANDT, H., [2]1952, 53–55

Hades, [1]48, 53

HADFIELD, J. A., [1]1935, 202–3

Hadrian, Emperor, [1]223*n*

Haeckel, Ernst Heinrich, [1]164 & *n*

HAEMMERLI, ARNIM, [2]1955, 273

Haemmerli, Theodor, [1]345 & *n*; [2]273

Haendler, Friedrich, [2]629 & *n*; *Grundriss der praktischen Theologie*, [2]629*n*

HAESELE, E., [1]1932, 112

Haggard, H. Rider, *She*, [1]305*n*

Hagia Sophia, Istanbul, [1]462

Hahnemann, Samuel, [1]429; *Organon of the Rational Art of Healing*, [1]429*n*

Haile, B., [2]287*n*

Hale, N. G., Jr., *Putnam and Psychoanalysis*, [1]33*n*

HALL, CALVIN S., [2]1954, 184–87, 191–92; *Theories of Personality* (with Lindzey), [2]184 & *n*, 185–87

Hall, G. Stanley, [1]531, pl. II

Hamburg, [1]176*n*

Hamburg University, [1]215*n*, 530*n*, 565*n*

HAMBURGER, CARL, [1]1943, 339

Hamburger, Michael, [2]37*n*

Hamelin, Pied Piper and children, [2]330–32

HANHART, ERNEST, [2]1957, 346–48, 349–50

happiness, [2]237–38; suffering and, [1]247; [2]268–69

HARDING, M. ESTHER, [1]1939, 276; 1947, 468–69; [2]1951, 29–30; 1957,

362–63; *The "I" and the "Not-I,"* [1]276*n*; *Journey into Self*, [1]276*n*; [2]362*n*; *The Parental Image*, [1]276*n*; *Psychic Energy*, [1]276*n*, 341*n*, 468*n*; *The Way of All Women*, [1]276*n*; *Woman's Mysteries*, [1]276*n*; [2]pl. VI

Harms, Ernest, "Carl Gustav Jung—Defender of Freud and the Jews," [1]160*n*

HARNETT, CHARLES B., [2]1957, 403–4

Harranites, [1]324*n*

Hart-Davis, Rupert, [1]75*n*

Hartmann, Eduard von, [1]87; [2]500 & *n*

Harvard Medical Library, [1]33*n*

Harvard Psychological Clinic, [1]42*n*

Harvard Tercentenary Conference of Arts and Sciences, [1]219*n*, 329, 489*n*

Harvard Theological Review, [1]419–20*n*

Harvard University, [1]xxiv, 42*n*, 198 & *n*, 222, 269*n*, 329, 431*n*, 531*n*; [2]232 & *n*, 354

Harvard University, Widener Library, [1]223

hashish, [2]222

Hasidim (Chassidim), [1]238; [2]205 & *n*, 359

Hatha Yoga, [1]67*n*, 310–11, 498

HAUER, J. WILHELM, [1]1932, 103; 1936, 209, 211–12; 1937, 233 — 113

Hauptmann, Gerhart, [1]60*n*

Hawaii University, [1]560*n*

healing: hypnosis and, [2]499, 613; miraculous, [2]498–500

healing function, [2]227–28

Heard, Gerald, *Is Another World Watching? The Riddle of the Flying Saucers*, [2]3 & *n*, 6

Hearst's International Cosmopolitan, [1]159*n*, 286*n*

Heaven, [1]387; journey to, [2]143; Kingdom of, [1]268

HEAVENER, ROSCOE, [1]1950, 557–58

Hebel, Johann Peter, [1]527

Hecate, [1]323, 462; [2]412

Hegel, Georg Wilhelm Friedrich, [1]61, 87, 194, 332, 532; [2]249, 500*n*, 501 & *n*, 502

Heidegger, Martin, [1]5*n*, 273, 330, 331,

J

chronology of his life, ¹xxi–xxv; death, ¹xxv; does not want biography, ²38–39, 106; evaluation of his own work, ²628–30; Freud's relationship with, *see* Freud, Sigmund; funeral, ²28n; illness: 1944, cardiac infarct, ¹343n, 345, 357–58, 379, 406, 518; ²273; 1946, embolism, ¹449, 450 & n, 451, 454–55, 473; 1952–53, tachycardia and arrhythmia, ²91, 93, 103–6, 108, 117, 125; 1960, ²544, 546, 554, 620–21; and Nazis in Germany, *see under* Germany; sculpture, ²83, 119n, 287 & n, 290–91, 317 & n, 527, 615–16, illus. facing p. 616; television interview, BBC, ²520 & n, 521n, 524, 525, 573 & n, 574

AWARDS AND HONOURS: honorary degrees, ¹xxi, xxiv, 305, 328–29; ²232n, 283n, 497, 579; Literature Prize of the City of Zurich, ¹xxiii, 109, 110n, 111; 70th birthday, ¹xxiv; 80th birthday, ¹xxv; ²270, 273, 276, 292; 85th birthday, ¹xxv; ²568, 577, 586

FESTSCHRIFTS FOR: *Komplexe Psychologie,* ¹562n; *Die Kulturelle Bedeutung der komplexen Psychologie,* ¹194 & n, 197; *Studien zum Problem des Archetypischen,* ¹374n, 376, 386

PORTRAITS: 1912, ¹frontispiece; 1928, ¹59; 1930, ¹pl. VII; 1936, ¹pl. VII; 1937, by M. Foote, ²xxxiv; 1939, ¹pl. V; 1945, ¹pl. I, pl. VI, pl. VII; 1950, ¹pl. VII; ²pl. I; 1954, ²pl. III; 1955, in *Time,* ²229 & n, 230, pl. II; 1959, ²frontispiece

SEMINARS AND LECTURES: Clark University, ¹11n, 531; Eranos Lectures, ¹xxiii, xxiv, xxv, 139n, 191n, 209, 245, 252, 300, 382, 435, 439, 449, 457n, 462, 525n, 530n; ²21; Fordham University, ¹xxii, 24n, 29n, 210n, 532; Psychological Club, Zurich, ¹xxiii, 188 & n, 300, 482; ²xxxin, xxxiiin; Swiss Federal Polytechnic (ETH), ¹xxiii, xxiv, xxv,

187, 281n, 286, 300 & n, 312, 345n, 506n; Tavistock Lectures, ¹xxiii; ²55n, 491n; Yale University, Terry Lectures, ¹xxiv, 234 & n, 235, 243, 378n; ²xxxviin, 520 & n

TRAVELS: Africa, ¹xxiii, 42–44, 399, 422, pl. IV; ²xxxix, 40, 201; Algeria, ¹xxii; Egypt, ¹xxiii, 42, 251n; ²xxxiiin; Germany, ¹62–63, 116, 120, 126; India, ¹xxiv, 239n, 241–42, 243, 244n, 247–48, 310, 345, 477n, 478; ²xxxiv, 6n, 129n, 247; Italy, ¹10; Kenya, ¹xxiii; London, ¹36–37, 50; Palestine, ¹251 & n; ²xxxiiin; Rhodes, ²xxxiii; Tunisia, ¹xxii; Uganda, ¹xxiii; United States, ¹xxi, xxii, xxiii, 11n, 27n, 101n, 198, 219, 220, 243, 378n, 530–32; ²xxxviin, 210

WORKS: "After the Catastrophe," ¹368n, 369n, 370n; "The Aims of Psychotherapy," ¹63n; *Aion,* ¹xxv, 62n, 69n, 234n, 371n, 402n, 413n, 416n, 417n, 478n, 480n, 497n, 502n, 507n, 516n, 527n, 539n, 540n, 541n, 553n, 565n; ²8n, 9, 13n, 14n, 49n, 52n, 53, 60 & n, 62, 64, 66, 85, 97, 114n, 117n, 118 & n, 134n, 135n, 136n, 143, 155, 157, 166n, 226, 236 & n, 257n, 259n, 267, 275, 281, 282, 301, 345, 427, 454, 483n, 490n, 510, 511, 558; *Alchemical Studies,* ¹63n, 240n, 305n; *Analytical Psychology: Its Theory and Practice,* ¹xxiii, 83n, 89n, 253n; ²55n; *Analytical Psychology and Education,* ¹xxiv, 363n, 365n; *Analytische Psychologie und Erziehung, see Analytical Psychology and Education;* "Answer to Job," ¹xxv, 414n, 527n; ²7n, 17–18, 20n, 21n, 29n, 33 & n, 35, 39 & n, 40, 51 & n, 59, 61 & n, 65n, 66 & n, 67, 68, 79, 80, 85, 92n, 97, 99 & n, 100 & n, 104 & n, 110 & n, 112 & n, 115, 116, 118, 151n, 152n, 153, 155 & n, 156n, 157, 158n, 163, 166n, 192 & n, 193, 196, 197, 199, 201, 213 & n, 231, 232, 238n,

[1]377–78; *The Form of Things Unknown*, [2]589 & *n*, 605, 606*n*; *The Green Child*, [1]509–10; *Zum 85. Geburtstag von Professor Carl Gustav Jung*, [2]586*n*; [2]pl. III
realism and nominalism, [1]496 & *n*
reality: absolute and relative, [1]57, 60; inner, [1]246; ultimate, [1]247*n*
rearmament, [1]536
Reason, Goddess, [2]209 & *n*, 286
rebirth, [2]148–49; rites, [1]260, 414
reciprocal effect: in parapsychology, [2]439–40; synchronicity and, [2]437 & *n*
reconciliation rites, [1]355, 356
Red Cross, [1]149*n*
Redemption, [2]281, 282, 303
Redlich, Monica, *The Various Light*, [1]516
Red Sea, [1]42–43
reductive standpoint, [1]172, 211
reflexology, [2]56
Reformation, [2]7, 8, 69, 334, 486
Regensburg, [1]293
Regina (queen, anima), [2]145*n*
Regina Coeli, *see* Queen of Heaven
regression: into childhood, [1]270; [2]148–49; Freud's concept, [1]13; rebirth and, [2]148–49
REH, VALERIE, [2]1952, 78
Reichard, G. A., *Navaho Religion*, [1]101*n*
Reichl (publisher), [1]119
REICHSTEIN, MEGGIE, [2]1957, 381
Reimer, Georg Andreas, [2]528 & *n*, 529
Reimer, Hermann, [2]528 & *n*; Georg Andreas Reimer, [2]528*n*, 529
Reimer-Jung, Anna, [2]528 & *n*, 529
reincarnation, [1]209; [2]103–4
Reinhold, H. A., [1]506
Reiter, Paul, [1]136
Reitzenstein, Richard, [1]352
relativity: of causality, [1]394; Einstein's theory, [2]109, 398*n*; of space and time, [1]176, 322, 327, 359, 365*n*, 389, 390, 394, 421, 432, 495, 522; [2]109, 127, 160
religion, [1]237; African sun worship, [1]44; American Indian, [1]101–2, 380,

381; American white sects, [1]380; anxiety and, [2]575 & *n*; definitions of *religio*, [2]272 & *n*, 283, 482 & *n*, 483 & *n*, 517; in dreams and fantasies, [2]56–57; faith without, [2]482 & *n*, 484–85; fear in, [1]399; [2]363; Freud's attitude toward, [2]204, 295–96, 575; future of, [1]158–59, 401–2; Germanic, primitive, [1]39–40; in healing of neuroses, [2]625; in individuation, [2]566; inner experience and, [2]183–84; Jung's answers to questions on, [2]273–76; Jung's principles of, [1]65–66, 123–27, 345–50, 359–62, 502; [2]257–58, 271–72, 482–88, 517–18; of modern man, [1]216–17, 386–87, [2]67–68, 75–77; mythological aspect of, [2]468; race and, [1]233, 380; science and, [1]118, 124–27, 327–28, 346, 350, 359–61; symbolism in, [1]383; transcendent function and, [1]268; world sanctuary proposed, [2]597–98; *see also* Buddhism; Christianity; Gnosticism; Hinduism; Islam; Judaism; Tao; Yoga
religiosity, [1]118
religious experience, psychology of, [1]98
religious movements of Middle Ages, [2]331
Renaissance, [1]79–80, 102, 226; [2]486
Renan, Ernest, [2]203; *Life of Jesus*, [2]87 & *n*
représentations collectives, [1]525
repression, [1]173*n*, 211, 564; sexual, *see* sexual repression
resistance, [1]54, 251–52; [2]555–56; to father, [1]73; to understanding, [1]30–31
res simplex, [1]171*n*
Revelation (Apocalypse), [1]125, 278*n*, 507; [2]7*n*, 118*n*, 134*n*, 152*n*, 157, 253*n*, 314 & *n*, 610*n*
revelation, [1]269, 453
Revue de culture européene, La, [2]115*n*
Revue de Genève, [1]482*n*
Revue metapsychique, [2]127*n*, 216
Rex (king, animus), [2]145*n*
Rhein Verlag, [1]103*n*; [2]424*n*
Rhenanus, Johannes, [1]449*n*; *Harmoniae*

T

Index by Delight Ansley

Library of Congress Cataloging in Publication Data

Jung, Carl Gustav, 1875-1961.
   Letters.

   Includes bibliographical references.
   CONTENTS: v. 1. 1906-1950.—v. 2. 1951-1961.
   1. Jung, Carl Gustav, 1875-1961. 2. Psychoanalysts—Corre-
spondence, reminiscences, etc. I. Series.
BF175.J8513   1973   150'.19'5408   74-166378
ISBN 0-691-09895-6 (v. 1)
      0-691-09724-0 (v.2)